The Spirit of C

An Introduction to Modern Programming

The Spirit of C

An Introduction to Modern Programming

Henry Mullish
New York University

Herbert L. Cooper

West Publishing Company
Saint Paul ■ New York ■ Los Angeles ■ San Francisco

Copyediting	Comptron Research, Inc.
Composition	WPT Services, Inc.
Cover design	Delor Erickson, Studio West

Library of Congress Cataloging in Publication Data

Mullish, Henry
 The spirit of C.

 Bibliography: p.
 Includes index.
 1. C (Computer program langauge) I. Cooper,
Herbert. II. Title.
QA76.73.C15M86 1987   005.13'3   86-33994
ISBN 0-314-28500-8

Contents

Preface

This is a book about the computer language called C. If you are seeking a book to increase your typing speed, expand on your knowledge of word processing, or learn the secrets of chip fabrication and design, this is not the one for you. However, if you want to become thoroughly familiar with the C programming language, then you have made a wise choice. For this book is devoted to just that—to help you become proficient in C.

It is one thing to read about a language; it is quite another to get involved in it. The best and most time-effective way to absorb a language such as C is to have a terminal or computer available to you, preferably at your fingertips. You will be exposed to well over one hundred C programs in this book.

You are encouraged to experiment with the programs illustrated in this text. Omit keywords, change a comma to a period, deliberately forget to terminate a statement with the required semicolon, etc. You can do whatever you want without having to worry about causing any damage to the computer, because you simply can't. Play "what if" games to your heart's content. Familiarity with the language will bring with it greater understanding; the more you understand about C, the more you will enjoy it.

You might be surprised to find out that C has a rather extensive variety of operators and data types designed specifically to offer you a greater range of options and to permit you to solve a multitude of problems with the minimum of effort. These may range in diversity from bookkeeping to accounting to problems of mathematics. There is no real limit to the areas in which C can be of use. The only limitation is your imagination. At the first opportunity, begin to write your own programs. This is an order!

This book is intended for the person with or without programming experience. No programming experience will be assumed, however, nor will we expect the reader to have any mathematical expertise above the standard high school level. The novice to programming will naturally move along at a slower pace than that of the more experienced, simply because there is often much transfer of knowledge when going from one language to another. The experienced person has the distinct advantage of at least knowing what to expect. Such people can probably skim over much of the more descriptive detail without any loss. Even so, C may have some unexpected surprises for the seasoned programmer too. Whatever your background, by the time you have finished reading this book, have answered the myriad of questions, and completed the suggested exercises, you will have come to know the essentials of the C language. That is the only purpose of this book.

To help get you involved—probably the most important ingredient to the effective learning of any subject material—each chapter is followed by a list of questions based on the text, for which answers are supplied.

Sometimes they are quite detailed, thereby reinforcing the concepts learned in the chapter. Secondly, you will find that every chapter contains many programs. This too is done to further your understanding of the language and its related concepts. Having to examine so many programs in minute detail, you will find yourself unconsciously absorbing the style of C until it becomes your own. Yes, C does have a very characteristic style. A further advantage of supplying so many different programs is that most people learn more effectively by reading programs, rather than reading descriptive text.

Finally, it should be emphasized that, regardless of the language, learning to program is not a spectator sport. Competency comes by actually doing it. The more programs you write, the sooner you will progress to greater heights—and the more fun it will be. Welcome aboard! Your trip should prove exciting and challenging. As you'll soon realize, programming is not only a science but an art, one which may bring you great satisfaction, intellectual challenge and enjoyment. Expertise in the field will probably not come instantly, however, so plan on some hard work. Above all, do not expect to understand every concept with a single reading. If you apply yourself, you can master each of the ideas, but it does take time and effort. Good luck on your voyage of discovery.

Prologue
The History of C

You are about to be introduced to a powerful programming language that is known cryptically as C. This language is attracting considerable attention worldwide because the software industry is adopting the language to great advantage. One reason for this popularity is portability. That is to say, a program written in C can be transferred easily from one computer to another with minimal changes or none at all. Programs written in C are fast and efficient. This versatility makes C a desirable language in the highly competitive software industry.

The C language was developed at Bell Laboratories in the early 1970's by a systems programmer named Dennis Ritchie. It was written originally for programming under an operating system[1] called UNIX, which itself was later rewritten almost entirely in C.

In case you have wondered why a language should be given such a cryptic name as C, it derives from the fact that it is based on an earlier version written by Ken Thompson, another Bell Laboratories systems engineer. He adapted it from a language that was known by the initials BCPL, which stand for Basic Combined Programming Language. To distinguish his version of the language from BCPL, Thompson dubbed it B, the first of the initials BCPL. When the language was modified and improved to its present state, the second letter of BCPL, C, was chosen to represent the new version. It is mere coincidence that the letters B and C are in alphabetic order. Some contend that the successor to C will be D, while others say it should be called P. You are left to ponder this weighty problem for yourself.

There is no single compiler for C. Many different organizations have written and implemented C compilers, which differ from one another to a greater or lesser extent. Even for the same computer, there may be several different compilers, each with its own particular requirements. As of this writing, C is in the process of being officially standardized. Even so, you should be prepared for minor variations that may become apparent. Compilers can be very sensitive even to minor differences of syntax. If you experience any difficulties, just consult the manual that comes with your version of C. Or better still, get help from someone with first-hand experience.

The C language is often described as a "middle-level" language. It permits programs to be written in much the same style as that of most modern high-level languages, such as FORTRAN, COBOL, BASIC, PL/I, and Pascal. Where it differs is that C permits very close interaction with the inner workings of the computer. It is anologous to a car that has the luxury of automatic gears, but at the option of the

---

[1] An operating system is a set of programs that enable the user to interact with the hardware components of a computer system.

driver, permits the manual shifting of gears. It is possible in C to deal with the machine at a fairly low level. Nevertheless, C is a general-purpose structured programming language that has much in common with the best of the high-level languages. Even though C is concise and terse (as its short name seems to suggest), it is also extremely powerful.

When you learn how to write programs in C, those programs will also have to be compiled and executed. For details on how to edit, compile, and run programs, consult the manuals for your particular compiler and computer. Whenever you feel you are ready, just start typing in your programs. You may proceed at your own speed. The chances are rather high that you will make mistakes at first, but this is par for the course. The more errors you make at the beginning, the fewer you will make later on, so don't get too depressed. Just rest assured that there is nothing that you can possibly do within a program to cause any damage to the computer, even if the results leave something to be desired.

1

Elementary Programming

This chapter presents several fairly simple programs, which are designed to acquaint you with the structure of the C language. These programs are worth your attention because the longer programs will be written in precisely the same format.

A Typical C Program

Program 1-1 is an interactive program that calculates the hypotenuse of a right triangle, after the user types in the lengths of the other two sides. (It is called "interactive" because the user interacts directly with the computer.) This program is presented to give you an idea of what a substantial C program looks like, since we won't be writing such involved programs until several chapters from now. At this stage, the chances are that much of the program will be difficult to understand. You might be able to discern the logic behind the program, however, particularly if you have been exposed to other programming languages.

```
/* An interactive program to calculate the hypotenuse of a right triangle */

#define square(x) ((x) * (x))     /* square(x) becomes x squared */

main()
{
    double a_leg, b_leg,          /* The two legs of the triangle, entered
                                     by the user (0 to quit) */
           hypotenuse,            /* The hypotenuse, calculated by the program */
           sqrt();                /* square root library function */

    printf("Enter the lengths of the two legs of a right triangle.\n");
    printf("The program will display the length of the hypotenuse.\n");
    printf("Enter zero or negative values to end program.\n\n");

/* Priming reads follow */

    printf("First leg (0.0 to quit)? ");
    scanf("%f", &a_leg);
    printf("Second leg (0.0 to quit)? ");
    scanf("%f", &b_leg);

    while (a_leg > 0.0 && b_leg > 0.0)
    {
        /* Hypotenuse = square root of a*a + b*b */
        hypotenuse = sqrt(square(a_leg) + square(b_leg));
        printf("The legs of the right triangle are %.2f and %.2f,\n",
            a_leg, b_leg);
        printf("   so the hypotenuse is %.2f\n\n", hypotenuse);

        printf("First leg (0.0 to quit)? ");
        scanf("%f", &a_leg);
        printf("Second leg (0.0 to quit)? ");
        scanf("%f", &b_leg);
    }

    printf("Thank you.\n");
}
```

Program 1-1

A sample run follows to help you understand how Program 1-1 operates. Throughout this book, the user's input is underlined to distinguish it from the program's output.

```
Enter the lengths of the two legs of a right triangle.
The program will display the length of the hypotenuse.
Enter zero or negative values to end program.

First leg (0.0 to quit)? 3
Second leg (0.0 to quit)? 4
The legs of the right triangle are 3.00 and 4.00,
    so the hypotenuse is 5.00

First leg (0.0 to quit)? 5
Second leg (0.0 to quit)? 12
The legs of the right triangle are 5.00 and 12.00,
    so the hypotenuse is 13.00

First leg (0.0 to quit)? 1.75
Second leg (0.0 to quit)? 6.00
The legs of the right triangle are 1.75 and 6.00,
    so the hypotenuse is 6.25

First leg (0.0 to quit)? 0.27
Second leg (0.0 to quit)? 1.23
The legs of the right triangle are 0.27 and 1.23,
    so the hypotenuse is 1.26

First leg (0.0 to quit)? 12
Second leg (0.0 to quit)? 35
The legs of the right triangle are 12.00 and 35.00,
    so the hypotenuse is 37.00

First leg (0.0 to quit)? 0.0
Second leg (0.0 to quit)? 0.0
Thank you.
```

Output 1—1

The Structure of a Simple Program

Program 1-2 is a very simple C program. Before we say anything at all about it, examine it for yourself and try to discover what it does.

```
main ()
{
    printf("Welcome to C programming!\n");
}
```

Program 1—2

Now here is the output that this program produced. It prints out the string of characters enclosed by the double quotation marks (but not the quotes themselves). How close did you come?

```
Welcome to C programming!
```

Output 1—2

If you are familiar with other programming languages, this program may look strange to you. One reason is that almost every character in the program is lowercase. In most other languages, uppercase letters are the rule. So if you come from a background of another high-level language, such as Pascal, you will have to become accustomed to lowercase. You should also remember that C (unlike Pascal) "knows" the difference between uppercase and lowercase letters. Lowercase letters are characteristic of the C language.

C program instructions, like those of Pascal, are written in free format. That is to say, they may appear anywhere on a line. Spacing generally is of no consequence in C, nor are there many restrictions on where to end a line. Program 1-2 could just as easily have been written as follows:

```
main(){printf("Welcome to C programming!\n");}
```

Needless to say, when written in this "scrunched-up" fashion, the program is not very easy to read. But, so far as the C compiler is concerned, the second version is perfectly valid and would produce the same output. Now let us examine the program very carefully.

The first line of Program 1-2 specifies a function (defined for now as a group of program statements) named *main*. This is a special name that is recognized by the system under which C runs: It points to the precise place in the program where execution begins. Every C program must have a *main* function.

The word *main* is followed by a pair of ordinary parentheses. Do not try to use square brackets ([ ]) or even curly braces ({ }). Although these other symbols are used in C, they are not used in this context. In the example, there is nothing enclosed within the parentheses. Later on we shall have much more to say about the significance of any information that may be contained within these parentheses.

Next comes the { symbol, called the left brace or left curly bracket. It matches the right brace, which is located all the way at the end of the *main* function. (It may be interpreted as meaning, "Brace yourself for the function which follows immediately!") The braces enclose the body of the function (that is to say, the statements that form the function). In this case, the body consists of only one statement, the one beginning with *printf*. In a short while, however, we shall be including many statements between the two braces.

The *printf* Function

The *printf* function is used to print out a message, either on screen or paper. (The letter "f" in *printf* could stand for either "formatted" or "function.") It is equivalent to the WRITE statement in Pascal, only more powerful.

The statement between the braces in Program 1-2 specifies that the function called *printf* is to be called into action. In C jargon, we say that the function is *called* (or *invoked*). In this example, the function has a single *literal*, or *character string* as its argument (the value upon which it operates). This string is the sentence contained within the parentheses following the word *printf.* The contents of this string, called the *control string*, are printed out.

Notice that a character string in C is a series of characters written within double quotation marks. These punctuation marks are not actually part of the literal, but serve to delimit it. For this reason, double quotation marks cannot be used directly within a literal, because their presence would confuse the compiler (if not the programmer).

If you need to include double quotes as part of a literal, you must precede it with a backward slash, also called a backslash. This symbol tells the compiler that the quotation marks are part of the string, as in the following example:

```
"He said, \"Hi!\""
```

Notice that the string ends with two double quotation marks. The first is part of the literal, whereas the second serves to delimit it. The backslash itself does not become part of the literal, but merely tells the compiler: "The following mark is *not* a delimiter." (Incidentally, when reading program listings, be sure not to confuse the double quote, which is a single character on the keyboard, with two adjacent apostrophes.)

Please note also that a blank space in a string counts as a character. After all, it is inserted in a program by pressing the space bar.

Unlike Pascal, C restricts the programmer to a single control string in the *printf* statement. That is to say, the statement

```
printf("Oh, ","say ","can ","you ","C?","\n");
```

would *not* work, even though it may look reasonable enough. All the strings except the first would be ignored.

The *newline* Character

In Program 1-2, the control string ends with the symbols \n. These two adjacent symbols together represent the *newline* character. (We will henceforth refer to them as the *newline* character, although strictly speaking, the character and its representation are not the same thing.) Even though the *newline* character is composed of two separate symbols, they are translated by the compiler into a single character.

The *newline* is analogous to a typewriter's carriage return, which advances to the beginning of the next line. The *newline* symbol instructs the computer to advance to the next new line before printing subsequent information. The *printf* function does not do this automatically. Note that the *newline* character is enclosed within the control string.

The *newline* character is an example of an escape sequence in C. We will have much more to say about escape sequences later on. Note the direction of the backslash symbol. C also uses another symbol called the slash (or forward slash). It is very easy to confuse these two symbols, so try to get them straight at the outset.

What do you think would be the result of having a succession of \n characters? You're absolutely right; it would cause blank lines to appear in the output.

The Use of the Semicolon

The end of the *printf* line is denoted by a semicolon. In C, *all* statements are terminated with a semicolon. Novices to C frequently forget to add the semicolon, so be on your guard!

The Use of Braces

The end of the program is marked off by the closing brace, which matches the opening brace we mentioned previously. Notice that these braces line up with the letter *m* of the word *main*. This alignment is not strictly necessary, but it makes the program more readable. A stranger to the program can see quickly what the program does by casting a glance at the contents of the program enclosed within these two braces. Positioning the braces in this way has now become conventional. Notice, too, that the body of the function is indented within the braces. Once again, this makes no difference to the computer or the compiler, but it helps us to read the program more easily.

We shall now expand our horizons and examine a C program containing two *printf* statements (Program 1-3). The first one does not contain the \n symbol. How do you think this will affect the way the output is printed?

```
main()
{
    printf("Give me land, lots of land");
    printf("And the starry skies above...\n");
}
```

Program 1—3

```
Give me land, lots of landAnd the starry skies above...
```

Output 1—3

It is clear that the appearance of the output leaves much to be desired. The output consists of a single line with the last word of the first *printf* statement (*land*) printed alongside the first word (*And*) of the second *printf*. This happened because the control string does not end with the \n symbol in the first *printf* statement. In its absence, the computer assumes that the next piece of information should be printed immediately after the first. To avoid this problem, all that is necessary is to rewrite the first line as follows:

```
printf("Give me land, lots of land\n");
```

As soon as the word *land* is printed, the *newline* character sends the printer to the beginning of the next new line.

An alternative is to place the *newline* character at the beginning of the literal in the second *printf* statement. If this is done, the carriage return is effected before the second literal is printed.

The Use of Comments in a Program

Program 1-4 prints a poem. It also demonstrates the method used in C to add a comment or a helpful remark to a program. This is done by beginning the comment with the two characters /* and ending it with the characters */. No space can be included between the two characters. Between these pairs of characters (delimiters), any characters may be included in either uppercase or lowercase. In other words, a comment appears as follows:

```
/* Whatever you want using any characters at all */
```

The only restriction is that a comment may not contain the closing delimiter */ as part of the comment's text.

All such comments are ignored by the compiler and have no effect on the way the program runs. So why include them at all? Because they serve as an excellent way of internally documenting the program. When a program is printed out, those comments appear along with the program instructions.

Comments may appear anywhere, except within a literal, and they may be of any length. That is to say, a comment may start on the same line as another statement or on a line of its own. It may also extend over any number of lines if the terminating delimiter is placed at the appropriate point. Should the delimiter be omitted, the rest of the program would become one long comment!

A word of caution to Pascal programmers: In Pascal, the curly braces are used to delimit comments. Be careful not to fall back into this habit when writing C programs.

If a general comment is required (for example, one describing the role of the entire program), usually it is placed on a line by itself. If the comment refers to a particular line only, it should be included on the same line as the statement, usually to the right of it. It is not unusual to phrase comments in terms of the instructions that one human being would give another.

Comments may not be essential in a simple program, but in more complex situations they are a veritable lifesaver. For any program, no matter how well written, the day will surely arrive when it must be amended in order to improve it, to allow for changing conditions, or to accommodate some governmental directive. The chances are quite high that the original author of the program will not be present when those changes have to be made. Even the original author may not remember the logic of a program that he wrote several months or years before.

In order to lessen the burden on the person who must amend the program, ample comments should be included at the time when the program is being written. Many programmers are tempted to postpone this obligation until the program has been checked out and passed, but then the task of including the comments is not very attractive.

Some programmers feel that C is such a concise language that every line of code should be accompanied by a comment. Too many comments actually can reduce the readability of the program. Even so, it is better to have too many comments than too few.

```
/* a short poem */

main()
{
    printf("Mary had a little lamb, ");
    printf("its fleece was white as snow.\n");
    printf("And everywhere that Mary went, ");
    printf("the lamb was sure to go.\n");
}
```

Program 1—4

```
Mary had a little lamb, its fleece was white as snow.
And everywhere that Mary went, the lamb was sure to go.
```

Output 1—4

Careful attention should be given to the first and third *printf* statements in Program 1-4. Notice that a space has been included at the end of those literals, so that when the lines are printed they will be correctly spaced.

You have now seen some elementary programs. Before long, we shall be examining more interesting ones, but first we have to become acquainted with some of the "nuts and bolts" of the C language. Among the most important of these are variables and the assignment statement, both of which are discussed in the next chapter.

The Spirit of C

This feature is included at the end of each chapter. Its purpose is to illustrate the material just covered, by demonstrating the solution of a realistic programming problem.

Suppose you were given the following text:

```
The rain in
Spain  stays

mainly on the
plain.
```

Your task is to devise a program that will display this text exactly as written, including the two spaces between the words *Spain* and *stays*.

Clearly, the program will consist of one or more *printf* statements. Theoretically, a whole page of text could be displayed with a single *printf* statement, but your compiler may impose limits on how long the control string may be. The limiting factor is the maximum length of a line for the compiler, because a string cannot extend over more than one line. For now, however, let us assume that the preceding text can fit into a single literal.

Remember that the number of lines displayed is determined not by how many *printf* statements are used, but by how many *newline* characters appear in the control string. The two statements

```
printf("The");
printf("rain");
```

will print only one line, namely

```
Therain
```

because neither of the statements contains a *newline* character. (Because no spaces are included either, the two words are joined into one.) The *printf* function in C enables the programmer to display a single line of text by using two or more printing statements, without having to resort to special carriage control symbols. By contrast, the single statement:

```
printf("The\nrain");
```

prints two lines:

```
The
rain
```

The *newline* character (\n) between the words *The* and *rain* causes a carriage return at this point.

In order to construct a control string to display a given text, it is necessary to place the *newline* characters correctly. Look at this text again:

```
The rain in
Spain  stays

mainly on the
plain.
```

Now mark the end of each line with a *newline* character. If a line is blank, it is marked with a *newline* character in the first position:

```
The rain in\n
Spain  stays\n
\n
mainly on the\n
plain.\n
```

The last line also is terminated by a *newline* character. This ensures that any text printed subsequently will begin on a new line, not on the same line that contains the word *plain*. The lines may now be linked together into a single control string and used in a *printf* statement:

```
printf("The rain in\nSpain  stays\n\nmainly on the\nplain.\n");
```

Notice that the text is written exactly as originally shown, including the two spaces between *Spain* and *stays*. It is important that the control string contain the same number of blank spaces which appears in the text.

The literal in the preceding statement can be split into two or more literals at any point (except, of course, between the \ and the n in the *newline* character, since they have meaning only when they are together). The text could be displayed just as well with the following statements:

```
printf("The rain in\nSpain");
printf("  stays\n\nmainly on the\nplain.\n");
```

or

```
printf("The rain");
printf(" in\nSpain  stays\n\nmainly ");
printf("on the\nplain.\n");
```

or even the more unsightly

```
printf("The ");      printf("rain ");    printf("in");    printf("\n");
printf("Spain  ");    printf("stays");    printf("\n");    printf("\n");
printf("mainly ");    printf("on ");      printf("the");   printf("\n);
printf("plain.");     printf("\n");
```

Notice that the spaces between the words are placed carefully in the literals, even when each word is in a separate *printf* statement. Clearly, such divisions can become confusing. The best policy is to place each line of text in a separate *printf* statement. This placement not only makes for more clarity but also assures that no control string will be too long:

```
printf("The rain in\n");
printf("Spain  stays\n");
printf("\nmainly on the\n");
printf("plain.\n");
```

The blank line after the second line of text was not given its own *printf* statement. Instead, the *newline* character that produces the blank line was placed at the beginning of the following line of text (before the word *mainly*) to indicate that the line is double-spaced relative to the previous line (the one starting with *Spain*).

You may, of course, exercise your own judgment in devising rules on how to split a literal. For example, you may think it better to include the double-spacing *newline* character in its own statement, as shown here:

```
printf("The rain in\n");
printf("Spain  stays\n");
printf("\n");
printf("mainly on the\n");
printf("plain.\n");
```

Remember that the most important goal is clarity.

The final step is to place the *printf* statements within the standard program "shell," along with an appropriate comment, and you are done:

```
/* Display the following text:
     The rain in
     Spain  stays

     mainly on the
     plain.
*/

main()
{
    printf("The rain in\n");
    printf("Spain  stays\n");
    printf("\nmainly on the\n");
    printf("plain.\n");
}
```

C Tutorial

1. What delimiters are used to specify the beginning and end of a literal (character string) in C?

2. What is the character string in a *printf* statement usually called?

3. What symbol terminates every C statement?

4. What delimiters are used to specify the beginning and end of a group of instructions to be executed?

5. How is the *newline* character formed?

6. What is the effect of executing the following statement?

```
printf("alpha\n\nbeta\n\ngamma\n"
```

7. What symbols are used to specify a comment?

8. What does one use to print out a literal?

9. What is the purpose of including comments in a program?

10. May comments extend beyond a single line?

11. Study the following C program carefully. It is possible you will detect some errors. Find them and state the reasons why they are in error.

```
mane{}  \* this is one grait program; stand buy... /*
(
        print('I think I am getting the hang of it./n')
```

12. What is printed by the following segments of C code:

```
(a) printf("Going, one, \ntwo,\nthree.\n");
(b) printf("An apple a day keeps the doctor\n");
    printf("\n\n\n                away.\n");
```

13. What is wrong with the following statement?

```
printf("c","o","m","p","u","t","e","r","\n");
```

14. What symbol cannot be used as part of a literal?

ANSWERS TO C TUTORIAL

1. Double quotation marks.

2. The control string.

3. The semicolon.

4. The left and right braces, { and }.

5. By the two adjacent symbols \ and n.

6. It prints these three lines, double-spaced:

alpha

beta

gamma

7. The /* symbol pair, followed by the comment and then terminated with */ .

8. The *printf* function.

9. To document the program internally.

10. Yes; they may be as long as you like.

11. The program is, of course, replete with errors. They are:
    (a) The word *main* is incorrectly spelled.
    (b) Parentheses should be used instead of braces after the word *main*.
    (c) The wrong slash symbol is used in the first comment symbol.
    (d) The spelling of the words *great* and *by* in the literal leaves something to be desired, but the computer gladly accepts this spelling.
    (e) The characters comprising the terminating comment symbols are reversed.
    (f) The body of the program should commence with a left brace, not a left parenthesis.
    (g) The function should be spelled *printf*, not *print*.
    (h) The literal should be delimited by double quotation marks, not by apostrophes.
    (i) The *newline* symbol has the wrong type of slash.
    (j) The terminating semicolon is missing from the *printf* statement.
    (k) The final right brace is missing.

12. (a) Going, one,
        two,
        three.
    (b) An apple a day keeps the doctor

                          away.

13. There can be only one control string in a *printf* statement. All but the first literal will be ignored.

14. Double quotation marks, because this symbol is used as the delimiter of a literal.

Exercises

1. Write a program that prints your name and address.

2. Write a program that prints any four-line poem (double-spaced).

3. Write a program to display the following text:

```
Mary had a
    Little lamb,
    Little lamb,
    Little lamb,
Mary had a little lamb,
And then she had
    Dessert.
```

4. What output is produced by the following program?

```
main()
{
    printf("    *\n      *\n");
    printf("  *   *  *\n*    ***     *\n");
    printf("*           *\n *         *\n");
    printf("    *****\n");
}
```

5. Using the principles of "typewriter art," write a C program consisting of a series of printf instructions to draw the following picture of the Big Dipper:

```
        *       *               *
    *
                        *           *
      *
```

6. Decide what the output of the following program will be, and then run it on a computer to confirm your answer:

```
main()
{
    printf("He who\n");
    printf("laughs last\nlasts\n");
    printf("last.\n");
}
```

2

An Introduction to Declarations, Assignments and Variables

Now *that you have seen some elementary C programs that print out character strings, it is time to explore the manner in which numeric information is handled.*

The Concept of an Integer

C deals with several different kinds of numbers. One of the most frequently used is the whole number, usually called an *integer*. The integer is one of the basic data types in C. It is characterized by the fact that it does not have either a decimal point or a fractional portion. Here are some examples of integer numbers:

123   -34   0   345   -57   98

A number such as 13.6 is not considered to be an integer, because it contains a decimal point. Such a number is described as *floating point* or *real*, a subject we shall cover very soon. (A number such as 15. or 15.0 also is considered a floating point number, even though its fractional part is zero. The critical consideration is whether the number contains a decimal point, regardless of what follows it.) Like Pascal, C makes a definite distinction between integer and floating point numbers.

The Concept of a Variable

Strings and numeric values can be stored in the memory of the computer for subsequent recall. Whenever the memory is used for this purpose, the programmer must assign a unique name to each such area in memory. If the arbitrary name *number* is used to refer to the area of memory in which a particular value is stored, *number* is called a *variable*. Variable names are used in a program in much the same way as they are in ordinary algebra.

In order to appreciate the significance of variables, consider for a moment the following instruction:

```
printf("%d", 23 + 17);
```

When this instruction is executed, the sum of 23 and 17 is calculated and displayed. (The %d following the left parenthesis is known as the *conversion specification*. Its role is to specify that the number is to be converted to decimal notation before being printed. We will discuss this later on.)

Once the sum is printed out, it is lost from the computer's memory. Should the need arise to evaluate the same expression again, both computer time and human effort would be wasted, because the same calculation would have to be programmed again. A better approach is to store the result in the computer's memory, from which it can be recalled as often as needed. Most programs use many memory locations, represented by variable names, for precisely this reason.

Declaring an Integer Variable

In C each variable used in a program must be *declared*. That is to say, the program must contain a statement specifying precisely what kind of information the variable will contain. This applies to every variable in the program, regardless of the type. The declaration statement is important in C because it helps to avoid many different types of errors.

If we wish to use the variable *number* to store an integer value, we must declare that *number* is of the type **int**. The abbreviated word **int** is one of about 30 *keywords* in C. These keywords appear and must always be typed in lowercase. (Keywords are reserved names that may never be used as variable names. More will be said about them later.)

The keyword **int** must always be written as shown in the following example. The full spelling, *integer*, is not allowed as a substitute and will cause an error.

```
int number;
```

In this example, *number* is the name of the variable that is declared to be of type **int**. Such a declaration is placed after the opening brace of the *main* function. All declarations must come before the first executable (non-declaration) statement of the program.

Later on, you will learn about data types other than integers. All types of variables in C must be declared before they are used. This is not an arbitrary decision on the part of the designers of the language. On the contrary, it was designed to assist the programmer. Here are some of the reasons:

1. It is good programming practice to collect all the variables used in a program together, so that a reader of the program can see its ingredients at a glance.
2. Requiring the programmer to declare the variables ahead of time often encourages him to refine his thinking about the logic used in the program.
3. If a variable is incorrectly spelled at some point in the program, the undeclared spelling will be flagged as an error, thus enabling the programmer to find and correct it. Otherwise, he might never be aware of the problem and the program could produce wrong results.
4. Declaring variables prevents the accidental or sloppy use of one variable type where another was intended.
5. As you will learn later on, declaring variables allows the programmer to conserve memory space.

The Rules for Naming Variables

The rules for naming variables are very simple:

1. Variable names must begin with a letter of the alphabet. In C, the underscore character (_) is considered a letter. It is legal to start a variable name with the underscore character, but this practice is discouraged to prevent possible conflict

with some special system names that begin with the underscore.

2. The first character may be followed by a sequence of letters and/or digits (0 through 9).

3. On most microcomputers, the first seven or eight characters (depending upon the version of C) of the name must be unique. That is, no other variable used in the program may begin with the same seven or eight characters. If it does, it will be treated as the same name and the program may produce questionable results. For example, the names *variable1* and *variable2* would not be distinguished by such compilers.

4. The compiler regards uppercase and lowercase letters as different, although both may be used in constructing variable names. Therefore, the variable names *NET*, *net*, and *Net* are regarded as three separate variables in C. Usually, however, variable names in C are entirely in lowercase.

5. No variable name may be a keyword. This rule means we cannot give a variable a reserved name such as *int*.

6. No special characters, such as a blank space, period, semicolon, comma, or slash, are permitted in variable names. (Remember that the underscore is not considered to be a special character in C.)

Here are some examples of valid variable names:

grosspay   *count*   *total*   *PI*   *average*   *top_value*

Now here are some invalid variable names. The reason why each is invalid is written beside the name.

Variable	Why it's invalid
int	keyword
1986TAX	begins with a numeric character
#profit	must begin with an alphabetic character
period.	contains a period
bad name	contains a space

Guidelines for Selecting Variable Names

When selecting variable names, you should observe certain guidelines that are regarded as good programming practice. (Of course, you must also follow the rules listed in the previous section.)

First, the name should be chosen to be descriptive of the role that the variable is designed to play. For example, if two values are to be added and their result stored, the variable containing the result might be called *sum*. Naming it *s* is not a good idea, because this could stand for just about anything.

It requires a certain amount of discipline to take the trouble to name the variables appropriately. If a computation calls for the calculation of an average, for instance, it would be foolhardy to name it something like *xyz123*, even though the computer wouldn't complain. (The programmer who might have to modify the program later might complain, though.) The purpose of naming a variable is to select a name that transmits as much information as possible to a reader of the program. Most good programmers simply resort to sound common sense.

Finally, it is best to avoid using the letter *O* in situations where it can be confused with the number 0. Such names as *LOGO* and *SOLO* should be avoided, because it is not clear that they are different from *LOG0* and *S0L0*. Similarly, the lowercase letter *l* can be mistaken for the number 1 and vice versa. (The lowercase 1 and the number 1 are two different keys on a computer keyboard.)

The Assignment Statement

The next program (Program 2-1) declares the variable *number* to be of type **int** and then assigns the number 7 to it. The latter operation requires an assignment statement, which has the following general format:

```
variable = expression;
```

The assignment statement is one of the basic building blocks of C. For example, the statement

```
number = 7;
```

assigns the value 7 to the variable *number*. By this we mean that the integer 7 is stored in the memory of the computer under the symbolic name *number*.

Notice that the variable named appears to the left of the equal sign, which is called the *assignment operator*. Assignment is a dynamic instruction; that is, it has the effect of changing the value of a variable. An assignment statement should not be read as if it were a simple algebraic statement of equality. Instead, it means: Take the value on the right side of the equal sign (in this case, 7) and store it in the variable specified on the left side of the equal sign.

If the expression on the right were 7 + 8, the computer would evaluate the expression, reduce it to the single number 15, and then store this result into the variable called *number*. Only one variable name may appear to the left of the equal sign. A statement such as

```
a + b = c;
```

which makes good sense from the point of view of algebra, is unacceptable in C.

Before proceeding further, we suggest that you examine Program 2-1 and its output. Then we shall discuss some of the other features it contains.

```
/* An introduction to variable declarations */

main()
{
  int number;

  number = 7;
  printf("There are %d days in a week.\n", number);
}
```

Program 2—1

```
There are 7 days in a week.
```

Output 2—1

After the opening brace, the variable named *number* is declared to be of type **int**. (This is the first statement in the body of the *main* function.) First the word **int** is specified, and then the variable name is written to its right. As is usual in C, the declaration statement (like other statements) is terminated by a semicolon. Then some white space (a blank line) is left so that the program is more legible. C encourages the use of white space to highlight specific parts of the program and its output, as well as to enhance the appearance of the program.

The second statement of the body of the *main* function is the assignment statement, which assigns the integer value 7 to *number*. Next comes the familiar *printf* statement which, this time, contains the characters %d. This is a composite symbol known as the *conversion specification*. These symbols mean that the value of the integer variable *number* which appears after the comma at the end of the statement, is to be converted to decimal (base 10) and inserted at the position within the literal where the symbols %d appear. Study this program carefully until you become used to the manner in which values are printed.

In Program 2-2, two variables are declared to be integers and there are two assignment statements. In order to declare two variables to be integers, you can write either two separate declarations or just one. The example has a single declaration, with the two variables separated by a comma. In other words, the two declarations

```
int minutes;
int hours;
```

act in exactly the same way as does the single declaration

```
int minutes, hours;
```

where the two variables, *minutes* and *hours*, are separated by a comma.

```
/* A simple program with two declarations */

main ()
{
  int minutes, hours;

  minutes = 60;
  hours = 24;

  printf("There are %d minutes in an hour.\n", minutes);
  printf("And %d hours in a day.\n", hours);

}
```

Program 2—2

```
There are 60 minutes in an hour.
And 24 hours in a day.
```

Output 2—2

In Program 2-2, you will notice that each of the *printf* statements commences with a string of characters (the control string), followed by a comma and the appropriate variable name.

In contrast, Program 2-3 is an example of how you should *not* write programs in C, even though there is really nothing wrong with the syntax. The compiler gladly accepts it and produces the correct results, but it is somewhat difficult to read.

```
/* How NOT to write a program */

main () { int year; year = 365
;
printf(
"There are %d days in a year.\n",
year)
;}
```

Program 2—3

```
There are 365 days in a year.
```

Output 2—3

As the final example in this chapter, Program 2-4 uses a variable to hold the result of a simple calculation. In the statement

```
units = dozens * 12;
```

the asterisk (*) is the symbol used in C to represent multiplication.

```
/* Prints values of two variables */

main()
{
  int units, dozens;

  dozens = 17;
  units = dozens * 12;

  printf("%d units is equivalent to %d dozen.\n", units, dozens);

}
```

Program 2—4

```
204 units is equivalent to 17 dozen.
```

Output 2—4

You will notice that this *printf* statement contains two conversion specifications within the control string. This is because we want to print out the values stored in the two variables, *units* and *dozens*, using a single *printf*. Both variable names must also be listed at the end of the *printf* statement. The variable names must be separated from each other and from the control string by commas.

The first listed variable (*units*) is associated with the first %d, and is therefore printed at the beginning of the line, whereas the second variable (*dozens*) is associated with the second conversion specification. Thus there is a one-to-one correspondence between conversion specifications and the variable names associated with them, as illustrated in Figure 2-1.

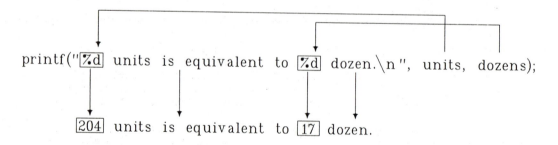

Figure 2—1

So far, we have seen the control string of the *printf* function used for two purposes: (1) as a literal to be printed out as written, and (2) as the location of conversion specifications. The contents of the control string are scanned from left to right by the *printf* function. As each regular character is encountered, it is printed out as written. When a conversion specification is found, the contents of the next variable in the list following the control string are printed out in accordance with the conversion specification. The scan of the control string is then resumed. Thus the control string is like an image of the line to be printed, with the positions in which variables are to be printed, marked by appropriate conversion specifications.

The ability to combine text and variable values in a line of output should be used to advantage by the programmer. The text should clearly describe the meanings of the displayed values, in a way that is clear to the user of the program. A program that spews out a bunch of numbers with no explanation is of little use to anyone; even the author of the program may forget the meaning of each number. Later on, when we show how a user can supply data interactively to a running program, you will see how necessary it is for instructions displayed by the program to be crystal clear.

The Four Arithmetic Operators

In C the four major arithmetic operations are those of addition, subtraction, multiplication and division. Each of the four arithmetic operators is sometimes called a *binary* operator because it operates on two terms or values at a time.

Addition is represented by the plus sign (+), subtraction by the minus sign (-), multiplication by the asterisk or star (*), and division by the slash (/). This slash is not the same symbol as we used for the *newline* character; that was the backslash, which slants in the opposite direction. The asterisk is used for multiplication because the letter x could easily be confused with a variable named x, and the period or dot could be confused with the decimal point.

These four symbols, +, -, *, and /, are used by the vast majority of computer languages. Like Pascal, C has no symbol for exponentiation. This operation can be coded by the programmer.

Here are some C statements using the arithmetic operators:

```
inches = 12 * feet;         /* Multiply variable feet by 12,
                               assigning result to inches */
miles = feet / 5280;        /* Divide variable feet by 5280,
                               assigning result to miles */
printf("%d\n", 12 * 16);    /* Display the product of
                               12 and 16 */
smaller = larger - 17;      /* Subtract 17 from larger,
                               assigning result to smaller */
distance = first_leg + second_leg;
                            /* Add variable first_leg to
                               second_leg, assigning result
                               to distance */
printf("%d\n", sum / items);
                            /* Divide sum by items,
                               displaying the result */
```

We will be talking a lot more about arithmetic operations in the next chapter.

You might have noticed that, whenever we have used an arithmetic operator, we have added a space both before and after it. This is not to satisfy any demand of the language, but rather to make it look more appealing to the eye. In C there is almost never any need for a space to appear anywhere, except to separate a keyword from a variable name (as in **int** *number;*).

In C, there is no such thing as implied multiplication; the asterisk has to be included at all times. If you wish to multiply together the variables *x,* *y,* and *z,* you must include two multiplication operators: $x * y * z$. The computer would take the expression xyz to mean the single variable name *xyz.*

Now that you have been introduced to the integer, the variable, and four basic arithmetic operators, it is time to study these areas in greater depth in the next chapter.

The Spirit of C ∎

In C, as in most other computer languages, an arithmetic expression or calculation is written differently from standard algebraic notation. We covered the arithmetic operators and the topic of implied multiplication in the preceding section.

An advantage that programming languages such as C have over algebra is that variables can be given meaningful names. Algebra requires that variables be indicated by single-letter identifiers, with textual explanations provided to clarify the meaning of each variable. C's variable naming abilities are helpful, however, only if you use them.

When converting an algebraic formula to C, do not use the single-letter names, but give the variables descriptive names where possible. In this text, single-letter variable names sometimes are employed in the illustrations for the sake of simplicity, if the quantities contained in the variables have no special meaning other than that they are numbers. In real-life programming situations, however, it is more important to choose variable names carefully.

Suppose you are given the following algebraic formula and are asked to convert it to a C assignment statement:

```
d = st
```

where s = speed of travel, t = elapsed time, and d = distance covered. The rules of algebra say that the right hand side of the equation, *st*, means "s multiplied by t." But there is no implied multiplication in C, so you must insert the multiplication operator:

```
d = s * t
```

The next step is to give the variables better names. The following are good selections:

```
distance = speed * time
```

Finally, don't forget the semicolon!

```
distance = speed * time;
```

Now, suppose you had to include this statement in a complete program. First you would place the statement within a *main* function:

```
main()
{
    distance = speed * time;
}
```

The most important thing to do next is to declare all your variables:

```
main()
{
    int speed, time, distance;

    distance = speed * time;
}
```

This would also be a good time to begin adding comments. Although they are not crucial to the successful execution of the program, they are an important part of good programming style. Furthermore, it is easier to put in the comments as you code the program rather than after the entire program has been completed.

```
main()
{
    int speed,       /* Speed of travel in miles per hour */
        time,        /* Elapsed time in hours */
        distance;    /* Distance covered in miles (result) */

    distance = speed * time;   /* Distance is equal to speed
                                  multiplied by time */

}
```

The last comment may be unnecessary, because it does not provide any information beyond what the C code states.

Next, values must be assigned to the variable *speed* and *time*, in order for there to be something with which to perform calculations (this is known as *initialization*):

```
main()
{
    int speed,       /* Speed of travel in miles per hour */
        time,        /* Elapsed time in hours */
        distance;    /* Distance covered in miles (result) */

    speed = 10;      /* 10 MPH */
    time = 3;        /* Travel for 3 hours */
    distance = speed * time;   /* Distance is equal to speed
                                  multiplied by time */

}
```

Finally, an appropriate *printf* statement is added, and the program is finished:

```
main()
{
    int speed,        /* Speed of travel in miles per hour */
        time,         /* Elapsed time in hours */
        distance;     /* Distance covered in miles (result) */

    speed = 10;       /* 10 MPH */
    time = 3;         /* Travel for 3 hours */
    distance = speed * time;   /* Distance is equal to speed
                                  multiplied by time */

    printf("Traveling at %d MPH for %d hours\n", speed, time);
    printf("    covers %d miles.\n", distance);
}
```

Notice that the first *printf* statement, which displays the values of *speed* and *time*, contains those variables within its parentheses. It would not be correct to place all three variables at the end of the second *printf* statement, unless that statement contained all three corresponding conversion specifications in its control string.

C *Tutorial*

1. What is an integer?

2. What is a variable?

3. What is the form of the assignment statement?

4. In order to store the result of a computation, what kind of statement must be used?

5. Why is the assignment statement regarded as dynamic?

6. How many variables may appear on the left of the equal sign in an assignment statement?

7. Which of the following variable names are valid in C?

   (a) bingo   (b) accts_payable   (c) total-revenue
   (d) ANNUAL REPORT   (e) acc'ts

8. What are the rules for the naming of variables?

9. What purpose is served by including white space in a program?

10. Comment briefly on the following assignment statement:
x + y = z;

11. What is the output produced by the following program segment?

```
int x;
x = 1;
x = 2;
x = 3;
printf("%d %d %d\n",x,x,x);
```

12. What is printed by the following program?

```
main()
    {
    int a, b, c;
    a = 4;
    b = a * 7;
    c = a + b;
    }
```

ANSWERS TO C TUTORIAL

1. It is a whole number; one without a decimal point.

2. It is a symbolic name for a memory location in which a value is stored.

3. variable = expression;

4. The assignment statement.

5. Because during execution of the program, the expression to the right of the equal sign is reduced to a single number which is then stored in the variable specified on the left.

6. Only one.

7. (a) and (b) only.

8. They must begin with a letter (including the underscore), may contain only letters and digits, may not include any special characters, may not be a keyword, and the first eight characters or so (depending upon the implementation) must be unique.

9. It highlights program statements and output, and makes the program listing easier to read.

10. It is invalid because in an assignment statement only one variable may appear to the left of the equal sign.

11. 3 3 3
[The variable x is first set equal to 1, then 2 and finally 3. This final value, 3, is printed three times.]

12. Nothing is printed, because the program does not include any statement (such as *printf*) to cause output to be displayed.

Exercises

1. Anticipate the results of the following program, and then run it on a computer to verify your prediction.

```
main()
{
    int a;
    a = 1;
    a = 2;
    a = 3;
    printf("%d %d %d\n", a, a, a);
}
```

2. Using the arithmetic operators provided in C, write a program that declares and assigns values to the variables *a*, *b*, and *c*, and then does the following:

   a. halves the value of *a*.
   b. doubles *b*.
   c. multiplies *c* by itself.
   d. prints out the results of the preceding operations.

3. Suppose you had to write a program to compute the volume of a cube. The values you would need are the three dimensions of the cube. Think up four appropriate variable names to be used in this program - three variables to hold the three dimensions, and one for the result. (You do not need to write the program, but nobody will stop you if you feel like taking a crack at it.)

4. Examine the following program, which is designed to calculate the distance covered by a car traveling at a certain speed for a given time:

```
main()
{
    int bingo, schmingo, zingo;

    bingo = 55;
    schmingo = 2;

    zingo = bingo * schmingo;
    printf("%d, %d, %d\n", bingo,
            schmingo, zingo);
}
```

Criticize this program and amend it appropriately. Points to look for are appropriate variable names, comments, and a meaningful display of the results.

5. The following program computes the perimeter of a rectangle. Add appropriate comments.

```
main()
{
    int length, width, perimeter;

    length = 13;
    width = 52;
    perimeter = 2 * length + 2 * width;

    printf("The perimeter of a rectangle with\n");
    printf("  length = %d and width = %d is %d\n",
                    length, width, perimeter);
}
```

3

Integer Arithmetic Expressions

Computers are renowned for their ability to calculate accurately and at phenomenal speed. They handle arithmetic calculations so efficiently that they are often referred to by the term "number-crunchers." In this chapter you will begin to learn how the computer manages its integer calculations.

The Combined Declaration— Initialization Statement

You have already seen how integer values are declared. C provides a neat way to combine a declaration with an assignment. For example, if the integer variable *a* is to have an initial value of 2, the combined statement is as follows:

```
int a = 2;
```

This single statement is equivalent to the two separate statements

```
int a;
a = 2;
```

It is not sufficient to declare a variable before it is used. The variable must also be initialized; that is to say, it must be given a value. The C compiler does not automatically place the value 0 in each variable when it is created. As we have just shown, both declaration and initialization can be accomplished by a single statement.

The initializing value in a combined declaration-initialization may be virtually any C expression. Both of the following declarations are valid:

```
int i = 2 * 3;
int j = 5 / (4 - 2);
```

The expression may contain references to other variables that have been previously declared and initialized. For example, the following statements are valid if written in the order specified:

```
int i = 7;
int j = i + 1;
```

If these two statements were reversed, however, the first statement would *not* be valid. The reason is that it refers to the variable *i* which must itself be initialized before it can be referred to in an initialization statement.

The Truncation Effect of Integer Division

In Program 3-1, the integer variables *a*, *b*, and *c* are initialized to 2, 3, and 4 respectively. Another integer variable, *answer*, is declared and its value is computed within the program. Four arithmetic operations are carried out, and the result of each is stored in *answer* and then printed.

If you carefully scrutinize the output produced by the program, you will agree with the first three answers but not with the fourth. The computer has printed 0 as the result of dividing 2 by 3, whereas we know full well that this isn't so.

Did the computer make a mistake?

```
/* An introduction to arithmetic */

main ()
{

  int a = 2, b = 3, c = 4, answer;


  answer = a + b;
  printf("a + b = %d\n",answer);

  answer = a - b;
  printf("a - b = %d\n",answer);

  answer = a * b;
  printf("a * b = %d\n",answer);

  answer = a / b;
  printf("a / b = %d\n",answer);

}
```

Program 3—1

```
a + b = 5
a - b = -1
a * b = 6
a / b = 0
```

Output 3—1

If you were to divide 2 by 3 on an ordinary pocket calculator, you would get the answer 0.6666667. In C, however, when one integer is divided by another integer, the result is also displayed as an integer. Any fractional part is discarded. Therefore, instead of printing 0.6666667, this program prints out only the integer portion, 0.

This process is called *truncation*. (Pascal programmers will recognize this as the result of using the DIV operator.) Sometimes truncation leads to horrendous errors, as it did in this case, but at other times it is very helpful.

For example, suppose we wanted to know whether a certain integer number was odd or even. (It is surprising how often this determination becomes necessary in computer programming.) We could simply divide that number by 2 and then multiply it by 2. Dividing an even number by 2 and multiplying it by 2 should return the original number. If the number is odd, however, dividing it by 2 and then multiplying it by 2 will *not* yield the original number, because dividing an odd number by 2 truncates the result.

The Relative Priority of the Arithmetic Operators

In Program 3-2, variables *a*, *b*, and *c* again are initialized to 2, 3, and 4 respectively. This time the program evaluates the expression a + b * c. This is a simple calculation, but the answer depends upon the sequence in which the arithmetic operations are performed. If the addition is done first, the answer is 5 * 4 = 20. If the multiplication comes first, then the answer is 2 + 12 = 14.

```
/* Illustration of mathematical hierarchy */

main()
{
  int a = 2, b = 3, c = 4, answer;

  answer = a + b * c;

  printf("a = %d, b = %d, c = %d\n", a, b ,c);
  printf("a + b * c = %d\n", answer);

}
```

Program 3—2

```
a = 2, b = 3, c = 4
a + b * c = 14
```

Output 3—2

Any computer language must have rules to determine which operation comes first. In C, multiplication and division are done before addition and subtraction. Therefore, the correct answer in this case is 14. The rules of precedence will be explained further in the next section.

The Use of Parentheses

Multiplication and division have the same precedence; so do addition and subtraction. If operators of the same precedence level appear in one expression, the order in which they are evaluated depends on their associativity (see Appendix A). To avoid this consideration, however, you are always free to surround any part of an expression with parentheses in order to override the hierarchy. Whatever is contained within the parentheses will be evaluated first, before the terms outside the parentheses. (Of course, whatever is within the parentheses will be evaluated in the order described above.)

Parentheses may also be nested; that is to say, one set may contain another set. In this case, the contents of the innermost set are evaluated first, and then the process continues to the outer parentheses. It is perfectly acceptable to use redundant parentheses if they help to make the expression more meaningful. Whenever parentheses are used, however, be sure that there are as many left parentheses as right.

In Program 3-3, which reinforces the concept of operator precedence, the three variables *a*, *b*, and *c* are initialized to 5, 10, and 15 respectively. Four separate calculations are performed on these values, and each time the result is printed out. When you examine the program, cover up the printed output and try to come to your own conclusion as to what it should look like.

You will find that the division in the expression a + b / c is done first, because division (as well as multiplication) has a higher precedence than addition. By this process, 5 + 10 / 15 reduces to 5 + 0 (because of the truncation effect) and then finally to 5, the answer returned by the program.

In the second expression, b * c - a, there are no surprises. The multiplication is evaluated before the subtraction.

The third expression, a * b / c, includes both multiplication and division (which have the same priority level). The calculation proceeds from left to right, but truncation takes place in the division operation. The expression goes from 5 * 10 / 15 to 50 / 15, and from there it is reduced to 3 because of truncation.

Finally, in the last case, (a + c) * b / a, the contents of the parentheses are evaluated first. After (5 + 15) has been reduced to the single number 20, it is multiplied by 10, producing 200. Finally, 200 is divided by 5 to yield the answer of 40. In this instance, no truncation takes place because 200 is evenly divisible by 5.

```
/* A more advanced illustration of mathematical hierarchy */

main()
{
  int a = 5, b = 10, c = 15, answer;

  answer = a + b / c;
  printf("%d + %d / %d = %d\n", a, b, c, answer);

  answer = b * c - a;
  printf("%d * %d - %d = %d\n", b, c, a, answer);

  answer = a * b / c;
  printf("%d * %d / %d = %d\n", a, b, c, answer);

  answer = (a + c) * b / a;
  printf("(%d + %d) * %d / %d = %d\n", a, c, b, a, answer);

}
```

Program 3—3

```
5 + 10 / 15 = 5
10 * 15 - 5 = 145
5 * 10 / 15 = 3
(5 + 15) * 10 / 5 = 40
```

Output 3—3

The Modulus Operator

The modulus operator is not available in all languages, although it also is supported by Pascal. In C the modulus operator is specified by the percent sign, %, the same symbol that we have been using as part of the conversion specification for the *printf* function. The percent sign serves both functions in C.

The modulus operator behaves as illustrated in the following example. If the integer 18 is divided by the integer 4, the result is 4 with a remainder of 2. The modulus is nothing other than the remainder. This binary operator is written as in the following example:

```
18 % 4
```

and is read as "18 modulo 4" or "18 mod 4." The modulus operator is restricted to integer quantities, so don't be tempted to use it with other data types. This operator can be useful, for example, in determining if a number is odd.

In Program 3-4, a single statement declares the integer variables a, b, and c and initializes them to the values 4, 8, and 13 respectively. The first *printf* statement evaluates the expression 8 % 4. Since 8 is exactly divisible by 4, the remainder (modulus) is 0, and the result that is printed is 0. The second calculation is 13 % 4. This yields the result 1, because when 13 is divided by 4 there is a remainder of 1. The result of 13 % 8 is 5, because when the division of 13 by 8 is performed, there is a remainder of 5.

You might well be wondering how the symbol % itself can be printed, should the need arise. The answer is simple — just follow it immediately with another % symbol. Two adjacent % signs are printed as a single %. This is confirmed by the last line of Output 3-4, in which no calculation is performed; just the symbol % is printed out.

With respect to its precedence level, the modulus operator is on the same level as the multiplication and division operators. Thus an expression such as

```
alpha + beta % gamma
```

is evaluated as though it were written

```
alpha + (beta % gamma)
```

The modulus operator does not work the same on all machines for the case in which one or both of the operands is negative. The difference will occur in the sign of the result. Check the manual for your particular compiler, or experiment with a test program, before using the modulus operator with negative values.

```
/* Illustration of the modulus operator */

main()
{
  int a = 4, b = 8, c = 13;

  printf("%d mod %d = %d\n", b, a, b % a);
  printf("%d mod %d = %d\n", c, a, c % a);
  printf("%d mod %d = %d\n", c, b, c % b);

  printf("The modulus operator is: %%\n");

}
```

Program 3—4

```
8 mod 4 = 0
13 mod 4 = 1
13 mod 8 = 5
The modulus operator is: %
```

Output 3—4

The Unary Minus Operator

Before you leave this chapter, you should become acquainted with the notion of the unary minus sign. The minus sign is nothing new to us. We have used it many times already, as a binary operator. But the minus sign may also be used as a unary operator, as in the following examples:

```
-3    -14    -123    -17
```

In each case, the value of the number is negated. Just as a number can be preceded by a minus sign, so can a variable. If the variable *net* has been set to the value 1000,

```
flip = -net;
```

assigns the value -1000 to the variable *flip*. It is equivalent to multiplying the value of *net* by -1.

Of all the arithmetic operators, the unary minus has the highest precedence level. Thus in an expression such as

```
z = w + x * -y;
```

evaluation commences with the unary minus, which negates the value of *y*. Then *x* is multiplied by -*y*, and finally the addition takes place. The resulting value is stored in the variable *z*. Incidentally, many programmers would recommend the use of parentheses to separate the two adjacent operators and avoid possible confusion:

```
z = w + x * (-y);
```

In Program 3-5, the three variables *a*, *b*, and *c* initially are set to -4, 5, and -6 respectively. Within the program, each of these values is negated by the unary minus and the new values are then printed out. The unary minus operator can be applied to negative values; that is to say, the expression --5 is equivalent to 5, and ---5 is the same as -5. If the variable *q* contains the value -23, the expression -*q* results in the positive value 23.

```
/* Illustration of the unary minus */

main()
{
  int a = -4, b = 5, c = -6;

  printf("a = %d, b = %d, c = %d\n\n\n",a, b, c);
  printf("      and now\n\n\n");

  a = -a;
  b = -b;
  c = -c;

  printf("a = %d, b = %d, c = %d\n\n\n",a, b, c);

}
```

Program 3—5

```
a = -4, b = 5, c = -6


      and now


a = 4, b = -5, c = 6
```

Output 3—5

We mentioned earlier that C permits variables to be of several different types. So far, we have described the **int** type in detail. The next chapter covers some of the other types, giving special attention to floating point numbers. Much of the material that we have covered with respect to integer variables applies equally to the other types of variables that are found in C.

The Spirit of C

The hierarchy of operators is of paramount concern not just in C, but in all programming languages. In C, there are more operators available to the programmer than in some other languages, so the issue assumes even greater importance.

Consider the trivial problem of calculating the average of three numbers, *a*, *b*, and *c*. In algebraic notation, the solution can be expressed as

$$\text{average} = \frac{a + b + c}{3}$$

How would this be translated into C? You might be tempted to write

```
average = a + b + c / 3;
```

The compiler would not treat this statement as an error, yet it is. Because of the rules of precedence, it calculates not the average, but the sum of *a* plus *b* plus one third of *c*. The correct statement is as follows:

```
average = (a + b + c) / 3;
```

where parentheses are placed around the additions so that these operations will be performed before the division by 3.

These parentheses are implied by the algebraic notation, because we assume that when a horizontal bar is used for division, the numerator and denominator are each calculated separately before the division is performed. C does not use a horizontal bar, however, so we have to respect the rules of C rather than those of algebra.

In algebra, it is assumed that all numbers are real, (as opposed to integer). Therefore, if the sum $a + b + c$ is not a multiple of 3, the result is a fractional number. For example, the average of 3, 5, and 6 is calculated as $4\,{}^2/_3$, or 4.6667 in decimal notation (depending on how many digits are used). In C, however, if the values involved are integers (the only type of number we have dealt with so far), the result is truncated to 4 in the example given. In such a case we either have to settle for an integer average, or use the modulus operator to calculate the remainder.

The following C program calculates the average of three numbers using truncated division. Notice that the variables are assigned their values using combined declaration and initialization.

```
/* Program to compute the average of three integers */

main()
{
    int a = 7,
        b = 12,
        c = 6;

    printf("The average of %d, %d, and %d is %d\n",
            a, b, c, (a + b + c) / 3);
}
```

What do you think the output will be? If you are not sure, why don't you run the program on your computer to find out.

There are several different ways in which this program could be written. For example, rather than calculating the average within the *printf* statement, we could have declared a variable *average* which would be assigned the result. The program would then look like this:

```
/* Program to compute the average of three integers */

main()
{
   int a = 7,
       b = 12,
       c = 6,
       average;

   average = (a + b + c) / 3;

   printf("The average of %d, %d, and %d is %d\n",
          a, b, c, average);
}
```

Perhaps you have guessed at yet another possible modification. (C permits you a wide range of options.) Since operators may be used in a combined declaration/initialization, we could declare *average* and assign it a value at the same time:

```
/* Program to compute the average of three integers */

main()
{
   int a = 7,
       b = 12,
       c = 6,
       average = (a + b + c) / 3;     /* Combined declaration
                                         and initialization */

   printf("The average of %d, %d, and %d is %d\n",
          a, b, c, average);
}
```

We mentioned earlier that the modulus operator can be used to give a more exact average. Here is a program employing that enhancement:

```
/* Program to compute the average of three integers */

main()
{
   int a = 3,
       b = 2,
       c = 6,
       average = (a + b + c) / 3,
       remainder = (a + b + c) % 3;

   printf("The average of %d, %d, and %d is %d and %d/3\n",
          a, b, c, average, remainder);
}
```

The control string is designed to display the average in fractional form. The output of the preceding program is:

```
The average of 3, 2, and 6 is 3 and 2/3
```

The observant programmer will notice that the sum of *a*, *b* and *c* is calculated twice. Such redundancy should be avoided in programs whenever possible. One solution would be to calculate the sum first, and then use it in further calculations. This is accomplished by the following set of declarations:

```
int a = 3,
    b = 2,
    c = 6,
    sum = a + b + c,     /* No parentheses needed now! */
    average = sum / 3,
    remainder = sum % 3;
```

C Tutorial

1. Which of the two operators, multiplication or division, has the higher precedence?

2. Distinguish between the binary and the unary minus.

3. How may the variable *x* be declared to be of type **int** and, at the same time, have the value 456 assigned to it?

4. What is meant by truncation?

5. What role is played by parentheses in evaluating expressions?

6. What is the modulus operator and how does it work?

7. How would you print out the % symbol?

8. What are the results of the following expressions?

   (a)   17 % 3
   (b)   20 % 4
   (c)   15 % 15
   (d)   6 % 5
   (e)   -(10 % 4)
   (f)   -10 % 4

ANSWERS TO C TUTORIAL

1. Neither; they have the same priority level. If they are both present, they are evaluated from left to right.

2. The binary minus has an operand before and after the minus sign, and is used for subtraction. The unary minus has only one operand — to its right — and serves to convert a positive value into its corresponding negative value and vice versa.

3. int x = 456;

4. It is the rounding–down effect achieved, among other times, when an integer is divided by another integer and the resulting fractional portion is chopped off.

5. They override the normal priorities. What is contained within the parentheses is evaluated first, in the normal order.

6. It is represented by the symbol %. It finds the remainder that is left when one integer is divided by another integer.

7. By including two adjacent % signs in the *printf* control string.

8. (a) 2   (b) 0   (c) 0   (d) 1   (e) −2
   (f) This will depend on the particular machine,
      but would be either 2 or −2.

Exercises

For each of the following exercises, ensure that all output is explicitly labeled and is replete with literals.

1. Write a program that computes the area of a square, whose length is defined in the program as some integer of your choosing. (Remember, the symbol for multiplication is the asterisk.)

2. Write a program that computes the perimeter and the area of a rectangle. Define your own values for the length and width.

3. Write a program that declares an integer variable called *num*, assigns a value to it, and computes and prints out the value of the variable itself, its square, and its cube.

4. The following formulas are used to convert a temperature in Fahrenheit (F) to its equivalent in Celsius (C) and vice-versa:
   C = (F - 32) * 5/9
   F = 9/5 * C + 32

Note that the above formulas are not necessarily in correct C syntactical form. Write a program to convert a temperature in Fahrenheit to its Celsius equivalent, and one to convert a Celsius temperature to Fahrenheit. Hint: Because of the truncation effect of integer division, C will always evaluate multiplication by 5/9 as equal to multiplication by zero, resulting in erroneous results. The solution to this is to multiply first by 5 and then divide the result by 9. Similar care should be taken in the second expression because, in integer division, 9/5 reduces to 1.

5. Write a program to convert a given number of days to a measure of time given in years, weeks, and days. For example, 375 days equals 1 year, 1 week, and 3 days. (Ignore leap years in this program.)

6. Write a program to convert a number of inches into yards, feet, and inches. Example: 123 inches equals 3 yards, 1 foot, and 3 inches.

7. It is possible to calculate easily the day of the week on which a given date falls, if one knows the Julian day for that date. For example, January 1 is always Julian day 1, since it is the first day of the year, whereas December 31 is day 365 in a non-leap year or day 366 in a leap year. The day of the week is calculated as follows:

year = year in question (all four digits)
Julian_day = Julian day of date in question (1 to 366)
fours = integer portion of (year - 1) / 4
hundreds = integer portion of (year - 1) / 100
four_hundreds = integer portion of (year - 1) / 400

day_of_the_week = (year + Julian_day + fours - hundreds + four_hundreds) % 7
where:

result	means
0	Saturday
1	Sunday
2	Monday
3	Tuesday
4	Wednesday
5	Thursday
6	Friday

Write a program to calculate the day of the week as described above. Verify its correctness by testing it on the current date.

4

Some More
Data Types

We have covered the subject of integer numbers fairly thoroughly. Later on in this chapter, we shall have a little more to say about them. The time has arrived to learn how to handle some additional data types.

Floating Point Numbers

Floating point numbers are numbers that have a decimal point. The compiler differentiates between floating point numbers and integers because they are stored differently in the computer.

Floating point numbers sometimes are referred to as *real* numbers—not that there is anything unreal about integers. Floating point numbers include all the numbers between the integers. Some examples are 1.234, -5746.8, 15. and 128.0. The major differences between integers and floating point numbers are as follows:

1. Integers include only whole numbers, but floating point numbers can be either whole or fractional.

2. Floating point numbers can represent a much broader range of numbers than can integers. Their range will depend upon the particular computer.

3. Floating point numbers sometimes can lead to loss of mathematical precision. The result may be slightly "off," (as in 4.2 being represented as 4.199999), whereas integers are always exact.

4. On most computers, floating point operations are slower in execution and often occupy more memory than integer operations.

5. Declaration of integers is accomplished by the use of the keyword **int**, whereas floating point declarations use the keyword **float**.

6. Integers are stored internally as ordinary binary numbers, whereas floating point numbers are broken up into a fractional portion (called the mantissa) and an exponent part. Both parts are stored in binary form.

7. The conversion specification %d is used to print out an integer. The %e or %f symbols are used for floating point numbers.

As with integer constants, floating point numbers may be declared and initialized in a single statement. The two statements

```
float a;
a = 123.45;
```

may be written as the following single statement:

```
float a = 123.45;
```

Some expressions using floating point values are included in Program 4-1.

```
/* An illustration of the use of floating point numbers */

main()
{
  float a = 246.8, b = 135.79, answer;

  answer = a + b;
  printf("%f + %f = %f\n", a, b, answer);

  answer = a - b;
  printf("%f - %f = %f\n", a, b, answer);

  answer = a * b;
  printf("%f * %f = %f\n", a, b, answer);

  answer = a / b;
  printf("%f / %f = %f\n", a, b, answer);

}
```

Program 4—1

```
246.800003 + 135.789993 = 382.589844
246.800003 - 135.789993 = 111.010010
246.800003 * 135.789993 = 33512.972656
246.800003 / 135.789993 = 1.817505
```

Output 4—1

Output 4-1 illustrates the loss of precision which was mentioned previously. For example, the value of *a*, 246.8, is displayed in the output as 246.800003, and the value of *b*, 135.79, appears as 135.789993. The results of the calculations also are a tad off. For most non-scientific applications, errors resulting from floating point calculations are tolerable.

Scientific Notation

Floating point numbers may also be expressed in what is called *scientific notation*. For example, the expression 123.45e6 represents a floating point number in scientific notation. It refers to the number ordinarily written as 123.45×10^6, which is equivalent to the number 123,450,000. (Incidentally, although we have shown this large number with the traditional commas, numbers in C must never include them.)

The letter e (the capital letter E will do just as well) stands for the word *exponent*. The exponent is the whole (integer) number following the letter e; the part of the number before the letter e is called the *mantissa*. The number 123.45e6 should be interpreted as: 123.45 times 10 to the 6th power. The exponent is positive in this case, so in order to write the number in the standard form, we move the decimal point six places to the right.

Scientific notation is convenient for expressing very small numbers too. If the exponent is negative, the decimal point is moved to the *left* the number of places indicated by the exponent. For example, 123.45e-6 is equivalent to 0.00012345. A floating point number may be printed out in scientific notation format by using the symbol %e in the *printf* control string, or in standard format by using the %f symbol. The two forms of floating point numbers are interchangeable.

The Type double

If the accuracy obtained using a variable of the type **float** is insufficient for the purpose at hand, it can be declared instead to be of the type **double**. This is very similar to the type **float**, except that it provides about twice the number of significant digits for the result. The exact number of significant digits varies from system to system, but usually if a **float** variable has seven digits, a **double** variable has 16 or 17.

Numbers of the types **float** and **double** are treated identically by the system in terms of calculations. As a matter of fact, all floating point numbers are converted to **double** values automatically before they are used in any operation. Using the type **float** saves memory, however, because a **float** variable takes up only half as much space as a **double**. To display a **double** value, the format characters %f (for standard floating point notation) or %e (for scientific or exponential notation) are used, just as with type **float**.

Converting Integers to Floating Point, and Vice Versa

C permits integer values to be stored into variables that have been declared to be floating point. The number is merely converted to its floating point equivalent; its value is not changed. By the same token, C also enables the programmer to store floating point values into variables declared to be integer. In the latter case, however, the value is changed because the number is truncated (its fractional portion is lost). For example, in the program segment

```
int a, c;
float b, d;

a = 3;
b = 987.654;

c = b;
d = a;
```

the integer 3 is assigned to the integer variable *a* and the floating point number 987.654 is assigned to the floating point variable *b*. After the value of *b* has been stored into *c*, printing or displaying the value of *c* shows that it has been truncated to 987. The final value of *d* is 3.0, however, which is equivalent to 3, the original value.

Mixed Mode Calculations

It is clear that C allows for a certain degree of flexibility. Consider the following statement:

```
x = 5 * 6.7;
```

The arithmetic expression contains one operand of type **int** and another of type **float**. In C, this is not considered an error. The integer value is automatically converted to type **double** for the calculation; this is known as *implicit conversion*. Program 4-2 further illustrates mixed-mode calculations.

```
/* Illustration of mixed mode expressions */

main()
{
  int a = 2, answer;
  float b = 12.34, result;

  result = a * b;
  printf("%d * %f = %f\n", a, b, result);

  printf("%f in scientific notation is %e\n", result, result);

  answer = a * b;
  printf("%d * %f = %d\n", a, b, answer);

}
```

Program 4—2

```
2 * 12.339996 = 24.679993
24.679993 in scientific notation is 2.467999E+01
2 * 12.339996 = 24
```

Output 4—2

Once again, it is clear that some of the values as displayed by the program are slightly inaccurate due to the error inherent in the use of floating point values.

Coercion and the Cast Operator

The C programmer also has the choice of explicitly specifying how the values are to be converted in a mixed-mode expression. This feature is known in C as *coercion*, and may be accomplished using what is called the *cast operator*. The name of the data type to which the conversion is to be made (such as **int** or **float**) is enclosed in parentheses and placed directly to the left of the value to be converted; the word "cast" never is actually used. Here is a simple example of casting:

```
int a = 7;
float b;
b = (float)a + 1.0;
```

The cast operator converts the value of *a* to its equivalent **float** representation before the addition of 1.0 is carried out. The precedence of the cast operator is the same as that of the unary minus operator.

The cast operator can be used on a constant or expression as well as on a variable:

```
(int)3.14159
(double)(4 * 3 / 7)
(float)(a + 3)
```

In the second example, the cast is performed only after the entire expression within the parentheses is evaluated. The expression

```
4 * 3 / 7
```

evaluates to 1 (due to integer truncation), so the resultant **double** value is equal to 1.0.

Using Qualifiers to Extend the Accuracy of Integers

Just as the programmer can extend the precision of a floating point variable by declaring it to be of type **double**, so it is possible to increase the number of digits in an integer variable. On many computers, if the qualifier **long** is placed before the **int** declaration, the range of the associated variables is extended. Here is a typical example:

```
long int x;
```

When it is desired that an integer constant be **long**, the letter L is affixed immediately after the constant, with no space between the last digit and the letter, as shown in the following example. (It is recommended that the uppercase letter L rather than lowercase l be used, to avoid confusion with the digit 1.)

```
long int x = 12345678L;
```

If an integer constant or variable is of type **long**, it can be displayed on the screen (or printed on paper) by changing the conversion specifier in the *printf* control string to %ld. (Some implementations may accept %Ld.)

Not only can **long** integers be declared, but so can **short** ones. As you will have guessed, the keyword this time is **short**, which is placed before the word **int**. This declaration saves memory space, because short integers take up less memory than long ones. The drawback is that the allowable range of values is reduced, so **short int** variables should be used only when a small range of integers is being used.

On virtually every computer, the type **int** is synonymous with either **long int** or **short int**. Which one depends on the particular computer. To have control over the size of the integer, the programmer should specify **long** or **short** explicitly.

Another type is called the **unsigned int**. This qualifier is used for variables that take positive values only, such as those used for counting. By prefixing the **int** declaration (or **long int** or

short int) with the word **unsigned**, the range of the positive numbers can be doubled.

In mixed-mode calculations involving several different-sized integers, all **short** values are converted into type **int**. The exception occurs when an operation involves both a **long int** and a shorter value, in which case the shorter operand is converted into a **long int**. In operations involving both a **signed** and an **unsigned** value, the **signed** value is converted into an **unsigned** value.

In all the preceding cases of integer modifiers, the word **int** can be omitted without any loss of meaning; in such cases, it is always assumed that the variable(s) is an integer. Thus the following examples are valid:

```
long x;
unsigned y;
unsigned short z = 15;
```

The first declaration creates a long, signed integer named x. The second creates an unsigned, standard-sized integer called y. The third declaration creates a short, unsigned integer named z and initializes it to the value 15.

The Type char

The type **char** is used to store a single character of information. As with **int**, **char** is the actual name of the data type, and must be written as such in the declaration. The word *character* cannot be substituted.

A character constant must be a single character enclosed between two single quotation marks (or apostrophes). Pay special attention to the fact that the single quotation mark is used, not the double quotation marks that we have used to enclose control strings in *printf* statements. Some examples of character constants are 'a', 'f', 'r', '*', ':', '#', '{', and even '\n' (as mentioned previously, the latter represents a single character). In order to display a character constant, the conversion specification %c is used in the corresponding *printf* statement.

It is possible to store single digits as characters by enclosing them in single quotation signs: '1', '6', and '9'. Care must be taken not to confuse these character constants with the numeric values 1, 6, and 9. Digits enclosed in apostrophes cannot be used in arithmetic expressions.

Through the control string of *printf*, you have already seen examples of character strings, which are simply collections of single characters. A character string may contain only a single character, but such a string is represented differently than a single character constant. Character strings are always enclosed by double quotation marks. That is, 'a' refers to a character constant, but "a" refers to a character string. Later on in this text, we will show how these strings can be stored in variables.

A simple illustration of the use of a character constant appears in Program 4-3. Both uppercase and lowercase letters and a punctuation symbol are used as character constants. Notice that even though only one blank space is assigned to ltr_2, two spaces appear in the printout. The reason is that the variable ltr_2 appears twice in the *printf* statement. (The two occurrences of ltr_2 have two separate conversion specifications within the control string.)　Notice also that, within the control string, each occurrence of %c is adjacent to the previous one, with no spaces in between. If spaces were included, they would appear in the output.

```
/* An illustration of the use of the type char */

main()
{
  char ltr_1 = 'C',
       ltr_2 = ' ',
       ltr_3 = 'i',
       ltr_4 = 's',
       ltr_5 = 'g',
       ltr_6 = 'r',
       ltr_7 = 'e',
       ltr_8 = 'a',
       ltr_9 = 't',
       ltr_10 = '!';

  printf("%c%c%c%c%c%c%c%c%c%c%c\n", ltr_1, ltr_2,
      ltr_3, ltr_4, ltr_2, ltr_5, ltr_6, ltr_7,
      ltr_8, ltr_9, ltr_10);

}
```

Program 4—3

```
C is great!
```

Output 4—3

Keywords

Although the C programmer can select a wide range of variable names, some names are reserved by the compiler for specific purposes and cannot be used by the programmer. Examples of keywords that we have already discussed are **int, unsigned,** and the other words used to declare variables. As we mentioned earlier in the book, a variable cannot be given a keyword as a name, because an error will be flagged by the compiler. In later chapters, several more keywords will be encountered; there are about 30 in all. Starting with this chapter, a cumulative list of keywords will be presented at the end of each chapter for easy reference and visual reinforcement. Throughout the text of the book, but not within the programs themselves, keywords are printed in boldface.

It is permissible for a variable or other programmer-selected name to contain a keyword. For example, *integer* is a perfectly valid variable name, even though it contains the keyword **int.** As long as the C compiler can distinguish between the variable name and the keyword, there is no danger of conflict.

Certain other words that we have encountered, such as *main* and *printf,* are not keywords. The *printf* function actually is a prewritten program and not part of C. Naming a variable *printf* does not cause the compiler to flag an error, but it prevents the *printf* function from being used for its normal purpose of producing output. Any name can be used only for one specific task at a time, so naming a variable *printf* prevents the C compiler from recognizing the word as the name of the standard printing function. The name *main* is even more crucial in C. If a program does not contain a section of code with this name, the program will not be able to run at all, since a program can start only at the section of code labeled *main*.

All keywords in C must be written entirely in lowercase. This means that it is perfectly valid to name a variable *Int*, even though **int** is a keyword. The capital letter will prevent the two from being confused. A conflict occurs only when the name of a variable exactly matches a keyword. It can sometimes be confusing to use a variable name that looks like a keyword, however, because even though the compiler will not be confused, a human reading the program might be.

Now that we have covered the fundamental mathematical capabilities of the C language, we can move on to the decision-making statements that are necessary to give any computer language real computing power. Such statements are the substance of the next chapter.

The Spirit of C

In the previous chapter, we showed various ways to write a program that finds the average of three integers. Now that we have covered floating point numbers, we can write a program that displays the average as a real number. Once again, there are various approaches we may take. These all involve the question of the proper way to do mixed-mode calculation in C.

The following program uses a floating point variable called *average* to hold the result of the calculation. The variable is declared to be of type **double** so that we can display more significant digits in the result. Will this program achieve the desired result?

```
/* Program to print the real average of three integers */

main()
{
    int i = 5,
        j = 8,
        k = 13;
    double average;

    average = (i + j + k) / 3;

    printf("The average of %d, %d, and %d is %f\n"),
        i, j, k, average);
}
```

If you feel uncomfortable about this program, you have good reason to. The calculation of the average is not really mixed-mode; all that happens is that the integer result of the expression on the right side of the assignment operator is assigned to a floating point variable *average*. Both the numerator $(i + j + k)$ and the denominator (3) of the division operator are integer values, so the division is done in integer mode and therefore truncates any fractional portion of the result. This defeats the purpose of using a floating point variable for the result. The answer will be the same as would have been produced using only integers, except that the result will be displayed with a decimal point and a fractional portion of zero. Although this might look satisfactory, for many purposes it is not precise enough.

In order to ensure floating point division in this program, either the numerator or the denominator (or both) must be floating point. The following statements all yield true floating point results:

```
average = (i + j + k) / 3.0;
average = (double)(i + j + k) / 3;
average = (double)(i + j + k) / 3.0;
```

Note that in the second and third statements, the cast operator (**float**) could also have been used.

The program could be rewritten as follows:

```
/* Program to print the real average of three integers */

main()
{
    int i = 5,
        j = 8,
        k = 13;
    double average;

    average = (double)(i + j + k) / 3.0;
    printf("The average of %d, %d, and %d is %f\n"),
        i, j, k, average);
}
```

C Tutorial

1. What is another name for floating point numbers?

2. Which of the following is not a floating point number?

   (a)   123
   (b)   987.0
   (c)   −425.7
   (d)   92.45e12
   (e)   10.23E−9

3. What is the keyword that is used to declare floating point variables?

4. What distinguishes floating point numbers from integers?

5. Write the following numbers in scientific notation, using a mantissa with a single non-zero digit to the left of the decimal point. The first one has been done for you:

   (a)   123.456   1.23456e2
   (b)   987.654
   (c)   .000123
   (d)   1230000

6. With what kind of number is the **double** declaration associated?

7. What is the effect of dividing an integer by a real quantity? Also, what is this effect called?

8. What is meant by the term *coercion*?

9. How would you use the cast operator to convert $(7 * 9 / 11)$ to **double**?

10. What is a character constant?

11. What is the maximum number of characters which a variable of type **char** can hold?

12. What do the following words have in common?

    main
    bingo
    printf

ANSWERS TO C TUTORIAL

1. Real numbers.

2. (a) is not.

3. **float** (or **double**)

4. Floating point numbers have a broader range; may have a fractional portion; are stored differently; use the %e or %f conversion specifier rather than %d; and may result in slower operations.

5. (b) 9.87654e2
   (c) 1.23e−4
   (d) 1.23e6

6. With a floating point number.

7. The integer is temporarily converted to its floating point equivalent before the calculation is performed. This automatic operation is known as implicit conversion.

8. Coercion refers to the use of the cast operator by the programmer to specify explicitly what type a value (or value of an expression) is to be converted to.

9. (double)(7 * 9 / 11)

10. It is a single character enclosed by single quotation marks (apostrophes).

11. One.

12. None of them are keywords in C.

Keywords

This list contains all the keywords encountered so far in this book. Keywords introduced in the current chapter are listed in boldface.

char	**double**	**float**	int	**long**	**short**
unsigned					

Exercises

1. Write a C program that evaluates the following arithmetic expression and prints out the result in scientific notation:

$$\frac{(\ 1.234 \times 10^7 \ + \ 3.2 \times 10^{-3}\ )}{(\ 9.81 \times 10^5 \ - \ 2.746 \times 10^7\ )}$$

2. Write a C program that calculates the circumference and area of a circle from its radius. The value of *pi* may be assigned to a variable or used as a constant in the calculation. C has no built-in constant *pi,* so a floating point approximation such as 3.1416 should be used.

3. Augment the program from Exercise 2 so that it calculates the volume and surface area of a sphere, given the radius.

4. Write a C program to add up five amounts of money (dollars and cents) represented as floating point numbers, and print the result as a truncated integer value.

5. Given that 39.37 inches are equivalent to 1 meter, write a program that converts a given number of inches to the equivalent length in centimeters.

6. To round off a floating point number to the nearest integer, one adds 0.5 to the number and truncates it to an integer. Using this knowledge, try to figure out how to round a floating point number to the nearest tenth, hundredth, etc.

7. In a program, store the five vowels (a,e,i,o,u) in five suitably declared variables. Then print out the contents of the variables on a single line.

5

Making Decisions in C

Computers are renowned not only for their ability to execute a large number of instructions at lightning speed, but also for their ability to make decisions. The decision—making constructs in the C language are easy to use, but they enable the computer to make some very sophisticated decisions.

Often it is convenient to write programs so that they interact with the user through the screen and keyboard. We have already seen how a program can display messages to the user; now we will see how the user can talk back to the computer.

The scanf Function

One of the primary advantages of modern computers is their ability to communicate with the user during program execution. This feature enables the programmer to enter values into variables as the occasion demands, without having to change the program itself. The disadvantage of this option is that execution stops each time the program needs to have a new value entered. Once the required value has been entered and the return key pressed, execution resumes from the point at which it stopped.

In C, the *scanf* function permits a program to be interrupted during execution in order to input required values. The name stands for "scan function" or "scan formatted." It is equivalent to the READ statement of Pascal.

An example of the *scanf* statement follows:

```
scanf("%d",&n);
```

where the variable *n* has previously been declared as an integer. This statement looks similar to the *printf* statement, and in a sense is its reverse. The conversion specification within the control string tells the computer that it should expect the user to type in an integer (decimal) number. The ampersand symbols (&) that precedes the variable *n* is mandatory whenever a single numeric value or character is to be read into a simple variable. We will discuss the actual meaning of the ampersand later on, but for now, always remember to use it in the *scanf* statement when data is being entered. If you forget, funny things will happen when you run the program.

The *scanf* function stops program execution until a value is typed in and the return key is pressed. The computer will not tell you that it is waiting for a value to be entered, however, so it may sit idle for a long time, until you realize that it is waiting for you to act. Therefore, the programmer should precede each *scanf* statement with an appropriate *printf* statement, specifying precisely what the user should do. Such a statement is called a prompt, and displaying such a message is known as prompting.

Program 5-1 introduces the use of the *scanf* function. It declares a variable *n* to be of type **int** and then asks the user to type in an integer, which is read by means of the *scanf*. Notice how the *scanf* function is preceded by a *printf* in order to alert the user that input is expected. Furthermore, these two statements are grouped to represent a unit. (This grouping was chosen by the programmer and has nothing to do with C syntax, but judicious use of C's free format makes programs considerably more readable.) By means of a second *printf* statement, the value of *n* and its square are printed out.

```
/* An illustration of the scanf statement.
   This program inputs a number and prints out its square. */

main()
{
   int n;

   printf("Please type in an integer: ");
   scanf("%d",&n);

   printf("The square of %d is %d.\n", n, n * n);
}
```

Program 5—1

```
Please type in an integer: 5
The square of 5 is 25.
```

Output 5—1

Decision Making in C

The **if** statement, as its name implies, is used to make decisions. *If* a certain condition is true, we direct the computer to take one course of action; *if* the condition is false, we direct it to do something else. This is one of the most fundamental concepts in computer science.

Before we can proceed to a detailed discussion of the **if** statement, however, we must explain the relational and logical operators that are used in defining the conditions on which the **if** statement acts. These operators will be the subject of the next two sections. The few **if** statements used as examples in these sections will be simple and largely self-explanatory, and will be clarified further by the discussion of the **if** statement which follows.

The Relational Operators

Relational operators are symbols that are used to test the relationship between two variables, or between a variable and a constant. The test for equality, for example, is made by means of two adjacent equal signs with no space separating them. C has six relational operators, as defined in the following table:

Operator	Meaning
==	equal to
>	greater than
<	less than
!=	not equal to (either greater than or less than)
>=	greater than or equal to
<=	less than or equal to

Notice that some of these operators consist of only one character, whereas others contain two. Those with two characters must not contain spaces.

The expression (n==7) means: "Is the value contained in the variable *n* equal to 7?" The answer to this question obviously is either yes or no. In programming, however, we use the terms *true* and *false* instead. In this example, if *n* is equal to 7, we say that the value of the expression is *true*.

A common error in C is to forget that the **if** statement's test for equality requires two consecutive equal signs, rather than the single one used in certain other languages. C does not consider a single equal sign in an **if** statement to be an error, but it will produce the wrong results, as you will see later on.

The Logical Operators

Logical operators are symbols that are used to combine or negate expressions containing relational operators. For example, you might want a program to perform certain steps if *n* is equal to 7 AND *x* is greater than 5. To code this type of expression, you use one of the logical operators, called AND, in conjunction with the relational operators. The AND operator is represented by a symbol, &&. (Do not confuse this operator with the single ampersand, which is used with the *scanf* function and for other purposes yet to be discussed.)

Another logical operator, called OR, is used when at least *one* of two conditions must be true in order for the compound condition to be true. The OR operator in C is represented by two consecutive vertical bars, ||. On most keyboards, the vertical bar is found on the same key as the backslash character.

A third logical operator, called NOT, is represented by a single exclamation point (!). This operator has the effect of reversing the truth value of the expression to its immediate right. It is possible to do the same thing by changing an expression so that it uses the inverse relational operator; for example, we could find the inverse of

```
if (n <= 4)
```

by changing it to

```
if (n > 4)
```

In some expressions that involve many relational operators, however, it can be very complicated to find the inverse by this method. At this point, we will not discuss why one would wish to replace a comparison with its logical inverse. The point we wish to make is that the NOT operator often is the simplest way to achieve this result:

```
if (!(n <= 4))
```

Those readers who are familiar with Pascal may wonder why C has no special data type for logical expressions or values. In C, all boolean values (as *true* and *false* sometimes are called) are represented by integers. The value 0 is interpreted as *false* when it is used with relational or logical operators, and any other integer is regarded as *true*. For example, an **if** statement that begins

```
if (n != 0)
```

could be abbreviated to the more succinct (though cryptic)

```
if (n)
```

because testing for truth can be interpreted as testing for a non-zero value.

Precedence of Operators

In C, every operator has its place in the order of precedence. We have already discussed the precedence of various mathematical operators. You will recall, for example, that multiplication and division take precedence over addition and subtraction. In the same way, mathematical operations are performed before the relational operators, and these in turn take precedence over the logical operators.

Within the logical operators, AND takes precedence over OR. As with mathematical operators, expressions within parentheses are evaluated before anything outside the parentheses. These rules are summarized in the following table, which lists the operators in descending order of precedence:

```
()
!   - (unary)
*  /  %
+   - (binary)
<  <=  >  >=
==  !=
&&
||
=
```

Notice that the assignment operator is included in this list. It is evaluated after all the others. Binary operators with the same precedence are executed from left to right in the expression being evaluated. Unary operators (more of which will be introduced later) are performed from right to left. Appendix A contains a table of all C operators and their precedence.

If you have trouble remembering all these rules of precedence, you can always resort to parentheses in order to express your intentions explicitly. For example, if you can't remember whether AND is evaluated before OR, just decide which one you want to come first and enclose it within parentheses.

The programs discussed in the following sections, which deal with the **if** statement, contain further examples of the relational and logical operators.

The if Statement

C allows decisions to be made by evaluating a given expression as true or false. Such an expression involves the relational and logical operators, which we discussed in the preceding sections. Depending on the outcome of the decision, program execution proceeds in one direction or another. The C construct that enables these tests to be made is called the **if** statement.

The simplest form of the **if** statement is as follows:

```
if (expression)

    statement;
```

The keyword **if** must be followed by a set of parentheses containing the expression to be tested. The parentheses are followed by a single C statement, which is executed only if the expression evaluates as *true*. If the programmer wants more than one statement to execute at this point, they may be grouped together to form a *compound statement* surrounded by paired curly braces. (In the following example of format, the braces are lined up to make them easy to read. They may be arranged differently if you prefer.)

```
if (expression)

{

    statement;

    statement;

}
```

compound

It is also acceptable to enclose a single statement within braces. This construction would simply be a compound statement made up of one statement.

Program 5-2 illustrates the use of the **if** statement. It asks the user to select an integer less than 10, and then determines whether the number selected was 7.

```
/* scanf and if together. */

main()
{
    int n;
    printf("Enter a positive integer under 10: ");
    scanf("%d",&n);

    if (n == 7)
        printf("I knew you'd select 7!\n");
    printf("Thank you for your cooperation.\n");
}
```

Program 5—2

```
Enter a positive integer under 10: 7
I knew you'd select 7!
Thank you for your cooperation.


Enter a positive integer under 10: 3
Thank you for your cooperation.
```

Output 5—2

There are two sets of output for Program 5-2, because we ran the program twice. We will do this whenever it is desirable to see the output from different sets of input values. In the first example, the expression was true because *n* contained the value 7, so the message in the first *printf* statement was output. In the second example, *n* contained a value other than 7, so the expression was false and only the second *printf* statement was executed.

The if...else Statement

In Program 5-2, only the general message is printed if the user selects a number other than 7. Suppose we wished to respond with a message such as: "How come you didn't pick 7?" One way of doing this would be to add another if statement after the first one:

```
if (n != 7)
    printf("How come you didn't pick 7?\n");
```

Were we to adopt this method, then only one of the **if** statements would be true for any value of *n* entered. Only one of the two messages would be printed, followed by the unconditional message, "Thank you for your cooperation."

It seems wasteful, however, to make two comparisons each time, knowing that only one expression will be true for any value of *n* entered. A better way to code the program is to use an optional feature of the **if** statement: the **else** clause. This feature permits the programmer to write a single comparison, and then execute one of the two statements depending upon whether the test expression is true or false.

The **if...else** statement looks like this:

```
if (expression)
  statement1;
else
  statement2;
```

Note that both the **if** clause and the **else** clause are terminated by semicolons. Even though these two clauses seem like two separate entities, there must be no other statements between them. Here is an example of an **if...else** statement:

```
if (a == b)
  printf("a is equal to b.\n");
else   /* Print warning message and make them equal */
{
  printf("a is not equal to b, but they will be.\n");
  b = a; /* Make them equal by assigning a to b */
}
```

Notice that the statements in the **if** and **else** clauses may be either simple or compound.

Here is an example of an **if...else** statement that is invalid:

```
if (c != d)
  printf("c is not equal to d, but they will be.\n");
  d = c;
else
  printf("c is equal to d.\n");
```

This is invalid because a statement intervenes between the **if** and **else** clauses. The first *printf* statement is part of the **if** clause, and the second one is part of the **else** clause, but the assignment statement (d = c) belongs to neither.

Note that indentation has no meaning in C syntax, so indenting the assignment statement to line up under the first *printf* would have no effect, even though it might look correct to the unsuspecting programmer. The proper correction is to place the first *printf* statement and the assignment statement within braces to form a compound statement.

Continuing with our modification of Program 5-2, we could rewrite the program with the following single **if** statement:

```
if (n ==7)
  printf("I knew you'd select 7!\n");
else
  printf("How come you didn't pick 7?\n");
```

The first *printf* is executed if and only if *n* is equal to 7, in which case the **else** clause is ignored. If *n* is not equal to 7, the first *printf* is ignored, and the second *printf*, the one following the word **else**, is executed.

Program 5-3 illustrates the use of the **if...else** structure and the logical operators AND (&&) and OR (||). The user is asked to type in any year, and the program determines whether it is a leap year or not. For your information, a leap year is one that is evenly divisible by 4, other than a century year (such as 1900); or a century year that is evenly divisible by 400 (such as 2000). Notice how succinctly this information is conveyed in the **if** statement of Program 5-3.

```
/* Testing for leap years */

main()
{
   int year;

   printf("Please enter a year: ");
   scanf("%d",&year);

   /* If "year" is divisible by 4 AND not divisible by 100,
        OR is divisible by 400, it is a leap year */

   if (year % 4 == 0 && year % 100 != 0 || year % 400 == 0)
      printf("%d is a leap year.\n",year);
   else
      printf("%d is not a leap year.\n",year);
}
```

Program 5—3

```
Please enter a year: 1986
1986 is not a leap year.


Please enter a year: 1948
1948 is a leap year.


Please enter a year: 1900
1900 is not a leap year.


Please enter a year: 2000
2000 is a leap year.
```

Output 5—3

Nesting of if Statements

The **else** clause, like the **if** clause, may contain a compound statement. This feature of C provides the programmer with a most flexible programming tool. Moreover, a clause of the **if** statement may itself contain another **if** statement. This construct, known as *nesting* of **if** statements, is illustrated by the following example:

```
if (n < 3)
  printf("%d is less than 3\n",n);
else
  if (n > 10)
  printf("%d is greater than 10\n",n);
else
  printf("%d is between 3 and 10\n",n);
```

In Program 5-3, we used the logical operators AND (&&) and OR (||) to determine whether an input year was a leap year or not. We could rewrite the **if** statement in Program 5-3 using nested **if...else** statements, as follows:

```
if (year % 4 == 0)
  if (year % 100 != 0)
      printf("%d is a leap year.\n",year);
  else
    if (year % 400 == 0)
        printf("%d is a leap year.\n",year);
    else
        printf("%d is not a leap year.\n",year);
else
  printf("%d is not a leap year.\n",year);
```

This revised version of Program 5-3 is considered to show a less sophisticated programming style than the original, because it is less concise; but it serves to illustrate two rules that pertain to the use of nested **if...else** statements.

- An AND (&&) operation can be replaced with an **if** statement nested within an **if** clause.
- An OR (||) operation can be replaced with an **if** statement nested within an **else** clause.

It is very important to be sure which **else** clause goes with which **if** clause. In our examples, we have lined up the **else** clauses with their corresponding **if** clauses. This indentation greatly aids the clarity of the code for a human reader. As previously mentioned, however, lining up the clauses does not determine the connection between them from the point of view of the compiler. The rule is that each **else** matches the nearest **if** preceding it which has not already been matched by an **else**.

Consider the following example:

```
if (n <= 10)
  if (n >= 3)
      printf("%d is between 3 and 10\n",n);
  else
      printf("%d is not between 3 and 10\n",n);
```

Which **if** does the **else** match? Do not assume that the indentation determines this; the compiler does not care about indentation. If the **else** clause matches the outer **if**, then the second *printf* is executed only if *n* is greater than 10. If the **else** matches the inner **if**, however, then the second *printf* executes when n is less than 10 but also less than 3.

Using the rule stated earlier, we determine that the **else** clause in fact matches the second **if**. But what if we want it to match the first **if** instead? We could write:

```
if (n <= 10)
{
  if (n > = 3)
      printf("%d is between 3 and 10\n",n);
}
else
  printf("%d is not between 3 and 10\n",n);
```

where the addition of braces prevents any association between the **if** statement within the braces and the **else** clause outside them. Even where braces are not necessary, they may still be used to promote clarity for the sake of the human reader.

Program 5-4 takes advantage of the **if...else** statement. Once again, the user is asked to type in an integer. The program examines the number to determine whether it is odd or even, and prints out an appropriate message to that effect.

```
/* Illustration of if with else clause.
   Tell whether a number is odd or even. */

main()
{
    int n;

    printf("Please enter an integer: ");
    scanf("%d",&n);

    if (n % 2 != 0)
        printf("%d is odd\n",n);
    else
        printf("%d is even\n",n);
}
```

Program 5—4

```
Please enter an integer: 13
13 is odd
```

```
Please enter an integer: 5746
5746 is even
```

Output 5—4

The program makes use of the % (modulus) operator to determine whether the number entered is odd or even. If an integer is divided by 2 and there is a remainder, the integer must be odd. No remainder (a remainder of 0) indicates that the integer is even. if *n* is odd (n % 2 != 0), then the first *printf* statement is executed; otherwise, the second *printf* is executed.

We could have changed the logic in the **if** statement slightly by testing

```
if (n % 2 == 0)
```

rather than

```
if (n % 2 != 0)
```

as shown in the program. In that case, we would also have to switch the two messages.

We can make this program more general by making it able to test whether any integer is evenly divisible by another integer. This is done in Program 5-5, which asks the user to enter an integer and then determines whether this number is evenly divisible by 7.

```
/* Testing if a number is divisible by 7 */

main()
{
    int n;

    printf("Enter an integer: ");
    scanf("%d",&n);

    if (n % 7 == 0)
        printf("%d is divisible by 7.\n", n);
    else
        printf("%d is not divisible by 7.\n", n);
}
```

Program 5—5

```
Enter an integer: 13
13 is not divisible by 7.
```

```
Enter an integer: 21
21 is divisible by 7.
```

Output 5—5

As another example of the **else** clause, consider Program 5-6, which asks the user to enter two numbers and then determines which of them is greater.

```
/* Determining which of 2 numbers is larger */

main()
{
   int a,b;

   printf("Enter an integer: ");
   scanf("%d",&a);

   printf("Enter another integer: ");
   scanf("%d",&b);

   if (a > b)
      printf("%d is greater than %d.\n",a,b);
   else
      printf("%d is smaller than %d.\n",a,b);
}
```

Program 5—6

```
Enter an integer: 4
Enter another integer: 7
4 is smaller than 7.




Enter an integer: 17
Enter another integer: 9
17 is greater than 9.
```

Output 5—6

In Program 5-6, the first of the two *printf* statements within the **if** statement is executed if *a* is greater than *b*. Otherwise, the second message is printed. The astute reader will notice that, if *a* and *b* are equal, the second message is printed. The reason is that the program tests whether *a* is greater than *b*. If *a* is equal to *b*, then obviously *a* is not greater than *b*, so the **else** clause is executed. The program as written does not take into account the possibility that *a* could be equal to *b*.

The relational and logical operators are used in several C statements other than the **if** statement. All of these statements are involved in decision making of some sort. Chapters 6 and 7 will introduce several statements that are concerned with repeating a sequence of steps until a certain condition is met. Such constructs, known as loops, are among the most important and fundamental constructs in computer programming.

The Spirit of C

The power of the **if...else** statement is that it can choose between two mutually exclusive directions for the program to take, based on the result of a test. The code in an **if** clause can be totally different from that contained in its corresponding **else** clause, so different input data can cause a program to perform completely different tasks. A nested **if...else** allows a large number of different possibilities. Nesting should be used with care, however, as too much of it can cause confusion.

Consider a program that tests a series of numbers to determine whether they are sorted in ascending order--that is, whether each number is greater than (or equal to) the one immediately preceding it. Suppose the program reads five numbers into five variables, called a, b, c, d, and e. First, a is compared to b. If a is less than b, then b is compared to c, and so forth. But if a is greater than b, we want the program to display a message to the effect that the second value is out of sequence. Furthermore, in this case, we do not want to compare c to b but rather to a, the last number known to be in correct order. This assumption is based on examining a series such as the following:

3 1 2 4 5

Clearly, the second number, 1, is out of order. It would appear that the third value, 2, is in order, since it follows 1. But, if the number 1 were placed in its proper place, at the beginning of the list, we would have

1 3 2 4 5

Now the number 2 is out of order, even though in the original series it followed 1.

Here is how we would begin the program described above:

```
/* A program to test five integers for ascending order */
                /* Stage 1 */

main()
{
   int a, b, c, d, e;

   printf("Please enter five integers, separated by a space.\n");
   scanf("%d %d %d %d %d", &a, &b, &c, &d, &e);

} /* Program not finished yet! */
```

You will notice that, for the first time, we are using a single *scanf* statement to read in several values at one time. Such a construct is not always desirable in a program, but here it serves our purpose. Each conversion specification has a matching variable into which a value is to be read. The first integer that the user enters is placed in *a*, the second in *b*, and so forth. As stated in the prompt, the integers are separated from each other by one or more blank spaces (a carriage return is also a valid separator).

When typing in the values, the user must be sure to supply five integers. If only four are typed in, the program will just sit there waiting for the fifth integer. Since only one prompt is displayed, and since the *scanf* statement cannot pass control to the next statement until all five numbers are entered, the program will not be able to alert the user to the problem.

The requirement of comparing *c* to *a*, in the case that *b* is less than *a*, would seem to call for an additional **if** statement. The result, however, could be a confusing tangle of nested **if...else** statements. We will therefore decide to pursue a different programming strategy.

One possible way of handling the case in which *b* is less than *a* would be to assign *a* to *b*, thereby forcing the required comparison of *c* to *a* with an **if** statement that compares *c* to *b* (remember, *b* now actually contains the value of a). Of course, if we wished to preserve all five values, this strategy would be unsatisfactory, since in the previous example the old value of *b* would be lost. This strategy is used in the next stage of the program.

We now add the statements required to compare the values with each other:

```
/* A program to test five integers for ascending order */
                  /* Stage 2 */

main()
{
   int a, b, c, d, e;

   printf("Please enter five integers, separated by a space.\n");
   scanf("%d %d %d %d %d", &a, &b, &c, &d, &e);

   if (b < a)
   {
      printf("The second number is out of order.\n");
      b = a; /* Value of "a" used for future comparisons */
   }
   if (c < b)
   {
      printf("The third number is out of order.\n");
      c = b; /* Value of "b" used for future comparisons */
   }
```

Program continued on next page

Program continued from previous page

```
   if (d < c)
   {
      printf("The fourth number is out of order.\n");
      d = c; /* Value of "c" used for following comparison */
   }
   if (e < d)
      printf("The fifth number is out of order.\n");
}
```

If all the numbers are out of sequence (that is, if they are initially in descending rather than ascending order), the first number is passed down as the comparison value until it ends up in *d*. The value of *d* is not assigned to *e* in the last **if** statement, because no more comparisons are done.

No message is displayed if the numbers are all in order. There should be a variable that keeps track of whether or not any values are out of order, or better yet, how many numbers are in order. The following revision uses such a variable:

```
/* A program to test five integers for ascending order */
                   /* Stage 3 */

main()
{
   int a, b, c, d, e,
       count = 1;       /* Counts how many numbers are in order
                           (automatically includes first number) */

   printf("Please enter five integers, separated by a space.\n");
   scanf("%d %d %d %d %d", &a, &b, &c, &d, &e);

   if (b < a)
   {
      printf("The second number is out of order.\n");
      b = a; /* Value of "a" used for future comparisons */
   }
   else count = count + 1;

   if (c < b)
   {
      printf("The third number is out of order.\n");
      c = b; /* Value of "b" used for future comparisons */
   }
   else count = count + 1;

   if (d < c)
   {
      printf("The fourth number is out of order.\n");
      d = c; /* Value of "c" used for following comparison */
   }
   else count = count + 1;

   if (e < d)
      printf("The fifth number is out of order.\n");
   else count = count + 1;

   printf("%d of the numbers are in ascending order.\n", count);
}
```

Note that this program uses the following assignment statement:

```
count = count + 1;
```

At first glance, this statement may seem somewhat ridiculous. How can *count* ever be equal to *count* plus 1? From an algebraic point of view, this makes no sense. But this is an assignment statement, not an algebraic statement. The same variable name, *count*, appears on both sides of the assignment operator. What this means is that each time the statement is executed, the old value (the one on the right) is incremented (or increased) by 1. The result is stored in the same variable, the one that appears on the left of the assignment operator.

The same rule holds in more complex assignments, such as the following:

```
count = z + 3 * count;
```

In this example, the value of *count* is multiplied by 3 and then added to *z*. The result is stored back in *count*, replacing its previous value. Incrementing by 1 is discussed further at the beginning of Chapter 6.

Returning to our problem of checking for ascending order: It could be argued that our method is faulty. Consider, for example, the following sequence:

```
20 3 4 5 6
```

The latest version of our program would consider the last four numbers to be out of sequence, because they are all less than the first number. It would probably be more correct, however, to say that the first number, 20, is out of order and that the rest are in order. Therefore, an intuitively correct solution to the problem would be more complicated than the one we have presented. At this stage, we are concerned mainly with showing you how to program an algorithm and not so much with correct formulation of the algorithm itself. The latter certainly is important, however, and is dealt with at other points in this book.

One way to improve the program would be to make it more general. Instead of storing the five values into five different variables, we could use only one variable and read in the five numbers one at a time. The resulting program would consist of several identical blocks of code, each one reading in a value and comparing it to the previous one. All that is necessary to allow for six variables would be to add another block of code.

Actually, at least two variables are required for this revised program. One contains the number most recently read in. Let's call it *number*. The other variable, which we shall name *previous_number*, contains the previous value read in, against which the current value of *number* is to be compared. A block of code reads in *number* and compares it to *previous_number*. If they are in ascending order, the value of *number* will be assigned to *previous_number*, and the program continues with another identical block of code. If the two values are out of order, a message to that effect is printed, and the value of *number* is discarded (it is not assigned to *previous_number*). To ensure that even the *printf* statements are general, a variable *index* will be added to keep track of the sequence number of the value currently being examined (first, second, and so on). The variable *count* will keep track of how many values are in order.

```
/* A program to test five integers for ascending order */
                        /* Stage 4 */

main()
{
    int number,             /* Number currently being examined */
        previous_number,    /* Last number that was in order */
        index = 1,          /* Which number is currently being
                               examined?  (1=first, 2=second, etc.) */
        count = 1;          /* Counts how many numbers are in order
                               (automatically includes first number) */

    printf("Please enter five integers, ");
    printf("separated by a carriage return.\n");
    scanf("%d", &previous_number);     /* First value used only to
                                          test others against */

    scanf("%d", &number);
    index = index + 1;     /* (Now index == 2) */
    if (number < previous_number)
        printf("The number in position %d is out of order.\n", index);
    else  /* In order */
    {
        count = count + 1;
        previous_number = number; /* number becomes new value
                                     for comparison */
    }

/* Repeat the above three more times */

    scanf("%d", &number);
    index = index + 1;     /* (Now index == 3) */
    if (number < previous_number)
        printf("The number in position %d is out of order.\n", index);
    else  /* In order */
    {
        count = count + 1;
        previous_number = number; /* number becomes new value
                                     for comparison */
    }

    scanf("%d", &number);
    index = index + 1;     /* (Now index == 4) */
    if (number < previous_number)
        printf("The number in position %d is out of order.\n", index);
    else  /* In order */
```

Program continued on next page

Program continued from previous page

```
{
    count = count + 1;
    previous_number = number; /* number becomes new value
                                 for comparison */
}

scanf("%d", &number);
index = index + 1;      /* (Now index == 5) */
if (number < previous_number)
    printf("The number in position %d is out of order.\n", index);
else  /* In order */
{            count = count + 1;
    previous_number = number; /* number becomes new value
                                 for comparison */
}

printf("%d of the numbers are in ascending order.\n", count);

}
```

One major problem with this version of the program is that the tests are interwoven with the inputting of the numbers. This means that, on some computers, a message about a number being out of order will be displayed as soon as that number is entered. (Some computers produce no output until after a line of input is entered, but some are totally interactive, meaning they can produce output after each number is entered.) This could distract the user, who presumably is concentrating on the task of inputting the values. It would be desirable to read in and store all five values before displaying any results.

Another problem is that, even though we tried to make the program general, it still operates on exactly five numbers. This limitation defeats much of the purpose of generality. In Chapters 6 and 7, which deal with loops, we will see how to adapt a program such as this one to accept as many values as the user chooses. Arrays, which will be introduced in Chapter 10, make it possible to store a variable number of values before operating on them.

When we first approached the problem of testing five numbers for ascending order, we considered nested **if** statements but rejected it in favor of another strategy. Experienced C programmers can predict the trouble that the first idea would cause, but a novice might spend considerable time and effort programming the first method before deciding against it. It is perfectly acceptable, and in fact desirable, to throw out a program and start over if it becomes clear that the method you are using is less than ideal.

Programming and Debugging *Hints*

Knowing the repertoire of a language is not quite the same as knowing how to program in that language. Programming is a skill that can be obtained only through study and experience. The newcomer to C or to programming in general has to recognize the fact that errors are bound to occur. In programming circles, errors are known as *bugs*, possibly because they seem to creep undetected into every program. The process of finding and eliminating bugs is known as *debugging*. The insidious manner in which bugs invade programs is so well recognized that many programmers believe there is no such thing as a debugged program.

The feature we are introducing now, called "Programming and Debugging Hints," is included in most of the remaining chapters of this book. It will help you to eliminate those inevitable bugs and to prevent them from occurring in the first place.

Syntactic vs. Logical Errors

Errors can be separated into at least two distinct classes: syntactic and logical.

Syntactic or syntax errors are those involving violations of the syntax of a language. Examples in C include using $=<$ instead of the $<=$ operator, or having unbalanced parentheses (more open parentheses than closed parentheses or vice versa). Fortunately, such errors are detected by the compiler when the statements are scanned during the compilation process.

This category usually is extended to include semantic errors. That is, errors that are syntactically correct but are contradictory. An example of a semantic error is a reference to a variable that doesn't appear in a variable declaration. Syntactic errors, then, are defined as those errors that can be detected during compilation.

When a syntax error is detected, the compiler prints out a diagnostic message specifying the nature of the error and the line on which it occurred. If an error is detected by the compiler, compilation may continue up to a point in order to detect further errors, but a compiled program is not produced. Such an error sometimes is known as a fatal error.

On occasion, the compiler displays a warning message to advise the programmer that a statement is technically acceptable, but is unusual enough to constitute a potential error. A warning does not prevent a compiled program from being produced, whereas a fatal error does.

Logical errors are capable of doing much more harm than syntax errors. Syntax errors are flagged by the compiler and may be eliminated from the program fairly quickly, but logical errors usually permit the program to run and produce the wrong results. Such errors cannot be detected by the compiler because they do not violate the rules of the language. Rather, they are caused by an incorrect algorithm or by a statement mistyped in such a way that it does not violate the syntax of the language, but nonetheless performs an unintended computation.

Sometimes these logical errors are very difficult to find and can prove to be quite frustrating to track down. In most programs, the final output is the result of many calculations performed by many program statements. It can be difficult to trace the cause of an error using only the final output of the program.

Clarity in Programming

The need for clear, understandable programs cannot be overstressed. Clarity is essential both for the internal documentation, which helps a reader understand the program logic, and for the manner in which the program communicates with the user.

We have spoken before about the elements of a clear program. Comments should be used generously, and placed so that they catch the eye of the reader. They should be intelligent, well placed, uncluttered and non-obvious. "Add 1 to a" is not a necessary comment, for example, since the reader can see this from the statement itself. A more useful comment would describe the significance of adding 1 to a, if such an explanation is necessary.

Modern computers have storage capacity that can easily handle this extra text. Comments are not included in the compiled program, so they do not affect the efficiency of the program. It is possible for badly conceived comments to mislead and confuse the reader, however, so all documentation should be appropriate and to the point.

Identifiers should be chosen to describe their function clearly. Fortunately, even though C sometimes truncates variable names, there is no limit to the length of names as written in the source program. A variable name should not take up an entire line, but excessive abbreviation should also be avoided.

The messages displayed by the program to the user should be given as much care as internal documentation, because some users may have little or no experience in computer programming. Even for a seasoned programmer, a message such as "Enter a value for variable pdq" is not very helpful. A program should explain its function, what input is expected, what the output will consist of, and other pertinent information. A prompt should specify clearly the nature of the desired input (for example, "length of the road," "number of children," or "your aunt's name") and, where applicable, the allowable values. The format of the input also should be specified when necessary (floating-point value, seven-digit integer, etc). Output from the program should be clearly labeled, because the results of the computations do a user very little good if he doesn't know what the results mean.

C *Tutorial*

1. What function enables a user to input information while the program is in execution?

2. What statement should precede every *scanf* statement, and why?

3. If numeric or single-character information is being entered by means of the *scanf* function, what symbol must precede the corresponding variable name?

4. What statement in C permits decisions to be made?

5. How many relational operators are there, and what are they?

6. What symbols are used for the logical operators AND and OR?

7. If two values are compared using a relational operator, what are the possible answers that can be produced?

8. In an **if** statement, if two separate statements are to be executed when the comparison is true, what must be done with them?

9. What is the function of the **else** clause in an **if** statement?

10. Which of the following statements are true, and which are false?

    a) An **if** statement must always include an **else** clause.
    b) An **if** statement may contain only an **else** clause.
    c) An **if** statement may include only simple statements.
    d) An **if** statement may contain compound statements only in the **else** clause.
    e) A semicolon may follow an **if** statement only if a compound statement is used.
    f) The **else** clause must always be indented to line up under the **if** clause.

11. What is a nested **if** statement?

12. How many semicolons must be included in an **if** statement that contains a single statement in the **if** clause and a single statement in the **else** clause?

13. When two **if** statements are nested, what is the rule that determines which **else** clause matches which **if**?

14. Is the following statement correct? If not, why?

```
if (q >= r)
    printf("q is greater than or equal to r");
    a = b;
else
    printf("r is less than q.");
    c = d;
```

15. What is the difference between the two operators = and == ?

16. What logical operator negates the truth value of the expression to its immediate right?

17. What integer value is equivalent to "false"?

ANSWERS TO C TUTORIAL

1. The *scanf* function.

2. A *printf*, advising the user that input is required, and specifying of what type it should be.

3. The ampersand (&) symbol.

4. The **if** statement.

5. Six, as follows:

==	equal to
!=	not equal to
<	less than
>	greater than
<=	less than or equal to
>=	greater than or equal to

6. && for AND, || for OR.

7. True and false.

8. They must be combined into a compound statement, using the curly braces { and }.

9. If present, it is followed by a statement that is executed only if the condition being tested proves to be false.

10. All the statements are false.

11. An **if** statement in which the **if** clause or the **else** clause contains another **if** statement.

12. Two.

13. Each **else** matches the nearest **if** before it which has not already been matched by a previous **else**.

14. The statement contains only one syntactic error: The first assignment statement (a = b;) is not part of the **if** clause, and therefore intervenes between the **if** and **else** clauses. This error can be corrected by joining the first *printf* statement and the first assignment statement within braces, to form a compound statement.
    In addition, there appear to be logical errors. The indentation has no effect on the compiler, but evidently the programmer intended both the second *printf* statement and the second assignment statement to be part of the **else** clause and therefore joined in a compound statement. It is also likely that both *printf* statements should contain *newline* (\n) characters at the end of their control strings. Finally, the second *printf* statement should read:

    ```
    "q is less than r."
    ```

15. The single equal sign means assignment, whereas the double equal sign is a relational operator used for testing purposes.

16. The NOT operator, symbolized by !

17. 0 (zero).

Keywords

char	double	**else**	float	**if**	int
long	short	unsigned			

Exercises

1. Write a program that enables a user to input an integer. The program should then state whether the integer is evenly divisible by 5.

2. Write a program that asks the user to input two integers, *a* and *b*, and then states whether or not *a* is evenly divisible by *b*.

3. Write a program that reads in two real numbers and tells whether the product of the two numbers is equal to or greater than 100.

4. Write a program that inputs two numbers, *a* and *b*, and then determines whether the product of the two numbers is greater than half of *a*.

5. Rewrite Program 5-6 to display a message stating whether *a* is less than, equal to, or greater than *b*.

6. Write a program that inputs an integer and determines whether it is evenly divisible by both 6 and 7.

7. Input a number and determine whether it is within a given range (for example, between 1 and 10). The low and high values of the range may be input by the user rather than fixed by the program.

8. Input three positive integers representing the sides of a triangle, and determine whether they form a valid triangle. Hint: In a triangle, the sum of any two sides must always be greater than the third side.

6

The while and do...while Loops

One of the most valuable characteristics of a computer is its ability to execute a series of instructions repeatedly. This chapter introduces the structures known as loops, which permit the programmer great flexibility in controlling how many times a series of C statements are executed.

The Updating Assignment Operators

The previous chapter included statements of the form

```
count = count + 1;
```

or

```
count = count - 1;
```

where 1 is either added to or subtracted from a given variable. Such statements are quite useful and are a feature of all languages. C has a number of ways of abbreviating these common operations. One way is through the use of *updating assignment operators*. For example, the first assignment statement above could be rewritten in C as

```
count += 1;
```

The operator (+=) may look like a typographical error to you at first, but it means: "Add the expression on the right to the variable named on the left." (There must be no space between the + and the =.) By the same token,

```
count -= 1;
```

is equivalent to

```
count = count - 1;
```

where the -= operator means: "Subtract the expression on the right from the variable named on the left."

The value to the right of the updating assignment operator can be any arithmetic expression. The expression is evaluated, and is then added to or subtracted from the variable to the left of the operator. There are also updating assignment operators to perform multiplication, division, modulus, and the other binary operations in C (including some we haven't covered yet). Here are some examples of their use:

Statement	Is Equivalent To:
a += b;	a = a + b;
c -= d;	c = c - d;
e *= f;	e = e * f;
g /= h;	g = g / h;
i %= j;	i = i % j;

As you can see, the abbreviated version is more compact. The abbreviated version also may compile faster, thereby saving computer time.

Another advantage of the updating assignment operator is that it is similar to human thought processes. For example, for the operation x += 5; we customarily say "add five to x" rather than "take the value x, add five to it, and store the result back into x."

Note that

```
a *= b + c;
```

is evaluated as

```
a = a * (b + c);
```

where *b* is added to *c* first, as if the variables were enclosed by parentheses. The reason is that the expression to the right of the updating assignment operator always is evaluated before the update. Therefore, the addition is performed before the multiplication, which constitutes the update.

If the variable being assigned a value appears more than once on the right-hand side of the simple assignment operator, then the programmer can eliminate only *one* of these occurrences by using the updating assignment operator. For example, the statement

```
a = a + a + 3;
```

can be rewritten as

```
a += a + 3;
```

Even with the updating assignment operator, *a* still appears once on the right side of the statement.

The Increment and Decrement Operators

Because the operation of adding 1 to or subtracting 1 from a variable occurs so frequently in programming, C provides an even more concise way of accomplishing this task. For example, if we wish to add 1 to the variable *bingo*, we can use the increment operator:

```
bingo++;
```

To subtract 1 from *bingo* (decrement it by 1), we use the decrement operator:

```
bingo--;
```

No spaces may be imbedded between the adjacent plus or minus symbols.

You will notice that these operators are different from the ones we have seen before. They are the only operators present in their respective statements; even the assignment operator has been eliminated. Also, these operators are written after the variable name instead of before. In these two examples, the statements also could have been written as follows:

```
++bingo;
--bingo;
```

In this case, the position of the increment and decrement operators does not make a difference. As you will soon learn, however, these operators can be used in other ways, and in some cases their positions are important.

The while Loop

A segment of code that is executed repeatedly is called a loop. The loop concept is fundamental to good programming. The simple programs we have shown so far do not contain loops, because their only purpose is to introduce you to C. Once you have mastered the C language, however, you will not be writing such elementary programs. The commercial world demands much more complex programs.

The general form of the **while** loop is

```
while (expression) statement;
```

The loop operates in the following fashion:

The value of the test expression enclosed in parentheses is evaluated. If the result is *true*, then the program statement (the body of the loop) is executed. The statement may be a compound statement. Then the test expression, which may be just as complex as any of those found in **if** statements, is evaluated again. If it is again true, the statement is executed once more.

This process continues until the test expression becomes false. At that point, the loop is terminated immediately, and program execution continues with the statement (if any) following the **while** loop. If there are no more statements, the program terminates.

In Program 6-1, a **while** loop is used to print out ten lines. Each line is numbered by printing out the value of *i* each time around the loop.

```
/* A first look at the while loop */

main()
{
    int i = 1;

    while (i < 11)
    {
        printf("This is line number %d\n",i);
        i++;
    }
}
```

Program 6—1

```
This is line number 1
This is line number 2
This is line number 3
This is line number 4
This is line number 5
This is line number 6
This is line number 7
This is line number 8
This is line number 9
This is line number 10
```

Output 6—1

All variables used in the test expression of the **while** statement must be initialized at some point before the **while** loop is reached. In addition, the body of the loop must do something to change the value of the variable(s) used in the expression being tested. Otherwise the condition would remain true and the loop would never terminate. This situation, known as an infinite loop, is illustrated in the following example:

```
while (i < 11)
    printf("Beware! This is an infinite loop!\n");
```

The loop is infinite because the value of i is never changed. If the test expression starts out being true, it remains true forever, and the cautionary message fills the screen in no time at all.

In Program 6-1, the value of i determines how many times the loop executes. Therefore, the second statement in the body of the loop (i++;) serves to increment i by 1. Since i starts out with a value of 1 and is incremented by 1, at some point it must become equal to 11. Then the condition in the **while** loop becomes false and the loop is terminated.

If i were initialized to a value of 11, the condition in the loop would be false to begin with, and the body of the loop would not be executed at all (no printout would be produced). It is clear, then, that the **while** statement employs a loop pre-test. The loop condition is tested *before* each iteration, and therefore before the loop is entered at all. If the condition initially fails, the loop is skipped entirely.

Suppose we were to add two more statements to the body of the loop in Program 6-1, as follows:

```
while (i < 11)
{
    printf("This is line number %d\n",i);
    i += 20;
    i -= 20;
    i++;
}
```

The two new statements have no effect on the value of i, because even though the first adds 20 to it, the second subtracts 20, leaving the value as it was. Between these two statements, however, i has a value greater than 11. This does not cause the loop to terminate, because the test is not made here; it is made before the first statement of the loop is executed or re-executed. At that point, the original value of i has been restored. In other words, if the test expression becomes false within the body of the loop, execution still continues for the entire body of the loop.

In the following **while** loop, the test expression involves not only i but also the variable a, which we will assume has been declared as **int**. The loop executes only while i is less than 11 and a is greater than 3. If at least one of these conditions becomes false, the loop terminates. If at least one of the conditions is false when the loop is first encountered, the loop is skipped entirely.

```
while (i < 11 && a > 3)
{
    printf("This is line number %d\n",i);
    i++;
}
```

The value of a is not changed in the loop, but the value of i is incremented in a way that will make the loop terminate eventually. The loop could therefore be rewritten as follows:

```
if (a > 3)
    while (i < 11)
    {
        printf("This is line number %d\n",i);
        i++;
    }
```

Notice that in either form of the loop, if the value of a is less than or equal to 3, then the initial test fails and the **while** loop is skipped entirely.

The numbers in Output 6-1 do not line up as we would like. The 0 in the number 10 should be directly under the numbers 1 through 9. Such alignment is called right justification. C provides a method for doing this, as we shall demonstrate in this chapter.

Just as the condition in the **while** loop may be as complex as desired, the variables used in the condition may be changed in any way that will eventually cause the condition to become false. In Program 6-1, i could have been incremented by 2 instead of 1; this still would cause it to attain a value greater than 11 eventually, causing the loop to terminate. Also, a loop can count down rather than up, as illustrated in Program 6-2.

```
/* Countdown to blastoff */

main()
{
    int i = 10;

    printf("Countdown\n");
    while (i >= 0)
    {
        printf("%d\n",i);
        i--;
    }
    printf("\n\nBlastoff!\n");
}
```

Program 6—2

```
Countdown
10
9
8
7
6
5
4
3
2
1
0


Blastoff!
```

Output 6—2

Notice that the initial value of *i*, as well as the test expression in the **while** loop, reflect the fact that we are now counting down. If the condition were the same as the one in Program 6-1, *i* < 11, then the loop would be infinite, because decrementing *i* does not make it greater than 11.

The next program illustrates another way of manipulating the variable used in the loop condition. The problem is based on an idea that was written up in the *Scientific American* in January 1984, in an article entitled "Hailstones." It states that any positive integer *n* will go to 1 if treated in the following fashion:

If *n* is even, it is divided by 2. If odd, it is multiplied by 3 and then incremented by 1. This process continues, using the generated number as the new value of *n*. It ceases only when *n* finally reaches 1 (if ever). For your information, no one has yet found an integer that does not go to 1 using this process, but no mathematician in the world has been able to prove that such a number does not exist. So if it is instant fame you seek, here is a golden opportunity. Try to find an integer that does not go to 1 under these conditions.

The **while** loop is ideally suited to the problem at hand. The loop will be repeated so long as *n* is greater than 1, and the body of the loop will modify the value of *n* as specified by the problem. Since nobody has been able to determine how many steps are required for any given number to go to 1, we have no way of predicting in advance how many iterations the loop will go through. This contrasts sharply with the loops previously shown, in which the loop variable was incremented or decremented by 1 and it was easy to determine how many times the loop would iterate.

```
/* Hailstones */

main()
{
int n, nsave, counter = 0;

 printf("Enter a positive integer: ");
 scanf("%d",&n);

 nsave = n;
 while (n > 1)
 {
    if (n % 2)              /* If (n % 2) is non-zero, "n" is not divisible
                               by 2 and therefore is odd */
        n = n * 3 + 1;
    else                    /* "n" is even */
        n /= 2;
    counter++;
    printf("Step %4d: n = %4d\n", counter, n);
 }

 printf("\n\n%d went to 1 in %d steps.\n", nsave, counter);
}
```

Program 6—3

```
Enter a positive integer: 51
Step     1: n =   154
Step     2: n =    77
Step     3: n =   232
Step     4: n =   116
Step     5: n =    58
Step     6: n =    29
Step     7: n =    88
Step     8: n =    44
Step     9: n =    22
Step    10: n =    11
Step    11: n =    34
Step    12: n =    17
Step    13: n =    52
Step    14: n =    26
Step    15: n =    13
Step    16: n =    40
Step    17: n =    20
Step    18: n =    10
Step    19: n =     5
Step    20: n =    16
Step    21: n =     8
Step    22: n =     4
Step    23: n =     2
Step    24: n =     1


51 went to 1 in 24 steps.
```

Output 6—3

An Enhancement of the printf Function

Output 6-3 shows that the integer 51 goes to 1 in 24 steps. The intermediate values of *counter* and *n* are printed with four column positions allocated to each, and within these four positions the number is right-justified.

This neat technique is accomplished by preceding the letter d in the conversion specification by an integer, which defines the field width for that number. If the field width specified is larger than the number of digits in the number being displayed, the number is right-justified. If the specified field width is smaller than the number of digits in the integer, the computer assigns sufficient space to accommodate the number.

For example, if the number 123 is printed out with a conversion specification of %2d, the computer prints the number 123 in three columns. The effect is as if a conversion specification of %3d had been used. The programmer should try to estimate the maximum width of the number to be printed, in order to obtain neat-looking output with numbers lined up in straight columns. (You will notice that the field width specifier feature is not used in the last *printf* of the program, since there is no need here to line up the numbers with anything.)

In the body of the **while** loop there are two assignment statements. In one, the value of *n* is tripled and incremented by 1. In the other, the value of *n* is divided by 2 with the updating assignment operator. The question arises: Could the updating assignment operator be used in the **if** clause?

The answer is no, because the statement

```
n *= 3 + 1;
```

would produce the wrong result, as mentioned earlier. The value of *n* would be multiplied by (3 + 1), rather than multiplied by 3 and then incremented by 1. Incidentally, it is syntactically incorrect to write

```
n++ *= 3;
```

With rare exceptions, no operator other than an assignment operator can be applied to a variable that is being assigned a value.

Boolean Values

A famous English mathematician and logician named George Boole (1815-1864) invented a deductive logical system that forms the basis for the logical operators used in C and other computer languages. In his honor, expressions involving true or false answers are called *boolean expressions*.

In C, there is no type called *boolean*. The boolean values *true* and *false* are represented by integers instead. The rule used in C is that the integer 0 represents the value *false*, and any other integer represents the value *true*. Thus, an integer value can be used anywhere a boolean test is required, in an **if** statement or a **while** loop, for example. If *n* is a variable of type **int**, the statement

```
if (n)
    a = b;
```

is perfectly valid. It means that the assignment statement is executed only if *n* has a non-zero value (corresponding to the boolean value *true*). The statement is equivalent to

```
if (n != 0)
    a = b;
```

As you might expect, many professional C programmers tend to use the former version because it is more concise.

In Program 6-3, the **if** statement tests the expression (n % 2). If *n* is odd, the value of the expression is 1, which is interpreted as *true*. Thus, the first clause of the **if** statement is executed. If *n* is even, the test expression yields 0, which is equivalent to *false*. In this case, the **else** clause is executed.

Program 6-4 also uses a **while** loop, this time to compute the factorial of an integer that is input by the user. As you may recall, the factorial of *n* (usually written *n!*) is the product of (n)(n-1)(n-2)...(1). For example, the factorial of 4 is (4)(3)(2)(1), or 24.

```
/* Computing the factorial */

main()
{
    int n, nsave, factorial;
    printf("Type in a positive integer: ");
    scanf("%d",&n);

    nsave = n;
    factorial = 1;
    while (n > 1)
    {
        factorial *= n;
        n--;
    }
    printf("Factorial of %d = %d\n",nsave, factorial);
}
```

Program 6—4

```
Type in a positive integer: 6
Factorial of 6 = 720
```

```
Type in a positive integer: 5
Factorial of 5 = 120
```

Output 6—4

Since the variable *n* changes its value with each iteration of the **while** loop, a copy of it is saved in *nsave* so that it can be displayed at the end of the program run. The variable n is then decremented, using a **while** loop with a decrement operator. The variable *factorial* is used as a sort of accumulator; at each iteration of the loop, the current value of n is multiplied into *factorial*.

Notice that *factorial* is initialized to 1. The reason is that any number remains unchanged when it is multiplied by 1. It is necessary to initialize *factorial* to some number, since it is being used in an updating assignment, and initializing it to 1 has no effect on the result.

In order to understand exactly how this program works, let us assume that the integer entered is 3. This value is copied into *nsave* and 1 is stored in *factorial*. Next, the **while** loop is encountered. It is executed only if n is greater than 1. At this point, n is equal to 3, so the loop is entered. The variable *factorial* becomes equal to *factorial* times n which equals (1)(3), or 3.

The value of n is decremented by 1, becoming 2, and the **while** expression is tested again. Since 2 is greater than 1, the body of the loop is executed a second time. This time *factorial* becomes (3)(2), or 6. The variable n again is decremented by 1, giving it a value of 1. When the loop condition is tested, it yields the value *false*, causing the loop to terminate and the results to be displayed.

The Position of the Increment and Decrement Operators

A slightly abbreviated version of the factorial program is now presented:

```
/* Computing the factorial, shorter version */

main()
{
    int n, nsave, factorial;
    printf("Type in a positive integer: ");
    scanf("%d",&n);

    nsave = n;
    factorial = 1;
    while (n > 1)
        factorial *= n--;
    printf("Factorial of %d = %d\n",nsave, factorial);
}
```

Program 6—5

```
Type in a positive integer: 6
Factorial of 6 = 720
```

```
Type in a positive integer: 5
Factorial of 5 = 120
```

Output 6—5

Once again, the input value of *n* is saved in *nsave* and *factorial* is initialized to 1. A **while** loop is used to decrement *n* by 1 and to multiply these intermediate values into *factorial*. This time, however, instead of using two separate statements, the multiplication and the decrement are done in a single statement. This involves a new use of the decrement operator.

The expression n-- means: "Use the current value of *n* in the expression, then decrement it." In other words, the first time the loop is executed, *n* (which initially is set to 1), is multiplied into *factorial*, and then *n* is decremented. This order of operation is known as post-decrement, because the decrement operator is written *after* the variable name and the operation is performed *after* the variable's value is used.

If we had written:

```
factorial *= --n;
```

then *n* would have been decremented *before* it was used in the updating assignment, since the decrement operator appears before *n*. This operation is said to be pre-decrement. The first iteration of the loop would set *factorial* equal to 2 instead of 3.

The same rules apply to the increment operator. The expression ++n (pre-increment) increments *n* before its value is used in an assignment operation or any other expression containing it. The expression n++ (post-increment) does the incrementing after the value of *n* is used.

This use of the increment and decrement operators can make programs very concise, as seasoned C programmers prefer. To the novice, however, such programming techniques can make a program hard to understand. One solution is to use clear comments describing what each statement or critical section of code does. A better solution, however, is to avoid complicated code until you become more experienced.

There are also some practical considerations to bear in mind. When using the increment or decrement operator, the programmer must carefully determine whether to place it before or after the variable in question. This decision can be complicated by situations such as those where the variable appears more than once in the statement. For example,

```
if (a++ == 7) b = a;
```

is equivalent to:

```
if (a == 7) {a++; b=a;}
```

The do...while Loop

The **do...while** loop (sometimes referred to simply as the **do** loop) differs from its counterpart, the **while** loop, in that it makes what is called a loop post-test. That is, the condition is not tested until the body of the loop has been executed once. In the **while** loop, by contrast, the test is made on entry to the loop rather than at the end.

The implication is that, even if the condition is false when the **do...while** loop is first encountered, the body of the loop is executed at least once. If the condition is false after the first loop iteration, the loop terminates. If the first iteration has made the condition true, however, the loop continues.

The general form of the **do...while** loop is as follows:

```
do
      statement;
while (expression);
```

The fact that the **while** clause is located after the statement reflects the fact that the test is made after the statement is executed.

Note that, if the body of the loop is a single statement, it must be terminated with a semicolon. For example:

```
do
      a += 7;
while (a < b);
```

This semicolon marks the end of the inner statement only, not of the entire loop construct.

In every situation that requires a loop, either one of these two loops can be used. Some types of problems, however, suggest one loop or the other as a more natural solution. A good example is Program 6-6, which adds up the values of the digits of any input integer. For instance, if the user enters the number 456, the computer adds $4 + 5 + 6$ and prints the sum, 15.

```
/* Illustration of do...while loop */

/* This program reads in an integer,
   then adds up the values of each of its
   individual digits, and prints out the sum. */

main()
{
 int n, sum = 0, rightmost_digit;

 printf("Type in an integer: ");
 scanf("%d",&n);

 do
 {
   rightmost_digit = n % 10;     /* Extract rightmost digit */
   sum += rightmost_digit;
   n /= 10;                      /* Move next digit into rightmost position */
 }
 while (n > 0);                  /* When "n" is zero,
                                    no more digits to extract */

 printf("The sum of the digits is %d\n", sum);
}
```

Program 6—6

```
Type in an integer: 1776
The sum of the digits is 21



Type in an integer: 390
The sum of the digits is 12



Type in an integer: 4
The sum of the digits is 4



Type in an integer: 0
The sum of the digits is 0
```

Output 6—6

This program uses the % operator which we have used on several previous occasions. The expression

```
n % 10
```

yields the rightmost digit of the number n. For example,

```
123 % 10
```

yields a remainder of 3, which clearly is the rightmost digit. This technique is used to extract the rightmost digit of the number n in the program. This digit is stored in a separate variable called *rightmost_digit*.

Once we have extracted the rightmost digit, the problem arises: How does the program get at the next digit? The solution is to make the next one the rightmost digit, by dividing the value of n by 10. For example, 123 / 10 yields 12 (since integer division truncates 12.3). Now the second digit can be extracted in the same way as the first one. This process terminates when the value of n becomes 0.

The process of extracting digits is destructive, in the sense that it causes the program to lose the original value of n. To display the original value of n at the end of the program, we would need to save its original value in some other variable.

Now we will explain why a **do...while** loop is preferable to a **while** loop in this problem. Look at the final run of the program, where the value entered is 0. If we used a **while** loop, the body of the loop would never be executed, because the condition (n > 0) would be false from the beginning. As the program stands, this is acceptable. If the program were amended to print out each digit, however (as will be done in Program 6-7), this termination would be premature, since the value 0 is commonly considered to have one significant digit, namely 0. Therefore, even if the input is 0, we want to execute the body of the loop once.

It would be possible to write the program using only a **while** loop, but the section would have to be rewritten as follows (adding the digit display feature):

```
rightmost_digit = n % 10;
printf("%d", rightmost_digit);
sum += rightmost_digit;
n /= 10;
while (n > 0)
{
    rightmost_digit = n % 10;
    printf("%d", rightmost_digit);
    sum += rightmost_digit;
    n /= 10;
}
```

Even though this solution works, such redundant coding usually is undesirable.

The advantage of the **do...while** loop over the **while** loop in this type of situation is more clearly illustrated in Program 6-7, which closely resembles Program 6-6. The technique used to extract the digits requires that they be removed from right to left. The next program exploits this fact to print the input number backwards.

```
/* This program reads in an integer
   and prints it out backwards. */

main()
{
 int n, rightmost_digit;

 printf("Type in an integer: ");
 scanf("%d",&n);

 printf("%d backwards is ",n);
 do
 {
   rightmost_digit = n % 10;
   printf("%d", rightmost_digit);
   n /= 10;
 }
 while (n > 0);
 printf("\n");
}
```

Program 6—7

```
Type in an integer: 5746
5746 backwards is 6475


Type in an integer: 60
60 backwards is 06


Type in an integer: 0
0 backwards is 0
```

Output 6—7

If a **while** loop were used in the above program, an input of 0 would cause the loop never to execute. The output of this program shows that a **do...while** loop is the way to go, because it produces the desired result of a single digit, 0, being printed out.

Notice how the *printf* statements are used in Program 6-7. The *printf* immediately preceding the **do...while** loop not only echoes the input but also prints the first part of the solution line. This literal does not end with \n, because the program is designed to print the reversed number on this same line. The *printf* in the loop does not contain \n either, because if one were included, each digit would be displayed on a separate line. The program ends with a *printf* that serves only to end the output line with a *newline* character.

The Trailer Technique

One of the most common uses of loops is to input a number repeatedly and perform some operation on it. For example, we might want to read in a series of radius values of circles and compute the corresponding circumferences and areas. We could take the statements of Program 6-7 and place them in a **while** loop, which would make it possible to print several numbers backwards without having to rerun the program for each number.

If we were to do this, however, a small problem would arise. Computers do not tire very easily; they can run continuously until there is a power failure or some other natural catastrophe. Unfortunately, humans are not so resilient. If we were to place Program 6-7 in a loop, the computer would merrily continue asking the user to enter numbers. We must provide the user with a way to tell the computer that there are no further problems to solve.

Every **while** loop requires that a test condition be provided. Therefore, the problem is merely one of designating a suitable condition that will terminate the loop when it becomes false. One way is to choose a number that the user normally would never ask the program to process.

For example, if the program requires that the user type in a radius, then entering a negative number might be a suitable way to terminate the program. Since this special end-of-data value trails all the meaningful data, the technique usually is referred to as the *trailer* technique. Program 6-8 illustrates its use:

```
/* A program to read in numbers
   and print out their squares */

main()
{
int n;

printf("Enter an integer (negative to quit): ");
scanf("%d",&n);              /* Get first number ("priming scanf") */
```

Program continued on next page

Program continued from previous page

```
while (n >= 0)
{
  printf("\n%d squared is %d\n",n, n * n);
  printf("\n\nEnter an integer (negative to quit): ");
  scanf("%d",&n);          /* Get next number */
}
}
```

Program 6—8

```
Enter an integer (negative to quit): 5

5 squared is 25


Enter an integer (negative to quit): 6

6 squared is 36


Enter an integer (negative to quit): 10

10 squared is 100


Enter an integer (negative to quit): -1
```

Output 6—8

The condition in the **while** loop in this program ensures that the loop will run as long as the value of n is non-negative. When the user enters a negative value, we want the program to terminate immediately. Therefore, we want to read in the value of n just before the test is made. That is why there are two *scanf* statements in the program.

The first *scanf* reads in the first value for n. If that value is negative, the loop does not execute at all. Otherwise, the calculation is performed and output is produced. The last action taken in the body of the loop is to read in the next value of n. If this is *still* not the trailer item, the body of the **while** loop is executed again, using that value of n.

Just about every program that uses the trailer technique requires two *scanf* statements. Since the first *scanf* reads in the first value for n, it is sometimes called the priming *scanf*.

Notice that the prompts preceding the *scanf* statement tell the user what to enter and also how to terminate the program. This type of prompt is considered good programming style.

Unlike previous programs, we are able to present the program with several input values without having to rerun the program each time. All this, thanks to the **while** loop!

A similar approach is adopted in Program 6-9, which reads in a radius and computes the circumference and area for the corresponding circle. In order to allow for non-integer values of the radius, the variable *radius* is declared to be of type **float**. A variable named *pi* is declared for the purpose of holding the value of *pi*. Since its value is real, *pi* has to be declared to be of type **float**.

We could have used the value 3.1416 in place of *pi* in the program, but keeping it in a variable makes for better program readability, since we can tell by the name *pi* exactly what its value means. It could be argued that, since the real purpose of variables is to contain values that change during the course of the program, it is bad practice to use one that remains constant. The value of this variable might be changed unintentionally during execution of the program. C provides a better method of handling constants, but we shall get to that in a later chapter.

```
/* A program to read in radius values
   and print out the circumference and area */

main()
{
  float radius, pi = 3.1416;

  printf("Enter radius (negative to quit): ");
  scanf("%f",&radius);

  while (radius >= 0.0)
  {
    printf("\nThe circumference is %f\n", 2.0 * pi * radius);
    printf("The area is %f\n", pi * radius * radius);
    printf("\n\nEnter radius (negative to quit): ");
    scanf("%f",&radius);
  }
}
```

Program 6—9

```
Enter radius (negative to quit): 4.5

The circumference is 28.274414
The area is 63.617432


Enter radius (negative to quit): 7.3

The circumference is 45.867402
The area is 167.416087


Enter radius (negative to quit): 2.0

The circumference is 12.566406
The area is 12.566406


Enter radius (negative to quit): -1.0
```

Output 6—9

In order to print out values of type **float**, we have used the %f conversion specification. You may remember from Chapter 4 that values of type **float** may be printed out in either of two ways: in standard notation with %f, or in scientific notation using %e. In this book we will mostly use %f, since that notation is more familiar.

C also offers a third choice, %g, which prints out the number in either scientific or standard notation, whichever is shorter. This option is not used nearly as frequently as either %e or %f, however, because most programmers seem to prefer using a predetermined format.

The numbers printed by Program 6-9 have six digits to the right of the decimal point. A programmer may not require this high level of accuracy. Later on, we shall show you a method that enables you to control the number of decimal places that are printed out, as well as the width of the field.

Our final illustration of the **while** loop, Program 6-10, uses two input values in the test condition. The program reads in two numbers at a time, and if at least one is the trailer value (a negative number), the loop terminates. The two values represent the length and width of a rectangle. The program computes the perimeter and area of the rectangle.

```
/* A program to read in length and width
   and print out the perimeter and area */

main()
{
 int length, width;

 printf("Enter length and width\n");
 printf(" (one or both negative to quit): ");
 scanf("%d %d",&length, &width);

 while (length > 0 && width > 0)
 {
    printf("\nThe perimeter is %d\n", 2 * (length + width));
    printf("The area is %d\n", length * width);
    printf("\n\nEnter length and width\n");
    printf(" (one or both negative to quit): ");
    scanf("%d %d",&length, &width);
 }
}
```

Program 6—10

```
Enter length and width
 (one or both negative to quit): 4   5

The perimeter is 18
The area is 20


Enter length and width
 (one or both negative to quit): 5   5

The perimeter is 20
The area is 25


Enter length and width
 (one or both negative to quit): -1    0
```

Output 6—10

In this program, the prompting *printf* tells what condition is necessary to stop the loop, and the loop expression tells what condition is necessary to keep it going. One is merely the logical inverse of the other. So long as *length* is greater than 0 and *width* is greater than 0, the program will calculate the perimeter and area.

Notice how multiple values are entered into a C program when they are included in a single *scanf* statement. The numbers must be separated by white space, which means at least one blank space, tab character, or carriage return. In Program 6-10, the conversion specifications in the *scanf* control string are separated by a blank, but it would not matter if the conversion specifications were separated by ten spaces or no spaces at all—the rule for entering more than one number would still be the same.

You have now been introduced to two of the fundamental loops used in C. It is clear that these are very powerful constructs. In both these loops, a variable often is initialized before the loop is executed, and is incremented or decremented at the end of each iteration. For this reason, C provides another equally powerful loop known as a **for** loop. This loop, as we shall see, serves as an abbreviated form of the **while** loop. Chapter 7 is devoted to a detailed study of the **for** loop.

The Spirit of C

Now that you have been introduced to loops, we can rewrite the program from Chapter 5 which tests for ascending order. Rather than repeating the main block of statements four times, we can place one copy of the block within a **while** loop that iterates four times. Without the loop condition, the loop would look like this:

```
while(...)
{
    scanf("%d", &number);
    index = index + 1;
    if (number < previous_number)
        printf("The number in position %d is out of order.\n", index);
    else  /* In order */
    {
        count = count + 1;
        previous_number = number; /* number becomes new value
                            for comparison */
    }
}
```

Rather than declare a new variable for use in the loop condition, it would be desirable to employ an existing variable that is incremented in the body of the loop. Clearly the candidate for this role is the variable called *index*, since it is unconditionally incremented each time around the loop (as opposed to *count*, which is incremented only when a number is in correct order).

We can guess that the loop condition will compare *index* to the value 5, because when the fifth number has been read in and tested, the program will have completed its work (except for displaying the final statistics). We must be careful to use the correct condition. Should it be (index < 5) or (index <= 5)? We must examine the loop carefully to determine, once the index reaches 5, whether the body of the loop should be repeated one more time.

Since the loop makes only four iterations, we can trace through the scenario one iteration at a time. The first time the loop is encountered, *index* has the value 1. The second time the loop test is made, it has the value 2. Before the third iteration, *index* is equal to 3. Before the fourth (and final) iteration, *index* has the value 4.

Now that all the iterations have been completed, we want the next test of the loop condition to fail (return a false value). This will have to occur when *index* has the value 5 (right before a possible fifth, undesired iteration). This means that a value of 5 for *index* should not be accepted by the condition. Therefore the correct expression is (index < 5).

Note that the expression (index != 5) would serve in this case, but is not the ideal choice because it does not reflect the fact that the values of *index* approach 5 from below.

Incorporating the loop condition we have just arrived at, the completed program reads as follows:

```
/* A program to test five integers for ascending order */
/* Final Version */

main()
{
    int number,          /* Number currently being examined */
        previous_number, /* Last number that was in order */
        index = 1,       /* Which number is currently being
                            examined?  (1=first, 2=second, etc.) */

        count = 1;       /* Counts how many numbers are in order
                            (automatically includes first number) */

    printf("Please enter five integers, ");
    printf("separated by a carriage return.\n");
    scanf("%d", &previous_number);    /* First value used only to
                                         test others against */

    while (index < 5)  /* Test the four remaining integers */
    {
        scanf("%d", &number); /* Input the next integer */
        index = index + 1;    /* Increment index to reflect new position */
        if (number < previous_number)
            printf("The number in position %d is out of order.\n", index);
```

Program continued on next page

Program continued from previous page

```
    else  /* In order */
    {
        count = count + 1; /* One more value is in order */
        previous_number = number; /* number becomes new value
                              for comparison */
    }
}

/* Print final statistics */

    printf("%d of the numbers are in ascending order.\n", count);

}
```

Now that we have modified the program to use a loop, it is possible to adapt it further so that it can test a sequence of any length. We leave it as an exercise for the reader to come up with the solution to this problem.

We would now like to propose a new problem to be solved using loops. This time, the input to the program is assumed to be in ascending order already, so no test for that condition will be made. Rather, we wish to compare each input number with some preselected number. All input values that are less than that value are to be displayed on the first output line. The remaining values, which are equal to or greater than the preselected number, should be displayed on the second line. For example, let us use the following input:

```
3 5 9 12 23 41 56 74
```

Now, if the test value is 20, the output will be:

```
3 5 9 12
23 41 56 74
```

All numbers less than 20 are on the first line, and all those greater than 20 are on the second line. Since the input values were already in ascending order, it was not necessary to reorder them; in fact, all that the program really needs to do is output a *newline* at the appropriate point.

We are assuming that the program will not produce any output until after the entire input line is entered. On computers that display output immediately (that is, as soon as it is generated by the program), the output would become interwoven with the input, causing some confusion to the viewer. For such computers, the program will need to be rewritten slightly. We will present versions of this program for both situations.

In our previous example above, the number 20 was not part of the input. Suppose that we change the test value to 12. Now the correct output is:

```
3 5 9
12 23 41 56 74
```

The input value that is equal to the test number is always displayed at the beginning of the second output line. We have not prohibited duplicate input values, so it might be possible to have an input with two consecutive copies of the test value. In this case, both copies of the value would be displayed at the beginning of the second line.

It is possible that all the input values would be less than or greater than the test value. In this case, all the input values would be displayed on a single line, either preceded or followed by a blank line. For example, again using the input sequence

```
3 5 9 12 23 41 56 74
```

if the test value is 2, the output will be a blank line followed by all the input values on the second output line. In order to distinguish the location of the blank line, you may wish to label the two output lines:

```
line 1>
line 2> 3 5 9 12 23 41 56 74
```

We can begin writing the program with the following loop:

```
while (input_value < test_value)
```

We know that there is no change in the program's activity until the test value has been reached or passed. Thus we can assume that all the program needs to do initially is read in and print out integers, all on the same line. The loop condition covers the case in which the first input value is greater than the test value; in that case, the loop is not executed at all and the first output line is left blank.

The case that is not handled is the one in which all the input values are less than the test value. In that situation, the loop condition remains true until all the numbers have been entered. We need a test for the end of input, which must be located within the **while** loop.

For the sake of simplicity, let us use a trailer to indicate the end of input. We will impose the additional constraint that all input values must be positive, thus allowing the trailer to be a zero or negative value. The **while** condition can now be rewritten as

```
while (input_value > 0 && input_value < test_value)
```

This assures loop termination as soon as the trailer value is read in, assuming that we place a priming *scanf* right before the loop and the loop's *scanf* statement at the end of the loop body. The result is that the loop test occurs immediately after either *scanf* is executed.

The body of the loop needs to contain only output and input statements. It can be written as follows, including the priming read:

```
    scanf("%d", &input_value);   /* Priming read */

    /* While the value is positive (not the trailer) and is less
       than the test value, echo it back */

    while (input_value > 0 && input_value < test_value)
    {
        printf("%d ", input_value);
        scanf("%d", &input_value);
    }
```

Notice that the *printf* control string includes a blank space so that the output values are separated by spaces. There is no *newline* character because all values echoed by this loop are to appear on the same line.

At this point we should add the variable declarations, which should be written as soon as possible so that they are not forgotten. It is perfectly permissible to add a previously undeclared variable to your code while writing a program, because that is how you decide what variables are needed. As soon as you discover that a new variable is required, however, you should add a declaration for that variable, because one undeclared variable is sufficient to terminate compilation of the program prematurely.

Our program so far looks like this:

```
/* This program divides a series of positive integers (in ascending
   order) into two lines, at a predetermined point */
                        /* Stage 1 */

main()
{
    int input_value,     /* Holds the value just read in */
        test_value;      /* This is the value that determines where
                            the output is divided */

    scanf("%d", &input_value);   /* Priming read */

    /* While the value is positive (not the trailer) and is less than
       the test value, echo it back */

    while (input_value > 0 && input_value < test_value)
    {
        printf("%d ", input_value);
        scanf("%d", &input_value);
    }
}
```

One thing we notice is that *test_value* must either be initialized or have its value read in during execution of the program. For flexibility, we will input its value. This will be seen in the next stage of the program.

The next situation to be handled is what to do once the **while** loop is completed. Clearly, the program must output a *newline*, and then enter a second loop which will echo the remaining numbers until the input is exhausted. A new priming *scanf* is not needed, because this purpose is served by the last *scanf* performed in the first loop. That value caused the first loop to terminate, so it was not displayed. Either that value is to be displayed on the second line of the output, or it is the trailer value, which means the second loop should test for it immediately.

The second loop needs only to test for the trailer, since all remaining values are known to be greater than or equal to the test value and should therefore be echoed. The second **while** loop looks like this:

```
while (input_value > 0)
{
    printf("%d ", input_value);
    scanf("%d", &input_value);
}
```

We can now present the second stage of the program, which includes both the second loop and the inputting of *test_value*. We have also included user prompts and labeling of the output lines.

```
/* This program divides a series of positive integers (in ascending
    order) into two lines, at a point determined by the user */
                        /* Stage 2 */

main()
{
    int input_value,    /* Holds the value just read in */
        test_value;     /* This is the value that determines where
                            the output is divided */

/* Input a positive value for test_value */

    do
    {
        printf("Enter a positive value for use in\n");
        printf("dividing the input into two lines: ");
        scanf("%d", &test_value);
    }
    while(test_value <= 0);

    printf("Enter a line of positive integers in ascending order,\n");
    printf("with zero (or negative) as a trailer:\n");

    scanf("%d", &input_value);  /* Priming read */
    printf("\nLine 1> ");           /* Label the first line */

/* While the value is positive (not the trailer) and is less than
    the test value, echo it back */

    while (input_value > 0 && input_value < test_value)
    {
        printf("%d ", input_value);
        scanf("%d", &input_value);
    }
```

Program continued on next page

Program continued from previous page

```
    printf("\nLine 2> ");        /* Start second line */

    while (input_value > 0)      /* Echo the remaining numbers */
    {
        printf("%d ", input_value);
        scanf("%d", &input_value);
    }

    printf("\n");      /* Finish off second line */

}
```

The test value is input within a **do...while** loop so that, if the user types a nonpositive number, the prompt is repeated until a positive number is entered. You may notice that the *printf* statement used to display the label for line 1 occurs after the priming *scanf*. This is done so that the label is not displayed until the input is typed in. Remember that we are assuming that once a *scanf* is executed, it waits until a line of input is typed before returning control to the program; any input it does not use is saved for the next *scanf*, which returns immediately since it already has input waiting for it. If the *printf* that displays the label for line 1 were placed before the *scanf* instead, it would be displayed right after the instructions to the user and would precede the input. Notice also that the second loop is followed by an output *newline*, so that anything displayed by the computer following the end of the program's execution occurs on a new line.

We should check the latest version of the program to see that it handles a typical input correctly. This can be done without actually running the program, by selecting a small input and "playing computer" to see that the output is what is expected. (see the description of the "walk-through" technique in *Programming and Debugging Hints* below).

Once we are certain that the program is correct for a typical input, we must check it for special cases. There are three such cases to consider:

a) All the input values are less than the test value.
b) All the input values are greater than the test value.
c) The input is empty (consists only of a trailer).

This last case is particularly important to examine at this point because we have not considered it up until now.

In the first special case, the first **while** loop is terminated by the reading in of the trailer value. The second loop immediately tests for the trailer value and therefore is not executed at all. The second output line is blank.

In the second special case, the first value read in (by the priming *scanf*) is greater than the test value, so the first loop is not executed at all and the first output line is blank. The second loop displays the first number that was read in, and then accepts and displays the remaining numbers.

In the third special case, the priming *scanf* reads in the trailer value. The first **while** loop tests for this value and fails immediately. The same occurs when the second loop is encountered. The result is two blank output lines.

We can now say that our program has been correctly designed. But we cannot be certain that it works entirely correctly until after it has been entered into the computer, run on a series of test inputs, and debugged if necessary. In fact, we cannot even assume that there are no syntactical errors in the above program (or in any programs presented in this book).

We promised earlier that we would rewrite the program so that it works on computers where the *scanf* returns immediately upon input of a value, even before a carriage return is entered. Input typed by the user is displayed automatically on the computer screen, whether or not the program itself echoes the input. Therefore, it is not necessary for the program to echo the input. It is necessary only for the program to output a *newline* at the correct point, causing the remainder of the numbers typed by the user to appear on the second line. The program must also display the line labels before the user's input for those lines is typed. The program therefore looks like this:

```
/* This program divides a series of positive integers (in ascending
   order) into two lines, at a point determined by the user */
                        /* Version 2 */

main()
{
    int input_value,      /* Holds the value just read in */
        test_value;       /* This is the value that determines where
                             the output is divided */

/* Input a positive value for test_value */

    do
    {
        printf("Enter a positive value for use in\n");
        printf("dividing the input into two lines: ");
        scanf("%d", &test_value);
    }
    while(test_value <= 0);

    printf("Enter a line of positive integers in ascending order,\n");
    printf("with zero (or negative) as a trailer:\n");
    printf("\nLine 1> ");          /* Label the first line */

    scanf("%d", &input_value);  /* Priming read */

/* While the value is positive (not the trailer) and is less than
   the test value, echo it back */

    while (input_value > 0 && input_value < test_value)
        scanf("%d", &input_value);

    printf("\nLine 2> ");          /* Start second line */
```

Program continued on next page

Program continued from previous page

```
while (input_value > 0)      /* Echo the remaining numbers */
   scanf("%d", &input_value);

printf("\n");    /* Finish off second line */

}
```

Notice that the label for line 1 is placed before the first *scanf* statement. It is necessary to label the first line before the user types input for that line.

As a final exercise you may wish to rewrite either version of this program so that it does something useful with the two lines of values, for example, so that it computes the sums of the numbers on each line. It may not be necessary to display the two resulting lines, so one version of the program will run on virtually any computer, whether or not its *scanf* function waits for a complete line of input before continuing.

Programming and Debugging *Hints*

In this chapter, we will examine some basic debugging techniques and some sources of error that are peculiar to the C language.

Basic Debugging Techniques

The technique known as walk-through is used to debug a program before it is actually run. The program is given to a programmer (preferably someone other than the original author), who then mentally executes the program as though he or she were the computer. This is done to ensure that the logic of the program is sound and that all possibilities have been covered.

Seasoned programmers are so convinced of the inevitability of errors that they incorporate defensive programming techniques into their initial draft of a program. These techniques aid in locating the errors. The easiest way to accomplish this task is to print out a number of intermediate results, suitably labeled, to identify the areas in which the errors begin to appear. This technique is known as tracing the execution of the program. Once a program has been debugged, these redundant *printf* statements are removed.

Possible Sources of Error in C

Unfortunately, a compiler is as error-prone as any other program. Companies that write compilers continually find and correct such errors, but it is still possible to possess a compiler that contains bugs. A word of warning is in order, however: It is too easy, when faced with a seemingly unexplainable error, to throw up one's hands and declare that the bug is the fault of the compiler. In fact, the vast majority of all program errors are the fault of the programmer. Before accusing the compiler, be sure that you have ample evidence to back up your claim.

In the early versions of C, updating assignment operators had the equal sign before the associated operator rather than after. For example, to add 7 to the variable *a*, one would write:

```
a =+ 7;
```

This led to ambiguity in a statement such as

```
a=-7;
```

Using the old form of the updating assignment operators, this statement could be interpreted to mean either "subtract 7 from *a*" or "assign -7 to *a*." Many C compilers still recognize the old form and choose the first interpretation. Therefore, when assigning a negative number, you should either place parentheses around the number or spaces on either side of the assignment operator:

```
a=(-7);
```

or

```
a = -7;
```

One of the tradeoffs inherent in the C language is that the programmer is granted great freedom and power, at the price of comprehensive error detection. In other words, C is very permissive. It accepts certain programming mistakes which it does not consider to be faulty. An example is the inadvertent use of the assignment operator (=) in place of the relational equals operator (==). Since C allows assignment to occur in any expression, an **if** statement whose condition reads

```
if (c = 0)
```

is accepted by the compiler, though not as a relational test. The compiler treats this operation as an assignment in which the value 0 is assigned to *c*. The test fails, because the value returned by an assignment is the assigned value, and 0 represents *false*.

One of several errors Pascal programmers may make in C is that of omitting the semicolon after the last statement before a closing brace. Whereas semicolons in Pascal separate statements, semicolons in C terminate statements.

One of the most frequent errors involving comments is the omission of the closing delimiter (*/). This error can lead to extreme headaches, because it may result in huge chunks of the program being unintentionally "commented out." The compiler does not indicate any sort of error until either the end of the program is reached (in which case the comment will never have been closed) or the closing delimiter of some other comment is detected.

This single error can lead to a cascade of error messages, perhaps none of which refers to a comment at all. An even worse result which may occur is that the compiler detects no error, and merely excludes a series of crucial statements from the program. The omission of the closing delimiter of a comment is harder to trace than the omission of a closing brace, because there is no such thing as a nested comment.

Very often, a programmer will purposefully place a comment around a series of statements, in order to exclude them temporarily from execution and yet retain them for possible use later on (simply by removing the comment delimiters). When this is done, the programmer should watch out for comments already present in the code. Examine the following code:

```
/*
    a = b * c;
    printf("a = %d\n", a);    /* Display "a" */
    if (a < c)
        scanf("%d", &c);
*/
```

When the programmer commented out the three statements shown above, using the delimiters seen at the left margin, he didn't notice that the second statement itself is followed by a comment. The compiler encounters the first opening comment delimiter and interprets the following code as a comment. When it encounters the second opening delimiter (the one to the right of the *printf*), it treats it as part of the comment. The only thing the compiler recognizes as a terminator for the comment is a closing delimiter. It finds one at the end of the line containing the call to *printf*. Now the compiler considers subsequent text (the if statement, including the *scanf*) to be part of the program. The compiler then encounters the final closing comment delimiter, but since the comment has already been closed, an error is flagged. Depending on how clear the compiler's message is, the programmer may or may not be able to locate the error quickly.

Another troublesome area for Pascal programmers is the formatting of input and output. In C, unlike Pascal, all formatting is done in the control string. Some programmers may confuse the slash (/) and backslash (\) characters, since the latter is not used in Pascal.

A final warning concerns the truncation of names as practiced by many C compilers. The danger here is that the compiler may not alert the programmer to possible ambiguities. Consider the following declaration, submitted to a C compiler that truncates all identifiers to eight characters:

```
int variable_1, variable_2;
```

The compiler should be able to tell that both variables names will be truncated to the same name, *variable*. Some compilers, however, say nothing about this, and merely treat references to both *variable_1* and *variable_2* as references to the same variable, called *variable*.

C *Tutorial*

1. Show two different ways to multiply the variable x by y, placing the result in x.

2. Which operations can be used with the updating assignment operator?

3. Write equivalent but more concise statements for the following:

   (a) s = s + x;
   (b) s = s - x;
   (c) s = s / x;
   (d) s = s * x;
   (e) s = s % x;

4. Write the C equivalents of the following:

   (a) Double the value of v.
   (b) Halve the value of x.
   (c) Triple the value of b.
   (d) Increment the value of r by 9.

5. What is the output from the following program?

```
main()
{
    int i, j;

    i = 7;
    j = ++i;
    printf("i=%d, j=%d\n",i,j);
}
```

6. Write an abbreviated form of:
   total = total - 1;

7. What is the difference between a pre-decrement and a post-decrement operation?

8. What is the essential difference between a **while** and a **do...while** loop?

9. What happens if the condition in a **while** loop is initially false?

10. What is the minimum number of times the body of a **do...while** loop is executed?

11. How can an integer be printed so that it is right-justified within a six-position field?

12. What happens if the field width specifier is too small for the number being printed?

13. Can more than one field width specifier be included in a single *printf?*

14. How are the boolean values *true* and *false* represented in C?

15. If the trailer technique is used in a program, how many *scanf* statements are necessary?

16. If a single *scanf* statement inputs more than one value, how must the user enter these values?

ANSWERS TO C TUTORIAL

1. (a) x = x * y;
   (b) x *= y;

2. All binary operators (+, -, *, /, %, and others yet to be described).

3. (a) s += x;
   (b) s -= x;
   (c) s /= x;
   (d) s *= x;
   (e) s %= x;

4. (a) v *= 2; or v += v;
   (b) x /= 2;
   (c) b *= 3;
   (d) r += 9;

5. i=8, j=8

6. total -= 1; or --total; or total--;

7. A pre-decrement operation, such as --a, decrements the value of *a* by 1 before *a* is used in a computation, while a post-decrement, like a--, uses the current value of *a* in a calculation, and then decrements it.

8. A **while** loop performs its test before the body of the loop is executed, whereas a **do...while** loop makes the test after the body is executed.

9. The whole loop is skipped over.

10. One

11. By using a conversion specification of %6d.

12. The computer will take as many columns (or print positions) as necessary to display the full number.

13. Certainly; we included two in Program 7-3.

14. The integer zero represents *false*, while any other integer represents *true*.

15. Two are necessary: one right before the **while** loop (the priming *scanf*), and one at the end of the body of the loop.

16. Separated by at least one blank space (or tab or carriage return).

Keywords

char	**do**	double	else	float	if
int	long	short	unsigned	**while**	

Exercises

1. Write a program that repeatedly asks the user to input a negative or positive number, and then echoes it. When the value 0 is entered, the program should terminate.

2. Amend the program in Exercise 1 so that it keeps a count of how many of the numbers are positive and how many are negative. The program should print out these two totals immediately before terminating.

3. Write a program that asks the user to enter a radius value, and computes the volume of a sphere with that radius. The program should terminate when a non-positive value is entered. (Volume of a sphere = $^4/_3$ * pi * r^3.)

4. Write a program containing a loop that counts from 1 to 1000 using a variable i, which is incremented each time around the loop. The program should print out the value of i every hundred iterations (i.e., the output should be 100, 200, etc.).

5. Write a program that examines all the numbers from 1 to 999, displaying all those for which the sum of the cubes of the digits equals the number itself. For example, given the number 563, $5^3 + 6^3 + 3^3 = 125 + 216 + 27 = 368$, which is not equal to 563. On the other hand, given 371, $3^3 + 7^3 + 1^3 = 27 + 343 + 1 = 371$.

6. The "Russian Peasant Problem" is a method of multiplying two numbers together, using only division by 2, multiplication by 2, and addition. For example, if the numbers 17 and 19 are to be multiplied together, they are put at the head of two columns:

17   19

The first number, 17, is divided by 2 (using integer division), and the result is placed below the original number in the first column:

17   19
 8

The second number, 19, is multiplied by 2:

17	19
8	38

This process is continued until the number on the left reduces to 1:

17		19
8		38
4		76
2		152
--> 1	<--	304

All those numbers in the righthand column which lie to the right of even numbers in the lefthand column are ignored:

17	19	
8	38	(ignore)
4	76	(ignore)
2	152	(ignore)
1	304	

The remaining numbers in the righthand column then are added together:

19
304
323

The result is the solution to the problem, 17 times 19.

Write a program to implement the Russian Peasant method for multiplying any two positive numbers. Hint: It will be necessary to eliminate or sum the numbers in the righthand column as they are generated.

7. Write a program that inputs pairs of integers, a and b, and divides the larger of the two by the smaller. Note that it will first be necessary to test for a zero value, since division by zero will cause your program to halt immediately.

8. A prime number is one that is not evenly divisible by any other number besides 1. Write a program to input numbers and determine whether they are prime or composite (non-prime). Perhaps the easiest (though not the fastest) way of doing this is to test whether the number is evenly divisible by all numbers between 2 and itself. The process can be shortened appreciably by not testing the number against any even numbers above 2. It also turns out that it is necessary to test the candidate only against numbers less than half of its own value.

7

The
for
Loop

So far we have discussed in detail two commonly used loops: the while loop and the do...while loop. There is a third extremely versatile loop structure called the for loop which we shall now explain.

The for Loop

Most of the **while** loops we have seen so far have been used as follows. First, the variable used in the loop condition is initialized. Next, execution of the loop begins. A test is made at the beginning of each iteration. The body of the loop ends with a statement that modifies the value of the test variable (or variables).

Because this looping method is so common, C provides a sort of abbreviated version of this construct, called the **for** loop. Its general form is as follows:

```
for (expression-1; expression-2; expression-3)
   statement;
```

Expression–1 is the initialization expression, usually an assignment, which is performed once before the loop actually begins execution. (Remember, every variable used in a loop must be declared in the ordinary way.) *Expression–2* is the test expression, exactly like the one used in the **while** loop, which is evaluated before each iteration of the loop and which determines whether the loop should continue or be terminated. Finally, *expression–3* is the modifier statement, which changes the value of the variable used in the test (or any other associated variable). This expression is executed at the end of each iteration, after the body of the loop is executed. *Statement* is the body of the loop, which may, as usual, be compound. The three loop expressions are separated by two semicolons. (No semicolon should be placed after *expression–3*).

The first expression of the **for** loop can be omitted if the variable is initialized outside the loop. The third expression can also be omitted, but this will probably occur far less frequently. If one or more expressions are omitted from the for loop, the two semicolons still must appear, even if they are not preceded or followed by anything.

In order to print out a literal exactly 100 times, the **for** loop could be used in the following way:

```
for (i = 1; i <= 100; i++)
   printf("This line is printed 100 times\n");
```

First, the value of the variable *i* is initialized to 1. A test is then made to determine whether the current value of *i* is less than or equal to 100. If it is, the condition is true and the body of the loop is executed. Then the value of *i* is incremented by 1.

The same loop could also have been written as a **while** loop:

```
i = 1;
while (i <= 100)
{
   printf("This line is printed 100 times\n");
   i++;
}
```

The advantage of the **for** loop is that it gathers the important parts of the loop construct into one place.

The form of loop to use is largely a matter of personal choice. Any loop that can be written as a **while** loop can be rewritten easily as a **for** loop and vice versa. A **do...while** loop can also be rewritten as either of the two other loops, but a slightly more complicated change would be involved, since the **do...while** loop makes one test fewer than the **while** and **for** loops.

In Program 7-1, which is a simple illustration of a **for** loop, the variable i is declared to be **int** and is initialized to 1 in the **for** statement. A test is made to determine whether i is less than or equal to 10. If so, the loop is executed (the *printf* function is executed, printing out the current value of i). The modifying expression is then executed, incrementing the value of i by 1. The net result is that ten lines of output are printed.

```
/* A simple illustration of a for loop */

main()
{
    int i;

    for (i = 1; i <= 10; i++)
        printf("This is line number %d\n", i);
}
```

Program 7—1

```
This is line number 1
This is line number 2
This is line number 3
This is line number 4
This is line number 5
This is line number 6
This is line number 7
This is line number 8
This is line number 9
This is line number 10
```

Output 7—1

It is important to note that, in order to print the tenth line, the test expression must use the $<=$ relational operator. If $<$ alone were used, the loop would print only nine lines. This difference can be confirmed easily by experimentation.

There is no need to restrict ourselves to counting from 1 to 10. We could just as easily have specified that the values of i go from -4 to 5, which would also produce ten lines of output, although the numbers printed on each line would be different.

You might not be surprised to learn that the **for** loop can count down as well as up. You may remember how we were able to accomplish this task using the **while** loop. Program 7-2 illustrates how this is done using the **for** loop.

```
/* Another simple illustration of a for loop */
main()
{
    int i;

    printf("Countdown\n");
    for (i = 10; i >= 0; i--)
        printf("%d\n", i);
    printf("\n\nBlastoff!\n");
}
```

Program 7—2

```
Countdown
10
9
8
7
6
5
4
3
2
1
0


Blastoff!
```

Output 7—2

In this program, i is initialized to 10 and the test expression reads $i >= 0$. Since the initial value of i is greater than its final value, *expression-3* (the modifying expression) must decrement the value of i each time around the loop. For this reason, the decrement operator (--) is used with i.

This program is not actually the opposite of Program 7-1, because it counts down to 0 and therefore prints eleven lines. If we wanted to count backwards from 10 to 1, the test expression would have to be $i > 0$ or $i >= 1$.

Program 7-3 takes advantage of the **for** loop by iterating the variable i from 1 to 10 and printing out each value of i and its corresponding square.

```
/* Calculating the squares of the integers 1 through 10 */

main()
{
    int i;

    for (i = 1; i <= 10; i++)
        printf("%d squared = %d\n", i, i * i);
}
```

Program 7—3

```
1 squared = 1
2 squared = 4
3 squared = 9
4 squared = 16
5 squared = 25
6 squared = 36
7 squared = 49
8 squared = 64
9 squared = 81
10 squared = 100
```

Output 7-3

The careful programmer probably would object to the appearance of the output. The columns of numbers are non-aligned, making for a somewhat messy-looking display. In Program 7-4, this problem is taken care of. The output is further enhanced by a general heading and two underlined column headings.

```
/* A better-looking program to calculate squares */

main()
{
    int i;

    printf("Table of Results\n\n");
    printf("   i      i squared\n");
    printf("   -      ---------\n");

    for (i = 1; i <= 10; i++)
        printf("%4d%13d\n", i, i * i);
}
```

Program 7-4

```
Table of Results

    i      i squared
    -      ---------
    1          1
    2          4
    3          9
    4         16
    5         25
    6         36
    7         49
    8         64
    9         81
   10        100
```

Output 7-4

In order to align the printed numbers with the right edge of the column heading, the field width specifiers 4 and 13 are used. Often it is a matter of simple experimentation to figure out the exact spacing that is required. After some practice, you will find yourself making these estimates automatically.

The purpose of the next program is to find the sum of the integers from 1 through 100. This can be done using the **for** loop, but you should be aware that this is not a particularly efficient method. As a matter of fact, it is known as a "brute force method," because it actually goes through the work of adding together all of the integers 1 through 100.

Legend has it that, when the famous German mathematician Karl Friedrich Gauss was a mere seven years of age, he was given the punishment in school of computing the sum of the integers 1 through 100. Rather than have to resort to a brute force method, he discovered that the sum of the integers 1 through n can be calculated immediately by the following method, now called the Gauss method:

```
sum = (n * (n + 1)) / 2
```

Both methods are used in Program 7-5, and as you can see, one confirms the results of the other.

```
/* Finding the sum of the integers 1 through 100 */

main()
{
    int i, sum = 0, n = 100;

    for (i = 1; i <= n; i++)
        sum += i;

    printf ("The sum of the integers from 1 to %d is %d\n", n, sum);
    printf ("\n\nThis is confirmed by the Gauss Method: %d\n",
                                    (n * (n + 1)) / 2);
}
```

Program 7—5

```
The sum of the integers from 1 to 100 is 5050


This is confirmed by the Gauss Method: 5050
```

Output 7—5

In this program, *sum* is used as an accumulator. This means the new numbers are added to this variable as they are generated (note the use of the updating assignment operator) until all the required numbers have been summed. Of course, before these additions can be done, *sum* must be cleared, or set to 0. This is done in a single statement, when *sum* is declared.

You may recall a similar method being used in Program 6-4, in which factorials were generated using a series of multiplications. In that program, the accumulator variable *factorial* was initialized to 1 because multiplication was used. With addition, the accumulator variable must be initialized to 0.

Like Program 6-9, which stored a constant in a variable, Program 7-5 stores the constant 100 in the variable *n*, rather than just using the value 100 wherever it is needed. As we mentioned earlier, this use of variables can be considered bad programming practice, particularly since C provides a special way of defining constants. We will discuss this topic in the next section.

Defining Constants, and the C Preprocessor

In certain types of programs, the same constant may be used many times. For example, in Program 6-9 the value of *pi* was used in two different calculations. It is considered good programming practice to define such a value as a constant, which means giving it a name. This method obviates the need to rewrite the constant value each time it is used. Defining constants save time if the value contains many digits or is difficult to remember. Also, if the value of a constant needs to be changed at any time, the change can be made in the single statement that defines the constant.

It is conventional in C to write the names of all constants in uppercase letters, so that the reader can distinguish them readily from variables. We suggest that you adhere to this convention. Moreover, constant definitions usually are placed at the beginning of the program, before the *main* function. The names of constants, like those of variables, should be descriptive of their functions.

The syntax of constant definitions differs somewhat from the usual C syntax. The definitions are not processed by the C compiler directly, but rather by what is known as the *preprocessor*. The preprocessor is a section of the compiler which "looks over" the C program before it is compiled. The format of a constant definition is

```
#define    constant-name    constant-value
```

where the first character (#) must be typed in column 1. The directive **#define** must be written as shown, starting in column 1, with no space between the number sign and the word **define**. This word is followed by one or more spaces and then by the name chosen for the constant.

Like variable names, constant names must begin with a letter and contain only letters, digits, or underscores. As we said previously, it is conventional in C to write all constants in capital letters.

The constant name is followed by one or more spaces and then by the value of the constant. In C, unlike some other languages, no equal sign is used when defining the value of a constant. Also, no type is specified for a constant; the type is determined automatically by the nature of the constant's value. Note that no semicolon is used at the end of the definition.

As an example, if we wished to assign a name to the constant 100 in Program 7-5, we could write the following:

```
#define MAX_VAL 100
```

Notice that the constant definition is *not* followed by a semicolon, since the definition is not part of the C language proper. The end of the line marks the end of the definition. Here are some more examples of constant definitions:

```
#define GRAVITY 9.81
#define LETTERS_IN_ALPHABET 26
#define SECONDS_IN_DAY 216000
#define PERCENT '%'
```

As the last example shows, constant definitions are not confined to numeric constants only.

Here is the previous program rewritten using a constant. Although Program 7-6 contains a single constant definition, a program may contain as many as are necessary. Each one takes the same form as shown here, and must be written on a separate line.

```
/* Finding the sum of the integers 1 through MAX_VAL */

#define MAX_VAL 100

main()
{
    int i, sum = 0;

    for (i = 1; i <= MAX_VAL; i++)
        sum += i;

    printf ("The sum of the integers from 1 to %d is %d\n", MAX_VAL, sum);
    printf ("\n\nThis is confirmed by the Gauss Method: %d\n",
                        (MAX_VAL * (MAX_VAL + 1)) / 2);
}
```

Program 7—6

```
The sum of the integers from 1 to 100 is 5050


This is confirmed by the Gauss Method: 5050
```

Output 7—6

The preprocessor first sees the constant definition, and makes note of the fact that the name MAX_VAL is just another name for the value 100. It then scans the program, replacing every occurrence of the name MAX_VAL with the constant 100. Finally it compiles the program in the ordinary way.

This process emphasizes the fact that a constant name can be used only in places that a constant (such as 100) can be used. It would make no sense to place the constant MAX_VAL to the left of an assignment operator, for example, just as it would make no sense to place 100 in that location. The preprocessor does not know that 100 is a value; it sees it merely as a group of characters. It substitutes 100 wherever MAX_VAL occurs, without regard for C syntax.

Program 7-7 allows the user to enter the value of n. In this case, it is necessary to use a variable rather than a constant to hold the upper bound, since this value is set by the user and therefore is not a constant in the program.

```
/* Calculating the sum of integers 1 through n */

main()
{
    int i, n, sum = 0;

    printf("Please type in a positive integer: ");
    scanf("%d", &n);

    for (i = 1; i <= n; i++)
        sum += i;

    printf("\nThe sum of the integers from 1 to %d is: %d\n", n, sum);
}
```

Program 7–7

```
Please type in a positive integer: 50

The sum of the integers from 1 to 50 is: 1275
```

Output 7–7

We have already illustrated two ways in which the sum of the integers from 1 through n can be calculated: by a brute force method that involves a **for** loop, and by the more efficient Gauss method. The problem presented in Program 7-8 is slightly different. It is designed to compute not the sum of the integers 1 through n, but rather the sum of the integers between any two arbitrary limits. These two values, which we call *low* and *high*, are typed in by the user, and the program uses the brute force method to calculate the desired sum.

```
/* Calculating the sum of integers low through high */

main()
{
    int i, low, high, sum = 0;

    printf("Please type in the low bound: ");
    scanf("%d", &low);
    printf("Please type in the high bound: ");
    scanf("%d", &high);

    for (i = low; i <= high; i++)
        sum += i;

    printf("\nThe sum of the integers from %d to %d is: %d\n",
            low, high, sum);
}
```

Program 7–8

```
Please type in the low bound: 3
Please type in the high bound: 9

The sum of the integers from 3 to 9 is: 42
```

Output 7–8

In this case, two separate sets of *printf* and *scanf* statements are used to input the two required values. This is done purely for aesthetic purposes; the program could easily be modified to read in both *low* and *high* with a single *scanf* statement.

A Word to the Wise

All programmers write code that contains errors. One of the most frequent sources of error is typing in the wrong values. Obviously, it is desirable to be able to trap such errors whenever possible. In Program 7-8, for example, the user is asked to type in two values, *low* and *high*. If the user inadvertently enters a larger number for *low* than for *high*, the sum computed by Program 7-8 will be 0, because the **for** loop will be skipped.

To prevent this error, we can test the value of *low* against that of *high* immediately after the two numbers are entered. If *low* is smaller than (or equal to) *high*, the logic of the program will permit it to compute the desired result. If the value of *low* is greater than that of *high*, however, various options are open to us.

The first option is to terminate the program immediately. This is not the best route to take, however, since the user would be at a loss to understand the nature of the problem. A more user-friendly approach is to print out a message explaining the nature of the error and then terminate the program. The message enables the user to examine the program (or program instructions), trace the source of the error, and type in the correct data the next time the program is run.

Yet another option is to attempt to recover from the error automatically. This means to have the computer correct the error as well as detecting it. In Program 7-8, the most logical correction would be to exchange the values of *low* and *high*.

How can one switch the value of *low* with the value of *high* within the program? At first glance, the following two statements might appear to accomplish the task:

```
low = high;
high = low;
```

Unfortunately, this will not do the job, because the value in *low* will be erased by the first statement when the value of *high* is stored there. Here is what actually happens, using arbitrary values for *high* and *low*:

```
                /* initially, low == 3, high == 2 */
low = high;  /* low gets the value of high (2) */
                /* now, low == 2, high == 2 */
high = low;  /* high gets the new value of low (2) */
                /* now, low == 2, high == 2 */
```

Another attempt might be to write

```
high = low;
low = high;
```

This too falls short of the mark, because the value of *high* is erased this time. The solution to this frequently occurring problem of swapping two values is to use an extra variable, which must be of the same type as the variables to be swapped. Such a variable often is called *temp*. Either one of the two items to be swapped, let us say *low*, is stored in *temp*. Next, the value of *high* is stored in *low* and the value of *temp* (the old value of *low*) is placed in *high*.

Thus, the segment of code to swap the two values *high* and *low*, is as follows:

```
temp = low;
low = high;
high = temp;
```

This segment of code is incorporated into Program 7-9, which has been run twice. In the first case, the two values entered are in the correct order. In the second case, they have been entered in the wrong order. In both cases, the computer prints out the correct result. In the second case, a message that the computer has detected the error, and is correcting the matter by exchanging the two values, is printed.

```
/* Calculating the sum of integers low through high
   with an exchange if necessary */

main()
{
    int i, low, high, temp, sum = 0;

    printf("Please type in the low bound: ");
    scanf("%d", &low);
    printf("Please type in the high bound: ");
    scanf("%d", &high);

    if (high < low)
    {
        printf("Oops! Wrong order.\n");
        printf("Never mind, I'll switch them.\n");

        /* swap the two values */
        temp = low;
        low = high;
        high = temp;
    }

    for (i = low; i <= high; i++)
        sum += i;

    printf("\nThe sum of the integers from %d to %d is: %d\n",
            low, high, sum);

}
```

Program 7—9

```
Please type in the low bound: 5
Please type in the high bound: 20

The sum of the integers from 5 to 20 is: 200



Please type in the low bound: 30
Please type in the high bound: 15
Oops! Wrong order.
Never mind, I'll switch them.

The sum of the integers from 15 to 30 is: 360
```

Output 7—9

Nesting of for Loops

Note that we had to run Program 7-9 twice in order to enter two sets of values. Another solution is to nest the **for** loop of Program 7-9 within a **while** loop or another **for** loop. In Program 7-10, we show an example of such nesting.

The program to find the sum of the integers 1 through n is repeated, but this time within a **for** loop with six iterations. This outer loop enables the user to enter six values of n without having to rerun the program.

```
/* Illustration of a nest of for loops */

main()
{
    int sum, i, j, n;

    for (i = 1; i <= 6; i++)     /* do the calculation 6 times */
    {
        printf("\n\nPlease type in a positive integer: ");
        scanf("%d", &n);

        sum = 0;
        for (j = 1; j <= n; j++)
            sum += j;

        printf("\nThe sum of the integers from 1 to %d is: %d\n", n, sum);
    }
}
```

Program 7—10

```
Please type in a positive integer: 5

The sum of the integers from 1 to 5 is: 15


Please type in a positive integer: 10

The sum of the integers from 1 to 10 is: 55


Please type in a positive integer: 15

The sum of the integers from 1 to 15 is: 120


Please type in a positive integer: 20

The sum of the integers from 1 to 20 is: 210


Please type in a positive integer: 25

The sum of the integers from 1 to 25 is: 325


Please type in a positive integer: 30

The sum of the integers from 1 to 30 is: 465
```

Output 7—10

Note that *sum* is initialized to 0 with an assignment statement, rather than in the declaration as in previous programs. The reason is that six sums are being calculated. The variable *sum* must be reset to 0 six times; otherwise, only the first result would be correct. When a variable is initialized in a declaration, the assignment occurs only once.

The trouble with Program 7-10 is that it restricts us to six values. A more flexible program would enable the user to determine how many times the calculation is to be done. One way we have seen to do this is the trailer technique. Another is for the program to ask the user how many values of *n* he wishes to enter, as shown in Program 7-11. This value then becomes the upper limit for the outer **for** loop.

```
/* Another illustration of a nest of for loops */

main()
{
    int sum, i, j, n, runs;

    printf("How many values of n do you wish to enter? ");
    scanf("%d", &runs);
    printf("\n\n");
```

Program continued on next page

Program continued from previous page

```
for (i = 1; i <= runs; i++)           /* do the calculation as many times
{                                        as specified by "runs" */

    printf("\n\nPlease type in a positive integer: ");
    scanf("%d", &n);

    sum = 0;
    for (j = 1; j <= n; j++)
        sum += j;

    printf("\nThe sum of the integers from 1 to %d is: %d\n", n, sum);
}
}
```

Program 7–11

```
How many values of n do you wish to enter? 3



Please type in a positive integer: 9

The sum of the integers from 1 to 9 is: 45


Please type in a positive integer: 53

The sum of the integers from 1 to 53 is: 1431


Please type in a positive integer: 127

The sum of the integers from 1 to 127 is: 8128
```

Output 7–11

In Program 7-11, the reader is first prompted to type in the number of runs required. This value is stored in the variable *runs*, which replaces the value 6 in the outer **for** loop of Program 7-10. The inner loop then executes as in the previous version. In the example shown, the value typed in for *runs* is 3, so three separate calculations of the sums of the integers are performed. Each time, the user is prompted for a value of *n*.

If you have had previous high-level programming experience, you may expect that all languages supply a function for finding the square root of a number. Unlike many languages, C does not support a built-in square root function—nor any other built-in function, for that matter. Your C compiler comes with several libraries of useful functions, however, including a mathematical library, which can be automatically or manually accessed when you compile your programs.

We have decided not to take advantage of the math library for the time being, in order to show you how a programmer can overcome the absence of a square root function. The method that is generally used for finding the square roots of numbers is the Newton-Raphson method, which is presented in Program 7-12.

You should not be concerned at this point if you do not fully understand this program. Its main purpose is to illustrate some C programming techniques.

```
/* Newton-Raphson method for calculating square roots */

#define EPSILON 0.0001
main()
{
  float n, guess;

  printf("What number do you want to take the square root of? ");
  scanf("%f", &n);

/* verify the input */
  while (n < 0.0)
  {
    printf("Please enter a non-negative number! ");
    scanf("%f", &n);
  }

/* calculate the square root */
  for(guess = n / 2.0;
      guess * guess - n > EPSILON || guess * guess - n < -EPSILON;
      guess = (guess + n / guess) / 2.0
     );

  printf("I calculate the square root of %f to be %.4f\n", n, guess);
}
```

Program 7—12

```
What number do you want to take the square root of? 100.0
I calculate the square root of 100.000000 to be 10.0000




What number do you want to take the square root of? 17.0
I calculate the square root of 17.000000 to be 4.1231




What number do you want to take the square root of? -3.0
Please enter a non-negative number! 0.0
I calculate the square root of 0.000000 to be 0.0000
```

Output 7—12

Validating Input

The programmer should not assume that the user of a program is going to type in a meaningful value. For example, it is impossible (for our purposes) to find the square root of a negative number. There is no guarantee, however, that a user of Program 7-12 will not enter a negative number. If the program did not test the input, serious problems could result.

To prevent this from occurring, a **while** loop has been used to *validate* the input. That is to say, the program verifies that the input is of the correct form, within the correct range, and so on. If *n* is less than 0.0, a cautionary message is printed, and the user is given another opportunity to enter a correct value. The **while** loop continues to iterate so long as a negative value is entered. If the user enters an acceptable value at the initial prompt, the **while** loop is skipped.

The Newton— Raphson Iteration Method

The first step in the Newton-Raphson iteration method is to guess the square root of the number. The closer the initial guess is to the correct square root, the fewer iterations will be required. In Program 7-12, we have chosen to set the initial guess equal to one-half of the number whose square root is required. This decision can be seen in the initialization expression of the **for** loop.

The formula for calculating the square root is as follows:

```
newguess = (oldguess + (n / oldguess)) / 2
```

where *oldguess* is the initial guess, *newguess* is the computed value, and *n* is the number whose square root is required. This process is then repeated, with the value of *newguess* becoming the value of *oldguess* for the next iteration. For this reason, both *newguess* and *oldguess* can be replaced by a single variable, *guess*. Thus, the modifying expression in the **for** loop reads:

```
guess = (guess + n / guess) / 2.0;
```

The new guess that is generated from repeated execution of this line is a value that increasingly approaches the true square root of *n*. We must be satisfied with an approximation of the true square root, because most square roots will require more than the available precision.

How can we tell the computer to stop iterating when it has arrived at a sufficiently accurate approximation? Let us arbitrarily decide that we are interested in an accuracy of about four decimal places. We define a constant EPSILON with the value 0.0001 to specify this tolerance. In order to know whether the desired approximation has been reached, we ask the question: Is the difference between *guess* squared and *n* smaller than the value of EPSILON? If the answer to this question is yes, then we have arrived at the desired accuracy. If the answer is no, then another iteration is required.

The difference between *guess* squared and *n* can be written in C as (guess * guess - n). The **for** loop must continue as long as this value is greater than EPSILON. If *n* happens to be greater than *guess * guess*, however, then the difference will be a negative number. In that case, we would continue the loop if the difference were less than -EPSILON (negative EPSILON). That is the reason for the two parts of the test expression in the **for** loop, joined by a logical ||.

The **for** loop actually has no body. A semicolon follows the parentheses, terminating the **for** statement, because all the calculation done in the loop happens within the parentheses.

Specifying the Number of Decimal Places to be Printed

In an earlier section of the book, we hinted that it is possible to control the number of decimal places printed in a floating point number. This is done by means of the *decimal places specifier*. To display three digits to the right of the decimal point in the number 123.45678, one would use the conversion specification %.3f. The printed value would be 123.457 (notice that this number is rounded, not truncated).

The number 3 in this conversion specification is the decimal places specifier. It is written after the field width specifier and is separated from it by a period. Since we do not choose to use the field width specifier in this example, however, it is omitted and only the period and the decimal places specifier are shown. We could have written %0.3f instead. In either case, the computer uses as many columns as are necessary to print the number, taking into account the required number of decimal places.

If we wanted to print the number in a field of ten spaces, we would write %10.3f. Keep in mind that the ten columns include the decimal point and the three decimal places. In Program 7-12, %.4f is used to display the value of the square root to four decimal places.

Expanding the for Loop By Using the Comma Operator

We now turn our attention to another way of increasing the power of the **for** loop. First, however, we will examine Program 7-13. This program accepts a number *n* and prints a table of sums that are equal to *n*.

```c
/* Generate addition table for a number n */

main()
{
    int i, j, n;

    printf("What number do you want a table for? ");
    scanf("%d", &n);
    printf("\n");

    j = n;
    for (i = 0; i <= n; i++)
    {
        printf("%3d + %3d = %3d\n", i, j, n);
        j--;
    }
}
```

Program 7-13

```
What number do you want a table for? 10
```

```
 0 +   10 =   10
 1 +    9 =   10
 2 +    8 =   10
 3 +    7 =   10
 4 +    6 =   10
 5 +    5 =   10
 6 +    4 =   10
 7 +    3 =   10
 8 +    2 =   10
 9 +    1 =   10
10 +    0 =   10
```

Output 7–13

In the output, as the first operand of the addition increases from 0 to 10, the second operand decreases from 10 to 0 so that the sum is always constant. In the program, the first operand is represented by i, which is incremented by the **for** loop. The variable j is used as the second operand, but it is decremented explicitly within the body of the loop rather than in the **for** statement itself.

The reader might question why j cannot be decremented as i is incremented—within the **for** statement itself. It is possible, and indeed preferable, to do so. Even though i and j are incremented and decremented in parallel with each other, they are not close enough together in Program 7-13 to give the reader a clear understanding of what is happening.

One *cannot* write the **for** statement as follows:

```
for ({i = 0; j = n;}; i <= n; {i++; j--;})... /* illegal!! */
```

Using braces in this manner to group together multiple expressions defies the syntax of the **for** statement. C does, however, provide a way of including more than one assignment-type expression as a single expression in a **for** loop. It is done by means of the *comma (,)* operator.

To increment i from 0 to n and at the same time decrement j from n to 0, the following modified **for** statement may be used. The two usual semicolons are included, in addition to two commas:

```
for (i = 0, j = n; i <= n; i++, j--)...
```

This version of the **for** statement is incorporated into Program 7-14, which produces the same output as Program 7-13.

```
/* Generate addition table for a number n, shorter loop */

main()
{
  int i, j, n;

  printf("What number do you want a table for? ");
  scanf("%d", &n);
  printf("\n");

  for (i = 0, j = n; i <= n; i++, j--)
          printf("%3d + %3d = %3d\n", i, j, n);
}
```

Program 7—14

What number do you want a table for? <u>10</u>

```
 0 +  10 =  10
 1 +   9 =  10
 2 +   8 =  10
 3 +   7 =  10
 4 +   6 =  10
 5 +   5 =  10
 6 +   4 =  10
 7 +   3 =  10
 8 +   2 =  10
 9 +   1 =  10
10 +   0 =  10
```

Output 7—14

In almost every program presented so far, we have used the *printf* and *scanf* functions for displaying and reading simple data in simple ways. These functions are capable of considerable flexibility in their use, as we will demonstrate in the next chapter.

The Spirit of C

One useful application for computers is the simulation of real-life events that we consider to be partially or totally random. An example is the simulation of the flow of customers into and out of a bank, to help determine service requirements. Such a program would model the random flow of customers, while compiling statistics about the flow.

Of course, certain events (such as an increase in customers at lunchtime) are far from random, but in general this simulation has no rules specifying exactly when a customer will arrive. The program therefore allows customers to arrive and leave at a rate roughly corresponding to what is expected or observed in real life, with the exact time of their arrival or departure being arbitrary. The use of simulation frees the programmer and user from having to observe a bank and keep track of exactly when each customer arrives and leaves.

A more familiar computer application of randomness is in computer games. If the sequence of events in such a game were predetermined, the player would quickly learn the sequence and become bored. One solution would be to have a large number of games stored in the program, but this could take up an inordinate amount of memory space. The usual solution is for the game program to choose its own moves at random. In most games, the total number of possible combinations of events or moves is so astronomically large that this method results in each game being unique.

There are two possible ways in which an element of randomness can be introduced into the actions of a computer. One method is to build into a computer a special circuit that produces random numbers. These numbers can then be used by the program to determine its next operation. Such a method has been tried, but the difficulty and cost involved in designing such a circuit has made it unpopular.

Most computers employ what is known as pseudorandomness. This means that the numbers used to determine a program's next step are generated by a series of specific operations. Each number is generated by performing these operations on the previous number. Even though the resulting numbers are not really random, for all practical purposes they work as well as truly random values.

The requirement for such a series of operations is that the numbers it produces should have an equal likelihood of being anywhere within the specified range. For example, suppose we wish to generate a series of four-digit pseudorandom numbers. The algorithm used to accomplish this should, in the long run, produce as many numbers between, say, 1000 and 2000 as it does between 8000 and 9000.

We will try to implement a simple random number generator. We start with a four-digit integer, which is called a seed (because all the subsequent random numbers will sprout from it). This number is then squared. When a number is squared, the result has about twice as many digits as the original, so we now have an eight-digit number. We extract the middle four digits of this number, and the result becomes our new random number. That value is then used as the seed for the next random number, and so on. This method is not the best random number generator, but it is a good example of a simple scheme that produces tolerable results.

The hardest part of the proposed algorithm is the extraction of the middle four digits of the squared value. This can be accomplished through a modification of the method used to extract the individual digits of an integer. First, the two rightmost digits are discarded, by dividing the number by 100. Then the rightmost four digits of the new number are extracted by using the modulus operator. For example, suppose our seed value is 4321:

1. Square the seed to get 18671041.
2. Divide by 100 to get 186710 (integer division discards the remainder).
3. Calculate 186710 % 10000 to arrive at 6710.

The new random number is 6710.

Steps (1) through (3) can be repeated almost indefinitely, until the middle four digits of the number become zeroes. Squaring the number 1000, for example, yields 1000000, where the middle four digits are 0000. This seed will cause all further calculations to return zero. It would be a good idea to test for such a case and to use a new seed if it occurs.

There might also be a four-digit number such that, when it is squared, the middle four digits are the original number. Thus the same non-zero value will be repeated over and over again. You should also test for this case. It is also possible to get into a cycle in which, say, the same sequence of four values are generated over and over again. This case is much harder to test for. That is why most real-life random number generators are based on more complicated schemes that are unlikely to suffer from these anomalies. Nonetheless, for illustrative purposes, we will go ahead and implement our simple generator, ignoring the possible difficulties that could arise.

We have already figured out the main body of the program. If the variable *random_number* contains the last value generated, the code to generate the next number is

```
random_number = ((random_number * random_number) / 100) % 10000;
```

We are able to perform all three steps (squaring, division, and modulus) in a single statement. This is placed in the body of a loop, along with a statement to print out each value (if desired). Here is what the loop will look like, excluding the expressions of the **for** statement:

```
for(...;...;...)
{
    random_number = ((random_number * random_number) / 100) % 10000;
    printf("%d\n", random_number);
}
```

The only remaining considerations are what seed to use and how many times to perform the loop body.

An important detail, which is too easily overlooked, is whether C will allow the storage of an eight-digit number. Even though the intermediate eight-digit value is not actually stored in a variable, the computer will have to keep it in memory. It is therefore necessary to know how large an integer the computer can support. It turns out that most machines can store eight-digit numbers in **long int** variables. We must therefore declare *random_number* to be a **long** variable, and rewrite the main calculation as:

```
random_number = ((random_number * random_number) / 100L) % 10000L;
```

Without these precautions, we could end up with bad results or even negative numbers. An execution error might occur, if the multiplication resulted in what is known as an overflow—a result that is too big to fit in the variable or memory space into which it is to be stored.

Before we say any more about our problem, here is what we have so far:

```
/* Program to generate 1000 random integers between 0 and 9999 (4 digits) */
main()
{
    long int random_number = 4321; /* Variable to hold random number
                                          (Initialized to seed) */
    int i;                         /* Loop index */

    for(i = 1; i <= 1000; i++)
    {
        random_number = ((random_number * random_number) / 100L) % 10000L;
        printf("Random number %d is %ld\n", i, random_number);
    }
}
```

Our program could use some improvements, such as allowing the user to choose the number of loop iterations and the initial seed. In actual use, one iteration would be made each time a random number is needed. Most random number functions actually used with various programming languages allow the programmer the option of selecting the seed. If this option is not taken, the seed is chosen by some other method.

This raises an interesting point: If our random number generator always starts out with the same seed, it will always produce the exact same sequence of numbers. A program using this generator will perform exactly the same steps each time it is run. This is a useful feature when debugging a program, because it is desirable to reproduce detected errors. This is not desirable, however, when the program is actually being used. You would not want a computer game you were playing to repeat exactly the same moves each time, nor would you want the same questions to come up in a computerized quiz.

Computers have several methods of assuring that a program uses a different seed each time it is run. Sometimes the last random value generated by a program is saved, to be used as the seed the next time the same program or a different program is run. Most computers contain built-in clocks that count very small units of time. The reading of such a clock can be used as the seed when a program begins execution. The units of time measured by such clocks are small enough that each program will have a different seed, even if they execute very quickly and are executed one after another. Many random number generators that use these methods still allow the programmer the option of specifying the initial seed for debugging purposes.

The previous program is used merely as a demonstration; normally we would not want to display every random value generated. You might be interested in running the program and observing the output, in order to decide whether the generated values form an even distribution (that is to say, the majority of the values do not occur in one specific part of the range 0 - 9999). You might wish to amend the program as suggested earlier, to allow interactive determination of the number of iterations and the initial seed, and to see how this affects the output.

It might also be interesting to modify the program to deal with random values of only two or three digits. This will make it easier to observe the distribution of the values. It will also simplify a method you could use to determine the distribution of values. Suppose the program were amended to generate two-digit values. You could add ten new variables, each of which represents a range of integers: 0-9, 10-19, ..., 90-99. When a random value is generated, the program would test it to determine which range it falls into and would then increment the appropriate variable (using it as a counter). Using the techniques covered up to this point in the book, such a test would involve a nested **if** statement of about ten levels. At the end of execution, the program would display the range corresponding to each variable and the number of values which fell in each range. The total of all ten variables should equal the number of random values generated.

Most random number-generating functions actually return a real value, ranging from zero to a value just less than 1 (for example, 0.999999 if six significant digits are used). Such a value can be "mapped" to any range of random values. That is to say, the returned value can be used to produce a number in the desired range, without resulting in an uneven distribution.

For example, suppose we want to generate random integers in the range 1 through 12 inclusive. We would take the random number generated by the routine just described and multiply it by 12, truncating the result to an integer. Since the routine can return a value from 0 to just less than 1, multiplying by 12 results in an integer between 0 and just less than 12—that is, 11. There are 12 integers between 0 and 11 inclusive, but they are not the integers we want. We therefore add 1 to the result of the previous step, and end up with a value that can range from 1 to 12.

The C random number function, called *random*, is slightly different from most random number functions. It returns a random integer (rather than a floating point number) ranging from the largest negative value to the largest positive value available on the computer. Using techniques described later in this book, this integer can be transformed, if desired, into a value of any other C data type.

By the time you finish this book, you should be able to use the *random* function to generate values in any range. For specific details of the *rando*m library function, see the user manual that accompanies your C compiler.

Programming and Debugging *Hints*

All but the most trivial programs require user input. Unlike computers, however, humans are prone to make errors. A well-written program must be able to deal with invalid input in a way that will benefit the user (in terms of informing him of the nature of the error) and perhaps even prevent the premature termination of the program. This and related topics will be covered in this section, including criteria for the selection of test data.

Robust Programs

The major criterion by which a program is judged is whether it produces the correct results. The question arises: What degree of confidence can one place in the results?

The debugging process described so far is a sound first step in the elimination of errors. But once the program is up and running, there still are several potential sources of error that can never be avoided. One of these sources is the possibility of the user entering unacceptable data. Whenever possible, a program should be designed so that invalid input will not cause it to crash.

One very effective technique that is available in C is to input all data as character strings (a topic we will soon cover) and examine the format of the input. This step prevents the errors that occur when, say, the program expects an integer but is given a floating point number. Once the data has been verified to be of the correct format, it can be converted to the desired form for storage.

Just because a value has been successfully read in does not mean it is harmless. It may still have to be tested to ensure that it is within the acceptable range defined by the algorithm. This cannot always be done immediately, because the separation between acceptable and unacceptable data is not always apparent until some elementary computation is carried out. All levels of the program must be "bullet-proofed" against bad data, not just the input functions.

Bad data may not only lead to incorrect results, but also may cause the program to crash. For example, suppose a program contains the expression:

```
a / b
```

This looks innocent enough to the programmer and even to the compiler, but if the executing program is given a value of 0 for *b* by mistake, then a "divide by zero" error will occur and the program will crash. Division by zero is the bane of programmers in almost every language yet invented.

Once the program has detected a data error, it should be able to recover. If the error is detected in the input function, the user should be informed that there is an error in the data. The erroneous data item should be clearly identified, along with the reason it is considered erroneous. The user should then be given an opportunity to re-enter some or all of the data. The function can contain a loop that continues to request input until the data is valid. A programmer might impose a limit on how many chances the user has to re-enter data; after that number of chances has expired, the program terminates.

An error detected farther along in program execution is more problematic. The program must undo all effects that the erroneous data has produced, and then allow the data to be re-entered. Sometimes this is just not possible, and the best thing the program can do is terminate after displaying a clear explanation of what caused the error.

The time to decide where to insert error-detecting functions is during the initial writing of the program. Including this additional code will make the program longer, will necessitate more time to complete the project, and might even result in a less efficient program. All the error-detecting techniques will have to be executed each time the program is run, regardless of whether any errors appear. Nevertheless, it is worth the extra effort and expense involved in building error traps into the program in order to avoid disastrous results later on.

Selecting Test Data

The most obvious way to check out a program is to use ordinary, reasonable data as input. The output should be checked against previously known results (a pocket calculator might be useful here). Once ordinary data has passed the test, it is advisable to use more maliciously contrived data. Data close to the edges of the allowable ranges should be used, as well as out-of-range data, which the program should be able to detect and reject before it leads to further errors.

The edge data is perhaps the most important, because it is the most frequently neglected. It is much more usual for the input to a program, either in actual use or during testing, to consist of either ordinary data or erroneous data. Yet the data on the edges of the ranges is just as important in testing as any other data.

As an example, consider the factorial program described in the previous chapter. This program does not work for negative numbers, because the factorial function in mathematics is not defined for negative numbers. Mathematicians define the factorial of 0 as having the value 1, however, and programs that calculate factorials often accept 0 as input. It is possible to write a factorial program that works correctly for 0 without explicitly testing for that value, but the only way to make sure is to test it with an input value of 0.

At first glance, it might appear a simple matter to develop a limited set of test data which will verify a program's correctness for all inputs. For all but the most trivial programs, however, this is a virtual impossibility. The number of combinations of possible inputs to a program can be astronomical. It may not even be possible to choose a truly representative subset of these inputs, because a particular datum that causes an error might not be included.

C *Tutorial*

1. Which is the better loop to use, the **for** loop or the **while** loop?

2. What is a special advantage of the **for** loop?

3. What separates the three expressions of a **for** statement?

4. How does the **for** loop operate?

5. Under what condition can the first expression of the **for** loop be omitted?

6. What is the C preprocessor?

7. How would you define the value of *pi*, which is 3.14159, as a constant?

8. Why are the names of constants usually capitalized?

9. What is wrong with the following constant definition? (After answering, try to write a corrected version.)

   # define x=123.4; y=9876;

10. How would you exchange the values of the two variables *bingo* and *shmingo*?

11. In order for the exchange described in Question 10 to work, what must be true about the types of the variables involved?

12. What is meant by a nested **for** loop?

13. Why is it a good idea to validate input data?

14. What is the name of the built-in function for finding square roots?

15. What conversion specification should be used to print out a floating point number in standard notation, in a field of 15 positions, with 6 decimal places displayed to the right of the decimal point?

16. How would the number 123.4235678 be displayed using the conversion specification described in Question 15?

17. When is the comma operator used?

ANSWERS TO C TUTORIAL

1. It depends on the nature of the problem to be solved, and upon the preference of the programmer.

2. The initialization, testing and modifier expressions of the loop all are specified within a single set of parentheses.

3. Semicolons.

4. The first expression is executed once. Then the second expression is tested, and if it evaluates as *true*, the body of the loop is executed. Then the third expression is executed (usually to change the value of the test variable). Once again, the second expression is evaluated. As long as the second expression is true, the body of the loop is executed, followed by the third expression. When the second expression evaluates as *false*, the loop terminates.

5. If the initialization for the loop is done before the loop is reached.

6. It is the first step in the compilation of a C program, which performs several initial tasks, including the processing of constant definitions.

7. `#define PI 3.14159`

8. This convention has developed to highlight the name of the constant and to avoid confusing it with a variable.

9. Plenty.

   (a) No space is allowed between the # sign and the word **define**.
   (b) According to convention, the name of the constant should be capitalized.
   (c) No equal sign should be used.
   (d) There should be at least one space between the constant name and its value.
   (e) A constant definition is not terminated with a semicolon.
   (f) Each constant definition must appear on a separate line.
   (g) Names such as x and y probably are not descriptive of the roles they play.

   Suggested corrected version:

   ```
   #define LENGTH 123.4
   #define POPULATION 9876
   ```

10. ```
    temp = bingo;
    bingo = shmingo;
    shmingo = temp;
    ```

11. All three variables must be declared to be of the same type.

12. The body of one **for** loop contains another **for** loop.
    ```

13. If bad data is allowed to slip through, it may create havoc with the program.

14. C has no built-in functions, but usually it has a math library which contains a square root function.

15. %15.6f

16.   123.423568
    (There are 5 leading blank spaces, and the number is rounded off.)

17. When the first (initializing) or third (modifying) expressions of the **for** statement contain more than one expression.

Exercises

1. Write a program that prints out the even numbers 2, 4, ..., 20, using a **for** loop.

2. Write a program to calculate the average of n numbers, with the value of n (and the numbers themselves) entered by the user.

3. Amend Program 7-8 to verify the result by using a modified form of the Gauss method. Use your own initiative in devising this formula.

4. Write a program that reads in a minimum and maximum value for a radius, along with an increment factor, and generates a series of radii by repeatedly adding the increment to the minimum until the maximum is reached. For each value of the radius, compute and print out the circumference, area, and volume of the sphere. (Be sure to include both the maximum and the minimum values.) Validate each of the input values to be sure they are positive. If the minimum is typed in place of the maximum, have the program print out an appropriate message, swap the values within the program, and continue execution. Produce a table of the desired results, suitably formatted and with headings.

5. Write a program that allows any positive integer to be typed in. The program should count how many times the number has to be doubled before it reaches 1 million.

6. A famous conjecture holds that all positive integers converge to one when treated in the following fashion:

   a) If the number is odd, it is multiplied by 3, and then 1 is added.
   b) If the number is even, it is divided by two.
   c) Continually apply the above operations to the intermediate results until the number reaches 1.

For example, if the number 7 is selected, the results will be:

```
 7
22      (7 * 3 + 1)
11      (22 / 2)
34      (11 * 3 + 1)
17      (34 / 2)
52      (17 * 3 + 1)
26      (52 / 2)
13      (26 / 2)
40      (13 * 2 + 1)
20      (40 / 2)
10      (20 / 2)
 5      (10 / 2)
16      (5 * 3 + 1)
 8      (16 / 2)
 4      (8 / 2)
 2      (4 / 2)
 1      (2 / 2)
```

So far, nobody has been able to come up with a number which does not converge to 1 in this way, but that does not mean such numbers do not exist. Write a program to test numbers that are selected and input by the user. It may be desirable to count the number of computations required. You may also wish to display the intermediate results. Caution: Some small numbers take a long time to converge to 1.

7. The formula used to calculate the amount of interest on a bank account that compounds interest daily is

$$i = p \ (1 + r)^d - p$$

where:

i is the total interest earned,
p is the principal (the amount originally deposited in the account),
r is the rate of interest as a decimal less than 1 (for example, 15 percent is expressed as 0.15), and
d is the number of days the money is earning interest.

Write a program that accepts values for p, r and d and calculates the interest earned (i). Since C does not have an operator for exponentiation (raising a number to a power), this will have to be simulated using a loop.

8. Write a program which accepts a number *n*, and then finds the sum of the integers from 1 to 2, then from 1 to 3, then 1 to 4, and so forth until it displays the sum of the integers from 1 to *n*. For example, if the input is 5, the output will be:

    1
    3
    6
    10
    15

    This can be done using a pair of nested **for** loops, but you may also wish to try it using Gauss' formula and another method of your own devising.

9. All of the preceding programs should have been written with some form of input validation. Modify one of them so that it limits the number of chances the user gets to correct errors, for example to 3. If the user does not enter a valid input after three tries, the program terminates.

10. Write a program that reads in a number, then reads in a single digit and determines whether the first number contains the digit. If it does, the program should display how many times the digit occurs in the number.

11. The Fibonacci series is an infinite series of numbers which starts out as follows:

    1, 1, 2, 3, 5, 8, 13, 21, ...

    As you may notice, each number in the series is the sum of the preceding two numbers. Write a program to generate the series to any length desired. This problem is not as easy to program as it looks, but a little creativity can lead to an elegant solution.

8

A Detailed Look at the *printf* and *scanf* Functions

*D*espite the fact that we have used the printf and scanf functions in almost every program, we still have not covered them in sufficient detail to do them justice. It is also important to be able to display messages and output in a manner that is clear, helpful, and attractive to the user. It is also desirable to be able to input data in a format that is convenient for the user as well as the programmer.

The printf and scanf functions are so useful for these purposes that we are devoting this whole chapter to an exploration of some of their other features. You might find that this chapter contains more detail than you need for the time being, but it will surely prove valuable at a later time.

The Conversion Specifications for *printf*

You will recall that, in order to print out a decimal number using the *printf* function, the conversion specification %d is used. Every conversion specification begins with a percentage sign and terminates with a lowercase letter such as *d, f, e,* or *c.* (In some versions of *printf,* uppercase letters have special significance.) Between the percentage sign and the letter, one can insert a number specifying the minimum field width. If the *e* or *f* format is used, the field width number (if any) may be followed by a decimal point and a number that specifies how many digits are to be displayed to the right of the decimal point in the output.

The conversion specification may also include a minus sign, immediately after the % sign. Ordinarily, numbers are right-justified in the output field. When the minus sign is included, however, the number is left-justified.

Program 8-1 illustrates various conversion specifications. To the right of each *printf* statement we have included a numbered comment. Colons have been inserted before and after each conversion specification in order to show in the output the exact limits of the field in which the number appears. We recommend that you read each example very carefully to ensure that the material is crystal-clear. There is nothing difficult about these conversions, but a certain amount of attention to detail is required.

```
/* A printf demo:
   The conversion specification for numbers. */

main()
{
 printf("Case  1 :%d:\n", 123);        /* 1) defaults to width of number */

 printf("Case  2 :%0d:\n", 123);       /* 2) equivalent to the above */

 printf("Case  3 :%2d:\n", 123);       /* 3) also defaults to width
                                              of number */

 printf("Case  4 :%8d:\n", 123);       /* 4) right-justified in a field
                                              of 8 */

 printf("Case  5 :%-8d:\n", 123);      /* 5) left-justified in a field
                                              of 8 */

 printf("Case  6 :%8d:\n", -123);      /* 6) negative number right-
                                              justified in a field of 8 */

 printf("Case  7 :%f:\n", 123.456);    /* 7) prints in "f" format with 6
                                              decimal digits */

 printf("Case  8 :%f:\n", 123.4567896); /* 8) prints in "f" format, rounding
                                              to 6 decimal digits */

 printf("Case  9 :%e:\n", 123.456);    /* 9) prints in "e" format */
```

Program continued on next page

Program continued from previous page

```
printf("Case 10 :%e:\n", 1.23456e2);      /* 10) prints in "e" format */

printf("Case 11 :%e:\n", 123.456e+0);      /* 11) prints in "e" format */

printf("Case 12 :%f:\n", 1.23456E+02);      /* 12) prints in "f" format */

printf("Case 13 :%4.2f:\n", 123.456);      /* 13) prints in "f" format with 2
                                                 decimal digits (rounded), but
                                                 needs (and gets) more than
                                                 4 columns total. */

printf("Case 14 :%8.2f:\n", 123.456);      /* 14) prints in "f" format with 2
                                                 decimal digits in a field
                                                 of 8 columns */

printf("Case 15 :%.3e:\n", 123.456);      /* 15) prints in "e" format
                                                 with 3 decimal places */

printf("Case 16 :%12.3e:\n", 123.456);      /* 16) prints in "e" format in a
                                                 field of 12 with 3 decimal
                                                 places */

}
```

Program 8—1

```
Case  1 :123:
Case  2 :123:
Case  3 :123:
Case  4 :     123:
Case  5 :123     :
Case  6 :    -123:
Case  7 :123.456000:
Case  8 :123.456790:
Case  9 :1.234560E+02:
Case 10 :1.234560E+02:
Case 11 :1.234560E+02:
Case 12 :123.456000:
Case 13 :123.46:
Case 14 :  123.46:
Case 15 :1.235E+02:
Case 16 :   1.235E+02:
```

Output 8—1

In the first example, the number 123 is printed out using the conversion specification %d. This situation is quite familiar to us by now. The three-digit number is printed out in a field width of three positions, since that is how many are needed to display the full number. In other words, the field width defaults to the width of the number. In the second case, the number 123 is printed using a specification of %0d, and the same result is obtained. Obviously, zero spaces are not sufficient to accommodate any number, let alone a three-digit number. The same result appears in the third example, for which the specification is %2d.

Case number 4 shows that, when the number 123 is printed with a conversion specification of %8d, eight columns are supplied and the number is right-justified within these eight columns. When the specification is changed to %-8d, as in case 5, the number is left-justified within the field.

In case number 6, the negative number -123 is printed using a specification of %8d. The number is printed right-justified in a field eight columns wide. Notice that -123 requires at least four positions, since the minus sign also occupies a position.

The next case, number 7, uses the %f conversion specification to print out the number 123.456. Notice that six decimal places are displayed in the output. This is the default when no decimal place count is explicitly specified, so there are three trailing zeroes. In case number 8, the %f specification again is used, but this time with the number 123.4567896. This number contains more than the output default of six decimal places. The result is that C rounds it off to 123.456790.

Case 9 uses the %e conversion specification to print out the number 123.456 in scientific (exponential) notation. The number is displayed as 1.234560E+02. When numbers are printed in e format, there is exactly one non-zero digit to the left of the decimal point. Again, the default is six digits to the right of the decimal point. The capital letter E is followed by a minus or plus sign and an exponent of exactly two digits. (On some computers, three digits are displayed.)

Case number 10 illustrates that there is flexibility in the manner in which a number in exponential format can be written. In this example, the number 1.23456e2 is printed using the %e conversion specification. It is printed out in the format described in case 9. The *printf* statement uses a lowercase e, with no plus sign and no zero preceding the exponent 2, but C converts it automatically to the standard exponential format as shown in the output.

Case number 11 is another example of a number expressed in scientific notation, but written in non-standard form. The number 123.456e+0 is converted automatically on output to 1.234560E+02, with only a single digit to the left of the decimal point.

Case number 12 illustrates that a number written in e format can be converted to standard notation by using a conversion specification of %f.

In case 13, the number 123.456 is printed with a specification of %4.2f. Since the conversion specifies that two decimal places should be displayed, the number 123.456 is rounded to 123.46. But such a number requires six positions, rather than the four specified in the field width specifier, so the total field width defaults to six positions.

A similar situation arises in case number 14, where the number 123.456 is converted using the specification %8.2f. Once again, the number is rounded to two decimal places, yielding the value 123.46, and this is right-justified within a field width of eight positions. Remember that, even though eight positions is wide enough to hold the original number 123.456, only two decimal places are permitted by the conversion specification, so the number printed is again the rounded value 123.46.

Careful attention should be paid to case number 15, in which the number 123.456 is converted using the specification %.3e. The number first is converted to scientific notation, and then only three decimal places are kept to the right of the decimal point. In other words, the number 123.456 gets converted to 1.234560E+02, but since the specification permits only three decimal places, the number is rounded to 1.235E+02. Even though the original number 123.456 had three digits to the right of the decimal point, if we wished to retain all these digits in scientific form, we would have had to resort to a conversion specification of %.5e.

In the last case, number 16, the same value as in case 15 is printed, but this time it is right-justified in a field width of twelve positions. Notice that the minimum number of positions needed for a number in exponential form includes exactly four positions for the exponent (the letter E, a sign, and two digits), plus two positions for the leading digit and the decimal point, plus the specified or default number of decimal places.

Type char and the ASCII Code

When a character is typed into the computer via the keyboard, the character itself is not recorded. Rather, a numeric version of that particular character is stored. Each character is assigned a number according to the ASCII (pronounced "ask-ee") code, which is the most popular code for representing characters on computers. ASCII is an abbreviation for American Standard Code for Information Interchange. (For a complete listing of the ASCII code, please see Appendix C.)

The capital letters A through Z are represented in ASCII by the numbers 65 through 90. The lowercase letters are represented by the numbers 97 through 122. The digits 0 through 9 are represented internally by the ASCII values 48 through 57, and the intervening values from 32 through 126 are various punctuation symbols. The values 0 through 31, and 127 (the highest ASCII number), represent what are called *control characters*. These are non-printable characters (such as the *newline* character) which perform special functions. More will be said about these control characters later.

If characters are stored in the computer as numbers (their ASCII code representation), how can one differentiate between a character and a number? The simple answer is that it is up to the programmer to maintain the conceptual separation. We have discussed the variable type **char**, which is used to hold single characters. In fact, a variable of type **char** simply holds a number, and it can be used in almost the same way as a variable of type **int**. The difference is that a variable of type **char** can hold only a small range of values, generally -128 through 127 (or 0 through 255 in the versions of C which allow type **unsigned char**). This is enough of a range to hold any one of the ASCII values. Since both characters and numbers are stored internally in the same form, the C programmer must keep track of the intended use of a particular variable.

Program 8-2 illustrates how a particular value can be interpreted in more than one way.

```
/* A printf demo:
   Interpretation of values */

main()
{
  int n = -123;
  char c = 'V';

  printf("%d\n", n);       /* 1) negative number correctly interpreted */
  printf("%u\n", n);       /* 2) negative number incorrectly interpreted */

  printf("%c\n", c);       /* 3) printing a character */
  printf("%d\n", c);       /* 4) printing ASCII value of a character */
  printf("%c\n", 86);      /* 5) printing a character by ASCII value */
}
```

Program 8—2

```
-123
65413
V
86
V
```

Output 8—2

In this program, the variable n is declared to be of type **int**, and is initialized to -123 in the same declaration. The variable c is declared to be of type **char**, and is initialized to the single character uppercase V. (You will recall that a variable of type **char** can hold only a single character.)

Within the program, the variable n is displayed using the standard conversion specification %d. The number -123 prints out as expected. Then the value of n is printed out using the specification %u, which tells the *printf* function to treat the corresponding value as an unsigned number. Note the output.

The error occurs for a reason that is a little more complicated than you might expect. The *printf* function does not know that the variable n is declared to be of type **int**. It only sees the series of bits representing -123 and the conversion specification. Because the conversion specification tells the computer to interpret the series of bits as an unsigned (positive) integer, the *printf* function dutifully goes ahead and misinterprets the value presented to it. The series of bits which represents the value -123, when interpreted as an unsigned integer, yields the value 65413 on the particular computer we are using. This number is of no concern to the C programmer.

In the third *printf*, the **char** variable c, into which the character 'V' has been stored, is printed out in c format. As expected, the letter V is printed without the apostrophes. In the fourth *printf*, the contents of this same variable are printed out using the %d conversion specification. This time, the contents of the variable c are interpreted as an integer rather than a character, and what is printed out is the ASCII equivalent of the letter V.

Finally, the value 86 is printed out using the %c conversion specification. Since 86 is the ASCII code for the letter V, that letter is displayed, rather than a number.

Program 8-3 enables a user to type in a character at the keyboard and have the equivalent ASCII code printed out.

```
/* Printing out the ASCII value of a character */

main()
{
  char in_char, answer;

  do    /* as many times as the user wants */
  {
      printf("\n\n\nEnter a character: ");
      scanf("%c", &in_char);

      printf("\nThe ASCII value of %c is %d.\n", in_char, in_char);

/* ask if the user wants to go again */
      printf("\nAnother? (y/n) ");
      scanf("%c", &answer);
  }
  while (answer == 'y');
}
```

Program 8—3

```
Enter a character: a
The ASCII value of a is 97.

Another? (y/n) y


Enter a character: V
The ASCII value of V is 86.

Another? (y/n) y


Enter a character: 6
The ASCII value of 6 is 54.

Another? (y/n) n
```

Output 8—3a

```
Enter a character: #
The ASCII value of # is 35.

Another? (y/n) Y
```

Output 8—3b

In this program, the variables *in_char* and *answer* are declared to be of type **char**. In response to a prompt, the user enters any character from the keyboard. The ASCII value of this character is stored into *in_char*. Like a numeric variable, *in_char* must be prefixed with an ampersand (&) in the corresponding *scanf* statement. (Actually, **char** variables are identical to other integer types, just smaller.) The contents of the variable *in_char* then are printed out in both character and decimal format.

At this point, the user is asked if another round is required. The response is y for *yes* or n for *no*. The response is stored in *answer*. Since both y and n have their own ASCII values, a relational operator (in this case ==) is used in the **while** clause of the **do...while** loop, where the y is enclosed in single quotation marks (apostrophes).

Any response other than lowercase y is regarded by this program as a negative response. In the second run of the program, the user responds with a capital Y to the prompt for y or n. This input terminates the program, because the Y is not lowercase.

One of the purposes of the next program is to illustrate the difference between a digit's ASCII representation and its integer equivalent. If one were to type the character 7 in Program 8-3, the output would be the ASCII value 55. But what if we wanted a program that could input a digit as a character and derive its integer equivalent, which is simply the number 7? This actually is what the *scanf* function does. When you type a number at the keyboard, it is just a string of characters, which the *scanf* function converts into the intended integer.

Fortunately, the ASCII codes for the digits are in the same order as the digits themselves. That is, the ASCII code for the character 0 is 48, the code for 1 is 49, and so forth. Therefore, if we subtract the number 48 from the ASCII code of each of the digits, the result is the equivalent integer. This method is used in Program 8-4, which accepts a digit, generates its integer equivalent, and prints out the resulting value.

```
/* Converting a digit to a number by using its ASCII value */

main()
{
  char digit;

  printf("Enter a digit: ");
  scanf("%c", &digit);                 /* digit is entered as a character */

  if(digit < '0' || digit > '9')
    printf("\nThat's not a digit!\n");
  else                                 /* digit's numerical equivalent is printed */
    printf("\nThe digit you typed is %d\n", digit - '0');
}
```

Program 8—4

```
Enter a digit: 7
The digit you typed is 7




Enter a digit: A
That's not a digit!
```

Output 8—4

The variable *digit* is declared to be of type **char**. In response to the prompt, the user types in a character, which may or may not be a digit. The ASCII value of this character is stored in *digit*. A test is made to determine whether the character is a digit by determining whether it falls within the range of characters '0' through '9'; that is, whether its ASCII value is in the range 48 through 57 inclusive. Note that the use of single quotation marks in the **if** statement specifies the characters '0' and '9', rather than their ASCII values. The effect is the same as if the ASCII values were given.

If the first expression OR the second expression of the **if** statement is true (both cannot be true simultaneously), the character typed in is not a digit, and a message to that effect is displayed. By using the characters '0' and '9' in the **if** expression, the programmer avoids having to remember the ASCII codes for those digits.

If the character typed in is a digit, the **else** clause of the **if** statement is executed. The *printf* contains the expression

```
digit - '0'
```

This is another example of using a character directly instead of its ASCII value. The expression subtracts the value 48 from the ASCII code for a digit and thereby generates the numeric equivalent of that digit. Again, this approach clarifies what is being done and also relieves the user of the chore of having to remember the ASCII codes.

The program was run two times. In the first case, a digit was entered, but on the second run the letter A was typed in. As the output clearly shows, the computer detected that the letter A is not a digit.

In Program 8-5, the computer distinguishes between uppercase and lowercase letters, and converts each input letter from one case to the other. We recommend that you study the program first and try to see how it operates before reading the detailed explanation which follows.

```
/* Converting a letter from lower to upper case, or vice-versa */

main()
{
  char letter, answer;

  do
  {
    printf("\n\n\nEnter a letter: ");
    scanf("%c", &letter);

    if(letter >= 'A' && letter <= 'Z')   /* letter is upper case */
      printf("\nLower case is: %c\n", letter + ('a' - 'A'));
```

Program continued on next page

Program continued from previous page

```
    else if(letter >= 'a' && letter <= 'z')   /* letter is lower case */
        printf("\nUpper case is: %c\n", letter - ('a' - 'A'));

        else printf("\nThat's not a letter!\n");


/* ask if the user wants to go again */
    printf("\nAnother? (y/n) ");
    scanf("%c", &answer);
  }
  while (answer == 'y');
}
```

Program 8—5

```
        Enter a letter: a
        Upper case is: A

        Another? (y/n) y


        Enter a letter: V
        Lower case is: v

        Another? (y/n) y


        Enter a letter: 7
        That's not a letter!

        Another? (y/n) n
```

Output 8—5

The variables *letter* and *answer* both are declared to be of type
char. At the beginning of the **do...while** loop, a prompt asks the
user to type in a letter, which is stored in the variable *letter*. In
order to determine whether the letter to be typed in is uppercase
or not, the first **if** clause tests whether its ASCII code is within
the range of characters A through Z inclusive. The two relational
expressions in the **if** statement are joined by the **&&** operator,
because if the character is uppercase, its ASCII value must be
greater than or equal to that of A and less than or equal to
that of Z. If this compound test condition proves to be true, the
lowercase equivalent is computed and printed out.

Lowercase letters have greater ASCII values than uppercase
letters. The constant value 32, when added to the ASCII value
of an uppercase letter, produces the ASCII value of the lowercase
equivalent of this letter. The expression ('a' - 'A'), which
appears in Program 8-5, is equivalent to 32 and thus can be
used to convert uppercase letters to lowercase and vice versa.

The **else** clause of the first **if** statement contains another **if**
statement to test whether the character contained in *letter* is a
lowercase letter. If it is, the corresponding uppercase letter is
generated by subtracting the value 32 ('a' - 'A') from *letter*.

The **else** clause of the inner **if** statement is executed if the
character in **letter** is neither an uppercase nor a lowercase letter.
In that case, an error message is displayed.

After the **if** statements are executed, the user is asked if another round is required. If the response is y, the loop is repeated. Otherwise, the program is terminated.

Escape Sequences and Control Characters

Certain ASCII characters are unprintable, which means they are not displayed on the screen or printer. These characters perform special functions other than producing text, such as backspacing, returning to the beginning of a line, advancing to a new line, tabbing, or ringing a bell. You have already seen many examples of one of these control characters—the *newline* character, represented by the escape sequence \n. The backslash character in C is called the escape character, because a character following immediately after it takes on a special meaning. Such characters may be used within apostrophes (when specifying a character constant) or within double quotes (such as in a control string). Here are some of the more commonly used escape sequences:

Escape Sequence	Meaning
\n	newline
\t	tab
\b	backspace
\r	carriage return
\f	form feed

The tab character moves over to the next preset tab stop, which may or may not be user-determined on your computer, terminal, or printer. The backspace character performs the same task as that key on your computer or typewriter. The carriage return character returns to the beginning of the current line, but your printer may not perform this task correctly unless specially set. (Notice that, when you press the carriage return key on your computer, what you see on your screen actually is a carriage return followed by a line feed.) Finally, the form feed character generally clears the screen or, in the case of a printer, advances it to the next new page.

Program 8-6 illustrates two of these escape sequences: the backspace and the tab. What is printed by the printer is different from what appears on the screen, because backspacing on the screen overwrites whatever character formerly resided in that position.

```
/* Example of using control characters */

main()
{
  printf("The word apple\b\b\b\b\b_____ is underlined.\n\n");

  printf("The last word in this sentence is way over\t\there.\n");
}
```

Program 8—6

```
The word apple is underlined.

The last word in this sentence is way over            here.
```

In this program, the five-letter word *apple* contained in the literal is followed by five successive \b control characters. Thus the next five characters (which are underscores) are printed exactly under the word *apple*.

The second *printf* statement contains two instances of the control character \t, which follow the word *over* in the literal. Notice how escape sequences can look confusing at times. The \t before the word *here* may look at first as if the word *there* is being printed. The compiler, however, recognizes the character immediately following the backslash (in this case *t*) as part of the escape sequence. Two tabs are used because the first tab stop follows too soon after the word *over*, and would have not been effective in illustrating the role played by the tab. The second tab allows a more conspicuous gap between the words.

The next program illustrates how escape sequences can be used to print certain characters that would otherwise be ambiguous. These are the double quotation marks, the apostrophe (or single quotation mark), the percent sign, and the backslash itself. In this case, the backslash actually performs the task of *removing* the special meaning of the symbol following it.

```
/* How to print special characters */

main()
{
  char c;

  printf("This is how to print a double-quote: \"\n");
  printf("This is how to print a backslash: \\\n");
  /* this is how to write an apostrophe character: */
  c = '\'';
  printf("c now contains: %c\n", c);
  printf("This is how to print a percent-sign: %%\n");
}
```

Program 8—7

```
This is how to print a double-quote: "
This is how to print a backslash: \
c now contains: '
This is how to print a percent-sign: %
```

There is one exceptional case in the above program: the percent sign (%). To print a percent sign in a control string, instead of preceding it by a backslash, you must use two adjacent percent signs.

You will notice that the \" sequence is necessary only within a string (between double quotes), since a double quote between apostrophes is not ambiguous. Similarly, \' is necessary only between apostrophes, such as in the assignment statement involving the variable *c* in Program 8-7. If the apostrophe were specified directly in the control string, rather than stored in a variable, the backslash would not be necessary, because the control string is delimited by double quotes rather than by apostrophes.

When a backslash is followed by any letter or punctuation mark other than those mentioned here, the character is printed as is. When a backslash is followed by a digit, however, it serves yet another purpose. A backslash followed by a one, two, or three digit number yields the character whose ASCII value is the number represented by those digits. This technique usually is used to represent control characters other than the five mentioned in the table in this chapter. The following two statements are equivalent (the variable *c* is declared to be of type **char**):

```
c = '\007';
c = 7;
```

Again, the escape sequence can be used only within single or double quotation marks. The form of the first statement, with the apostrophes and backslash, merely accentuates the fact that a character rather than a number is intended. The leading zeroes in the first statement are optional.

The ASCII code 7 represents the control character that causes a bell to ring in your computer or terminal, and sometimes on your printer. Try running the following program and see (and hear) what happens:

```
main()
{
    printf("Ding!\007\n");
}
```

Octal and Hexadecimal Notation

In the escape sequence that specifies an ASCII value, the three-digit number is always interpreted as being in *octal* or *base 8*. In base 8, the rightmost digit represents ones, the next digit represents 8's, and the next represents 64's. For example, the octal number 123 represents $(1)(64)+(2)(8)+(3)(1)$, or 83 in decimal (base 10) notation. The character '\123' would be printed out as uppercase S, which has the ASCII value 83 (in decimal notation).

C allows us to work entirely in base 8 and/or base 16 notation, known as *octal* and *hexadecimal* respectively. Octal notation uses only the digits 0 through 7; the number 8 in octal is specified as 10, which is equal to $(1)(8)+(0)(1)$ or 8 in decimal. Each digit in an octal number, starting at the right, represents a progressively higher power of 8 ($64 = 8^2$, $512 = 8^3$, etc.) Similarly, each digit in base 10 represents a higher power of 10 ($100 = 10^2$, $1000 = 10^3$, etc.).

In the hexadecimal system (commonly called hex), the rightmost digit represents ones (as in all systems). The next digit represents 16's, the next represents 256's (16^2), and so on. Therefore, each of the numbers up through 15 must be represented by a single digit. Hex uses all the digits 0 through 9, and also uses the letters A through F as digits representing the decimal numbers 10 through 15.

In the escape sequence specifying an ASCII value, the number is always octal. In other situations, however, it is necessary to specify the base of a number. For example, in the statement

```
n = 23;
```

is this the number 23 in base 10, the number 19 in base 8, or the number 35 in base 16?

The C compiler assumes that a number beginning with one of the digits 1 through 9 is in decimal (base 10). A number beginning with a leading 0, such as 023, is assumed to be in octal (base 8). A number beginning with the two characters 0x (a zero followed by the letter x), such as 0x23, is assumed to be in hex (base 16). The letter x may optionally be capitalized. Also, the letters a through f, when used as hex digits, may be either uppercase or lowercase.

Program 8-8 shows how octal and hex numbers can be represented and printed in C.

```
/* Octal and hexadecimal notation */

main()
{
 int a, b, c;

 a = 27;
 b = 033;
 c = 0x1b;

 printf("a = %d, b = %d, c = %d\n", a, b, c);
 printf("a = %o, b = %o, c = %o\n", a, b, c);
 printf("a = %x, b = %x, c = %x\n", a, b, c);
}
```

Program 8–8

```
a = 27, b = 27, c = 27
a = 33, b = 33, c = 33
a = 1b, b = 1b, c = 1b
```

Output 8–8

In the first assignment statement, the value 27 is represented in decimal. In the second, the same value is represented in octal, and in the third assignment, the equivalent value is written in hex. Although the three representations appear quite different, they are all stored in the computer identically.

The equivalence of all three representations is demonstrated when the values of the three variables are printed in decimal notation, then in octal, and finally in hex. Within each row of the output, the same values for *a*, *b* and *c* are displayed, because all three variables contain the identical number and are displayed with the identical conversion specification in a given row.

The conversion specification for printing a number in octal is %o, while that for printing in hex is %x. You will notice that the 0 (for octal) and 0x (for hex) prefixes are not printed out when these conversion specifications are used.

In an assignment, the notation used to represent a number has nothing to do with the type of the variable to which the number is being assigned. The variables *a*, *b*, and *c* in the above program all are of type **int**. The value assigned to all of them is represented in the computer's memory in the same way, regardless of the base. In later chapters, we will explain how numbers are stored internally.

Character Strings and How to Print Them

If you have used a word processor, you are aware of the fact that computers manipulate text as well as numbers. It has already been shown that characters are stored within the computer as numeric values. Nevertheless, it is always more convenient for a programmer to represent a string of characters as a string of characters.

The control string used in conjunction with the *printf* and *scanf* functions is a special-purpose string. In fact, a string is any group of characters enclosed within double quotation marks. Strings can be stored and manipulated in various ways in C, but this requires techniques we have not yet covered. At this point, we will only show how strings can be printed with the *printf* function.

The conversion specification used to print strings is %s. The specification %c cannot be used for strings, because %c is reserved for single characters only. Also, whereas characters of type **char** are embedded in single quotation marks, strings are always enclosed by double quotes. Although this distinction may seem trivial to you at this point, it is a critical difference which you should bear in mind as you proceed through this book. Even though the string

```
"p"
```

contains a single character, it still is considered to be a string rather than a simple character by virtue of the fact that it is within double quotes. Therefore, the %s conversion specification must be used to print it.

Program 8-9 is designed to introduce you to the concept of strings and how they are printed. It also demonstrates some subtleties in their use.

```
/* Illustration of some ways to print a string */

main()
{
  printf("This is simply a control string.\n");

  printf("%s\n", "The control string just tells how to print this.");

  printf("%s", "Newline may be put here, instead!\n");

  printf("%s %s %s %s %s\n", "This", "is", "valid", "in", "C.");

  printf("%s %s also %s %s %s\n", "This", "is", "valid", "in", "C.");

  printf("%s %s %s %s %s %s %s", "This", "is", "valid", "in", "C",
                            "also.", "\n");
}
```

Program 8—9

```
This is simply a control string.
The control string just tells how to print this.
Newline may be put here, instead!
This is valid in C.
This is also valid in C.
This is valid in C also.
```

Output 8—9

The first *printf* statement is familiar to us by now. It consists of the control string, which contains no conversion specifications, only a line of text. In the second example, however, the control string is the first of the two strings specified. It contains the conversion specification %s, followed by the *newline* character. The presence of one conversion specification means that the control string must be followed by another item in the *printf*, namely a string. This too is enclosed in quotation marks.

The only difference between the second and third *printf* statements is that the *newline* character has been relocated from the first string to the end of the second. The net effect is the same, because in both cases the *newline* is the last character to be printed. The fourth example shows that the control string may specify that more than one string is to be printed. There are five %s conversion specifications, which mean that five strings follow the control string. They are associated in a one-to-one correspondence between string and conversion specification.

Since the conversion specifications are separated by spaces, these spaces are printed out during execution of the function. Therefore, it is unnecessary (and incorrect) to include spaces in the corresponding strings. Of course, if the spaces were omitted from the control string (the first string), they would have to be included in the strings containing the text. You should also note that strings in *printf* statements, like their numeric counterparts, must be separated from one another by commas.

The last two examples are merely variations on the fourth one. The fifth statement shows how conversion specifications and literal text can be combined in the control string. Note that the word *also* is embedded between the second and third %s specification. It is printed as shown, as the fourth word in the sentence. The last example, which contains seven %s specifications, shows that the *newline* character itself can be a string, with its own associated conversion specification.

The control string contains the conversion specifications and thereby directs the entire operation of the *printf* function. The control string must always appear in a *printf*, and must always be the first item specified after the left parenthesis.

Program 8-10 concentrates on the possible variations of the %s conversion specification. Like the other specifications, it can be used with a field width specifier and the minus sign for left-justification. The decimal places specifier is replaced by the *maximum characters specifier*, which limits the number of characters from the string which are displayed.

```
/* %s conversion specification demonstrated */

main()
{
  printf("Case 1 :%s:\n", "A string");      /* 1) normal printing */
  printf("Case 2 :%3s:\n", "A string");     /* 2) minimum field width,
                                                   which is too small */

  printf("Case 3 :%12s:\n", "A string");    /* 3) printed in a field
                                                   wider than the string */

  printf("Case 4 :%-12s:\n", "A string");   /* 4) left-justified in a
                                                   field of 12 columns */

  printf("Case 5 :%12.6s:\n", "A string");  /* 5) truncated to 6 charac-
                                                   ters, printed in a
                                                   field of 12 */

  printf("Case 6 :%12.12s:\n", "A string"); /* 6) "truncated" to 12
                                                   characters (which is
                                                   more than enough)
                                                   printed in a field
                                                   of 12 */

  printf("Case 7 :%.6s:\n", "A string");    /* 7) truncated to 6
                                                   characters */

  printf("Case 8 :%-12.6s:\n", "A string"); /* 8) truncated to 6 charac-
                                                   ters, left justified
                                                   in a field of 12 */
```

Program 8—10

```
Case 1 :A string:
Case 2 :A string:
Case 3 :     A string:
Case 4 :A string     :
Case 5 :      A stri:
Case 6 :     A string:
Case 7 :A stri:
Case 8 :A stri       :
```

Output 8—10

In case number 1, the literal is printed in the ordinary way, taking as many print positions as are needed to accommodate the string. In case 2, a field width of 3 is requested. Since the string requires more than three positions to be displayed, this width of 3 is overruled, and the minimum field necessary is used by default.

In the third case, where the field width used to display the string is 12, the string is right-justified in a field of 12 positions. This rule differs from most other languages, in which strings invariably are left-justified. In C, a string is left-justified only if the field width is preceded by a minus sign, as demonstrated in case 4.

The specification used in example 5 may appear to include a decimal places specifier, but the number after the decimal point has a different meaning in the %s conversion specification. It means that no more than six characters of the literal should be printed, within a field width of 12 (right-justified). Therefore, even though 12 spaces are more than enough to hold the entire string, it is truncated because the maximum characters specifier limits it to six characters.

Case number 6 is a little more subtle. The maximum characters specifier is 12, meaning that no more than 12 characters from the string are to be printed. Since the string actually contains only eight characters, including the space, all eight characters from the string are used. There is no truncation, nor is the string stretched to 12 characters. The field width specifier causes the string to be printed right-justified in a field of 12 spaces.

In case 7, where the field width specifier is omitted, the maximum characters specifier truncates the string to six characters. They are printed in a field wide enough to accommodate all six characters. Finally, in case 8, where the specification is %-12.6s, the string is truncated to six characters and then printed left-justified in a field of 12 spaces.

Some Final Comments on the printf Function

We conclude our discussion of the *printf* function with Program 8-11, which illustrates a few additional conversion specifications.

```
/* Some miscellaneous conversion specifications */

main()
{
long a = 123456789L;
printf("%d\n", a);        /* 1) Wrong way to print a long integer */
printf("%ld\n", a);       /* 2) Right way to print a long integer */
printf(":%c:\n", 'V');    /* 3) Printing a character */
printf(":%0c:\n", 'V');   /* 4) Printing a character
                                with a 0 field width specified */
printf(":%5c:\n", 'V');   /* 5) Printing a character right-justified
                                in a field of 5 spaces */
printf(":%-5c:\n", 'V');  /* 6) Printing a character left-justified
                                in a field of 5 spaces */
}
```

Program 8—11

```
-13035
123456789
:V:
:V:
:     V:
:V     :
```

The variable *a* is declared to be a **long** integer with the value 123456789L. You will recall that the letter L at the rightmost end of a number signifies that it is a **long** integer. The L can be written in either uppercase or lowercase, but using the uppercase letter avoids confusion with the digit 1. On some computers, type **int** is the same as **long int**, whereas on others, including many personal computers, type **int** is the same as **short int**. The latter is true for the computer on which we are running these programs. It is therefore necessary to declare a variable explicitly to be of type **long int** for it to be able to hold a number as large as 123456789.

When a **long** integer is being printed, it is necessary to inform the *printf* function that a **long** integer is being supplied. The *printf* function cannot figure this out by itself, any more than it can figure out whether a value is of type **int** or **float**, without a conversion specification.

In example 1 of Program 8-11, the **long** integer is printed using a regular specification of %d. As the output shows, the *printf* misinterprets the number and prints some seemingly arbitrary value. Example 2 shows the right way to print a **long** integer. A lowercase letter l (it should always be lowercase, unlike the L used to specify a **long** integer constant) is added immediately before the letter d in the conversion specification to form the specification %ld.

There is no corresponding provision for helping *printf* distinguish between **float** and **double** values. The reason is that values of type **float** are converted automatically to type **double** in most C operations, even when no mixed-mode is involved. Therefore, *printf* receives all floating point numbers as type **double**.

The last four examples in this program show how the field width specifier and the minus sign can be used with the %c conversion. We leave it to the reader to examine each of these cases carefully in order to understand exactly how they operate.

There also is a *printf* conversion specification %g, which displays a floating point number in either decimal or scientific notation, whichever uses fewer output columns. This is useful when numbers of a wide range of magnitudes are displayed in the same table.

The Conversion Specifications for *scanf*

Most of the rules controlling the *scanf* function are similar to those governing the *printf* function. Both have control strings (enclosed by double quotation marks) which contain conversion specifications. The conversion specifications used in both are basically the same: %d is used for integers, %f or %e for floating point numbers, and so forth. If more than one conversion specification is present in the control string, the same number of variables must follow the control string, so there is a one-to-one correspondence between conversion specifications and variables.

There are several differences, however, between the format of *scanf* and that of *printf*. For example, the *scanf* function may contain only variables following the control string, not constants or values. The reason is that *scanf* reads in values, and values may be placed only into variables. The variables listed must be preceded by the & operator (which will be described fully in Chapter 11) if they hold numbers or characters. Also, any white space (blanks, tabs, and *newline* characters) included in the control string for *scanf* is usually ignored.

Program 8-12 illustrates most of the features of the *scanf* function. Since the program consists of eight separate cases, it is rather long, but we shall discuss each case separately.

```
/* A scanf demo */

main()
{
  int a, b;
  char c, d;
  float x;

  /* Case 1: */

  printf("Case 1: Please enter an integer: ");
  scanf("%d", &a);
  printf("         You entered %d\n", a);

  /* Case 2: */

  printf("\nCase 2: Please enter 2 integers: ");
  scanf("%d%d", &a, &b);
  printf("         You entered %d and %d\n", a, b);

  /* Case 3: */

  printf("\nCase 3: Please enter 2 integers,\n");
  printf("            the first no longer than 5 digits: ");
  scanf("%5d %d", &a, &b);
  printf("         You entered %d and %d\n", a, b);

  /* Case 4: */

  printf("\nCase 4: Please enter a floating point number: ");
  scanf("%f", &x);
  printf("         You entered %f\n", x);
```

Program continued on next page

Program continued from previous page

```
/* Case 5: */

printf("\nCase 5: Please enter 2 consecutive characters: ");
scanf("%*c %c %c", &c, &d);
printf("\n         You entered %c and %c\n", c, d);

/* Case 6: */

printf("\nCase 6: Please enter 2 integers,\n");
printf("          separated by the word, \"fred\": ");
scanf("%d fred %d", &a, &b);
printf("         You entered %d and %d\n", a, b);

/* Case 7: */

printf("\nCase 7: Please enter an integer, a character and an integer: ");
scanf("%d%c%d", &a, &c, &b);
printf("         You entered %d, %c and %d\n", a, c, b);

/* Case 8: */

printf("\nCase 8: Please enter 2 integers,\n");
printf("          separated by a character: ");
scanf("%d %*c %d", &a, &b);
printf("         You entered %d and %d\n", a, b);
}
```

Program 8—12

```
Case 1: Please enter an integer: 34
            You entered 34

Case 2: Please enter 2 integers: 3 4
            You entered 3 and 4

Case 3: Please enter 2 integers,
            the first no longer than 5 digits: 123456
            You entered 12345 and 6

Case 4: Please enter a floating point number: 13.3
            You entered 13.300003

Case 5: Please enter 2 consecutive characters: as
            You entered a and s

Case 6: Please enter 2 integers,
            separated by the word, "fred": 65 fred 1
            You entered 65 and 1

Case 7: Please enter an integer, a character and an integer: 7n8
            You entered 7, n and 8

Case 8: Please enter 2 integers,
            separated by a character: 2x5
            You entered 2 and 5
```

Output 8—12

The variables a and b are declared to be of type **int**, c and d of type **char**, and x of type **float**.

In case number 1, the user is asked to enter an integer. In this and all the other cases, the program echoes the number to show that it was input correctly. When *scanf* reads in an integer using the %d format, it first skips over all leading white space (blanks, tabs, and *newline* characters). It then reads in all the consecutive digits forming the number. This process ends when *scanf* reaches white space, or a character that is not a digit. The digits read in then are combined internally to form an integer, which is stored in the corresponding variable (preceded by an &)—in this case, the variable *a*.

If the first non white-space character *scanf* encounters is not a digit or a plus or minus sign, one of two things may happen, depending on the version of the *scanf* function you are using. The *scanf* function may be aborted immediately, even if there are more conversion specifications following in the control string; in this case, execution resumes with the next statement in the program. The other possibility is that *scanf* may assume the value is omitted, assign 0 to the corresponding variable, and continue reading in values. The non white-space character at which it stopped is considered to be part of the next value in the input.

The only way to find out what your compiler does is to test it. The *scanf* function returns a value, so you could write a statement like this:

```
b = scanf("%d", &a);
```

The value returned in *b* is the number of values successfully read by *scanf*. If the character typed in is invalid (say, a letter instead of a digit), and the value returned in *b* is 0, this means that the version of *scanf* you are using took the first option previously described. If the returned value is 1, that indicates the *scanf* function took the second option and assigned the value 0 to *a*.

In the second case in Program 8-12, two integers *a* and *b* are requested. The conversion specifications are written adjacent to each other, without any intervening space, but the two values must be entered with at least one space between them. Otherwise, the two digits would be read in as a single number. In general, white space should be used to separate all input numbers.

In case number 3, the user is asked to enter two integers, the first of which is to be no more than five digits long. In the conversion specification for the variable *a*, %5d, the number 5 is a *maximum field width* rather than a minimum as it would be in *printf*. It specifies the maximum size of the number to be entered. Notice that a single six-digit number has been typed in, contrary to the program instructions. The *scanf* function accepts the first five digits as the value for *a* and the sixth digit as *b*.

To summarize, we now have three rules for determining when *scanf* stops reading in digits of an integer.

1. When white space is reached.
2. When a non-digit is reached.
3. When the maximum field width is exceeded.

In this case, there is white space between the conversion specifications. This does not mean that there must be spaces between the inputted numbers, however, because the field width specifier is used.

We can also type in floating point values, as in case number 4. Although the conversion specification in the *scanf* statement reads %f, C permits the flexibility of typing in a value in either *e* or *f* format. The conversion specification %e can also be used for floating point input, again allowing the input to be typed in either *e* or *f* format. In neither case, however, may the variable listed in the *scanf* statement be of type **double**. Only variables of type **float** can be read in directly. (Similarly, on systems where type **int** is different from **long int**, only variables of type **int** can be read in.)

Note that the input value 13.3 is echoed back as 13.300003. This is not the result of any programming error, as you might assume. It shows the kind of computational error that invariably creeps in when floating point numbers are used. The number 13.3 is converted into binary when it is read in, then converted back to decimal when printed out. Every integer number has an exact binary equivalent, but most floating point numbers do not. Thus 13.300003 happens to be the closest number to 13.3 that can be stored in the computer's memory. On larger computers, this type of error generally is much smaller because they can store floating point numbers to a much higher precision.

Case number 5 involves the reading in of single characters, and it illustrates several new concepts. The most important point is that *scanf* reads in characters much differently from the way it reads numbers. The *scanf* simply reads in the next character in the input, including white space characters. This, however, leads to some complications. The previous case involved the reading in of a number which was terminated with a *newline* (the pressing of the return key). A terminating *newline* is not part of the number, so it is not read in. That means it is left over for the next *scanf* statement. An attempt to read in a character using the %c conversion specification would read in the *newline* rather than the character typed by the user.

For this reason, there has to be a way to skip over the *newline* character and read in the next two printable characters as the values for the variables *c* and *d*. This is accomplished by the first conversion specification, as illustrated in the control string of case 5, %*c. When an asterisk follows the % in a *scanf* conversion specification, it means the *scanf* should find and skip over the described value in the input (in this case a single character), without reading it into any variable. Thus a conversion specification containing an asterisk should have no corresponding variable in the *scanf* statement. The *scanf* statement in case 5 can be interpreted to mean: "Skip over the next character in the input, assign the following character to *c*, and assign the one following that to *d*."

This "leftover *newline*" concept can be critical in some programs. It is also very machine dependent. On some computers, when the *scanf* function causes the computer to pause for input, execution does not resume until the user enters a *newline* (return), no matter what input was requested. On other computers, including the one on which our programs were run, this input is not necessary. If a *scanf* requests the input of a single character, execution resumes immediately, and the user need not enter a *newline* or even a blank space. That is why in Programs 8-3 through 8-5 there was no need to skip over *newline* characters, since only characters were input. In case 4, however, the floating point number had to be followed by some terminating character to indicate the end of the number. On our computer, this could have been the letter *a*, which would have been left over for the *scanf* of case 5. This would not have made sense, however, because the prompt had not yet asked for a character. Thus some form of white space was required. A blank would have sufficed, but then the output of the following *printf* would have appeared on the same line as the number, so a *newline* was the best idea. On some computers, a *newline* would have been the only option. Therefore, a *newline* was left over for the *scanf* of case 5; this was foreseen, and the %*c conversion specification was included to skip over it.

You will notice that the conversion specifications in case 5 are separated by blanks. As before, this does not mean that a blank space was required between the *a* and *s* that were entered. Including a space would have been incorrect, because then a blank space would have been placed in variable *d*, and the *s* would have been left over.

Case 6 presents an interesting feature of the *scanf* control string. When non white-space characters are included in the control string, *scanf* expects those characters to appear in the input at the corresponding place. Therefore, the control string in case 6 expects the input to consist of an integer, followed by the word *fred*, followed by another integer. The specified characters must appear as written, so *fred* must be in lowercase letters with no embedded blanks. If the input does not correspond to this expected pattern, the result is the same as if invalid input were specified, as described in connection with case 1 above.

Once again, the blank spaces in the control string do not mean that there must be spaces at the corresponding locations in the input. The input could just as well have been *65fred1*. If the control string were

```
"%d 5 %d"
```

it would be necessary to include the blanks, so that the digit 5 would not be taken as part of the first or second integer. If the control string of case 6 were

```
"%dfred%d"
```

without any blank spaces, different versions of *scanf* would treat it differently. Some versions don't care whether there are blanks in the input between the word *fred* and the two integers. Others require that there be no blanks between the word and the integers.

Case 7 is fairly straightforward. The prompt requests an integer, followed by a character, followed by another integer. No spaces were included in the input. There could have been spaces after the character, because the *scanf* function skips over white space to find an integer in the input. No blank could have been typed between the first integer and the character, however, since *scanf* does not skip over white space *after* an integer. A blank would have been read in erroneously as the character and assigned to *c*.

Case 8 is very similar to case 7, except that this time the character is skipped over and not assigned to a variable. Notice that the variable list contains only two variables, *a* and *b*, to receive the two integers that are actually read in.

The final program in this chapter, Program 8-13, demonstrates how octal and hexadecimal numbers are read in.

```
/* Reading decimal, octal and hex numbers */

main()
{
  int a;

  printf("Enter a number in decimal: ");
  scanf("%d", &a);
  printf("You entered %d\n", a);

  printf("\nEnter a number in octal: ");
  scanf("%o", &a);
  printf("You entered %o, or %d in decimal\n", a, a);

  printf("\nEnter a number in hex: ");
  scanf("%x", &a);
  printf("You entered %x, or %d in decimal\n", a, a);
}
```

Program 8—13

```
Enter a number in decimal: 27
You entered 27

Enter a number in octal: 33
You entered 33, or 27 in decimal

Enter a number in hex: 1B
You entered 1b, or 27 in decimal
```

Output 8—13

Like *printf*, the *scanf* function uses %o to indicate that an octal number is expected, and %x to indicate a hex number. It is not necessary to precede the octal value with a leading 0, or the hex value with 0x, because the conversion specification determines how the input digits should be interpreted, and this cannot be overruled. Note that, even though the B in the hex number was entered as an uppercase letter, it was printed out in lowercase. The *scanf* function permits the digits a through f of a hex number to be entered in either uppercase or lowercase, but the %x conversion specification always prints them in lowercase.

The digits that are accepted as part of an octal or hex number are different from those accepted as part of a decimal number. For example, *scanf* accepts the letter b as part of a hex number, but stops at 8 when reading an octal number (since octal numbers include only the digits 0 through 7).

The official definition of *scanf*, as specified by Kernighan and Ritchie[2] (the recognized authority on the C language), permits a hexadecimal number to be input with the 0x prefix included. Of course, this would be acceptable only if the %x conversion specification were being used to read in the number. We have found, however, that some versions of *scanf* do not permit this. In all versions of *scanf*, an octal number (or any number, for that matter) may be input with a leading 0, because it is a valid digit and does not change the value of the number in any base.

The conversion specification %h is used to read in a short integer. This is useful on computers where the size of **short int** variables is different from the size of regular **int** variables. There is no corresponding conversion specification for *printf*, because short integers automatically are cast to regular integers, just as **float** values are cast to **double** values.

We have now covered some of the basic tools of the C programmer. The time has arrived to learn how to make the standard modules of which all professional C programs are composed—functions. That is the subject of the next chapter.

The Spirit of C

Any useful computer language should be able to handle character data as easily as it can perform numerical calculations. C, of course, can handle character information very well. In this section, we will develop a program that combines the use of numeric data and calculation with character data.

In Chapter 6, we developed a program to divide a list of numbers into two parts based on a test value. To refresh your memory, here is that program again:

---

[2] *The C Programming Language*, by Brian W. Kernighan and Dennis M. Ritchie. Prentice–Hall: 1978

```
/* This program divides a series of positive integers (in ascending
   order) into two lines, at a point determined by the user */

main()
{
    int input_value,     /* Holds the value just read in */
        test_value;      /* This is the value that determines where
                            the output is divided */

/* Input a positive value for test_value */

    do
    {
        printf("Enter a positive value for use in\n");
        printf("dividing the input into two lines: ");
        scanf("%d", &test_value);
    }
    while(test_value <= 0);

    printf("Enter a line of positive integers in ascending order,\n");
    printf("with zero (or negative) as a trailer:\n");

    scanf("%d", &input_value);    /* Priming read */
    printf("\nLine 1> ");          /* Label the first line */

    /* While the value is positive (not the trailer) and is less than
       the test value, echo it back */

    while (input_value > 0 && input_value < test_value)
    {
        printf("%d ", input_value);
        scanf("%d", &input_value);
    }

    printf("\nLine 2> ");          /* Start second line */

    while (input_value > 0)        /* Echo the remaining numbers */
    {
        printf("%d ", input_value);
        scanf("%d", &input_value);
    }

    printf("\n");       /* Finish off second line */

}
```

We now propose that this program be amended to divide any list of numbers (not necessarily in ascending order) into two parts, based on the presence of some special character in the input. For example, suppose the comma is used as a delimiter. An input of

7 3 21 18 33, 67 92 11

where the number 33 is followed by a comma, will be displayed as:

7 3 21 18 33
67 92 11

The *newline* occurs at the point formerly occupied by the comma.

This program could be written so that it simply accepts and prints characters one at a time, displaying a *newline* when a comma is entered. (This allows for the division of the input into more than two lines, if more than one comma appears.) We want to add an additional feature to the program; namely, we would like it to add up the numbers on each line, and display the totals at the end of the lines.

This feature makes it desirable to be able to input the numbers so that they are readily available as numbers, without the need to convert a series of digits into an integer. Since the input (other than the comma) consists only of numbers and white space, it is possible to read in the numbers using the %d conversion specification.

In order to be able to read in integers and at the same time detect a comma, it is necessary to input two values with each *scanf* statement: an integer and then a character. The *scanf* statement would look something like this:

```
scanf("%d%c", &number, &delimiter);
```

If the integer read into *number* is followed only by a space, that space is read into *delimiter*. If only one space separates the number from its successor, the input is positioned at the beginning of the next integer. Otherwise, the input contains some blank spaces before the next number, and these are ignored. Either way, the same *scanf* statement can again be used. If the integer is followed by a comma, the comma is read into *delimiter*. (This requires that a comma must immediately follow a number, with no intervening blank spaces. Can you figure out why?) The final number in the input is followed by a *newline* (a carriage return). Since only one line is required for the input, the *newline* character can be used as a trailer, thus eliminating the need for an explicit trailer number.

Let us first construct a program that merely inputs and echoes numbers, ignoring any commas, until a *newline* character is read in:

```
/* This program inputs and echoes back a lineful of integers */
                    /* Stage 1 */

main()
{
    int number;        /* Holds the integer just read in */
    char delimiter;    /* Holds the character immediately following
                          the integer */

    printf("Enter a line of positive integers:\n");
    scanf("%d%c", &number, &delimiter);    /* Priming read */
```

Program continued on next page

Program continued from previous page

```
    /* While the delimiter is not a newline (that is, while the end
       of the line has not yet been reached), echo back the number */

    while (delimiter != '\n')
    {
        printf("%d ", number);
        scanf("%d%c", &number, &delimiter);    /* read a new number */
    }

    printf("\n");      /* Finish off the last line */
}
```

Notice that the integers can be negative or even zero, since the value of a number no longer is used as the trailer.

The next step to add to the program is to check for commas and, if they are found, to output *newline* characters. Remember that any number of commas, including none, may appear in the input. There is no efficiency to be gained by terminating a **while** loop when a comma is detected and entering another loop. Since it is always necessary to test for commas as well as for the *newline*, a single loop will suffice. The comma may be detected by an **if** statement within the loop:

```
/* This program inputs and  echoes back integers, beginning a new output
   line  at  each  point where  a comma appears in the input.  The input
   itself  must  consist  of only  one line, any commas must immediately
   follow an integer with no intervening spaces, and the carriage return
   to end the input line must immediately follow the final integer, with
   no intervening spaces */
                         /* Stage 2 */

main()
{
    int number;         /* Holds the integer just read in */
    char delimiter;     /* Holds the character immediately following
                           the integer */

    printf("Enter a line of positive integers:\n");
    scanf("%d%c", &number, &delimiter);    /* Priming read */

    /* While the delimiter is not a newline (that is, while the end
       of the line has not yet been reached), echo back the number */

    while (delimiter != '\n')
    {
        printf("%d ", number);
        if (delimiter == ',')    /* Comma indicates end of output line */
            printf("\n");
        scanf("%d%c", &number, &delimiter);    /* read a new number */
    }
    printf("\n");      /* Finish off the last line */

}
```

Notice the positioning of the **if** statement. This causes the current output line to be terminated *after* the number preceding the comma is displayed.

Now we can add a variable that accumulates the sum of all the numbers on an output line. Since a line ends when a comma is detected, the **if** statement in this program also can be used to cause the display of the final total at the end of the line. Remember that the accumulator must be initialized, since numbers are being added to it. It must also be reset to zero after it is displayed, or the totals will be cumulative from the beginning of the input rather than from the beginning of the current line. The final version of this program includes the accumulator.

```
/* This  program  inputs and echoes back integers, beginning a new output
   line  at each point where a comma appears in the input.  At the end of
   each  output  line,  the  total  of  all  the integers on that line is
   displayed.  The input itself must consist of only one line, any commas
   must immediately follow an integer with no intervening spaces, and the
   carriage  return  to  end  the  input line must immediately follow the
   final integer, with no intervening spaces. */
                         /* Stage 3 */

main()
{
    int number;          /* Holds the integer just read in */
    char delimiter;      /* Holds the character immediately following
                            the integer */
    int accumulator;     /* Accumulator for the total of all integers
                            on a line */

    printf("Enter a line of positive integers:\n");
    scanf("%d%c", &number, &delimiter);    /* Priming read */
    accumulator = number;             /* Initialize accumulator */

    /* While the delimiter is not a newline (that is, while the end
       of the line has not yet been reached),  echo back the number */

    while (delimiter != '\n')
    {
        printf("%d ", number);

        if (delimiter == ',')    /* Comma indicates end of output line */
        {
            /* Print total for this line, start next line */

            printf(" < total: %d\n", accumulator);
            accumulator = 0;        /* Reset accumulator */
        }

        scanf("%d%c", &number, &delimiter);    /* read a new number */
        accumulator += number;                 /* Add it to accumulator */
    }

    /* Finish off the last line */

    printf(" < total: %d\n", accumulator);

}
```

This program takes advantage of the necessity for a priming read to initialize *accumulator* to the first number on the first line. This is an alternative to initializing *accumulator* to zero and then adding the first value of *number* to it. Usually no extra efficiency is gained by using the first method, but it may be considered more elegant. In all cases other than the first, the value of *number* is added to the accumulator as soon as it is read in. One advantage of this approach is that it makes it clear, both to the reader and to the programmer, that each value is indeed being added to the accumulator and not ignored. If the adding statement were placed at the top of the loop instead of at the bottom, several changes would have to be made elsewhere in the program. It is left to the reader to determine what these changes would be.

Notice that, within the **if** statement, a single *printf* is used both to finish off the current line, with the displaying of the total, and to start the next line with a *newline* character.

C *Tutorial*

1. What conversion specifications are used to print out the following?

    (a) an integer
    (b) a floating point number in decimal form
    (c) a floating point number in scientific notation
    (d) a single character

2. What is the minimum field width specifier, and where is it located?

3. What is the effect of a negative number in a field width specifier?

4. Is it wrong to omit a field width specifier entirely? If not, what is the effect?

5. When the conversion specification is %d, what is its default field width?

6. How would the number 9876 appear if printed with the following conversion specifications?

    (a) %0d
    (b) %3d
    (c) %4d
    (d) %10d

7. How would the number −456 be printed if the conversion specification were %10d?

8. What general statement can be made about the conversion specifications %e and %f?

9. How many decimal places are displayed when a number has a conversion specification of %f?

10. What happens if a number being printed by a conversion specification of %f has more than six decimal places?

11. How would the number 987.65 be printed if the conversion specification were %10.1?

12. What does the word ASCII stand for?

13. How is a character (printable or otherwise) stored in the memory of the computer?

14. What are the ASCII codes for A and Z?

15. Which letters have the higher ASCII values, uppercase or lowercase?

16. What is the difference in the ASCII values between the letters T and t?

17. What are control characters?

18. Give some examples of control characters.

19. How can a % sign be printed within a control string?

20. What significance does a backslash character have when placed immediately before a one-, two- or three-digit number?

21. What conversion specifications are used for the printing of octal and hexadecimal numbers?

22. True or false: C ignores leading zeroes, so that 123 is the same as 0123.

23. True or false: When specifying a hexadecimal number in C, the letters A through F and also X may be written in uppercase or lowercase as desired.

24. What is a string, and what conversion specification can be used to print it out?

25. What is the essential difference between %c and %s?

26. What is the critical difference between 'x' and "x"?

27. What does the conversion specification %.6s mean?

28. What conversion specification ensures that a **long** integer is printed correctly?

29. True or false: %d is equivalent to %D.

30. What is the difference between the conversion specification letters used in *printf* and those used in *scanf*?

31. If a program contains the statement

    `scanf("%3d", &n);`

    and the input for this scanf is

    12345 6

    a) What value is assigned to *n* (assuming *n* was declared to be of type **int**)?
    b) What value would be assigned to *n* if the control string were changed to "%7d"?

32. If a scanf contains the control string

    "%d \n %d"

    which of the following sets of inputs will allow the *scanf* function to read in two integers successfully?

    a) 4
       5

    b) 23   4

    c) 19
          18

33. If the following scanf statement is executed:

    `scanf("%d%c", &n, &c);`

    where *n* is of type **int** and *c* is of type **char**, and the input is

    23
    x

    what values are read in for *n* and *x*?

34. How could the *scanf* statement in the previous problem be rewritten so that the letter x is read into the variable *c*?

35. If a scanf statement is written as

    ```
    scanf("%f bingo %d", &x, &n);
    ```

    where x is of type **double** and n is of type **int**, which of the following sets of input are valid?

    a) 34 bingo 45
    b) 12.3 bingo 12.4
    c) 2.1 bingo 9
    d) 3.2 bingo7
    e) 1.9bingo2

36. True or false: The conversion specification %h is used to read in values in hexadecimal format.

ANSWERS TO C TUTORIAL

1. (a) %d   (b) %f   (c) %e   (d) %c

2. It specifies the smallest field in which a value is to be printed. It is used in a conversion specification, and if present, it is placed immediately following the % sign.

3. The value being displayed is left-justified instead of right-justified within the field.

4. It is perfectly acceptable. The effect is as if 0 had been specified, which means the value is displayed in as many columns as necessary (and no more).

5. The size of the number being printed (including a minus sign, if the number is negative).

6. (a) 9876   (b) 9876   (c) 9876   (d) 9876 preceded by six spaces

7. It would be printed in a field width of 10 positions, with the negative number right-justified.

8. Either one may be used to print out any floating point number, regardless of how that number is written in the program or entered by the user. Similarly for input.

9. Six places are displayed, even if they are all zero.

10. It is rounded to the sixth decimal place.

11. It would not be printed, because %10.1 is an invalid specification. It does not end with e or f (or any other letter, for that matter).

12. American Standard Code for Information Interchange, which is the most popular code used for microcomputers.

13. It is stored as a number.

14. 65 and 90 respectively.

15. Lowercase.

16. 32

17. They are unprintable characters that play a special role of some kind.

18. Backspace, tab, newline, carriage return, form feed, and bell ('\007'), to name a few.

19. By using two adjacent % signs.

20. It refers to the ASCII character with that particular value, when the three digits are interpreted as an octal number.

21. %o for octal and %x for hexadecimal.

22. False; the leading zero indicates that the number is expressed in octal. The number 0123 is interpreted as an octal number whose value is equal to 83 in decimal. (This does not apply to input).

23. True. You may even mix uppercase and lowercase letters in the same number.

24. A string is any group of characters enclosed by double quotation marks. The conversion specification %s is used to print it out.

25. The conversion specification %c is used for printing a single character, whereas %s must be used for a string of characters.

26. The first is a single character, whereas the second is a string.

27. Print the first (leftmost) six characters of the corresponding string (or the entire string if it has six or fewer characters).

28. %ld

29. False; some *printf* functions do not accept uppercase conversion specifications. Those that do give them special significance (see your user manual for details).

30. Generally, there is no difference in the set of letters used. There is some difference in operation, however; for example, %f used in *printf* always displays a floating point number in decimal notation, but when it is used in *scanf* it is equivalent to %e, both of which accept a number in either decimal or scientific notation.

31. a) 123
    b) 12345

32. All three sets of input are acceptable.

33. The variable *n* gets the value 23, whereas x gets the value '\n' (or ASCII code 10 or '\012'), since that is the character immediately following the integer 23 in the input.

34. `scanf("%d %*c %c", &n, &c);`
    `/* The blanks in the control string may be omitted */`

35. a, b, d, and e are valid. Note that in (b), the value 12 is read into *n*. This may cause the next *scanf* to fail, but that is another matter.

36. False; %h is used to read in short integers, whereas %x is used to read in hexadecimal values.

Keywords

(No new keywords were introduced in this chapter)

char	do	double	else	float	for
if	int	long	short	unsigned	while

Exercises

1. Rewrite the compound interest exercise from Chapter 7 so that the monetary values are displayed in dollars and cents. That is to say, the values should be preceded by the dollar sign and rounded to two decimal places.

2. Write a program that inputs single characters and prints out the sum of their ASCII values. The program can display a running total, or just the grand total at the end of the run. In either case, you will need to include some method of indicating the end of input.

3. A popular method of message encryption involves replacing each letter of the message by the one that follows it in the alphabet. For example, the word HAL becomes IBM, since I follows H, B follows A, and M follows L. Since no letter follows Z, it is replaced with A, so that ZAP becomes ABQ. Write a program to encrypt and/or decrypt such messages. You can do this easily by using what you know about the ASCII code.

4. Write a program to read in an integer by reading in its digits one by one, as characters. Convert each digit to its numerical value, and shift it into a variable that eventually will hold the actual integer. This is the inverse of the method previously shown for extracting the digits of an integer one by one. The program should check for invalid characters, that is, non-digits. You might also have the program accept (and handle correctly) an optional leading negative sign, or you could modify this program to work with floating point numbers.

9

User—Defined Functions

*U*ntil now, we have been introduced to only two C functions: printf and scanf. The system supplies both these functions, thus freeing the programmer from the responsibility of having to write C statements to perform certain operations. Other C library functions are available as well, as you will learn in future chapters. In this chapter, you will learn how C provides you with the option of writing any function of your own design.

What is a Function?

On the highest level, a function can be thought of as a way to extend the repertoire of a language. Once a function has been written to play a particular role, it can be called upon repeatedly throughout the program. Whereas constructs such as **for** loops are built into the C language, functions must be either created by the user or supplied by the system under which C is running.

Both *printf* and *scanf* are examples of functions. Other functions are supplied by the system in what are called *libraries*. One library, the standard C library, is automatically attached to your program each time it is processed, so that you can refer to the functions in this library whenever you need to. We will introduce other standard C library functions in later chapters.

There also is another library, called the math library, which you must tell the system to attach to your program when you need to use its included functions. (Consult the manual supplied with your compiler or operating system for details on how to do this.) One function available in the math library is *sqrt*, which returns the square root of a number. Some others are *sin*, *cos*, *tan*, and *log*. All these functions are discussed in Appendix B.

Let us examine the way the *printf* and *scanf* functions typically are used in a program. First the name of the function is specified, followed immediately by parentheses, which contain information that tells the function how to perform its task. Sometimes the function is just written as a C statement followed by a semicolon. As was mentioned earlier, however, the *scanf* function returns a value that can be used by the programmer. The *printf* function also returns a value, though this is rarely used. If the programmer wants to store these values, statements such as the following can be used:

```
n = scanf("%d", &a);
q = printf("%d", e);
```

In these cases, the function (with its parenthetical information) is used in an expression to the right of an assignment operator, in much the same way as is a variable. The function performs its task and then returns a value. The *scanf* function returns the number of items successfully read in and the *printf* function returns the number of characters output.

The *printf* and *scanf* functions display or read values as well as return values. Some functions, however, only perform the task of calculation. For example,

```
y = sqrt(144.0);
```

calculates the square root of 144.0, the floating point argument, and returns the result (12.0), which is stored in the variable *y*. We could also use the function in an expression, such as the following:

```
y = 3.0 + sqrt(x);
```

It would be meaningless, however, to write:

```
sqrt(144.0);
```

as a statement. C would compile and execute it, but the result of the calculation would be lost, because it is not stored anywhere. When a function is written as a statement rather than as part of an assignment or expression, it performs its defined task, but its returned value is lost.

Some functions, such as *printf* and *scanf*, typically are used in this manner. A function with a returned value that is not significant often is called a *procedure* in other languages. We shall concentrate initially on this type of function.

Why Use Functions?

In all areas of life, we try to find ways of simplifying tasks that would otherwise be repetitious. Functions frequently are used in C as abbreviations for a series of instructions that are to be executed more than once. Do not confuse this concept with that of a loop. A loop can repeat a series of instructions only if each iteration immediately follows the previous one. Calling a function, by contrast, can cause a series of instructions to be repeated at any point within the program. Thus the use of functions generally results in a shorter, less expensive program that is quicker to write and easier to debug.

Functions and Structured Programming

In the early days of computer programming, the structure of programs often left much to be desired. Programs were considered acceptable so long as they worked; indeed, the only criterion used in those days was whether the program accomplished its task in a reasonable time. It soon became evident, however, that programs had to be amended periodically to respond to changing conditions or government requirements. Because the programs were poorly structured, often this was a difficult, tedious, and time-consuming chore. Sometimes the program had to be rewritten from scratch.

Rewriting programs led to a serious waste of manpower and computer time. Beginning in the mid-60's there was a movement to include specially designed structures in programming languages, to encourage programmers to adopt a more disciplined approach to program writing. This practice lead to more readily understandable programs. The techniques that were adopted are known as *structured programming*.

Structured programming includes several different features. Each of them was designed not only to solve the problem at hand, but also to make the logic clear to someone reading the program. One feature of most computer languages which helps achieve clarity is the comment. We have used at least one comment in each of our program examples in this book. The level of complexity of the program dictates how detailed the comments should be. Your solutions to the more difficult programming exercises in each chapter should include comments. A program of up to 20 lines often does not require comments.

Modern programming languages such as C provide constructs that lend themselves to structured programming. These constructs include the **while** and **for** loops, which we have already encountered. They are used to encapsulate a portion of the program which represents a specific task.

Most modern programming languages also provide ways to break up a long, continuous program into a series of individual modules that are related to each other in a specified fashion. Usually, it is easier to break down a difficult task into a series of smaller tasks and then to solve those sub-tasks individually. In C, such modules are called functions. Indeed, C is a language whose building blocks are functions. The *main* function, as we have said before, must be included in every complete C program. Any executable statements not located within the *main* function must be part of some other function.

The term *top-down programming* means that the programmer begins writing a program by thinking about how it can be divided into sub-tasks. He writes the *main* function so that it consists almost entirely of calls to functions, which represent the initial set of sub-tasks.

The programmer then writes these functions. This stage may itself involve dividing a module into sub-tasks; thus a function may consist of calls to other functions. Eventually, the programmer decides that the sub-tasks he has yet to code are small enough to be written as series of C statements without calling other user-supplied functions.

In the following simple program, we show how a function can be used as an abbreviation for a series of repeated C statements.

```
/* Using a function as an abbreviation */

main()
{
    printf("This old man, he played one,\n");
    printf("He played knick-knack on my thumb,\n");
    chorus();

    printf("This old man, he played two,\n");
    printf("He played knick-knack on my shoe,\n");
    chorus();

    printf("This old man, he played three,\n");
    printf("He played knick-knack on my knee,\n");
    chorus();

    /* And so on */
}
```

Program continued on next page

Program continued from previous page

```
chorus()
{
   printf("%60s\n", "With a knick-knack-paddy-whack,");
   printf("%60s\n", "Give the dog a bone,");
   printf("%60s\n\n", "This old man went rolling home.");
}
```

Program 9—1

```
This old man, he played one,
He played knick-knack on my thumb,
                              With a knick-knack-paddy-whack,
                                    Give the dog a bone,
                           This old man went rolling home.


This old man, he played two,
He played knick-knack on my shoe,
                              With a knick-knack-paddy-whack,
                                    Give the dog a bone,
                           This old man went rolling home.


This old man, he played three,
He played knick-knack on my knee,
                              With a knick-knack-paddy-whack,
                                    Give the dog a bone,
                           This old man went rolling home.
```

Output 9—1

The format of Program 9-1 is not very different from those of all the preceding programs. As usual, it has an explanatory comment, followed by the word *main* and its empty parentheses. Next comes an opening brace, followed by the body of the *main* function. This consists of a series of *printf* statements, interspersed with calls to the function *chorus*. After the first closing brace is the word *chorus*, followed by an empty pair of parentheses. This, in turn, is followed by a pair of braces containing three *printf* statements (or, more accurately, three calls to the *printf* function).

The *chorus* function is written in a manner analogous to that of the *main* function. Both begin with the name of the function, followed by a pair of parentheses. The rules for naming functions are the same as those for naming any other entity in C, such as variables. Although the parentheses following the names are empty in both of these cases, they must be included anyway. These parentheses are followed by a pair of braces containing statements.

Braces are used to surround not only a compound statement but also the body of a function. In fact, both constructs are almost the same in C. A function definition could be thought of as being a large compound statement with a name attached. The name should represent the action performed by the function, just as the name of a variable should be selected to reflect the role that it plays.

The *chorus* function is invoked, or called into execution, when *main* mentions the name *chorus*. The invocation of the function's name must be followed by a pair of empty parentheses, to match the empty parentheses in the function definition. No semicolon is written after the set of parentheses where the function is defined, but it must be present in the calling function (in this case, *main*) to indicate the end of the statement that calls the *chorus* function.

It is not necessary to place the definition of the *chorus* function after the *main* function. Unlike the rule in Pascal, functions in C can be defined in any order. Therefore, the program listing could have begun with the definition of the *chorus* function and followed by *main*. Usually, however, the *main* function is listed first. It is not permitted in C to define a function within another function.

Keep in mind that a function is executed only when it is invoked by another function. Even though the *chorus* function is defined in the program listing, its statements would never be executed if the *main* function did not invoke *chorus*. The definition of a function is remembered by the computer and executed only when it is actually called.

One might wonder, then, how the *main* function is executed, since it is not invoked anywhere in the program. The answer is that the operating system automatically calls the *main* function upon execution of the program. For this reason, there must always be a *main* function present; otherwise, the program cannot run.

All functions, including *main*, finish execution by default when the last statement in the function body is executed, or more specifically, when the closing brace of the function body is reached. At that point, control returns from the called function to the calling function. Execution continues at the statement that logically follows the one that made the call. (If the calling statement is the last in the calling function, the function terminates.)

In Program 9-1, each time the statement

```
chorus();
```

is executed within *main*, it is conceptually replaced by the three *printf* statements contained within the definition of the *chorus* function. The program output confirms this fact. Since each invocation effectively represents three *printf* statements, the program becomes more concise and far easier for a human to read and comprehend. Also, it saves the programmer the trouble of having to type the three *printf*s each time they are required.

Whenever a string is printed, it is right-justified by default. Since the conversion specification in each of the *printf* statements in the *chorus* function of Program 9-1 is %60s, each of the lines is printed right-justified in a field of 60 spaces.

Returning A Value From a Function

Program 9-1 illustrates some of the important features of a user-defined function. It suffers, however, from the fact that it does not illustrate how to return a value to the calling function. The function *chorus* does not communicate in any way with the *main* function. A major advantage of functions is that they can return a value to the calling function. This concept is incorporated into Program 9-2.

```
/* Demonstration of one use of a function */

main()
{
  int length, width;

  printf("Enter the length of a rectangle: ");
  length = get_an_int();

  printf("Enter the width: ");
  width = get_an_int();

  printf("\nThe area is %d.\n", length * width);
}

/* The following function inputs an integer and returns its value */

get_an_int()
{
  int a;

  scanf("%d", &a);
  return(a);
}
```

Program 9—2

```
Enter the length of a rectangle: 5
Enter the width: 17

The area is 85.
```

Output 9—2

In order for a function to return a value to the calling function, the last statement executed in the function must be the C **return** statement. This statement consists of the keyword **return**, followed by the value to be returned. This value may be an expression, variable, constant, or even another function call. The returned expression may be enclosed within parentheses; this is often done even though it is not necessary. (In this book, the parentheses are always used.)

A function can return only a single value each time it is called. As soon as a **return** statement is executed, the function terminates, so following this statement with any other statements (including other **return**s) is meaningless. An exception to this rule is when the **return** ends one clause of an **if** statement. In this case, the other clause may include alternate statements, including another **return**. For example:

```
if (a < 7) return (a);
else a++;
```

It is also permissible to use the **return** statement to force termination of a function that returns no value, as in the following example:

```
if (i == 0) return;
```

which returns control to the calling program if *i* is equal to zero.

The function *get_an_int* in Program 9-2 reads in an integer and returns this value to the *main* function by way of the **return** statement. The variable *a* is used merely to receive the value read in, before that value is returned to the *main* function; it has nothing to do with the variable that finally receives this value. The function is called twice by *main* to get two integers, a length and a width. The *main* function then computes and prints out the area of a rectangle with this length and width.

Unlike Pascal, the C language makes no distinction between procedures and functions. A function returns a value if it contains a **return** statement that specifies a value to be returned; otherwise, it simply terminates without returning any value. The calling function can ignore a returned value, or it can expect a value even when the called function returns none (the latter case is considered an error).

In Program 9-2, the function does not save much effort, because the reading in of an integer can be accomplished by a single call to *scanf*. The function does, however, enable the programmer to read values into the variables *length* and *width* by placing them on the left side of an assignment operator. This seems a good deal clearer than placing the variable name within the parentheses of a *scanf* statement.

Local and Global Variables

Another feature introduced in Program 9-2 is the declaration of a variable within a function. This is not really a new feature, however, because we have already mentioned that *main* is syntactically a function and that variables can be declared in *main*.

Variables declared within functions are called *local* variables; such a variable is is said to be local to the function in which it is declared. The names of local variables have meaning only within the function in which they are declared. The *scope* of a variable means the range within a program over which that variable has meaning. Statements within the *get_an_int* function can refer to the variable *a*, but statements in *main* cannot; if a reference is made to *a* in the *main* function, it is flagged as an error. Similarly, *get_an_int* cannot refer directly to the variables *length* and *width*. These variables can be referred to only within the *main* function, in which they have been declared.

A variable exists only while the function that contains it is executing. The variable *a* in Program 9-2 does not even exist until the function *get_an_int* is called. When the function finishes executing, the variable *a* passes into oblivion.

Declaring a variable of the same name in each of the two functions does *not* make it possible to use that variable for the purpose of communication between functions. Program 9-3 illustrates this principle.

```
/* An attempt at communication between functions */

main()
{
  int i;

  i = 1;
  printf("i is now equal to %d\n", i);

  modify_i();
  printf("i is now equal to %d\n", i);
}

modify_i()
{
  int i;

  i = 3;
}
```

Program 9—3

```
i is now equal to 1
i is now equal to 1
```

Output 9—3

In Program 9-3, the *main* function declares a variable named *i* and assigns to it the value 1. It then calls the function *modify_i*. This function creates its own local variable *i*, and assigns the value 3 to it. This assignment has no effect, however, on the variable named *i* that was created in the *main* function.

When control returns to the *main* function, the variable *i*—the one local to the *main* function—still contains the value 1. A function does not terminate its execution when calling another function; it only suspends it. Therefore, the variable *i* local to the *main* function remains in existence while the function *modify_i* is executing. The variable *i* in the function *main* disappears only when *main* finishes execution, which is at the end of the entire program's execution.

It might appear at first that, even though a function can return a value to its calling function, the calling function has no way to communicate a value to the function it calls. As the next program will show, C provides ways to do this. For example, if we have a function that calculates square roots, we need to be able to tell the function the number whose square root is required. Also, sometimes it is useful for a function to produce two or more values. For example, it might be desirable to have a function which, given the radius of a circle, produces both the circumference and the area of the circle.

One way of implementing two-way communication among functions is through the use of *global* variables. These variables are not declared within a specific function, so they are accessible to all functions in the program. If a global variable named *i* is declared, then all functions can refer to it. A function can assign a value to *i*, and then call another function, which uses the value contained in the same variable *i* to produce a result. Global variables are illustrated in Program 9-4, which is a modified version of Program 9-2.

```c
/* Demonstration of the use of a global variable */

int length, width, area;

main()
{
  printf("Enter the length of a rectangle: ");
  length = get_an_int();

  printf("Enter the width: ");
  width = get_an_int();

  calc_area();
  printf("\nThe area is %d.\n", area);
}

/* The following function inputs an integer and returns its value */

get_an_int()
{
  int a;

  scanf("%d", &a);
  return(a);
}

/* The following function  calculates the area of a rectangle.
   It uses the values in global variables "length" and "width"
   and places the result in global variable "area" */

calc_area()
{
  area = length * width;
}
```

Program 9—4

```
Enter the length of a rectangle: 11
Enter the width: 7

The area is 77.
```

Output 9—4

In this program, three global variables are declared—*length*, *width*, and *area*. We know they are global variables because they are not declared within the body of any function. Usually, global variables in C are declared at the beginning of a program, before the definition of the *main* function. Thus the *main* function need not (and should not) declare the variables *length* and *width*, as was done in the earlier version of the program. The "scope rules" of C—the rules that determine where any given variable can be used—state that, if a local variable is given the same name as a global variable, the function declaring the local variable can refer only to the local variable and never to the global variable of the same name. Therefore, declaring *length* and *width* within the *main* function would defeat their purpose, which is to provide communication between functions.

The values for *length* and *width* are read in the same way as before. The *get_an_int* function does not refer to any global variables, because it is called twice. During execution, there is no way the function can know for which variable a particular value is being read. Therefore, it uses the one-way communication powers of the **return** statement. This example illustrates another advantage of returning values from functions: the function can operate independently of the context in which it is called.

The major difference between Program 9-4 and Program 9-2 is that, in Program 9-4, the area is calculated by calling the *calc_area* function. This function uses the values that already have been placed in *length* and *width* in order to calculate the area. The result then is placed in the global variable *area*. This variable is accessible by the *main* function, so its value can be printed by a *printf* located in *main*.

In a sense, the logic of Program 9-4 is *less* clear than that of Program 9-2. In the original version, one could look at the *main* function and see exactly how the area was calculated. The latter version is less readily understood because all one sees is a call to the function *calc_area*. The problem is not the use of a function per se, but the fact that it is difficult to see what is going on. One could never guess that *calc_area* is using the global variables *length* and *width*, or that it is placing its result in *area*, unless one looks directly at the definition of *calc_area*. One of the rules of structured programming is that one should be able to figure out what a function does without having to look elsewhere.

For example, when we see the statement

```
printf("Hello.\n");
```

it is evident that the function *printf* prints out the contents of the control string and does nothing else. A function should be a self-contained entity.

Furthermore, the function *calc_area* has what are called *side effects*. This expression means that the function affects the state of the program as a whole, in a way that is not evident from the way the called function is used by the calling function. The function *calc_area* actually relies on side effects to operate, despite the fact that structured programming discourages the use of them.

For the reasons we have discussed, structured programming frowns on the overuse (or abuse) of global variables. One of the criteria for a well-written program is that most functions that return a value should produce only one result, which they send back to the calling function using the **return** statement. This means we should, so far as possible, avoid the use of global variables.

How then, can the calling function send a value to the function it calls without the use of global variables? This topic is discussed in the next section.

Parameters

A calling function can send a "package" of values for the called function to operate on, or to control how the function is to operate. Each value passed in this manner is called a *parameter* or *argument*.

You already have seen many examples of parameters. One familiar example is the information included between the parentheses in a call to *printf* or *scanf*. The first value passed to *printf* is the control string, which tells *printf* how many other parameters are being passed and how to convert each of the other parameters to the appropriate form for printing. Another illustration of parameter passing is the *sqrt* function illustrated earlier. In the statement

```
y = sqrt(144.0);
```

the value 144.0 is the parameter passed to the function. It represents the value for which the function is to find a square root.

When a function is called, the parameter specified within the parentheses of the calling statement is known as an *actual* parameter or argument, because it is the value that is actually transmitted to the function. This is in contrast with what is called the *dummy* or *formal* parameter, which is the name of the corresponding parameter in the called function.

Program 9-5 illustrates this concept, by showing the several forms an actual parameter may take.

```
/* Introduction to parameters */

main()
{
  int n = 3;

  printf("Passing a constant: ");
  print_an_int(5);

  printf("\n\nPassing a variable's value: ");
  print_an_int(n);

  printf("\n\nPassing the value of an expression: ");
  print_an_int(n * 4 + 1);
}
```

Program continued on next page

Program continued from previous page

```
/* The following function prints an integer
      passed as a parameter */

print_an_int(i)
int i;
{
  printf("%d", i);
}
```

Program 9—5

```
Passing a constant: 5

Passing a variable's value: 3

Passing the value of an expression: 13
```

Output 9—5

This program introduces the function *print_an_int*, which, in a sense, is the opposite of the function *get_an_int* used in previous programs. What it does is to print out an integer that is passed to it as a parameter. The function *print_an_int* returns no value.

In the function definition, note that a variable named *i* is written within the parentheses following the function name. This variable is a dummy parameter. It is similar to a local variable except that, when the function *print_an_int* begins execution, the variable *i* is initialized automatically to the value passed to it.

Following the closing parenthesis in the function definition is what looks like a variable declaration for the dummy parameter *i*. It is unlike the variable declarations we have seen before, however, because it occurs between the function name and the function body. Each dummy parameter must be declared in this way. Just as a type must be specified for each regular variable, so must the type of a parameter be specified in a declaration that occurs before the open brace of the function body. The dummy parameter must be included within the parentheses following the function name. It also must have its type declared after the function name; undeclared dummy parameters are assumed to be **int**, but should be declared anyway for the sake of clarity. Note that there is no semicolon between the closing parenthesis and the parameter declaration, but that the parameter declaration *is* terminated with a semicolon.

In the first call to *print_an_int*, the parameter passed is the value 5. When the function begins execution, it knows that whatever value was passed is contained within the dummy parameter *i*, which otherwise is treated as a local variable. The value contained in *i* is printed out, and control returns to the *main* function.

Next, *print_an_int* is called again, but this time the parameter is a variable. The value contained in the variable *n* is copied into the dummy parameter *i*, and the function executes as before.

Finally, *print_an_int* is called with an expression as a parameter. The expression is evaluated, the resulting value is copied into *i*, and the function is executed for the last time.

In all cases, the parameter passed to *print_an_int* must evaluate to an integer value, because the dummy parameter *i* has been declared to be of type **int**. If one were to attempt to pass a **float** value to *print_an_int*, havoc would result. The programmer must make sure that the types of the actual parameters passed to a function always match the types of the corresponding dummy parameters.

If a variable can be passed as a parameter (as in the second call to *print_an_int*), can its value be changed by the called function? Since the value is only copied from the variable to the dummy parameter, the answer is no. Program 9-6 demonstrates this fact.

```
/* Demonstration of how a  procedure  cannot modify
   the contents of a variable passed as a parameter */

main()
{
  int i;

  i = 1;
  printf("i is now equal to %d\n", i);

  modify(i);
  printf("i is now equal to %d\n", i);
}

modify(i)
int i;
{
  i = 3;
}
```

Program 9—6

```
i is now equal to 1
i is now equal to 1
```

Output 9—6

In this program, the value 1 is assigned to the variable named *i* in the *main* function. This value is passed as a parameter to the function *modify*. In other words, it is copied into the dummy parameter *i* (which is *not* the same variable as the local variable *i* in *main*).

At this point, dummy parameter *i* contains the value 1. After the assignment statement in the function assigns the value 3 to *i*, dummy parameter *i* contains 3. Then the function has no more statements to execute, so dummy parameter *i* disappears. Control returns to the *main* function, in which the local variable *i* still contains the value 1. Thus the assignment statement in the function *modify* has no effect on the *main* function's variable *i*, even though it is used as an actual parameter passed to *modify*.

This program is identical to Program 9-3, except that i is now a formal parameter rather than a local variable. Normally one would not want to assign a value directly to a dummy parameter, since all that would be accomplished would be the loss of the value that originally was passed.

In Program 9-7, we present a new version of the "hailstones" program from Chapter 6. In this version, a function named *step* carries out the operations on the variable n which need to be performed at each step. The old value of n is passed as a parameter to the function, where it is stored in the dummy parameter i. It then is divided by 2, or multiplied by 3 and incremented by 1, and the resulting value is returned as the value of the function. Back in the *main* function, this value is stored as the new value of n. Notice that, in the function *step*, the parameter helps determine what operation is performed on it.

```c
/* Hailstones, demonstrating the use of a parameter */

main()
{
 int n, nsave, counter = 0;

 printf("Enter a positive integer: ");
 scanf("%d",&n);

 nsave = n;
 while (n > 1)
 {
    n = step(n);
    counter++;
    printf("Step %4d: n = %4d\n", counter, n);
 }

 printf("\n\n%d went to 1 in %d steps.\n", nsave, counter);
}

/* This function returns a value which is either:
    1) Its parameter "i" divided by 2, if "i" is even, or
    2) Its parameter "i" multiplied by 3 and incremented by 1,
        if "i" is odd.
*/

step(i)
int i;
{
    if (i % 2)
        return(i * 3 + 1);
    else
        return(i / 2);
}
```

Program 9-7

```
Enter a positive integer: 25
Step     1: n =    76
Step     2: n =    38
Step     3: n =    19
Step     4: n =    58
Step     5: n =    29
Step     6: n =    88
Step     7: n =    44
Step     8: n =    22
Step     9: n =    11
Step    10: n =    34
Step    11: n =    17
Step    12: n =    52
Step    13: n =    26
Step    14: n =    13
Step    15: n =    40
Step    16: n =    20
Step    17: n =    10
Step    18: n =     5
Step    19: n =    16
Step    20: n =     8
Step    21: n =     4
Step    22: n =     2
Step    23: n =     1

25 went to 1 in 23 steps.
```

Output 9—7

This program does not introduce any new concepts, but it illustrates how the use of functions and parameters can make a program more attractive and orderly, two of the features that mark a well-written structured program. It also affords us an opportunity to show one way in which C programs can be made more concise. One of the desirable features of C is that it can be used to write programs that are very elegant and efficient. C affords one the opportunity to write clear, structured code, or to write a program in as few lines as possible. In some cases, these two goals may be mutually exclusive.

It would be constructive to examine the body of the **while** loop in Program 9-7. You may discover how the program can be shortened by eliminating one statement. The variable *counter* can be incremented within the *printf* statement, so that the body of the loop contains only two statements:

```
n = step(n);
printf("Step %4d: n = %4d\n", ++counter, n);
```

Since pre-increment is used on the variable *counter*, its value is incremented to 1 before being printed out the first time. When a separate statement was used to increment *counter*, it did not matter whether pre- or post-increment was used, since either way the incrementing happened before the printing. Here, however, the distinction is crucial.

We can reduce the size of the body of the loop even further. Unlike other computer languages, C treats the assignment operator as just another binary operator. This means that an assignment can be made within the context of an expression. The body of the **while** loop can therefore be written as a single statement:

```
printf("Step %4d: n = %4d\n", ++counter, (n = step(n)));
```

This means the pre-increment is performed before the *printf* function is called. Then the *step* function is called, and the returned value is assigned to the variable *n*. This value also becomes the value of the expression (n = step(n)), so the new value of *n* is passed as the parameter to *printf*, which is precisely what is intended.

The assignment expression is enclosed in parentheses because assignment is very low in the order of operations. Whenever assignment is done within a larger expression or statement, it should always be surrounded by parentheses to prevent ambiguity. Note that this last form of the body of the **while** loop is not any more efficient than the original form. It is more concise, but possibly less clear.

Declaring the Type of a Function

At the end of Chapter 7, we illustrated a program for calculating the square root of a number. The math library also supports a square root function, which is called *sqrt*. This function takes as an argument a value of type **double** and returns a value of type **double**. The purpose of presenting the next program is to show how such a function can be custom-made if it is not included in the supplied library of functions.

Even if a function is included in a C library, we can still define a function with the same name in our program. In such a case, the function definition in the program takes precedence over the library version.

The following program will introduce you to several features that are important to know when writing functions. Program 9-8 uses the Newton-Raphson iteration method, and uses as its initial guess *n/2*, where *n* is the value passed to the function.

```
/* Square root program demonstrating a non-integer
   function and parameter */

main()
{
  float x, sqrt();

  printf("Enter the number whose square root you want: ");
  scanf("%f", &x);

  printf("The square root of %f is %f\n", x, sqrt(x));
}
```

Program continued on next page

Program continued from previous page

```
/* Newton-Raphson method for calculating square roots */

#define EPSILON 0.0001

float sqrt(n)
float n;
{
  float guess;

    /* verify the input */
  if (n >= 0.0)
  {
    /* calculate the square root */
      for(guess = n / 2.0;
          guess * guess - n > EPSILON || guess * guess - n < -EPSILON;
          guess = (guess + n / guess) / 2.0);
      return (guess);
  }
  else return (-1.0);
}
```

Program 9—8

```
Enter the number whose square root you want: 17.1
The square root of 17.100006 is 4.135208
```

Output 9—8

Just as the type of a variable must be explicitly declared, so must the type of a function. By the type of a function, we mean the type of the value returned by the function.

C allows us one shortcut: If the type of a function is **int**, one need not declare this explicitly. Since the functions we have illustrated so far have returned either integer values or no values at all, we have not had to declare the types of functions. Here, however, our function is to return a value of type **float**. (We have decided not to use type **double** and settle for a little less precision than that given by the library *sqrt* function.)

The type of a function (other than **int**) must be declared in at least two places: in the function definition, and in every calling function. In Program 9-8, the name of the function is preceded by the word **float** when the function is defined. If the **return** statement in the function specifies a non-**float** value, this value is cast automatically into the correct type, namely **float**. The type of the function also must be declared in every function that calls it. In this case, the only function that calls *sqrt* is *main*. Therefore, among the local variable declarations for the *main* function, we find *sqrt()* declared to be of type **float**. Such a declaration does not allocate any memory, but merely informs the *main* function that, when the function *sqrt* is called, it will return a value of type **float**.

The *sqrt* function attempts to verify the validity of its parameter, just as programs we have seen previously have attempted to verify their input. This function considers a negative value to be an invalid parameter, since it is impossible to take the square root of a negative number without resorting to complex arithmetic. A function is limited, however, in the action it can take when it receives an invalid parameter. According to the accepted rules of good programming, having a function display an error message (or any other message) is considered a side effect and is therefore discouraged.

Thus our *sqrt* function resorts to a commonly used method, which is to return a signal value, -1, to indicate that an error has occurred. This value was chosen because the function normally would not return a negative number. The programmer who uses our *sqrt* function must be made aware that, if the function returns a value of -1, this means the parameter passed to the function was invalid.

Note that the constant EPSILON is defined not at the beginning of the program, but immediately before the *sqrt* function. This practice is justified by the fact that the constant is used only by the function and should be defined near the function definition. It is permissible to define a constant anywhere within a program, even within the body of a function, as long as the constant is not used prior to its definition in the program.

Boolean Functions

Since boolean values are represented by integers in C, it is very easy to write a function that returns a *true* or *false* value. Such a function is useful when a particular test is used many times, especially when the test is somewhat complex. It can save considerable programming effort and can also make a program look a lot neater.

As a simple example, the following program is a rewrite of the leap year program illustrated in Chapter 5. In the revised version, the lengthy test has been placed within a function.

```
/* Testing for leap years using a "boolean" function */

main()
{
    int year;

    printf("Please enter a year: ");
    scanf("%d", &year);

    if ( is_leap(year) )
        printf("%d is a leap year.\n",year);
    else
        printf("%d is not a leap year.\n",year);
}

/* "Boolean" function is_leap returns true if year is a leap year */

is_leap(year)
int year;
{
    return (year % 4 == 0 && year % 100 != 0 || year % 400 == 0);
}
```

Program 9—9

```
Please enter a year: 1986
1986 is not a leap year.



Please enter a year: 1948
1948 is a leap year.



Please enter a year: 1900
1900 is not a leap year.



Please enter a year: 2000
2000 is a leap year.
```

Output 9—9

In Program 9-9, the function *is_leap* returns a value by placing the boolean expression used to test for a leap year directly within the **return** statement. This placement allows the function to return whatever integer is generated by the boolean expression: 0 for *false* or non-zero for *true*. A specific non-zero value is always generated when a boolean expression is true, but this value often depends on the version of C, and in any case it is not of any particular interest to the programmer. If the expression in the **return** statement is true, a non-zero value is returned to the calling function and is correctly interpreted.

Functions With More Than One Parameter

So far we have shown how a single parameter can be passed to a function. Oftentimes, however, it is necessary to pass more than one parameter to a given function. Program 9-10 illustrates how C enables us to do this. It is almost identical to Program 9-4, except that it uses parameters and the **return** statement instead of global variables.

```
/* Demonstration of the use of multiple parameters */

main()
{
  int length, width;

  printf("Enter the length of a rectangle: ");
  length = get_an_int();

  printf("Enter the width: ");
  width = get_an_int();

  printf("\nThe area is %d.\n", area(length, width));
}
```

Program continued on next page

Program continued from previous page

```
/* The following function inputs an integer and returns its value */

get_an_int()
{
  int a;

  scanf("%d", &a);
  return(a);
}

/* The following function calculates the area of a rectangle.
   It uses the values of its parameters "length" and "width"
   and returns the result */

area(length, width)
int length, width;
{
  return(length * width);
}
```

Program 9—10

```
Enter the length of a rectangle: 7
Enter the width: 9

The area is 63.
```

Output 9—10

In Program 9-10, the calculation of the area of the rectangle is done by calling the *area* function inside the call to *printf*. The *area* function is passed the values of *length* and *width* (which are assigned to formal parameters of the same name), and calculates the area within the **return** statement that passes the final result back to the *main* function.

The next program further explores the passing of two parameters.

```
/* Illustration of a 2-parameter function:
   raising a number to a power */

main()
{
    int  number,     /* Number to be raised to power */
         exponent;   /* Power to raise number to */
    long power();    /* (See below) */
    char answer;     /* Y or N, whether user wants to go again */

    do
    {

        printf("\nPlease enter an integer: ");
        scanf("%d", &number);

        printf("Please enter a non-negative integral power\n");
        printf("    to which the first number is to be raised: ");
        scanf("%d", &exponent);
```

Program continued on next page

Program continued from previous page

```
/* Make sure exponent is non-negative */

        while (exponent < 0)
        {
            printf("*** \7Please make that a non-negative integer: ");
            scanf("%d", &exponent);
        }

        printf("%d raised to the power %d is %ld.\n", number, exponent,
                power(number, exponent));

/* See if user wants to keep going */

        printf("\nAnother calculation? (y/n) ");
        scanf("%*c %c", &answer);
    }
    while (answer == 'y' || answer == 'Y');
}


long power(i, x)
int i, x;
    /* Function to raise i to the x power (x must be non-negative) */
{
    int index;              /* loop index */
    long accum = 1;         /* accumulator for final product */

/* If x < 0 (invalid), return 0.  This is not a very good error
    indication, but since this routine might generate any value,
    there is no integer which would be any better */

    if (x < 0) return(0);

/* Loop x times; if x is zero, return 1. */

    for (index = 0; index < x; accum *= i, index++);

    return(accum);
}
```

Program 9—11

```
            Please enter an integer: 4
            Please enter a non-negative integral power
                to which the first number is to be raised: 2
            4 raised to the power 2 is 16.

            Another calculation? (y/n) y

            Please enter an integer: 3
            Please enter a non-negative integral power
                to which the first number is to be raised: 4
            3 raised to the power 4 is 81.

            Another calculation? (y/n) y
```

Output continued on next page

Output continued from previous page

```
Please enter an integer: -3
Please enter a non-negative integral power
    to which the first number is to be raised: 2
-3 raised to the power 2 is 9.

Another calculation? (y/n) y

Please enter an integer: 2
Please enter a non-negative integral power
    to which the first number is to be raised: -3
*** Please make that a non-negative integer: 3
2 raised to the power 3 is 8.

Another calculation? (y/n) Y

Please enter an integer: 2
Please enter a non-negative integral power
    to which the first number is to be raised: 10
2 raised to the power 10 is 1024.

Another calculation? (y/n) y

Please enter an integer: 190
Please enter a non-negative integral power
    to which the first number is to be raised: 2
190 raised to the power 2 is 36100.

Another calculation? (y/n) n
```

Output 9—11

In Program 9-11, the user is prompted to type in the base number, which is read into the variable *number*. The user is then asked to enter a non-negative integer, which represents the power to which the first number is to be raised. This second number is stored in the variable named *exponent*.

The exponent cannot be negative, because raising a number to a negative exponent yields a value less than 1, which would be interpreted as zero because we are dealing only with integers. In case the user enters a negative value, the value of *exponent* is validated with a **while** loop, which keeps prompting for a value until the user enters one that is greater than or equal to zero. In order to draw attention to this error, the bell connected to the computer is sounded by use of \7 in the *printf* statement. (As you may remember, \7 is the octal code for sounding the bell or beeper.)

Once the input values have been validated, a call to the function *power* is made in which *number* and *exponent* are passed as parameters. Notice that the corresponding formal parameters in the function *power* have different names than the variables in the *main* function used as actual parameters. This underscores the fact that the matching between actual and formal parameters depends upon position and not name.

When two or more parameters are required by a function, the calling function must pass its parameters in the correct order. The variable *number* is passed as the value for the function's formal parameter *i*, and *exponent* is the value placed in formal parameter *x*. If the function were called instead as

```
power(exponent, number)
```

the parameters would be assigned incorrectly. There is a one-to-one correspondence between the actual parameters passed to a function and the dummy parameters specified in the function heading. If a function requires two parameters, the calling function must pass two parameters to match the formal parameters within the function. The parameters also must match in type.

The function *power* is declared to return a value of type **long**. This declaration must be made both within the *main* function and in the actual definition of *power*. This declaration is necessary because exponentiation tends to produce very large results. Also, *power* is written in a way that allows it to be used with any calling function. This generality is reflected in the fact that no assumption is made about whether the calling function has validated the parameters. Even though the *main* function makes sure the exponent is non-negative, the function makes its own test.

Unfortunately, there is not much the function can do if the value of *x* passed to it is negative. There is no return value that can unambiguously indicate an error, since the function can generate both positive and negative values as results of its calculation. The only really effective indications of an error condition would involve side effects, such as printing an error message, placing a special value in a global variable, or stopping the program. The use of these devices is discouraged, so we merely return zero as an error indicator, in the hope that the calling function will take this as a possible indication of an error condition. A really good calling function would verify the data beforehand, which is exactly what our *main* function does.

The function *power* declares a **long** variable *accum* and initializes it to 1 (no L is needed after the value 1, since a **long** 1 is always represented the same as an **int** 1). The function performs its calculation by repeatedly multiplying the value of *i* into *accum* as many times as indicated by the value *x*. If *x* is 0, the loop never is executed and the value returned is 1. This is perfectly acceptable, since any number raised to the power 0 is 1.

Getting back to the *main* function: The result is displayed using the conversion specification %ld to display the **long** value returned by *power*. The whole process is then repeated so long as the user responds positively to the prompt, "Another calculation?" The prompt itself suggests a response of *y* or *n*. If the test compared the response with *y* only, a response of *Y* would be treated as a negative response. In order to prevent this from happening, a two-part test is made, one part for *y* and the other for *Y*. The || operator enables us to accept either one of these two responses. Any other character, even if it is not *n* or *N*, will lead to termination of the program.

You will notice that the *scanf* used to input *answer* contains the conversion specification %*c. This skips over the carriage return following the value for *exponent*. Of course, this works only if there is a single white space character between the values of *exponent* and *answer*. It would also be possible to examine the value of *answer* and, if it is a white space character, attempt to read in another character until a non white-space value for *answer* has been obtained. In the next chapter, we shall learn another method of handling this situation which allows for greater flexibility.

There is no need to worry about the carriage return (if any) following the input value for *answer*, since the next item read is an integer, and the %d conversion specification skips over white space. The user must not, however, enter a value for *answer* containing more than one character. If a response of *yup* were typed in by the user, the *y* would be read in successfully, but when the time came to read *number*, a *u* would be encountered, instead of a digit as expected. The result would be an incorrect computation or some other unpredictable occurrence. This problem is solvable in several other ways, one of which will be described in the next chapter.

An initializing expression used in a variable declaration can contain a function call. Of course, any variables used as arguments to the function must be declared first. If the function returns a non-**int** value, its type must also be previously declared. For example, the following is syntactically valid:

```
int a, func(), b = func(a);
```

The modularization of programs—that is, the process of dividing them into simpler subtasks—is implemented in C by means of functions. But functions alone are not sufficient to manipulate data efficiently. C provides other constructs that add greatly to the usefulness of functions. One of these constructs is the array, which is the subject of the next chapter.

The *Spirit of* C

Now that you have learned about functions, you should design all future programs as collections of functions. This probably is not a drastic departure from the style you are already accustomed to. In previous chapters of this book, we have designed individual program segments separately. Functional programming simply means that each subsection of the program is placed in a separate function. For more on this topic, see the

Programming and Debugging Hints section of this and the next chapter.

Suppose we wish to write a program similar to the one created in Chapter 8's *Spirit of C* section, which accepted a line of integers with one or more commas between numbers. Now, however, we wish to remove the restriction that a comma must immediately follow a number with no intervening blanks. We also wish to permit characters other than digits and commas to appear in the input; such characters are to be ignored.

Removing the requirement that commas must immediately follow numbers means that the numbers have to be read in as individual characters and then converted to integers within the program. To illustrate why this is so, consider the input:

    3 , 4

where the 3 is followed by a space and then a comma, followed in turn by another space and the 4. Suppose we have just read the number 3. We now expect to find one of the following characters in the input: a blank, a comma, or some other character. A digit is not expected, since we just read in a number, and at least one non-digit character must separate numbers in the input.

We therefore read in the next character, using the %c conversion specification. If the next character is a comma, we start a new line; otherwise we ignore the character. Now, however, the next character in the input could be a digit or any of the other characters mentioned above. Since we don't know whether or not it will be a digit, we again input a character using %c. If it is a non-digit character, we have acted appropriately. If it is a digit, however, then it is too late to read in the next number using %d, since we have just removed the first digit of that number from the input by reading it in as a character.

It would be nice if there were a facility to restore that first digit to the input. Such a function will be described in Chapter 14; meanwhile, we will resort to the solution of reading in the number as a series of characters. This means we can still make use of the first digit, since all the digits will be read in as characters.

The first part of the program we will write is the code to convert a series of characters to an integer. We may as well make this section a function. A difficulty that occurs is that each digit read in must be added to the part of the number read in up until that point. For example, if the number is

    123

the program will first read in the character '1' and convert it to the number 1. Let us say this number is stored in a variable *shifter* (we will soon see the reason for this). Next, the character '2' is read in. We now need to shift the value in *shifter* to the left by 1 decimal place, so that the value 2 can be attached on the right. This can be done by multiplying *shifter* by 10, yielding the value 10. We then add 2, giving 12.

Next, the character '3' is read in and converted to the number 3. The variable *shifter* is multiplied by 10, giving 120, and 3 is added to that value, giving 123. This clearly is a general algorithm, since any number of digits can be handled. The function that performs it cannot be passed all the characters at once, however, and should not be required to read them in. We therefore require a function that can append one digit at a time to the accumulating variable.

We could write this function by using a global variable for *shifter*, so that as soon as all the digits have been read in, the calling function can have access to the final value. But since we wish to avoid global variables, a better solution is to have the function return the intermediate value it generates each time it is called. This solution requires that the function be passed not only the new digit, but also the value returned the last time the function was called. (The first time the function is called, it must be passed 0.) Such a function can be written with only one statement:

```
shift_in (old_value, new_digit)
int old_value;
char new_digit;

    /* Attach "new_digit" to the right of "oldvalue". For example,
       if old_value == 123 and new_digit == '6', result is 1236 */

{
    return(old_value * 10 + (new_digit - '0'));
}
```

No test is made to be sure the character passed as *new_digit* is a digit; we assume the calling function is behaving correctly. This is a permissible assumption at this point (considering that we have not written the calling program yet), but we must remember to write the calling program so that it passes only digits to the *shift_in* function.

Now, we can write a function to start a new line, which is called when a comma is read in. The function needs to know the sum of all the integers on the current line, as well as the ordinal number of the next line. This function also is easy to write:

```
end_line (line_total, next_line)
int line_total,      /* Total of all integers on this line */
    next_line;       /* Ordinal of the next line */

    /* Print total for this line, start next line */

{
    printf(" < total: %d\nLine %d> ", line_total, next_line);
}
```

Notice that the function does not reset the value of *line_total* or increment *next_line*. These actions are left to the calling program.

It is perfectly acceptable for functions to be small, so long as they divide the problem into its component tasks, are easy to understand, and can be combined to form complex programs.

The next function we can write will read in characters and call the two functions we have already written where appropriate. It would be possible to write a function that reads in only one character each time it is called, but at this point, this solution would require the use of several global variables. It would be easier to write the function so that it reads all the input using a loop. This last function will be *main*:

```
/* This program inputs and echoes back integers, beginning a new output
   line at each point where a comma appears in the input. Each line is
   labeled, and at the end of each output line, the total of all the integers
   on that line is displayed. The input itself must consist of only one line.
   Any characters other than digits and commas are ignored, except as
   delimiters for the numbers. The newline is used to detect the end of the
   line. */


                        /* Stage 1 */

main()
{
    char character;         /* Holds the character just read in */
    int line_total = 0,     /* Accumulator for the total of all integers
                               on a line */
        next_line = 2,      /* Number of the next line (start with 2,
                               because that is the first value to be
                               passed to the "end_line" function) */
        current_number = 0; /* Accumulator for the number currently
                               being read in character-by-character */

    printf("Type a line of integers, with commas everywhere\n");
    printf("the line is to be split. Any other characters\n");
    printf("are ignored:\n");

    scanf("%c", &character);        /* Priming read */
    printf("Line 1> ");             /* Initial line label */

    /* Read and process characters until end of line */

    while (character != '\n')
    {

        if (character == ',')       /* Split the line */
        {
            end_line(line_total, next_line);
            line_total = 0;         /* Reset total of all numbers on line */
            next_line++;            /* Increment line number */
        }
```

Program continued on next page

Program continued from previous page

```
    /* If a digit, shift into the integer */

    else if (character >= '0' && character <= '9')
            current_number = shift_in(current_number, character);

}

    printf(" < total: %d\n", line_total);      /* Finish off last line */

}
```

Notice in the above function that *next_line* starts out as 2. This is because the first time *end_line* is called, the new line being started is line number 2. We could instead initialize *next_line* to 1 and increment it before *end_line* is called. This would not be any more or less efficient than the method we have used, because both versions perform an unnecessary increment; either when the loop begins, or before it terminates.

One possible objection to this function is that it prints the label for the first line and the line total for the last line, operations that otherwise are performed by the *end_line* function. In other words, the same task is being performed at different times by two different functions. It would be possible to modify *end_line* so that, if it is called with a line number of 1, it prints only the line label, and if it is called with a line number of 0, it displays only the line total. This solution might lead to other complications, however. It is up to you, the programmer, to make these decisions.

Actually, the function just illustrated will not work correctly. Even though it shifts in digits correctly, it does not check for the end of an integer, the signal to add the completed number to the line total and reset the variable *current_number*. This problem requires testing for a non-digit following a digit. That is, it depends on the character read in during the previous loop iteration. We must therefore add a variable to hold the character previously read in, and an extra nested **if** test:

```
/* This program inputs and echoes back integers, beginning a new output
   line at each point where a comma appears in the input. Each line is
   labeled, and at the end of each output line, the total of all the integers
   on that line is displayed. The input itself must consist of only one line.
   Any characters other than digits and commas are ignored, except as
   delimiters for the numbers. The newline is used to detect the end of the
   line. */

                            /* Stage 2 */

main()
{
    char character,         /* Holds the character just read in */
        last_char = ' ';    /* Saves the character read in before the
                               current one (initialized to a non-digit
                               for correct program operation) */
```

Program continued on next page

Program continued from previous page

```
int line_total = 0,        /* Accumulator for the total of all integers
                              on a line */
    next_line = 2,         /* Number of the next line (start with 2,
                              because that is the first value to be
                              passed to the "end_line" function) */
    current_number = 0; /* Accumulator for the number currently
                              being read in character-by-character */

printf("Type a line of integers, with commas everywhere\n");
printf("the line is to be split. Any other characters\n");
printf("are ignored:\n");

scanf("%c", &character);        /* Priming read */
printf("Line 1> ");             /* Initial line label */

/* Read and process characters until end of line */

while (character != '\n')
{

    if (character == ',')       /* Split the line */
    {

        /* If this immediately follows a digit, a number has just
           been finished and should be added to line total */

        if (last_char >= '0' && last_char <= '9')
        {
            line_total += current_number;
            current_number = 0;   /* Reset for next number */
        }

        end_line(line_total, next_line);
        line_total = 0;             /* Reset total of all numbers on line */
        next_line++;                /* Increment line number */
    }

    /* If a digit, shift into the integer */
    else if (character >= '0' && character <= '9')
            current_number = shift_in(current_number, character);

        else      /* Some other character */

        /* If this immediately follows a digit, a number has just
           been finished and should be added to line total */

        if (last_char >= '0' && last_char <= '9')
        {
            line_total += current_number;
            current_number = 0;  /* Reset for next number */
        }

        /* Else, ignore this character */

    last_char = character;      /* Save this character for the next
                                    time around */
}

printf(" < total: %d\n", line_total);      /* Finish off last line */

}
```

This solution will do the trick. Notice, however, that the new code (to add the current number to the line total) must be written twice, for the two cases in which it must be used. The only case in which this code is *not* performed is when a digit is read in. Therefore, the case of a digit being read in should be tested first within the loop. If it fails, the code to add the number to the current line total (if necessary) is executed before any of the other tests are made. This change will avoid the duplication of code. It is implemented in the next version of the function:

```
/* This program inputs and echoes back integers, beginning a new output
   line at each point where a comma appears in the input. Each line is
   labeled, and at the end of each output line, the total of all the integers
   on that line is displayed. The input itself must consist of only one line.
   Any characters other than digits and commas are ignored, except as
   delimiters for the numbers. The newline is used to detect the end of the
   line. */

                        /* Stage 3 */

main()
{
    char character,         /* Holds the character just read in */
         last_char = ' ';   /* Saves the character read in before the
                                current one (initialized to a non-digit
                                for correct program operation) */
    int line_total = 0,     /* Accumulator for the total of all integers
                                on a line */
        next_line = 2,      /* Number of the next line (start with 2,
                                because that is the first value to be
                                passed to the "end_line" function) */
        current_number = 0; /* Accumulator for the number currently
                                being read in character-by-character */

    printf("Type a line of integers, with commas everywhere\n");
    printf("the line is to be split. Any other characters\n");
    printf("are ignored:\n");

    scanf("%c", &character);    /* Priming read */
    printf("Line 1> ");         /* Initial line label */

    /* Read and process characters until end of line */

    while (character != '\n')
    {

        /* If a digit, shift into the integer */

        if (character >= '0' && character <= '9')
            current_number = shift_in(current_number, character);

        else        /* Not a digit */
        {

            /* If this immediately follows a digit, a number has just
               been finished and should be added to line total */
```

Program continued on next page

Program continued from previous page

```
    if (last_char >= '0' && last_char <= '9')
    {
        line_total += current_number;
        current_number = 0;   /* Reset for next number */
    }

    /* Is it a comma? */

    if (character == ',')    /* Split the line */
    {
        end_line(line_total, next_line);
        line_total = 0;           /* Reset total of all numbers on line */
        next_line++;              /* Increment line number */
    }

    /* Else, ignore this character */

    }

    last_char = character;     /* Save this character for the next
                                  time around */
    }

    printf(" < total: %d\n", line_total);     /* Finish off last line */

}
```

Now we need only attach the definitions of the two smaller functions, *shift_in* and *end_line*, and the program is complete.

Programming and Debugging *Hints*

What is a well-written program? From the point of view of the programmer, it is a program written in such a way that the debugging process is as painless as possible. This cannot be done effectively without utilizing the techniques of modular programming.

Modular Programming, Part I

Modular programming is a broad topic, but basically it means that each individual subtask of a programming problem is performed by a function. Ideally, each function is as small as possible or reasonable. It is far easier to write and debug 10 functions consisting of 20 lines each than it is to write and debug a single function consisting of 200 lines.

In modular programming, most functions consist of calls to other functions. The *main* function is composed almost entirely of calls to other functions, which in turn may call still other functions, as illustrated in the following figure.

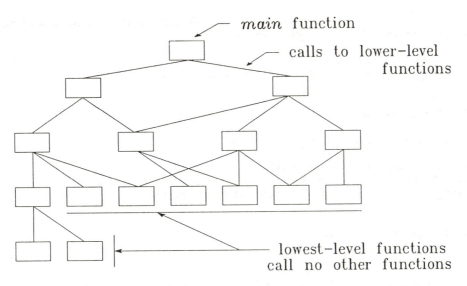

Figure 9—1

Only functions on the lowest level do not call other functions. These functions perform relatively simple tasks that are used by higher-level functions.

The advantages of modular programming are many. Each small, manageable subtask of the program can be isolated and tested individually. Each subtask can easily be found and modified. It is easier to identify which part of a program is responsible for a particular error when each part is clearly defined and separate from the rest of the program. Furthermore, modular programming makes it easier to amend the program or add new code at some later stage.

A necessary feature of modular programming is the use of good interfaces between functions. This means, among other things, that one should try to avoid the use of global variables for communication between functions. Side effects, defined as non-obvious effects of a function, also should be avoided. Usually these effects are purposeful, but they leave the program wide open to undesired bugs.

For example, suppose a global variable is used for communication between two functions, but the programmer inadvertently allows a third function to use that variable as temporary storage. The three functions will interfere with each other's communication, and disaster will result. If global variables are not used, a whole class of errors is automatically avoided and the program is a lot clearer to the reader.

Preprocessor constants are global by nature, so they must be used with care. A constant should not be used where a parameter would be clearer. For example, the value of a constant should be passed to a function rather than having the function refer to it directly. Use of the argument makes the function more general.

Another characteristic of a clear interface is that each function should begin with a comment that describes exactly what the function does, what its arguments are, what values are permissible as arguments, and what value is returned. This last item should include values returned as indications of an error condition. If a function returns error codes, the calling function should always test for these codes.

C Tutorial

1. Distinguish between a user-defined function and one supplied in the C library.

2. In what sense does the user-defined function feature of C extend its repertoire?

3. Name two common functions supplied in the standard C library.

4. Name a commonly used function that resides in the C math library.

5. When is the execution of a function terminated?

6. What is the essential difference between a function call written as a solitary statement and one that is part of an expression or statement?

7. How many values can a function return?

8. What is the major difference between a function and a procedure?

9. What distinguishes a call to the function *bingo* from its definition?

10. Why is it a good idea to use functions when programming in C?

11. What is the meaning of the term *debugging*?

12. What are some of the primary features of structured programming?

13. What is a module, and what is an example in C?

14. What are the rules regarding the naming of a function?

15. How often can a function be called?

16. What is meant by modular programming?

17. What is meant by a side effect? Give an example.

18. What symbols are used to encompass the body of a function?

19. Where in a C program is the *main* function generally located, and what difference does its position make?

20. How is a function invoked?

21. How is the *main* function normally invoked?

22. What role does the **return** statement play?

23. Where are global variables placed within a program?

24. Distinguish between local and global variables.

25. What is a formal or dummy parameter?

26. What is the difference between an actual parameter and a formal or dummy parameter?

27. What would be the effect of passing a parameter of type **float** to a function whose dummy parameter is declared to be of type **int**?

28. What special advantage does a function whose type is **int** have?

29. Where in a program can a constant be defined?

30. What values are returned by a boolean function?

31. How many parameters can be passed to a function?

32. What are the rules regarding the relationship between the actual parameters that are passed to a function and its formal parameters?

ANSWERS TO C TUTORIAL

1. The statements of a user—defined function are written as part of the program itself, according to the programmer's requirements.

2. A function may be designed to carry out some frequently used task, and called upon when needed merely by specifying the name of the function.

3. *printf* and *scanf*

4. *sqrt* (or *sin*, *cos*, etc.)

5. When it executes the **return** statement or when the last statement in the body of the function is executed.

6. When a function call is written as a statement, any value returned is discarded.

7. One.

8. A procedure does not return a value, while a function does. In C, the term procedure is not used, since functions that return values are identical in overall structure to those that do not.

9. The call to the function ends with a semicolon following the parentheses, since it is a complete statement. When *bingo* is defined, the parentheses are not followed by a semicolon.

10. Functions enable the programmer to divide the program into smaller, more easily managed segments.

11. It is the finding and elimination of errors in programs.

12. Modular programming; avoidance of side effects and global variables; well—chosen use of comments; intelligently selected variable and function names; use of self—contained units of code, such as loops and **if** statements.

13. A module is a section of code which performs its own subtask. In C, these are written as functions.

14. They are the same as for naming variables:

    a) The name must begin with a letter or an underscore.
    b) The name may contain only letters, digits, or underscores.
    c) The name should not be in all capitals, to avoid confusion with constants.
    d) The name should not begin with an underscore, to avoid conflict with system names.
    e) The first eight characters should not be the same as those of another entity in the program, to avoid system—dependent problems.
    f) The name should be descriptive of the role played by the function; in other words, it should be self—documenting.

15. As many times as needed.

16. A program should be broken down into smaller sub—tasks, which in turn may be broken down again, so that the lowest—level functions are as simple as possible (within reason).

17. This term describes the situation that results when a function performs an operation that is not evident from the way the function is used. Examples are the placing of values into global variables, or printing an error message in a function that returns a value.

18. The curly braces, { and }.

19. The *main* function generally is placed at the beginning of the program, but the position makes no difference whatever.

20. Its name is specified, followed by a pair of parentheses which contain the parameters, if needed.

21. This is done automatically by the operating system when the program is executed.

22. It specifies the value to be returned by the function. It also terminates the execution of the function.

23. Outside all function definitions, usually at the beginning of the program.

24. Local variables are declared within the body of the function. They can be referred to only within the function, and they disappear once the function finishes execution. Global variables are declared outside the function definitions, can be referred to from any function, and remain in existence for the entire execution of the program.

25. It is like a local variable but is used to hold a value passed from the calling function when a function is called.

26. A dummy parameter is the local variable that holds the value of the actual parameter.

27. Utter chaos.

28. Its type need not be declared, either when the function is defined or in other functions that call it.

29. Anywhere, as long as it is on a separate line, but it cannot be referred to until after it is defined.

30. Zero, representing *false*, or a non–zero value, representing *true*.

31. As many parameters as are specified in the function definition.

32. (a) There must be a one–to–one correspondence between the actual and formal parameters.
    (b) Corresponding parameters must be of the same type.

Keywords

char	do	double	else	float	for
if	int	long	**return**	short	unsigned
while					

Exercises

The following exercises all require the writing of functions, rather than entire programs. In order to test the correctness of a function, however, a *main* function must be written to call the function being tested, using different test parameters each time, and displaying the returned results. Test values should be chosen intelligently. For example, to test the *abs* function in Exercise 1, the function should be called with the values -1, 0, and 1, to assure that it works properly for all these cases. Further testing may be done by calling the function with arbitrary values to assure correctness.

1. Write a function *abs* which returns the absolute value of an integer that is passed as a parameter.

2. Write a function *min* which returns the smaller of its two parameters. You may also write the function *max* which returns the larger of the two, even though the two functions are nearly identical. You can expand on these functions so that they return the maximum or minimum (as appropriate) of three or more numbers passed as arguments.

3. In Chapter 5, Exercise 8, you were asked to write a program that tests for a valid triangle. You are now in a position to write a function that does the same. The function should take three arguments, the sides of the triangle. It should return a boolean value: *true* if the triangle is valid, *false* otherwise. To refresh your memory, a triangle is valid if the length of each side is less than the sum of the lengths of the other two sides.

4. The area of any triangle can be calculated by Heron's formula, which defines the semiperimeter, *s*, as half of the sum of the sides of the triangle. The area of the triangle then is given by the formula

    Area = the square root of $(s(s-a)(s-b)(s-c))$

    where *a*, *b*, and *c* are the sides of the triangle. Write a function which, when passed the sides of a triangle, returns the area using Heron's formula. The function should first make sure the triangle is valid; if it is not, the function can return zero or a negative value as an error indicator. To calculate the square root, you can either write a *sqrt* function using the Newton-Raphson method, or use the *sqrt* function supplied in the math library if you know how to link in the library (check the user manual for your C compiler).

5. The problem of solving for the roots of a quadratic equation involves finding values of *x* for which an equation of the following form is true:

    $$ax^2 + bx + c = 0$$

    The values *a*, *b* and *c* are numeric constants known as *coefficients*. For example, given the equation

    $$x^2 - 6x + 5 = 0$$

    where the coefficients are 1, -6, and 5, substituting 1 for *x* makes the equation true, as well as substituting 5 for *x*. In general, quadratic equations have two roots, or solutions. The formulas for finding the roots are:

    $$x_1 = \frac{-b + \sqrt{b^2 - 4ac}}{2a}$$

    $$x_2 = \frac{-b - \sqrt{b^2 - 4ac}}{2a}$$

where *a*, *b* and *c* are the coefficients of the quadratic equation. Notice that the two formulas are identical, except for the plus or minus sign to the left of the square root. The portion of the formula under the square root sign is known as the *discriminant*.

Two cases must be tested for before the calculation is made. In the *linear* case, the coefficient *a* is 0, resulting in an equation of the form

bx + c = 0

Since *a* is zero in this case, dividing by 2a as required by the standard formula would result in a division-by-zero error. A linear equation has only one root, which is calculated by the formula

x = -c / b

The other special case occurs when the discriminant (b^2 - 4ac) is negative. Since the square root of the discriminant is required, but negative numbers do not have real square roots, the roots of the quadratic equation are in this case referred to as complex.

Write a function that solves for the roots of a quadratic equation. The function should take three arguments, the values of the coefficients. Since two values (the two roots) need to be returned, global variables should be used to return the results. (This is not the best way to return values; Chapter 11 will introduce a better method.) Again, either the Newton-Raphson function or the library *sqrt* function may be used.

The quadratic roots function should test for the linear and complex cases. In the former case, it should calculate the linear root using the alternate formula. In the latter case, no roots need to be calculated. The function should notify the calling function if a special case has been detected. This can be done by returning a value via the **return** statement. A returned value of zero can indicate that the two quadratic roots were calculated. A value of 1 can indicate that the case was linear, and that only one root was calculated. A returned value of -1 can be used to indicate that the case was complex and no roots were calculated. The calling program should check this returned value before attempting to use the calculated roots. (The *main* function you write should test the quadratic roots function with sample data from all three cases.)

6. In Chapter 3, Exercise 4, you were asked to write programs to convert temperatures in Fahrenheit to their Celsius equivalents and vice versa. You should now be able to write a temperature conversion function. The function should take two arguments, the first being a temperature and the second being a letter or a number (as you prefer) which indicates whether the temperature is in Fahrenheit or Celsius. If the temperature is in Fahrenheit, the function should calculate and return the Celsius equivalent. Similarly, a Celsius temperature should be converted to Fahrenheit.

7. During the winter, the United States meteorological office often includes with its weather forecasts an index known as the *wind chill factor*. This reflects how cold the air feels when the wind is blowing, based on the actual coolness of the air and the wind speed. As you probably are well aware, the stronger the wind, the colder it feels. The wind chill temperature may be calculated by means of the following formula:

$$W = 33 - \frac{(10\sqrt{v} - v + 10.5)(33 - t)}{23.1}$$

where

v = wind velocity in meters per second
t = outside temperature in degrees Celsius
W = wind chill temperature in degrees Celsius

Write a function that returns the wind chill temperature, given the temperature and wind velocity. Since the formula is valid only up to 10 degrees Celsius, ensure that the temperature does not exceed this limit. As an added challenge, you could modify the function to accept temperatures in Fahrenheit. It can call the temperature conversion function from Exercise 6 to convert from Fahrenheit to Celsius, which is necessary for the formula to work.

8. In *The Spirit of C* section in Chapter 7, we demonstrated the construction of a random number generator. Write a pair of functions, *seed* and *ran*. The *seed* function sets the value of the random number seed, which is stored in a global variable. The *ran* function generates and returns the next random number. Note that the *ran* function needs no parameters. It is called simply as

```
ran()
```

You may wish to combine *seed* and *ran* into a single function. In this case, *ran* takes one argument. If *ran* is called with an argument of 0, it returns the next random number. If any other argument is used, that number becomes the new seed, which is returned by the function.

Another possibility is for the *ran* function to be called with two integer parameters, specifying a range of integers from which the random number is to be selected. In that case, *ran* calculates the new random number and then converts it to a number in the desired range. You may also wish to try another algorithm for generating random numbers, or write the function so that it returns a real number in the range from 0.0 up to, but not including, 1.

Write a *main* function to test whether your random number function is returning a good distribution of values.

10

Arrays

As you have seen in previous chapters, variables are the entities in C which are used to hold data in memory. So far, it has been necessary to know how many items are to be stored and to declare a variable for each item. This method does not allow for the common case in which an indeterminate number of values is to be stored and operated upon. Furthermore, if a large amount of data is to be stored, it would be a long and tedious task to think of a separate variable name for each datum, and then to type the declaration for each one of these variables.

Arrays are the solution to this problem. They are such an important part of the art of programming that they are included in every high—level language.

What is an Array?

In C, as in other computer languages, it is possible to assign a single name to a whole group of similar data. For example, if we are interested in a large number of recorded Celsius temperatures, we can assign a common name such as *C_temp* to all of the data. Then we can refer to each element in terms of its position within the list of items. This is done in mathematics, as well as in computer programming, using an entity called an *array.*

An array is a group of elements that share a common name, and that are differentiated from one another by their positions within the array. For example, if we have five numbers, all of which are named x, they may be listed:

$$\begin{array}{c} \underline{\quad \textbf{x} \quad} \\ 58 \\ 63 \\ 49 \\ 18 \\ 7 \end{array}$$

The position of each of these elements can be indicated by means of a subscript:

$$x_1 = 58$$
$$x_2 = 63$$
$$x_3 = 49$$
$$x_4 = 18$$
$$x_5 = 7$$

In mathematics, a subscript is a number written to the right of the variable name, slightly below the line, and usually in small type. The subscript indicates the position of the particular element with respect to the rest of the elements.

For those movie buffs who are fans of the old Charlie Chan detective movies, you will remember that whenever it became necessary for Mr. Chan to introduce his sons to clients, he would always introduce them as: "This is my number one son...my number two son..." etc. It is clear from this that even though computers were a long way from being invented at the time those movies were made, Mr. Chan actually resorted to the method of introducing his sons by their subscripts!

Since it is impossible to display subscripted numbers on the standard computer terminal, the usual recourse is to enclose the subscript in parentheses or brackets. In C (as in Pascal), square brackets are used. The following five statements are valid in C:

```
x[1] = 58;
x[2] = 63;
x[3] = 49;
x[4] = 18;
x[5] =  7;
```

Declaring an Array

An array must be declared, since it is a type of variable. An array containing five elements, all of which are integers, can be declared as follows:

```
int x[5];
```

An array name must be chosen according to the same rules used for naming any other variable. The name of the array cannot be the same as that of any other variable declared within the function. The size of the array (the number of elements) is specified using the subscript notation; in our example, the subscript 5 indicates how many elements are to be allocated to array x.

The subscript used to declare an array sometimes is called the *dimension*, and the declaration itself often is called *dimensioning*. As with regular (or *scalar*) variables, the declaration does not assign values, but simply sets aside memory for the array. The dimension used to declare an array must always be a positive integer constant, or an expression that can be evaluated to a constant when the program is compiled.

The method of subscripting arrays in C is different from that used in many other programming languages. The elements of a five-element array in C are numbered starting with 0, not with 1. Therefore, the assignment statements for this example actually should be written

```
x[0] = 58;
x[1] = 63;
x[2] = 49;
x[3] = 18;
x[4] =  7;
```

There is no element named $x[5]$. The reason for this unusual numbering scheme is that C was designed to model the operation of the computer at a level lower than that dealt with by most programming languages. The calculation of the address corresponding to a subscript is simpler when the first array element is numbered 0.

If the programmer attempts to access an element outside the legal subscript range of an array (for example, $x[8]$ when the array x has only five elements, with subscripts 0 through 4), it is not considered an error so far as the C compiler is concerned. In fact, the program may even run without crashing (coming to a halt). This fact is related to the flexibility of C, which we will discuss further in the next chapter. It is almost always a logical error to do this, however, so it is up to the programmer to ensure that all subscripts are within the correct limits.

All elements of an array are of the same type. In other words, if an array is declared to be of type **int**, it cannot contain elements that are not of type **int**. Each element of an array can be used anywhere that a variable name is allowed or required. (With few exceptions, the unsubscripted array name cannot be used in this way.)   The following assignment statements are all valid in C:

```
x[0] = 4;
x[1] = x[0] - 2;
x[2] = x[1] + 5 + x[0];
x[3] += 7;
```

The feature that makes arrays such powerful tools is that the subscript used to reference a particular array element can be any integer expression. For example, if the variable i has the value 3, $x[i]$ refers to array element number 3 (which is actually the fourth array element, since the numbering of array elements in C starts from 0). Thus the ideal C construct to manipulate arrays is the **for** loop.

The following loop reads six integers into an array a, which consists of six elements (assuming all variables have been properly declared):

```
for (i = 0; i < 6; i++)
    scanf("%d", &a[i]);
```

The variable i in this loop often is called the *index* variable, because it is used to "index" the desired element of the array. The body of the loop is executed six times. The first time, i has the value 0. The second time, i has the value 1, and so forth. The sixth and last time the loop executes, i has the value 5. When i is incremented to 6, the loop test fails and the loop terminates.

This form of the **for** loop is used so often with arrays that it is almost worth memorizing. All that is necessary to customize it for a particular array is to replace 6 with the number of elements in the array. This loop also illustrates an important fact about arrays: An entire array (with one exception, to be described later) cannot be read in all at once. Each element of an array must be read in separately, either with a loop as shown above or with a call to *scanf* in which each element is specified separately. Also, an entire array cannot be assigned to another array (this rule has no exceptions). Even if both x and y are declared to be arrays of the same type and size, and all the elements of x have been assigned values, a statement such as

```
y = x;
```

is illegal in C. An attempt to write such an assignment would cause the compiler to signal an error. Each element of x must be assigned separately to the corresponding element of y.

Program 10-1 is a simple illustration of the way in which an array of five elements can be stored in memory and printed out again.

```
/* Introduction to arrays */

main()
{
    int array[5], i;

    printf("You are to enter 5 integers.\n\n");

/* Input the 5 integers into array "array" */

    for (i = 0; i < 5; i++)
    {
        printf("Enter integer #%d: ", i + 1);
        scanf("%d", &array[i]);
    }

    printf("\nThank you.\n\n");

/* Print out the integers stored in array "array" */

    for (i = 0; i < 5; i++)
        printf("Integer #%d = %d.\n", i + 1, array[i]);
}
```

Program 10—1

```
You are to enter 5 integers.

Enter integer #1: 3
Enter integer #2: 12
Enter integer #3: 8
Enter integer #4: 63
Enter integer #5: 0

Thank you.

Integer #1 = 3.
Integer #2 = 12.
Integer #3 = 8.
Integer #4 = 63.
Integer #5 = 0.
```

Output 10—1

The integer array *array* is declared to contain five elements. ("Array" is not a reserved word in C, but it is not a very original name to give to an array.) The variable i is declared for use as an index. (All index variables must be of type **int** or a compatible type, such as **short** or **char**.)

A prompt is displayed, asking the user to enter five integers. A loop is then executed to read in the integers. The user is prompted for each integer, and each one read in is assigned to the array element subscripted by i. Notice that the prompt for the individual elements uses the expression $i + 1$ rather than i, as you might have expected, when printing the element number. This approach enables the user to see the numbering of the elements in the natural way, starting with 1 rather than 0.

When the body of the loop has been executed five times, the user is thanked, and the elements of the array are displayed using another **for** loop. Again, the element number is printed out using $i + 1$, though i still is used as the actual subscript.

Initializing an Array

In the next program, an array of five integers is declared as a global array. As you will recall, a global variable is one that is declared outside any function (usually before *main*). It exists throughout the execution of the program, and is accessible from any function within the program.

A special feature of global arrays is that they can be initialized when they are declared. This is done by following the array name and dimension with an equal sign (as used to initialize variables), followed by a pair of braces. These braces contain a series of constant values separated by commas. Since the array in Program 10-2 is an integer array of five elements, the braces contain five integers.

```
/* Initializing a global array */

int array[5] = { 4, 6, 5, 7, 2 };

main()
{
    int i;

/* Print out the integers stored in array "array" */

    for (i = 0; i < 5; i++)
        printf("Integer #%d = %d.\n", i + 1, array[i]);
}
```

Program 10—2

```
Integer #1 = 4.
Integer #2 = 6.
Integer #3 = 5.
Integer #4 = 7.
Integer #5 = 2.
```

Output 10—2

Arrays can be initialized at declaration time when their initial values are known in advance, as is done in this program. Using the concepts we have shown you so far, only global arrays can be initialized at the time of declaration. Initializing a local array requires a concept that we will cover in a later chapter. The values used to initialize an array must be constants—never variables or function calls.

It is not always necessary to specify the dimension of an array if it is being initialized. For example, C would allow *array* to be declared as follows:

```
int array[] = { 4, 6, 5, 7, 2 };
```

Since the square brackets following the array name are empty, the compiler determines how many elements to allocate for the array by counting the number of values within the curly braces. This approach can help avoid errors. If the dimension is specified explicitly, and the curly braces contain more initialization values than are needed, a syntax error is flagged by the compiler.

It is not necessary to fill all the elements of an array if fewer elements than the maximum are needed. Sometimes it is not known in advance how many elements will be needed until execution time, at which point the array has already been dimensioned. When dealing with arrays, it is easiest to occupy as many low-numbered elements as are needed and leave the rest unused.

In a local array, the unused elements are uninitialized, meaning they contain unpredictable values. For this reason, care must be taken not to use an uninitialized element in an expression. The C compiler does not regard the use of an uninitialized variable as an error. (This is also true for scalar variables that are not initialized.) You should be on your guard against this possible source of programming error.

It is legal to initialize only some of the elements of an array. If an element of a global array is not explicitly initialized, it is set to 0 automatically by the compiler. For example, the statement

```
int array[5] = { 1, 2, 3 };
```

allocates five elements to *array*, and then initializes *array[0]* to 1, *array[1]* to 2, and *array[2]* to 3, setting the remaining elements to 0.

In such a declaration, the dimension of the array must be explicitly specified, since if the compiler counted the initializing values, it would allocate only three elements. Moreover, the programmer cannot arbitrarily choose the elements to be initialized. The specified values are assigned to consecutive elements of the array, beginning with the 0th element. The example initializes elements 0 through 2. It would not be possible to initialize only elements 1 through 3 or 2 through 4 within the declaration; that would have to be done using either individual assignments or *scanf* statements.

In Program 10-3, the constant MAX_ARRAY_SIZE is defined to be 20. In the declaration of the integer array *array*, this constant is used to dimension the array. The variable *array_size* is used to store the actual size of the array, however, as specified by the user of the program in response to the initial prompt. The variable *array_size*, rather than the constant MAX_ARRAY_SIZE, is used in both **for** loops as the upper limit of the index.

```
/* The number of array elements actually used may vary */

#define MAX_ARRAY_SIZE 20

main()
{
    int array[MAX_ARRAY_SIZE];
    int array_size, i;

/* Read in the size of the array */

    printf("How many integers will you enter? ");
    scanf("%d", &array_size);

/* Read in the integers */

    printf("\nPlease enter %d integers:\n", array_size);
    for (i = 0; i < array_size; i++)
        scanf("%d", &array[i]);

/* Print out the integers */

    printf("\n");
    for (i = 0; i < array_size; i++)
        printf("Integer #%d = %d.\n", i + 1, array[i]);
}
```

Program 10—3

```
How many integers will you enter? 6

Please enter 6 integers:
12 3 -5 21 0 899

Integer #1 = 12.
Integer #2 = 3.
Integer #3 = -5.
Integer #4 = 21.
Integer #5 = 0.
Integer #6 = 899.
```

Output 10—3

After the user is prompted to enter the number of elements to be stored into the array, a further prompt asks the user to enter the actual elements of the array. In contrast to the first program in this chapter, a prompt is not issued for each individual integer. Instead, they must be entered at the same time, separated either by blank spaces, tabs, or *newline* characters (carriage returns typed at the keyboard). The number of integers must correspond to the number specified at the beginning of the program by the user. If too few numbers are entered, the computer waits for the remainder to be typed in. If too many are provided, the extra ones are ignored. After the elements of the array have been entered, a blank line is printed by outputting a single *newline* character, and the elements of the array are displayed in the usual manner.

Program 10-4 takes a different approach to determine how many elements are to be stored in the array. Sometimes a user may have a large amount of data to enter into an array, and does not want to be concerned with counting how many values there are. Once a maximum number has been established, an arbitrary trailer number (see Chapter 6) can be selected, such as -9999. As each element is entered, it is tested to see whether it is equal to the trailer item. If it is not, it is entered into the array, and the next number is input.

A running count is kept of the number of items currently in the array. This information is readily available, since it is necessary to keep track of the subscript of the next available array element. In C, this subscript is equal to the number of elements read in so far. As soon as the program detects the fact that the number entered is the trailer item, reading ceases, and the number of elements read in is contained in the loop index. This method is employed in Program 10-4.

```
/* The trailer method */

#define MAX_ARRAY_SIZE 20
#define TRAILER -9999

main()
{
    int array[MAX_ARRAY_SIZE];
    int array_size, item, i;

/* Read in the integers */

    printf("Please enter up to %d integers, using %d as a trailer:\n",
        MAX_ARRAY_SIZE, TRAILER);
    for (array_size = 0; array_size < MAX_ARRAY_SIZE; array_size++)
    {
        scanf("%d", &item);
        if (item == TRAILER) break;
        array[array_size] = item;
    }

/* Print out the integers */

    printf("\nYou have entered %d integers.\n", array_size);
    for (i = 0; i < array_size; i++)
        printf("Integer #%d = %d.\n", i + 1, array[i]);
}
```

Program 10—4

```
        Please enter up to 20 integers, using -9999 as a trailer:
        3 75 -34 6 -1 2 41 0 90 -9999

        You have entered 9 integers.
        Integer #1 = 3.
        Integer #2 = 75.
        Integer #3 = -34.
        Integer #4 = 6.
        Integer #5 = -1.
        Integer #6 = 2.
        Integer #7 = 41.
        Integer #8 = 0.
        Integer #9 = 90.
```

Output 10—4

In this program, a maximum size for the array again is specified using the constant MAX_ARRAY_SIZE. Another constant, TRAILER, is defined to specify the number used as the trailer item. Both of these constants can be changed if necessary, so it is easy to modify the program as conditions change. The variables *array_size* and *i* serve the same purpose as in the previous program. An additional variable, *item*, also is declared. This variable is used to hold each integer before it is stored in the array, in order to allow a comparison to be made with TRAILER.

The user is prompted to enter the integers. The program specifies the maximum number of elements and the trailer value. Notice that the constants are placed not within the control string, but after it. This is necessary because a constant name placed within a string is not converted to its corresponding value, but is just treated as a set of characters. The statement

```
printf("TRAILER");
```

would print out the following:

```
TRAILER
```

not the value -9999. The same rule holds for variables. You would not consider printing out the value of a variable *n* using the statement

```
printf("n");
```

because the literal "n" would be displayed, rather than the contents of a variable named *n*.

The break Statement

Within the first **for** loop of Program 10-4, each of the elements of the array is entered into the variable *item*. (The use of a **for** loop assures that no more than MAX_ARRAY_SIZE integers are read in, even if the trailer number never is entered.) The value of *item* then is compared to the constant TRAILER. So long as they are not equal, the value of *item* is regarded as the next element to be appended to the array.

If the value of *item* is the trailer number, -9999, execution of the loop is terminated. In Program 10-4, this is done by means of the statement, **break**. This statement immediately terminates execution of any **while**, **do...while**, or **for** loop in which the **break** statement appears, continuing execution with the statement following the loop. That is why no **else** clause is used in this particular **if** statement. If the **break** statement is executed, control will not fall through to the next statement, because control will already have been sent elsewhere. The **break** statement can be used in any C loop, not just the **for** loop.

As useful as the **break** statement is, it is not above criticism. It violates the rules of structured programming, because it necessitates a jump from one part of the program to another, thus detracting from the organization of the code. Any loop containing a **break** can be rewritten using an appropriate test to control the loop. It would be an instructive exercise for the reader to rewrite the first **for** loop in Program 10-4 without the use of the **break** statement.

In the first **for** loop, *array_size* is used as the index. When the loop terminates—due to the **break** statement or the failure of the loop test—*array_size* reflects the correct number of elements in the array. (You can prove this to yourself by going through the loop by hand, using a small number of input items.) A *printf* statement informs the user of this number. A **for** loop then repeats the items entered.

The next program finds the average of an array of real numbers. Once again, an arbitrary maximum of 20 elements is assigned to the array, and a trailer of -9999 is used to indicate the end of data.

```
/* Calculating the average grade for a class */

    /* The class may have up to 20 students */
#define MAX_GRADES 20
    /* -9999 marks the end of the grade list */
#define TRAILER -9999

main()
{
    float grades[MAX_GRADES],    /* Holds grades for the class */
          item,                  /* Used to read in a grade */
          sum = 0.0;             /* Used to calculate sum of all grades
                                    in order to find average */
    int num_grades,              /* Number of grades entered */
        i;                       /* A loop index */

/* Read in the grades */

    printf("Please enter up to %d grades, using %d as a trailer:\n",
        MAX_GRADES, TRAILER);

    scanf("%f", &item);
    for (num_grades = 0;
        num_grades < MAX_GRADES && item != TRAILER;
        num_grades++)
    {
        grades[num_grades] = item;
        scanf("%f", &item);
    }

    printf("\nYou have entered %d grades.\n", num_grades);

/* Find the average */

    for (i = 0; i < num_grades; sum += grades[i++]);
    printf("\nThe average grade is %f.\n", sum / num_grades);
}
```

Program 10—5

```
Please enter up to 20 grades, using -9999 as a trailer:
41
92
15
65
0
78
81
96
-9999

You have entered 8 grades.

The average grade is 58.500000.
```

Output 10—5

There are only a few differences between Program 10-5 and its predecessor. More comments than usual have been included, because the programs are becoming a trifle more complicated. Comments are placed near each constant and variable declaration to explain their roles clearly. Also, the name of the array has been changed to *grades* to reflect the fact that it will hold student grades for a class. The constant MAX_ARRAY_SIZE has been renamed MAX_GRADES for the same reason.

The array is declared to be of type **float**, thereby allowing for non-integer grades (although the input used in this execution consists of whole numbers only). The type of *item* also is changed to **float**, since its contents are transferred to array *grades*. The variable *num_grades* performs the same role as *array_size* in the previous program. A variable *sum* is introduced and initialized to zero. It is used to add up all the values in the array.

The loop to read in the array elements compensates for the avoidance of the **break** statement. This method is similar to the one used in Program 6-8, in which the priming *scanf* technique was introduced. Here, however, a **for** loop is used to ensure that the loop will end when 20 grades have been input, regardless of whether the trailer item has been entered. Thus there are two tests in the loop: one comparing *num_grades* to MAX_GRADES and one comparing *item* to TRAILER.

Notice that, even though *item* is of type **float**, the value of TRAILER, -9999, is an integer constant. When integers and real numbers are mixed in an expression (including a boolean expression), the **ints** are converted to **floats**. This is why it is possible to type integers as input to the program. It would not be permissible, however, to type in real values if integers were called for.

After the grades are read in, and the user is informed of the number of grades, a **for** loop is used to add up all the grades in the array. This is accomplished entirely within the loop heading, by virtue of the third expression. This expression adds the value of the array element indexed by *i* into *sum* (which was initialized to 0.0). At the same time, it increments the value of *i* using the post-increment operator. The average grade then is found by dividing the sum of the grades (the final value of *sum*) by the number of grades (the value of *num_grades*). The real result is displayed in the default format of six decimal places.

None of the programs illustrated so far in this chapter requires the use of arrays. Reading in and echoing numbers, and finding the average of a series of numbers, always can be done without arrays, even though the steps involved might be somewhat less elegant. In the next program, however, the need for arrays is clear. The average of an array of grades again is computed, using the same techniques as in the previous program. In this case, however, it is necessary to print out those grades that are greater than the computed average. There is no alternative to using an array, because it is necessary to keep the entire array in memory after computing the average, in order to compare each element to the average.

```c
/* Determining which grades in a class are above the average */

    /* The class may have up to 20 students */
#define MAX_GRADES 20
    /* -9999 marks the end of the grade list */
#define TRAILER -9999

main()
{
    float grades[MAX_GRADES],    /* Holds grades for the class */
          item,                  /* Used to read in a grade */
          sum = 0.0,             /* Used to calculate sum of all grades
                                    in order to find average */
          avg_grade;             /* Holds average grade */
    int num_grades,              /* Number of grades entered */
        i;                       /* A loop index */

/* Read in the grades */

    printf("Please enter up to %d grades, using %d as a trailer:\n",
        MAX_GRADES, TRAILER);

    scanf("%f", &item);
    for (num_grades = 0;
         num_grades < MAX_GRADES && item != TRAILER;
         num_grades++)
    {
        grades[num_grades] = item;
        scanf("%f", &item);
    }

    printf("\nYou have entered %d grades.\n", num_grades);

/* Find the average */

    for (i = 0; i < num_grades; sum += grades[i++]);
    printf("\nThe average grade is %f.\n", (avg_grade = sum / num_grades));
```

Program continued on next page

Program continued from previous page

```
/* Find who got above average */

    printf("\nThe following grades were above average:\n");
    for(i = 0; i < num_grades; i++)
        if (grades[i] > avg_grade)
            printf("%f (student #%d)\n", grades[i], i + 1);
}
```

Program 10—6

```
        Please enter up to 20 grades, using -9999 as a trailer:
        41
        92
        15
        65
        0
        78
        81
        96
        -9999

        You have entered 8 grades.

        The average grade is 58.500000.

        The following grades were above average:
        92.000000 (student #2)
        65.000000 (student #4)
        78.000000 (student #6)
        81.000000 (student #7)
        96.000000 (student #8)
```

Output 10—6

The Assignment Operator Within an Expression

When the average is computed in Program 10-6, it is stored in the variable *avg_grade* so it can be used in subsequent comparisons. Notice that this assignment is done within the *printf* statement:

```
printf("\nThe average grade is %f.\n",
                    (avg_grade = sum / num_grades));
```

Assignment operators, including the updating assignment operators, are treated just like any other operator. They can be used in any expression, so it is possible to use them in the first and third expressions of a **for** loop heading. When an assignment operator is used in an expression, the assignment is made, and the value returned by the operator is the value assigned. The assignment is enclosed within parentheses for clarity, and also because assignment operators have one of the lowest levels of precedence (second only to the comma operator).

This unusual feature is peculiar to C. As a further example of its use, consider the following code:

```
int a, b = 3, c;
a = c = ((b += 3) * 4);
```

In the statement following the declarations, the first operation performed is contained in the inner parentheses, the incrementing of *b* by 3. The value returned by this operation is the new value of *b*, which is 6. Next, this value of 6 is multiplied by 4, giving 24, which then is assigned to *c*. The new value of *c*, 24, is assigned to *a* (assignment operators are evaluated from right to left, unlike other binary operators).

Notice the importance of the parentheses. If the statement in question had been written instead as:

```
a = c = b += 3 * 4;
```

it would be evaluated as

```
a = (c = (b += (3 * 4)));
```

which would have resulted in all the variables getting the value 15, a decidedly different result.

The program ends with a loop that examines each element of the array *grades*. Each time a grade is encountered which is greater than the average, the grade is printed out, along with the sequential number of the student associated with that grade. If a grade is lower than or equal to the average, nothing is printed for that grade.

In the next program, no major computation is done. Instead, an array is read in, echoed back, and printed out again in reverse order. We suggest that you examine the program carefully yourself and try to trace through its logic.

```
/* Reversing an array */

    /* The array has 10 elements */
#define ARRAY_SIZE 10

main()
{
    int array[ARRAY_SIZE];    /* An array */
    int i;                    /* A loop index */

/* Read in the array */

    printf("Please enter %d integers:\n", ARRAY_SIZE);
    for (i = 0; i < ARRAY_SIZE; i++)
        scanf("%d", &array[i]);

/* Echo the array */

    printf("\nThe original array was:\n");
    for (i = 0; i < ARRAY_SIZE; i++)
        printf("%d ", array[i]);
    printf("\n");
```

Program continued on next page

Program continued from previous page

```
/* Print the array in reverse */

    printf("\nThe reversed array is:\n");
    /* Index goes from highest to lowest */
    for (i = ARRAY_SIZE - 1; i >= 0; i--)
        printf("%d ", array[i]);
    printf("\n");
}
```

Program 10—7

```
Please enter 10 integers:
10 42 7 0 923 13 -5 6 19 3

The original array was:
10 42 7 0 923 13 -5 6 19 3

The reversed array is:
3 19 6 -5 13 923 0 7 42 10
```

Output 10—7

The array of integers is read in the usual manner, although the limit this time has been defined as 10 elements, and all 10 must be read in. After the array has been echoed back, a blank line is printed. The array then is displayed backwards by a **for** loop, which instead of incrementing its index from 0 to ARRAY_SIZE - 1, decrements it from ARRAY_SIZE - 1 to 0. This demonstrates that the elements of an array do not have to be accessed in any specific order. The order is determined by the programmer, based on the requirements of the problem at hand.

Strings and Character Arrays

Each of the arrays illustrated so far has contained numeric elements. Arrays are not confined to numeric elements, however; they also may consist of characters. In C, a string is stored internally as an array of characters. Since a string can be of any length, the end of the string is marked with the single character '\0', the *null* character, with ASCII value 0. (For this reason, a string cannot contain the *null* character.) For example, the string "bingo" is stored as shown in Figure 10-1.

0	1	2	3	4	5
'b'	'i'	'n'	'g'	'o'	'\0'

Figure 10—1

In this diagram, each box represents a memory location containing one character. If this string were stored in an array, it would require six elements: five for the letters in the string and one for the *null* character. (Notice that the double quotes delimiting the string are not stored as part of the string.)

The most obvious way to assign a string to an array would be to assign the characters to the elements one at a time, including the *null* character. This is somewhat tedious. Several easier methods are beyond the scope of this chapter, but there is one method we can use here: A string can be read directly into an array of characters.

Assuming that an array *c_array* has been declared to be of type **char**, one could read a string into it using the following *scanf* statement:

```
scanf("%s", c_array);
```

It is clear that the %s conversion specification is used for both reading in and printing out strings. There are two unusual details about this *scanf* statement which deserve your attention. First, the array name is used without a subscript. This is the rule when reading a string into a character array. Second, there is no ampersand (&) before the array name. When an array name is specified in the manner shown here, no ampersand should be used. This will be explained in detail in the next chapter when we discuss pointers.

There are two restrictions to note when reading in strings. The first is that *scanf* defines a string as being delimited by white space. When reading in a string, *scanf* skips over all leading blanks, tabs, and *newline* characters, and then reads in all the characters up to the next blank, tab, or *newline* character. For this reason, %s can be used only to read in a single word at a time, where a word is defined as being a sequence of characters without any imbedded white space.

If you wish to read in blanks as part of a string, you must use the %c conversion specification. Remember that if %c is used, the corresponding variable must be a single (subscripted) array element preceded by an &.

The second restriction is that the array of characters must be large enough to hold the longest string that is to be read in, plus one extra element to hold the *null* character. If the array is too short to hold the input string, the results are unpredictable and most certainly undesirable. Fortunately, the %s specification can be used with a maximum field width specifier. For example, if the array into which a string is being read consists of 11 elements, %10s will read in no more than 10 characters, thus ensuring against overflow of the array.

The ability to read in strings also can be used to solve a problem posed in the previous chapter. When the user is prompted for a y/n response, and a single character is read in, the program must skip over the carriage return before the character, and only one character may be typed by the user. The first of these difficulties is overcome by the use of the %s conversion specification, which automatically skips over any leading white space. Thus the y/n response can be read into an array of two characters (one for the response, and one for the *null* character) using the conversion specification %1s. The second difficulty can be solved by using a larger character array, together with the conversion specification %s. That way, the user may type the entire word *yes* or *no*, or even *yup* or *nope*. The program checks only the first letter of the string, which is contained in the 0th element of the array.

In Program 10-8, the user is prompted to enter a word of up to 10 characters, which then is printed out in reverse.

```
/* Reversing a character string */

    /* The word may have up to 10 characters */
#define MAX_STRING_SIZE 10

main()
{
    char word[MAX_STRING_SIZE + 1];    /* Holds the string */
    int string_size,                   /* Holds actual string length */
        i;                             /* A loop index */

/* Read in the word */

    printf("Please enter a word of up to 10 letters:\n", MAX_STRING_SIZE);
    scanf("%s", word);

/* Echo the word */

    printf("\nThe word is %s.\n", word);

/* Find the word length */

    for (string_size = 0; word[string_size] != 0; string_size++);

/* Print the word in reverse */

    printf("\nThe reversed word is ");
    /* Index goes from highest to lowest */
    for (i = string_size - 1; i >= 0; i--)
        printf("%c", word[i]);
    printf("\n");
}
```

Program 10—8

```
        Please enter a word of up to 10 letters:
        bingo

        The word is bingo.

        The reversed word is ognib
```

Output 10—8

The *scanf* statement uses the conversion specification %s to read the string into the character array *word*, which is declared to be of size MAX_STRING_SIZE + 1. The extra element is allocated to hold the terminating *null* character, which is placed after the string automatically by the *scanf* function. The word in question then is echoed back, again using the %s conversion specification and the unsubscripted array name *word*. The printing of strings is the only situation in which an entire array can be displayed all at once. If the array consisted of integers instead of characters, each element would have to be printed out individually.

The string is reversed in the same way the integer array is reversed in Program 10-7. In order to do this, however, it is necessary to know the length of the word. There is a library function to find the length of a string, but the function will not be described until the next chapter, so Program 10-8 contains the necessary code instead. It consists of a bodyless **for** loop that continually increments the value of *string_size* until the *null* character is found in the array *word*. Notice how the loop is written so that the *null* character itself is not counted as part of the string.

Once the length is found, it is possible to print out the string in reverse order, using the same technique as was used in Program 10-7. Since the characters are not being printed out in their normal order, it is necessary to print them one at a time, using the %c conversion specification rather than %s. The array name *word* therefore is subscripted with index *i*.

Finding the Minimum and Maximum of an Array

Often it is necessary to find the minimum and maximum of a set of values. If these values are stored in an array, the minimum can be found by the following method:

The first value in the array is stored in a variable, say *min*, which represents a temporary minimum. Then *min*'s value is compared successively with each of the remaining elements of the array, beginning with the second and ending with the last element. Each time an element is found which is smaller than the current value of *min*, it replaces the current minimum, and the comparison continues from that point in the array. When the end of the array is reached, its minimum value will be contained in *min*. The maximum can be found in the same way, except that instead of searching for smaller elements, the loop searches for elements larger than the original value.

The following program reads in an array of grades (with values of type **float**) using the trailer method, and then finds and prints out the minimum and maximum values. The two values are found in separate loops, for reasons of clarity, but in fact both the minimum and maximum can be found in a single loop. As a challenge, you might try writing such a loop.

```
/* Calculating the minimum and maximum grade in a class */

    /* The class may have up to 20 students */
#define MAX_GRADES 20
    /* -9999 marks the end of the grade list */
#define TRAILER -9999

main()
{
    float grades[MAX_GRADES],    /* Holds grades for the class */
          item,                  /* Used to read in a grade */
          min, max;              /* Used to find the minimum and maximum */
    int num_grades,              /* Number of grades entered */
        i;                       /* A loop index */

/* Read in the grades */

    printf("Please enter up to %d grades, using %d as a trailer:\n",
        MAX_GRADES, TRAILER);
    scanf("%f", &item);
    for (num_grades = 0;
        num_grades < MAX_GRADES && item != TRAILER;
        num_grades++)
    {
        grades[num_grades] = item;
        scanf("%f", &item);
    }
    printf("\nYou have entered %d grades.\n", num_grades);

/* Find the minimum grade */

    min = grades[0];
    for (i = 1; i < num_grades; i++)
        if (grades[i] < min) min = grades[i];
    printf("\nThe lowest grade is %f\n", min);

/* Find the maximum grade */

    max = grades[0];
    for (i = 1; i < num_grades; i++)
        if (grades[i] > max) max = grades[i];
    printf("\nThe highest grade is %f\n", max);
}
```

Program 10—9

```
            Please enter up to 20 grades, using -9999 as a trailer:
            41
            92
            15
            65
            0
            78
            81
            96
            -9999

            You have entered 8 grades.

            The lowest grade is 0.000000

            The highest grade is 96.000000
```

Output 10—9

Sorting an Array

In order for human beings to make sense of large amounts of data, it is often a good idea to arrange the values in some specified way. One of the most common ways is to sort the values into either ascending order (the numbers go from smallest to largest) or descending order (the numbers go from largest to smallest). In many industrial computing centers, as much as 30 percent of the total computer time is devoted to sorting data. Many different approaches have been adopted to expedite sorting as much as possible. Unfortunately, the most efficient sorting techniques are rather subtle and beyond the scope of this text. We will demonstrate a sorting technique that is satisfactory for modest jobs, although it may not be efficient enough for large amounts of data. The method we shall describe is known as the *exchange sort.*

The exchange sort, shown in Program 10-10, is based on an extension of the minimum/maximum technique implemented in the previous program. By means of a nest of **for** loops, a pass through the array is made to locate the minimum value. Once this is found, it is placed in the first position of the array (position 0). Another pass through the remaining elements is made to find the next smallest element, which is placed in the second position (position 1), and so on. Once the next-to-last element has been compared with the last one, all the elements of the array have been sorted into ascending order.

```
/* Sorting an array */

    /* The array may have up to 20 elements */
#define MAX_ARRAY_SIZE 20

main()
{
    int array[MAX_ARRAY_SIZE],    /* An array */
        array_size,               /* Actual number of integers in array */
        i, j;                     /* Loop indices */

/* Read in the size of the array (until a valid value is entered) */
    do
    {
        printf("How many numbers? ");
        scanf("%d", &array_size);
    }
/* Size must be at least 1 and at most MAX_ARRAY_SIZE */
    while (array_size < 1 || array_size > MAX_ARRAY_SIZE);

/* Read in the array */
    printf("Please enter the integers:\n");
    for (i = 0; i < array_size; i++)
        scanf("%d", &array[i]);

/* Echo the array */
    printf("\nThe original array is:\n");
    for (i = 0; i < array_size; i++)
        printf("%d ", array[i]);
    printf("\n");
```

Program continued on next page

Program continued from previous page

```
/* Sort the array */

    for (i = 0; i < array_size - 1; i++)
        for (j = i + 1; j < array_size; j++)
            if (array[i] > array[j])
            {
                int temp = array[i];
                array[i] = array[j];
                array[j] = temp;
            }

/* Print the sorted array */

    printf("\nThe sorted array is:\n");
    for (i = 0; i < array_size; i++)
        printf("%d ", array[i]);
    printf("\n");
}
```

Program 10—10

```
How many numbers? 10
Please enter the integers:
10 42 7 0 923 13 -5 6 19 3

The original array is:
10 42 7 0 923 13 -5 6 19 3

The sorted array is:
-5 0 3 6 7 10 13 19 42 923
```

Output 10—10

The array in this program is dimensioned to 20 elements, but this can always be extended at the discretion of the programmer. The user is prompted to type in the number of elements to be sorted. This value is validated to ensure that it is not less than 1 or greater than the maximum, as specified by the constant MAX_ARRAY_SIZE. Next, the array is read in and echoed back by means of two separate but similar **for** loops.

The sorting itself is done in the nest of **for** loops. The index i of the outer loop is used to indicate the array element that will receive the next minimum value. The element *array[i]* plays the same role as did *min* in the previous program, when the minimum of an array was being sought. The index j of the inner loop points to the elements to be compared with *array[i]*.

To see exactly what happens in the exchange sort, consider Figure 10-2, which traces the sorting of an array of five elements into ascending order.

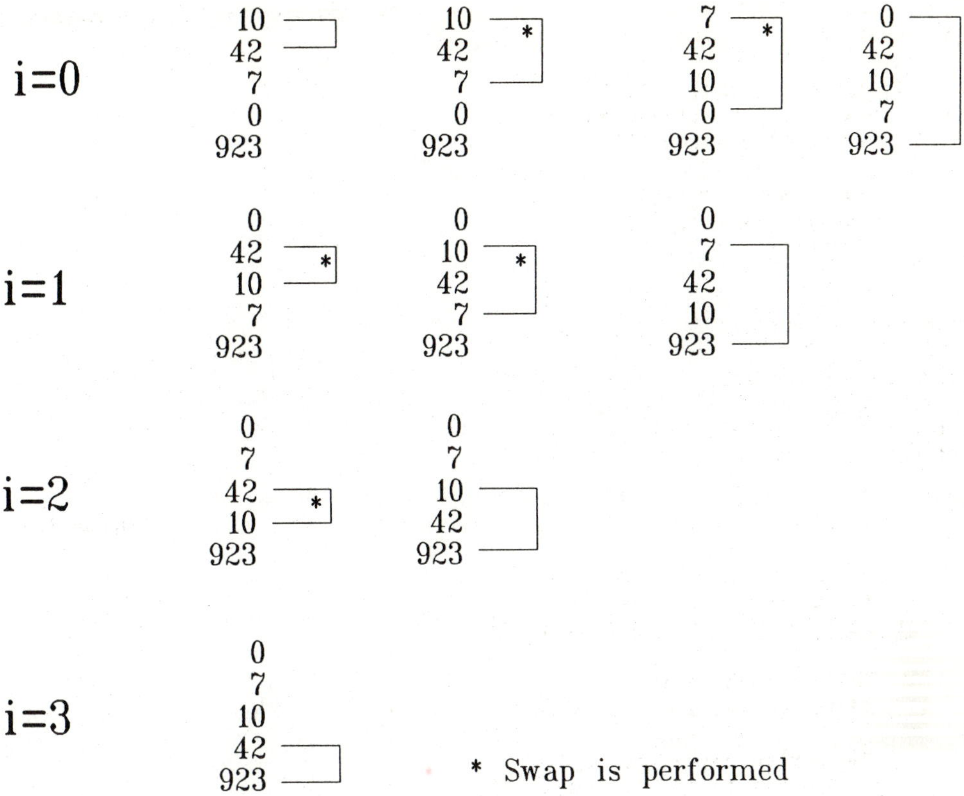

i=0

```
10 ⌐        10 ⌐ *     7 ⌐ *      0 ⌐
42          42         42         42
7           7 ⌐        10 ⌐       10
0           0          0 ⌐        7
923         923        923        923 ⌐
```

i=1

```
0           0          0
42 ⌐ *      10 ⌐ *     7 ⌐
10 ⌐        42         42
7           7 ⌐        10 ⌐
923         923        923 ⌐
```

i=2

```
0           0
7           7
42 ⌐ *      10 ⌐
10 ⌐        42
923         923 ⌐
```

i=3

```
0
7
10
42 ⌐
923 ⌐
```

* Swap is performed

Figure 10—2

The array consists of the five elements 10, 42, 7, 0, and 923. In the first pass (i has the value 0), the first element is compared with the second. Since they are already in ascending order, nothing is done. The first element then is compared with the third. Since 10 is greater than 7, the two elements are exchanged, so that the first element of the array is the value of the newly-found minimum. Then, it is compared with the fourth element. Since 7 is greater than 0, an exchange again is made, placing 0 in the position of the first element. Next, the value 0 is compared with the last element of the array. Since 0 is less than 923, no swap is made.

At the end of the first pass, therefore, the smallest number, 0, is located in the first position of the array as desired. It is no longer necessary to examine the first element, since we know that it is smaller than any other element within the array. The second pass ignores the first position of the array and starts making comparisons with the second element.

Subsequent passes perform the same comparisons with the remaining array elements, as shown in Figure 10-2. An array of n elements requires $n-1$ passes to be sorted by the exchange sort method.

In order to convert this sorting technique so that it sorts the numbers in descending order, all that is necessary is to change a single character in the program. Examine the program carefully and try to decide which character this is.

One advantage of the exchange sort is that the sorted elements are rearranged within the same array. Some other sorting methods require the declaration of a second array into which the sorted elements are stored. These methods work well, but require more memory than the exchange method. Their advantage is that they allow the program to retain both the original array and the sorted array simultaneously.

Declaring Variables Within Compound Statements

In the segment of the program that exchanges two elements of the array, note that the variable *temp* is declared (and initialized to the value *array[i]*) within the compound statement connected with the *if* statement, rather than at the beginning of the function where declarations are normally found. This is syntactically correct, because as we have mentioned previously, the body of a function is syntactically identical to a compound statement.

Since one may declare local variables at the beginning of a function, one should also be able to do this at the beginning of any compound statement. The rules governing variables declared within a compound statement are basically the same as those governing all local variables: The variables can be referenced only within the compound statement in which they are declared. Such variables come into existence when the compound statement is entered, and disappear when the compound statement has completed execution.

The variable *temp* is declared here rather than at the beginning of the program only for the sake of clarity. Since *temp* is used only for the exchange itself, it is more helpful to the reader of the program to include its declaration at this point. It may well be argued, however, that this is not a good place to declare *temp*, since it is recreated each time the exchange is made, sometimes involving extra work on the part of the computer. It is up to the programmer to resolve this problem based on the tradeoff between clarity and efficiency.

Once an array of numbers has been sorted in some order, it becomes much easier to perform certain operations on the contents of the array. A statistic that is often used in place of the average is known as the *median*. The median is defined as the value above and below which are an equal number of values. That is to say, in an array of nine numbers (assuming they are sorted into either ascending or descending order), the median is the middle number, the one in the fifth position. If the number of elements is even rather than odd, the median is defined as the average of the middle two elements of the sorted array.

The program that follows permits the user to read in a maximum of 20 elements for a given array. Once the array has been typed in, echoed back to the screen, and sorted, the median is calculated. The complete program consists of a *main* function, a function called *get_size*, one called *read_array*, another called *write_array*, and finally one called *sort_array*. There is also a boolean function called *even*, which returns a value of *true* if its argument is even.

```
/* Finding the median of an array */

    /* The array may have up to 20 elements */
#define MAX_ARRAY_SIZE 20

int array[MAX_ARRAY_SIZE],      /* an array */
    array_size;                 /* actual number of integers in array */

main()
{
/* Read in the size of the array */

    get_size();

/* Read in the array */

    read_array();

/* Echo the array */

    printf("\nThe original array is:\n");
    write_array();

/* Sort the array */

    sort_array();

/* Print the sorted array */

    printf("\nThe sorted array is:\n");
    write_array();

/* Print the median */

    printf("\nThe median is ");
    printf("%.1f\n", even(array_size) ?
                    (array[array_size / 2 - 1] + array[array_size / 2]) / 2.0
                    : (float)array[array_size / 2] );
}

get_size()
    /* Read in the size of the array (until a valid value is entered) */
{
    do
    {
        printf("How many numbers? ");
        scanf("%d", &array_size);
    }
/* Size must be at least 1 and at most MAX_ARRAY_SIZE */
    while (array_size < 1 || array_size > MAX_ARRAY_SIZE);
}
```

Program continued on next page

Program continued from previous page

```
read_array()
    /* Read in the array */
{
    int i;                      /* loop index */

    printf("Please enter the integers:\n");
    for (i = 0; i < array_size; i++)
        scanf("%d", &array[i]);
}

write_array()
    /* Write out the array */
{
    int i;                      /* loop index */

    for (i = 0; i < array_size; i++)
        printf("%d ", array[i]);
    printf("\n");
}

sort_array()
    /* Sort the array */
{
    int i, j;                   /* loop indices */

    for (i = 0; i < array_size - 1; i++)
        for (j = i + 1; j < array_size; j++)
            if (array[i] > array[j])
            {
                int temp = array[i];
                array[i] = array[j];
                array[j] = temp;
            }
}

even(n)
int n;
    /* Returns non-zero (true) if n is even; zero (false) otherwise */
{
    return((n / 2) * 2 == n);
}
```

Program 10-11

```
How many numbers? 10
Please enter the integers:
10 42 7 0 923 13 -5 6 19 3

The original array is:
10 42 7 0 923 13 -5 6 19 3

The sorted array is:
-5 0 3 6 7 10 13 19 42 923

The median is 8.5
```

Output continued on next page

Output continued from previous page

```
How many numbers? 9
Please enter the integers:
15 29 6 -34 8 -7 0 61 4

The original array is:
15 29 6 -34 8 -7 0 61 4

The sorted array is:
-34 -7 0 4 6 8 15 29 61

The median is 6.0
```

Output 10—11

In this program, the variables *array* and *array_size* are declared as global variables. (We need to resort to this method, because we have not yet discussed the methods of passing arrays as parameters or changing the values of parameters.) The array *array* is dimensioned to MAX_ARRAY_SIZE elements, specified to be 20. The actual number of elements stored in the array is indicated by the value of *array_size*.

At the beginning of the *main* function, a call is made to the function *get_size*. This function reads in the number of elements to be input and stores the validated value into *array_size*. The value could also have been returned using the **return** statement, but since *get_size* uses input and output, it does not conform to the strict definition of a function specified by the rules of structured programming. In the next chapter, we will demonstrate how this function can be written without using a global variable.

The function *read_array* is called to input the array, and *write_array* is invoked to output it. Since *write_array* is used twice, once to print the original array and again to print the sorted one, it does not print a message before the array. The task of specifying which version of the array is being displayed is left instead to the *main* function. The function *sort_array* is basically the same set of statements which was used in the previous program to sort the array.

The final statements of Program 10-11 involve several new concepts, which we shall address in the next section. The function *even(n)* determines whether its argument *n* is odd or even by testing its divisibility by 2. The value returned is taken directly from the boolean expression by including the entire test within the **return** statement. If *n* is even, a value of *true* is returned; otherwise, a value of *false* (0) is returned.

The Conditional Expression

The value returned by *even* in Program 10-11 is used as part of a new operator. This operator, called the *conditional expression*, is represented by the ? and : symbols. This operator is different from the others we have encountered so far, because the ? and the : are not adjacent. They constitute an example of a rare entity known as a *ternary* operator, meaning it operates upon three values rather than one or two. The form of the conditional expression is as follows:

```
e1 ? e2 : e3
```

The expression *e1* is interpreted as a boolean expression. It is a sort of switch, in that it determines which of the two expressions, *e2* or *e3*, is to be returned. This is similar to the way the condition in an **if** statement determines which of two statements will be executed. If the value of *e1* is *true*, the value returned by the ?: operator is that of the expression *e2*, located after the ? symbol but before the : symbol. If *e1* evaluates to *false*, the value returned is that of *e3*.

As an example, examine the following program:

```
main()
{
    int i, j;
    scanf("%d", &i);
    j = (i > 4) ? 200 : 100;
    printf("%d\n", j);
}
```

Suppose the value entered for *i* is 3. Since the expression (i > 4) evaluates to *false*, the value 100 (the value after the colon) is returned by the ?: operator, and is therefore assigned to *j*. If the input value is, say, 7, the expression (i > 4) evaluates to *true*. Therefore, 200 (the value specified before the colon) is returned and assigned to *j*. The parentheses around the boolean expression are included merely for the sake of clarity, since the > operator is evaluated before ?:, which itself is evaluated before the assignment is made.

The operation of the conditional expression is illustrated in Figure 10-3.

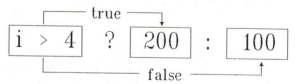

Figure 10—3

Getting back to Program 10-11: The final *printf* statement in the *main* function contains a formidable-looking conditional expression. The first (boolean) sub-expression is a call to the *even* function. If the value of *array_size* is even, the expression following the ? is evaluated. This expression calculates the average of the two middle elements of the array. You should examine the code very carefully so that you are completely satisfied that, regardless of the size of the array, if the number of elements is even, the middle two elements are averaged.

If the value returned by *even* is false, the array has an odd number of elements. In this case, the expression following the colon is returned. This is simply the value of the middle element.

Since the median of an even-numbered array is the average of two integers, the result may be a fractional value. Thus the median should be printed as a real value. Because the average of the two middle elements is calculated by dividing their sum by the real value 2.0, the expression before the : in the conditional expression automatically evaluates to a value of type **double**. (When C automatically converts an integer value to a real one, it chooses **double** rather than **float**.)

The next program consists of a *main* function only. It inputs a series of values in a predefined range, and then displays how many of each number were entered. In other words, it plays the role of a frequency counter.

The program makes use of three constants, thus allowing for greater flexibility. The first two, RANGE_LOW and RANGE_HIGH, define the lowest and highest value in the range. If these values are modified, the programmer must be sure that RANGE_LOW is indeed smaller than RANGE_HIGH. In the program, these constants are defined as the values 1 and 10 respectively.

A third constant, TRAILER, defines the end-of-data indicator. This number must not lie within the range specified by RANGE_LOW and RANGE_HIGH, so it has been given the value -1.

```
/* Tally how many of each number within a range are entered */

#define RANGE_LOW 1
#define RANGE_HIGH 10
    /* Tallies numbers between RANGE_LOW and RANGE_HIGH */
#define TRAILER -1
    /* TRAILER marks end of data */

main()
{
    int tally[RANGE_HIGH - RANGE_LOW + 1],
                    /* One bin for each number in the range */
        num,        /* Holds the inputted value */
        i;          /* Your all-purpose loop index */

/* Initialize the array to zero */
    for (i = 0; i <= RANGE_HIGH - RANGE_LOW; tally[i++] = 0);

/* Input numbers */
    printf("Please enter a number between %d and %d (%d to quit): ",
                        RANGE_LOW, RANGE_HIGH, TRAILER);
    scanf("%d", &num);
```

Program continued on next page

Program continued from previous page

```
        while (num != TRAILER)
        {
            if (num < RANGE_LOW || num > RANGE_HIGH)   /* Out of range */
                printf("%d is not between %d and %d.\n",
                        num, RANGE_LOW, RANGE_HIGH);
            else      /* Tally "num" */
                tally[num - RANGE_LOW]++;
            printf("\nEnter another number: ");
            scanf("%d", &num);
        }

    /* Print totals */

        printf("\n------------\n\nYou entered:\n");
        for (i = 0; i <= RANGE_HIGH - RANGE_LOW; i++)
            printf("%2d %2d's\n", tally[i], i + RANGE_LOW);

        printf("\nThank you.\n");
    }
```

Program 10—12

```
Please enter a number between 1 and 10 (-1 to quit): 3

Enter another number: 5

Enter another number: 1

Enter another number: 10

Enter another number: 8

Enter another number: 5

Enter another number: 10

Enter another number: 6

Enter another number: 2

Enter another number: 11
11 is not between 1 and 10.

Enter another number: 4

Enter another number: 9

Enter another number: -2
-2 is not between 1 and 10.

Enter another number: 3

Enter another number: 2

Enter another number: 9

Enter another number: -1
```

Output continued on next page

Output continued from previous page

```
------------

You entered:
  1  1's
  2  2's
  2  3's
  1  4's
  2  5's
  1  6's
  0  7's
  1  8's
  2  9's
  2  10's

Thank you.
```

Output 10—12

The integer array *tally* must contain one element for each number in the range. Therefore, its size must be determined by the difference between RANGE_LOW and RANGE_HIGH. An extra 1 is added to make the range inclusive.

The array *tally* is initialized to all zeroes by means of a bodyless **for** loop designed to cover all elements of *tally*. Once again, the difference between RANGE_LOW and RANGE_HIGH is used. The array is initialized to zeroes to indicate that no numbers have been entered yet. Then the user is prompted to enter a number in the specified range. The prompt includes a reminder of the trailer value. A priming *scanf* is executed, reading an integer into *num*. If this value is not the trailer, a **while** loop is entered which processes the entered number and then inputs another one.

Within the **while** loop, the entered number is validated. If it is outside the allowable range, a message to this effect is printed and the number is ignored. Otherwise, the number is accepted and used to locate an element of the array *tally*. Each integer in the range is represented by an element of *tally*. The index, or subscript, of this element is determined by subtracting from *num* the value RANGE_LOW, so that the lowest value in the range is always represented by element 0. The element so located then is incremented to indicate that the integer represented by this element has been entered. If this integer is entered again at a later time, the same element is incremented again.

After the number has been tallied, the user is prompted to enter another integer, and the loop prepares for another iteration.

As soon as the trailer value has been entered, the **while** loop terminates and the final section of the program is encountered. It is here that, with the aid of a **for** loop, the tally of all the entered numbers is printed out. The value RANGE_LOW is added to the index *i* so that the actual range is displayed, rather than the array indices.

Multi— dimensional Arrays

The arrays we have used so far have been one-dimensional. That is to say, the elements of the array could be represented either as a single column or as a single row. Many applications, however, revolve around arrays that have more than one dimension.

A typical two-dimensional array is the common railroad or airplane timetable. To locate a particular piece of information, you determine the required row and column, and then read the location where they meet. In the same way, a two-dimensional array is a grid containing rows and columns, in which each element is uniquely specified by means of its row and column coordinates.

Figure 10-4 is a representation of a two-dimensional matrix (multidimensional array) named *a*, of type **int**, with 3 rows and 4 columns. The number 9 is stored in the element of array *a* designated as row 1, column 2. (Both rows and columns are numbered from 0.)

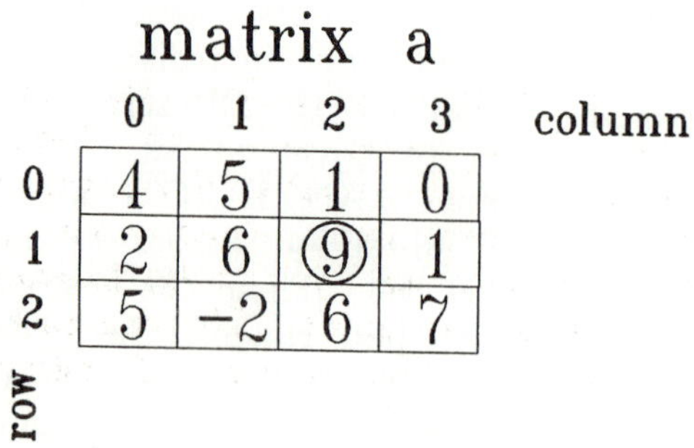

Figure 10—4

When dealing with one-dimensional arrays, you specify a single subscript to locate a specific element. Because elements of two-dimensional arrays are located by means of a row and a column, two subscripts are required. The row subscript generally is specified before the column subscript. Thus, the element containing the value 9 in Figure 10-4 would be referred to in C as *a[1][2]*. Unlike most other languages, C requires that each subscript be written within its own separate pair of brackets.

In C, as in Pascal, a two-dimensional array actually is an array of arrays. In other words, one can think of *a* as being an array of 3 elements, each of which is an array of 4 integers, as shown in Figure 10-5:

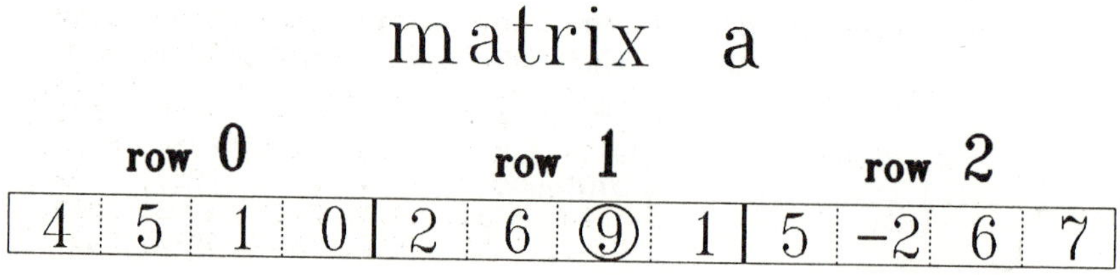

Figure 10—5

In array notation, *a[1]* represents a row, and *a[1][2]* represents a column within that row. This definition of a two-dimensional array will become more significant in the next chapter. Right now, all you need to remember is that each subscript must be contained in its own pair of square brackets, and that the order of the row and column subscripts should be consistent.

The last comment in the preceding paragraph is particularly noteworthy. One can decide whether the first subscript of a two-dimensional array is the row or the column, but once the decision has been made, consistency must be maintained throughout the entire program. For example, in Figure 10-4, *a[2][1]* is not the same element as *a[1][2]*. The former is the element located in the third row (row 2) and second column (column 1), whereas the latter is the element in the second row (row 1), third column (column 2). In this book, we will consistently specify the row before the column.

You can probably guess how array *a* would be declared:

```c
int a[3][4];
```

Arrays of more than two dimensions can be declared in C, merely by adding more subscripts, but these are used less frequently than one- or two-dimensional arrays. If you ever need to use arrays containing more than two dimensions, the principles described in this section can be extended to arrays of as many dimensions as required. The number of dimensions usually is limited only by the amount of memory available to the program.

The next program illustrates the use of a two-dimensional matrix. It consists of 4 rows and 12 columns, in which each row represents a particular make of car, and each column represents a year between 1975 and 1986. Each element contains the fictitious price in dollars of the car represented by the row and column in which the element is located.

To find the price of a 1975 Volkswagen, for example, one would look in row 0 (representing Volkswagen) and column 0 (representing 1975). The value is 4775, so a 1975 Volkswagen costs $4775. The program simply prints out the price of a car whose make and year are entered by the user.

```c
/* Program to report car prices.  User enters car make by number, and
   car year.  Program reports price.  All data is fictitious. */

int price_list [4] [12] =     /* 2-D array of prices:
                                 row = make, column = year */
    {
        /* Volkswagen */      { 4775, 4980, 5222, 5305, 5483, 5547,    /* 75-80 */
                                5596, 5713, 5842, 5903, 6043, 6230 },   /* 81-86 */
        /* Chevy */           { 4853, 5140, 5413, 5590, 5723, 5848,
                                5762, 5944, 6104, 6255, 6370, 6526 },
        /* Cadillac */        { 5627, 5772, 5973, 6210, 6539, 6720,
                                6792, 6930, 7054, 7202, 7365, 7562 },
        /* Honda */           { 1576, 1738, 1970, 2161, 2205, 2280,
                                2442, 2580, 2814, 2953, 3078, 3201 }
    };
```

Program continued on next page

Program continued from previous page

```
                              /*********************/
   main()
   {
       int make,                 /* Make of the car as a number 1 - 4
                                    (see "print_make" routine for
                                    number-name correspondence) */

           year;                 /* Year of the car, 1975-1986 */

       make = get_make();        /* Priming read */

       while (make != 0)         /* 0 indicates end of input */
       {
           year = get_year();
           printf("The price of a %d ", year);
           print_make(make);
           printf(" is $%d.\n\n", price(make, year));
           make = get_make();    /* For the next time around */
       }
       printf("\nThank you for buying all those cars!\n");
   }


                              /*********************/

   get_make()

   /* Read in and return the number (make) of the desired car */

   {
       int i, make;

       /* Print the choice numbers and names */
       for (i = 1; i <= 4; i++)
       {
           printf("%d=", i);     /* The number */
           print_make(i);        /* The name   */
           printf(", ");
       }
       printf("0=END\n");

       /* Read in the selection by number */
       do
       {
           printf("    Which car do you want? ");
           scanf("%d", &make);
       }
       while (make < 0 || make > 4);

       return(make);
   }


                              /*********************/
```

Program continued on next page

Program continued from previous page

```
get_year()

/* Read in and return the year of the desired car */

{
    int year;

    do
    {
        printf("    What year (1975-1986)? ");
        scanf("%d", &year);
    }
    while (year < 1975 || year > 1986);

    return(year);
}

                      /********************/

price (car, yr)
int car, yr;

/* Use "car"and "year" to generate an index into "price_list"
   and return the corresponding entry */

{
    return(price_list [car-1] [yr-1975]);
}

                      /********************/

print_make(car)
int car;

/* Print the make of "car" according to its value */

{
    if (car == 1)
        printf("Volkswagen");
    else if (car == 2)
            printf("Chevy");
        else if (car == 3)
                printf("Cadillac");
            else
                    printf("Honda");
}
```

Program 10—13

```
1=Volkswagen, 2=Chevy, 3=Cadillac, 4=Honda, 0=END
     Which car do you want? 2
     What year (1975-1986)? 1980
The price of a 1980 Chevy is $5848.

1=Volkswagen, 2=Chevy, 3=Cadillac, 4=Honda, 0=END
     Which car do you want? 3
     What year (1975-1986)? 1974
     What year (1975-1986)? 1976
The price of a 1976 Cadillac is $5772.

1=Volkswagen, 2=Chevy, 3=Cadillac, 4=Honda, 0=END
     Which car do you want? 5
     Which car do you want? 4
     What year (1975-1986)? 1982
The price of a 1982 Honda is $2580.

1=Volkswagen, 2=Chevy, 3=Cadillac, 4=Honda, 0=END
     Which car do you want? 1
     What year (1975-1986)? 1982
The price of a 1982 Volkswagen is $5713.

1=Volkswagen, 2=Chevy, 3=Cadillac, 4=Honda, 0=END
     Which car do you want? 4
     What year (1975-1986)? 1986
The price of a 1986 Honda is $3201.

1=Volkswagen, 2=Chevy, 3=Cadillac, 4=Honda, 0=END
     Which car do you want? 0

Thank you for buying all those cars!
```

Output 10—13

Since the matrix *price_list* in Program 10-13 must be initialized, it must be declared globally. The initialization of *price_list* is somewhat more involved than the initialization of a one-dimensional array, partly because it contains a lot of data and partly because it is two-dimensional. In the initialization of a two-dimensional matrix, each row must be contained within a pair of curly braces, as if each row were a separate array. Then all the rows, separated by commas, are enclosed within an outer pair of braces. (If all the elements in the rows are being initialized, the inner braces can be omitted, but we recommend that you retain them for clarity.)

Since each row of the matrix in this program is too long to fit on a single line, each has been split into two lines. The data for the first row are followed by comments indicating the years represented by each line, again for the sake of clarity. Each row is preceded by a comment specifying the make represented by that particular row.

In declaring *price_list*, it would have been permissible to omit the row dimension and leave the first set of square brackets empty, since the compiler would count the number of rows to which *price_list* is being initialized. It is never permissible to omit the second subscript, the column dimension. This is because, in some situations, it is not possible for the compiler to count the columns as well. The syntax of C allows only the first set of square brackets to be left empty when a multidimensional array is being declared and initialized. As with one-dimensional arrays, all dimensions must be specified if only part of the array is initialized.

In the *main* function, the priming read is carried out by calling the function *get_make* to get the first piece of input as the initial value of *make*. The make of the car is represented by a number between 1 and 4. 1 represents Volkswagen, 2 represents Chevy, 3 is Cadillac, and 4 is Honda. The value 0 indicates that the user wishes to terminate the run.

If a zero is entered, the **while** loop in the *main* function does not execute and the program ends. Otherwise, the loop begins execution. The *get_year* function is called to read in and return the year, which is stored in the variable *year*, and the price of the car is printed out using the *print_make* and *price* functions (to be described below). The *get_make* function again is called. If the user enters zero this time, the loop terminates execution; otherwise, the body of the loop is again executed.

The *get_make* function first prints out an information line, specifying all the valid inputs and their meanings. For the values 1 through 4, the function *print_make* is called from within a **for** loop. The *print_make* function prints out the name of the car corresponding to the integer passed to it as a parameter. Only the *print_make* function needs to know the actual names corresponding to makes 1 through 4. Therefore, to change the names of the cars handled by this program, the programmer needs to change only the function *print_make*. If you find the coding difficult to follow, look at the output, which will help to explain what is going on.

Finally, *get_make* prompts the user to enter one of the numbers listed in the information line, and reads in a value for *make*. If the integer is not one of the legal values, the loop continues execution until a valid integer is entered. When that occurs, the value is returned.

The function *get_year* reads in the car's year, validating the input to ensure that the year in question is between 1975 and 1986. The valid year is then returned.

The function *price* returns the price of the car represented by its two parameters *car* and *yr*, representing the make of the car and the year. These two parameters are converted to valid subscripts of the matrix *price_list*. The value of *car* is decremented by 1, because its original value is between 1 and 4, but the matrix *price_list* needs a value between 0 and 3 as a subscript. The year is decremented by the value 1975, so that 1975 corresponds to column 0, 1976 corresponds to column 1, and so forth. This function does not validate its parameters, because it is assumed that they were already validated by the functions *get_make* and *get_year*. There would be no point in revalidating the same data. Assuming that a program is correctly written, usually only those functions that actually read in data need to validate it.

The final function, *print_make*, prints out the actual name of the car represented by its parameter, *car*, which is a value between 1 and 4. A nest of **if** statements is used to accomplish this step. Notice that none of the *printf* control strings contains a *newline* character. The *newline* is omitted so the control strings can be used to print part of a single line, the rest of which is printed by other *printf* statements. This is exactly what is done when *print_make* is called from *main* and *get_make*. The function *print_make*, like the function *price*, does not revalidate its parameters.

Even though it might not be apparent to the casual observer, arrays depend to a considerable extent on the class of C data types known as *pointers*. Values and variables of these types make it possible to manipulate memory addresses, thereby giving the C programmer low-level access that is not present in most other languages. Pointers are the subject of the next chapter.

The Spirit of C

Now that we have covered arrays, we could rewrite all our earlier *Spirit of C* programs so that they store all of their input in an array before generating any output. Besides avoiding the interleaving of input with output, this technique also makes possible the implementation of certain algorithms, such as sorting, which require the processing of an entire group of input values at once. Such algorithms are not easily programmable without arrays.

Our illustrative program for this chapter is related to the program in the previous chapter's *Spirit of C*. Here is the problem:

When short sections of a poem are quoted in a prose text, the lines often are not written in verse form. Instead, slashes are used to separate the lines. We wish to write a program that will read in a poem in this format and print it out in the correct verse form. This is similar to the program from the last chapter, but there are several differences. First, we are not concerned with numbers, so the problem is basically one of entering, storing, and printing characters. Second, a slash rather than a comma is used to indicate line breaks. Third, the input may be somewhat long, so more than one line of input should be acceptable to the program. Any *newline* characters in the input should be ignored, with only the slashes signalling line breaks in the output. This also means that a *newline* can no longer be used as the trailer, so some other indication of the end of input must be used.

In the last chapter, we constructed the program by writing the low-level routines before the *main* function that used them. This sometimes is called the bottom-up method. This time, we will use top-down programming, in that we will write the *main* function before the lower level ones. More will be said about this subject in the *Programming and Debugging Hints* section.

The first part of our program will consist of a loop to read in characters and store them in a character array until some end-of-input condition is detected. Let us say that the end of input is marked by a period at the end of an input line (a period followed by a *newline*, not a slash). Since this process will be performed by a function other than *main*, the array in which the characters are stored will have to be global. The code in the main function which handles this subtask is

```
get_input();
```

It calls a function, to be written later, which will input the array. (Much of the initial work of top-down programming consists of "passing the buck" to lower-level functions.)

To make the situation symmetric, the only other action performed by the *main* function is to call a function that outputs the array contents in the correct format. The completed *main* function is as follows:

```
main()
{
    get_input();

    produce_output();
}
```

The only operations performed on the input are the conversion of slashes to *newlines* and the discarding of *newlines* in the input. This could be done in any of several places. The conversion could be made as soon as the character is read in, so that the *newlines* actually are stored in the array. It could also be done by the *produce_output* function as the characters are read from the array. We could even include a third function call in the *main* function, between the call to *get_input* and the call to *produce_output*, to perform the conversion on the array contents. We have chosen to do the conversion in the *get_input* function.

Before we continue, we should write the declarations for the global variables we know we will need. We need a character array, which we shall call *input_text*. The declaration

```
char input_text[500];
```

should do the trick. Even though an array of 500 characters is not very big compared to the memory sizes of today's personal computers, one must be careful when declaring arrays, especially two-dimensional arrays, on small computers. A 500 by 500 character array may be too large for many personal computers. A 1000 by 1000 array requires one megabyte (1 million bytes) of memory, which is too much to handle for most personal computers. An oversized array may not be caught by your C compiler. Probably an execution error will occur instead, and when that happens, usually the computer does not provide too much information regarding what caused the error.

Now we can write the *get_input* function. It will contain a loop that calls lower level functions to input a character, convert it, and store it in the array. The test for the end of input will be made by saving the previous character read in. If the current character is a *newline* and the previous one was a period, the end of input has been reached.

The *get_input* function must have a local variable (let's call it *next_avail*) which is used to keep track of the array element into which the next character is to be stored. Note that *next_avail* need not be global, since it is used only when entering the text. The array will be terminated with a *null* character, thus making it possible to output the entire array as a string using the %s conversion specification. It is not necessary for the output routine to know the length of the string. The value of *next_avail* is passed to the function that stores the character in the array.

Here is how the *get_input* function may be written:

```
get_input()

/* This function inputs characters, converts them, and places them in
   global array "input_text". All operations are actually performed by
   lower level functions, except testing for end of input. This is done
   by saving the last inputted character in "last_char" before reading a
   new one. If the new character is a newline and the old one is a
   period, the end of input has been detected. */

{
    int next_avail = 0;         /* Array location in which to place
                                   next character */
    char new_char,              /* Holds the character just read in */
         last_char = ' ';       /* Holds the previous character.  May be
                                   initialized  to anything but a period */

    /* Loop until this character is a newline
       and the last was a period */

    scanf("%c", &new_char);     /* Priming read */
    while (new_char != '\n' || last_char != '.')
    {

        /* Convert the character, and store it in element "next_avail" */

        store_char (convert (new_char), next_avail++);

        last_char = new_char;

        scanf("%c", &new_char);

    }

    store_char('\0', next_avail);   /* Terminate "input_text" so
                                       that it becomes a string */

}
```

In the above, you will notice that the functions used to convert and store the character are called in the same statement. This is possible because *convert* returns the character to be stored by *store_char*. The value of *next_avail* also is incremented in that statement.

Pay particular attention to the **while** condition in the above. It is important to understand why the || operator is used rather than &&. If && were used, then both conditions would have to be true for the loop to continue. That is, the current character could not be a *newline* AND the previous one could not be a period. As soon as the current character became a *newline*, the expression

```
new_char != '\n'
```

would become false, making the entire condition false (this is the nature of the && operator). The loop would terminate regardless of what the previous character was.

Now we can write the *convert* function. This function will return the character passed to it unchanged, unless it is a slash or a *newline*. It converts slashes to *newlines*, and converts *newlines* into spaces (since it is necessary to separate the last word on a line from the first word on the next line). This is the mechanism by which input *newlines* are ignored by the program. Remember that *convert* is of type **char**, so we must add the following declaration to *get_input*:

```
char convert();
```

We will add that line when we return to *get_input*, but for now, let us just write *convert*:

```
char convert(in_char)
char in_char;                /* Character to be converted */

/* This  function returns  the character  "in_char"  unchanged
   unless it is a slash or  a  newline. Slashes are  converted
   to newlines, and newlines into spaces */

{
   if (in_char == '/')
      return('\n');

   else if (in_char == '\n')
      return(' ');

      else
         return(in_char);
}
```

In this function, the **else** keywords are not really necessary. If any **if** test succeeds, the function returns immediately, so none of the subsequent **if** statements are encountered. Nevertheless, the use of the **else** clauses are considered good form. In fact, some proponents of structured programming frown upon the use of multiple **return** statements in a function, since this can create confusion as to where and when the function returns. In a function as small as *convert*, the way we have written it is the most expedient.

Now comes the *store_char* function:

```
store_char (character, position)
char character;              /* Character to store */
int position;                /* Location in array where character
                                is to be stored */

/* This function stores "character" in global array "input_text",
   in element  "position". */

{
     input_text[position] = character;
}
```

None of the functions we have written so far tests to see whether *input_text* is full (contains more than 500 characters). We are assuming that no input will have 500 characters. If we wish to add a test, this can be done within either the *get_input* function or the *store_char* function. In the latter case, *get_input* will have to test for an error code being returned from *store_char*. The alternative would be for *store_char* to ignore all characters after 500, without informing *get_input*. This would be a bad way to write the program. Either *get_input* or *store_char* should print an error message, informing the user that all but the first 500 characters will be excluded. The program might even forego displaying any of the poem, because the output would not be complete.

The only function that remains to be written is *produce_output*. But because of the way we have constructed the other functions, *produce_output* will consist only of a *printf* function that outputs the entire string. Therefore, we will dispense altogether with the reference to *produce_output* in the *main* function, replacing it with

```
printf("%s\n", input_text);
```

We assume that the string does not end with a *newline*, since it would be unnatural for the user to place a slash at the end of the text.

Now we can put it all together. Notice how rows of asterisks (bounded by slashes, so they become comments) are used to separate sections of the program.

```
/*
When short sections of  a poem  are quoted in  a prose text, the lines are often not
written in verse form, but  rather  slashes  are used  to  separate the lines.  This
program reads in a poem in  this  format  and  print  it out  in  the  correct verse
form. A slash is  used to  indicate  line breaks.  More  than  one  line  of input is
acceptable by the program. Newlines in the input are  ignored, with only the slashes
signalling line  breaks in the output. The end of  input  is marked by a  period  at
the  end  of  an input line (a period followed by a newline, not a slash).
*/

/*********************************************************************/
char input_text[500];  /* Array to store converted text */
/*********************************************************************/

main()
{
   get_input();

   printf("%s", input_text);
}


/*********************************************************************/

get_input()

/* This  function inputs  characters, converts them, and  places them in
   global array "input_text". All operations are  actually performed  by
   lower level functions, except testing for end of input. This is  done
   by saving the last inputted character in "last_char" before reading a
   new one. If the new  character is a  newline  and  the  old  one  is a
   period, the end of input has been detected. */

{
   int next_avail = 0;          /* Array location in which to place
                                   next character */
   char new_char,               /* Holds the character just read in */
        last_char = ' ',        /* Holds the previous character. May be
                                   initialized to anything but a period */
        convert();              /* Function to convert input characters
                                   to desired output characters */

   /* Loop until this character is a newline
      and the last was a period */

   scanf("%c", &new_char);      /* Priming read */
   while (new_char != '\n' || last_char != '.')
   {

      /* Convert the character, and store it in element "next_avail" */

      last_char = new_char;

      store_char (convert (new_char), next_avail++);

      scanf("%c", &new_char);

   }
```

Program continued on next page

Program continued from previous page

```
    store_char('\0', next_avail);    /* Terminate "input_text" so
                                        that it becomes a string */
}

/*********************************************************************/

char convert(in_char)
char in_char;                    /* Character to be converted */

/* This  function returns  the character  "in_char"  unchanged
   unless it is a slash or  a newline.  Slashes are  converted
   to newlines, and newlines into spaces */

{
    if (in_char == '/')
        return('\n');

    else if (in_char == '\n')
        return(' ');

        else
            return(in_char);
}

/*********************************************************************/

store_char (character, position)
char character;                  /* Character to store */
int position;                    /* Location in array where character
                                    is to be stored */

/* This function stores "character" in global array "input_text",
   in  element "position" */

{
    input_text[position] = character;
}
```

Programming and Debugging *Hints*

We continue our discussion of modular programming with a comparison of the top-down and bottom-up techniques of program design.

Modular Programming, Part II

Two methods may be used for modular programming. They are known as *top−down* and *bottom−up*. The bottom-up method is the easier from the point of view of testing, because each of the lowest-level functions is written and tested first. This testing is done by special test functions that call the low-level functions, providing them with different parameters and examining the results for correctness. Usually, it is the responsibility of the programmer to examine the results produced, and to determine whether they are correct by means of test data. The programmer chooses data to submit to the functions being tested and determines what the correct results should be. These results are compared with the actual results produced by the functions.

Once the lowest-level functions have been tested and verified to be correct, the next level of functions may be added. These functions are then tested by making available to them all the functions that they call. Since the lowest-level functions already have been tested, any detected errors are probably due to the higher-level functions. This process continues, moving up the levels, until finally the *main* function is tested.

The top-down method of programming is just the opposite. The higher-level functions are written first, which consist of calls to the lower-level functions. Testing these functions is somewhat problematic because their functioning depends on lower-level functions that have not yet been written. The solution is to use fake lower-level functions, sometimes called *stubs*. These functions simulate the operations of the actual functions.

For example, suppose a high-level function makes use of a square root function, which has not yet been written. Now let us suppose that the programmer is testing the high-level function such that it calls the square root function only with the arguments 9, 25, and 64. The stub version of the square root function merely contains a table, such as an array, which it uses to look up the correct values to be returned. In this example, the table would need only three entries and the stub function would be simple indeed. Another method would be for the stub function to print out its argument and ask the programmer to enter the value to be returned.

The use of stubs is perfectly valid, because only the higher-level functions are being tested. Once the lower-level functions are ready for testing, the stubs are replaced with the actual functions. This process continues until the lowest-level functions have been added and tested.

The top-down method is easier to implement from the point of view of program design. This method is often called *stepwise refinement*, for it involves the breaking down of more complex modules into simpler ones until each one is eventually of manageable size. The programmer begins by defining the task of the *main* function. This task then is broken down into a series of function calls. This stepwise refinement is performed on each function, continuing until the low-level functions are simple enough that they can be coded without the use of other functions. By that time, they should be so small that this step will not pose any difficulty.

Regardless of whether the top-down or bottom-up method is used, the end result is a modular program. This end result is as important as the creation process, because not all errors may be detected at the time of the initial testing. It is possible that there are still bugs in the program. If an error is discovered after the program supposedly has been fully tested, then the modules concerned can be isolated and retested by themselves.

It may seem easier to write all the functions at once, put them together, and test the program as a whole. Sometimes this method is successful, particularly if the program is short and uncomplicated.

Usually, however, this is not the case. Regardless of the design method used, if a program has been written in modular form, it is easier to detect the source of the error and to test it in isolation than if the program were written as one function.

C Tutorial

1. What is an array?

2. How is the integer array *a*, containing 100 elements, declared in C?

3. What is the subscript of the first element of an array in C?

4. What are the rules for naming arrays?

5. How would you declare an array *x* containing 50 integer elements followed immediately by 50 real elements?

6. What is the purpose of initializing an array?

7. Is it possible to declare and initialize an array in C simultaneously? If so, how?

8. If *array1* and *array2* are dimensioned as follows:

   ```
   char array1[10], array2[10];
   ```

   and *array1* has been initialized, what is the effect of the following?

   ```
   array2 = array1;
   ```

9. What purpose is served by the **break** statement?

10. What criticism can be levelled against the **break** statement?

11. Explain the operation of the following expression (assume *y* has the value 5):

    ```
    x = (y *= 2) + (z = a = 4);
    ```

12. How is a string stored in an array in C?

13. What declaration would be used for the array *bingo*, into which the string "I love C" is to be stored?

14. What conversion specification usually is used to read in a string?

15. When the conversion specification %s is used in a *scanf* statement to read in a string, what is unusual about the way the name of the array is specified?

16. How can one ensure that a *scanf* statement used to read in a string does not read in more characters than the corresponding character array can hold?

17. Is it obligatory to use all the elements of an array?

18. When a one-dimensional array is being declared, under what condition may the dimension be omitted, with the array name followed by an empty pair of square brackets?

19. What happens if an array is being initialized within its declaration, and too few initialization values are specified within the curly braces?

20. What happens if the number of initializing values is greater than the dimension specified for the array?

21. Must the elements of an array be read in or printed out in order of subscript?

22. When sorting the elements of an array, is it necessary to use another array to store the sorted elements?

23. Where is it legal to declare a new variable?

24. What is the name of the construct used in the following statement, and how does it operate?

    a = (b > c) ? b : c;

25. What is the maximum number of dimensions an array in C may have?

26. True or false: If all the elements of a two-dimensional array are initialized in the declaration of the array, both subscripts may be omitted.

ANSWERS TO C TUTORIAL

1. An array is an ordered collection of elements that share the same name.

2. int a[100];

3. 0 (zero)

4. The same as for naming regular variables or functions. An array cannot have the same name as a variable or function within the same program.

5. It can't be done. (All elements of a single array must be of the same type.)

6. Before any element of an array can be used, it must have a value. Initializing an array gives a value to each of its elements.

7. Yes. The array declaration is followed immediately by an equal sign. This is followed by the list of values to be assigned (separated by commas) enclosed in braces.

8. A syntax error is flagged by the compiler. One array cannot be assigned to another using the assignment operator. Each element must be assigned individually.

9. It provides a means of immediately terminating the execution of a loop.

10. It violates the tenets of structured programming, in that it permits a jump to another part of the program.

11. The first set of parentheses is evaluated first, multiplying the value of *y* by 2; the new value of *y*, 10, is returned by the sub-expression. The second set of parentheses is then evaluated, assigning 4 to *a* and *z* and returning that value. The values returned by the two sub-expressions (10 and 4) then are added together to produce the result of 14, which is assigned to *x*.

12. It is terminated by the *null* character, which has the ASCII value 0 and is written in C as '\0'.

13. `char bingo[9];` /* One element is reserved for the null character, '\0' */

14. %s

15. The ampersand (&) is not used, and the array is not subscripted.

16. A maximum field width specifier should be used with the %s conversion specification; for example, %10s.

17. No, but the program must keep track of how many elements are being used, and which ones.

18. If the entire array is being initialized within the declaration.

19. This is perfectly acceptable, as long as the dimension is specified explicitly in the declaration. The initialization values that are specified are assigned to consecutive elements of the array, starting with element 0. The remaining elements are initialized to zero.

20. A syntax error occurs during compilation of the program, and the compilation is aborted.

21. No. The elements of an array (even a character array) may be accessed in any order at all.

22. Not always. In this chapter, the method employed did not use another array. The advantage to using another array is that the original array is retained. Its disadvantage is that it uses extra memory.

23. At the beginning of the body of a function, and at the beginning of a compound statement.

24. The statement makes use of the conditional expression. If b is greater than c, the conditional expression returns the value of b (the value following the ?); otherwise, it returns the value of c (the value following the :). The returned value is assigned to a. The overall effect is that the larger of the two variables b and c is assigned to a.

25. Theoretically, there is no limit. The only practical limits are memory size and the restrictions imposed by the compiler being used.

26. False. Only the first (row) subscript can be omitted, with the first pair of square brackets left empty. The second subscript must always be explicitly specified.

Keywords

break	char	do	double	else	float
for	if	int	long	return	short
unsigned	while				

Exercises

1. A *palindrome* is a word that is spelled the same forward and backward, such as *level*, *radar*, etc. Write a program to read in five-letter words and determine whether they are palindromes. There are several different ways of doing this.

2. Modify the palindrome program to accept variable-length words, up to a predetermined length. This requires determining how many characters are read in.

3. Write a program to read in a number and print it out digit by digit, as a series of words. For example, the number 523 would be printed as "five two three."

4. A harder version of Exercise 3 involves reading in a number and printing it in "true" English; for example, 523 would be displayed as "five hundred twenty-three." This problem is more difficult because it is necessary to take into account the digit's position within the number. If your program accepts large numbers, the digits also must be grouped into threes. For example, 1,234,517 would be displayed as "one million, two hundred thirty-four thousand, five hundred seventeen." Hint: One function can be used to convert a set of three digits into words, for example "two hundred thirty-four," and that function can be called by another which adds the appropriate word ("thousand", "million", etc), for example "two hundred thirty-four thousand." In this way, numbers of virtually any length can be handled.

5. Read in an array of numbers or characters and print out its contents backwards. For example, the array of four integers:

23 34 123 7

would be displayed as:

7 123 34 23

6. Write a program that reads in short strings, say four characters long, and prints out the characters in all possible permutations. For example, an input of *abcd* would result in an output that begins:

abcd
abdc
acbd
acdb
. . . .

Warning: This is a bit harder than it looks.

7. Modify Program 10-9 to print out the number of students with the highest and lowest grades.

8. Write a program to read in grades and print out the top five. Hint: One way to do this is to sort the grades and choose the top five. You may, however, prefer a different method.

9. Write a program that sorts an array of numbers, and not only prints out the maximum and minimum but also calculates the difference between them.

10. Write a function that reverses an array in memory. Either reverse the elements in place (within the array they are originally stored in), or reverse them into a second array.

11. The transpose of a two dimensional array is a second array containing the same elements as the first, but in which the rows become columns and vice versa. For example, given the array

```
 1  5  7
 9  6  3
52 11  9
```

the transpose would be:

```
1  9 52
5  6 11
7  3  9
```

Write a program to read in a square, two-dimensional array and display its transpose.

12. Write a program that reads in an array (not necessarily square) of numbers, and calculates and displays the row and column sums, as well as the grand total. If possible, place the sums next to their respective rows and columns. For example, an output might look like the following:

```
                               |  SUMS
------------------------------ |-----
    5    3    4    8    2    6  |   28
    1    0    7    7    4    3  |   22
    6    9    2    5    1    3  |   26
    3    8    4    9    2    1  |   27
------------------------------ |-----
   15   20   17   29    9   13  |  103
```

13. On the standard telephone, each of the digits 2 through 9 is associated with a group of three letters. For example, the number 2 is associated with the letters A, B, and C, 3 with D, E, and F, and 9 with W, X, and Y. The letters Q and Z are not used. Thus it is possible to translate telephone numbers into words. For example, the number 776-4726 can be represented by the word PROGRAM, since P and R appear above the digit 7 on the telephone, O appears above the digit 6, G appears above 4, and so on. Such words often make it easier to remember a telephone number.

Not all phone numbers can be translated in this fashion; since no letters are associated with 1 or 0, a phone number must not contain these digits if it is to be converted to a word.

Write a program that reads in a seven-digit telephone number, tests to ensure that it does not contain either a 0 or a 1, and if it does not contain these digits, displays a list of all possible words that can be formed from the number. Of course, the program cannot be made to discriminate between real and "phony" words, so you are required only to display all possible combinations of the associated letters. For example, the list for 776-4726 begins:

PPMGPAM   PPMGPAN   PPMGPAO   PPMGPBM   PPMGPBN   PPMGPBO
PPMGPCM   ...

The user then reads the whole list to find real words that are easy to remember.

14. Program 10-12 showed how to use bins to record how many of each value in a range were read in. The lower and upper bounds of the range could be changed, but not the size of the bins. For example, suppose we wish to accept numbers between 1 and 50, using only 10 bins. The first bin records how many of the numbers between 1 and 5 are read in, the second records how many numbers between 6 and 10 are read in, and so on up to the tenth bin, which records the numbers 46 through 50. The "width" of each bin, in this case 5, is the total number of values in the range divided by the number of bins.

Write a program similar to Program 10-12, but which uses ten bins and permits the user to input the lower and upper bounds of the range. The only restriction is that the number of values in the range should be a multiple of 10, so that all ten bins can have the same width. Try to figure out how the program must calculate to which bin each value belongs. You can then modify this *main* function so that it tests your random number generator from Exercise 8 of the previous chapter.

11

Pointers and Indirection

O*ne of the major features that distinguishes the C language from most others is the abundant use of pointers, a data type which will be introduced in this chapter.*

The Concept of Pointers

As you know by now, variables are stored in memory. Each memory location has a numeric *address*, in much the same way that each element of an array has its own subscript. Variable names in C and other high-level languages enable the programmer to refer to memory locations by name, but the compiler must translate these names into addresses. This process is automatic, so the programmer need not be concerned with it. However, the kind of problems for which C is particularly noted requires that the user be able to refer to those addresses indirectly, in order to manipulate the contents of the corresponding memory locations. In a sense, the address or name of a memory location points to whatever is contained within that memory location.

You might well ask why variable names are not sufficient to provide the kind of manipulations required in C. One reason is that memory addresses are global to all functions, whereas local variable names are meaningful only within the functions in which they are declared. A function can pass the address of a local variable to another function, and the second function can use this address to access the contents of the first function's local variable.

Passing addresses does not violate the rules of modular programming, as does the use of global variables. The addresses are passed only to the functions that need to access those memory locations. Passing a local variable's address is analogous to passing a key: only the functions possessing the key can access the variable in question, so some measure of protection is involved.

At any given moment in a program's execution, each existing variable has a unique address associated with it. As we have explained, local variables disappear when the functions in which they are declared finish execution. The memory location formerly occupied by such a local variable then is freed and can be allocated to another local variable later in the program.

The Address Operator

In this section we will explain how the address of a variable can be determined. Actually, we have been using this technique all along. The ampersand (&) immediately preceding a variable name in a call to the *scanf* function returns the address of the variable associated with it. This operator is known as the *address operator*, and it is not restricted to the *scanf* function. It may precede only a variable name or array element, never a constant, an expression, or the unsubscripted name of an array. The & operator can be used with any item that can be placed on the left side of an assignment operator.

Addresses themselves can be stored in variables. Addresses are a separate data type in C, distinct from the other types introduced so far. There are, in fact, several types of address; the address of an **int** variable is of a type distinctly different from that of a **char** variable. A variable *a* that can hold the address of an integer can be declared as follows:

```
int *a;
```

The asterisk is not part of the variable name; rather, **int** * (read "pointer to **int**") is the type of variable *a*. If we were to declare the following:

```
int *a, b;
```

only *a* would be of type **int** *. The variable *b* would simply be of type **int**. In this text, sometimes we shall refer to the type of item pointed to by a pointer variable as the *target type*. For example, the target type of **int** * is **int**.

Pointer variables are named in the same manner as any other variable. Since the asterisk is not part of the name, the following example is illegal, since it is an attempt to declare the same variable twice with two different types:

```
int a, *a;    /* illegal */
```

When a variable is declared as a pointer, it is not automatically initialized to any value. In this respect, it is just like any other variable. Initially, then, the pointer does not point to anything. To assign an address to a pointer, the programmer must assign it a value. For example, the following statement:

```
a = &b;
```

may be interpreted as, "assign the address of *b* to *a*." The ampersand operator applied to a variable of type **int** returns a constant value of type **int** *, which can be assigned to a variable of type **int** *.

C actually allows the assignment of an address to a pointer variable of a different target type, through the use of the cast operator. For example, if *c* is of type **char** * and *d* is of type **int**, the following is legal:

```
c = (char *) &d;
```

In this statement the address of *d* is converted from type **int** * to type **char** * and assigned to *c*. Most versions of C allow the cast operator to be omitted in such a case, but they may print a warning message.

Do not confuse the preceding example with the statement

```
c = &(char)d;    /* illegal */
```

which is illegal. The cast operator returns a *value* (the contents of *d* cast into a **char**), whereas the & operator can be applied only to a variable.

A pointer variable can be initialized in its declaration. It can be set to the address of any variable already declared. For example, the following is perfectly acceptable in C:

```
int a, *b = &a;
```

It declares *a* as a variable of type **int**, declares *b* as a pointer to **int**, and initializes *b* to the address of *a*.

The Indirection Operator

Once the address of integer variable *i* has been assigned to the pointer variable *j*, *j* can be used to manipulate the contents of *i*. This is illustrated in the following program.

```
/* An introduction to pointers */

main()
{
    int i = 3, *j, k;   /* "j" is a pointer to integer */

    j = &i;                 /* "j" points to the location of "i" */
    k = *j;                 /* Assign to "k" the value pointed to by "j"
                               (== the value of "i") */
    *j = 4;                 /* Assign 4 to the location pointed to by "j"
                               (that is, to "i") */

    printf("i = %d, *j = %d, k = %d\n", i, *j, k);
}
```

Program 11—1

```
i = 4, *j = 4, k = 3
```

Output 11—1

In Program 11-1, the variable *i* is declared to be of type **int** and is initialized to 3. The variable *j* is of type **int** * ("pointer to int"), and the variable *k* is of type **int**. The actions performed by the program are illustrated in Figure 11-1.

In the first statement, *j* is assigned the address of *i*. The second statement contains an example of what is called the *indirection operator*. When an asterisk is placed before a pointer variable in an expression, the value returned is not the value of the pointer variable, but rather the value contained in the memory location pointed to by the pointer variable's value. Since *j* was assigned the address of *i* in the first statement, the second statement assigns to *k* the value of *i*, which happens to be 3.

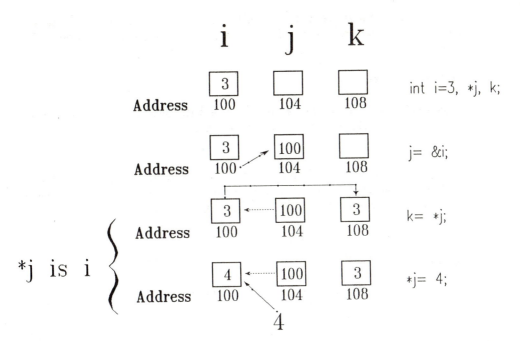

Figure 11—1

The reason the syntax for declaring a pointer variable uses an asterisk next to the variable name is that the declaration

```
int *p;
```

could be read as, "declare *p to be an **int**." Memory is allocated for p, however, not for *p. This is reflected in the fact that the declaration

```
int q, *p = &q;
```

assigns the address of q to p, not to *p, which does not exist before the assignment is made.

In the third assignment statement of Program 11-1, the indirection operator is used on the left-hand side of the assignment operator (it is one of the few operators that can be used there). Here, the value 4 is assigned not to j but to the memory location whose address is contained in j — again, i. Thus the third statement has the effect of assigning 4 to i. These claims are verified by Output 11-1.

The output of the *printf* function reads *j = 4. Sometimes, however, a memory location is accessible only through a pointer variable. In such a case, the name of the pointer variable may be used informally as the name of the location it points to. In other words, the output might instead have read j = 4. This usually would not cause any confusion, since one rarely needs to print out the memory address contained in a pointer variable. On most machines, memory addresses are simply integers, so a pointer value may be cast automatically into an **int** or some other compatible type. As we shall see later, however, pointers are treated differently from integers in the way calculations are performed with them.

Passing Pointers as Parameters

The next program demonstrates how a pointer can be passed to a function, thereby allowing the receiving function to modify the value of the variable being pointed to. (A call to the *scanf* function uses the & operator to pass the addresses of the variables being read in.) The program is a rewrite of Program 9-6, which illustrated the fact that a function cannot change the value of a variable whose *value* is passed as a parameter. In Program 11-2, however, instead of the *main* function passing *i*, it passes the address of *i*, which is accessible under the name &*i*.

To accommodate the change of the parameter value, the function *modify* had to be rewritten, since now it must be prepared to accept an address passed to it. The dummy parameter *i* in *modify* therefore is declared as a pointer to an **int**. Now *modify* can change the value of *main*'s local variable *i* through the process of indirection described in the previous section. The technique of making a variable accessible to a function by passing its address is often referred to as *passing by reference*.

```
/* Demonstration of passing by reference
   for a function to be able to modify its parameters */

main()
{
  int i;

  i = 1;
  printf("i is now equal to %d\n", i);

  modify(&i);
  printf("i is now equal to %d\n", i);
}

modify(i)
int *i;
{
  *i = 3;
}
```

Program 11–2

```
i is now equal to 1
i is now equal to 3
```

Output 11–2

As a further illustration of passing by reference, Program 11-3 includes a *swap* function to exchange the values of two variables.

```
/* Pointer parameters in action: the swap routine */

main()
{
    int i, j;

    i = 1;
    j = 9;
    printf("i = %d and j = %d\n", i, j);

/* Now exchange them */

    swap(&i, &j);
    printf("\nnow i = %d and j = %d\n", i, j);
}

swap(i, j)

/* Exchange "*i" with "*j" by swapping values of "i" and "j" */
int *i, *j;
{
    int temp = *i;      /* Create "temp" and store into it the value pointed to
                           by "i" */
    *i = *j;            /* The value pointed to by "j" is stored in the location
                           pointed to by "i" */
    *j = temp;          /* Assign "temp" to the location pointed to by "j" */
}
```

Program 11-3

```
        i = 1 and j = 9

        now i = 9 and j = 1
```

Output 11-3

If the formal parameters *i* and *j* of the *swap* function were declared merely as integers, and the *main* function passed only *i* and *j* rather than their addresses, the exchange made in *swap* would have no effect on the variables *i* and *j* in *main*, just as *modify* in Program 9-6 did not affect the variable *i* in its *main* function.

Notice that the variable *temp* in the *swap* function is of type **int**, not **int ***. The values being exchanged are not the pointers, but the integers being pointed to by them. Notice also that *temp* is initialized immediately upon declaration to the value pointed to by *i*.

Arrays and Pointers

Pointers are intimately associated with arrays. The address operator is not used with an array name because when the unsubscripted name of an array is written in a C program, it is evaluated as a *constant* pointer. Therefore, if *array* is the name of an integer array and *i* is an integer variable, the expression

```
    array = &i;
```

is illegal in C, since a constant cannot be placed to the left of an assignment operator. The name of an array points to its first element, the one with the subscript 0. Since the elements of an array always are stored contiguously (adjacent to one another) and are all of the same type, only the address of the first element is needed to access an entire array.

For example, suppose array *bingo* is declared as follows:

```
int bingo[10];
```

Let us assume that a variable of type **int** takes up four bytes of memory on the machine you are using. (A byte is the smallest addressable unit of memory.) Let's suppose further that the address of *bingo* is memory location 100. The address of *bingo[0]* would be 100. Since *bingo[0]* is, like all the other elements of *bingo*, a variable of type **int**, it takes up four memory locations, 100 through 103. That means *bingo[1]* is located at memory location 104. By the same reasoning, *bingo[2]* is located at location 108. This is illustrated in Figure 11-2.

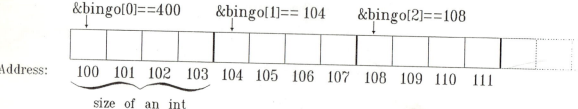

Figure 11—2

The concept of array names as pointers is illustrated in Program 11-4.

```
/* Array names are constant pointers */

int an_array[2] = { 3, 7 };

main()
{
    int *also = an_array;          /* "also" is a pointer to the array
                                      called "an_array" */

    also[0] = 14;
    printf("an_array = { %d, %d }\n", an_array[0], an_array[1]);
}
```

Program 11—4

```
an_array = { 14, 7 }
```

Output 11—4

In this program, an integer array called *an_array* is initialized to the two elements 3 and 7. Within the *main* function, the variable *also* is declared as a pointer to an integer, and is initialized to the address of *an_array*. Notice that *also* is of type **int** **; in C, there is no special type for an **int** array, so a pointer to an array has as its target type the type of the elements in the array.

Once *also* has been assigned the address of *an_array*, it can be used to manipulate the elements of the array. This means *also* can be subscripted. The element *also[0]* is exactly the same as *an_array[0]*, since *also* is declared as a pointer to **int** and *an_array* is an **int** array.

In C, any pointer variable can be subscripted. As with arrays, it is up to the programmer to be sure that the subscript is within the proper limits. In the case of a pointer, the programmer must also be sure that the pointer actually points to an array. (Of course, a scalar variable may be thought of as an array of one element.) The contents of the first (0th) element of *an_array* may therefore be replaced by assigning the new value, 14, to *also[0]* (see Figure 11-3).

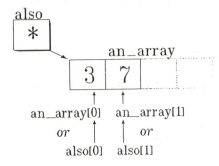

Figure 11—3

Since *also* points to the first location of *an_array*, the assignment just described could have been written as follows:

```
*also = 14;
```

In fact, it is even syntactically correct to write

```
*an_array = 14;
```

because *an_array* also is a pointer to the first element of the array.

Finally, the values of *an_array* are printed out to show that a change has indeed taken place. Notice that each element must be listed individually in the call to *printf*, since only a string array can have all its elements displayed with a single conversion specification (and then only if the elements are to be printed as characters, as opposed to ASCII values).

In the next program, we present an exchange sort that is not fundamentally different from the one shown previously (Program 10-10). What is different, however, is the general structured approach taken in the organization of the program itself. Instead of using global variables and arrays, the program accesses these structures by passing their addresses to the functions that handle them. This program also serves to introduce several key C programming features related to pointers.

```c
/* Sorting an array revisited:
   Passing an array as a parameter */

     /* The array may have up to 20 elements */
#define MAX_ARRAY_SIZE 20

     /* Message flags for "print_array" */
#define ORIGINAL 0          /* Display original array */
#define SORTED   1          /* Display sorted array */

main()
{
    int numbers[MAX_ARRAY_SIZE],    /* An array */
        array_size;                 /* Actual number of integers in array */

    /* Read in the array's size */

    get_size(&array_size);

    /* Read in array "numbers" of size "array_size" */

    get_array(numbers, array_size);

    /* Echo the array */

    print_array(numbers, array_size, ORIGINAL);

    sort_array(numbers, array_size);

    /* Print the sorted array */

    print_array(numbers, array_size, SORTED);
}

get_size(size)
int *size;

/* Read the size of the array into "*size" (until a valid value is entered) */

{
    do
    {
        printf("How many numbers? ");
        scanf("%d", size);
    }
    /* "*size" must be at least 1 and at most MAX_ARRAY_SIZE */
    while (*size < 1 || *size > MAX_ARRAY_SIZE);
}
```

Program continued on next page

Program continued from previous page

```c
get_array(array, size)
int array[], size;

/* Read in the array called "array" of size "size" */

{
    int i;

    printf("Please enter the integers:\n");
    for (i = 0; i < size; i++)
        scanf("%d", array+i);
}

print_array(array, size, message)
int array[], size, message;

/* Print out "array" of size "size" on a single line.  "message" is a flag
   indicating which message to display (ORIGINAL or SORTED) */

{
    int i;

        /* Print the appropriate message */
    if (message == ORIGINAL)
        printf("\nThe original array is:\n");
    else
        printf("\nThe sorted array is:\n");

    for (i = 0; i < size; i++)
        printf("%d ", array[i]);
    printf("\n");
}

sort_array(array, size)
int array[], size;

/* Sort "array" of size "size" */

{
    int i, j;

    for (i = 0; i < size - 1; i++)
        for (j = i + 1; j < size; j++)
            if (array[i] > array[j])
                element_swap(array, i, j);
}

element_swap(array, i, j)
int array[], i, j;

/* Swap elements "i" and "j" of "array" */

{
    int temp = array[i];
    array[i] = array[j];
    array[j] = temp;
}
```

Program 11-5

```
How many numbers? 10
Please enter the integers:
10 42 7 0 923 13 -5 6 19 3

The original array is:
10 42 7 0 923 13 -5 6 19 3

The sorted array is:
-5 0 3 6 7 10 13 19 42 923
```

Output 11–5

Once again, the constant MAX_ARRAY_SIZE is defined to be 20. Two new constants, ORIGINAL and SORTED, are defined. These are called *flags* because they are used to signal a special condition, as will be explained shortly. ORIGINAL is set to 0, whereas SORTED is defined as 1. It is permissible to follow constant definitions with comments, as long as the entire comment fits on the **#define** line. (The reason for this restriction will be explained in Chapter 15.)

Passing by Value and Reference

Within the *main* function, the variable *numbers* is declared to be an integer array with space for MAX_ARRAY_SIZE elements. The actual number of elements stored in the array is specified by the value of *array_size*. This value is read in by the function *get_size*, which essentially is the same as the function of the same name in the previous version of the sorting program.

This program differs from the earlier version in two respects. First, *array_size* is passed by reference to the *get_size* function, meaning that its address is passed using the address operator, &. This allows the function to change the value of *array_size*. The alternative to passing by reference is called *passing by value*, in which only the value stored in the variable is passed.

The second difference between this version of *get_size* and the previous one also is related to the fact that *array_size* is passed by reference: In the *scanf* invocation within *get_size*, no address operator is used before the formal parameter *size*. This is because *size* already is pointing to the location where the value read in is to be stored. The C compiler will not alert you if you inadvertently use an address operator here (since that would be syntactically acceptable). The results produced would be incorrect, however, because the value read in would be assigned to *size* rather than **size*. Using an address operator here would be as disastrous as omitting it in the *scanf* calls we have shown previously.

The actual elements of the array are read in by invoking the function *get_array*. The address operator is not used with *array_size* this time (it is passed by value), since its value is not being modified by the function. The array *numbers* also is passed to the *get_array* function as the first parameter. In C, arrays always are passed by reference.

Notice how the dummy parameter *array*, corresponding to *numbers*, is declared in the function. When a dummy parameter corresponds to an array, it is not necessary to specify the array's size when declaring the dummy parameter. A set of empty square brackets may be written after the parameter's name. It is not necessary for the function to know the exact size of the array when it is written, so the function can be used without modification in different programs or with arrays of different sizes. It *is* necessary, however, for the function to know how many elements are stored in the array when the function is executed. That is why *array_size* is passed to the function and stored in the formal parameter *size*.

The formal parameter *array* could also have been declared as follows:

```
int *array;
```

since the address of an array is a pointer to its first element. Note that a declaration such as

```
int size, array[size];    /* illegal */
```

is illegal in C, because a variable (even a parameter) cannot be used to define the size of an array. It is not an error to declare *size* first, however, as in the following:

```
int size, array[];
```

The parameters of a function can be declared in any order, as long as they are specified in the correct order within the parentheses following the function name.

Address Arithmetic

The call to the *scanf* function in Program 11-5 contains an unusual expression:

```
array + i
```

This addition of a pointer and an integer is one of the few arithmetic operations allowed on pointers. It is not a case of mixed-mode, because the two operands are supposed to be of different types, and no casting is done.

When an integer is added to a pointer of any target type, the result is a pointer of the same target type as the pointer operand. The value is the pointer operand incremented by as many target units as indicated by the integer operand. As an illustration: If *p* is of type **int ***, and we write

```
p = array + 3;
```

p ends up pointing to the third **int** past the location pointed to by *array*. Since *array*, being the name of an array, points to the 0th element, the expression returns a pointer to the 3rd element. In other words, the above assignment is equivalent to

```
p = &array[3];
```

The pointer–integer addition version was used in Program 11-5 because it is more concise and direct. The expression

```
array + i;
```

is equivalent to

```
&array[i];
```

and

```
*(array+i);
```

is equivalent to

```
array[i];
```

This form of addition works with any array or pointer target type. If *array* were an array of type **char**, "*array* + 3" would return the value of *array* incremented by **3 chars**, which would still be equivalent to

```
&array[3];
```

Just as with regular addition, neither of the operands is changed by the operation.

Two more arithmetic operations are possible using pointers. One is the subtraction of an integer from a pointer. This operation decrements the pointer, just as addition increments it. If we write

```
p = array + 3;
```

and then follow it with the expression

```
p - 3
```

the same value as *array* is returned.

The third possible operation is the subtraction of a pointer from another pointer, which, as you may have guessed, returns an integer. The resulting value is the distance, expressed in target units, between the two pointers. For example, if *p* is assigned a value as shown above, the expression

```
p - array
```

returns the value 3. If *p* points to an element in an array, subtracting the address of the array from *p* yields the subscript of the element pointed to by *p*. The first pointer should always be greater than the second, meaning it should point to a memory location farther ahead than that pointed to by the second pointer. A pointer subtraction that yields a negative value does not work on some computers, but such a subtraction rarely is required.

The relational operators can also be used with pointers, but the < and > operators are meaningful only when both pointers point to elements within the same array.

In Program 11-5, the function *print_array* also has been modified. In the sort program of Chapter 10, the *print_array* function was used to print both the original and sorted versions of the array. A message was printed in the *main* function to indicate which version was being displayed. In the revised version, Program 11-5, these messages are instead printed in the *print_array* function itself. The *main* function passes a third parameter: a flag that indicates which version of the array is to be printed and, therefore, which message is appropriate. The flag is received in the dummy parameter *message*. A value of 0 indicates that the original array is being passed, and a value of 1 signifies that the sorted array is being passed. These flag values have been given the constant names ORIGINAL and SORTED to make it easier for readers to remember their meanings.

An **if** statement is used to determine which message is to be displayed, based on the value of *message*. Any value other than 0 (ORIGINAL) indicates a sorted array; since the *print_array* function may be modified later, however, the programmer should stick with the values ORIGINAL and SORTED. Finally, the array itself is printed. Notice that, as in the *get_array* function, the size of the array must be passed along with a pointer to the array.

The function *sort_array* in Program 11-5 is basically the same as in Program 10-10 except that, instead of exchanging the elements itself, it calls the function *element_swap* to do this. The function *element_swap* is slightly different from the *swap* function in Program 11-3. Instead of its parameters being pointers to the two elements to be swapped, one parameter points to the array, while the other two are the subscripts of the two elements to be swapped.

Words, like numbers, often are most useful when sorted. Since computers represent letters as numeric values, there is a direct correspondence between the processes of sorting numbers in ascending order and alphabetizing words. The ASCII value for 'z', for example, is greater than that for 'a', so a word starting with 'a' would be placed before one starting with 'z', provided that strings could be sorted like numbers.

Dealing with words, however, is a little more complicated in C than dealing with numbers. Entire strings can be read in and printed out, but they cannot be assigned to each other using a simple assignment statement. Thus the process of swapping strings is somewhat difficult. Even the process of comparing one string to another requires something more than an **if** statement.

Pointers and Two-Dimensional Arrays

An array of strings can be represented in C as a two-dimensional array of characters, as shown in Figure 11-4. Each row of the matrix represents a separate string.

row \ column	0	1	2	3	4	5	6	
0	'z'	'e'	'r'	'o'	'\0'			string 0
1	'o'	'n'	'e'	'\0'				string 1
2	't'	'w'	'o'	'\0'				string 2
3	't'	'h'	'r'	'e'	'e'	'\0'		string 3
4	'f'	'o'	'u'	'r'	'\0'			string 4

Figure 11–4

The name of a two-dimensional array in C is also evaluated as a pointer. The name of a matrix of type **char** is of type **char ***, and it points to the element in the 0th row and the 0th column. Since the type of an unsubscripted name of a two-dimensional array is the same as that of a one-dimensional array, it seems logical that the name of a two-dimensional array can be followed by a single subscript. This is in fact permissible in C. For example, if an array is declared as

```
char c[5][7];
```

then the expression

```
c[3]
```

is evaluated as a constant pointer to the first (0th) element of the fourth row (the row with subscript 3) of the matrix. This pointer may be interpreted as the name of a one-dimensional array of seven elements (the number of columns in matrix *c*). Like the name of an array, the name of a row of a two-dimensional array cannot be placed on the left side of an assignment operator. For example, using array *c* described above, it is not permissible to write the following:

```
c[3] = "abc";     /* illegal */
```

If the matrix *c* is being treated as an array of strings, using a single subscript allows the programmer to treat a string as a single array element. Thus, array *c* could be treated for most of the program as if it were a one-dimensional array with *c[3]* as its fourth element.

The switch Statement

Program 11-6 is used to sort an array of strings. It introduces a new feature of C called the **switch** statement, which we shall discuss before presenting the program.

The **switch** statement is in effect an extension of the familiar **if...else** statement. Rather than permitting a maximum of only two branches, the **switch** statement permits virtually any number of branches. The direction of the branch taken by the **switch** statement is based on the value of any **int** (or **int**-compatible) variable or expression. This variable or expression is placed in parentheses following the keyword **switch**.

For example, if the variable *n* is of type **int** and has already been assigned a value, one could write the following **switch** statement:

```
switch (n)
{
    case 0:
        printf("BASIC is easy\n");
        break;  /* "break" jumps out of the switch */
    case 1:
        printf("FORTRAN is fun\n");
        break;  /* "" */
    case 2:
        printf("Pascal may be structured\n");
        break;  /* "" */
    default:
        printf("But C is the one!\n");
}
```

The body of a **switch** statement is enclosed in braces. The form of the statement is unique. It consists of **case** labels, which take the form of the keyword **case** followed by a constant value. This value should be of the same type as the switch variable (or expression); it must be an **int** or **int**-compatible value (such as **long** or **char**). The **case** label is followed by a colon. The preceding example contains three **case** labels:

```
case 0:
case 1:
case 2:
```

Other possible **case** labels include the following:

```
case 4:
case BIG:     /* Assuming BIG has been defined as a constant */
case BIG+3:   /* Must evaluate to a constant at compile time */
```

The constants in the **case** labels need not be consecutive, nor must they be in any particular order. It is perfectly legal for a **switch** statement to have the following as labels:

```
case 9:
case 96:
case -4:
case 0:
```

If the switch variable were of type **char**, the **case** labels might include the following:

```
case 'a':
case 'a'+4:    /* Evaluates to the ASCII value of 'e' */
case 64:       /* Evaluates to the ASCII value of '@' */
case '\007':
```

The **case** labels usually are followed by C statements. The **switch** works as follows: When the statement is encountered, the **switch** variable or expression is evaluated to yield a specific value. Program control is transferred to the statement immediately following the **case** label whose constant is equal to the value of the **switch** variable or expression. This statement is executed, followed by all the succeeding statements in the body of the **switch** statement. These steps are illustrated in Figure 11-5:

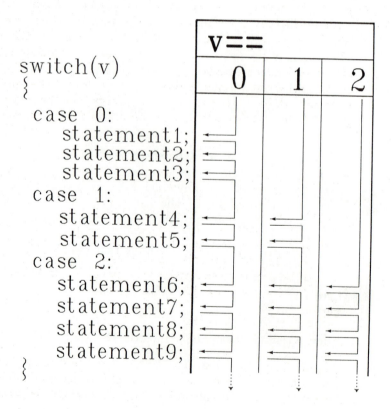

Figure 11—5

A special label, **default**, can also be used. It is a "catch-all" label to allow for the possibility that the value of the **switch** expression does not match any of the **case** labels. In such a situation, control transfers to the **default** label if it is present. If it is not present and there is no match, the entire **switch** statement is skipped.

The **default** label can be placed anywhere within the body of the **switch** statement; it need not be the last label. In fact, the labels of a **switch** statement can appear in any order, depending on the logic of the program.

In C, one is not restricted to a single statement for a given label. Any number of C statements can appear between two labels. If more than one statement follows a label, it is *not* necessary to group them together with curly brackets, although it is not an error to do so.

In the preceding example, the objective was to print one line, depending on the value of n, and to skip all other statements in the **switch** body. For that purpose, the **break** statement is permitted in a **switch** statement. This is one use of the **break** statement that does not violate the principles of structured programming.

When the **break** statement is encountered, the **switch** statement is terminated immediately, and any remaining statements in the body are ignored. (If the **switch** is nested within another **switch** or a loop, the outer **switch** or loop is not affected; only the one immediately containing the **break** statement is terminated.)

Assuming that the value of n is 2 in the preceding **switch** example shown above, control passes to the **case 2** label. The *printf* function is called, producing the following output:

```
Pascal may be structured
```

The next statement encountered is the **break**, which causes the **switch** to terminate. Execution resumes with the next statement (if any) following the **switch** statement.

If the **break** statements were omitted from this switch statement, execution would proceed as follows: After the *printf* function printed out the line about Pascal, the next statement encountered and executed would be the one following the **default** label. The output would be as follows:

```
Pascal may be structured
But C is the one!
```

Labels are not executable, so the fact that the **default** label comes between the two *printf* calls has no effect on program execution. The **default** label, or any label for that matter, does not prevent control from falling through to the remaining statements. After control branches to a label, all the statements following that label are executed, unless a **break** statement intervenes.

Often, it is desirable for several different values of the **switch** variable to cause execution of the *same* set of statements. This can be accomplished by including several labels in succession with no intervening statements, as in the following example:

```
switch (digit)
{
        case 0:
        case 1:
        case 2:
        case 3:
        case 4:
            printf("Round down\n");
            break;
        case 5:
        case 6:
        case 7:
        case 8:
        case 9:
            printf("Round up\n");
}
```

In this example, if *digit* has the value 0, 1, 2, 3, or 4, the first *printf* statement is executed. The rest of the **switch** statement is ignored, due to the **break** statement. If, however, the value of *digit* is 5, 6, 7, 8, or 9, the second *printf* is executed and the switch statement is terminated. No **break** is needed after the second *printf*, since there are no further instructions left to execute in the **switch** statement.

This example does not include a **default** label. This fact implies that the value of *digit* has been validated previously. If it were necessary to have a **default** label, it could be placed in either group of labels.

Program 11-6, which sorts an array of strings, starts out very much like the program for sorting an array of integers. One new constant is introduced: MAX_STRING_SIZE, which specifies the maximum number of characters in the strings (or the number of columns in the two-dimensional array of characters).

```
/* Sorting an array revisited:
   Two-dimensional char array (array of strings) */

    /* The array may have up to 20 elements */
#define MAX_ARRAY_SIZE 20
    /* Each string may have up to 10 characters */
#define MAX_STRING_SIZE 10

    /* Message flags for "print_array" */
#define ORIGINAL 0          /* Display original array */
#define SORTED   1          /* Display sorted array */

main()
{
    char words[MAX_ARRAY_SIZE][MAX_STRING_SIZE+1];      /* An array of strings */
    int array_size;                                     /* Actual number of
                                                           strings in array */
```

Program continued on next page

Program continued from previous page

```
/* Read in the array's size */

    get_size(&array_size);

    /* Read in the string array "words" of size "array_size" */

    get_array(words, array_size);

    /* Echo the array */

    print_array(words, array_size, ORIGINAL);

    sort_array(words, array_size);

    /* Print the sorted array */

    print_array(words, array_size, SORTED);
}


get_size(size)
int *size;

/* Read the size of the array into "*size" (until a valid value is entered) */

{
    do
    {
        printf("How many words? ");
        scanf("%d", size);
    }
    /* "*size" must be at least 1 and at most MAX_ARRAY_SIZE */
    while (*size < 1 || *size > MAX_ARRAY_SIZE);
}

get_array(array, size)
char array[][MAX_STRING_SIZE+1];
int size;

/* Read in the string array called "array" of size "size" */

{
    int i;

    printf("Please enter the words:\n");
    for (i = 0; i < size; i++)
        scanf("%s", array[i]);
}
```

Program continued on next page

Program continued from previous page

```
print_array(array, size, message)
char array[][MAX_STRING_SIZE+1];
int size, message;

/* Print out string array "array" of size "size".  "message" is a
   flag indicating which message to display (ORIGINAL or SORTED) */

{
    int i;
        /* Print the appropriate message */
    switch (message)
    {
        case ORIGINAL:
            printf("\nThe original array is:\n");
            break;
        case SORTED:
            printf("\nThe sorted array is:\n");
            break;
    }
    for (i = 0; i < size; i++)
        printf("%s\n", array[i]);
}

sort_array(array, size)
char array[][MAX_STRING_SIZE+1];
int size;

/* Sort string array "array" of size "size" */
{
    int i, j;
    for (i = 0; i < size - 1; i++)
        for (j = i + 1; j < size; j++)
            if (bigger(array[i], array[j]))
                string_swap(array[i], array[j]);
}
bigger(a,b)
char *a, *b;

/* Return true if string a is "greater" than string b */

{
    int i;
    for (i = 0; a[i] != 0 && b[i] != 0 && a[i] == b[i]; i++);
    return(a[i] > b[i]);
}

string_swap(string1, string2)
char *string1, *string2;

/* Swap two strings, character by character */

{
    int i;
    char temp;

    for (i = 0; i <= MAX_STRING_SIZE; i++)
    {
        temp = string1[i];
        string1[i] = string2[i];
        string2[i] = temp;
    }
}
```

Program 11-6

```
How many words? 8
Please enter the words:
cat
pig
dog
earlobe
bingo
elbow
likely
radar

The original array is:
cat
pig
dog
earlobe
bingo
elbow
likely
radar

The sorted array is:
bingo
cat
dog
earlobe
elbow
likely
pig
radar
```

Output 11—6

The *main* function looks almost the same as the one for sorting integers, except that the array *words* is declared as a two-dimensional array of type **char**. (Notice that the number of columns is one more than MAX_STRING_SIZE, to allow room for the terminating '\0'.) The *get_size* function contains no new features.

In the *get_array* function, the *array* parameter is declared as a two-dimensional array. This must be done, even though the array is being treated as a one-dimensional array of strings, so that C can interpret the subscripts correctly. Notice that, although the first (row) subscript is empty, the second (column) subscript must be specified explicitly. When multi-dimensional array parameters are declared, only the first subscript can be left empty. This limitation is also required so that subscripts can be handled correctly. The function is therefore less general than might be desired, but a solution to this problem will be presented shortly.

When the words are entered, they must be separated from each other by a carriage return, spaces, or some other form of white space. Notice that the *scanf* function is passed a pointer to a single row of the array.

In the function *print_array*, the *message* parameter again is used to specify which descriptive message should be displayed before the contents of the array. On this occasion, a **switch** statement is used. A **switch** statement often is used where a nested **if** would otherwise be required, specifically when each **else** clause consists of another **if** statement. This equivalence can be seen by comparing the nested **if** in Program 11-5 with the **switch** statement that replaces it in this program. The **switch** statement employed here hardly seems worth the rewrite, but its advantage is that, if more message options were to be added later, the program could easily be modified by expanding the **switch** statement.

The *printf* function is passed a pointer to the string being displayed. Pointers always are used in connection with the *scanf* function, but the *printf* function usually does not use them, since it does not change any of its parameters. As indicated previously, however, an array cannot be physically passed by value; it can only be passed by reference. Therefore, when the *printf* function finds a %s conversion specification in the control string, it assumes that the corresponding parameter is not the value to be printed, but rather a pointer to the string.

The function *sort_array* is deceptively short, because it uses the function *bigger* to compare two strings and the function *string_swap* to exchange two strings.

The function *bigger* is the counterpart to the > operator used to compare two integers in the number sorting program. It returns *true* if the first string passed to it is "greater" than the second one, but this is not just a question of size. If, for example, the second string is longer than the first, and contains the first string as its initial portion, as shown here:

```
lever
leverage
```

then the second string is considered bigger than the first, and the function will return *false*. If, however, the first string starts with a higher letter (one with a greater ASCII value) than the second string, as here:

```
radar
lever
```

then regardless of the sizes of the two strings, the first one will be considered "bigger" than the second. The function *bigger* returns *true* if its two parameters are not in alphabetical order. Its first parameter should come after the second in an ascending alphabetic sort.

The function *bigger* works as follows: The **for** loop increments the parameters *a* and *b* (if necessary) until they point to corresponding positions in the two words containing unequal characters. (Incrementing the dummy arguments will not affect the strings being pointed to. It will, however, prevent the function from finding the beginnings of the strings again.) For example, given the following words:

```
table
tabulate
```

pointers *a* and *b* would both be incremented until *a* points to the *l* in *table* and *b* points to the *u* in *tabulate*. These are the first columns in which the letters of the two words differ. The returned value then depends on whether or not the ASCII value of the character pointed to by *a* is greater than the ASCII value of the character pointed to by b.

The **for** loop will also terminate if it encounters the *null* character marking the end of one or both of the strings. This happens if the two strings are identical, or if one string contains the other as its initial portion (like lever and leverage). The correct result still is produced. In the first case, both pointers point to *null* characters, which are equal; in the second case, the shorter string's pointer will point to a *null* character which has a value smaller than that of any other character.

The function *string_swap* differs from the swap function in Program 11-5 in that it takes as parameters pointers to the two strings to be exchanged, rather than a pointer to the whole array and two indices. An entire array cannot be assigned all at once, so a loop is used to exchange one element at a time. The loop is very simple but not very general, because it uses the value of MAX_STRING_SIZE. Besides swapping the strings themselves, it also swaps the unused trailing elements of the rows containing the strings. This is perfectly acceptable under the circumstances, since it is a small price to pay for the simplicity it affords.

If the function were really general, however, it would allow for the possibility of its two strings residing in different arrays with different numbers of columns. One proper method of making the exchange would be to exchange corresponding elements until a *null* character is encountered, and then move the remaining characters of the longer string into the other string. Both arrays containing the strings would need enough columns to hold the longer of the two strings.

Another acceptable method would be to declare a local array *temp*. Three loops would perform the following actions: (1) copy the entire first string into *temp* (only up to the *null* character); (2) copy the second string into the first; and (3) copy *temp* into the second string. This solution would require that *temp* be dimensioned to some maximum possible size, which could be considered a violation of the generality principle.

The C standard library contains functions to perform comparisons and assignments of strings. These functions will be described in the next chapter.

Arrays of Pointers, and Pointers to Pointers

As Program 11-6 demonstrated, sorting strings is no trivial task. In order to exchange two character strings, each element of each string must be manipulated individually. The computer does all this work, but this translates directly into computer time. Cost and delays due to processing time often are important considerations.

One way to minimize the amount of data swapping required when sorting an array of strings (and thereby minimizing execution time) is to use an array of pointers. Since pointers are treated by C as just another data type, it is perfectly permissible to have an array of pointers. The following declaration creates an array named *point* containing ten elements, each of which is of type **int ***:

```
int *point[10];
```

The name of the array, *point*, written without a subscript, is interpreted by C as a constant of type **int ****, or a "pointer to pointer to **int**." C allows for pointers to pointers, pointers to pointers to pointers, and so forth.

If one were to write:

```
int **point;
```

this would declare a variable of type **int ****, but it would not set aside space for an array. Similarly the statement

```
int *array;
```

does not allocate an array of integers.

Figure 11-6 shows how an array of pointers works:

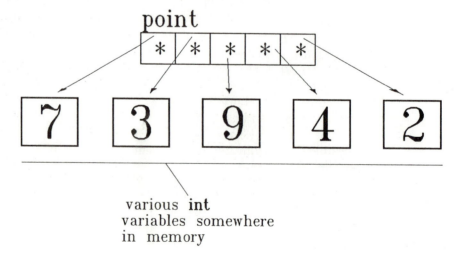

various **int**
variables somewhere
in memory

Figure 11—6

The element *point[0]* is itself a pointer. To access the memory location to which it refers, it is necessary to write

```
*point[0]
```

Since subscripting has a higher precedence than indirection, the preceding expression is evaluated as

```
*(point[0])
```

This is in contrast to

```
(*point)[0]
```

which refers to "the zeroth element of the array pointed to by *point*." This, in turn, really means "the zeroth element of the array pointed to by the pointer pointed to by *point*," which happens to be the same location as **point*.

If this seems somewhat confusing, keep track of the depth of the pointers in question. In other words, be sure you understand whether you are dealing with type **int *** or type **int **** or even type **int *****. Also remember that a subscript adds one more level of indirection. In other words, *a[i]* is the same as **(a+i)*.

Sorting by Pointer

One advantage of pointers is that, instead of having to move a data item around in memory, one can just move the pointer to the item in question.

If an array contains pointers to values to be sorted, then instead of exchanging the values, the programmer need only exchange the pointers. Since all pointers are of the same size, regardless of the sizes of the items to which they point, this feature allows voluminous data, such as long strings, to be sorted with a minimum of effort. (Such a sort is also called an *index sort*.)

In the following program, the concept of sorting by pointers is introduced with a simple example, in which an array of integer numbers is sorted into ascending order using the exchange sort. The program also demonstrates another advantage of sorting by pointers: If the original numbers are placed in an array, and the elements of the array are pointed to by the elements of a pointer array, then one can display the sorted array as well as the numbers in their original unsorted order (since the integer array containing the actual values is never rearranged).

```
/* Sorting an array revisited:    Sorting by pointer */

    /* The array may have up to 20 elements */
#define MAX_ARRAY_SIZE 20

main()
{
    int i;

    int numbers[MAX_ARRAY_SIZE],        /* An array of integers */
        *pointers[MAX_ARRAY_SIZE],      /* Pointer array, points to elements of
                                           "numbers" */
        array_size;                     /* Actual number of integers in array */

    /* Read in the array's size */

    get_size(&array_size);

    /* A pointer to each element of "numbers" is assigned to the
       corresponding element of pointer array "pointers" */

    for (i = 0; i < array_size; i++)
        pointers[i] = &numbers[i];

    /* Read values into locations pointed to by elements of array "pointers" */

    get_array(pointers, array_size);

    /* Sort the array first */

    pointer_sort(pointers, array_size);

    /* Echo the original array */

    print_original(numbers, array_size);

    /* Print the sorted array */

    print_sorted(pointers, array_size);
}


get_size(size)
int *size;

/* Read the size of the array into "*size" (until a valid value is entered) */

{
    do
    {
        printf("How many numbers? ");
        scanf("%d", size);
    }
    /* "*size" must be at least 1 and at most MAX_ARRAY_SIZE */
    while (*size < 1 || *size > MAX_ARRAY_SIZE);
}

get_array(array, size)
int *array[], size;
```

Program continued on next page

Program continued from previous page

```
/* Read in the array called "array" of size "size" */

{
    int i;

    printf("Please enter the integers:\n");
    for (i = 0; i < size; i++)
        scanf("%d", array[i]);
}

pointer_sort(array, size)
int *array[], size;

/* Sort "array" of size "size" by pointer */

{
    int i, j;

    for (i = 0; i < size - 1; i++)
        for (j = i + 1; j < size; j++)
            if (*array[i] > *array[j])
            {
                /* Swap elements "i" and "j" of "array" */

                int *temp = array[i];
                array[i] = array[j];
                array[j] = temp;
            }
}

print_original(array, size)
int array[], size;

/* Print out the original array "array" of size "size", on a single line */

{
    int i;

    printf("\nThe original array is:\n");

    for (i = 0; i < size; i++)
        printf("%d ", array[i]);
    printf("\n");
}

print_sorted(array, size)
int *array[], size;

/* Print out the numbers pointed to by the elements of array "array" of size
   "size", on a single line.  These numbers form a sorted array. */

{
    int i;

    printf("\nThe sorted array is:\n");

    for (i = 0; i < size; i++)
        printf("%d ", *array[i]);
    printf("\n");
}
```

Program 11—7

```
How many numbers? 10
Please enter the integers:
10 42 7 0 923 13 -5 6 19 3

The original array is:
10 42 7 0 923 13 -5 6 19 3

The sorted array is:
-5 0 3 6 7 10 13 19 42 923
```

Output 11-7

In Program 11-7, the maximum dimension for the array is restricted to 20. As was mentioned earlier, however, this can be changed at the discretion of the programmer. In the *main* function, two arrays are declared. One of them, *numbers*, with dimension MAX_ARRAY_SIZE, holds the actual integer values to be sorted. The other array, *pointers*, is an array of type **int ***, which is used to hold the pointers to the values. (It is also dimensioned to MAX_ARRAY_SIZE elements, because there must be one pointer per item of data.) The variable *array_size* is used to hold the number of elements actually used when the program is run.

As in most of our previous sorting programs, the *get_size* function is called to read in a value for *array_size*. After that, however, a **for** loop is executed. This loop assigns to each element of array *pointers* the address of its corresponding element in the array *numbers*. It is not necessary for a variable or array element to be initialized in order for its address to be assigned to a pointer variable or array element.

C allows the array *pointers* to be initialized upon declaration instead of resorting to a loop. It is legal to write a declaration of the following form:

```
int *pointers[] =
    {
        &numbers[1],
        &numbers[2],
              .
              .
              .
    };
```

The disadvantage of this form is that it is necessary to write as many address values as there are elements in the array. Since it is not known in advance how many elements are needed, all the array locations must be initialized. Therefore, in such a case, use of a loop is the preferred method.

The function *get_array* is called next in the program, but it is passed array *pointers* instead of the array that contains the integers. Thus the function has been modified so that it declares parameter *array* to be of type **int ***. The *scanf* statement also has been modified, so that the element *array[i]* is not preceded by the address operator. As we stated previously, *scanf* requires parameters that are pointers to the locations into which it is to read data. Since *array[i]* is itself a pointer, using the & operator would cause the integer to be read into *pointers[i]* rather than *numbers[i]* where it belongs.

Before the array is printed at all, the sort function *pointer_sort* is called, again with *pointers* rather than *numbers* as the first parameter. In the **if** statement, the integers themselves are compared, so the indirection operator must be applied to the array elements. The corresponding pointers (rather than the integers) are exchanged when two elements of the array have to be swapped, so the indirection operator is not used. This difference is illustrated in Figure 11-7.

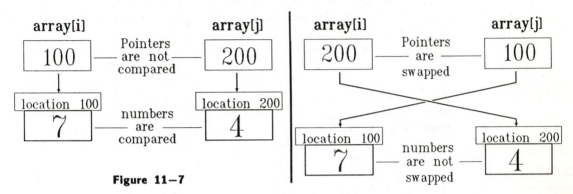

Figure 11—7

In the *pointer_sort* function, the temporary variable *temp* is declared to be a pointer to **int**.

After the numbers are sorted by pointer, both the original array and the sorted array are displayed. Two separate functions are required, since one is passed the array *numbers* (of type **int**) as a parameter and the second is passed *pointers* (of type **int ***). The integers in array *numbers* are still in their original order, even after their corresponding pointers have been rearranged. The pointers in array *pointers*, however, have been sorted as shown in Figure 11-8.

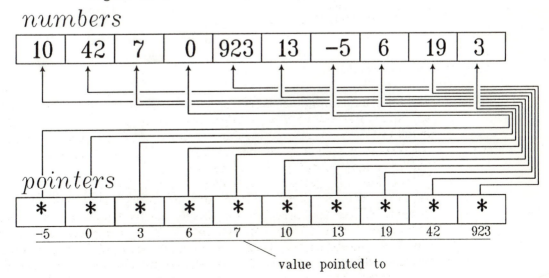

Figure 11—8

The differences between the functions *print_original* and *print_sorted* are:

1. Their explanatory messages are different.
2. The *print_original* function declares its parameter *array* to be an array of integers, whereas *print_sorted* declares *array* to be an array of pointers to integers.
3. The *print_original* function prints *array[i]*, whereas *print_sorted* prints **array[i]*.

Sorting a String Array by Pointer

Now that the concept of sorting by pointer has been introduced, we will explain how to sort strings by pointer. Assume we have two arrays:

```
char strings[5][10];
char *point[5];
```

If we were to write

```
for (i = 0; i < 5; i++)
    point[i] = strings[i];
```

which assigns to each element of *point* a pointer to its corresponding row of *strings*, then we could refer to the fourth row (subscript 3) of array *strings* as either

```
strings[3]
```

or

```
point[3]
```

In other words, the fact that *strings* is an array of strings, whereas *point* is an array of pointers to strings, makes little difference. Similarly, one could refer to the fifth character (subscript 4) of the fourth row of *strings* as either

```
strings[3][4]
```

or

```
point[3][4]
```

Since *point[3]* is a pointer, and every pointer can be subscripted, *point[3][4]* refers to the fourth character from the location to which *point[3]* points. This fact is illustrated in Figure 11-9.

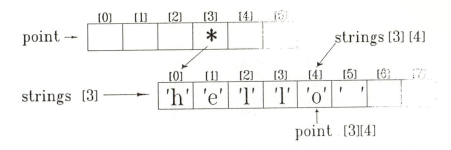

Figure 11—9

In case you are wondering how C can tell the difference between a subscripted pointer (as in *point[3][4]*) and a reference to an element of a two-dimensional array (such as *strings[3][4]*), remember that the two arrays are declared differently.

Much of the preceding discussion applies to Program 11-8. It differs from the previous program in that, instead of sorting an array of integers by pointer, it sorts a string array into ascending order.

```
/* Sorting an array revisited:    Sorting a string array by pointer */

    /* The array may have up to 20 elements */
#define MAX_ARRAY_SIZE 20
    /* Each string may have up to 10 characters */
#define MAX_STRING_SIZE 10

    /* Message flags for "print_array" */
#define ORIGINAL 0        /* Display original array */
#define SORTED   1        /* Display sorted array */

main()
{
    int i;

    char words[MAX_ARRAY_SIZE][MAX_STRING_SIZE+1];    /* An array of strings */
    char *pointers[MAX_ARRAY_SIZE];      /* Pointer array, points to rows in
                                            "words" ("pointers[n]" is the same as
                                            "words[n]") */
    int array_size;                      /* Actual number of strings in array */

    /* Read in the array's size */

    get_size(&array_size);

    /* Read in the string array "words" of size "array_size" */

    get_array(words, array_size);
```

Program continued on next page

Program continued from previous page

```
    /* A pointer to each string in "words" is assigned to the
       corresponding element of pointer array "pointers" */

    for (i = 0; i < array_size; i++)
        pointers[i] = words[i];

    /* Echo the original array */

    print_array(pointers, array_size, ORIGINAL);

    pointer_sort(pointers, array_size);

    /* Print the sorted array */

    print_array(pointers, array_size, SORTED);
}


get_size(size)
int *size;

/* Read the size of the array into "*size" (until a valid value is entered) */

{
    do
    {
        printf("How many words? ");
        scanf("%d", size);
    }
    /* "*size" must be at least 1 and at most MAX_ARRAY_SIZE */
    while (*size < 1 || *size > MAX_ARRAY_SIZE);
}

get_array(array, size)
char array[][MAX_STRING_SIZE+1];
int size;

/* Read in the string array called "array" of size "size" */

{
    int i;

    printf("Please enter the words:\n");
    for (i = 0; i < size; i++)
        scanf("%s", array[i]);
}


print_array(array, size, message)
char *array[MAX_ARRAY_SIZE];
int size, message;
```

Program continued on next page

Program continued from previous page

```
/* Print out string array "array" of size "size".  "message" is a
   flag indicating which message to display (ORIGINAL or SORTED) */

{
    int i;

        /* Print the appropriate message */
    switch (message)
    {
        case ORIGINAL:
            printf("\nThe original array is:\n");
            break;
        case SORTED:
            printf("\nThe sorted array is:\n");
            break;
    }

    for (i = 0; i < size; i++)
        printf("%s\n", array[i]);
}


pointer_sort(array, size)
char *array[MAX_ARRAY_SIZE];
int size;

/* Sort string array "array" of size "size" by pointer */

{
    int i, j;

    for (i = 0; i < size - 1; i++)
        for (j = i + 1; j < size; j++)
            if (bigger(array[i], array[j]))
            {
                /* Swap strings "i" and "j" of "array" by pointer */

                char *temp = array[i];
                array[i] = array[j];
                array[j] = temp;
            }
}

bigger(a,b)
char *a, *b;

/* Return true if string a is "greater" than string b */

{
    int i;

    for (i = 0; a[i] != 0 && b[i] != 0 && a[i] == b[i]; i++);

    return(a[i] > b[i]);
}
```

Program 11–8

```
How many words? 8
Please enter the words:
cat
pig
dog
earlobe
bingo
elbow
likely
radar

The original array is:
cat
pig
dog
earlobe
bingo
elbow
likely
radar

The sorted array is:
bingo
cat
dog
earlobe
elbow
likely
pig
radar
```

Output 11—8

Much of the program probably looks familiar. Once again, the array to be sorted has a maximum size of 20 elements (rows), and each string element within the array has a maximum of 10 characters. The flag constants ORIGINAL and SORTED have been resurrected from previous programs, as we are returning to the method of using a single function to print both the original array and the sorted array.

In the *main* function, the array *words* is declared as a two-dimensional array to hold the strings. The pointer array *pointers* is declared to provide pointers to the rows of the array *words*. The variable *array_size* is declared to hold the count of the number of elements contained in the arrays.

After the value of *array_size* is read in by the *get_size* function, the strings are read into the array *words* by the *get_array* function. At this point, the array *pointers* is set to point to the rows of *words* with the aid of a **for** loop. The array is echoed before it is sorted, by means of a call to the *print_array* function. The array *pointers* is passed by reference to this function. It would be erroneous to pass *words* as a parameter, because the formal parameter *array* is declared as an array of pointers, not as a two-dimensional array. The value ORIGINAL also is passed as a flag, to indicate which of the two messages is to be displayed by the function.

Next, the array is sorted by pointer. The sorting function is similar to the one used in the previous program, except a special boolean function is called to compare the two strings. This function, *bigger*, is identical to the one used in Program 11-6.

Finally, the sorted array is displayed by another call to *print_array*. This time, the flag SORTED is used.

Now that we have covered the concepts of arrays and pointers, it is possible to discuss strings and string variables in full detail. The following chapter contains a thorough exposition of the uses of strings in C.

The Spirit of C

The C language is adequate for applications involving mathematical calculations, but it offers little in that area that is not available in other computer languages. C's strength lies in its ability to operate close to the fundamentals of the computer, and this is perhaps most useful in the area of symbol manipulation.

One such application is the manipulation of words, as in understanding human language. Such programs are too complex to be presented in this book, but we will present one mechanism that is useful in the handling of words and sentences. The program will be developed in steps through each of the remaining chapters in this book, as more features of the C language are introduced.

Consider the following program: A sentence is typed in by the user. The program separates the words from the punctuation, and stores the words as an array of strings, so that the individual words can be manipulated. We propose that the sentence be divided into a subject and a predicate. Normally this would be a very difficult task, but we will make a few assumptions about the sentences submitted to the program: The subject will never end in an *s*, will always be singular third person, and the verb will be in the present tense, therefore ending with an *s*. For example, the sentence

The cat eats the dog.

could be input to the program. The program would look for the first word ending in an *s*, in this case the word *eats*. The output would be

subject: The cat
predicate: eats the dog

We can begin thinking of what functions are needed by the program:

1) *find_verb*, to return the position of the verb in the array of words.

2) *is_verb*, a boolean function to return the value *true* if the word passed to it is a verb (ends in *s*).

3) *store_word*, to store a string in the string array.

4) *filter*, to which will be passed a character and a string. If the character is a letter or number (we will allow numbers as words), it is appended to the end of the string. Otherwise, the character is ignored. A value is returned by the function to let the calling function know what action *filter* has taken.

5) *process_input*, to read in the sentence character by character, and to call *filter* to process the character. This function must also assemble the words, calling *store_word* when the end of a word is reached.

6) *divide_sentence*, to find the verb, split the sentence into subject and predicate, and output the two parts of the sentence.

It is also desirable to decide what major variables are needed by the program:

1) *word_list*, the array of strings to hold the words from the sentence.

2) *word_count*, to hold the number of words in *word_list*

3) *word*, to hold the word currently being assembled by *process_input*.

4) *word_length*, the number of characters in *word*.

5) *verb_location*, the index of the verb in *word_list*.

6) *current_character*, the character that was just read in.

These variables are not necessarily global, and in fact they can be declared as local variables in several different functions. When the same local variable name is used by several functions, all the variables should be used for the same purpose.

Many of the operations in this program will be simplified once the material in the next chapter has been covered. Until then, however, we can make do with what we have.

Here is the function *find_verb*:

```
find_verb(word_list, word_count)
char word_list[][MAX_WORD_LEN + 1];    /* String array containing words */
int word_count;                        /* Number of words (strings) in
                                          "word_list" */

/* Search for the verb in "word_list", return the index of the verb
   or -1 if no verb found */

{

    int i;
```

Program continued on next page

Program continued from previous page

```
    /* Loop until either i == word_count (meaning the end of the
       list has been reached), or is_verb(word_list[i]) (meaning the
       current word is a verb) */

    for (i = 0; i < word_count && !is_verb(word_list[i]); i++);

    /* Did the loop stop because of the end of the list or because
       a verb was found? */

    if (i == word_count)    /* End of list */
        return(-1);         /* Return error code -- no verb found */

    else                    /* Verb found */
        return(i);          /* Return index of verb */

}
```

We must remember to define MAX_WORD_LEN, a constant specifying the row width in *word_list*, which is a two-dimensional character array.

Examine the test expression in the **for** loop. A condition is tested only up to the point where failure is detected. That is, if the test (i < word_count) fails, the second half of the expression is not evaluated, so the function call

```
is_verb(word_list[i])
```

is never made when *i* equals *word_count*.

The function *is_verb* must locate the end of the word. It searches for the terminating *null* character and then backs up by one character to the end of the string:

```
is_verb(word)
char word[];

/* Returns true if the last character in "word" is a letter "s". That
   means "word" is a verb. */

{
    int i;

    /* Locate end of word (loop while word[i] != 0) */

    for (i = 0; word[i]; i++);

    /* Now "i" is the index of the terminating null character,
       so "i - 1" is the last non-null character */

    return (word[i - 1] == 's');   /* Returns the result of the test */
}
```

In order to avoid the need for *word_count* to be global, it must be passed to *store_word*. Actually, *word_count* must be passed by reference, because it must be incremented after the new word is stored:

```
store_word(word, word_list, word_count)
char word[],                          /* Word to be stored */
     word_list[][MAX_WORD_LEN + 1];   /* String array containing words */
int *word_count;                      /* Number of words (strings) in
                                         "word_list" */

/* Store "word" in the next free row of "word_list". The next available
   index  is in "word_count", which is incremented by one after the word
   is stored. */
{
    int i;
    /* Assign characters from "word" to "word_list[*word_count]"
       until a null is assigned */
    for (i = 0; (word_list[*word_count][i] = word[i]); i++);

    (*word_count)++;
}
```

Notice the test used in the **for** loop. Again the loop is
terminated when *word[i]* is the *null* character, but the test is
made only after the assignment, so the *null* character is copied
into *word_list*. Compare that loop with the following:

```
for (i = 0; word[i]; i++)
    word_list[*word_count][i] = word[i];
```

Now comes the *filter* function, which is no more complicated
than any of the preceding functions:

```
filter(current_character, word, word_length)
char current_character,    /* Character to be tested */
     word[];               /* String to which the character is to be
                              appended, if the character is a letter
                              or digit */
int *word_length;          /* Length of "word" */

/* Test "current_character". If it is a letter or digit, append it
   to "word", otherwise ignore  it. Return  0 if the character is
   ignored, 1  if  it  is  appended. The variable "word_length" is
   incremented if the character is appended */

{
    if (current_character >= '0' && current_character <= '9'
        || current_character >= 'A' && current_character <= 'Z'
        || current_character >= 'a' && current_character <= 'z')

    /* Append it to the word */

    {
        /* "word_length" is the next available index. Notice that it
           is postincremented */

        word[(*word_length)++] = current_character;
        return(1);
    }

    else

    /* Ignore it */

    return(0);

}
```

With the function *process_input*, we begin to tie everything together. Our trailer character for the input is simply a period:

```
process_input(word_list, word_count)
char word_list[][MAX_WORD_LEN + 1];    /* String array containing words */
int *word_count;                        /* Number of words (strings) in
                                           "word_list" */

/* The input is a sentence, terminated by a period. Characters are
   read in from the input and grouped into words. The words are
   stored in "word_list". */

{
    char word[MAX_WORD_LEN + 1],   /* Holds the word currently being
                                       assembled */
        current_character;          /* The character that was just
                                       read in */
    int word_length = 0,            /* The number of characters
                                       in "word" */
        i;                          /* Return code from filter (1 if
                                       a letter or digit was processed,
                                       0 otherwise) */

    *word_count = 0;       /* Clear the word list */

    printf("Please enter a sentence (terminated by a period):\n");

    do                              /* Process characters */
    {
        scanf("%c", &current_character);

        /* Process character, adding it to "word" if it is a letter
           or digit (filter returns 1 in that case, 0 otherwise) */

        i = filter(current_character, word, &word_length);

        /* If the character is not a letter or digit (i == 0),
           and if there is a word in "word" (word_length > 0),
           then the end of a word has just been passed. In
           that case, store "word" in "word_list" */

        if (i == 0 && word_length > 0)
        {
            store_word(word, word_list, &word_count);
            word_length = 0;    /* Clear out "word" */
        }
    }
    while (current_character != '.');  /* End after the period has been processed */

}
```

Notice the use of a **do...while** loop. It ensures that the loop terminates only after the period is processed. When the period is read in, the last word is stored and the loop ends. If a loop structure were used which terminated as soon as the period was read in, then the last word would not be stored. An extra statement would be needed to store it.

Since the input must consist of at least one character, it is safe to process the first character before any test is made. At worst, if the input consists of only one character, that character is ignored. Remember, however, that the program will keep waiting for input until a period is entered.

Next comes the function *divide_sentence*. It is presented with a completed word list, which it processes:

```
divide_sentence(word_list, word_count)
char word_list[][MAX_WORD_LEN + 1];     /* String array containing words */
int word_count;                         /* Number of words (strings) in
                                           "word_list" */

/* Locate the verb in "word_list", and output the sentence with the
   subject (all words before the verb) on the first line and the
   predicate (the verb and all following words) on the second */

{
    int verb_location,      /* Index of verb in "word_list" */
        i;                  /* Loop index */

    /* "find_verb" returns the index of the verb, -1 if no verb
       is found */

    verb_location = find_verb(word_list, word_count);

    if (verb_location >= 0)      /* Verb was found */
    {
        printf("\nsubject:     ");
        for (i = 0; i < verb_location; i++)
            printf("%s ", word_list[i]);

        printf("\npredicate:  ");
        for (i = verb_location; i < word_count; i++)
            printf("%s ", word_list[i]);
        printf("\n\n");
    }

    else                          /* No verb */
        printf("\nThat sentence has no verb!\n\n");

}
```

Notice that, if the sentence has no subject (no words before the verb), the subject line is empty.

Finally, we can write the *main* function:

```
/* This program reads in sentences, locates their verbs, and displays the
   subject and predicate (without punctuation) on separate lines. The
   sentences must be in the present tense, with singular, third-person
   subjects. Based on these criteria, a verb is defined as any word that
   ends with an "s" */

   /* Maximum number of words that can be stored in "word_list": */
#define MAX_WORDS 50
   /* Maximum number of characters per word: */
#define MAX_WORD_LEN 20
```

Program continued on next page

Program continued from previous page

```
main()
{
    char word_list[MAX_WORDS][MAX_WORD_LEN + 1],    /* String array
                                              containing words */
         reply[10];           /* Holds user reply to "Another?" query */
    int word_count;           /* Number of words (strings) in "word_list" */

    do
    {
        process_input(word_list, &word_count);

        divide_sentence(word_list, word_count);

        printf("Another (y/n)? ");
        scanf("%9s", reply);
    }
        /* Repeat until user says "n" */
    while (reply[0] == 'y' || reply[0] == 'Y');

}
```

Perhaps a test should be added to make sure that neither MAX_WORDS nor MAX_WORD_LEN is exceeded. The values of these constants are large enough, however, that this probably will not happen.

Throughout the program, if a function requires a parameter to be passed by reference, the calling function uses the & operator in the actual parameter (unless an array is being passed). You must be very careful not to pass by reference when a value is expected or vice versa. That is a major source of error in C programming.

It is left up to the reader to assemble and test this program.

Programming and Debugging *Hints*

The abundance of C operators, each with its own syntax, sometimes can lead to confusion on the part of the programmer. For example, a novice programmer can easily forget whether the expression

```
*p++
```

is evaluated as

```
*(p++)
```

or

```
(*p)++
```

The precedence and associativity rules of C, as illustrated in Appendix A, specify that the first interpretation is correct. If a programmer is unsure, parentheses should be used.

The forgiving nature of most C compilers often makes it possible for programmers to commit errors they would not have made otherwise. For example, suppose p is a pointer to an **int** and i is an **int** variable. The programmer intends to assign $*p$ to i, but accidentally omits the $*$ and instead assigns the pointer p to the integer variable i. C compilers allow this, some without even displaying a warning. As a result, the unfortunate programmer may have to spend a long time tracking down this single mistake.

Usually, very little can be done to remedy this situation. There is, however, a program called *lint* which can be found on most computers running the UNIX operating system. This program does not compile a C source program, but rather examines it for adherence to a strict version of the semantic rules of C (it "picks lint" out of the program). For example, it requires cast operators to be used anywhere data types are mixed (as when pointers are assigned to integer variables, or when integers are assigned to floating point variables). Whenever *lint* detects a violation of its rules, it displays a message describing the location and nature of the problem. The *lint* program helps the programmer to get into the habit of using pristine code that is easier for the human reader to understand. Unfortunately, however, not too many C compilers for microcomputers come with the *lint* program.

The C compiler does not automatically check whether the correct number of parameters is being passed to a function, even if the calling and called functions are defined in the same program file. It is therefore easier to pass the wrong number of arguments to a C function than to make the same error in Pascal. This error is probably easiest to detect when it occurs in conjunction with the *printf* function, because the mistake can be seen clearly from the output.

Neither does the C compiler automatically check for the data types of parameters, so a common error that is not flagged by the compiler is the omission of the address operator (&) before a variable name in a call to *scanf*. To the compiler, *scanf* is just another function, so any sort of parameter is acceptable. Very often, especially on larger computers, the omission of the address operator, or of an entire argument to *scanf*, results in the function attempting to store a value at a nonexistent address. This often leads to a runtime error generated by the operating system, which usually says something about an illegal address or a segmentation error, but is never very clear in terms of the cause of the error. This message also will occur when a value other than a true address is stored inadvertently in a pointer variable.

It is also an error to use the address operator when it should not be used, such as when a pointer variable is used as an argument to *scanf*. If the address operator is placed before the pointer variable, the program will not crash immediately, but the input value will be stored in the pointer variable rather than at the location the variable was pointing to. This error may later cause the program to crash when the pointer variable is used. A similar problem may arise if the indirection operator (*) is omitted before a pointer variable when indirection is called for.

C *Tutorial*

1. What numeric value is associated with every memory location?

2. How are variable names translated to their corresponding addresses?

3. Why is it desirable in C to be able to refer to a particular memory location by its address?

4. Why is it necessary to distinguish between a variable's address and the contents of that location?

5. What can be said about the addresses of all the variables in a program?

6. Why can a function refer to a local variable in another function only by its address?

7. What must be done to a pointer variable before it can be put to use?

8. Why is it preferable to pass the address of a local variable for the purpose of communication between functions, as opposed to using a global variable?

9. What is the role played by the & operator in a call to the *scanf* function?

10. What are the restrictions regarding the use of the & operator?

11. Can addresses be stored? If so, where?

12. What are the effects of the following C declarations?

    (a) `int *x;`
    (b) `int *y;`
    (c) `int z;`
    (d) `int p, *p, q, *q;`
    (e) `int x, *y = &x;`

13. What are the meanings of the following assignment statements?

    (a) `q = &r;`
    (b) `s = &t;`

14. Are the following statements legal? If so, explain their meanings.

    (a) `m = (char *)&n;`
    (b) `o = (float *)&p;`

15. Complete the following sentence:

    Once the address of the integer variable *m* has been assigned to the pointer variable *n*, *n* may be used...

16. What is the indirection operator, and what role does it play?

17. Since memory addresses are merely integers on most computers, in what sense are they different from integers in C?

18. What is meant by *passing by reference*?

19. What is the fundamental difference between passing by value and passing by reference?

20. When a function is written to swap the values of two variables, what special provisions must be made?

21. In what ways are arrays and pointers involved with each other?

22. Why isn't the & operator used with array names in a *scanf* statement?

23. If *ary* is the name of an array, what can be said about the following statement?

    ```
    ary = &x;
    ```

24. Why is only the address of an array's first element necessary in order to access the entire array?

25. In what order must the parameters of a function be declared?

26. What can be said about adding an integer to a pointer?

27. Under what circumstances can a pointer be subtracted from an integer?

28. What is returned when a pointer is subtracted from a pointer, and under what conditions is this permitted?

29. What can you say about pointer multiplication and division?

30. What are the conditions under which the < and > operators are meaningful when used with pointers?

31. Without referring to the actual values, what can be said about the ASCII values for 'p' and 'q'?

32. Why is it harder in C to compare strings than numeric values?

33. How can an array of strings be represented in C?

34. How is the unsubscripted name of a two-dimensional array interpreted in C?

35. If an array is declared as

    `char z[10][12];`

    what is referred to by $z[5]$?

36. What is the maximum number of labels permissible in a **switch** statement?

37. What is the purpose of the **switch** statement?

38. What is the role played by the **break** statement within a **switch** statement?

39. What symbols are used to group together the statements comprising the body of a **switch** statement?

40. What keyword is always used in the body of a **switch** statement?

41. What connection is there between the **switch** variable or expression and the constants in the **case** labels?

42. What role is played by the **default** label in a **switch** statement?

43. In what order can the **case** labels be specified?

44. If a particular **case** label has several statements associated with it, how must the statements be grouped together?

45. Explain the action of the **switch** statement.

46. How can it be arranged that different values of the **switch** variable or expression cause the same set of statements to be executed?

47. Why does it require more time to sort an array of strings than a numeric array?

48. How can a string sorting technique be improved by resorting to pointers?

49. True or false: A pointer variable can be at most two levels deep (as in **int** **a;)

50. Given the following declaration:

```
int a, *b = &a, **c = &b;
```

what is the effect of the following statments?

```
a = 4;
**c = 5;
b = (int*)**c;
```

51. How would one declare an array *fred* of seven elements, each of which is a pointer to a variable of type **float**?

52. Show how one would declare an array *high* of 3 integers, and another array *low* of pointers to integers, each of whose elements points to the corresponding element of array *high*. (Initialize array *low* in its declaration.)

53. What, if anything, is wrong with the following section of code?

```
int *a;
*a = 7;
```

54. What is the advantage of representing an array of strings by an array of pointers to strings?

55. When an array of pointers is used to represent a string array, what extra steps must be taken which are not necessary when using a two-dimensional character array?

56. What is the meaning of the expression *array[4][3]*?

ANSWERS TO C TUTORIAL

1. Its address.

2. With the & (address) operator.

3. That is the only way a function can reference another function's local variables.

4. A variable's contents may change during execution of the program, but its address cannot be changed.

5. Each variable has a unique address at any given moment.

6. The name of a local variable is meaningful only within the function in which it is declared.

7. After it has been declared, it must be initialized.

8. The local variable can be accessed only by the function that contains it and the function that receives its address.

9. It passes the address of the variable being input, making it possible for the contents of that location to be changed.

10. It can be used only before the name of a scalar variable or a subscripted array element, not before an unsubscripted array name or an expression.

11. Addresses can be stored in pointer variables.

12. (a) Declares variable x as a pointer to **int**.
    (b) Declares variable y as a pointer to **int**.
    (c) Declares variable z as an **int**.
    (d) Illegal, since the * is not part of a pointer variable's name, and therefore this statement tries to declare p and q twice.
    (e) Declares variable x as an **int**, declares variable y as a pointer to **int**, and initializes y to the address of x.

13. (a) Assign the address of r to q.
    (b) Assign the address of t to s.

14. They are both legal.

    (a) Takes the address of n, casts it into a pointer to **char**, and assigns this pointer to m.
    (b) Takes the address of p, casts it into a pointer to **float**, and assigns this pointer to o.

15. ...to access and/or change the contents of m by use of the * operator.

16. The indirection operator is the asterisk (*). When placed before the name of a pointer variable, it means that the location being referred to is not the pointer variable, but the location pointed to by the pointer variable.

17. C treats addresses (pointers) and integers as different data types.

18. Passing by reference is the term used to refer to the passing of a variable's address to a function.

19. When a variable is passed by value to a function, only its value is passed. The function cannot change the contents of the variable. Passing by reference means that the variable's address is passed, giving the function the power to change the contents of that variable.

20. The parameters must be the *addresses* of the variables, and the contents of the locations pointed to by the addresses must be exchanged.

21. The unsubscripted name of an array is interpreted as a constant pointer; only a pointer to an array can be passed to a function; any pointer variable can be subscripted.

22. Since the name of an array is already a constant pointer, the & would be both illegal (you can't take the address of a constant) and redundant.

23. It is illegal; *ary* is a constant pointer, and therefore cannot have its value redefined.

24. Since all the elements of an array are of the same type, and all the elements are stored contiguously in memory, the location of the first element can be used to find the second element, the third element, and so forth.

25. They may be declared in any order.

26. It is perfectly legal. It returns a pointer, which is the original pointer incremented by the number of *target units* specified by the integer.

27. Under no circumstances is it legal. (The pointer can be cast into an integer, but this rarely would have any value.) It is, however, legal to subtract an integer from a pointer.

28. The result is the distance between the pointers expressed in target units. The two pointers must be of the same type, and the first pointer must have a greater value than the one being subtracted from it.

29. There is no such thing.

30. The two pointers must point to elements of the same array.

31. The value for 'p' is less than that for 'q', since 'p' precedes 'q' in the alphabet.

32. Strings cannot be compared in a single operation; each character must be compared to its corresponding element in the other array.

33. As a two-dimensional array of characters, in which each row is a separate string.

34. The same as a one-dimensional array name - as a constant pointer to the array's type.

35. *z[5]* is a *pointer* to the sixth row (row #5) of the array.

36. There is virtually no limit.

37. The **switch** statement allows execution of its body to begin at one of several points, based on the value of an **int** (or **int**-compatible) variable or expression.

38. It causes the remaining statements in the body of the **switch** statement to be skipped.

39. The braces { and }.

40. **case.**

41. Program control is transferred to the statement immediately following the **case** label whose constant equals the value of the **switch** variable or expression.

42. If it is present, control transfers to the statement immediately following that label, if the value of the **switch** variable or expression does not match any of the **case** labels.

43. In any order that suits the logic of the program.

44. The statements just have to follow each other; it is not necessary to place them within a compound statement.

45. When the **switch** statement is encountered, the **switch** variable or expression is evaluated. Program execution then continues at the **case** label whose constant is equal to the value of the **switch** variable or expression. If no such **case** label exists, execution continues at the **default** label, if one is present. If neither a matching **case** label nor a **default** label is present, the statements in the **switch** statement body are skipped and execution continues at the statement following the **switch**. If a **break** statement is encountered during execution of the **switch** body, the rest of the statements in the body are skipped and execution resumes after the **switch** statement.

46. The **case** labels of all the values involved must be placed one after the other, with no intervening statements, before the statements to be executed.

47. To compare two strings, it may be necessary to examine all elements of both character arrays. If the strings are being directly exchanged, the characters must be moved individually.

48. Each string can be represented by a pointer in an array of pointers. Instead of physically exchanging two strings when necessary, the pointers are exchanged.

49. False. It is permissible to declare pointers of any depth (limited only by the compiler), but pointers more than two levels deep rarely are used.

50. The first statement assigns 4 to a.

    The second statement assigns 5 to the location pointed to by the location pointed to by c. Since c points to b, this is the same as assigning 5 to the location pointed to by b. Since b points to a, this statement is equivalent to assigning 5 to a.

    The third statement casts $**c$, which is the value of a, into type **int ***, and assigns this value to b. The result is meaningless, since location 5 (5 is the value of a) has no significance.

51. `float *fred[7];`

52. ```
    int high[3],
        *low[3] = { &high[0], &high[1], &high[2] };
    /* The dimension 3 may be omitted from the declaration of "low".
       Also, the notation &high[n] may be replaced with high+n */
    ```

53. Since *a* is not initialized, **a* does not refer to any location, and so the value 7 has nowhere to go.

54. It allows for easy moving of the strings by moving their pointers (as in a sort). It also allows for the possibility that all the **char** arrays being pointed to may be of different maximum lengths, thus allowing for more efficient use of memory.

55. Space must be allocated to hold the actual strings (for example, a two-dimensional array of characters). The pointer array must be initialized so that its elements point to the allocated areas.

56. It could mean either of two things:

    (a) Column 3 of row 4 of a two-dimensional array *array*, or
    (b) Element 3 of the array pointed to by element 4 of a pointer array *array*.

    The correct interpretation is determined by how *array* is declared.

Keywords

break	**case**	char	**default**	do	double
else	float	if	for	int	long
return	short	**switch**	unsigned	while	

Exercises

1. Write a program to emulate the workings of a simple pocket calculator. The user enters a problem, such as 3 + 2. The program extracts the two operands and the operator, and performs the appropriate calculation, displaying the result in a clear form, such as 3 + 2 = 5. The program may be restricted to the five operators +, -, *, /, and %. Hint: use a **switch** statement.

2. Write a program to read in an array of integers. Instead of using subscripting, however, employ an integer pointer that points to the element currently being read in, and which is incremented each time.

3. Exercise 5 in Chapter 9 asked you to write a function to calculate the roots of a quadratic equation. Now that you are familiar with the method of how to change the values of parameters through passing by reference, rewrite the function so that it returns the roots via arguments rather than through global variables. You may wish to try passing the coefficients in one array and receiving the roots in another. That way, the function is
    ```

called with two arguments, one representing input and the other representing output.

4. Write a function that is passed an array, the array's length, and a constant value. The role of the function is to multiply each element of the array by the constant (actually modifying the array).

5. Write a function that is passed an array and a constant, and counts how many elements of the array are less than the constant, equal to it, and greater than it. Return these three values either by way of passed-by-reference parameters or a three-element array parameter.

12

Strings and String Functions

One of the features of computers that makes them so valuable is that they can process entities other than numbers. Since the introduction of low−cost word processing programs, the number of users has increased by leaps and bounds. Whereas some computers are dedicated word processing machines, the microcomputer is a general−purpose machine. When a word processing program is stored in its memory, it becomes a word processing machine with many, if not all, of the advantages of the dedicated word processor.

A Brief Review of Character Strings

As you learned from our discussion of **char** values, a character, at the lowest level, is really stored as a number. The compiler and the programmer make it possible to treat certain values as characters and to manipulate them accordingly. C allows arrays of type **char** to be treated as unified entities called *strings*.

There is no string type in C; strings are merely a sort of abbreviated notation for specifying character arrays. For a character array to be treated as a string, its last meaningful character must be followed by the ASCII value 0, known as the *null* character and indicated in C by '\0'. For example, the string "review" would be stored as shown in Figure 12-1.

| r | e | v | i | e | w | \0 |

Figure 12—1

The length of a string is the number of non-*null* characters it contains, so the number of locations needed to store a string is one more than the string's length.

The Concept of a Literal

Character strings also can be expressed as constants, sometimes referred to as literals. These take the form of characters enclosed within double quotation marks. The quotes are not part of the literal, but merely serve as delimiters. All of the following are valid C literals:

```
"bingo"
"1234"
"So shaken as we are, so wan with care...\n"
"\007"
"\"\n"
"Evil to him who evil thinketh"
""
```

A double quote included in the literal as \" is regarded as part of the literal and not as a delimiter. A pair of double quotes with nothing between them is called the *null string*. It is stored as a *null* character with nothing preceding it, and has a length of 0.

Literals in C are enclosed within *double* quotes, not *single* quotes (apostrophes). In C, single quotation marks are used only around (single) character constants. Since these two symbols are so close in both meaning and appearance, it is very easy to mistake one for the other.

When a literal is included in a C program, it is actually stored somewhere in memory. We are not concerned with its exact location, so long as it is accessible. To access a literal, all that is necessary is to refer to its pointer. Each time the literal is referred to in the course of the program, it is replaced by the pointer pointing to that literal in memory. For example, when a control string is passed to the *printf* function, as in

```
printf("a = %d\n", a);
```

what is actually passed as the first parameter is a pointer to the literal, "a = %d\n". In effect, the type of a literal is **char ***.

One exception to the above rule occurs when a literal is used in initializing an array. The declaration

```
char str[] = "bingo";
```

actually is an abbreviation for the declaration

```
char str [] = { 'b', 'i', 'n', 'g', 'o', '\0' };
```

where *str* is declared as a character array and dimensioned to enough elements to hold all the characters, including the *null* character. In this case, *str* would have six elements. In both forms of the declaration, an explicit dimension can be specified, which must be equal to or greater than the number of characters in the initializer, including the *null* character.

These concepts are employed in Program 12–1, which uses a string variable (an array of characters) to store the control string for a *printf* call.

```
/* The control string is just a string */

char format[] = "%s\n",        /* Control string for printf        */
     message[] = "hello";      /* String to be displayed by printf */

main()
{
    printf(format, message);
}
```

Program 12–1

```
hello
```

Output 12–1

In this program, two strings are declared and initialized. The array *format* holds a string, which takes the form of a control string as used by the *printf* function. The other array, *message*, holds a string to be printed out. The body of the *main* function consists entirely of a call to the *printf* function, in which a string variable is used instead of a literal control string. This *printf* is equivalent to

```
printf("%s\n", message);
```

where a literal is used. It has the effect of printing out the contents of the string array *message*, followed by a *newline* character.

A two-dimensional array of characters, or an array of pointers to strings, can be initialized to a list of strings, as shown in the following example:

```
char word_list[10][20] =
{
    "hello",
    "goodbye",
    "nice day",
    "it's raining"
};
```

Since only four literals are specified, only the first four rows of the array are initialized. The row dimension (but not the column) could be omitted, in which case the number of allocated rows would be equal to the number of initializing strings. The preceding statement is equivalent to the following:

```
char word_list[10][20] =
{
    { 'h', 'e', 'l', 'l' 'o', '\0' },
    { 'g', 'o', 'o', 'd' 'b', 'y', 'e', '\0' },
    { 'n', 'i', 'c', 'e', ' ', 'd', 'a', 'y', '\0' },
    { 'i', 't', '\'', 's', ' ', 'r', 'a', 'i', 'n', 'i', 'n', 'g', '\0' }
};
```

A one-dimensional array of pointers to characters also can be initialized using a list of strings, as shown here:

```
char *word_list[4] =
{
    "hello",
    "goodbye",
    "nice day",
    "it's raining"
};
```

In this case, the initializing strings are treated as constants, with each array element set to point to its corresponding string constant.

The static and auto Storage Classes

So far, we have assumed that only global arrays can be initialized. This is not exactly true. Global variables are classified in C as **static** variables, meaning they come into existence when the program is executed and continue to exist until the entire program terminates. Local variables, by contrast, usually are created each time a function is executed and disappear when the function terminates. Local variables are by default classified as **auto** variables, because they are allocated automatically when a function is executed and deallocated automatically when the function terminates. The classes **static** and **auto** are called *storage* *classes*, because they determine how storage is allocated to the variable.

For reasons of efficiency, only **static** arrays can be initialized in C. It is possible to initialize local arrays by declaring them to be **static**. When this is done, the variable exists from the start of program execution to the finish, just like a global variable. Local **static** variables remain local, however, in that they can be referenced by name only within the function in which they are declared.

To declare a local variable as **static**, the keyword **static** is placed at the head of the declaration, as in

```
static int a;
```

If the keyword **static** is replaced with the keyword **auto**, the variable is declared to be of storage class **auto**. Since **auto** is the default storage class for local variables, that keyword usually is omitted. (Incidentally, global variables cannot be declared **auto**.)

If a **static** local variable is assigned a value the first time the function is called, that value is still there when the function is called a second time. Examine the following function:

```
print_num()
{
    static int num = 1;
    printf("num = %d\n", num);
    num++;
}
```

The first time *print_num* is called, it prints the value 1, to which *num* is initialized. Then *num* is incremented to 2, and terminates. The second time *print_num* is called, it prints the value 2. On the third call, the value printed is 3, and so forth. Note that the initialization is not performed after the first call. An initialization used in a declaration occurs only once—when the variable is allocated. Since a **static** variable is allocated only once (when program execution begins), the initialization occurs only once during the entire program, no matter how many times the function is called. When the *print_num* function in the example is called the second time (and in every subsequent call), the value found in the variable *num* is the value left there by the previous call to the function.

Any **static** variable, be it scalar or array, local or global, can be initialized only to a constant value or values. Variables and function calls cannot be used to initialize a **static** variable. The reason is that the initializing value must be known at compilation time.

Storing the control string for a *printf* or *scanf* function call in a local array provides the programmer with a useful tool. Since the contents of an array can be changed while the program is running, the control string may be modified at execution time. The following program illustrates the concept of the *variable format*, in which the format of a line of output can be determined by user input that modifies the control string.

```
/* The control string is just a string - part 2 */

main()
{
    static char format[] = "%.15s\n",      /* Control string for printf */
           message[] = "hellohellohello";  /* String to be displayed
                                              by printf */
    int size;                              /* number of characters to
                                              print from "message" */

/* Read in the number of characters to be displayed from "message" */
    printf("How many characters do you want displayed? ");
    scanf("%d", &size);

/* Convert "size" to 2-digit number in format[2] and format[3] */
    format[2] = (size / 10) + '0';
    format[3] = (size % 10) + '0';
    printf("The format is: %s\n", format);

/* Print the string */
    printf(format, message);
}
```

Program 12—2

```
How many characters do you want displayed? 5
The format is: %.05s


hello



How many characters do you want displayed? 7
The format is: %.07s

hellohe
```

Output 12—2

In this program, both *format* and *message* are declared to be static arrays of type **char**. The array *format* is initialized to the control string "%.15s\n" whereas *message* is initialized to "hellohellohello". The user is prompted to enter (into the variable *size*) the number of characters to be printed from the string *message*. The input is not validated, but it should be a positive integer of up to two digits and no greater in magnitude than 15.

This value of *size* then is converted to character form. This is done by extracting the high-order and low-order digits, using the / and % operators, and adding the ASCII value for '0' to both these values. The results are cast automatically into type **char**, and the two resulting digits are placed in the string *format* at the positions occupied by the number "15" in the original string. These locations follow the one occupied by the decimal point, and therefore form the maximum characters specifier. This process is illustrated in Figure 12-2.

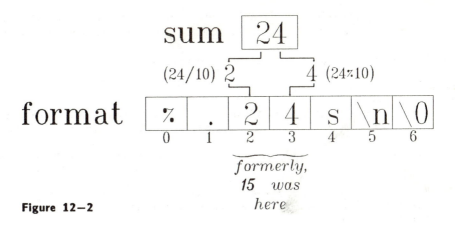

Figure 12-2

The use of 15 as the initial maximum characters specifier is arbitrary; any two characters could have been used as place-holders for the two digits that are actually placed there during program execution.

After the appropriate digits are placed in *format*, the string is printed out to illustrate what was done. The line is followed by two *newline* characters, rather than one; the first comes from the control string of the *printf*, and the second from *format* itself.

Finally, the *printf* function is called again, this time printing the contents of *message* with *format* used as the control string. The value entered for *size* determines how many characters from *message* are printed. The two executions of the program demonstrate how this value can be changed.

When the value of *size* is less than 10, the number in the control string *format* has a leading zero. In a control string, this is not interpreted as signifying an octal number. All field specifiers in a control string are interpreted as being in decimal.

The *sprintf* Function

Even though Program 12-2 works within satisfactory limits, the technique is rather cumbersome. Converting an integer to its character representation requires too much effort on the part of the programmer. The conversion performed in this program is not too taxing, because there are only two digits, but much more work would be required if more digits were involved.

C provides a function in its standard library which makes this same conversion trivial. It is called the *sprintf* function, which stands for *string printf*. It performs all the same conversions as the *printf* function, but instead of displaying its results on the standard output device (usually a screen), it stores the results in a string. The resulting string is an exact image of what would have been displayed had the *printf* function been used instead of *sprintf*.

Consider the following invocation of the *sprintf* function:

```
sprintf(string, "The integer is %d, the real number is %f\n",
5, 2.1);
```

The *sprintf* function has an extra parameter preceding the control string. This is the array that will receive the resulting string. It must be a character array large enough to hold the maximum number of characters which the *sprintf* function might generate, including the terminating *null* character. A common error is to omit this parameter, since it is not present in *printf*.

The preceding *sprintf* statement generates the string:

```
"The integer is 5, the real number is 2.100000\n"
```

where \n is stored as a single character, as usual. This is exactly what you would see on your screen or printer if *printf* were called with the same control string and values. (The first parameter, *string*, would of course be omitted.)

Program 12-3 is a simple illustration of *sprintf*. An integer is read into the variable *number* and converted to its character representation, with a preceding message, by a call to *sprintf*. The result is stored in *string*, and is displayed using *printf*. The whole process could have been accomplished with a single call to *printf*, but this program serves merely as an illustration of *sprintf*'s operation.

The value of *string* is displayed in two ways. The first time, it is displayed by use of the %s conversion specification in a literal control string. The second time, *string* itself is used as the control string. Since there are no conversion specifications in *string* (*sprintf* took care of that), no other variables are needed following *string*.

```
/* The sprintf function */

main()
{
    char string[80];
    int number;

    printf("Please enter a number: ");
    scanf("%d", &number);

    sprintf(string, "The number is %d\n", number);

    printf("%s", string);

/* OR */

    printf(string);
}
```

Program 12-3

```
Please enter a number: 17
The number is 17
The number is 17



Please enter a number: -143
The number is -143
The number is -143
```

Output continued on next page

Output continued from previous page

```
Please enter a number: 0
The number is 0
The number is 0
```

Output 12—3

The *sprintf* function clearly makes programming easier. Program 12-4 is the variable format program, rewritten to use the *sprintf* function. The array *format* no longer needs to be declared as **static**, since it is not initialized; *sprintf* does the job of filling in all the characters. The array *message* still is initialized, so it remains **static**. The control string generated by *sprintf* and placed in *format* is echoed before it is used in the subsequent call to *printf*.

```
/* Variable control string using the sprintf function */

main()
{
    char format[20];                                /* Control string for printf */
    static char message[] = "hellohellohello";      /* String to be displayed
                                                        by printf */

    int size;                                       /* Number of characters to
                                                        print from "message" */

/* Read in the number of characters to be displayed from "message" */
    printf("How many characters do you want displayed? ");
    scanf("%d", &size);

/* Create format in "format" using "size" */
    sprintf(format, "%%.%ds\n", size);
    printf("The format is: %s\n", format);

/* Print the string */
    printf(format, message);
}
```

Program 12—4

```
How many characters do you want displayed? 7
The format is: %.7s

hellohe



How many characters do you want displayed? 13
The format is: %.13s

hellohellohel
```

Output 12—4

The *sprintf* statement in Program 12-4 performs the awkward task of using a control string to generate another control string. The double % symbol is used in the literal control string of the *sprintf* because a % symbol must be transferred to the string *format.* If a single % were used, the *sprintf* function would see "%.%ds\n" and assume that "%." is a conversion specification for *sprintf*'s use. Most versions of *sprintf* would recognize that "%." is not a valid conversion specification, and would transfer the % directly to the result string anyway. It is preferable, however, to use the double %.

The *strcpy* Function

In the previous chapter, we faced the problem of having to copy one string into another. This cannot be done directly with an assignment statement, so we used pointers. Sometimes, however, it is necessary to *move* the contents of a character array.

The first version of the string sorting program presented a function that accomplished this task. Program 12-5 uses a more succinct version of that function, called *strcpy* (*string copy.*)

```
/* A terse string copy function */

main()
{
    char string1[20], string2[20];

    strcpy(string1, "This is a message");
    printf("String 1 = %s\n", string1);

    strcpy(string2, string1);
    printf("\nString 2 = %s\n", string2);
}

strcpy(copy, original)
char *copy, *original;

/* Copy "original" into "copy" */

{
    while (*copy++ = *original++);
}
```

Program 12—5

```
String 1 = This is a message

String 2 = This is a message
```

Output 12—5

The function *strcpy* copies the string pointed to by its second argument (*original*) into the array pointed to by its first argument (*copy*). Thus the copy is performed in the same direction as in an assignment statement: transfer the value on the right to the location on the left.

The first call to *strcpy* copies the literal "This is a message" into *string1*. If the literal were given as the first parameter, the function would be passed a pointer to the location where the literal is stored and would attempt to do the copy. It might succeed, but this would change the literal and would probably wreak havoc with the program, since the compiler translates a program in a way that relies on constants not changing. On some computers, an execution error results if an attempt is made to overwrite a constant string.

After the first copy is completed, the contents of *string1* are displayed to demonstrate that the copy succeeded. Then the function is called again, this time to copy *string1* into *string2*. Finally, the contents of *string2* are displayed.

The *strcpy* function itself is quite brief, because it makes good use of various operators provided in C. When the function is called, *copy* and *original* point to the first character positions of their respective strings. The assignment operator transfers the character pointed to by *original* to the location pointed to by *copy*. The post-increment operators then increment both pointers, after the assignment is made.

The assignment operator returns the value that it assigned to **copy*. Since every non-*null* character has a non-zero ASCII value, this value is interpreted as *true* by the **while** loop. The **while** loop has no body, so it merely evaluates its test expression. The copy-and-increment process therefore is repeated a second time, but this time both pointers reference the second character positions of their respective arrays. The process is repeated until the *null* character that terminates the string indexed by *original* is copied. When this happens, the value returned by the assignment operator is 0 (the ASCII value of the *null* character). The **while** loop interprets this value as *false*, and the loop is terminated.

One unusual feature found in the body of the *strcpy* function is the use of an increment operator on the left side of an assignment operator. If non-pointer variables were involved, this would be illegal, but the precedence rules for C determine that "**copy++*" is evaluated as "**(copy++)*". This means that, although *copy* is incremented, the location *pointed to* by *copy* (before the increment) is assigned a value. Therefore, there is no conflict.

Once *copy* and *original* are incremented, there is no way to determine their original values. The function has, in effect, lost the beginnings of the strings. Fortunately, this is not important to the function. Since *copy* and *original* are local variables, the *main* function does not suffer such a loss. If it were necessary for the *strcpy* function to keep pointers to the beginnings of the strings, it would have to copy the parameters into local storage variables.

This program has been presented to give the reader a better understanding of how strings are manipulated. The *strcpy* function is available in the standard C function library, along with some other useful string functions that will be presented in this chapter.

Using *sscanf* to Validate Input

Most programs, regardless of the language in which they are written, require the cooperation of the user. More often than not, a microcomputer program is interactive. This means the user must supply the program with appropriate data. A well-written program prompts the user with messages, specifying precisely the nature of the input that is required.

Even if such prompts are well constructed, however, at some point or other the user will enter inappropriate data. Perhaps the message is misread, or the user makes a typographical error. In such a case, the program should be able to detect the error, correct it if possible, and continue execution. It should inform the user that an error occurred and specify the nature of the error. The detection of erroneous input is a very important feature of interactive programming. It is usually called validation of data.

We have already seen some simple examples of input validation. These examples consisted of checking that the values fell within the required range. We have not yet seen a test designed to ensure that if (say) an integer is required, the user does not input a string. Although C is liberal in its treatment of erroneous input, in that program execution continues, it still is somewhat difficult to detect or correct such an error.

The *sscanf* (*string scanf*) function provides a useful tool in the detection and correction of incorrect input. It operates exactly like the *scanf* function except that, instead of reading data from the standard input device (usually a keyboard), it inputs from a string. The source string is provided as the first parameter to *sscanf*, immediately preceding the control string.

It is possible to input all data as strings and then use the *sscanf* function to convert it to the required data type. Before this conversion takes place, however, the input string can be checked character by character to make sure it is valid. For example, if the required data item is an integer, the input string can be checked to make sure it contains only digits. If it passes this test, it can be converted to an **int**, using the *sscanf* function with the %d conversion specification. Otherwise, the program can tell the user why the input is invalid, even displaying the non-digits and their positions.

Program 12-6 makes use of the technique just described, with a few modifications. The user is asked to enter an integer, which initially is stored as a string. The input string is validated to determine that the characters form an integer number. If the string is valid, it is converted to an integer and printed out in that form (rather than as the original character string). Otherwise, the user is informed of the error and is given a chance to re-enter the number. In either case, the user is then asked if another number is to be entered.

```
/* Using sscanf to validate input */

main()
{
    int number,          /* Holds numeric version of inputted integer */
        i,               /* Loop index */
        start_scan;      /* Character position at which to start digit scan */
    char input[40];      /* Holds input in string form (both the integer
                            and the yes/no response) */

    do          /* Loop for entering integers */
    {
        do      /* Loop for re-entering mistyped integers */
        {
            printf("Please enter an integer: ");
            scanf("%s", input);

        /* Allow for sign */
            start_scan = (input[0] == '+' || input[0] == '-') ? 1 : 0;

        /* Make sure all characters are digits */
            for (i = start_scan; input[i] >= '0' && input[i] <= '9'; i++);

        /* Accept only if first non-digit is null character */
        /* ((i == start_scan) eliminates null string, "+" and "-") */
            if (input[i] != '\0' || i == start_scan)
                printf("%s is not an integer!\n\n", input);
        }
        while (input[i] != '\0' || i == start_scan);    /* Again if input
                                                           was non-integer */

        printf("\nThank you.\n");

    /*  Convert string to integer */
        sscanf(input, "%d", &number);
        printf("You typed the number %d.\n", number);

    /*  Go round again? */
        printf("\n\nWould you like to enter another number? ");
        scanf("%s", input);  /* Outer loop condition checks input */
    }
    while (input[0] == 'y' || input[0] == 'Y');
}
```

Program 12—6

```
            Please enter an integer: 7

            Thank you.
            You typed the number 7.


            Would you like to enter another number? yes
            Please enter an integer: 4*5
            4*5 is not an integer!

            Please enter an integer: -
            - is not an integer!

            Please enter an integer: -2

            Thank you.
            You typed the number -2.
```

Output continued on next page

Output continued from previous page

```
Would you like to enter another number? yup!
Please enter an integer: zero
zero is not an integer!

Please enter an integer: 0

Thank you.
You typed the number 0.


Would you like to enter another number? Yeah
Please enter an integer: +
+ is not an integer!

Please enter an integer: +4

Thank you.
You typed the number 4.


Would you like to enter another number? y
Please enter an integer: 16w
16w is not an integer!

Please enter an integer: 16

Thank you.
You typed the number 16.


Would you like to enter another number? nope.
```

Output 12-6

In this program, the variables *number*, *i*, and *start_scan* are declared to be of type **int**, whereas *input* is declared to be a character array of 40 elements. The uses of these variables will be discussed as they are encountered in the program.

The body of the program consists of a **do...while** loop. Each time around this loop, the user enters a valid integer. The body of this loop consists mostly of another **do...while** loop, which reads in an integer as a string and then proceeds to validate it.

After the user is prompted to enter an integer, the *scanf* statement inputs the user's response as a string, storing it in the array *input*. The statement following the *scanf* is included because a valid integer may start with a plus or minus sign, indicating a positive or negative value. This statement contains a conditional expression. If the first character in the string is a plus or minus sign, the variable *start_scan* is set equal to 1. This indicates that the loop which scans for digits in the input string should start with character 1, skipping over character 0, which has already been validated (it contains a plus or minus sign). Otherwise, *start_scan* is set equal to 0, meaning that the first character is neither a plus nor a minus sign, and therefore all the characters are assumed to be digits.

Next comes the test for validity. It consists of two parts. The first is a **for** loop with no body. Its effect is to scan through the string, stopping when a non-digit character is encountered, and leaving the current value of the index in *i*. If the string contains all digits (not including the plus or minus sign, if any), the loop stops when it encounters the terminating *null* character, which is not a digit.

The second step of validation consists of a two-part test, embodied in the **if** statement following the loop. The first part tests whether the character indexed by *i* is the *null* character. If it is, then the end of the string has been reached without encountering a non-digit. Otherwise, the test

```
(input[i] != '\0')
```

succeeds, indicating that a non-digit has been encountered before the end of the string, and so the input is invalid. The second part of the test checks to see whether *i* is equal to *start_scan*. This can occur under two different sets of circumstances: if the input is the null string (unlikely, since there really is no way to input the null string), or if the input consists of only a plus sign or a minus sign. Since the two tests in the **if** statement are joined by the || operator, the *printf* in the **if** statement is executed if either of these two tests succeeds. This *printf* statement informs the user that an error has occurred.

If the input is found to be invalid, the test controlling the inner **do...while** loop succeeds, and the loop is repeated, requesting another input value. The test in the **do...while** loop is identical to that made in the **if** statement. This may seem redundant, but it makes the program a little simpler and clearer. An alternative would be to set the value of a flag variable to the result of the test made by the **if** statement, and then to use this variable to control the **do...while** loop.

Once the input is found to be valid, the inner **do...while** loop terminates. The program then thanks the user for entering a valid number, and converts it from its string form to a true integer using the *sscanf* function. The integer is stored in the variable *number*, the value of which is printed to verify that the input was converted correctly.

Finally, the user is asked if another round is required. This part of the program uses a method discussed in Chapter 10: The user's response is read in as a string, and then the first character is checked to see whether it is a 'y' or a 'Y'. Only the first letter is used to determine whether the user's response is positive. Therefore, responses such as *yes, yup!, Yeah,* or just *y* (in fact, any response beginning with y) all cause the outer **do...while** loop to repeat.

The next program illustrates the difference between a constant string and a variable string. Despite their outward similarity, these strings have some important differences that are highlighted in the program.

```
/*  Pointers to constant strings
    vs. constant pointers to strings */

main()
{
    char string_vari[10], *string_point;

    string_point = "hello";

    strcpy(string_vari, string_point);

    printf("%s\n%s\n", string_point, string_vari);
}
```

Program 12—7

```
hello
hello
```

Output 12—7

The comment at the beginning of Program 12-7 refers to the fact that *string_vari* is a constant pointer (since it is an array name), but it points to a string (character array) whose contents can be changed in the ordinary way. The variable *string_point*, on the other hand, is a variable pointer that can be set to point to any string.

The assignment statement in the program is one we have not used before. It assigns a literal to a string pointer. The string "hello" is considered to be a constant and is stored somewhere in memory. The variable *string_point* is set to point to that location, wherever it happens to be. This arrangement is illustrated in Figure 12-3.

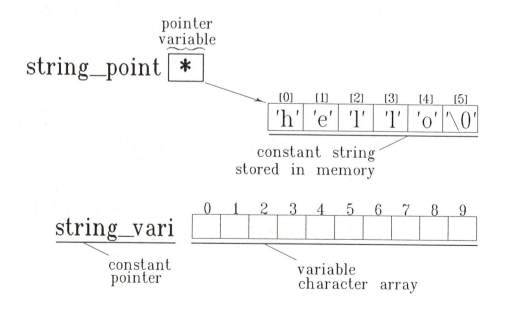

Figure 12—3

The characters that constitute *string_point* can be accessed in the same manner as *string_vari* or any other string. They can be copied to another string or printed out, as in this program. The copying process cannot be done in the opposite direction to that shown in the program; that is, the contents of *string_vari* cannot be copied into *string_point*. The memory locations pointed to by *string_point* should not be modified in any way, because a constant literal was assigned to *string_point*. Even if the compiler or the computer does not explicitly prevent such a modification, unpredictable side effects could result. The value of pointer variable *string_point* can be changed, but if a constant string is assigned to *string_point*, that string itself should be treated as a constant. In contrast, *string_vari* can never be placed on the left side of an assignment operator, but the string it points to, or specifically the array containing the string, can be altered.

The similarities between the two strings outnumber the differences. This fact is illustrated when both are printed out after the call to *strcpy*. Their contents after the *strcpy* are identical, as would be the case if they were both character arrays.

The *strcat* Function

We have already seen how one string can be copied into another. Now we illustrate another important string operation: that of joining two strings to form a third. This operation, known as *concatenation*, is demonstrated in Figure 12-4.

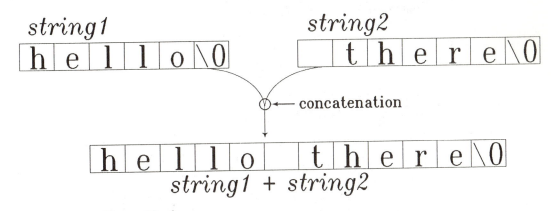

Figure 12—4

Program 12-8 illustrates one way in which concatenation can be accomplished. It uses a user-defined function called *strcat* (*string concatenation*) to concatenate two strings.

```
    /* String functions return pointers */
    /* (strcat version 1) */

main()
{
    static char string1[] = "hello";
    char *string2,
         *strcat();

    string2 = strcat(string1, " there");

    printf("string1 = %s\nstring2 = %s\n", string1, string2);
}


char *strcat(first, second)

/*  Returns pointer to concatenation of
    "first" and "second" strings */

char *first, *second;
{
    static char result[100];        /* Holds result of concatenation */
    auto char *ptr = result;        /* Points to "result", used because
                                       "ptr" can be incremented */

    while (*ptr++ = *first++);       /* Copy "first" to "*ptr" ("result").
                                       Finish when '\0' copied */
    ptr--;                          /* Back up to '\0' so that next
                                       character is copied over it */
    while (*ptr++ = *second++);      /* Copy "second" to "*ptr" (end of
                                       "result").  Finish when '\0' copied */
    return(result);
}
```

Program 12—8

```
            string1 = hello
            string2 = hello there
```

Output 12—8

In the *main* function, *string1* is declared to be **static** and is initialized to the string "hello". The variable *string2* is declared to be a character (string) pointer. The function *strcat* must also be declared in the *main* function, since it returns a non-integer value. The declaration

```
    char *strcat();
```

indicates that *strcat* returns a value of type **char ***.

The function *strcat* is called to concatenate the value of *string1* ("hello") with the string " there" (which starts with a blank space to separate it from "hello"). The function returns a pointer to the result of the concatenation; in the *main* function, this is assigned to *string2*. Both *string1* and *string2* are then displayed.

The function *strcat* returns a string that is the result of the concatenation of the function's two parameters, *first* and *second*. Of course, it cannot physically return the contents of a string (since arrays cannot be returned by functions), so it must return a pointer to the character string. But where is the concatenated string located? As is probably evident by now, it is not possible to take the memory locations in which two strings are stored and physically join them. It is clear that some form of copying must take place.

This version of *strcat* is written so that it does not actually change the contents of *first* or *second*. This feature allows both parameters to be either constant or variable strings. It also means, however, that the result of the concatenation must be stored in a third location. The array *result* is declared for this purpose. The result of the concatenation is stored in *result*, and the address of this array is returned by the function. The array *result* must be declared as **static**, so that it still exists after control returns to the calling function.

The only disadvantage presented by this method is that, when *strcat* is called subsequently, the contents of *result* are changed. For this reason, if the *main* function needed to call *strcat* a second time, it would first be necessary to copy the string pointed to by *string2* into another array. (Remember that *string2* actually points to *result*.)

In Program 12-8, the local variable *ptr* in *strcat* is declared to be of type **auto char ***. As we have said before, the storage class **auto** is automatically given to local variables, so the keyword **auto** could have been omitted. It is used here only to contrast *ptr* with *result*, which is static.

The variable *ptr* is initialized to point to the beginning of *result*. Thus, the first **while** loop in the body of *strcat* serves to copy the string *first* into the beginning of *result*. Since the value returned by an assignment is the assigned value, the loop will terminate when the *null* character terminating *first* is assigned to the corresponding element of *result* (the value 0 is interpreted by C as *false*).

It is not really necessary to copy the *null* character from *first*. That character will be overwritten when *second* is copied into *result*. The *null* character is copied only to make the **while** loop simpler. After the first **while** loop has finished execution, *ptr* points to the element of *result* following the one in which the *null* character was stored. This is the case because, after the *null* character is copied, *ptr* is post-incremented. Therefore, after the first copy, the value of *ptr* is decremented so that it points to the *null* character. (The reason the *strcpy* function is not called to perform the copy is that it would still be necessary to increment *ptr* to point to the end of the string just copied.)

Finally, the string *second* is copied into *result* using a **while** loop, starting at the location pointed to by *ptr*. As mentioned previously, this operation replaces the *null* character with the first character of *second*, so the only *null* character present in *result* is the one copied from *second*. (The reader might try to write a call to the *strcpy* function which would accomplish this second copy.) The string *result* now contains the concatenation of *first* and *second*.

There are problems associated with the use of **static** array *result* to return the concatenated string from *strcat*, but there are several other ways of implementing this function. One of these is shown in Program 12-9, in which the second string is copied to the end of the first string. This technique has two requirements:

1) The first parameter to the *strcat* function must be a variable string (an array).

2) The array in which the first string is stored must be large enough to hold the concatenated string (that is, both the first and the second string together).

In this version, the first string is modified by the *strcat* function, and it is unnecessary to introduce any other arrays. This is the method used by the *strcat* function that is supplied in the function library of most C compilers. Program 12-9 includes a user-defined function *strcat* in order to illustrate how such a function may be written. Like the library function, this one returns as its result the address of the first parameter.

```
/* strcat version 2 */

main()
{
    static char string1[15] = "hello";
    char *string2,
         *strcat();

    string2 = strcat(string1, " there");

    printf("string1 = %s\nstring2 = %s\n", string1, string2);
    if (string1 == string2)
        printf("string2 points to string1\n");
    else
        printf("string2 does not point to string1\n");
}


char *strcat(first, second)

/* Concatenates "second" string to end of "first",
   returns pointer to "first" */

char *first, *second;
{
    strcpy(first + strlen(first), second);
    return(first);
}
```

Program 12—9

```
string1 = hello there
string2 = hello there
string2 points to string1
```

Output 12—9

The *strlen* Function

In the *main* function, *string1* is explicitly dimensioned to 15 elements, since otherwise the compiler would make it only large enough to hold the string "hello". The number 15 is somewhat arbitrary; it merely ensures that there is enough room to hold the concatenated string. In a program in which the sizes of the strings are not known in advance, an array used as the first parameter of the *strcat* function should be large enough to hold all concatenated strings. (Multiple calls to *strcat* can result in an array holding the concatenation of more than two strings.)

The new version of *strcat* seems much shorter than the first version. The reason is that it makes use of two library functions. We have already encountered one of them, *strcpy*. The other one is named *strlen*. This function takes as its argument a string (pointer), and returns an integer specifying the number of characters in the string, excluding the *null* character. (The function *strlen* is not declared in *strcat* since it returns an integer.) The expression

```
first + strlen(first)
```

returns a pointer to the *null* character terminating *first*. The *strcpy* function therefore accomplishes the task of copying *second* into the end of *first*. This entire process is illustrated in Figure 12-5.

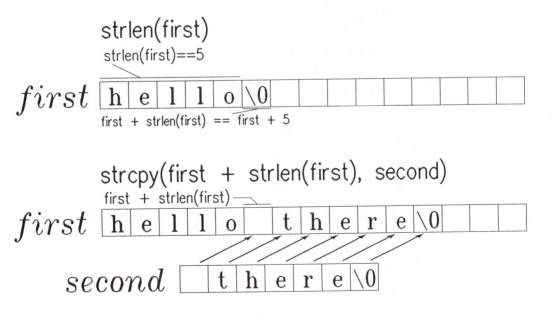

Figure 12—5

The **if** statement at the end of the *main* function is used to verify that the pointer returned by *strcat* is a pointer to *string1*. Since *string1* is modified, it is not really necessary to use *string2* to receive the returned value. If the value returned by *strcat* were not used, it would not be necessary to declare its type in the *main* function.

The official library version of the *strcpy* function also returns a pointer to the first parameter. Since we have not needed to make use of this returned value, the *strcpy* function has not been declared to be of type **char *** in any of the above programs.

The *malloc* and Related Functions

Every year, computers are being produced with more and more memory. It is not unusual for small computers to come equipped with 1M (1 megabyte, or 1 million bytes) of memory. Large mainframe computers generally have considerably more memory. It is also not unusual for business and scientific programs to handle millions of data items. Thus it is important for programmers to write programs that use a minimum of memory, as well as programs that are fast. Usually it is not possible to maximize a program's speed while also minimizing its memory requirements, but the conscientious programmer strives to achieve the most efficient program possible.

In many of the programs illustrated in the past few chapters, it has been necessary to dimension arrays to some maximum size. This technique can waste memory if the amount of data is much less than the maximum, but it is not always possible to predict what the array size will be. It would be desirable to be able to start a program with the smallest amount of memory necessary, and then allocate extra memory as the need arises. This capability is provided by the C library function *malloc* (*memory allocation*).

When a C function is executed, the computer must allocate memory for the local variables. This memory is taken from a pool of *free* memory, or memory that is not being used by the program. When the function finishes execution, this memory is returned to the pool for subsequent use. The *malloc* function permits allocation of memory from a similar pool. The parameter for the *malloc* function is an integer that specifies the number of bytes (or, more generally, the number of **char**-sized units) needed. The function returns a pointer to a block of contiguous memory of the size specified. The pointer actually is of type **char ***, but it can be cast into any other type as appropriate. The memory so allocated can be returned to the free pool by passing the pointer to the *free* function.

As an example of the use of the *malloc* function, suppose we need a character array whose size is not known until execution. We declare a pointer, say *string*, to be of type **char ***. The *malloc* function would also be declared to return a value of the same type:

```
char *string, *malloc();
```

Once the array size needed has been determined (during program execution), we would execute the following statement:

```
string = malloc(n);
```

where *n* is a variable containing the number of bytes (**char**s) needed. Now *string* can be used just as if it had been declared to be an array. Even though it is a pointer variable, its value should not be changed, because that would cause the program to lose track of the location of the allocated array. (Of course, if the value of *string* is first copied into another pointer variable, this restriction does not apply.)

When the array is no longer needed, the program would execute the following statement:

```
free(string);
```

which returns the allocated memory to the free pool. Now the value of *string* should *not* be used, since the memory it points to no longer belongs to the program. (This is also the reason a pointer to a local variable should not be returned by a function.) At this point, a new value can be assigned to *string*.

Several other standard functions related to memory allocation may be included in your C library. The function *calloc* (*clear and alloc*ate) is used both to allocate memory and to initialize it to 0. Its parameters differ slightly from those of *malloc*. Another standard function is *realloc* (*re-alloc*ate), which is used to enlarge the size of a previously allocated block. You should check the manual for your particular C compiler to find out which functions are available and how they are used.

The following version of the alphabetizing program makes use of the *malloc* and *free* functions, in order to conserve memory. It also makes use of another string function, *strcmp*, and a new operator, **sizeof**, both of which will be described after you have had a chance to examine the program.

```
/* Alphabetizing program using dynamically allocated arrays */

    /* The array may have up to 20 elements */
#define MAX_ARRAY_SIZE 20
    /* Each string may have up to 10 characters */
#define MAX_STRING_SIZE 10

    /* Message flags for "print_array" */
#define ORIGINAL 0          /* Display original array */
#define SORTED   1          /* Display sorted array */

main()
{
    int i;
    char *words[MAX_ARRAY_SIZE];    /* An array of pointers to strings */
    int array_size;                 /* Actual number of strings in array */

    /* Read in the array's size */

    get_size(&array_size);

    /* Read in the string array "words" of size "array_size" */
```

Program continued on next page

Program continued from previous page

```
    get_array(words, array_size);

    /* Echo the original array */

    print_array(words, array_size, ORIGINAL);

    pointer_sort(words, array_size);

    /* Print the sorted array */

    print_array(words, array_size, SORTED);

    /* Free the malloc'd arrays */

    release(words, array_size);
}


get_size(size)
int *size;

/* Read the size of the array into "*size" (until a valid value is entered) */

{
    do
    {
        printf("How many words? ");
        scanf("%d", size);
    }
    /* "*size" must be at least 1 and at most MAX_ARRAY_SIZE */
    while (*size < 1 || *size > MAX_ARRAY_SIZE);
}

get_array(array, size)
char *array[];
int size;

/*  Read in the string array called "array" of size "size".  Space is
    allocated to store each string,  the address of the string stored
    in "array" */

{
    int i;
    char *malloc();

    printf("Please enter the words:\n");
    for (i = 0; i < size; i++)
    {
        /* Allocate space for string before reading it in */

        array[i] = malloc((MAX_STRING_SIZE + 1) * sizeof(char));

        scanf("%s", array[i]);
    }
}

print_array(array, size, message)
char *array[];
int size, message;
```

Program continued on next page

Program continued from previous page

```
/*  Print out string array "array" of size "size".  "message" is a
    flag indicating which message to display (ORIGINAL or SORTED) */

{
    int i;
    static char *printout[] =
    {
        "\nThe original array is:\n",
        "\nThe sorted array is:\n",
        "\n"
    };

    /* Print the appropriate message */

    printf("%s", printout[message]);

    for (i = 0; i < size; i++)
        printf("%s\n", array[i]);
}


pointer_sort(array, size)
char *array[];
int size;

/* Sort string array "array" of size "size" by pointer */

{
    int i, j;

    for (i = 0; i < size - 1; i++)
        for (j = i + 1; j < size; j++)
            if (strcmp(array[i], array[j]) > 0)
                swap(array + i, array + j);
}

swap(i, j)
int *i, *j;

/* Exchange strings "i" and "j" by pointer */

{
    int temp = *i;
    *i = *j;
    *j = temp;
}

release(array, size)
char *array[];
int size;

/* Free memory space pointed to by pointer array "array" of size "size" */

{
    int i;

    for (i = 0; i < size; i++)
        free(array[i]);
}
```

Program 12—10

```
How many words? 8
Please enter the words:
cat
pig
dog
earlobe
bingo
elbow
likely
radar

The original array is:
cat
pig
dog
earlobe
bingo
elbow
likely
radar

The sorted array is:
bingo
cat
dog
earlobe
elbow
likely
pig
radar
```

Output 12—10

The first noteworthy point about Program 12-10 is that only one array is declared: a pointer array called *words*. There is no array to hold the actual strings, only a pointer array to point to them. The *malloc* function is used to allocate the storage space for the actual strings. This operation can be seen in the *get_array* function. Before a string is read in, *malloc* is called to allocate enough memory to store a string of size MAX_STRING_SIZE + 1.

The sizeof Operator

The call to *malloc* in the *get_array* function contains a new keyword, **sizeof**. The reader may be surprised that it is referred to as an operator, because syntactically it looks like a function. The **sizeof** operator is part of the C language, however, not a library function. Its returned value is determined at compilation time, even before the program is executed.

The **sizeof** operator returns the size in bytes (**char**s) of its operand. The operand can take either of two forms. In Program 12-10, it is a parenthesized data type name. When **sizeof** operates on a data type, it returns the number of bytes which a variable of that type occupies in memory. For example,

```
sizeof(int)
```

would return a value of 2 or 4, depending on the computer. This fact indicates that **sizeof** can be used to make programs machine independent. If it is necessary to allocate memory to store an integer, the programmer can write

```
int *i, *malloc();
i = malloc(sizeof(int));
```

to allocate memory for an integer without actually knowing how long an integer is. (The integer variable allocated in this example would be referred to as $*i$, since i points to it.)

The **sizeof** operator can also be used with a variable as an operand. In this case, it returns the size of the operand. If a variable i is declared as

```
int i;
```

then the expression

```
sizeof i
```

returns the same value as

```
sizeof(int)
```

Notice that, when the **sizeof** operator is applied to a variable, no parentheses are necessary. It is necessary, however, to leave at least one space between the operator and the variable name. For the sake of clarity, this text will henceforth always use parentheses with the **sizeof** operator.

The **sizeof** operator can even be used with arrays. For example, if an array is declared as

```
int q[12];
```

the expression

```
sizeof(q);
```

returns 24 if the size of an **int** is 2, or 48 if the size of an **int** is 4. The expression

```
sizeof(q) / sizeof(int)
```

returns the number of elements in q (12). The **sizeof** operator could also be applied to a single subscripted element of q. It cannot be applied to an array passed as a parameter, however, unless that array is explicitly dimensioned in the function. In other words, **sizeof** cannot be used to determine the size of an array passed as a parameter.

When the **sizeof** operator is applied to a pointer variable, it returns the size of the target type of that pointer.

Multiplying *MAX_STRING_SIZE + 1* by **sizeof(char)** in the call to *malloc* in Program 12-10 ensures that the function allocates the right number of bytes. The expression **sizeof(char)** always returns 1, but if the function were allocating an array of MAX_STRING_SIZE + 1 integers, it would be necessary to use

```
(MAX_STRING_SIZE + 1) * sizeof(int)
```

as the operand of **sizeof**.

Since the *get_size* function inputs the number of strings to be alphabetized, it would be possible to allocate the string space there instead of in *get_array*. Deferring this operation to the *get_array* function avoids the necessity of adding a **for** loop.

The function *print_array* employs a new method of selecting the correct message based on the *message* parameter. An array of string pointers, called *printout*, is declared and initialized. The form of initialization used is a special form usable only with such an array. Its effect is to declare an array of three elements (since it is initialized to three strings) and then set the three elements to point to constant strings. The declaration is equivalent to the following:

```
static char *printout[3];
printout[0] = "\nThe original array is:\n";
printout[1] = "\nThe sorted array is:\n";
printout[2] = "\n";
```

The *print_array* function chooses the desired message by using the parameter *message* directly to index the array *printout*. This method requires fewer statements than the *switch* statement used in the previous version of this program. A string containing only a *newline* is used as the third possible message, allowing a value of 2 for *message* to indicate the choice of no message at all. It would be easy to add some statements to validate the parameter if necessary.

The *strcmp* Function

The *pointer_sort* function compares two strings, using the library function *strcmp* (*string comparison*). This function returns an integer. If the first string argument is *less* than the second, *strcmp* returns a value *less* than zero. If the first argument is *equal* to the second, the function returns a value *equal* to zero. If the first is *greater* than the second, a number *greater* than zero is returned.

The comparison is performed by moving along the two strings and comparing the characters in corresponding positions. Whenever the two characters differ, the function returns a value specifying that the first string is either greater than or less than the second, depending on which of the two characters is greater. If the end of the string is reached without detecting unequal characters, then the two strings are equal.

The value returned by *strcmp* usually is the difference between the ASCII values of the unequal characters, but since this function is implementation-dependent, a program should not depend on *strcmp* returning a particular value less than or greater than zero. (Sometimes we speak of one string being *lexically* less than, equal to, or greater than another. A string is said to be lexically less than another when it comes before the other in an alphabetized listing.)

The last statement executed by the *main* function in Program 12-10 is a call to the *release* function, which is a new addition to the alphabetizing program. This function *frees* each allocated array. This step is not strictly necessary, since all memory allocated by a program is freed upon program termination, but it is a good practice to free unneeded memory space that has been allocated dynamically. (The *free* function should never be used to free memory not allocated by *malloc* or one of its related functions.) A common error is to include a call to *malloc* within a loop, where the allocated space is needed during only one iteration of the loop, and then to forget to *free* the memory. If the loop runs for many iterations, or if the allocated blocks are large, it is possible to run out of memory.

If *malloc* runs out of memory, or if some other error occurs, it returns a special value referred to as NULL (not to be confused with the *null* character). More will be said about this value in Chapter 14, but usually it is equal to 0. This is a suitable value for *malloc* to return as an error code, since no memory pool will include location zero. In fact, no variables are put at location zero. For this reason, most functions that return pointers will return the NULL value as an indication that some error has occurred, such as invalid parameters.

In this chapter, we have covered the fundamental string functions of the standard C library. Several more functions are available, some of which are variations on those already described. The manual for your C compiler will describe these in detail. If you need a function that is not provided in your function library, you can always write your own.

As you know, all the elements of an array are of the same type. There are times, however, when it is desirable to combine values of different types in a single entity of some sort. For such situations, C provides a construct known as the *structure*, which is the subject of the next chapter.

The Spirit of C

The string functions covered in this chapter, such as *strcmp* and *strlen*, can be used to simplify the program in the previous chapter's *Spirit of C*. We leave it up to the reader to make these modifications, but we suggest an improvement to the program: Instead of using the dubious technique of determining whether a word is a verb by examining its last letter, why not maintain a list of verbs against which a word can be compared? Such a list can contain all forms and tenses of a verb, so that no restrictions need be made on the input sentences, except that they must contain verbs in the verb list.

Such a change will affect only the *is_verb* function. Let us look at that function again, for the sake of review:

```
is_verb(word)
char word[];

/* Returns true if the last character in "word" is a letter "s". That
   means "word" is a verb. */

{
   int i;

   /* Locate end of word (loop while word[i] != 0) */

   for (i = 0; word[i]; i++);

   /* Now "i" is the index of the terminating null character,
      so "i - 1" is the last non-null character */

   return (word[i - 1] == 's');   /* Returns the result of the test */
}
```

The verb list should be a string array. It could be a **static** array that is local to the function, but we will declare it as a global array instead. This will make it possible to place the array at the top of the program, so that it is easily located and modified if necessary. Since the array is used only for comparison and is not modified by the program, we consider this acceptable.

A real-life verb list would be very large, but for purposes of illustration we will make ours very small:

```
char *verb_list[] =
{
   "eat", "eats", "ate",
   "run", "runs", "ran",
   "sleep", "sleeps", "slept",
   "laugh", "laughs", "laughed",
   "am", "are", "is", "was", "were"
};
```

It is also necessary to know how many words are in the list. We could declare a constant containing the number of verbs:

```
#define VERB_COUNT 17
```

If verbs were added to or removed from the list, however, the programmer would have to remember to change the value of VERB_COUNT. Instead, we will use the expression

```
sizeof(verb_list)/sizeof(char*)
```

which, as shown in this chapter, evaluates to the number of elements in *verb_list*. We can define VERB_COUNT as follows:

```
#define VERB_COUNT sizeof(verb_list)/sizeof(char *)
```

The number of words in the list can now be determined by the value of VERB_COUNT. The *is_verb* function compares the word being tested to each verb in the list:

```
is_verb(word)
char word[];

/* Returns true if "word" is a verb. That means "word"
   is in "verb_list" */

{
    int i;

    /* Scan through "verb_list" until a verb is found that is equal
       to "word" (strcmp(word, verb_list[i])).  Scan ends  when
       i == VERB_COUNT (the end of the list is reached) */

    for (i = 0; i<VERB_COUNT && strcmp(word, verb_list[i]); i++);

    /* If  (i<VERB_COUNT),  "word" is a verb. If no match was
       found, i==VERB_COUNT (the end of the list was reached). */

    return(i<VERB_COUNT);
}
```

The **for** loop test continues as long as both i is less than *VERB_COUNT* and *strcmp(word, verb_list[i])* is not zero. The boolean value returned by the function is (i<VERB_COUNT). If a match between *word* and *verb_list[i]* is not found, i is incremented until it indexes past the last element of *verb_list* and the **for** loop terminates because $i ==$ VERB_COUNT. If a match is found, the loop terminates with i equal to the index of the verb in *verb_list*, which is always less than VERB_COUNT.

Note that if we wrote the program so that verbs can be added dynamically (added by the user as the program runs), it would be necessary to use a variable to hold the current number of verbs in *verb_list*.

In Chapter 14, which introduces files, you will see how a longer list of verbs can be stored on a magnetic disk or other mass storage device.

C *Tutorial*

1. What is another name sometimes given to arrays of type **char**?

2. What type in C corresponds to strings?

3. How is the string "take care" stored in C?

4. How is the end of a string recognized in C?

5. What is the length of the string in Question 3?

6. What is another name for a character string expressed as a constant?

7. In what way is a literal handled differently than an array of type **char**?

8. What is the difference between \" and "\ ?

9. How is a literal accessed within a program?

10. What is the null string?   What is its length?

11. What is a more elaborate way of stating the following?

    ```
    char string[] = "computer";
    ```

12. What are **static** variables? Compare them with standard local variables.

13. Explain the meaning of an **auto** variable.

14. Why is the keyword **auto** generally omitted from a C program?

15. What is the role of the *sprintf* function?

16. What is the purpose of the *strcpy* function?

17. How does the *sscanf* function operate?

18. As a general concept, why is the validation of data so important?

19. In what ways are a constant string and a variable string similar?

20. What is meant by *concatenation*?   What function is used to achieve this operation?

21. What is the result of the concatenation of "bingo" with "shmingo"?

22. What is the restriction regarding the returning of strings by functions?

23. What function returns the length of a string?

24. What is an easy way of locating the end of a string?

25. Under what circumstances is the *malloc* function useful?

26. How does the *malloc* function operate?

27. What is the purpose of the *free* function?

28. As mentioned in the answer to Question 22, a function can return only a pointer to a string. Name four ways such a string can be stored so that the returned pointer is meaningful.

29. What role is played by the **sizeof** operator?

30. Does the **sizeof** operator return the same values on all computers?

31. What are the two different kinds of operand that **sizeof** can take?

32. How is the **sizeof** operator useful in conjunction with the *malloc* function?

33. How can an array of string pointers be initialized? Illustrate your answer with an example.

34. What are the possible values the *strcmp* function can return, and what do they mean?

ANSWERS TO C TUTORIAL

1. Strings (if they are used to store data in string format).

2. Type **char ***.

3.

t	a	k	e		c	a	r	e	\0

4. By the *null* character ('\0').

5. 9. The *null* character is not included in a string's length; spaces, on the other hand, always are.

6. A literal.

7. A literal string should not be modified in any way, while an array can be modified at will.

8. In C, \" is used to include a double quote as part of a literal. There is no such thing as "\ in C.

9. By a pointer to the literal.

10. The null string is an empty pair of double quotation marks (""). It is stored as a *null* character with no preceding characters. Its length is zero.

11. `char string[] = {'c', 'o', 'm', 'p', 'u', 't', 'e', 'r', '\0' };`

12. A **static** variable is created when the program begins execution, and remains in existence until the program terminates. A local variable declared as **static** does not disappear when the function in which it is declared terminates. A standard local variable, by contrast, disappears when the function terminates.

13. An **auto** variable comes into existence when the function in which it is declared is executed. It disappears (along with its contents) when the function returns. The next time the function is called, it is recreated.

14. The default class for local variables (and variables declared in a compound statement) is **auto**. Global variables can never be of that class. Therefore, it is never necessary to specify **auto** as a storage class.

15. It stores its output in a string (its first argument) instead of displaying or printing it directly.

16. It stores one string, its second argument, into the array which is its first argument.

17. It operates exactly like the *scanf* function, except that it draws its input from a string specified as its first argument instead of from the keyboard.

18. When implemented to the fullest, it assists the user in preventing errors from occurring in the input, alerts the user to the nature of the error, and also enables recovery from the error to take place.

19. They are stored in exactly the same format, and are both accessed by pointers.

20. Concatenation is the joining together of two or more strings so that one begins where the other ends. The *strcat* function concatenates its second argument to the end of its first argument, which must be a variable string (an array).

21. "bingoshmingo"

22. A function can only return a pointer to a string. Since a string is an array, the function cannot directly return the body of the string.

23. The *strlen* function.

24. Add the value returned by *strlen* to the pointer to the string. For example, if *string_pointer* points to the beginning of a string, *string_pointer* + *strlen(string_pointer)* points to the *null* character, the character that terminates the string. This is equivalent to &*string_pointer[strlen(string_pointer)]*.

25. When it is not known in advance how large an array will be, and there is a need to conserve memory.

26. Its parameter is the number of bytes (or **char**-sized units) to be allocated. It returns a pointer to a vacant area of memory of the specified size, or a value of 0 (NULL) if the specified amount of memory cannot be allocated.

27. It returns the memory allocated by the *malloc* function to the pool of free memory. It is especially important to do this in programs that place heavy emphasis on memory allocation.

28. (a) In a global array.
    (b) In a local **static** array.
    (c) In an array passed to the function
    (d) In an array allocated with the *malloc* function.

29. It returns the size in bytes (or, more generally, **char**-sized units) of its operand.

30. No. The **sizeof** operator is machine-dependent, because different computers or compilers assign different sizes to various data types. The exception is that, by definition, the **sizeof** operator always returns 1 as the size of a **char** operand.

31. (a) The name of a data type.
    (b) The name of a variable.

32. The **sizeof** operator can determine how many bytes are to be allocated. For example, to allocate an array of 10 elements of type **int**, with the pointer to this array assigned to *p*, one could write:

```
p = malloc(10 * sizeof(int));
```

33.
```
char *array[] =
{
    "hello",
    "there",
    "y'all",
    "have a nice day."
};
```

34. If *strcmp* returns zero, it means that its two arguments are identical. A negative value indicates that the first argument is alphabetically (lexically) less than the second. A positive value means the first argument is lexically greater than the second.

Keywords

auto	break	case	char	default	do
double	else	float	for	if	int
long	return	short	**sizeof**	**static**	switch
unsigned	while				

Exercises

1. Imagine a function that accepts a string of n characters and exchanges the first character with the last, the second with the next-to-last, and so forth until n exchanges have been made. What will the final string look like? Write a program to verify your conclusion.

2. Write a function that accepts strings of any length and determines whether they are palindromes. As an enhancement, allow the function to accept sentences, ignoring spaces when determining whether the sentence is a palindrome.

3. Rewrite Program 12-10 to use memory more efficiently, by determining in advance how many words are to be sorted and allocating the array *words* dynamically. Also, when allocating an array for a single word, make the array just large enough to hold the word (including the terminating *null* character). Hint: This will require that the word be held first in a temporary holding array. (This modification will make the program more space-efficient, but may slow down execution, since more operations will be performed. Often a programmer will allow some waste of space for the sake of fast execution, but the reverse sometimes is also true.)

4. Write a function that, given two strings a and b, returns the position at which a occurs in b. For example, if a is "cat" and b is "concatenate", the value returned is 4, since the substring "cat" is found starting at the fourth character of "concatenate". If a does not occur at all in b, the value zero should be returned. This value also should be returned if a is longer than b. If a occurs more than once in b, only the first occurrence need be considered.

5. As an enhancement of the previous exercise, write a function that accepts three strings, a, b and c. If a occurs in c, not only is its position returned, but the first occurrence of a is replaced by b. For example, if the strings passed are

   a: "cat"
   b: "dog"
   c: "concatenate"

   then after the function returns, the string c will contain

   condogenate

Note that, since *c* is modified, it must be a character array rather than a constant string. Also note that *a* and *b* might not be of the same length, so *c* must have enough space to contain a larger string than the original.

6. Write a function that reads an entire line of input into a string, which is passed as a parameter. The function must read in single characters until a *newline* is read. It is up to the programmer to decide whether the *newline* is to be included in the string. (Remember to add the terminating *null* character.)

7. Implement a user-written version of *realloc* making use of the *malloc* and *free* functions. The function is passed the address of the old block of memory, the size of the old block, and the new size to which it is to be increased. The function must attempt to allocate a block of memory of the required (new) size and, if successful, must copy the contents of the old block into the new one. It must then free the old block. Finally, it must return the pointer to the new block. The following special cases must be dealt with:

   a) The new size is the same as the old. In this case, the function merely returns the old pointer.
   b) The new size is less than the old. The function returns a negative value to indicate an error condition, without freeing the old block.
   c) The new block cannot be allocated (not enough memory). The function returns an error code without freeing the old block.
   d) The old block cannot be freed (it was not allocated with *alloc* in the first place). The new block is discarded and an error code is returned.

   Note that this is *not* the specification of the library version of *realloc*. It has been simplified for easy implementation.

8. Rewrite the calculator program from Chapter 11, Exercise 1, so that it evaluates more complicated expressions. Each expression should occupy one line of input. The program should be able to handle all the operators from the first version of this program. It is not necessary to handle operator precedence correctly at this point; you may simply perform each operation as it occurs. For example, if the line contains

   `3 + 2 * 4`

   the program would calculate 3 + 2, for a result of 5, and then multiply this by 4 to yield 20. You might try writing the program so it can handle floating point numbers. Also, you might wish to implement "variables," such that an expression can be assigned to a memory location of your calculator referred to by a single letter that can be accessed in later expressions. This enhancement should not be terribly difficult at this point, but you will need to scan a line of input before attempting to extract numbers or symbols from it.

13

Structures

In many real—life situations, it is desirable to store data of different types, say strings and integers, in one data structure. It is not possible, however, to use a single C array for this purpose. As we have seen, elements of an array must be homogeneous. This chapter introduces us to a feature of C which helps to solve this type of problem.

The Concept of a Structure

At the lowest level, a computer represents all data items in the same way—as groups of *bits* (*b*inary dig*its*), usually organized into sets of eight bits, known as *bytes*. If the programmer were restricted to writing programs that dealt only with bits and bytes, programming would be an arduous task indeed. Most fortunately, computer languages such as C allow the programmer to deal with data on a higher level. Thus it is usually possible to design a solution without having to get involved with the intimate architectural structure of the machine. Data items in memory can be described in terms of integers, floating point numbers, characters, and even arrays. Such realistic data structures help to make it easier for programs to be written.

Under most circumstances, if all the data elements of a program are of the same type, they can be represented as an array. If the elements are of different types, however, the array is inadequate to the task. We resort instead to an entity known in C as a *structure*.

The concept of a structure may be familiar to those readers who know Pascal. Structures constitute a sort of super-data type, which can represent several different types of data in a single unit. For example, a single catalog card from a library might be represented by the following individual variables:

```
char title[30];
char author[20];
int catalog_number;
int year_published;
int number_of_copies;
```

These variables can be grouped together into a single structure, using the following definition:

```
struct
{
    char title[30];
    char author[20];
    int catalog_number;
    int year_published;
    int number_of_copies;
}
```

A structure definition is specified by the keyword **struct**. This is followed by a *template*, surrounded by braces, which describes the *members* of the structure. A member of a structure is a single unit, so the structure shown here has five members. In the example above, two of them, *title* and *author*, are **char** arrays of 30 and 20 elements respectively. The remaining three members, *catalog_number*, *year_published*, and *number_of_copies*, are **int** variables. Every member of a structure must have its own name. The template can be pictured as shown in Figure 13-1.

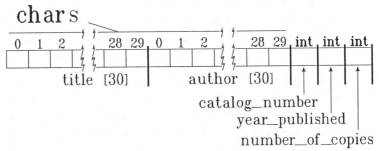

Figure 13—1

This construct is not complete. It defines the form of the structure, but does not declare any variables to be of that structure type. The declaration could be completed as follows, where the name *card* follows the template:

```
struct
{
    char title[30];
    char author[20];
    int catalog_number;
    int year_published;
    int number_of_copies;
}
card;
```

In this case, the structure declaration is delimited by the semicolon following *card*, which is the first semicolon after the template. Now the variable *card* is a structure variable with five members.

Note that, contrary to appearances, the members of a structure are not variables. Only when a structure variable (like *card*) is declared do the members come to represent locations in memory.

The Period Operator

Each member of a structure variable is specified by following the variable name with a period and the member name. The period is the *structure member* operator, which we shall hereafter refer to simply as the *period* operator. For example, the five members of *card* would be referred to in a program as

```
card.title
card.author
card.catalog_number
card.year_published
card.number_of_copies
```

Each of these members can have a value (or values) of the appropriate type assigned to it, and can be used like an ordinary variable.

Unlike array indexes, the members of a structure must be named explicitly. The period operator following the structure variable name can be followed only by a member name. It must be the name of a member actually defined in the structure template, and it cannot be a string variable containing the name of a member. In other words, the members of a structure must be accessed directly and explicitly. A **switch** statement or some similar structure can be used to choose between members.

When a structure member is named using the period operator, the variable name and member name are still separate identifiers. Thus the entire construct is not subject to the name truncation effect which otherwise would apply. That is, *card.author* is not a single identifier, so a compiler that truncates identifiers to eight characters will not reduce *card.author* to *card.aut*.

Program 13-1 illustrates the use of a structure. It is even simpler than the card catalog example. All it does is to declare two structures, assign values to them, and print them out.

```
/* Introduction to structures */

main()
{
    struct
    {
        int integer;
        float real;
    }
    first_structure, second_structure;

    first_structure.integer = 7;
    first_structure.real = 3.14;

    second_structure.integer = first_structure.integer;
    second_structure.real = first_structure.real;

    printf("integer = %d, real = %f\n",
        second_structure.integer, second_structure.real);
}
```

Program 13—1

```
integer = 7, real = 3.139999
```

Output 13—1

In this program, the structure template specifies two members: an **int** member called *integer* and a **float** member called *real*. Within the program, two variables, *first_structure* and *second_structure*, are created. Both are structures, and each contains a member called *integer* and a member called *real*. This may seem to violate the restriction that all variables must be uniquely named. Remember, however, that a structure member is not a variable in its own right, but part of a structure variable. The *integer* member of the variable *first_structure* is called *first_structure.integer*, whereas the *integer* member of *second_structure* is *second_structure.integer*. The structure name is qualified by the period and the member name.

In Program 13-1, the value 7 is assigned to the data item *first_structure.integer*, and the value 3.14 is assigned to *first_structure.real*. Then these members are copied individually into their member counterparts, *second_structure.integer* and *second_structure.real*, the contents of which are then printed out.

According to the original definition of the C language, structures cannot be assigned to one another as entire units, nor can they be passed to or returned from functions. Many C compilers, however, allow structures to be handled like scalar variables, with direct assignments and passing by value permitted. Since structures can be very large, such operations may be both time- and space-consuming, so compilers for microcomputers tend to treat structures according to the original definition. In this book, we shall assume that structures are subject to the same restrictions as arrays.

You will notice that the output of the program represents 3.14 as 3.139999. This slight error, of a type we have encountered before, is due to the need to convert the number from decimal to binary notation and then back to decimal again.

Initializing a Structure

Defining a structure is a way of creating a new data type. It may have virtually any design of your choosing. As with any other data type, a structure variable can be initialized. In keeping with the array analogy, a structure must be **static** in order for it to be initialized. The following program illustrates this feature.

```
/* Initializing a structure */

main()
{
    static struct
    {
        int integer;
        float real;
    }
    structure =
        {
            7,
             3.14
        };

    printf("integer = %d, real = %f\n",
        structure.integer, structure.real);
}
```

Program 13—2

```
integer = 7, real = 3.139999
```

Output 13—2

The initializer for a structure must be enclosed within a pair of braces. The constants to be assigned to the members of the structure must be in the same order as that in which the members are specified. That is to say, there must be a one-to-one correspondence between the members and their initializing values. If too few initializing values are specified, the remaining members are left uninitialized.

The syntax of the C language prevents the programer from initializing individual structure members within the structure template. The initialization must be done in the declaration of the actual variables.

In Program 13-2, the same two values are printed out as before. Once again, the same slight conversion error occurs with the value 3.14.

The Structure Tag

In any non-trivial program employing structures, it is necessary to pass a structure (by reference) to a function. Therefore, the function must be able to declare its parameters using the same template by which the structure being passed is declared. C simplifies this process by allowing a structure template to be given its own name, called a *structure tag*. The structure tag can be substituted for the structure template in subsequent declarations, as shown in Program 13-3.

```
/* The structure tag */

main()
{
    struct two_numbers
    {
        int integer;
        float real;
    }
    first_structure;
    struct two_numbers second_structure;

    first_structure.integer = 7;
    first_structure.real = 3.14;

    second_structure.integer = first_structure.integer;
    second_structure.real = first_structure.real;

    printf("integer = %d, real = %f\n",
        second_structure.integer, second_structure.real);
}
```

Program 13—3

```
integer = 7, real = 3.139999
```

Output 13—3

In the declaration of *first_structure*, the tag *two_numbers* follows the keyword **struct**, right before the structure template. The next statement can declare *second_structure* by using this tag. In effect, **struct** *two_numbers* has become a new data type, and the variable *second_structure* is declared to be of that type.

It is possible to define a structure type without declaring a variable. For example, in the above program, the declarations of *first_structure* and *second_structure* could be written as follows:

```
struct two_numbers
{
    int integer;
    float real;
};
struct two_numbers first_structure, second_structure;
```

No variables are declared until the second statement, which declares both *first_structure* and *second_structure* to be of type **struct** *two_numbers*. The first statement merely defines the structure type. If the programmer wishes to use the definition of *two_numbers* in another function, it is necessary to define *two_numbers* globally. That is, the first statement of this example would have to be written outside any function body. The type **struct** *two_numbers* then can be used in any function of the program, thus eliminating the need to respecify the template.

Since **struct** *two_numbers* is considered a data type, it can be used as an operand to the **sizeof** operator. The expression

```
sizeof(struct two_numbers)
```

returns the same value as

```
sizeof(first_structure)
```

which in turn is (usually) equal to

```
sizeof(int) + sizeof(float)
```

In terms of **sizeof**, a structure is not always equal to the sum of its parts. A structure may contain unused bytes, which are detected when the size of the entire structure is compared to the sum of the sizes of its members. This discrepancy occurs because of a requirement known as *alignment*. For example, some computers have the requirement that an integer must begin in a byte with an even address. Assume that a structure contains a character followed by an integer, and that the character is located at an even address. Since the integer also must begin at an even address, the compiler inserts an unused byte (with an odd address) between the character and the beginning of the integer so that the integer starts at an even address. This operation is shown in Figure 13-2.

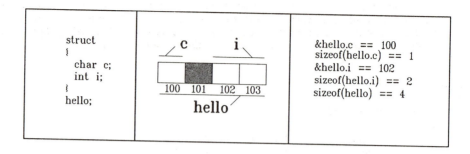

Figure 13—2

In this case, assuming that an integer is two bytes long, the size of the entire structure is 4: a character, an unused byte, and two bytes for an integer. For this reason, when determining the true amount of memory needed to hold an entire structure, generally it is not correct to add only the sizes of the structure members. The safest method is to apply the **sizeof** operator to the entire structure (or to the structure tag; all structures with identical templates have identical sizes).

A **struct** declaration that contains a template (rather than a predefined structure tag) must also contain a structure tag, one or more variable names, or both a tag and a variable name or names. It cannot contain only a template. If only a tag is present, the declaration serves to define a structure type without actually allocating any variables of that type. If only a variable name (or names) is specified, the variables are declared to be structures as specified by the template, but the template is not named (since it is given no tag). Therefore, it must be respecified if variables of the same type are to be declared later on in the program.

Arrays of Structures

In a program using structures to represent a card catalog, for example, it would not be sufficient to declare one or two structure variables. A whole array of structures would be needed. It is easy to declare an array of structures, each element of which is a structure of the specified template.

Program 13-4 incorporates an array of structures. The problem is analogous to that of a supermarket in which the check-out clerk, using a bar-code reader, scans each item to access its price. In our program, all the information must be typed in by hand. Each product is represented by a single character code. The user types in the code for the product desired and the number of units to be purchased. The program prints out the unit cost of the item and the total cost of the purchase (unit cost times quantity).

```
/* An array of structures.
     Each structure contains an item code (a letter) along with the price
     of one unit of the item.  User enters an item code and the  quantity
     to be purchased.  Program prints out unit price and total price.  It
     looks for the item code in "table", the array of structures.
*/

main()
{
    static struct item
    {
        char code;         /* Letter code for item */
        float price;       /* Unit price of item */
    }
    table[] =
        {
            { 'a', 3.29 },
            { 'b', 2.99 },
            { 'c', 0.59 },
            { 'd', 1.59 },
            { 'e', 2.39 }
        };
    char item_code[2];    /* Inputs user's choice of item (an array because
                             "%1s" is used to read it in) */
    int quantity,         /* Inputs quantity desired */
        i;                /* A loop index */

    do
    {
        printf("Enter item code: ");
        scanf("%1s", item_code);     /* Skip white space */

        if (*item_code != '.')       /* (Skip this last time around loop) */
        {

            /*  Search for "*item_code" in "table", or end of "table",
                whichever comes first */

            for (i = 0;
                i < sizeof(table)/sizeof(struct item)
                   && table[i].code != *item_code;
                i++);

            if (i < sizeof(table)/sizeof(struct item))    /* Found */
            {
                printf("Enter quantity: ");
                scanf("%d", &quantity);

                printf("\nUnit price = %.2f, total price = %.2f.\n\n\n",
                    table[i].price, quantity * table[i].price);
            }

            else    /* Not found */
                printf("\nItem code %c does not exist.\n\n\n", *item_code);

        }   /* end if */
    }   /* end do */
    while (*item_code != '.');     /* Loop until user enters '.' */

    printf("Thank you.\n");
}
```

Program 13—4

```
Enter item code: a
Enter quantity: 1

Unit price = 3.29, total price = 3.29.


Enter item code: c
Enter quantity: 5

Unit price = 0.59, total price = 2.95.


Enter item code: f

Item code f does not exist.


Enter item code: b
Enter quantity: 3

Unit price = 2.99, total price = 8.97.


Enter item code: .
Thank you.
```

Output 13—4

The program creates a **static** array of structures by following the template with the implicitly dimensioned array name, *table[]*. The array is **static** because it must be initialized, and the number of elements in the array is determined during this process. The array is initialized in the usual manner, except that each pair of inner braces represents the initializer for a single element. Each element, being a structure, contains several members of different types. Therefore, *table[0]* is initialized to the structure

```
{ 'a', 3.29 }
```

table[1] is initialized to

```
{ 'b', 2.99 }
```

and so on.

It would be permissible to omit the inner braces of the array initializer, since all the members of all the elements are initialized. Just as with two-dimensional arrays, however, it is recommended that the inner braces be used for clarity. Sometimes it is desirable to initialize only a few members of the elements of a structure array. In such a case, the inner braces must be used. If only some of the members of a structure are initialized, those members must be in consecutive order, starting with the first member of the structure. Fortunately, unlike arrays, structure members are accessed by name rather than position. The members therefore can be safely rearranged so those to be initialized precede the others.

The two-element array *item_code* is used to input the character code. An array, rather than a single **char** variable, is used because the conversion specification %1s is employed to read in the character while ignoring any leading white space. This operation requires an extra memory location to accept the *null* character appended to the input.

Within a **do...while** loop, the user is prompted to enter an item code. This code is read in and tested to determine whether it is a period. The entry of a period by the user signifies the end of input.

The input character is accessed as **item_code*. This is the same as *item_code[0]*, but the former method is shorter and perhaps more appropriate in this case.

If the entered character is a period, the rest of the body of the **do...while** loop is skipped. The loop is then terminated because the loop condition is false. This is equivalent to a **break** statement, but is preferable in structured programming.

The next step in the program is a bodyless **for** loop, which serves the purpose of searching for the input value of *item_code* in *table*. The condition of the loop specifies that the loop terminates either when the end of the table is reached (indicating that the input code does not exist in the table) or when the input code is found. Notice that the number of elements in *table* is determined by dividing the size of *table* by the size of a single element. This makes it possible to add items to *table* without having to change any constants in the program.

Notice how the *code* members are accessed. The element indexed by *i* is represented as *table[i]*. Within this indexed element, the *code* member is referred to as *table[i].code*.

If the item code selected by the user is found in the table, the variable *i* indexes the element containing that code. Otherwise, *i* indexes past the last element of the table, and has the value **sizeof** (*table*) / **sizeof** (**struct** *item*)). If the code is found in the table, the user is prompted to enter a value for *quantity*, indicating how many units of the item are being purchased. The program then prints out the unit price (*table[i].price*) and the total cost of the purchase. (Multiplying *quantity*, an **int**, by the *price* member, a **float**, causes *quantity* to be cast automatically into a **float** value before the multiplication is performed.)

If the input code is not in *table*, the program displays a message to this effect, echoing the character for the benefit of the user.

The loop condition causes termination when the user enters a period. This test is redundant, since it is made earlier in the body of the loop, but it makes for simpler code and is preferable to using a **break**.

Program 13-4 is restrictive in many ways. One obvious improvement would be the identification of items by descriptive strings rather than by single-character codes. The member *code* could be replaced with a member called *name*, defined to be a string pointer, as shown in Program 13-5.

```
/*  A pointer in a structure.
    Each structure contains an item name along with the price of one
    unit of the item.  User enters an item name  and the quantity to
    be purchased. Program prints out unit price and total price.  It
    looks for the item name in "table", the array of structures.
*/

main()
{
    static struct item
    {
        char *name;      /* (Pointer to) name of item */
        float price;     /* Unit price of item */
    }
    table[] =
        {
            { "pickles", 2.29 },
            { "soda", 0.99 },
            { "yogurt", 0.59 },
            { "bread", 1.09 },
            { "milk", 0.69 }
        };
    char item_name[21];   /* Inputs user's choice of item */
    int quantity,         /* Inputs quantity desired */
        i;                /* A loop index */
    do
    {
        printf("Enter item name: ");
        scanf("%s", item_name);

        if (*item_name != '.')    /* (Skip this last time around loop) */
        {

            /* Search for "*item_name" in "table", or end of "table",
               whichever comes first */

            for (i = 0;
                 i < sizeof(table)/sizeof(struct item)
                    && strcmp(table[i].name, item_name);
                 i++);

            if (i < sizeof(table)/sizeof(struct item))    /* Found */
            {
                printf("Enter quantity: ");
                scanf("%d", &quantity);

                printf("\nUnit price = %.2f, total price = %.2f.\n\n\n",
                    table[i].price, quantity * table[i].price);
            }

            else    /* Not found */
                printf("\nItem \"%s\" does not exist.\n\n\n", item_name);

        }    /* end if */
    }    /* end do */
    while (*item_name != '.');    /* Loop until user enters '.' */

    printf("Thank you.\n");
}
```

Program 13—5

```
Enter item name: pickles
Enter quantity: 1

Unit price = 2.29, total price = 2.29.


Enter item name: bread
Enter quantity: 2

Unit price = 1.09, total price = 2.18.


Enter item name: juice

Item "juice" does not exist.


Enter item name: milk
Enter quantity: 0

Unit price = 0.69, total price = 0.00.


Enter item name: .
Thank you.
```

Output 13—5

The initializer for the new version of the array *table* contains strings to be assigned to the *name* members of the array elements. These strings are stored in memory, and pointers to them are assigned to the *name* members of the corresponding elements.

The array *item_name* replaces *item_code* of Program 13-4, and is dimensioned to 21 elements, large enough to hold a string of length 20. Its value is read in using the conversion specification %s. Strictly speaking, a conversion specification of %20s should be used. If the user were to enter a string of more than 20 characters, however these would cause an error when *quantity* is read in, unless steps were taken to discard the excess characters. Therefore, to avoid the need for validation, it is assumed that the user always types in a string of 20 characters or fewer.

As in the previous version of this program, the user's input is tested to determine whether it is a period. Since only the first character need be checked, it is not necessary to use the *strcmp* function here. Instead, the first character of *item_name*, accessed as **item_name*, is compared with the period character.

The loop used to search for *item_name* in *table* makes use of the *strcmp* function. If *table[i].name* matches *item_name*, the *strcpy* function returns a value of zero, which causes the entire condition to become false, terminating the loop immediately. If the strings do not match, *strcmp* returns a non-zero (true) value, permitting the loop to continue. The loop also is terminated if the end of the table is reached. The remainder of the program is basically the same as in Program 13-4, except for the slight modification of the data structures used.

Arrays Within Structures

Program 13-5 solves the problem of restricting item names to single characters. Were this function incorporated into a larger program, however, another problem might arise. Many programs that use arrays of structures need to store these arrays into disk files. Files (which are discussed more fully in the next chapter) enable a program to store information outside the computer, to be read in later, often by a different program. When this is done, however, pointer values lose their meaning. If an array contains a pointer to a string, there is no guarantee that the string will be at the same location in memory when the array is read back in. In fact, the string probably will not be there, since the execution of a new program causes memory to contain totally different values. Therefore, it would be necessary to store the strings with the arrays, or more specifically, to store the strings physically within each structure rather than just storing a pointer.

C allows structures to contain arrays. The structure template in Program 13-5 could be rewritten as

```
{
    char name[21];
    float price;
}
```

in which case the structure would be stored in memory as shown in Figure 13-3.

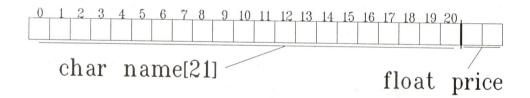

Figure 13—3

The array *table* can be initialized in the same manner as before. Since the compiler detects that the *name* member is an array rather than a pointer, however, it will copy the initializing strings directly into the *name* member.

Program 13-6 includes the modification just described. Except for the redefinition of the *name* member, the program is identical to Program 13-5, but the strings are stored directly in the array *table* instead of elsewhere in memory.

```
/*  An array in a structure.
    Each structure  contains an  item name along  with the  price of
    one unit of the item.  User enters an item name and the quantity
    to be purchased.  Program prints out unit price and total price.
    It looks for the  item name in "table", the array of structures.
*/

main()
{
    static struct item
    {
        char name[21];      /* Name of item */
        float price;        /* Unit price of item */
    }
    table[] =
        {
            { "pickles", 2.29 },
            { "soda", 0.99 },
            { "yogurt", 0.59 },
            { "bread", 1.09 },
            { "milk", 0.69 }
        };
    char item_name[21];     /* Inputs user's choice of item */
    int quantity,           /* Inputs quantity desired */
        i;                  /* A loop index */

    do
    {
        printf("Enter item name: ");
        scanf("%s", item_name);

        if (*item_name != '.')    /* (Skip this last time around loop) */
        {

            /*  Search for "*item_name" in "table", or end of "table",
                whichever comes first */

            for (i = 0;
                 i < sizeof(table)/sizeof(struct item)
                    && strcmp(table[i].name, item_name);
                 i++);

            if (i < sizeof(table)/sizeof(struct item))     /* Found */
            {
                printf("Enter quantity: ");
                scanf("%d", &quantity);

                printf("\nUnit price = %.2f, total price = %.2f.\n\n\n",
                    table[i].price, quantity * table[i].price);
            }

            else    /* Not found */
                printf("\nItem \"%s\" does not exist.\n\n\n", item_name);

        }    /* end if */
    }    /* end do */
    while (*item_name != '.');    /* Loop until user enters '.' */

    printf("Thank you.\n");
}
```

Program 13-6

```
Enter item name: milk
Enter quantity: 5

Unit price = 0.69, total price = 3.45.


Enter item name: yogurt
Enter quantity: 2

Unit price = 0.59, total price = 1.18.


Enter item name: fish

Item "fish" does not exist.


Enter item name: soda
Enter quantity: 14

Unit price = 0.99, total price = 13.86.


Enter item name: .
Thank you.
```

Output 13—6

Structures Within Structures

As you may have guessed by now, the structure is recursive. By this we mean that, since it can include members of any legal C type, it also can contain other structures. In the library problem, for example, suppose that we wish to record the last date on which a book was borrowed in addition to the other information. (This modification requires that each copy of the same book have its own card, so a copy number member also is added to the structure.) Such a structure might look like this:

```
struct card    /* This time "card" is the structure tag */
{
      char title[30];
      char author[20];
      int catalog_number;
      int year_published;
      int copy_number;
      char month_borrowed[3];    /* A 3-character name with
                                      no terminator */
      int day_borrowed;
      int year_borrowed;
      int number_of_copies;
}
one_card;    /* This is the variable name */
```

This arrangement contains the required information, but it obscures the logical association of the *month_borrowed*, *day_borrowed*, and *year_borrowed* members. It would be better to group these three into a substructure:

```
struct card
{
    char title[30];
    char author[20];
    int catalog_number;
    int year_published;
    int copy_number;
    struct
    {
        char month_borrowed[3];
        int day_borrowed;
        int year_borrowed;
    }
    date_borrowed;   /* member name goes here, not as tag */
    int number_of_copies;
}
one_card;
```

In the above example, the structure contains a member named *date_borrowed*. This member also is a structure, and it contains three members: *month_borrowed*, *day_borrowed*, and *year_borrowed*. We could say that *date_borrowed* is nested in *one_card* (or in **struct** *card*, for that matter). Notice that the name *date_borrowed* is specified in the position where the variable normally is located (after the template), rather than in the structure tag position.

The three members of the *date_borrowed* member are referred to as

```
one_card.date_borrowed.month_borrowed
```

```
one_card.date_borrowed.day_borrowed
```

and

```
one_card.date_borrowed.year_borrowed
```

A submember must be specified by the full path needed to access it; it is not legal, for example, to refer to *one_card.year_borrowed*, since *year_borrowed* is not a direct member of *one_card*. Because of this requirement, it is possible to have two sub-members of the same name if they are part of different substructures. Consider the following example:

```
struct card
{
    char title[30];
    char author[20];
    int catalog_number;
    int year_published;
    int copy_number;
    struct
    {
        char month_borrowed[3];
        int day_borrowed;
        int year_borrowed;
    }
    date_borrowed,
    first_borrowed;   /* Same structure type as "date_borrowed" */
    int number_of_copies;
}
one_card;
```

A new member, *first_borrowed*, has been added which represents the date the book was first borrowed. This new member has the same structure template as *date_borrowed*, which means that its members have the same names, but this fact creates no ambiguity. For example, the *year_borrowed* member of *date_borrowed* is referred to as

```
one_card.date_borrowed.year_borrowed
```

whereas the *year_borrowed* member of *first_borrowed* is referred to as

```
one_card.first_borrowed.year_borrowed
```

Pointers to Structures

The one restriction on structure nesting is that a structure cannot contain an image of itself. That is, a structure cannot contain a member defined with the same tag as the outside structure. Such a construct would be an infinite recursion. It is legal, however, to have a structure contain a pointer to a structure of the same type, as shown here:

```
struct card
{
    char title[30];
    char author[20];
    int catalog_number;
    int year_published;
    int copy_number;
    struct
    {
        char month_borrowed[3];
        int day_borrowed;
        int year_borrowed;
    }
    date_borrowed,
    int number_of_copies;
    struct card *next_card;    /* Points to next card in the
                                  catalog */
}
one_card;
```

Each *card* structure contains a member that is a pointer to another *card* structure. This does not cause infinite recursion, since a pointer to a structure is always the same size and does not physically contain any members.

The Arrow Operator

Suppose we wish to refer to the *title* member of the structure to which *one_card.next_card* points. One way is to refer to the whole structure as

```
*(one_card.next_card)
```

and therefore to the title member as

```
(*(one_card.next_card)).title
```

The period operator has a precedence value as high as that of parentheses, so we could write the following instead:

```
(*one_card.next_card).title
```

Fortunately, C provides an abbreviation for such an operation.

One can refer to the title member of one_card.next_card as

```
(one_card.next_card)->title
```

where the -> operator returns the member named on its right side from the structure pointed to by the pointer to its left. This operator, which resembles an arrow, consists of a minus sign followed immediately by a greater-than sign. It is called the *structure pointer* operator, but we shall refer to it as the *arrow* operator. It has the same high precedence as the period operator.

Linked Lists

In the preceding example, the member *next_card* was used to point to the *card* structure that logically followed it in the card catalog that was being simulated in the computer. That structure in turn pointed to the one following it, and so forth. The structures that made up the catalog therefore were linked together in a chain. Such a chain is known as a *linked list* (see Figure 13-4).

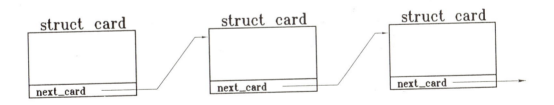

Figure 13—4

In computer programming, each structure of a *singly linked list* contains a single link that attaches it to the following structure in the chain. A *doubly linked list* contains pointers to both the following and the preceding structure. (A single element of a linked list is called a *node*.)

One of the advantages of a linked list is that it is easier to use than a dynamically allocated array. Whereas it would be necessary to know the number of elements needed before allocating an array, a linked list can be expanded as necessary, allocating additional structures only as they are needed.

The following program illustrates a simple use for a linked list. It is an inventory program that could be used in a store. Each node of the linked list featured in the program represents one product received by the store. Members of the structure include the product name, the number of units received, the cost per unit, and so on. Each time a shipment of a product is received, the information about the product is stored in a node of the list. The node also has a field that could be used to keep a running count of how many units of the product are on hand at any given time. Since there is no need to keep the nodes in any particular order, each new node is added to the beginning of the list. (As we will explain, it is easier to add a node to the beginning of a linked list than to the end.)

We have not yet discussed files, so this program performs only a subset of the functions it would have in real life. The program reads in the information about each product, stores the information in a node, and stores the node in the linked list. Once all the products have been entered, the program prints out a table of all the information in the linked list.

```
/*  Store inventory program.
    This program records information about stock received at a store.  The
user enters information about each product received -- the item name, the price
per unit (jar of jelly, can of tuna, etc.), the quantity and date received, and
the supplier.  Each product is represented by a  structure which is stored as a
node  in a linked list.  The structure  also contains  a member  named "count",
which  (theoretically) is  used  to record  the  number of units of the product
in the  store at any time.  This member is  initialized  to "quantity_received"
and would  be  decremented by 1  each time a unit  of  the product is purchased
(this latter process is not performed by this program). */

#define NULL 0

struct inventory     /* Represents a stock item */
{
    char item[15];
    float unit_price;
    int count;                  /* Number currently in store at any time */
    int quantity_received;      /* Number originally received */
    struct
    {
        int month;
        int day;
    }
    date_received;
    char supplier[15];
    struct inventory *next;
};

main()
{
    struct inventory *inv_list = NULL,      /* Pointer to linked list */
                     *p,                    /* Pointer to structure being added */
                     *new_node();           /* (See below) */
    char reply[10];                         /* Holds user's response as to whether
                                               another item is to be entered */
```

Program continued on next page

Program continued from previous page

```
    do
    {
        p = new_node();              /* Get a new structure */
        if (p == NULL)               /* Terminate if no more structures available */
        {
            printf("Out of memory.  Cannot add any more items\n");
            *reply = 'n';      /* Force termination of loop */
        }
        else
        {
            get_info(p);     /* Read in member values for structure */
            add_node(p, &inv_list);    /* Add node to list */

            printf("\nItem %s entered.\n", p->item);
            printf("\n\nDo you wish to enter another item (y/n)? ");
            scanf("%s", reply);
        }
    }
    while (*reply == 'y' || *reply == 'Y');
    printf("\nThank you.\n");

    print_inventory(inv_list);            /* Print out final inventory */
}

struct inventory *new_node()

/* Allocate a new inventory structure */

{
    struct inventory *malloc();

    return(malloc(sizeof(struct inventory)));
}

get_info(node)
struct inventory *node;

/* Read in member values for "node" (inventory information) */

{
    printf("\tItem? ");
    scanf("%s", node->item);

    printf("\tUnit price (no dollar sign)? ");
    scanf("%f", &node->unit_price);

    printf("\tQuantity received? ");
    scanf("%d", &node->quantity_received);

    /* Initialize "count" to "quantity_received" */

    node->count = node->quantity_received;

    printf("\tDate received (month#/day#)? ");
    scanf("%d/%d", &node->date_received.month, &node->date_received.day);

    printf("\tSupplier? ");
    scanf("%s", node->supplier);
}
```

Program continued on next page

Program continued from previous page

```
    add_node(node, header)
    struct inventory *node,
                    **header;

/* Add node pointed to by "node" to beginning of list pointed to by "*header"
   (*header is modified) */

{
    node->next = *header;
    *header = node;
}


    print_inventory(header)
    struct inventory *header;

/* Nicely print linked list pointed to by "header" */

{
    char price[10],        /* Holds string version of "unit_price" */
         date[10];         /* Holds string version of "date_received" */
    int i;                 /* Loop index */

    /* Print heading */

    printf("\n\n%-14s%11s%17s%17s      %-14s\n",
        "Item", "Unit Price", "Quantity Rec'd", "Date Rec'd", "Supplier");
    for (i = 0; i < 78; i++)
        printf("-");
    printf("\n");

    for (; header != NULL; header = header->next)
    {

        /* Make "unit_price" and "date_received" into nice strings */

        sprintf(price,"$%.2f", header->unit_price);
        sprintf(date,"%d/%d",
            header->date_received.month, header->date_received.day);

        printf("%-14s%11s%17d%17s      %-14s\n",
            header->item, price, header->quantity_received, date,
            header->supplier);
    }
}
```

Program 13—7

```
    Item? Happy_Cow_Milk
    Unit price (no dollar sign)? 0.70
    Quantity received? 500
    Date received (month#/day#)? 10/4
    Supplier? Judy's_Dairy

Item Happy_Cow_Milk entered.
```

Output continued on next page

Output continued from previous page

```
Do you wish to enter another item (y/n)? y
    Item? Marvel_Bread
    Unit price (no dollar sign)? 1.09
    Quantity received? 300
    Date received (month#/day#)? 10/12
    Supplier? IBC

Item Marvel_Bread entered.



Do you wish to enter another item (y/n)? y
    Item? noodles-1lb.
    Unit price (no dollar sign)? 0.59
    Quantity received? 350
    Date received (month#/day#)? 9/17
    Supplier? Mom's

Item noodles-1lb. entered.


Do you wish to enter another item (y/n)? n

Thank you.
```

Item	Unit Price	Quantity Rec'd	Date Rec'd	Supplier
noodles-1lb.	$0.59	350	9/17	Mom's
Marvel_Bread	$1.09	300	10/12	IBC
Happy_Cow_Milk	$0.70	500	10/4	Judy's_Dairy

Output 13—7

Program 13-7 begins with an extensive comment that details the purpose of the program. It is always a good idea to include descriptive information in comments within a program.

The constant NULL is defined to be the value 0. This is the same NULL that was described in the previous chapter. NULL is useful with linked lists, since it can be used to indicate the end of the list.

A structure named *inventory* is defined, with no variables yet declared. It is defined globally so that the tag (*inventory*) is meaningful throughout the program. The structure has a *next* member defined to be of type **struct** *inventory* * so that the structure can be used as a linked list node.

In the *main* function, a variable *inv_list* is declared to be a pointer to **struct** *inventory*. This variable is called the *header* of the linked list, since it will be used to point to the first node in the list. In a sense, the header is the first link in the chain; if you have the header, you have the key to the entire linked list. For this reason, the header variable can be identified with the entire list. That is why the name *inv_list* is used rather than, say, *inv_header*. The variable *inv_list* is initialized to NULL, indicating that there are no nodes in the list initially.

The variable *p* also is a structure pointer. It is used to point to a newly allocated structure before that structure is added to the linked list. The function *new_node*, which is specified within the program, is defined in the *main* function as returning a pointer to **struct** *inventory*.

The array *reply* is used to read in the user's response to the prompt that asks whether another item is to be entered. It allows for a response of up to nine characters (the *null* character takes up one element at the end).

Most of the *main* function consists of a **do...while** *loop*. Each time through the loop, one structure's worth of information is read in. The first step is a call to the *new_node* function to allocate a new structure. A pointer to the new structure is returned and assigned to *p*. If there is not enough memory left to allocate another structure, the *new_node* function returns NULL. In that case, a suitable message is printed and the loop is forced to terminate. This is accomplished by setting the first character of *reply* to 'n' and skipping the rest of the **do...while** loop body (by enclosing it in an **else** clause). The loop test is then made, and the first character in *reply* is found to be 'n'. This causes the loop to be exited, and no more data is read in. (Even though computers rarely run out of memory, it is always a good idea to prepare for unlikely as well as common errors.)

If the value of *p* is not NULL, the *get_info* function is invoked to read in the information. The value of *p* is passed as a parameter so that the function knows where to put the data. The function *add_node* is then called to add *p* (or rather, the structure pointed to by *p*) to the list headed by *inv_list*. Notice that the address of *inv_list* is passed, since the value of *inv_list* (the address it points to) is changed by the function.

After adding the new node to the list, the program informs the user of its actions and asks if there are more items to be entered. If there are, the loop goes through another iteration. Otherwise, the program thanks the user and calls the *print_inventory* function to print out the contents of the linked list.

The function *new_node* calls the *malloc* function, to allocate additional memory for a new structure, and returns the pointer that *malloc* returns. Since *malloc* returns NULL when it runs out of memory, the *new_node* function merely passes that value along to the *main* function.

The function *get_info* reads in values for the various members of the structure pointed to by the *node* parameter. The *count* member is set equal to the *quantity_received* member, as described in the comment at the beginning of the program. Notice how the *date_received* structure members are read in. The user is required to include the slash at the appropriate point in the date, and the *scanf* function "filters out" the slash because the control string passed to the *scanf* function contains a slash. The *get_info* function includes no data validation features, but many provisions could be included to ensure that the strings are of the correct length, the month and day values are meaningful, and so on.

The *add_node* function inserts the structure pointed to by *node* into the linked list pointed to by **header* (as you recall, *inv_list* was passed by reference). The argument *header* is declared to be of type **struct** *inventory* **, since it is the address of a variable that points to a structure. The *add_node* function adds the new node to the beginning of the list rather than to the end, because the former is easier. To find the end of a singly linked list, it is necessary to search through the list, starting from the header, until the end of the list is reached. The beginning of the list is merely the node pointed to by the header.

The process of adding a node to the beginning of a linked list is illustrated in Figure 13-5.

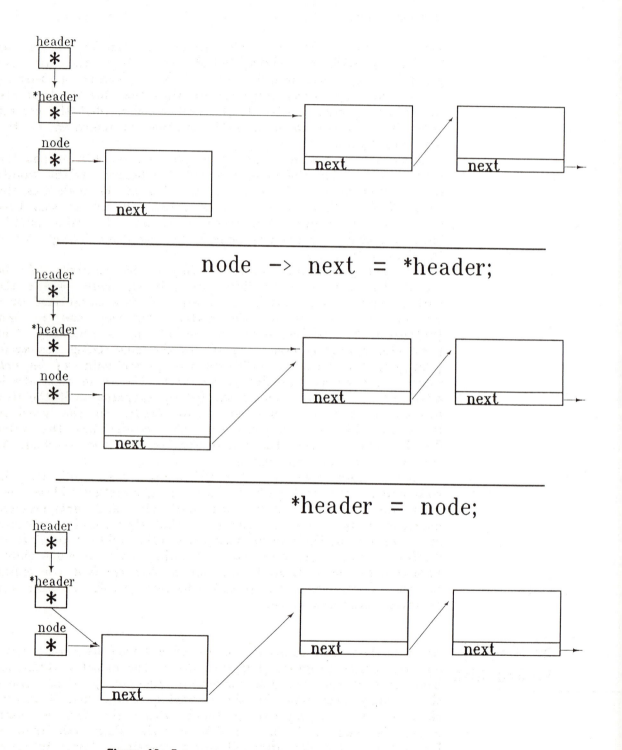

Figure 13—5

Consider what would happen if the two statements were reversed. If the statement

```
*header = node;
```

were executed first, the old value of *header* would be lost—along with the entire linked list! Only the structure pointed to by *node* would be left. When inserting or deleting nodes, the programmer must ensure that the correct steps are taken in the correct order. If you are not sure what the correct order is, just try to picture the process as indicated in the preceding figure.

When the first node is added to the list, the header has the value NULL. After the node is added, the header variable points to this first node, while the *next* member of the node has the value NULL. Since all new nodes are added behind this first node, its *next* member will continue to have the value NULL, indicating that it is the last node in the list (even though it was the first to be added).

The *print_inventory* function displays the contents of the linked list. First the headings are printed, under which the various items of information are listed. This is accomplished by a **for** loop that prints out the nodes. This loop has no first (initializing) expression, since no initializing is necessary. The parameter *header* is used to point to the node being displayed. (Changing this parameter will not change the value of *inv_list*, since it is a passed-by-value parameter.) The value of *header* is advanced to the next node in the list by assigning to it the *next* member of the node pointed to by *header* on the previous iteration. This process continues until *header* has the value NULL, indicating that the end of the list has been reached. At this point, the loop terminates.

This function uses two character arrays, *price* and *date*, in conjunction with two calls to the *sprintf* function. These two calls are used to convert the *unit_price* and *date_received* members of the node into strings so that they can be displayed more readily. In the case of *unit_price*, this makes it possible to display a dollar sign immediately preceding the price while right-justifying the entire field. In the case of *date_received*, conversion to string form enables the program to right-justify the date and eliminate unwanted spaces.

Sorting by Linked List

As a further illustration of the use of a linked list, we present another sorting program (Program 13-8). The essential difference between this and the store inventory program is that, rather than adding new nodes to the beginning of the list, it inserts them in their appropriate positions within the list. As each integer is read in, it is stored in a node. This node then is inserted into the list after all nodes containing lesser integers, but before all nodes containing greater integers. After all numbers are read in and inserted, the numbers contained in the list will be in ascending order.

```
/*  Sorting by linked list.
    The sort is accomplished by inserting each new number at the right place
    in the linked list. */

#define NULL 0

struct list_node      /* List node: datum is integer to be inserted */
{
    int number;
    struct list_node *next;
};

main()
{
    struct list_node *sorted_list = NULL,   /* Points to linked list */
                     *p,                    /* Node being added to list */
                     *q,                    /* Node after which "p" is to be
                                               added to list */
                     *new_node();           /* (See below) */

    int i,            /* Loop index */
        n;            /* Number of integers to be sorted */

    printf("How many numbers? ");
    scanf("%d", &n);

    printf("Please enter the integers:\n");
    for (i = 0; i < n; i++)
    {
        p = new_node();      /* Get a new node */
        if (p == NULL)       /* Terminate if out of memory */
        {
            printf("Out of memory.  Cannot add any more items\n");
            i = n;           /* Force termination of loop */
        }
        else
        {
            scanf("%d", &p->number);             /* Input the number */
            q = insert_point(p, sorted_list);    /* Find node after which to
                                                    insert "p" in "sorted_list" */
            if (q == NULL)    /* Insert "p" at front of list */
            {
                p->next = sorted_list;
                sorted_list = p;
            }
            else             /* Insert "p" after "q" */
            {
                p->next = q->next;
                q->next = p;
            }
        }
    }

    printf("\nThe sorted list is:\n");
    print_list(sorted_list);
}
```

Program continued on next page

Program continued from previous page

```
struct list_node *new_node()

/* Allocate a new node */

{
    struct list_node *malloc();

    return(malloc(sizeof(struct list_node)));
}


struct list_node *insert_point(node, header)
struct list_node *node,
                *header;

/* Returns  a  pointer  to the node after which "node" is  to be inserted in
   linked list "header", based on ordering the "number" members in ascending
   numerical order.  NULL  is  returned  if  "node"  is  to  be inserted at
   beginning of list. */

{
    struct list_node *p = NULL;          /* Follows one node behind "header" */

    for (; header != NULL && header->number < node->number;
            p = header, header = header->next);
    return(p);          /* NULL if "node" goes at beginning of list, or if
                            list is empty */
}


print_list(header)
struct list_node *header;

/* Prints the "number" members of the nodes of linked list "header" */

{
    for (; header != NULL; header = header->next)
        printf("%d ", header->number);
    printf("\n");
}
```

Program 13–8

```
How many numbers? 10
Please enter the integers:
10 42 7 0 923 13 -5 6 19 3

The sorted list is:
-5 0 3 6 7 10 13 19 42 923
```

Output 13–8

The user is asked by the program to enter the number of integers to be sorted. This value is stored in the variable n, which controls the number of times the ensuing **for** loop iterates. If the program runs out of memory, the termination of this loop is forced by setting i, the loop index, equal to n.

Each time around the loop, one integer is read in and inserted into the linked list headed by the variable *sorted_list*. The insertion consists of two steps. First, the function *insert_point* is called to find the location where the node pointed to by p is to be inserted. The function returns a pointer to the node in the list, at the point after which the new node is to be inserted. This pointer is stored in the variable q. The second step is the actual insertion.

Inserting a node into a linked list is similar to adding a node to the beginning of a list, except that three nodes are involved rather than two. The new node must be inserted between two other nodes, so it is necessary to know the addresses of these two nodes. Since the node before the insertion point contains a pointer to the node after the insertion point, however, it is suficient to know the address of the node before the insertion point. The insertion process is illustrated in Figure 13-6.

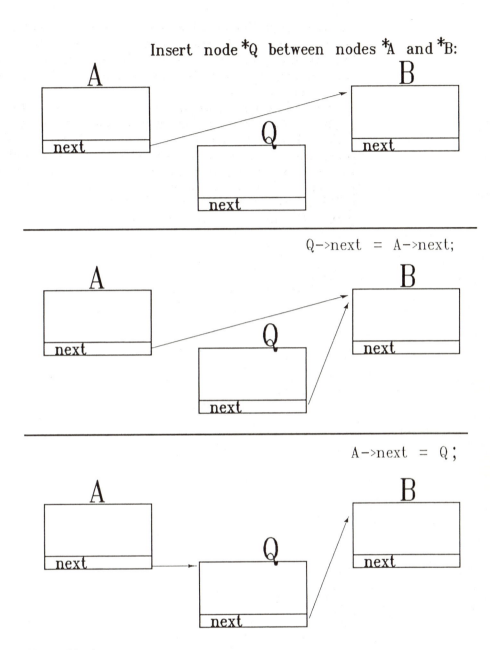

Figure 13—6

In Program 13-8, the *insert_point* function returns NULL if the new node is to be inserted at the beginning of the list. This occurs either when the new node is the first to be read in, or when it is the smallest to be read in so far. The insertion method is the same as the one used in Program 13-7 to add a node to the beginning of the list. If the new node is to be inserted at any point other than the beginning, the *insert_point* function returns a pointer to the node preceding the insertion point, and the method illustrated in Figure 13-6 is used.

The need for two separate insertion methods could be eliminated if the list header, instead of being a variable, were itself a structure with an unused *number* member. Inserting a new node at the beginning of the list would be identical to inserting it between two nodes, except that one node would be the list header.

After the **for** loop of the main program terminates, the *print_list* function is called to display the contents of the linked list, which at this point is the sorted set of numbers.

The *insert_point* function works by searching through the list until a node is found which contains an integer greater than that being inserted. The new node is inserted before this node. The function cannot return a pointer to the node located *after* the insertion point, however, since it would then be impossible to locate the node positioned *before* that point. This problem is solved by using two pointers to search through the list. The parameter *header* is used to index the node whose *number* member is currently being examined. Whenever the value of *header* is changed, its old value is assigned to the variable *p*. In this way, *p* always points to the node preceding the one pointed to by *header*. When the insertion position is located, the value of *p* is returned by the *insert_point* function.

Note the conditional test made by the **for** loop in *insert_point*. The loop continues execution as long as *header* is not equal to NULL, and as long as the number contained in the node pointed to by *header* is less than the number being inserted. It is not sufficient to write

```
header->number < node->number
```

because, if *header* is equal to NULL, an attempt to access *header−>number* may cause an execution-time error, since the value NULL does not point to a structure. It is therefore necessary to test the value of *header* first.

If the first part of the test, namely *header* != NULL, returns a value of *false*, the second part of the test is not made, since the && operator returns *true* only if both of its operands are true. If the first part of the test is found to be false, the entire test is false. In many other computer languages, a conditional test is evaluated in its entirety before its truth value is determined. The *"short−circuiting"* effect that is found in C helps to speed up program execution, and in some cases it helps to simplify the logic of the program.

After a node has been examined in the *insert_point* function, the variable *header* is assigned the address of the next node in the linked list, and *p* is assigned the old value of *header*. If the list is empty, or if the first number in the list is not less than the new number being inserted, the **for** loop is bypassed, and the value of *header* is never assigned to *p*. For this reason, *p* is initialized to NULL when it is declared. If this value is returned by the function, it indicates that the new node is to be inserted at the beginning of the linked list.

Now that we are familiar with the flexibility and data-handling power afforded by the use of arrays and structures, the time has arrived to learn more about ways of communicating with the outside world in order to exploit this power. The next chapter will explain more about the input/output functions that are available in the C library.

The Spirit of C

Let us again consider the division of a sentence into subject and predicate. We can represent the sentence by a structure with two members, *subject* and *predicate*. Both of these members are pointers to dynamically allocated string arrays. That is, the list of input words is split into two separate lists. The program could place each divided sentence into a different structure, and these structures could be joined in a linked list.

Programs that analyze natural language go through several stages of processing sentences. For example, suppose our program divides all the sentences of a story. Perhaps we could then examine the subject of every sentence to determine the protagonist of the story. Such a project is well beyond the scope of this text, but it illustrates the potential advantages of forming a linked list of divided sentences.

We will need new functions to allocate a linked list node and to insert a node into the linked list. These two operations can be combined into one function, since every allocated node is destined to be added to the end of the list. We require a template for the structure and a pointer to the head of the list. We will also maintain a pointer to the end of the list, so that nodes can be appended to the end of the list rather than the beginning.

```
#define NULL (struct sentence *)0

struct sentence
{
    int subj_len;                /* Number of words in subject */
    char (*subject)[MAX_WORD_LEN + 1];
    int pred_len;                /* Number of words in predicate */
    char (*predicate)[MAX_WORD_LEN + 1];
    struct sentence *next;    /* Link */
};

struct sentence *story = NULL,        /* Points to sentence list
                                         representing a story */
               *end_of_story = NULL;  /* Points to the end of the list */
```

Program continued on next page

Program continued from previous page

```
struct sentence *new_node()

/* Allocate a new "sentence" node, place it at the end of
   the "story" list, and return its address */

{
    struct sentence *malloc(),          /* Memory allocator */
                     *i;                 /* Points to new node */

    i = malloc(sizeof(struct sentence)); /* Assume always enough memory */
    i->next = NULL;                      /* This will be the last node */

    if (story == NULL)                   /* First node */
        story = i;

    else
        end_of_story->next = i;          /* Link to end of list */

    /* In either case, "i" is last node in list: */

    end_of_story = i;

    return(i);
}
```

It is permissible to define NULL as (**struct** *sentence* *)0, even before *sentence* is defined.

The members *subject* and *predicate* are defined in an unfamiliar way:

```
char (*subject)[MAX_WORD_LEN + 1];
```

where MAX_WORD_LEN was defined in the last chapter's version of this program. The definition reads: "*subject* is a pointer to an array of MAX_WORD_LEN + 1 characters." This is different from

```
char *subject[MAX_WORD_LEN + 1];
```

where the parentheses are omitted. This latter definition means: "*subject* is an array of MAX_WORD_LEN + 1 **char** pointers." It is also different from

```
char *subject;
```

which merely defines a pointer to characters. Even though a simple character pointer can point to a two-dimensional array of characters, we could not use two-dimensional subscripting with it. The C compiler must know the column dimension of a two-dimensional array in order to be able to interpret the subscripts correctly. The way we have defined *subject*, the size of its target type is MAX_WORD_LEN + 1 characters. If it were incremented by 1, it would point to the second row of the two-dimensional character array with MAX_WORD_LEN + 1 columns and an unknown number of rows. If there were a data type called *string* which was equivalent to a character array, *subject* would be a pointer to a variable of type *string*. (All this discussion applies to *predicate* as well.) Note that it is syntactically incorrect to use

```
char subject[][MAX_WORD_LEN + 1];
```

in a member definition. That notation can be used only in the declaration of an initialized array or an array passed to a function.

The changes to the original program occur only in the *divide_sentence* function. It must allocate string space and copy each word of the sentence into the proper string array (*subject* or *predicate*). It must determine beforehand the size of the two arrays, which it can do based on the values of *verb_location* and *word_count*:

```
divide_sentence(word_list, word_count)
char word_list[][MAX_WORD_LEN + 1];    /* String array containing words */
int word_count;                        /* Number of words (strings) in
                                            "word_list" */

/* Locate the verb in "word_list", and output the sentence with the
    subject (all words before the verb) on the first line and the
    predicate (the verb and all following words) on the second */

{
    int verb_location,      /* Index of verb in "word_list" */
        i, j;               /* Loop indices */
    struct sentence *new_node(),   /* Allocates a new node */
                    *node;         /* Holds allocated node */
    char *malloc();         /* Memory allocator */

    /* "find_verb" returns the index of the verb, -1 if no verb
        is found */

    verb_location = find_verb(word_list, word_count);

    if (verb_location >= 0)      /* Verb was found */
    {
        node = new_node();       /* Get a sentence node */

        /* Allocate a string array  for  the subject. The number
            of strings happens to equal the value of "verb_location".
            If  there  is  no  subject, then "verb_location" == 0 and
            "malloc"  returns  NULL. */

        node->subj_len = verb_location;
        node->subject = (char (*)[MAX_WORD_LEN + 1])   /* Cast it */
                    malloc(node->subj_len * (MAX_WORD_LEN + 1));

        printf("\nsubject:    ");
        for (i = 0; i < verb_location; i++)
        {
            printf("%s ", word_list[i]);
```

Program continued on next page

Program continued from previous page

```
        /* Copy the word into the "subject" list. */
        strcpy(node->subject[i], word_list[i]);
    }


    /* Allocate a string array for the predicate */

    node->pred_len = word_count - verb_location;
    node->predicate = (char (*)[MAX_WORD_LEN + 1])   /* Cast it */
        malloc(node->pred_len * (MAX_WORD_LEN + 1));

    printf("\npredicate:  ");

    /* In the following loop, "j" is used so the words are stored
       in "predicate" starting with element 0 */
    for (i = verb_location, j = 0; i < word_count; i++, j++)
    {
        printf("%s ", word_list[i]);

        /* Copy the word into the "subject" list */
        strcpy(node->predicate[j], word_list[i]);
    }
    printf("\n\n");
  }

  else                          /* No verb */
    printf("\nThat sentence has no verb!\n\n");
}
```

When the string arrays (two-dimensional **char** arrays) for the subject and predicate are allocated in the *divide_sentence* function, the pointer returned by the *malloc* function is cast into the same type as *subject* and *predicate*. The cast operator used is

```
(char (*)[MAX_WORD_LEN + 1])
```

which may be translated as: "a pointer to a **char** array of MAX_WORD_LEN + 1 elements."

Since it is not possible to determine the number of words in *subject* and *predicate* by using the **sizeof** operator, these numbers are stored in the numbers *subj_len* and *pred_len*.

The divided sentence is displayed here at the same point in the program as in the last chapter's version. You could amend the program so that it displays all the divided sentences at one time, only after they have all been processed. This would require the design of a function that goes through the linked list, displaying each subject and each predicate. We will not illustrate such a function; you can try to write it if you like. Consider also how the program could be expanded so that, once the list is formed, other functions could use it for further processing.

Programming and Debugging *Hints*

Runtime errors often result from the internal limitations of the program. To increase the reliability of the program, the programmer must give it the ability to survive its own errors as well as the errors of the user.

Consider a program that accepts data from the user and stores it in a linked list. We have seen in the description of the *malloc* function that there is a limit on how much memory can be allocated. Generally it is not possible for the program to predict in advance how many list nodes can be allocated before memory runs out. The programmer must decide what steps should be taken when the program attempts to allocate memory for a new node, and finds that there is no more memory to be had. Does the program crash? Does it reject the user's input and refuse to accept any more? Or does it somehow manage to readjust its data structures so that the new request can be accommodated?

There is no right or wrong answer to these fundamental questions. The programmer must decide what the best course of action is for a given situation. Sometimes cost, measured in terms of execution and programming time, is a dominant factor, whereas at other times, the available memory may be a more important consideration. It is important to remember that these sources of error are not the fault of the user, and therefore can occur no matter how much validation of input is performed.

More Possible Sources of Error in C

Perhaps the most frustrating syntax errors that can occur in C are those that occur when a semicolon or closing brace is omitted. Such errors are flagged by the compiler, but the line identified in the error message may not be the one where the omission occurred. The reason is that the compiler may not detect the missing symbol until one or more lines past the point of error. Also, the error message may be misleading.

For example, consider the following code, found at the beginning of a function:

```
static int a[] =
{
   2,
   3,
   4
float b;
```

It is relatively easy to spot the error: the closing brace and semicolon that should terminate the array initializer have been omitted. Yet the compiler does not detect this omission until the **float** keyword is encountered. The compiler is likely to display an error message indicating that an illegal keyword is being used in an initializer, rather than detecting the true nature of the error.

Another related error, often made by Pascal programmers, is the omission of the semicolon before the **else** clause of an **if** statement. This error is relatively easy to trace. Remember: A simple C statement that precedes a closing brace must end with a semicolon; an array or structure initializer must have a semicolon *after* the closing brace; a structure template requires a semicolon before the closing brace, and after the brace as well if no variables are being declared.

C *Tutorial*

1. What is a set of eight contiguous bits generally called?

2. What is the chief reason for using structures?

3. What distinguishes an array from a structure?

4. What special keyword is used in defining a structure?

5. What is a template, and how does it relate to a structure?

6. What is a structure tag and what is its purpose?

7. In what two ways can a structure variable be declared?

8. What rules govern the use of the period (.) operator?

9. What is the connection between a structure and a new data type?

10. What is the relationship between members of a structure being initialized, and their initializing values?

11. What is meant by an array of structures?

12. What characteristic must a structure have in order to be initialized within its declaration?

13. In what sense can a structure be recursive?

14. What is meant by the nesting of structures?

15. What is the one restriction that applies to the nesting of structures?

16. What is the meaning of the arrow (->) operator?

17. What is a linked list?

18. What must a structure include if it is to be a node in a linked list?

ANSWERS TO C TUTORIAL

1. A byte.

2. In everyday applications, it is helpful to group together non-homogeneous data into a single entity.

3. Whereas the elements of an array are always of the same data type, the members of a structure can be of different types.

4. **struct**.

5. A template is a list of the members of a structure, along with their type specifications, enclosed in braces.

6. A structure tag is a name associated with a structure template. This makes it possible later to declare other variables of the same structure type without having to rewrite the template itself.

7. By preceding the variable name with the keyword **struct** and either (1) a previously defined structure tag or (2) a template (optionally preceded by a tag not previously defined).

8. An individual member of a structure is accessed by following the name of the structure variable with the period operator and the member name. The member name must be explicitly specified.

9. Associating a tag with a template makes it possible to use the tag (preceded by the keyword **struct**) in the same way a type keyword is used, for example, to declare variables or the types returned by functions.

10. There must be a one-to-one correspondence between them.

11. It is an array in which each element is a structure.

12. It must be of the **static** storage class.

13. It can contain other structures as members.

14. It describes a situation in which a structure contains another structure as a member.

15. A structure cannot contain a member that is itself a structure of the same type (defined with the same tag) as the outer structure.

16. The notation $a \rightarrow b$ means $(*a).b$, that is, "the member named b of the structure pointed to by a."

17. A linked list is a group of structures in which the first one points to the second, the second points to the third, and so forth.

18. It must include a member that is a pointer to another structure of the same type.

Keywords

auto	break	case	char	default	do
double	else	float	for	if	int
long	return	short	sizeof	static	**struct**
switch	unsigned	while			

Exercises

1. Write a function to delete a node from a linked list. Remember that, to do this, it is necessary to know the location of the node *before* the one being deleted.

2. Design a structure to store a length in yards, feet and inches (for example, 7 yards, 2 feet, 3 inches). Write a function to find the difference between two measurements as represented by these structures.

3. Write a series of functions to implement a doubly linked list. Nodes in such a list contain pointers not only to the next node in the list, but also to the previous one. Such a list must have both a head pointer and a tail pointer. Doubly linked lists can be processed in both directions, thus simplifying operations on the list. A minimum set of functions will allocate a node, insert a node into the list, delete a node, and search the list for a particular node. A doubly linked list makes it possible to search the list starting from any internal node, rather than just the header node. A further challenge is to implement a *circular* linked list. This is a singly or doubly linked list in which the last node points to the first one (and vice versa, in the case of a doubly linked list). A header pointer can be used to determine the beginning of the list, but it is also possible to treat the list as if it has no beginning or end. You may wish to come up with some uses for such data structures.

4. Write a program to implement the card catalog system used as an example at the beginning of this chapter. The program should be able to handle browsing through the catalog, searching for a particular title, author, or (optionally) subject, as well as the borrowing and returning of books, charging of late fines, and acquisition of new titles. Use modular programming techniques to add one feature at a time.

5. Modify the store inventory program so that it maintains two lists with two different structure types. One list will contain general information about an item, including the item name, unit price, and supplier. The second list will contain inventory information such as the date the last shipment was received, the quantity received in the last shipment, and the number of units currently on hand. It is necessary to know which structure in the first list corresponds to which structure in the second. Since the two structures are added to their respective lists at the same time, a structure in the first list will correspond to the structure at the corresponding position in the second list. For added security, however, you may wish both structures to contain the item name or an ID number. In order to find out all information about a particular item, it is necessary to examine both lists.

   As a further enhancement, when the program displays the final list, have it calculate and display the purchase price for each shipment (unit price multiplied by quantity received) and also display a grand total for all shipments in the list.

6. [Note: This exercise is a challenge!] Modify the calculator program from Chapter 12, Exercise 8 so that it handles operator precedence and parentheses correctly. To do this, it is necessary to use a data structure known as a *stack*.

   A stack is just what it sounds like: nodes are said to be *pushed* onto the top of the stack and *popped* off. This data structure is often referred to by the term LIFO, or Last In, First Out. In other words, the last item pushed onto the stack is the first to be popped off.

   For example, suppose we push the value 3 onto the stack:

   3

   Now we push the value 2:

   2
   3

   Notice that values are pushed onto the top of the stack. The value 2 is at the top. Now we pop a value off the top of the stack. The stack now appears as follows:

   3

   Notice that 2 was the last value to be pushed, but the first to be popped. Stacks are easy to implement using linked lists. Pushing an item onto the stack is equivalent to placing a node at the beginning of the list, and popping an item means deleting the first node in the list.

   Here is a simple illustration of how a stack will be used in your program. In the following illustrations, a caret (^) is used to indicate the character of the input expression currently being scanned. Suppose the input line is:

   3 + 2 * (4 + 1)

The program inputs the first two items in the expression. In this case, they are the number 3 and the addition operator. The program stores them together in a structure:

expression	just read in	stored
3 + 2 * (4 + 1)	3 +	3 +

The program now reads in the next two items. These are the number 2 and the multiplication operator:

expression	just read in	stored
3 + 2 * (4 + 1)	2 *	3 +

Since multiplication must be performed before addition, the program must set aside the 3 and the + for now. It does this by pushing them on the stack (remember, each node contains a value and an operator):

expression	just read in	stored	stack
3 + 2 * (4 + 1)	2 *	2 *	3 +

Now the program must read in the next two items:

expression	just read in	stored	stack
3 + 2 * (4 + 1)	(4	2 *	3 +

Since a parenthetical expression takes highest precedence, it is also necessary to push the 2 and the * onto the stack:

expression	just read in	stored	stack
3 + 2 * (4 + 1)	(4	(4	2 *
			3 +

Now, since a parenthesis was just read in, only one more item is scanned:

expression	just read in	stored	stack
3 + 2 * (4 + 1)	+	4 +	2 *
			3 +

(Notice that the 4 was retained.) Since the addition operator must be followed by a second operand, two more items are scanned:

expression	just read in	stored	stack
3 + 2 * (4 + 1)	1)	4 +	2 *
			3 +

The closing parenthesis indicates that the expression within the parentheses can now be fully evaluated. This means that the stored 4 (the first operand) is added to the 1 just read in, yielding 5. The addition operator is discarded, and only the 5 is retained:

expression	just read in	stored	stack
3 + 2 * (4 + 1)	1)	5	2 *
^			3 +

There are no more characters on the line, so now it is necessary to pop an operator from the stack:

stored	popped	stack
5	2 *	3 +

The program now uses the stored operand and the popped operator and operand to perform the calculation 2 * 5 = 10:

stored	popped	stack
10		3 +

We now pop another node:

stored	popped	stack
10	3 +	

We perform another calculation, 3 + 10 = 13. Since the stack is now empty, 13 is the final result.

Note that a more complicated expression with more operators may require several stages of pushing and popping. Try a few more examples for yourself until you understand how the program must operate.

14

Input/Output and Files

*T*he manner in which information enters the computer is known as input, whereas the manner in which results are displayed or stored for use by the user is called output. This chapter discusses the standard C library functions that assist the programmer in handling input and output in a simple, device—independent manner.

I/O Devices

On most microcomputers, the usual input medium is the keyboard. The output usually is displayed on the computer screen, sometimes called the monitor. Output also can be printed, stored on a floppy disk, or transmitted via a modem to another computer.

These various forms of input and output, abbreviated as I/O, obviously are very different. The programmer's job is easier, however, if all these devices can be handled in a similar manner. In some cases, the programmer may not even know which I/O devices a program is using. Thus C provides convenient library functions that handle I/O devices in a standard way.

Disks and Files

A *disk* is a circular piece of metal or plastic, whose surface is coated with a magnetically-chargeable substance, similar to the coating on an audio tape. Data is stored on a disk by magnetizing certain sections of it. This is done automatically by means of the read/write head of the *disk drive*. On large computers, disks are made of metal and organized into groups. On microcomputers, including home computers, the most common form of disk is the diskette or floppy disk. It is a flexible plastic disk, encased in a square protective envelope as illustrated in Figure 14-1.

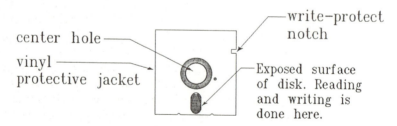

center hole

vinyl
protective jacket

write-protect notch

Exposed surface of disk. Reading and writing is done here.

Disk itself is circular and plastic. Surfaces are coated with metallic oxide which is magnetized by the disk drive's read/write head.

Figure 14—1

When data is stored on a medium such as a disk, this packet of information is called a *file*. It is analogous to the customary office file, in which related information is stored according to title or some other convenient label. In many programming situations, it is easier to access a file than to enter a succession of individual items of data from the keyboard.

In C jargon, the term *file* often refers to any device used for I/O. The reason is that C treats a file as a stream of characters, analogous to an array of characters. A file, however, can contain more characters than would fit at one time into a computer's memory. A file resides on a storage medium, not in memory. One or more characters are read in from a file, and after they have been processed, they may be discarded from memory as new characters are read in. Thus an entire file can be processed without having to store it in memory.

A keyboard can be thought of as a file, because it provides a stream of characters to the program. Characters can only be read *from* the keyboard, however; it would be meaningless to try to send output *to* the keyboard. In the same way, the computer screen can be sent a stream of characters as output, but most screens cannot be used as input devices. (An exception is the so-called *touch screen* available on some computers, which serves as both an input and an output device.) A file on disk can be both read from and written to.

Standard Input and Output

When a C program begins execution, it has access to three files. The first, known as the *standard input*, is the file from which input is received by default. This file usually is the keyboard, but it can also be redirected to obtain input from a disk file or other device. As long as the program only reads this file once from beginning to end, it need not be concerned about where the characters are coming from.

The second file, the *standard output*, is the default output file. This is usually the screen, but it can be redirected to another device such as a disk file. Usually the program need not be concerned about the identity of this file, unless special operations are required which can be performed only on disk files.

The third file available to the program is known as *standard error*. This file will scarcely be mentioned in this book. Its purpose is to keep error messages separate from other program output. For example, if standard output is going to a disk file, the standard error file can be the screen, so that the user sees error messages immediately.

We have been using standard input and standard output extensively throughout this book. The *printf* function sends its results to standard output, whereas *scanf* receives its characters from standard input. Since files in C are streams of characters, the *scanf* function serves to decode the input characters into the various internal representations needed by the program. The *printf* function encodes the data into character format before sending the characters to the standard output file. We will describe some additional functions that give the programmer more direct access to standard input and output.

The *putchar* and *getchar* Functions

The standard C function that prints or displays a single character (by sending it to standard output) is called *putchar*. This function takes one argument, which is the character to be sent. It also returns this character as its result. If an error occurs, an error value is returned. Therefore, if the returned value of *putchar* is used, it should be declared (explicitly or implicitly) as a function returning an int.

Program 14-1 demonstrates the use of this simple function. It is assumed that no output error will occur, so the returned value is ignored.

```
/* Demonstration of putchar */

main()
{
    putchar('H');
    putchar('e');
    putchar('l');
    putchar('l');
    putchar('o');
    putchar('\n');
}
```

Program 14—1

```
Hello
```

Output 14—1

Program 14-1 produces the same result as the statement

```
printf("Hello\n");
```

When *putchar* is used, however, each character must be output separately. The parameters to the function calls in Program 14-1 are character constants, represented between apostrophes as usual. Of course, the arguments could be character variables instead.

The *getchar* function is the counterpart to *putchar*. It reads a single character from standard input. It takes no parameters, and its returned value is the input character.

The next program illustrates the use of *getchar*. In Program 14-2, the *getchar* function is used to read a string from standard input into an array. The string is then echoed back to standard output.

```
/* Demonstration of getchar */

main()
{
    char input[200];       /* Holds input */
    int c,                 /* Receives one character of input */
        i = 0;             /* Index for "input" */

    printf("Enter text:\n");
```

Program continued on next page

Program continued from previous page

```
/* Get  characters  and place  them in "input", until a
   period, question mark, or exclamation point is typed */

do
    input[i++] = c = getchar();
while (c != '.' && c != '?' && c != '!');

input[i++] = '\n';      /* Add a final newline */
input[i] = '\0';        /* Terminate the string */

/* Display the string */

printf("\nYou entered:\n");
printf(input);          /* Use "input" as control string */
}
```

Program 14—2

```
Enter text:
BASIC is easy,
FORTRAN is fun,
Pascal may be structured,
But C's the one!

You entered:
BASIC is easy,
FORTRAN is fun,
Pascal may be structured,
But C's the one!
```

Output 14—2

Program 14-2 raises a question regarding the handling of files. The *null* character is used to mark the end of a string in C, but this rule does not apply to files. In a file, the *null* character is just another character that can be embedded in the middle of meaningful data. So how is it possible to detect the end of input?

In Program 14-2, the solution is simply to choose an arbitrary character and designate it as the delimiter. The program accepts an exclamation point, period, or question mark as an indication that input is finished. Therefore, input is limited to a single sentence.

After the user is asked to enter the text, a **do...while** loop is executed. This loop reads in a character and assigns it both to the variable *c* and to the element of the array *input* which is indexed by *i*. (Neither *input* nor *output* is a keyword in C.) The index *i* is post-incremented so that it always indexes the next available element of *input*. The value of *c* is then tested to see whether it is a terminating character. The use of a **do...while** loop, rather than a **while** or **for** loop, ensures that the terminating character is accepted into the array before the loop is terminated. In this case, the terminating character is a meaningful part of the data (unlike the *null* character, which is strictly a delimiter).

After the loop terminates, a final *newline* character is added to the end of the string so that the text looks correct when printed out. Then a *null* character is added so that *input* has the standard string form. (In this last assignment, *i* is not incremented because no further characters are to be added.) Finally, the input string is printed out using *printf*. Since the output consists only and entirely of the string stored in *input*, the control string to the final *printf* is *input* itself.

This program points out a definite advantage of *getchar* over *scanf*. When a string is read in using *scanf* together with the %s conversion specification, the delimiter of the string is always white space. In Program 14-2, however, the delimiter is chosen by the programmer. (With a small amount of modification to the program, it could even be chosen at execution time.) This allows the input string to include spaces and *newline* characters.

Note that the variable *c* is declared as an **int**, even though it is used to hold a character. The *getchar* function is not declared to return a **char**, and is therefore assumed to return an **int**. This is in fact correct, as we will explain shortly. The mixing of modes causes no problems; when the result of *getchar* is assigned to an element of *array*, it is cast into a **char** without having to be modified.

The I/O functions in C provide choices in processing input and output. The *getchar* function, for example, can be used to do anything that *scanf* can do, although a little more programming effort is required. Usually *getchar* is reserved for tasks that require character-level input manipulation, whereas *scanf* is used for higher-level chores, such as reading in strings or numbers. A similar distinction applies to *putchar* and *printf*. Most real-life programming situations require that I/O be handled on both these levels. Fortunately, *getchar* and *putchar* can appear with *printf* and *scanf* in the same program.

Every file that is used by a program can be thought of as having a pointer associated with it—not the kind of pointer we talk about in C, but rather a marker indicating where the next character is to be read from or written to. This concept applies to keyboard input and screen output as well as to disk files. As an example, suppose the input to a program consists of the line

```
Hello there.
```

Initially the marker points to the first character on the line, so the first character the program reads from the standard input file will be the H. Suppose the program executes the statement

```
scanf("%s", input);
```

where *input* is a character array. The *scanf* function reads in the string "Hello", which leaves the marker pointing to the space following that string. If a call is now made to *getchar*, the character returned will be a space. Therefore, both *getchar* and *scanf* can be used in a program, if the programmer pays attention to the current location of the marker.

The following program illustrates the combination of *scanf* and *getchar*. It stores the first word on each line of the input file, and then prints out this list of words at the end of the program.

```
/* I/O functions may be mixed.
      This program reads the first word of each line of input and
      prints them out at the end */

main()
{
    char input[20][20],      /* Holds input words */
         flag = 0;           /* Set to 1 when terminator is reached */
    int c,                   /* Receives one character of input */
        i = 0,               /* Row index for "input" */
        j;                   /* Loop index */

    printf("Enter text:\n");

    /* Get initial words until "flag" is set */

    do
    {
        scanf("%s", input[i++]);    /* Read in first word on line */

        /* Get characters until newline is input.  This has the
           effect of skipping the remainder of the line */

        while ((c = getchar()) != '\n')

            /* If a terminator is encountered, set "flag" */

            if (c == '.' || c == '?' || c == '!')
                flag = 1;
    }
    while (!flag);

    /* Display the words */

    printf("\nThe initial words of each line were:\n");
    for (j = 0; j < i; j++)
        printf("%s\n", input[j]);
}
```

Program 14—3

```
Enter text:
BASIC is easy,
FORTRAN is fun,
Pascal may be structured,
But C's the one!

The initial words of each line were:
BASIC
FORTRAN
Pascal
But
```

Output 14—3

The *scanf* and the %s conversion specification, as used in this program, provide the simplest method of reading in a single word. The word is stored in the row of *input* (which is now two-dimensional) indexed by the variable *i*.

The *scanf* function makes the task of searching for the end of a line somewhat difficult. Depending upon the conversion specification used, the *scanf* function usually ignores white space such as the *newline* character (the exception is the %c conversion specification). For this reason, *getchar* is the preferred method of locating the beginning of the next line. The statement

```
while (getchar() != '\n');
```

would suffice to skip to the beginning of a new line of input. The loop terminates when a *newline* is read in, and since the *newline* has already been read, the next character in the input stream will be the first character of the next line.

Since the program must also detect the end of the input, the **while** loop just shown is inadequate and must be modified. The character read in is assigned to *c*, and in addition to being compared to the *newline* character, it is also compared to the terminating punctuation characters. If the character is found to be a terminator, the variable *flag* is set to the value 1, which indicates a value of true. The reason *flag* is used is to avoid a redundant test in the **do...while** loop; technically, the inner **while** loop could be written to terminate immediately upon detecting a terminating character.

When the variable *flag* is set to 1, the conditional test *!flag* returns a value of *false*, and the **do...while** loop terminates. The words stored in the array *input* (the initial word of each line) then are displayed.

The *stdio.h* Header File

In order to make full use of the I/O functions of the standard C library, certain definitions must be included in the program. The programmer should include the following line at the beginning of the program:

```
#include <stdio.h>
```

The number sign at the beginning of the line indicates that this is a preprocessor directive. The **#include** must start in column 1 and must have no embedded spaces. When the preprocessor detects this directive, it inserts the contents of the named file into the program at the point where the directive is written. In this case, the file is called *stdio.h* (*standard I/O*). Although it is not part of the C language proper, it is included with C as the standard library is. The *.h* suffix indicates that the file is a *header file*, meaning that it is included at the head of a program for the purpose of defining certain values and symbols.

The file name is included in angle brackets to indicate that it is located in a special location on the disk. The angle brackets are meaningful only on computers that have directory structures, another name for a hierarchical organization of files.

On such computers, the *stdio.h* file resides in a special public directory. On microcomputers that do not have directory structures, or any system where *stdio.h* resides in a predetermined default directory, the **#include** directive can be written simply as

```
#include "stdio.h"
```

where the angle brackets have been replaced by double quotes.

The next chapter will say more about the **#include** directive. For now, we will merely describe the effect of including *stdio.h* in a program. This file defines certain constants, thus saving the programmer the trouble of having to do this explicitly. One of those constants is NULL, usually defined as the value 0. This is the same NULL we have been using with linked lists and strings. Since some I/O functions return pointers, the value NULL is used as an error indicator. Another value defined in *stdio.h* is EOF, which stands for *end of file*. On most computers, EOF has the value -1 and is an error value returned by I/O functions that normally return integers greater than or equal to zero. Since these constants already are defined in *stdio.h*, the programmer should avoid defining them explicitly in the program (unless, of course, *stdio.h* is not included).

Several other symbols are defined in *stdio.h*. Some of them will be covered later in this chapter. You should consult the documentation for your particular C compiler to find out exactly what features are provided by *stdio.h*, as well as which functions are available in the standard library. Though this chapter covers the standard functions, certain compilers for microcomputers diverge from the norm in this regard.

In most C standard libraries, the functions *printf*, *scanf*, *putchar*, and *getchar* are designed so that they can be used by a program without including *stdio.h*. Many of the new functions introduced in this chapter, however, require the definitions provided by *stdio.h*. This file therefore will be included in subsequent programs. You should include *stdio.h* in every program you write, even though it may not be necessary at first. As you develop your program, you may find it necessary to add features for which *stdio.h* is needed. It is a common error to omit *stdio.h*, so it is best to include it as the first line of your program.

The FILE Type, and the Constants *stdin* and *stdout*

The file *stdio.h* also defines a new data type, called FILE. (Chapter 16 describes how new types are defined in C). The word FILE must always be in capitals as shown. Just as constants usually are capitalized, new types also may be capitalized to distinguish them from native C types.

The data type FILE is used to describe various features of a file. Each file used in a program must have associated with it a *pointer* to this type. Two constants of type *FILE ** are defined in *stdio.h*. These are *stdin* and *stdout*, and they represent the standard input and standard output. (A constant *stderr* also is defined to represent the standard error file). In functions that require a FILE pointer as a parameter, these constants can be used if the function is to operate on the standard input or output.

The Functions *getc* and *putc*

Two functions that require FILE pointers are *getc* and *putc*. These functions are analogous to *getchar* and *putchar*, except that they can operate on files other than the standard input and output. The *getc* function is called with one argument, which is a FILE pointer representing the file from which the input is to be taken. The expression

```
getc(stdin)
```

is equivalent to

```
getchar()
```

because it says: "Get a character from the file represented by FILE pointer *stdin*." In a similar manner, the expression

```
putc(c, stdout)
```

is the same as

```
putchar(c)
```

because the former expression states: "Put the character stored in *c* into the file represented by *stdout*."

It is illegal to try to write to a file that can be used only for input, or to read from a file that is restricted to output. For example, you could not read from a printer or from most computer monitors, nor could you write to the keyboard. Therefore, it is illegal to write

```
putc(c, stdin)
```

or

```
getc(stdout)
```

Those function calls would return EOF as an indication of error.

In many versions of C, *getc* and *putc* are not functions. They are examples of what are called *macros*, which will be described fully in the next chapter. A macro cannot have its type declared, as in

```
int getc();
```

As you will learn in the next chapter, such a declaration is both unnecessary and illegal for macros. In most other respects, however, macros behave like functions. Often, when *stdio.h* is included, *getchar* and *putchar* also are defined as macros in terms of *getc* and *putc*. When *stdio.h* is not included, the function versions of *getchar* and *putchar* are used.

End of File

The manner in which the end of a file is indicated internally depends on the device the file is on. The *getc* and *getchar* functions translate these various terminators into a single, standard error indication. When a program tries to get a character from a file in which no characters remain, the *getc* or *getchar* function returns the value EOF, or -1. Note that this value is of type **int**. The functions *getc* and *getchar* return integer values. If the value is positive, it represents an ASCII value, which may be cast into a **char**. If the value is negative, it is an EOF indication. The value EOF must be tested for before the casting is done. Otherwise, a returned EOF is treated as an ordinary ASCII number.

As previously mentioned, EOF also is returned to indicate an error in the function parameters or some other error. To differentiate between the two causes of a returned EOF, *stdio.h* provides two macros, *ferror* and *feof*. These macros take one argument, a file pointer:

```
ferror(fp)
```

The value returned by *feof* is *true* (non-zero) if the last operation on the file reached the end of the file; otherwise, *false* (zero) is returned. The *ferror* macro returns *true* if the last operation on the file resulted in an error; otherwise, *false* is returned.

Program 14-4 makes use of several of the concepts introduced in this chapter. Since it deals only with the standard input and output, the functions *getchar* and *putchar* could have been used instead of *getc* and *putc*, but the use of the latter functions serves to illustrate their equivalence to the former. The program reads in a string and then echoes it back, but instead of using particular characters to indicate the end of input, it uses EOF. This technique removes the restriction as to which characters can be used where in the input.

```
/* Introduction to stdio.h: EOF, stdin, stdout, getc and putc */

#include <stdio.h>

main()
{
    char input[200];        /* Holds input */
    int c,                  /* Receives one character of input */
        i = 0,              /* Index for "input" */
        j;                  /* A loop index */

    printf("Enter text:\n");

    /* Get characters and place them in "input", until EOF */

    while ((c = getc(stdin)) != EOF)
        input[i++] = (char)c;

    /* Now i == strlen(input). */

    /* Display the string, one character at a time */

    printf("\nYou entered:\n");
    for (j = 0; j < i; j++)
        putc(input[j], stdout);
}
```

Program 14—4

```
Enter text:
BASIC is easy,
FORTRAN is fun,
Pascal may be structured,
But C's the one!

You entered:
BASIC is easy,
FORTRAN is fun,
Pascal may be structured,
But C's the one!
```

Output 14—4

Since the input is typed at the keyboard, the user must be able to tell the computer when typing is finished by providing the EOF indication. The manner in which this is done varies from computer to computer, but usually an EOF from the keyboard is indicated by the key combination *control—d* or *control—z* typed at the beginning of a line. (This cannot be seen in Output 14-4, unfortunately.) After the exclamation point was typed, the return key was pressed, and then *control—d* was entered. The program immediately resumed running and echoed the input text. The *getc* function translated the *control—d* into the standard EOF value. (Notice that the **while** loop is written so that the EOF is not included in the string.)

In this program, the string is echoed back one character at a time (rather than all at once with a call to *printf*). For this reason, it is not necessary to append a *null* character to the end of the input. The variable *i* ends up being equal to the length of the string, and this value is used in a **for** loop that prints out the string.

It would have been permissible instead to append a *null* character to the end of the string, and display the characters in a **while** loop that terminated when the *null* character was detected. In fact, if the input were to be used anywhere a string is required, such as in a *printf*, it would be necessary to add a *null* character to the end of the string.

The Functions *fopen* and *fclose*

We now address the problem of how to handle file I/O other than from the standard input and to the standard output. This topic requires an understanding of the concept of an *open* file.

Before a program can read from or write to a file, the file must be *opened* by the program. This process establishes a connection between the file and the program, in a manner dictated by the requirements of the operating system and the C library functions. Once the file has been opened, the program can perform I/O processes on the file. In C, a file is opened by the *fopen* (*file open*) function. This function returns a FILE pointer, which must be provided to all I/O functions that operate on the file.

The *fopen* function requires two arguments, both strings. These strings may be literals or variables. The first string is the name of the file to be opened. The second string specifies the file's *mode*, which determines how the file is operated upon. The two most common mode strings are "r" and "w", which stand for *read* and *write* respectively. A disk file opened with mode *r* must already exist, since there must be something to read from. If the file does not exist, NULL is returned by *fopen*. If a disk file is opened with mode *w*, either the file must already exist or it must be possible to create the file. If the file already exists, its former contents are erased. Otherwise, the file is created. If for some reason the file cannot be created, NULL is returned.

Several other modes can be used to open the file. They will be described later in this chapter. The *fopen* function of your particular compiler may accept modes not described here, or it may not recognize some modes that are standard. You should consult your C manual for this information. The modes described here probably are available to you and will be sufficient for most of your programming needs.

The function *fclose* (*file close*) is used to *close* a file. A file is closed when no more I/O is to be performed on it. All files are closed automatically when a program terminates, so that if a programmer forgets to close a file, no damage is done. The *fclose* function should be used for many of the same reasons that *free* should be used after *malloc*: There is a restriction on how many files can be open at any one time, and it is possible to reach this limit in a large program. Also, it is clearer to the reader of a program if files are closed when they are no longer needed. This serves as an indication that no more I/O is to be done on those files. There are some situations in which a file must be closed temporarily. The parameter to *fclose* is the file pointer representing the file to be closed (the value returned when the file was opened). A pointer to a file that is already closed cannot be supplied as an argument to *fclose* unless the file has first been reopened, just as the same block of memory cannot be freed twice.

Devices such as the keyboard or printer are represented by special file names, which vary widely from machine to machine. These devices can be opened in the same manner as disk files, but usually there is a restriction on the modes with which a device can be opened. For example, a printer can only be opened with mode *w*. The standard input and output are opened and closed automatically, so no attempt should be made to use *fclose* with *stdin* or *stdout*. (You could not use *fopen* with *stdin* or *stdout*, because they are constants and cannot have new values assigned to them.)

Program 14-5 reads in a string from the standard input and stores it in a file called *first_file*. The contents of that file then are displayed by the program.

```
/* Files and fopen, fclose */

#include <stdio.h>

main()
{
    FILE *fopen(),          /* File opening function, returns FILE pointer */
         *file_pointer;     /* Holds pointer to the open file */
    int c;                  /* Receives one character of input */

    /* Open the file for writing (create or erase old contents) */

    file_pointer = fopen("first_file", "w");

    printf("Enter text:\n");

    /* Get characters and place them in the file until EOF */

    while ((c = getc(stdin)) != EOF)
        putc(c, file_pointer);

    /* Close the file and reopen to read (file is "rewound" to beginning) */

    fclose(file_pointer);
    file_pointer = fopen("first_file", "r");

    /* Display the string, one character at a time */

    printf("\nYou entered:\n");
    while ((c = getc(file_pointer)) != EOF)
        putchar(c);

    fclose(file_pointer);
}
```

Program 14—5

```
Enter text:
BASIC is easy,
FORTRAN is fun,
Pascal may be structured,
But C's the one!

You entered:
BASIC is easy,
FORTRAN is fun,
Pascal may be structured,
But C's the one!
```

Output 14—5

In this program, *fopen* is declared to return a pointer to type FILE. A variable *file_pointer* also is declared as a pointer to type FILE. This variable holds the value returned by *fopen*. The first statement in the program opens the file *first_file* with mode *w* (since it will be written to) and assigns the file pointer to the variable *file_pointer*. This assignment could have been done in the declaration of *file_pointer*, since a variable can be initialized with a function call. In many programs, however, the file name and mode are not known until program execution, in which case the call to *fopen* might be possible only after the program has determined the file name or mode.

A **while** loop is used to read in the text and transfer it immediately to the disk file. Notice that the second parameter of *putc* is *file_pointer* rather than *stdout*, since the output is to be sent to *first_file* rather than to the standard output.

To prove that the text was transferred to the disk file, the program concludes by displaying the contents of *first_file*. (Actually, every operating system contains a command which allows a file to be displayed immediately, so this part is not strictly necessary.) To display the text, it is necessary to read the contents of *first_file*. But the file has been opened for writing, so an attempt to read from it would result in an error. The solution is to close the file and then reopen it with mode *r*.

When the file is reopened, the marker is positioned at the beginning of the file. A **while** loop gets the characters from the file one at a time until EOF is detected, sending the characters to the standard output using *putchar*. The argument to *getc* this time is *file_pointer*, since it takes its input from *first_file*. Notice that *control—d* is not stored in the file. The end of a disk file is indicated in a different way, which *getc* is also able to detect.

Reading the contents of a disk file does not destroy the contents, just as playing a cassette tape does not erase its contents. The contents of a file can be changed only by writing to it. In this respect, there is a difference between a disk file and a device such as a keyboard. When characters are read from a keyboard, they are not stored in the keyboard itself. It is not possible to "rewind" the keyboard and reread its input. As will be seen later, however, rewinding is possible with disk files.

The following program illustrates how more than one file can be used. It performs the simple task of copying the contents of one file to another. Both files must be open at the same time,

one for reading and one for writing. Two file pointer variables
must be declared, one for each file.

```
/* Using several files */

#include <stdio.h>

main()
{
    FILE *fopen(),
        *first_file_pointer,      /* Holds pointer to the "source" file */
        *second_file_pointer;     /* Holds pointer to the "destination" file */
    int c;                        /* Receives one character of input */

    /* Open the source file for reading ("first_file" must already exist) */

    first_file_pointer = fopen("first_file", "r");

    /* Open the destination file for writing */

    second_file_pointer = fopen("second_file", "w");

    /* Transfer characters from source to destination file until EOF */

    while ((c = getc(first_file_pointer)) != EOF)
        putc(c, second_file_pointer);

    /* Close both files */

    fclose(first_file_pointer);
    fclose(second_file_pointer);

    /* Open the second file to display contents */

    second_file_pointer = fopen("second_file", "r");

    /* Display the file contents */

    printf("'second_file' contains:\n");
    while ((c = getc(second_file_pointer)) != EOF)
        putchar(c);

    fclose(second_file_pointer);
}
```

Program 14—6

```
'second_file' contains:
BASIC is easy,
FORTRAN is fun,
Pascal may be structured,
But C's the one!
```

Output 14—6

Program 14-6 requires that the file *first_file* already exist. It
does not matter whether *second_file* exists, since it would be
rewritten anyway. To be perfectly safe, the program should test
whether either of the two calls to *fopen* (or at least the first)
returns NULL; this step is omitted here for the sake of
simplicity. After the files are opened, the contents of *first_file* are
copied into *second_file* using a **while** loop. Notice that the call to

getc uses *first_file_pointer* as its file pointer, whereas the call to *putc* uses *second_file_pointer*. After EOF is detected on *first_file* (the input file sends the EOF), both files are closed.

The contents of *second_file* are displayed, just as the contents of *first_file* were displayed in Program 14-5. The file is reopened, this time with mode *r*, and the contents are copied character by character to the standard output. Then the file is closed again.

The *fprintf* and *fscanf* Functions

The next program introduces a new library function, *fprintf* (file printf). This function behaves almost the same as *printf*, except that it sends its output to a specified file rather than to the standard output. The parameters to this function are the same as for *printf*, except that there is one additional parameter: the FILE pointer associated with the file to which the output is to be sent. This parameter is specified first, immediately before the control string. Using the constant FILE pointer *stdout* with *fprintf* is equivalent to using *printf*. The standard error file can be written to by specifying *stderr* as the first parameter to *fprintf*.

C also has an *fscanf* function, in which input is taken from the file specified by a FILE pointer as the first parameter. This function is not used in the following program, but will appear later in the chapter.

Append Mode

Program 14-7 also introduces another mode that can be used with the *fopen* function: *a*, for *append* mode. In append mode, a file is opened for writing, just as with write mode. If the file does not exist, it is created. Unlike write mode, however, if a file opened under append mode already exists, the previous contents of the file are not erased. Instead, new characters written to the file are appended to the end of the text that is already in the file.

Program 14-7 illustrates the difference between the write and append modes. The program opens the two files *first_file* and *second_file*. These are assumed to be the two files that would remain after Program 14-6 is run, and they both contain identical copies of the short poem we have been using in this chapter. The file *first_file* is opened in *w* mode, whereas *second_file* is opened in *a* (append) mode. The same string—an attribution for the poem—is written to each file, using the *fprintf* function twice. Both files are then closed, and the function *file_display* is called to print out the contents of each file. This function opens the file whose name is passed to it, displays the contents character by character, and then closes the file.

```
/* Append mode */

#include <stdio.h>

main()
{
    FILE *fopen(),
         *first_file_pointer,      /* Holds pointer to first file */
         *second_file_pointer;     /* Holds pointer to second file */

    /* Open the first file for writing (it already exists) */

    first_file_pointer = fopen("first_file", "w");

    /* Open the second file for appending (it already exists) */

    second_file_pointer = fopen("second_file", "a");

    /* Write line to both files */

    fprintf(first_file_pointer, "\n--Anonymous\n");
    fprintf(second_file_pointer, "\n--Anonymous\n");

    /* Close both files */

    fclose(first_file_pointer);
    fclose(second_file_pointer);

    /* Display contents of first file */

    printf("After write, 'first_file' contains:\n");
    file_display("first_file");

    /* Display contents of second file */

    printf("\n\nAfter append, 'second_file' contains:\n");
    file_display("second_file");
}


file_display(name)
char name[];

/* Display the contents of the file named by "name" */

{
    FILE *fopen(),
         *file_pointer;      /* Holds pointer to file */
    int c;                   /* Receives one character of input */

    file_pointer = fopen(name, "r");
    while ((c = getc(file_pointer)) != EOF)
        putchar(c);
    fclose(file_pointer);
}
```

Program 14—7

```
After write, 'first_file' contains:

--Anonymous


After append, 'second_file' contains:
BASIC is easy,
FORTRAN is fun,
Pascal may be structured,
But C's the one!

--Anonymous
```

Output 14-7

As the output shows, *first_file*, which is opened with *w* mode, has its contents entirely overwritten by the string written to it by the program. In *second_file*, which is opened in *a* mode, the original contents are retained and the new line is appended to the end of the file.

The *fseek* Function

One advantage of disk files over files on other devices (such as printers) is that a disk is what is known as a *direct access* device. This means that a character can be written to or read from a disk file by specifying the exact location where this operation is to take place. It is possible, for example, to read the fifth character in a disk file without first having to read the first four characters. A disk file is much like an array in that it can be indexed directly. In C, the analogy between files and arrays is further reenforced by numbering the characters of a file consecutively from 0.

Because of these disk file features, an array that is too large to fit in memory can be written to a disk file and accessed selectively as needed. Admittedly, it takes longer to access a character from a disk file than it does to access an array element in memory. This is another example of how programming involves tradeoffs between speed and memory usage.

The C library function used to index a file is called *fseek*, because it is used to seek a specific position or location in the file. This function can be thought of as manipulating a marker of the kind we spoke of earlier. This marker determines the character or location of the file that will be acted upon by the next read or write. Normally, a read or write of a single character increments the marker by 1. The *fseek* function can be used to increment or decrement the marker by any amount, or to reposition the marker relative to the beginning or end of the file. (The *fseek* function serves only to reposition the file marker, not to perform any actual I/O.)

The *fseek* function takes three arguments. The first is the FILE pointer of the (open) file that is to be operated upon. The second and third parameters are used to specify the repositioning, according to the following rules (the second parameter is a **long** integer):

1. If the third parameter is 0, the second parameter specifies the character to which the file is to be positioned, relative to the beginning of the file (In C we usually speak of "positioning a file," without referring to the concept of a marker.) The second parameter in this case must be equal to or greater than 0. For example, the statement

```
fseek(fp, 7L, 0);
```

positions the file associated with *fp* to the eighth character of the file (Remember, the first character is at position 0.) This is the mode in which *fseek* is closest to array indexing.

2. If the third parameter is 1, the second parameter specifies an increment or decrement to the current position of the file. For example, the statement

```
fseek(fp, 3L, 1);
```

skips ahead three characters in the file, whereas

```
fseek(fp, -3L, 1);
```

moves back three characters.

3. If the third parameter is 2, the second parameter specifies how many characters the file is to be positioned from the *end*. The second parameter must be equal to or greater than 0. For example,

```
fseek(fp, 5L, 2);
```

positions the file to the fifth character from the end of the file. The statement

```
fseek(fp, 0L, 2);
```

in which the second parameter is equal to zero, positions the file to the end, past the last character of the file (in other words, to the point where the EOF would be if it were actually in the file).

The user should avoid attempting to use *fseek* to seek before the beginning or after the end of the file. The results of such attempts depend on the computer, but are not meaningful.

The values for the third parameter are arbitrary. You can remember which number results in which operation by remembering the mnemonic "0-1-2, beginning-middle-end." The file *stdio.h* supplied with some compilers defines constants to represent these values. With other compilers, you are free to define your own constants. The second and third parameters may both be variables, but the third parameter rarely is. A variable used for the second parameter must be a **long int**, or must be cast explicitly into one.

Program 14-8 illustrates a simple use of the *fseek* function. The file *second_file*, assumed to contain a copy of the poem, is opened for reading. The *fseek* function is used to skip the first six characters of the file, namely the word BASIC and the space that follows it. The file is then positioned at the seventh character, the letter 'i'. As the output shows, the first call to *getc* returns the seventh character, so the output of the program consists of the entire poem except for the first word.

```
/* The fseek function */

#include <stdio.h>

main()
{
    FILE *fopen(),
         *file_pointer;        /* File pointer */
    int c;                     /* Receives one character of input */

    /* Open the file for reading */

    file_pointer = fopen("second_file", "r");

    /* Terminate if file can't be opened */

    if (file_pointer == NULL)
        printf("'second_file' does not exist.\n");

    else
    {
        /* Skip the first 6 characters */

        fseek(file_pointer, 6L, 0);

        /* Display the file contents */

        while ((c = getc(file_pointer)) != EOF)
            putchar(c);

        fclose(file_pointer);
    }
}
```

Program 14—8

```
is easy,
FORTRAN is fun,
Pascal may be structured,
But C's the one!

--Anonymous
```

Output 14—8

In this program, the value returned by *fopen* is tested. If it is NULL, the rest of the program is skipped. This step ensures that the program runs only if *second_file* actually exists.

Of course, skipping the first six characters of a file could be accomplished simply by calling *getc* six times and discarding the results. This method would be inefficient, however, if it were desired to skip to the thousandth character of a large file. The *fseek* function need be called only once to position the file at any point. Furthermore, the *fseek* function can backspace or rewind a file.

Write/ Read (w+) Mode

Rewinding a file can be accomplished by the statement

```
fseek(fp, 0L, 0);
```

where *fp* is a pointer to the file. (Some C libraries contain a macro or function called *rewind*, which accomplishes the same task.)   This operation allows a file to be read and reread without the need to close and reopen it. It can also be used to write a file and then read it back, as was done in Program 14-5.

If a file is opened with the mode string "w+", the file can be written to and read from without the need to close and reopen the file. The mode *w+* signifies "writing plus (reading)."   As with *w* mode, the file is created if it does not exist, and the contents are erased if the file already exists. After text is written to the file, however, the *fseek* function can be used to reposition the file to a point before the current end of the file, so that the contents can be read. The program then can reposition to the end of the file and continue adding characters, or even write over characters that were previously written. All this can be done without closing and reopening the file.

When a file is open for both writing and reading, a single marker is used for both reading and writing. That is, if *getc* is called when the file is positioned to the first character, the first character is returned and the file is positioned to the second character. A call to *putc* immediately following this operation writes the new character in place of the second character. The file then is positioned to the third character. Writing over a character changes only that character, and does not affect any other characters. Some versions of C require that a call to *fseek* be made when switching from reading to writing (or vice versa) on a single file, even if no repositioning is required.

Program 14-9 illustrates the use of *fseek* to rewind a file. It is identical to Program 14-5, except that the file is opened only once, in *w+* mode.

```
/* The "w+" mode, and using fseek to rewind a file */

#include <stdio.h>

main()
{
    FILE *fopen(),
         *file_pointer;        /* File pointer */
    int c;                     /* Receives one character of input */

    /* Open the file for read/write (create or erase old contents)
*/

    file_pointer = fopen("first_file", "w+");

    printf("Enter text:\n");

    /* Get characters and place them in the file until EOF */

    while ((c = getc(stdin)) != EOF)
        putc(c, file_pointer);

    /* Rewind file (fseek to beginning) */

    fseek(file_pointer, OL, 0);

    /* Display the file */

    printf("\nYou entered:\n");
    while ((c = getc(file_pointer)) != EOF)
        putchar(c);

    fclose(file_pointer);
}
```

Program 14—9

```
Enter text:
BASIC is easy,
FORTRAN is fun,
Pascal may be structured,
But C's the one!

You entered:
BASIC is easy,
FORTRAN is fun,
Pascal may be structured,
But C's the one!
```

Output 14—9

The *ftell* Function

The C library contains a function called *ftell* which returns the current position of the file whose pointer is supplied as the function argument. The function returns a **long int** (recall that a **long int** is used to position the file with *fseek*). The *ftell* function should therefore be declared as returning a **long int**. Some versions of *stdio.h* perform this declaration globally and also declare *fopen* as returning a FILE pointer. If you are not sure what your version does, it is safe to declare these two functions explicitly within a function.

Perhaps the most common use of *ftell* is to determine the size of a file. Suppose *fp* is a FILE pointer for an open file, and *size* is a **long int**. The statements

```
fseek(fp, OL, 2);
size = ftell(fp);
```

will result in *size* containing the number of bytes currently in the file. The call to *fseek* positions the file past the last character, and *ftell* returns this position. For example, if the file contains 100 characters, the last character is numbered 99. Since this call to *ftell* positions *past* the last character, it positions the file at character position 100. This is the value returned by *ftell*.

Read/ Write or Update (r+) Mode

Another mode in which a file may be opened is *r+* ("reading plus (writing)"). This mode also allows a file to be read from or written to without closing and reopening. The letter *r* signifies that this mode operates like the *r* mode, in that the file being opened must already exist and its contents are not erased. After the file is opened, however, it can be operated upon as in the *w+* mode. The file can even be extended by positioning to the end and writing. Because this mode is useful in modifying or adding to a file that already exists, it sometimes is called *update* mode.

Program 14-10 uses several of these above concepts to modify a file. The file called *first_file* is assumed to contain the same poem used in previous examples. It is opened in *r+* mode. The program then looks for the first occurrence of the word "may" in the file and replaces it with the word "can". The updated file is displayed.

```
/* Update ("r+") mode: Replace a word in the file with one of equal
length */

#include <stdio.h>

main()
{
    FILE *fopen(),
         *file_pointer;          /* File pointer */
    char word[20];               /* Holds one inputted word */
    int c;                       /* Receives one character of input */

    /* Open the file for reading and writing (update) */

    file_pointer = fopen("first_file", "r+");
```

Program continued on next page

Program continued from previous page

```
        /* Terminate if file can't be opened */

        if (file_pointer == NULL)
            printf("'second_file' does not exist.\n");
        else
        {

            /* Display the file contents */

            printf("File originally contained:\n");
            while ((c = getc(file_pointer)) != EOF)
                putchar(c);

            /* Rewind file */

            fseek(file_pointer, 0L, 0);

            /* Look for the word "may" */

            do
                fscanf(file_pointer, "%s", word);
            while (strcmp(word, "may"));

            /* Rewind to beginning of word */

            fseek(file_pointer, -3L, 1);

            /* Replace "may" with "can" */

            fprintf(file_pointer, "can");

            /* Rewind file and display the file contents */

            printf("\nFile now contains:\n");
            fseek(file_pointer, 0L, 0);
            while ((c = getc(file_pointer)) != EOF)
                putchar(c);

            fclose(file_pointer);
        }
}
```

Program 14—10

```
File originally contained:
BASIC is easy,
FORTRAN is fun,
Pascal may be structured,
But C's the one!

File now contains:
BASIC is easy,
FORTRAN is fun,
Pascal can be structured,
But C's the one!
```

Output 14—10

In this program, the value returned by *fopen* is tested to ensure that the file exists. If it does, the contents are displayed character by character. The file is then rewound (using *fseek*), and a loop is executed which reads in words from the file using *scanf*. This loop continues until the word "may" is read in. Notice the loop condition: The *strcmp* function returns a non-zero (*true*) value as long as the string contained in *word* is not equal to "may". When the strings match, *strcmp* returns 0 (*false*) and the loop terminates. This loop is not the ideal method of locating the word "may", because a punctuation mark following the word "may" would result in the word being skipped. The reader might try writing a function that detects a word in a file while ignoring all punctuation.

After the word "may" is read in, the file is positioned at the space immediately following the word. To write the word "can" over the word "may", first it is necessary to backspace to the beginning of the word. Since "may" has three letters, the file is backspaced three characters by the program's second call to *fseek*. The function *fprintf* can be used to write the new word over the old one. Since *fprintf* does not output the *null* character terminating a string, only the three characters constituting the word "may" in the file are affected. The file is rewound by a third *fseek*, the new contents are displayed, and the file is closed.

A series of characters in a file can be replaced by another string of the same length. To replace the word "may" with a longer word such as "might", or with a word containing fewer than three characters, it would be necessary to move the succeeding characters in the file, since characters cannot be inserted into or deleted from the middle of a file. (The same problem occurs when it is necessary to insert a number into, or delete a number from, an array.)

Program 14-11 illustrates a practical application of the various I/O functions covered so far. It is the store inventory program previously seen as Program 13-7. In the new version, the inventory structures are stored in a disk file instead of a linked list located in memory. When a series of structures is stored in a file, the individual structures often are called *records*. In this program, each record contains information about a single product. The records are stored consecutively in the file.

This program illustrates how a structure can be written directly into a file. When writing a numeric variable (such as the member called *count* of the *inventory* structure) into a file, it is not necessary to convert the number to its character representation in order to store it. Such a conversion is necessary only if the file is to be viewed by a human. Character representation of a number often takes up more space than the amount of memory needed to store the binary number itself. A number is stored in memory as a series of bytes, which can be thought of simply as characters.

As an example, suppose that an **int** variable takes up two bytes of memory on a particular computer. If the variable contains the number 1234, that number still takes up only two bytes. If 1234 is converted to its character representation, namely the string "1234", it takes up four bytes (five if you include the terminating *null* character). Therefore, it is more efficient to store the number on disk exactly as it is stored in memory, namely as two bytes. Of course, if the contents of the file were printed as is, the string "1234" would not be seen in the file. The two bytes making up the binary representation of the number 1234 would be seen but would have no connection to the ASCII values representing the characters 1234. However, if the number were read back from disk into an **int** variable, the *printf* function could then be used to convert the number to its string form and display this number for the user.

```
/* Store inventory program.
    This program  records  information  about  stock  received at  a store. The
user enters information about each product received -- the item name, the price
per unit (jar of jelly, can of tuna, etc.), the quantity and date received, and
the supplier.  Each product is represented by a structure which  is stored as a
record in  a  file called "inventory".   The  structure also contains a member
named "count", which  (theoretically) is  used to record the number of units of
the product  in  the  store  at  any  time.   This  member  is  initialized  to
"quantity_received"  and  would  be  decremented  by  1 each time a unit of the
product is purchased (this latter process is not performed by this program). */

#include <stdio.h>

struct inventory             /* Represents a stock item */
{
    char item[15];
    float unit_price;
    int count;               /* Number currently in store at any time */
    int quantity_received;   /* Number originally received */
    struct
    {
        int month;
        int day;
    }
    date_received;
    char supplier[15];
};

main()
{
    struct inventory inv_item;                /* Holds info for one item */
    char *inv_bytes = (char *)&inv_item,      /* Points to structure so it can
                                                 be accessed byte-by-byte */
        reply[10];                            /* Holds user's y/n response */
    FILE *fopen(),
        *inv_file = fopen("inventory", "a+");

    do
    {
        get_info(&inv_item);     /* Read in member values for structure */
        add_record(inv_bytes, inv_file);    /* Add record to file */

        printf("\nItem %s entered.\n", inv_item.item);
        printf("\n\nDo you wish to enter another item (y/n)? ");
        scanf("%s", reply);
    }
```

Program continued on next page

Program continued from previous page

```
        while (*reply == 'y' || *reply == 'Y');

        printf("\nThank you.\n");

        print_inventory(inv_file);          /* Print out final inventory */

        fclose(inv_file);
}

get_info(record)
struct inventory *record;

/* Read in member values for "record" (inventory information) */

{
        printf("\tItem? ");
        scanf("%s", record->item);

        printf("\tUnit price (no dollar sign)? ");
        scanf("%f", &record->unit_price);

        printf("\tQuantity received? ");
        scanf("%d", &record->quantity_received);

        /* Initialize "count" to "quantity_received" */

        record->count = record->quantity_received;

        printf("\tDate received (month#/day#)? ");
        scanf("%d/%d", &record->date_received.month, &record->date_received.day);

        printf("\tSupplier? ");
        scanf("%s", record->supplier);
}


add_record(pointer, file)
char *pointer;
FILE *file;

/* Write record pointed to by "pointer" to file pointed to by "file" */

{
        int i;
        for (i = 0; i < sizeof(struct inventory); i++)
                putc(pointer[i], file);
}
```

Program continued on next page

Program continued from previous page

```
print_inventory(file)
FILE *file;

/* Nicely print records of file pointed to by "file" */

{
    struct inventory record;          /* Holds a record from file */
    char *bytes = (char *)&record,    /* Used to read in record byte-by-byte */
        price[10],                    /* Holds string version of "unit_price" */
        date[10];                     /* Holds string version of "date_received" */
    int i,                            /* Loop index */
        c;                            /* Receives initial character for EOF test */

    /* Print heading */

    printf("\n\n%-14s%11s%17s%17s     %-14s\n",
        "Item", "Unit Price", "Quantity Rec'd", "Date Rec'd", "Supplier");
    for (i = 0; i < 78; i++)
        putchar('-');
    putchar('\n');

    /* Rewind file */

    fseek(file, OL, 0);

    /* Loop to read in records */

    while ((c = getc(file)) != EOF)
    {
        bytes[0] = (char) c;     /* Put character in structure */

        /* Read in the rest of the record */

        for (i = 1; i < sizeof(struct inventory); i++)
            bytes[i] = (char) getc(file);

        /* Make "unit_price" and "date_received" into nice strings */

        sprintf(price,"$%.2f", record.unit_price);
        sprintf(date,"%d/%d",
            record.date_received.month, record.date_received.day);

        printf("%-14s%11s%17d%17s     %-14s\n",
            record.item, price, record.quantity_received, date,
            record.supplier);
    }
}
```

Program 14—11

```
    Item? Happy_Cow_Milk
    Unit price (no dollar sign)? 0.70
    Quantity received? 500
    Date received (month#/day#)? 10/4
    Supplier? Judy's_Dairy

Item Happy_Cow_Milk entered.


Do you wish to enter another item (y/n)? y
    Item? Marvel_Bread
    Unit price (no dollar sign)? 1.09
    Quantity received? 300
    Date received (month#/day#)? 10/12
    Supplier? IBC

Item Marvel_Bread entered.


Do you wish to enter another item (y/n)? n

Thank you.


Item            Unit Price   Quantity Rec'd      Date Rec'd    Supplier
-----------------------------------------------------------------------

Happy_Cow_Milk     $0.70         500               10/4       Judy's_Dairy
Marvel_Bread       $1.09         300               10/12      IBC
```

Output 14—11a

```
    Item? noodles-11b.
    Unit price (no dollar sign)? 0.59
    Quantity received? 350
    Date received (month#/day#)? 9/17
    Supplier? Mom's

Item noodles-11b. entered.


Do you wish to enter another item (y/n)? n

Thank you.


Item            Unit Price   Quantity Rec'd      Date Rec'd    Supplier
-----------------------------------------------------------------------

Happy_Cow_Milk     $0.70         500               10/4       Judy's_Dairy
Marvel_Bread       $1.09         300               10/12      IBC
noodles-11b.       $0.59         350               9/17       Mom's
```

Output 14—11b

Because program 14-11 does not use a linked list, the *next* member has been removed from the *inventory* structure. In the *main* function, a single variable of type **struct** *inventory* named *inv_item* is declared. Each structure is written to disk after its members are assigned their values, so only a single structure is needed in memory at any one time.

A character pointer named *inv_bytes* is declared and initialized to the address of *inv_item*. By indexing *inv_bytes*, the programmer can access the individual bytes of *inv_item* as an array of characters. It is as though an array of characters is being mapped onto a structure. This principle can be understood more clearly from Figure 14-2.

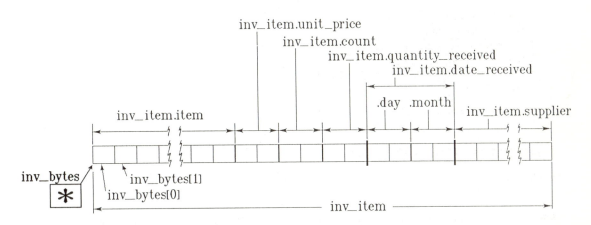

inv_bytes sees inv_item as an array of characters

Figure 14—2

Using the I/O functions described so far, the only way to write a structure directly to disk is to write its individual bytes one at a time.

Append/ Read (a+) Mode

A FILE pointer named *inv_file* is declared and initialized by a call to *fopen*. The mode specified is *a+*. Since we have already discussed the modes *r+* and *w+*, you can probably guess how the *a+* mode operates. The file is opened as in *a* mode, but it can be read from as well as written to. If the file *inventory* does not exist, it is created. If it already exists, the new records written to the file are added to the end.

The function *get_info* is called with a pointer to *inv_item*. Since a pointer to a structure is passed, this function is identical to the version in Program 13-7. The *add_record* function in the new program replaces the *add_node* function. This new function is passed two arguments: *inv_bytes*, the address of the structure, and *inv_file*, the file pointer. On most computers, the address of *inv_item* could instead be passed directly to the function and be cast automatically into a character pointer (since *add_record* expects the first parameter to be a character pointer). This method would eliminate the need for *inv_bytes*. Since *add_record* treats its first parameter as a character array pointer, it uses *putc* to write the elements of the array, one at a time, to the file specified by the *file* argument. The size of this array is simply **sizeof(struct** *inventory*). In this way, the complete structure is written to disk. The character array in question cannot be treated as a string because it is not terminated by a *null* character, since the structure itself does not have one.

The version of *print_inventory* used in Program 14-11 is passed a file pointer, namely the one associated with the (open) file containing the records. A single structure variable (named *record*) is declared, just as in the *main* function, and a character pointer (named *bytes*) is declared and assigned the address of the structure, also as in the *main* function. After printing the header lines, the *print_inventory* function rewinds the file and begins reading in the records. The file may have contained records before it was opened, so the function does not know automatically how many records are in the file. There are several ways this can be determined. One way is to calculate the size of the file by using *fseek* and *ftell*, and then divide this number by the size of one record.

The method used in Program 14-11 to ensure that all the records are displayed is simpler and sufficient for the application at hand. A single character is read into the integer variable *c*. If the value is EOF, the end of the file has been reached. Otherwise, it is assumed that at least one more structure remains in the file. This structure is read byte by byte into character array *bytes*. The effect of this operation is to read the structure into *record*. During these calls to *getc*, the value EOF is not tested for. It is assumed that the file contains an integral number of records of equal length, so if the first byte (initially read into *c* and then copied into *bytes[0]*) is in the file, the remaining bytes of the record are also in the file. There must be no extra characters in the file. If there are, after the last complete record is read in, the next *getc* will not return EOF.

On some computers, a normal text file cannot contain *null* characters. If this is true on your computer, you may have to modify Program 14-11 slightly to make it work since the structure may contain bytes with values of zero. Your system may support *fopen* modes that make it possible to open a binary file that can contain *null* characters.

After the record has been read in, the members of the structure *record* can be displayed. Notice that the period operator rather than the arrow operator is used, since *record* is a structure and not a structure pointer.

Program 14-11 was run twice. The first time, two records were entered; the second time, only one. The second run of the program was made immediately after the first. The output of the second run (Output 14-11) shows that the new record was added to the file after the two which were already stored in the file. The records are printed in the order in which they were entered. The use of the file makes it possible not only to add new records, but also to write another program that modifies the records. For example, such a program might decrement the *count* member of the *inventory* structure each time an item is purchased.

The *item* and *supplier* members of the record are still read in from the keyboard using *scanf*, so they still cannot contain spaces. With the I/O functions that have been introduced, however, you probably could write a function that reads in all characters up to a *newline* character and avoids reading in more characters than can fit into the destination array. Most C libraries contain functions that can be do this. (See Appendix B.)

The *ungetc* Function

The *ungetc* function works with virtually all types of input files. What it does is to "push back" a character into the input stream. As an example, suppose our input consists of the number 123 surrounded by various non-blank characters:

```
xw.&as123;asd
```

We wish to be able to input 123 as an **int**, meaning we will use the %d conversion specification. In order to be able to do that, however, we must skip over all the non-numeric characters that precede it. We could input characters one at a time until the first digit, 1, is found. But once we read in the 1, it is no longer in the input stream, and a *scanf* at this point will input only the number 23. We wish to back up by one position. If the file is a disk file, we can use *fseek*, but the *fseek* function does not work with keyboard input. Here is a program that uses the *ungetc* function to push the first digit back into the input stream.

```
/*  Illustration of the ungetc function.

    Scans the  input until a digit is found.  The digit is
    pushed back, and the whole integer is read in with %d.
*/

#include <stdio.h>

main()
{
    int number,                     /* Holds inputted numeric value */
        character;                  /* Holds inputted character */

    printf("Please enter a bunch of characters with an imbedded integer:\n");

    /* Keep getting characters while not EOF and not a digit */

    do
        character = getchar();
    while (character != EOF && (character < '0' || character > '9'));

    if (character == EOF)
        printf("No number found.\n");
```

Program continued on next page

Program continued from previous page

```
    else
    {
        /* Push back the first digit */

        ungetc((char)character, stdin);

        /* Read in the number as an int and echo it back */

        scanf("%d", &number);
        printf("\nThe number is %d\n", number);
    }
}
```

Program 14—12

```
Please enter a bunch of characters with an imbedded integer:
xw.&as123;asd
The number is 123
```

Output 14—12

To illustrate how the above program operates, here is the input just before the *ungetc* function is called. The caret (ˆ) indicates the position of the marker:

```
xw.&as123;asd
   ^
```

The *ungetc* function pushes the 1 back into the input. In effect, it backs up one character and writes a 1 over it (even though a 1 is already there):

```
xw.&as123;asd
   ^
```

Any character can be pushed back, so if we replaced the *ungetc* statement in Program 14-12 with

```
ungetc('9', stdin);
```

then, regardless of what character was last read from the input, a '9' character would be pushed back. Here again is the input before the *ungetc*:

```
xw.&as123;asd
   ^
```

Here it is after the statement *ungetc('9', stdin)*:

```
xw.&as923;asd
   ^
```

Once the first digit has been "ungotten," it can be reread by the *scanf* function as the first digit of the integer. Any input function on the same file will reread the character. It is not necessary for the read to appear immediately after the *ungetc*. In fact, you can place read operations from other files between the call to *ungetc* and the read from the file that the *ungetc* was performed upon.

The *ungetc* function takes two arguments: the character to be pushed back, and the FILE pointer of the file being operated upon. It returns an integer value, which is either its first argument or, if the *ungetc* was unsuccessful, EOF. You can push back only one character per file, so once you push back a character into a specific file, you must read from that file before calling *ungetc* again on the same file.

The standard C library contains many more functions than are described here. Some are described in Appendix B. The exact set varies according to the C compiler. Most of those functions can be written in terms of the functions *getc*, *putc*, and *fseek*, so any standard functions not provided in a particular C library can be written based on the material covered in this book. You should read the description of the function library provided with your compiler to determine the functions available and their permissible arguments.

The services provided by the C preprocessor, such as constants and file inclusion, make the programmer's job much easier. The next chapter describes the full range of the preprocessor's directives.

The Spirit of C

Mass storage devices such as disks or tapes are important because they retain their data even when the computer is turned off. Because of their large capacity, however, they would be necessary even if all computer memories had this same retention ability (such memories are known as *non−volatile*). Large databases (organized collections of data), which are used by just about every major organization, require immense amounts of storage. So do artificial intelligence programs, whose powers lie in their ability to make human-like decisions based on large amounts of stored information. Such programs often need to use large quantities of external intermediate storage, which is used only for the calculations the program needs while it is running (the same role played by variables in memory) and not for long-term storage.

Our sentence-dividing program could use files not only to hold a large list of verbs, but also as storage for the sentence list which the program generates. That list could later be used by another program.

In previous versions of the program, we have searched the entire verb list from beginning to end. This is the only effective way to find a word in an arbitrary list. If the word list were sorted, however, we could use much more efficient methods of locating a word. One such method is a *binary search*, in which the list to be searched is repeatedly divided in two. We compare the word we are testing with the verb in the *middle* of the list. If that verb is the one we are looking for, our search is over. Otherwise, if the word being tested is lexically less than the middle verb, we know that, if the word is in the verb list, it is in the first half of the list. If the word is lexically greater than the middle verb, we know that it would lie in the second half of the list.

This process is repeated, using only the half of the list in which the word is expected to be found. We compare the word to the middle verb in the half of the list we have chosen. Each time the process is repeated, the sublist being examined is halved. When we are down to only one or two verbs, we will either find the word in the list or discover that it is not a verb. If our verb list is large, a binary search is much faster than examining every verb in the list. Remember, however, that the binary search can be performed only on a sorted list.

Another method is called an *indexed search*. Again the verb list must be sorted. We also have a list of 26 pointers in memory. The first pointer points to the first verb in the list that begins with the letter *a*, the second points to the first verb beginning with *b*, and so on. By examining the first letter of the word being tested, we can find the portion of the verb list containing words that start with the same letter, thus reducing the list to be searched to a fraction of its original size. Now a binary search can be used to locate the word, or, if the sublist is small enough, an exhaustive search might suffice.

These two search methods can be used whether the verb list is in memory or in a file. In the indexed search, if the verbs are in a file, the pointers also are stored on disk, perhaps at the beginning of the verb file or in a separate index file. Their values refer to locations within the data file (the one with the verbs). If the number of indices is small, they can be kept in memory during program execution. If the data file is modified in any way, however, the updated indices must be stored back on disk. Our sentence-dividing program does not modify the verb list.

In this chapter, we will illustrate how the *is_verb* function can be modified to make use of a sorted verb file. We will use the binary search method. As an illustration of this method, consider a binary search of a sorted array of integers:

2 5 11 23 55 129 284 297 331 402

where the numbers are sorted in ascending order. Suppose we are searching for the number 23. Let us indicate the range being searched by two indices *lo* and *hi*, which define the lowest number and highest number in the range. Initially, our range is this:

2 5 11 23 55 129 284 297 331 402
lo⌃   ⌃hi

We will use an unlabeled caret to indicate the middle of the range. If the range has an even number of integers, as in this case, the middle value is the one just to the left of the center of the range:

```
2 5 11 23 55 129 284 297 331 402
lo^        ^              ^hi
```

Since 23 is less than 55, our next range to search is below 55, so we move down the *hi* pointer to the number just before 55:

```
2 5 11 23 55 129 284 297 331 402
lo^      ^hi
```

Again we find the middle number, which is 5:

```
2 5 11 23 55 129 284 297 331 402
lo^ ^    ^hi
```

23 is greater than 5, so we move the *lo* pointer to the number to the right of 5:

```
2 5 11 23 55 129 284 297 331 402
  lo^  ^hi
```

At this point, our range consists of only two values, so we could stop here and test both of them. To make the algorithm more general, we could go through another step in which *lo* is moved up one more time. Now both *lo* and *hi* point to 23:

```
2 5 11 23 55 129 284 297 331 402
     lo^hi
```

The number 23 is also the middle value, being the only one in the range, and it is the number we have been searching for. We found our number in five steps. If we had been looking for a number not in the list, such as 24, the search still would have ended here, but it would have ended in failure.

Presumably, the verb file we will use was prepared by some other programmer or typist so we can decide upon a format that is as convenient as possible. The file consists of verbs separated by white space. At the very beginning of the file is an integer in character form (it must be read in using %d) which represents the number of words in the file. This number not only eliminates the need for a trailer, but also makes it easier to decide the initial size of the search range.

In order to find the middle of any range quickly, we need to know where each word begins. This is very difficult unless each word is of a fixed length. Therefore, we determine that each word is MAX_WORD_LEN characters long, with any trailing characters being blank spaces (which will be skipped over if the words are read in using *fscanf*). In addition to any trailing blanks, the words are separated by one blank space or *newline* character. Therefore, the distance between the beginnings of any two adjacent words is MAX_WORD_LEN + 1 characters.

To determine the location of the beginning and end of the verb file, we first read in the list size as *list_size*. We initially set *lo* to 1 and *hi* to *list_size*. We also need to map these indices to actual locations in the file. For this reason, we set *list_start* to the result of a call to *ftell*. Assuming *list_size* is followed immediately by the first word, with no intervening white space, this call can be made right after reading in *list_size*. The location of the word indexed by *lo* is

```
list_start + (lo - 1) * (MAX_WORD_LEN + 1)
```

The same method is used to locate the word indexed by *hi* and the middle word in the list. We can write a function *locate* which positions the file to the word indexed by its parameter. Actually, it should be passed four parameters: the word index, the FILE pointer, the value of *list_start*, and the word size (MAX_WORD_LEN + 1):

```
locate(index, filep, list_start, word_len)
int index;                  /* Index of the word (1 through list length) */
FILE filep;                 /* Pointer for the verb list file */
long list_start;            /* Location in the file of word 1 */
int word_len;               /* Length of each word, including separators */

/* Position file "filep" to the word indexed by "index" (the first word
   has index 1). The first word is at file position "list_start", and
   the words are "word_len" characters apart. */

{
    fseek(filep, list_start + (long)(index - 1) * word_len, 0);
}
```

Notice how (*index* - 1) is cast into a **long**. This step ensures that a **long** multiplication is performed.

Next, let us construct the loop to perform the binary search. The loop continues either until *lo* passes *hi* or until the middle verb is equal to the word being searched for:

```
while ( lo < hi && (result = strcmp(word, middle_word)) )
```

where *middle_word* is a string containing the middle word of the current range and *result* stores the result of the comparison. Before the loop is entered, we must initialize *lo*, *hi*, and *middle_word*:

```
fseek(verb_file, OL,0);               /* Go to start of file */
fscanf(verb_file, "%d", &list_size);  /* Read # of words */
lo = 1;                               /* Initial search range starts
                                         at word 1 */
hi = list_size;                       /* End of range to search
                                         is last word */
list_start = ftell(verb_file);        /* File location of first word */

/* Position file to middle word */

locate((lo + hi) / 2, verb_file, list_start, MAX_WORD_LEN + 1);

fscanf(verb_file, "%s", middle_word);  /* Read in middle word */
```

We assume that all new variables have been declared. Notice that the index of the middle word is calculated by the expression

```
(lo + hi) / 2
```

Try this formula with a few values to satisfy yourself that it works.

Much of the initializing code shown here will have to be repeated within the loop. Since the loop condition includes a test for whether the word has been found, the body of the loop merely calculates the new values of *hi, lo,* and *middle_word*:

```
{
   if (result < 0)    /* Use lower half of range */
 hi = (lo + hi) / 2 - 1;

   else               /* Use upper half of range */
 lo = (lo + hi) / 2 + 1;

   /* Position file to middle word */

   locate((lo + hi) / 2, verb_file, list_start, MAX_WORD_LEN + 1);

   fscanf(verb_file, "%s", middle_word);    /* Read in middle word */
}
```

At the end of a search for a verb not in the list, the value of *lo* may be decremented to 1 less than *hi*. In this case, the call to *fseek* within the *locate* function and the call to *fscanf* both return error codes, but the program will still function correctly.

Once the loop terminates, we must determine whether it did so because the word was found in the list or because *lo* became equal to *hi* and the word was not found. To do this, we can check the value of *result*. If the word was found, *result* will equal zero; otherwise it will not. The *is_verb* function should return *true* (non-zero) if the verb is found, so we will return the complement of the value of *result*:

```
return(!result);
```

If *result* is zero, the NOT operator returns *true*. If *result* is non-zero, the NOT operator returns *false*. Thus the function returns the correct truth value.

Here is the complete *is_verb* function:

```
is_verb(word, verb_file)
char word[];
FILE verb_file;

/* Returns  true  if  "word"  is  a verb. That means "word" is in the
   file  represented  by "verb_file". The file contains a word count,
   followed by that many  words of length MAX_WORD_LEN. The words are
   padded  with  blanks and separated by one white space character. A
   binary search is used to find "word" in the file. */

{
  int list_size,        /* Holds the word count */
      lo,               /* Beginning of range for binary search */
      hi,               /* End of range for binary search */
      result;           /* Holds the result of the "strcmp" */
    char middle_word[MAX_WORD_LEN + 1];       /* Holds the verb that is in
                                                 the middle of the range */
    long list_start,      /* Holds the file position at which the first
                             verb is located */
    ftell();

    fseek(verb_file, OL, 0);                /* Go to start of file */
    fscanf(verb_file, "%d", &list_size);    /* Read # of words */
    lo = 1;                                 /* Initial search range starts
                                               at word 1 */
    hi = list_size;                         /* End of range to search
                                               is last word */
    list_start = ftell(verb_file);          /* File location of first word */

    /* Position file to middle word */

    locate((lo + hi) / 2, verb_file, list_start, MAX_WORD_LEN + 1);

    fscanf(verb_file, "%s", middle_word);     /* Read in middle word */

    /**********************************************************/
    /* Now do a binary search for the word. Search ends when  */
    /* "lo" reaches "hi" or a match is found.                 */
    /**********************************************************/

    while (lo < hi && (result = strcmp(word, middle_word)))
      {
if (result < 0)    /* Use lower half of range */
   hi = (lo + hi) / 2 - 1;

else               /* Use upper half of range */
   lo = (lo + hi) / 2 + 1;

/* Position file to middle word */

locate((lo + hi) / 2, verb_file, list_start, MAX_WORD_LEN + 1);
fscanf(verb_file, "%s", middle_word);    /* Read in middle word */
  }

  /* If "result" is 0, a match was found, so return true (non-zero).
     Otherwise, "return" is non-zero, so return false (zero). */
  return(!result);
}
```

The function is passed the FILE pointer *verb_file*, indicating that the file itself was already opened by the calling function or even by the *main* function. Clearly, some of the functions of the program have to be rewritten so that they pass the value of *verb_file* down to the *is_verb* function. One function also must open and close the verb file.

You might prefer to write the program so that the values of *list_size* and *list_start* are found when the file is opened, and are passed to *is_verb*. Actually, *verb_file*, *list_size*, and *list_start* could be global, by the same justification we used to make *verb_list* global.

As an exercise, you may wish to write a version of *is_verb* which uses the indexed search with an indexed file. You might also wish to rewrite the *divide_sentence* function so that it saves the divided sentences in a file rather than a linked list.

Programming and Debugging *Hints*

Sometimes a program contains an *execution* error, which is an error that occurs when the program is run, thus making it impossible for execution to continue. In such an instance, tracing *printf* statements can be used to determine at what point the program crashed (terminated immediately with an error condition). These statements tell what point has been reached in the program, and perhaps the values of key variables. In order for this method to be reliable in C, it is necessary to follow each call to *printf* with a call to the *fflush* function (see Appendix B). Often the standard output file is *buffered*, meaning that the output to those files is collected in memory but not actually displayed until the buffer becomes full. If the program suddenly crashes, some undisplayed characters may still be in the buffer. The result is that the program appears to have terminated earlier than it actually did. The *fflush* function, as its name might suggest, flushes out the buffer. This function requires the inclusion of *stdio.h*, as its argument is a FILE pointer (such as *stdout* or *stderr*).

Often the standard error file is not buffered. If you know this to be the case with your compiler, you can output tracing messages through *stderr* using the *fprintf* function, without the need to call *fflush*. Sometimes the standard error file is line buffered, meaning it stores characters only until a *newline* is output and then displays the line.

C *Tutorial*

1. Distinguish briefly between input and output.

2. Under what circumstances is a file more useful than an array?

3. On what medium is a file generally stored?

4. What kind of information is generally associated with (a) the screen? (b) the keyboard?

5. What three files are automatically associated with every C program?

6. What are the names of the files that are normally associated with the *printf* and *scanf* functions?

7. What are the restrictions related to the *putchar* function?

8. Name and describe the counterpart to the *putchar* function.

9. What is the major difference between the end of a string and the end of a file?

10. In what way is a file more flexible than a string in C?

11. Are the words *input* and *output* significant as keywords in C? If so, explain.

12. Name a possible advantage of the function *getchar* over *scanf*.

13. What is the significance of the following?

    #include <stdio.h>

14. What is the significance of the angle brackets in Question 13?

15. How does <stdio.h> differ from "stdio.h" in operating systems that do not support directories ?

16. What is EOF, and what value does it usually have?

17. Why is it recommended that *stdio.h* always be used?

18. What must each file have associated with it?

19. What do the functions *getc* and *putc* have in common?

20. What is the effect of trying to write to the keyboard, an input device?

21. What is *control—d*, and to what use is it placed in C?

22. What must be done to a file before it can be used?

23. How does the *fopen* function work?

24. What happens in a C program if a file is opened by the *fopen* function and the file is not found?

25. When and how is a file closed?

26. What is the effect of neglecting to close the files before terminating a C program?

27. What are the two common file modes, and what are they used for?

28. What is the only method of altering information in a file?

29. Distinguish between the *printf* and *fprintf* functions.

30. What is append mode, and what letter is used to specify it?

31. How does write mode differ from append mode when an existing file is being written to?

32. In what sense is a disk a direct access device?

33. What role does the *fseek* function play, and how many arguments does it have?

34. If a C library does not contain a *rewind* function, how can it always be implemented?

35. What is the significance of the *w+* mode string?

36. What does the *ftell* function do, and what is one of its most common uses?

37. What does the *r+* mode string accomplish, and how does it work?

38. What is special about *a+* mode?

ANSWERS TO C TUTORIAL

1. Information that enters the computer from the outside is called input, whereas information produced by the computer and sent to the outside world is known as output.

2. A file not only can store more data than an array but retains its contents even when the computer is turned off.

3. A file generally is stored on a disk.

4. The screen normally is used for output, and the keyboard is used for input.

5. Standard input, standard output, and standard error.

6. Standard output and standard input.

7. It can output only one character at a time, and only to the standard output.

8. The *getchar* function inputs a single character from the standard input.

9. The end of a string is always indicated by a *null* character, whereas the manner in which the end of a file is indicated depends on the storage device and the computer.

10. A file can contain the *null* character as part of its actual data, whereas a string cannot.

11. The words *input* and *output* are not keywords in C.

12. The *getchar* function can be used to input a string that includes white space characters.

13. It inserts the file *stdio.h* in the program, thereby making available all the definitions included in *stdio.h*.

14. On some computers, it indicates that the file *stdio.h* is to be found in a special directory rather than in the programmer's own directory.

15. In such a case there is no difference.

16. EOF is a constant returned by many I/O functions to indicate that the end of an input file has been reached. Its value on most computers is -1.

17. Even if the programmer does not plan to use special I/O functions at the time the program is written, such functions may have to be added later on. If the programmer remembers to add *stdio.h* at the beginning, it will not be omitted later.

18. A pointer of target type FILE.

19. They both deal with a single character, and both may be used on any file opened by the program.

20. An error code probably would be returned by the I/O function.

21. The character *control−d* (obtained by holding down the *control* key while at the same time pressing the *d* key) is usually used to indicate end of file on a keyboard.

22. It must be opened by the program.

23. The *fopen* function has two parameters. The first is a string specifying the file name. The second is a string that specifies the mode in which the file is to be opened (read is *r*, write is *w*, and so on). The function returns a FILE pointer associated with the opened file.

24. If the file is being opened for reading, NULL is returned by *fopen*. If the file is being opened for writing, the file is created.

25. A file is closed when it is no longer needed by the program. Closing the file is accomplished by calling the *fclose* function.

26. Nothing untoward; all files are closed automatically upon program termination.

27. The mode *r* is used for opening a file for reading, and *w* is used to open a file for writing.

28. The contents of a file can be altered only by writing, never by reading.

29. The *printf* function can send output only to the standard output file, whereas *fprintf* can send its output to any opened output file (including *stdout*).

30. Append mode is used to add characters to the end of a file that already exists. It is specified by using the mode string "a" as the second parameter to *fopen*.

31. When write mode is used, the former contents of the file are erased. With append mode, the contents of the file are retained and new information is added to the end of the file.

32. A program can read a character from any point in a file without having to read all preceding characters. The same statement applies to writing information to the file.

33. The *fseek* function is used to position the file (or the file's marker) to a specified location in the file. This function has three parameters: the first is the file pointer, and the second and third specify the new position.

34. A file can be rewound by the statement

    fseek(fp, 0L, 0);

    where *fp* is the file pointer.

35. A file opened with *w+* mode is opened in the same manner as with *w* mode (it is erased or created), except that the file can be both read from and written to without the necessity of closing and reopening it.

36. The *ftell* function returns the current position in the file. It is useful in determining the size of the file.

37. In *r+* mode, a file is expected to exist already. Its contents are retained, and it is opened for both reading and writing.

38. It is used to open a file for appending, but also permits the file to be read without the need to close and reopen the file.

Keywords

(No new keywords were introduced in this chapter)

auto	break	case	char	default	do
double	else	float	for	if	int
long	return	short	sizeof	static	struct
switch	unsigned	while			

Exercises

1. Write a program that uses the inventory file produced by Program 14–11. The user presents the program with a shopping list of items to be purchased. The program inputs the stored inventory file, and then it decrements the count for each item on the shopping list and charges the customer appropriately. The program must check for the presence of the item and for sufficient quantities in stock. Before terminating the program, it must update the inventory file to reflect the depletion in stock. It might also print a list of items that need to be restocked.

2. Implement your own versions of the *gets* and *puts* functions. The *gets* function returns a pointer to **char**, and takes one argument, a character array. The function reads in a line from *stdin*, placing it in the array and terminating it with a *null* character. The *newline* used to terminate the input line is not itself stored in the array. The function returns the address of the array. If an error or end of file occurs, the function returns NULL. The *puts* function takes one argument, a string to be sent to *stdout* as a single line. After the function writes the string, it writes a *newline* (so this character need not be included in the string). The function returns EOF if an error occurs.

3. Implement the *printf* and *scanf* functions, using only *getchar* and *putchar*. Do not use *sprintf* or *sscanf* to do the formatting, but rather try to implement at least some of the control string features on your own.

4. Write a program to change all uppercase characters in a file to lowercase, and vice versa. (Make the actual modifications to the stored file.)

5. Space can be saved in a file if numbers are stored in their internal form rather than as displayable numbers (see Program 14–11). Write a function that stores integers on disk in their internal form, and one that reads in those numbers. You may wish to use *fseek* in these functions in order to access the file like an array. The function could be passed an index, which would then be converted into a byte address in the file.

6. The sorting techniques we have seen so far have required that all the data to be sorted be kept in memory. In the real world, however, it is frequently necessary to sort files that are so large that they cannot be stored in their entirety in the computer's memory. One solution to this problem is the *mergesort* technique. The data are read in from the file in chunks of a fixed size, sorted, and stored in temporary files. For example, suppose we have a file called *data* containing the following data:

data: 7 3 14 22 9 16 3 17 2 14 9 27

This file is not large, but it would be inconvenient to illustrate the technique with a file containing thousands of numbers. We can divide the file *data* conceptually into chunks, each containing three numbers:

data: 7 3 14   22 9 16   3 17 2   14 9 27

Now the computer reads in the first three numbers of the file and sorts them:

input: 7 3 14
sorted: 3 7 14

This sorted chunk is stored in a file called *data1*. A similar process is performed on the second, third and fourth three-number chunks of the file *data*, resulting in the following four files:

data1: 3 7 14
data2: 9 16 22
data3: 2 3 17
data4: 9 14 27

Each of these files has been sorted, but if the four files were merely joined together, they would not form a sorted sequence. It is necessary to merge the files into a single, sorted file.

First, all four files need to be open at the same time. We also open an output file, called *sorted*, to hold the fully sorted data. The first numbers in each file are read in. We will show the contents of all the files, with arrows indicating the numbers that are in memory:

```
    data1      data2      data3      data4
    -----      -----      -----      -----
 -> 3       -> 9       -> 2       -> 9
    7          16         3          14
    14         22         17         27
```

Since 2 (from file *data3*) is the smallest value, it is written first into the file *sorted*. (We know that none of the other files contains a smaller value, because they are all sorted and begin with values greater than 2.) Since the first value came from *data3*, we read in the next number from that file:

```
    data1      data2      data3      data4
    -----      -----      -----      -----
 -> 3       -> 9          2       -> 9
    7          16      -> 3          14
    14         22         17         27
```

sorted: 2

The smallest values in memory are the two 3's, so they are written to *sorted*. Since the two numbers were from files *data1* and *data3*, the next values are read in from those two files:

```
   data1      data2      data3      data4
   -----      -----      -----      -----
     3       -> 9          2       -> 9
  -> 7         16          3         14        (now 7 is smallest)
    14         22       -> 17        27
```

sorted: 2 3 3

This process continues until all files are depleted. The subsequent steps are as follows:

```
   data1      data2      data3      data4
   -----      -----      -----      -----
     3       -> 9          2       -> 9
     7         16          3         14        (now the 9's are smallest)
  -> 14        22       -> 17        27
```

sorted: 2 3 3 7

```
                  *********************************
```

```
   data1      data2      data3      data4
   -----      -----      -----      -----
     3          9          2          9
     7       -> 16         3       -> 14        (now the 14's are smallest)
  -> 14        22       -> 17        27
```

sorted: 2 3 3 7 9 9

```
                  *********************************
```

```
  data1       data2      data3      data4
  -----       -----      -----      -----
  (end          9          2          9
   of         -> 16         3         14        (now 16 is smallest)
  file)         22       -> 17       -> 27
```

sorted: 2 3 3 7 9 9 14 14

```
                  *********************************
```

```
  data1       data2      data3      data4
  -----       -----      -----      -----
  (end          9          2          9
   of           16         3         14        (now 17 is smallest)
  file)       -> 22      -> 17      -> 27
```

sorted: 2 3 3 7 9 9 14 14 16

The last three numbers are 17, 22 and 27, resulting in the file *sorted* containing:

2 3 3 7 9 9 14 14 16 17 22 27

In summary, the steps of sorting and merging are:

1. Divide the unsorted file up into smaller chunks that fit in memory. Sort each chunk and store it in a separate file.
2. Read the first value from each file into memory.
3. Select the smallest value(s) in memory and write it (them) to the sorted file.
4. Read in the next value from each file for which a value was just written to the sorted file. If the end of a file is reached, make sure to indicate this so its last value is not reused.
5. Repeat steps 3 and 4 until the end of all input files has been reached. At this point, the output file is the sorted version of the unsorted file.

It should be relatively easy to implement a mergesort program if you are familiar with I/O techniques.

7. Rewrite Program 14-11 so that it maintains two files, representing the two lists described in Chapter 13, Exercise 5. As a further modification, before adding a new item, have the program check to see whether the item exists in the first file (the one containing constant information, such as the item name). If it does, have it update the information in the corresponding record of the second file. Otherwise, add new records to both files. This can be implemented by reading both files into linked lists at the beginning of the program, adding to or updating the lists as necessary, and writing both lists back to the file at the end of the program run. The first file need be rewritten only if records have been added to it. Note, however, that when making only a few modifications to a large file, it can sometimes be more efficient to update the files directly.

   When updating the *count* member of an already-existing record, the program should add the quantity received to the value already in the *count* member.

8. Rewrite the program from Exercise 1 to handle the two files described in Exercise 7. You will probably want to read both files into memory. Remember that it is never necessary in this program to rewrite the first file.

15

The
C
Preprocessor

*O*ne of the features not included in the original C language was constants. In order to accommodate various features (including constants), the authors of C developed the C preprocessor. None of the services provided by the preprocessor is indispensable for writing C programs, but these services make the task considerably easier.

Portability

The authors of any new programming language must decide on the general nature of the language, as well as the specific features it should include. These decisions usually are based on the constructs the authors believe are required and on their experience with other languages. As the new language comes into general use, however, its users discover various shortcomings and suggest enhancements to the language. New versions appear, written by people other than the original authors. Usually these new versions are made *portable*, meaning that a program written in the original version of the language runs on all compilers for the newer versions.

If a C program compiles and runs correctly on an Apple //e, for example, it would be desirable for it to compile and run correctly on an IBM PC that has a C compiler. Complete portability, however, is an ideal that is not always attained. Most computer languages have an official standard version, and programs written strictly according to the rules of this version are expected to run on all compilers of the language. The original text on C, *The C Programming Language*, usually is regarded as the authority. Yet most C compilers include more features than are mentioned in that text, and occasionally there are contradictions. A C standard has been proposed which includes many of the features added since the original creation of the language. At the time of this writing, however, the standard has not yet been officially accepted.

How the Preprocessor Works

When you issue the command to compile a C program, the program is run automatically through the preprocessor. The preprocessor is a program that modifies the C source program according to directives supplied in the program. An original source program usually is stored in a file. The preprocessor does not modify this program file, but creates a new file that contains the processed version of the program. This new file is then submitted to the compiler. Some compilers enable the programmer to run only the preprocessor on the source program and to view the results of the preprocessor stage.

If a program contains the directive

```
#define NULL 0
```

and the statement

```
x = NULL;
```

the preprocessor replaces every occurrence of NULL following the **#define** directive with 0. The resulting program no longer includes the directive (since directives are only for the preprocessor, not the compiler), and the preceding statement now reads as follows:

```
x = 0;
```

Constants, therefore, are abbreviations supplied for the convenience of the programmer. Each occurrence of a constant is translated by the preprocessor so that the program is comprehensible to the C compiler. The preprocessor also can add or delete C program statements.

All preprocessor directives begin with the number or sharp sign (#). They must start in the first column, and on most C compilers there can be no space between the number sign and the directive. The directive is terminated *not* by a semicolon, but by the end of the line on which it appears. Only one directive can occur on a line.

The #define Directive

The **#define** directive is used to define a symbol to the preprocessor and assign it a value. The symbol is meaningful to the preprocessor only in the lines of code *following* the definition. For example, if the directive

```
#define NULL 0
```

is included in the program, then in all lines following the definition, the symbol NULL is replaced by the symbol 0. If the symbol NULL is written in the program before the definition is encountered, however, it is not replaced.

A preprocessor symbol is never replaced if it occurs within single or double quotation marks.

The **#define** directive is followed by one or more spaces or tabs and the symbol to be defined. The syntax of a preprocessor symbol is the same as that for a C variable or function name. It cannot be a C keyword or a variable name used in the program; if it is, a syntax error is detected by the compiler. For example, suppose a program contains the directive

```
#define dumb 54
```

which in turn is followed by the declaration

```
int dumb;
```

This would be translated by the preprocessor into

```
int 54;
```

which would be rejected by the compiler. The preprocessor does not check for normal C syntax, except for identifying quotation marks. It merely substitutes symbols where it finds them.

The symbol being defined is followed by one or more spaces or tabs and a value for the symbol. The value can be omitted, in which case the symbol is defined but not given a value. If this symbol is used later in the program, it is deleted without being replaced with anything. A symbol defined with no value is useful with the conditional compilation directives (see below).

If a **#define** directive does not fit on a single line, it can be continued on subsequent lines. All lines of the directive except the last must end with a backslash (\\) character. A directive can be split only at a point where a space is legal.

Constants

A common use for defined symbols is the implementation of named constants. The following are examples of constants in C:

```
25
1.23
'a'
"hello"
-6
```

Any of these can be assigned to a defined preprocessor symbol:

```
#define INTEGER 25
#define CHARACTER 'a'
```

When we use the word "assign" in relation to defined symbols, we mean the association of a value with a symbol, not the sort of assignment accomplished by the C assignment operators.

A defined symbol can specify only a complete constant. For example, if a program contains the definition

```
#define NULL 0
```

the number 120 cannot be represented by 12NULL. A defined symbol can be recognized only if it is delimited by white space, punctuation, or operators. (This rule also applies to C identifiers, such as variable or function names.)

Macros

When a constant is associated with a defined symbol, the characters making up the constant are assigned, not the numeric value of the constant. The definition

```
#define EOF -1
```

really assigns the string "-1" to EOF. That is why constants have no innate type. The preprocessor replaces the symbol EOF by the characters "-1" without any consideration of the meaning of the two characters. In fact, a preprocessor symbol can be assigned any string at all.

The following is a valid preprocessor directive:

```
#define TEST if (a > b)
```

The symbol TEST is defined to be the entire contents of the directive following the symbol TEST; that is, the string

```
if (a > b)
```

The statement

```
TEST  printf("It worked\n");
```

would be translated to

```
if (a > b) printf("It worked\n");
```

When a preprocessor symbol is defined as a segment of text, it is more generally called a *macro*. Macros are very useful in making C code more readable and compact. For example, some programmers include the following definitions in all their programs:

```
#define and &&
#define or ||
```

These definitions enable the programmer to write more readable code, such as the following:

```
if (a < b or c > d and e < f)
```

A macro also can be used to define descriptive words. For example, the definition

```
#define local /**/
```

makes possible the declaration of a local variable as

```
local int i;
```

in which the proprocessor replaces the word *local* with an empty comment. This makes C more wordy, but helps clarify the meaning of statements that might otherwise be unclear to the reader of the program.

A comment can be included at the end of a macro or constant definition:

```
#define STUFF 1     /* Nothing in particular */
```

A comment can be inserted at any point in a C program where white space is permitted (except, of course, within a literal) without adverse effect to the program. Remember, however, that the comment is part of the definition, so if it is continued onto the following line, the first line must end with a backslash.

Macros also can be used as abbreviations for lengthy and frequently used statements. The one restriction on macros is

that, even though their definitions can occupy more than one
line, they cannot include a *newline*. That is, when a macro is
expanded (when the symbol is replaced by the text it
represents), all the resulting text is placed on the same line.

Macros With Arguments

The brief description of macros given in the preceding section
does not do them justice. In some cases a certain construct is
used frequently in a program but the details of the statement
vary. As an example, suppose a program contains the statement

```
if (a > 0) a -= 1;
```

and the statement

```
if (b > 0) b -= 1;
```

Aside from the different variables, the statements are identical
in form. It would be convenient to have a single macro that can
represent both statements. The preprocessor permits macros to
have arguments, just as functions do; the difference is that the
arguments are strings rather than values. Consider the following
definition:

```
#define   DECREMENT(x)   if (x > 0) x -= 1
```

When this macro is expanded, the string passed to the
argument x replaces all occurrences of x in the symbol's value.
That is, the statement

```
DECREMENT(a);
```

is expanded to

```
if (a > 0) a -= 1;
```

and the statement

```
DECREMENT(b);
```

becomes

```
if (b > 0) b -= 1;
```

Notice that the macro definition itself (the line containing the
word **#define**) does not include a semicolon. When the macro is
invoked later, it is followed by an explicitly specified semicolon:

```
DECREMENT(a);
```

The argument names used in a macro are local to the macro.
Thus there is no conflict between a macro's formal parameter
names and identifiers used in the program itself. In the definition

of DECREMENT, it does not matter if x is a variable used in the program, because the parameter x is replaced by the preprocessor. Any symbols used in the macro definition which are not argument names or names of other macros are left unchanged, and are assumed to be variable names or other C symbols.

The argument supplied to a macro can be any series of characters. For example, the definition

```
#define   NUM_PRINT(value, spec)   printf("value = %spec\n", value)
```

can be invoked as

```
NUM_PRINT(p+q*r, d);
```

which is expanded to

```
printf("p+q*r = %d\n", p+q*r);
```

Notice that the actual parameters are substituted for the dummy parameters in a macro expansion even though they are within quotation marks. The preceding macro could not have a parameter called n, because then the n in the control string that follows the backslash would be replaced by the value specified for n. That is, if the macro were defined as

```
#define   NUM_PRINT(n, spec)   printf("n = %spec\n", n)
```

then the expression

```
NUM_PRINT(p+q*r, d);
```

would be expanded to

```
printf("p+q*r = %d\p+q*r", p+q*r);
```

The comma is the delimiter that separates arguments in a macro. Therefore, there are only two cases in which a comma can be included as part of an argument: (1) when the comma is located between quotation marks, and (2) when the comma is used within parentheses, as in a function call or when the comma operator is used. For example, consider the following macro:

```
#define   LOOP(x, y, z)   for(x; y; z)
```

If it is necessary to use the comma operator in one of the arguments, this could be done by writing

```
LOOP((i = 0, j = 1), i < 10, (i++, j++))
```

which would be expanded to

```
for((i = 0, j = 1); i < 10; (i++, j++))
```

Notice the use of the parentheses in the arguments. It would be illegal to write

```
LOOP(i = 0, j = 1, i < 10, i++, j++)
```

since the preprocessor would interpret this as the specification of five arguments. The macro is defined with only three arguments, so this would be treated as an error.

The preceding technique works only with the comma operator. If one were to define a macro as follows:

```
#define   Print(format, value)   printf(format, value)
```

and then try to print two variables by writing

```
Print("%d %d", (q, r));
```

the preprocessor would produce the following statement:

```
printf("%d %d", (q, r));
```

Syntactically, the compiler interprets the comma between q and r as the comma operator. Since the comma operator returns the value of its second operand, the *printf* function would be passed the control string "%d %d" as its first parameter and the value of r as its second parameter. No third parameter would be passed.

The importance of parentheses in macro definitions cannot be overstressed. Consider the following macro:

```
#define   sqr(a)   a * a
```

Now consider the expansion of the following:

```
sqr(x+4)
```

The result is

```
x+4 * x+4
```

which states that 4 is multiplied by x and the result is added to x and 4. The macro should have been defined instead as

```
#define   sqr(a)   ((a) * (a))
```

which would result in the correct expansion:

```
((x+4) * (x+4))
```

The outer set of parentheses is useful in a case such as

```
(char)sqr(x)
```

which, without the outer parentheses, would be expanded to

```
(char)(x) * (x)
```

The cast operator has a higher precedence than multiplication. Assuming x is an **int**. The result would be to cast the first x to a **char** and then multiply this value by the **int** value of x, producing an **int** result. The outer parentheses in the macro definition result in the multiplication being performed first, with the result cast into a **char** as intended. Notice that the *sqr* macro uses no type-dependent operators, so even if x were of type **float**, the macro invocation

```
sqr(x)
```

still would produce the correct expression, namely

```
((x) * (x))
```

As an example of a useful macro, consider the following:

```
#define   until(x)   while(!(x))
```

The loop heading

```
until(a > 7)
```

is converted to

```
while (!(a > 7))
```

Notice that, in the macro value field, the argument x is enclosed in parentheses to separate it from the ! operator. If the macro had been defined as

```
#define until(x) while(!x)
```

then the statement fragment

```
until(a > 7)
```

would be converted to

```
while(!a > 7)
```

Since the ! operator has a higher precedence than the > operator, this would be interpreted by the compiler as equivalent to

```
while ((!a) > 7)
```

which is not the intended result.

Another often-defined macro is the one used to find the smaller of two numbers:

```
#define   MIN(a,b)   ((a) < (b) ? (a) : (b))
```

This operation is considered too simple to define as a function, but the conditional expression required can seem complicated if a and b are non-trivial expressions. The MIN macro makes an expression look like a function call.

A warning about macros is in order at this point. Consider the following use of the MIN macro:

```
z = MIN(++x,y)
```

The intention seems to be to increment the value of x, and then to assign x or y, whichever is smaller, to z. But look at the macro expansion:

```
z = ((++x) < (y) ? (++x) : (y))
```

If x is less than y, the value of x is incremented *twice*, because the dummy parameter a, which is substituted by $++x$, appears twice in the macro definition. Such a problem would not occur with an actual function, since in that case x would first be incremented, and then its value would be passed to the function. It is necessary to be careful in defining and using macros. If you write macros to be used by other people (or even by yourself at a later time), make sure to specify clearly any restrictions on the macro arguments.

Macros such as *until*, which was illustrated earlier, can radically alter the syntax used in a program, possibly rendering it unintelligible to a reader other than the original programmer. Macros such as MIN, however, which could be considered pseudo-functions, do not suffer from this problem because they adhere to the standard function-call syntax.

A macro can be defined in terms of another macro, as in the following example of nested macros:

```
#define   CONTROL   "%d\n"
#define   printint(x)   printf(CONTROL, x)
#define   TEST(x)   if (x > 0) printint(x)
```

If the program contains the statement

```
TEST(w);
```

where w is an integer variable, the statement goes through the following conversion steps:

```
1) if (w > 0) printint(w);
2) if (w > 0) printf(CONTROL, w);
3) if (w > 0) printf("%d\n", w);
```

A macro definition cannot contain itself, as in

```
#define  INFINITY  INFINITY x
```

since that construct would lead to an infinite recursion, which is physically impossible. The preprocessor would flag this as an error. For the same reason, the following is illegal:

```
#define  A  B
#define  B  A
```

The last two examples are simple instances of infinite recursion, but this error can have more complicated forms that are harder to recognize. There are also serious limits to the preprocessor's ability to detect hidden recursion, so these errors might not be detected until the preprocessor attempts to make the substitutions and finds itself in an infinite loop. A preprocessor can avoid getting caught in such a loop by limiting the depth to which it will nest macros.

The advantages of macros vs. functions depend on the situation. A function that would consist of only one line of code usually should be implemented as a macro, to save computing time. If memory space is the primary consideration, however, a macro may not be the best choice. It is expanded wherever it is invoked, whereas the code for a function appears only once in a program.

Macros are more powerful than functions in that their arguments can be any strings at all. As we have seen, they also can be used with arguments of different types. Some disadvantages of macros also have been illustrated. The programmer must not treat macros syntactically like functions; for example, he must not declare the type of a macro or take its address.

The #undef Directive

It may be necessary to redefine a macro at some point in a program. For example, the user may wish to redefine a macro or constant specified in a header file such as *stdio.h*. If only a few macros from such a file need to be redefined, the easiest way to do this is to #include the entire file and then redefine the macros in question.

For example, suppose a programmer wishes the constant EOF to have the value -2. (In practice, it would be dangerous to redefine the value of EOF; it is done here merely as an example.) The program could begin with the following directives:

```
#include <stdio.h>
#undef EOF
#define EOF -2
```

If a preprocessor symbol has already been defined, it must be undefined before being redefined. This is accomplished by the **#undef** directive, which specifies the name of the symbol to be undefined.

It is not necessary to perform the redefinition at the beginning of a program. A symbol can be redefined in the middle of a program, so that it has one value in the first part and another value at the end.

A symbol need not be redefined after it is undefined. If the program uses the symbol in a statement after the point at which it is undefined, however, the symbol is not replaced. A defined symbol will be replaced before the point (if any) at which it is undefined.

As mentioned in the previous chapter, there may be two versions of the *getchar* and *putchar* functions. Each can be a library function as well as a macro defined in *stdio.h*. If *stdio.h* is included in the program, the macro versions are used. If the programmer wishes to use the function versions they can be undefined after the #include <*stdio.h*> directive. Then, when the preprocessor sees the symbols *getchar* and *putchar*, it does not replace them with anything, but passes them on to the compiler. The compiler interprets the identifiers *getchar* and *putchar* as function names, since they are followed by argument lists.

The #include Directive

Often a programmer accumulates a collection of useful constant and macro definitions that are used in almost every program. It is desirable to be able to store these definitions in a file that can be inserted automatically into every program. This task is performed by the #include directive.

A file is inserted at any point where the #include directive is encountered. Usually, however, files are included at the beginning of a program. Such files are called *header files*, and by convention their names end with the characters *.h* (as in *stdio.h*).

Header files can contain any text at all. Aside from preprocessor directives to define macros, they may also contain C code to define structure templates, global variables, or function definitions. Header files usually do not contain function definitions, however, as it is more efficient to store these in function libraries set up by the user. Global variables sometimes are included. Even though strict followers of structured programming frown on the use of global variables, often such variables are useful in simplifying various tasks. For example, the I/O functions described in the previous chapter depend on the existence of a global array of type FILE.

An example of an inclusion you have already seen is

```
#include <stdio.h>
```

in which *stdio.h* is the file to be included. The angle brackets tell the preprocessor to search for the file in one or more standard directories. These directories contain header files that are provided by the system, and those commonly used by several programmers (if the computer is a multiple-user machine). If the brackets are replaced with double quotation marks, as in

```
#include "stdio.h"
```

the preprocessor looks first in the programmer's own directory, or the same one that contains the program file. If it is not found there, then the standard directories are searched. In operating systems in which directories do not exist as separate entities from disks, the header file is searched for on the current disk, regardless of whether the angle brackets or quotation marks are used.

Another common use for header files is to provide consistency among several program files. Often a program is so large that it is convenient to break it down into smaller units, each of which is stored in a separate file. After these separate program files are compiled, they must somehow be linked together to form a single program. This linking is usually accomplished by a program called the *linkage editor*, which is often run automatically when a program is compiled. It is desirable, however, that the separate program files be able to use the same macros and structure definitions and even have access to a common pool of global variables. This can be facilitated by the inclusion of the same header files in each program file.

For example, suppose an array is declared in one program file and passed to a function in another program file. The function might need to know the exact dimensions of the array. Therefore, the header file defines a constant equal to the dimension of the array, and each function that uses the array has this constant available. If it becomes necessary to change this dimension, only the header file needs to be modified. The same global variables are declared in each file, which would seem to create the undesirable situation of having multiple copies of the same variable. Some linkage editors combine multiple instances of a variable name into a single variable, provided that all the copies are declared in the same way; however, this is not the case with all linkage editors. For a more universal approach to shared global variables, see the description of the **extern** storage class in the next chapter.

A header file can contain other **#include** directives. It cannot include itself, because this would lead to infinite recursion. It cannot include another file that includes the first file, either, as this would also be an infinite recursion.

Conditional Compilation: #ifdef, #ifndef, and #endif

Sometimes it is necessary to have two different versions of a program. For example, suppose we are selling the store inventory program shown in the previous two chapters as a piece of commercial software. Some stores may want the version that saves the records on a disk, and others may want the linked list version. The two versions of the program are more alike than they are different, so it would be redundant to maintain both.

One solution would be to combine the code for both versions into a single program file, and then remove the portions not required for the version being sold to a particular customer.

Removing statements by hand would be rather tedious and could also lead to error. For this reason, the preprocessor provides directives for selectively removing sections of code, or choosing between two possible sections. This process is known as *conditional compilation*. Two of these directives are introduced in the following section of code, which might be part of the inventory program:

```
#ifdef RECORD_FILE
    add_record(inv_bytes, inv_file);
#endif
```

The function *add_record* is used only in the file version of the program. This code serves to accomplish the following task: If the preprocessor symbol RECORD_FILE has been defined before this code is reached, the code between the two directives **#ifdef** and **#endif** is included in the translated program that is passed by the preprocessor to the C compiler. Otherwise, the statement is removed from the program by the preprocessor. Conditional compilation usually involves large blocks of code; for the sake of brevity, our examples involve only one or two statements.

The **#ifdef** directive tests whether a particular symbol has been defined before the **#ifdef** is encountered. It does not matter what value has been assigned to the symbol. In fact, a symbol can be defined to the preprocessor without a value:

```
#define RECORD_FILE
```

If the **#ifdef** directive is encountered after this definition, it produces a true result. If, however, the directive

```
#undef RECORD_FILE
```

is encountered before the directive

```
#ifdef RECORD_FILE
```

then the preprocessor considers the symbol RECORD_FILE to be undefined, and the **#ifdef** directive returns a *false* value. If an **#ifdef** returns a *true* value, all the lines between the **#ifdef** and the corresponding **#endif** directive (or the **#else** directive, as discussed in the next section) are left in the program. If those lines contain preprocessor directives, the directives are processed. In this way, conditional compilation directives can be nested. If the **#ifdef** evaluates as *false*, the associated lines are ignored, including any preprocessor directives that are included.

Even though we talk about conditional compilation directives in the same terms as the C **if** statement, the preprocessor directives are executed *before* compilation is initiated. Thus there can be no overlap between C code and preprocessor directives. For example, the **#ifdef** directive cannot be used to test for the declaration of a variable.

In the inventory program, all statements that pertain only to the file version are enclosed between the directives

```
#ifdef RECORD_FILE
```

and

```
#endif
```

The statements need not all be grouped in one place. The **#ifdef** and **#endif** directives can be used as many times as required.

If the version being sold is the file version, then we insert the following directive at the beginning of the file:

```
#define RECORD_FILE
```

Now all the code pertaining to the file version is passed on to the compiler. It is also necessary to perform the same modification on the code pertaining to the linked list version. All code pertaining only to the linked list version is enclosed in directives testing for the symbol LINKED_LIST, as shown here:

```
#ifdef LINKED_LIST
    add_node(p, &inv_list);
#endif
```

This code is kept only if LINKED_LIST is defined; otherwise, it is removed. To produce the linked list version, we must place the directive

```
#define LINKED_LIST
```

at the beginning of the program.

All code common to both versions of the program is left as unconditional, meaning that it is not placed between an **#ifdef** and **#endif** pair. To make a meaningful version of the program, however, either RECORD_FILE or LINKED_LIST (but not both) must be defined. Once this is done, the program can be compiled to produce the desired version. It is possible to switch between versions by modifying one line in the program file, a **#define** directive.

On some computers, it is possible to define a preprocessor symbol as part of the command that tells the computer to compile (and preprocess) a program. In such a case, it is not even necessary to change the program file. Only the symbol being defined in the compile command needs to be changed.

The preprocessor also provides the directive **#ifndef**, which produces a *true* result if a symbol is *not* defined. This makes it possible to use a single symbol to switch between two versions. Consider the following:

```
#ifdef RECORD_FILE
    add_record(inv_bytes, inv_file);
#endif
#ifndef RECORD_FILE
    add_node(p, &inv_list);
#endif
```

In this example, the call to *add_record* is included only if RECORD_FILE is defined, and the call to *add_node* is included only if RECORD_FILE is not defined. Therefore, to produce the file version, we define RECORD_FILE. To produce the linked list version, we leave RECORD_FILE undefined. In this way, we are able to avoid the problem presented by the two-symbol method—namely, that we might forget to define either symbol, or that we might inadvertently define both. In the one-symbol version, RECORD_FILE always is either defined or not defined, so no matter what we do, a usable version of the program is produced.

There may be some code in the file version which has no counterpart in the linked list version or vice versa. It is not necessary to include a section of code for every section that is removed. We may just want to say: "If this is the file version, include the following code; otherwise, just forget it."

Conditional compilation can be used to select preprocessor directives as well as C code. For example, suppose a header file is included in a program, and a certain preprocessor symbol (say, FLAG) may or may not be defined in that header file. (Perhaps the header file is subject to frequent modifications.) If the programmer wants FLAG never to be defined, then the **#include** directive can be followed by

```
#ifdef FLAG
#undef FLAG
#endif
```

This ensures that, even if the symbol is defined in the header file, its definition is removed. It is not sufficient merely to write

```
#undef FLAG
```

because if FLAG is not defined, the directive is erroneous. If FLAG should always be defined, then we would write

```
#ifndef FLAG
#define FLAG
#endif
```

We could, of course, give FLAG a value. We cannot simply write

```
#define FLAG
```

since if FLAG is already defined, an error probably will result.

The #else Directive

Since the **#ifdef** and **#ifndef** directives often are used to choose between two sections of code, the preprocessor provides the **#else** directive. This directive functions in much the same way as the **else** clause of an **if** statement. The code in the previous section could be written as

```
#ifdef RECORD_FILE
    add_record(inv_bytes, inv_file);
#else
    add_node(p, &inv_list);
#endif
```

If the symbol RECORD_FILE is defined, the line before the **#else** directive is included and the line between the **#else** and the **#endif** is ignored. Otherwise, the line before the **#else** directive is ignored, and the line between the **#else** and the **#endif** is included. In general, all lines between an **#ifdef** or an **#ifndef** directive and the corresponding **#else** clause are included if the **#ifdef** or **#ifndef** is true. Otherwise, the lines between the **#else** and the corresponding **#endif** are included. One of the two sets of lines always is passed on to the compiler, but never both. The **#else** directive and the lines that follow it can be omitted, but never the **#endif** directive. No other text can be included on the same line as the **#else** or **#endif** directive.

Conditional compilation constructs can be nested. In this case, **#ifdef**s (or **#ifndef**s) and **#else**s and **#endif**s are associated in the same way that **if** and **else** clauses are matched in nested **if** constructs. The disadvantage of nesting conditional compilations is that, since preprocessor directives usually must start in column 1, it generally is not possible to use indenting to highlight the nesting structure. Therefore, such code is prone to errors.

The #if Directive

There are two disadvantages to the **#ifdef** and **#ifndef** directives. Although it is possible to test whether a symbol is defined, it is not possible to test whether that symbol has a specific value or to compare it to another symbol. Also, it is not possible to test for the case in which several symbols are defined simultaneously, or one of several symbols is defined; that is, there is no connecting logical AND or OR operator. These two problems are overcome by the more general **#if** directive.

The **#if** directive tests an expression. This expression can be of any form used in a C program, with virtually any operators, except that it can include only integer constant values. No variables or function calls are permitted, nor are floating point, character, or string constants.

The **#if** directive is true if the expression evaluates to *true* (non-zero). For example, suppose we wish to select a version of the inventory program based on the value of a symbol called VERSION. We could write

```
#if VERSION == 0
    add_record(inv_bytes, inv_file);
#else
    add_node(p, &inv_list);
#endif
```

This code would choose the file version if VERSION has the value zero, or the linked list version if VERSION has any other value. We could also use this method to choose among three or more groups of lines. Suppose we were to add a third version that stores the records in an array, and makes use of a function called *add_element*. The program file might include the following:

```
#if VERSION == 0
    add_record(inv_bytes, inv_file);
#else
#if VERSION == 1
    add_node(p, &inv_list);
#else
    add_element(p, inv_array);
#endif
#endif
```

The outer **#else** clause contains a nested **#if** construct; notice that there are two **#endif** directives, one for the outer construct and one for the inner. In this example, the file version is created if VERSION has the value 0; the linked list version is created if VERSION equals 1; and the array version results in all other cases. To avoid nesting, we could rewrite the code as follows:

```
#if VERSION == 0
    add_record(inv_bytes, inv_file);
#endif
#if VERSION == 1
    add_node(p, &inv_list);
#endif
#if (VERSION != 0 && VERSION != 1)
    add_element(p, inv_array);
#endif
```

Such a construct would be inefficient if applied to an **if** statement in a C program, because if the first test succeeds, the second one still is made. Since the **#if** tests are made only during the preprocessor stage, however, and not during execution, the program is not adversely affected.

Any undefined preprocessor symbol used in the **#if** expression is treated as if it has the value 0. Using a symbol that is defined with no value does not work with all preprocessors, and an attempt to do so might result in an error. The same rule applies to symbols defined to have non-numeric or non-integer values, unless those symbols' values can be evaluated as constant integers. For example, if three macros are defined as

```
#define A 4
#define B 5
#define SUM A + B
```

then SUM can be used in an **#if** expression, since $A + B$ evaluates to $4 + 5$, which in turn evaluates to 9. A symbol defined as follows, however, cannot be used in an **#if** directive:

```
#define TEXT   @#$
```

The **if...else** statement of C could be used to choose between two blocks of code, based on the value of one or more preprocessor symbols. For example, the block of C statements

```
if (VERSION == 0)
    add_record(inv_bytes, inv_file);
else
    add_node(p, &inv_list);
```

selects one of the two function calls at execution time. If VERSION is **#define**d as 0, the **if** clause is converted by the preprocessor into

```
if (0 == 0)
```

If VERSION is **#define**d as 1, the statement becomes

```
if (1 == 0)
```

Therefore, the compiler is presented with an **if** condition that is either always true or always false. However, unnecessary variables and functions may have to be compiled. In the preceding example, both *add_record* and *add_node* are compiled along with the rest of the program, even though one of them is never used. This results in the program occupying more memory space than needed. The use of conditional compilation results in extra preprocessing time, in return for slightly faster execution and conservation of memory.

Most of the problems for which C is a valuable tool can be solved with the information already presented. The next chapter will discuss some advanced features that will serve to round out your knowledge of the C language.

Programming and Debugging *Hints*

We have mentioned that *printf* statements can be used to examine the values of variables for debugging purposes. For example, consider the following version of the *is_verb* function. Several *printf* statements have been placed in the function to trace its execution. These statements are flush with the left margin so that they stand out, but they could be highlighted even more by using comments containing asterisks. Each *printf* is followed by a call to *fflush* so that, if an execution error occurs, the debugging message is printed.

```
is_verb(word, verb_file)
char word[];
FILE verb_file;

/* Returns  true  if  "word" is  a verb. That means "word" is  in the
   file  represented  by "verb_file". The file contains a word count,
   followed by that many  words of length MAX_WORD_LEN. The words are
   padded  with  blanks and separated by one white space character. A
   binary search is used to find "word" in the file. */

{
    int list_size,        /* Holds the word count */
        lo,               /* Beginning of range for binary search */
        hi,               /* End of range for binary search */
        result;           /* Holds the result of the "strcmp" */
    char middle_word[MAX_WORD_LEN + 1];    /* Holds the verb that is in
                                              the middle of the range */
    long list_start,      /* Holds the file position at which the first
                             verb is located */
    ftell();

printf("***** entering is_verb(word = %s, verb_file = %d\n",
word, verb_file); fflush(stdout);

    fseek(verb_file, OL,0);              /* Go to start of file */
    fscanf(verb_file, "%d", &list_size); /* Read # of words */

printf("***** list_size = %d\n", list_size); fflush(stdout);

    lo = 1;                              /* Initial search range starts
                                            at word 1 */
    hi = list_size;                      /* End of range to search
                                            is last word */
    list_start = ftell(verb_file);       /* File location of first word */
```

Program continued on next page

Program continued from previous page

```
    printf("***** list_start = %ld\n", list_start); fflush(stdout);

       /* Position file to middle word */

       locate((lo + hi) / 2, verb_file, list_start, MAX_WORD_LEN + 1);

    printf("***** middle position = %ld\n", ftell(verb_file)); fflush(stdout);

       fscanf(verb_file, "%s", middle_word);      /* Read in middle word */

    printf("***** middle word = %s\n", middle_word); fflush(stdout);

       /**********************************************************/
       /* Now do a binary search for the word. Search ends when  */
       /* "lo" reaches "hi" or a match is found.                 */
       /**********************************************************/

       while (lo < hi && (result = strcmp(word, middle_word)))

       {
           if (result < 0)    /* Use lower half of range */
               hi = (lo + hi) / 2 - 1;

           else               /* Use upper half of range */
               lo = (lo + hi) / 2 + 1;

    printf("***** lo = %d, hi = %d\n", lo, hi); fflush(stdout);

           /* Position file to middle word */

           locate((lo + hi) / 2, verb_file, list_start, MAX_WORD_LEN + 1);

    printf("***** middle position = %ld\n", ftell(verb_file)); fflush(stdout);

           fscanf(verb_file, "%s", middle_word);      /* Read in middle word */

    printf("***** middle word = %s\n", middle_word); fflush(stdout);

       }

       /* If "result" is 0, a match was found, so return true (non-zero).
          Otherwise, "return" is non-zero, so return false (zero). */

    printf("***** is_verb returning !result = %d\n", !result); fflush(stdout);

       return(!result);

    }
```

Once the above function is debugged and ready to be used, the *printf* statements must be removed. One way of expediting this is to place the debugging statements within conditional compilation blocks:

```
is_verb(word, verb_file)
char word[];
FILE verb_file;

/* Returns   true  if  "word"  is  a verb.  That means "word" is in the
   file  represented  by "verb_file". The file contains a word count,
   followed by that many  words of length MAX_WORD_LEN. The words are
   padded  with  blanks and separated by one white space character. A
   binary search is used to find "word" in the file. */

{
    int list_size,      /* Holds the word count */
        lo,             /* Beginning of range for binary search */
        hi,             /* End of range for binary search */
        result;         /* Holds the result of the "strcmp" */
    char middle_word[MAX_WORD_LEN + 1];      /* Holds the verb that is in
                                                the middle of the range */
    long list_start,    /* Holds the file position at which the first
                            verb is located */
    ftell();

#ifdef DEBUG
printf("***** entering is_verb(word = %s, verb_file = %d\n",
word, verb_file); fflush(stdout);
#endif

    fseek(verb_file, 0L,0);                  /* Go to start of file */
    fscanf(verb_file, "%d", &list_size);     /* Read # of words */

#ifdef DEBUG
printf("***** list_size = %d\n", list_size); fflush(stdout);
#endif

    lo = 1;                             /* Initial search range starts
                                           at word 1 */
    hi = list_size;                     /* End of range to search
                                           is last word */

    list_start = ftell(verb_file);      /* File location of first word */

#ifdef DEBUG
printf("***** list_start = %ld\n", list_start); fflush(stdout);
#endif
```

Program continued on next page

Program continued from previous page

```
      /* Position file to middle word */

      locate((lo + hi) / 2, verb_file, list_start, MAX_WORD_LEN + 1);

#ifdef DEBUG
printf("***** middle position = %ld\n", ftell(verb_file)); fflush(stdout);
#endif

      fscanf(verb_file, "%s", middle_word);      /* Read in middle word */

#ifdef DEBUG
printf("***** middle word = %s\n", middle_word); fflush(stdout);
#endif

      /************************************************************/
      /* Now do a binary search for the word. Search ends when   */
      /* "lo" reaches "hi" or a match is found.                  */
      /************************************************************/

      while (lo < hi && (result = strcmp(word, middle_word)))

      {
          if (result < 0)    /* Use lower half of range */
             hi = (lo + hi) / 2 - 1;

          else               /* Use upper half of range */
             lo = (lo + hi) / 2 + 1;

#ifdef DEBUG
printf("***** lo = %d, hi = %d\n", lo, hi); fflush(stdout);
#endif

          /* Position file to middle word */

          locate((lo + hi) / 2, verb_file, list_start, MAX_WORD_LEN + 1);

#ifdef DEBUG
printf("***** middle position = %ld\n", ftell(verb_file)); fflush(stdout);
#endif

          fscanf(verb_file, "%s", middle_word);     /* Read in middle word */

#ifdef DEBUG
printf("***** middle word = %s\n", middle_word); fflush(stdout);
#endif

      }
```

Program continued on next page

Program continued from previous page

```
/* If "result" is 0, a match was found, so return true (non-zero).
   Otherwise, "return" is non-zero, so return false (zero). */

#ifdef DEBUG
printf("***** is_verb returning !result = %d\n", !result); fflush(stdout);
#endif

   return(!result);

}
```

The debugging statements are compiled only when the first line in the program is

```
#define DEBUG
```

If that line is omitted, the debugging statements are not compiled. If the function is modified at a later time and new bugs show up, the debugging statements again can be activated merely by putting the **#define** line back into the program.

C *Tutorial*

1. What is meant by a C program being *portable*?

2. How many versions of C conform strictly to the official standard?

3. What, in general terms, is the role played by the C preprocessor?

4. What symbol always precedes preprocessor directives?

5. Where on the line must all preprocessor directives begin?

6. If preprocessing is separate from compilation, why must identifiers in both be named differently?

7. How can a **#define** directive be continued to a new line?

8. Where can a preprocessor directive be written?

9. Where can a preprocessor directive be split?

10. What is a macro, and what is it used for?

11. What symbol is used to separate the arguments of a macro?

12. What can a macro argument consist of?

13. What is meant by a nested macro?

14. What role is played by the **#undef** directive?

15. How is the **#include** directive used?

16. What are common uses of a header file?

17. What is conditional compilation?

18. State the reason for using the **#ifdef** directive.

19. How is the **#ifndef** directive used?

20. When a C program is compiled, at what point are the preprocessor directives processed?

21. What directive is used to terminate the scope of an **#ifdef** or **#ifndef** (or **#if**) directive?

22. How is the **#else** directive used?

23. What is characteristic of the **#else** and the **#endif** directives?

24. How does the **#if** directive operate?

25. What happens if a preprocessor symbol in the **#if** expression is undefined?

26. What preprocessor symbols, if any, cannot be used in the expression of an **#if** directive?

ANSWERS TO C TUTORIAL

1. The program can be compiled and run on any C compiler with identical results.

2. There is as yet no official C standard.

3. It provides for the implementation of macros and conditional compilation.

4. The # sign.

5. The first column.

6. The preprocessor must be able to distinguish between C identifiers and preprocessor symbols. If, for example, a preprocessor constant has the same name as a C variable, then the preprocessor replaces each occurrence of the variable name with the constant value, even though this was not intended.

7. The line that is to be continued is ended with a backslash.

8. Anywhere at all in a program, so long as it starts in the first column of a line and is not on the same line as another directive or C statement.

9. Wherever a blank space could safely be placed.

10. A macro is an abbreviation for a segment of code. It is useful when a sequence of code is repeated often (with few if any modifications), but is too small to warrant the creation of a function. In such a case, a macro saves the programmer typing effort.

11. The comma.

12. Any series of characters (except that the comma can be used only within quotation marks or parentheses).

13. A macro whose definition includes a reference to another macro.

14. It undefines a preprocessor symbol, meaning that it makes the preprocessor forget that the symbol was defined. It is necessary if one wishes to change the value of a preprocessor symbol.

15. The file named in the directive is inserted into the program at the point where the directive occurs.

16. To include various definitions that the programmer uses often; to include definitions needed for certain operations, such as I/O; and to facilitate communication between program files through the use of shared global variables.

17. The including or excluding of certain program lines, depending on the values of specified preprocessor symbols.

18. The **#ifdef** directive is used in order to pass certain lines of code to the compiler, only if the specified preprocessor symbol is defined before the **#ifdef** directive is encountered.

19. It passes lines of code to the compiler only if the specified preprocessor symbol is *not* defined.

20. The preprocessor runs first, before the program reaches the actual C language compiler.

21. The **#endif** directive.

22. If an **#ifdef** or **#ifndef** (or **#if**) directive returns a *false* result, the **#else** directive specifies lines to be passed to the compiler in place of those following the **#ifdef** or **#ifndef** directive. The **#else** directive and its associated lines must follow the lines associated with the **#ifdef** or **#ifndef** directive, and must precede the **#endif** directive.

23. They are the only text permitted on the lines they occupy.

24. The **#if** directive is followed by an integer constant expression. If the expression evaluates to a *true* (non-zero) value, the lines following the directive are passed on to the compiler. Otherwise (if the expression evaluates to zero, or *false*), the lines are omitted.

25. It is treated as having the value zero.

26. Symbols defined to be anything other than integer constants or expressions that evaluate to integer constants.

Keywords

(No new keywords were introduced in this chapter. Remember that the preprocessor is not part of the C language, and so its directives are not reserved keywords. Indeed, they are recognized by the preprocessor only on lines beginning with the # sign).

auto	break	case	char	default	do
double	else	float	for	if	int
long	return	short	sizeof	static	struct
switch	unsigned	while			

16

Miscellaneous Features and Advanced Topics

Outline

C *has several powerful features that have not yet been covered, for the following reasons:*

(1) these constructs violate the usual rules of structured programming;
(2) they involve machine—specific information; or
(3) they are specialized, advanced topics.

The typedef Declaration

C enables the user to define individualized type names. For example, if it is desirable to have *integer* be a synonym for **int**, you could write:

```
typedef int integer;
```

After this declaration is made, the word *integer* can be used anywhere that **int** can be used, with the same effect. A similar substitution could be performed using the **#define** preprocessor directive, except that **typedef** (*type def*inition) is part of the C language. Furthermore, user-defined types obey the same scope rules as variables, so if one is defined in a function, it is recognized only within that function.

The syntax of a **typedef** is identical to that of a variable declaration. In the preceding example, if you consider **typedef** to be a storage class, the syntax is similar to that of declaring a variable called *integer* of type **int** and storage class **typedef**.

A storage class can never be included in a type declaration. For example, it would be legal to write

```
typedef long int integer;
```

but it would *not* be legal to write

```
typedef static int integer;
```

This rule is easy to remember if you think of **typedef** syntactically as a storage class. A variable cannot be declared with more than one storage class (in this case, **typedef** and **static**). Of course, what is being declared is not a variable, but a data type.

The declaration:

```
typedef int *int_point;
```

causes *int_point* to be equivalent to the data type **int** *, or pointer to integer. Thus, the subsequent declaration

```
int_point a, *b;
```

declares *a* as a pointer to integer, and *b* as a pointer to a pointer to integer. The cast operators associated with these variables are (*int_point*) and (*int_point* *) respectively. The declaration

```
typedef char *string;
```

can be used to define *string* as a type equivalent to a pointer to **char**, thus making possible the declaration of string pointers as if they were of a special data type. Alternately, we could use the definition:

```
typedef char string[10];
```

This definition means that a variable *word* declared as:

```
string word;
```

is a character array of 10 characters. The dimension becomes part of the defined type. The declaration

```
string sentence[20];
```

creates a two-dimensional (10 by 20) character array *sentence*, which can be interpreted as a 20-element array of type *string*.

User-defined types are useful for documentation. A variable declared to be of type **char** * could be a pointer to a string, or merely to an array of **char**-sized values. A declaration using type *string* would make it clear that the variable points to a string.

Another application of user-defined types is to give a single name to a structure. Normally, a structure template defined as

```
struct node
{
    int value;
    struct node *next;
}
```

must always be referred to as **struct** *node*. If one were to follow this declaration with

```
typedef struct node NODE;
```

or simply rewrite the declaration as

```
typedef struct node
{
    int value;
    struct node *next;
}
NODE;
```

then a structure variable of this type could be declared as

```
NODE p;
```

If the structure did not contain the member *next*, which points to a structure of the same type, then even the structure tag *node* could have been omitted. (The pointer cannot be declared as NODE *next*, because the type NODE is not mentioned until after the template.) Remember that *node* and *NODE* are different identifier names in C, but using both in one program could cause confusion.

The type FILE defined in *stdio.h* is specified in a manner similar to the preceding example. It describes a structure that contains information about an open file.

A **typedef** can include a previously defined type, as in this example:

```
typedef struct node
{
    int value;
    struct node *next;
}
item;
typedef item *item_ptr;
```

The register and extern Storage Classes

The **register** storage class can be specified only for local variables. A computer contains a small number of *registers*, or individual storage units. They are similar to memory except that they are part of the computer processor itself, so operations on registers are faster than those involving memory. The **register** storage class is used in programs for which speed is of the utmost importance. Registers are more expensive than memory, however, so computers have relatively few of them. Some machines possess as few as three.

A variable declaration with the **register** storage class is a suggestion to the compiler that the variable be assigned to a register rather than to a location in memory. The reason we say "suggestion" is that the number of **register** variables in existence at any time is limited by the number of registers available. The C compiler tries to accommodate as many **register** variables as possible. A good compiler gives priority to the most frequently used variables.

Since a register is not located in memory, it is syntactically illegal to apply the address (&) operator to a **register** variable. (It is assumed that all **register** variables are stored in registers, although this may not be the case.) It is perfectly legal to apply the indirection (*) operator, however, since a register can hold a pointer. A **register** variable must be scalar; it cannot be a structure or an array, although it can be a pointer to one.

The **register** storage class also can be applied to a formal parameter in a function. Since parameters are passed to functions through memory, the supplied parameter value is loaded into a register when the function is executed.

The **extern** storage class does not create a variable, but merely informs the compiler of its existence. If a variable is declared globally, it can be referenced by any function in the same program file. If it is declared in the middle of the program, however, after a function that references it, the function must declare the variable to be **extern**:

```
main()
{
    extern int i;
    printf("i = %d\n", i);
}

int i = 4;
```

This program prints

```
i = 4
```

since the i referred to in *main* is the global variable i; no local i is declared. An **extern** declaration may never include an initialization, since the variable is not created when it is declared as **extern**.

Since an **extern** declaration is not needed when a global variable is used after it is declared, most programmers place all global declarations at the beginning of the program and dispense with the **extern** declaration. Even if an **extern** declaration is not necessary, however, it can still be useful as documentation. If a function contains declarations for all global variables used in the function, a reader can see all the variables used by the program merely by examining the declaration section at the beginning of the function.

When a global **extern** declaration is made (outside a function), it indicates that the variable referred to is declared in another file, which will be linked with the file containing the **extern** declaration. For example, the global declaration

```
extern int fred;
```

states that (1) within this program file, *fred* is a global variable; (2) the actual storage for *fred* is allocated in another program file, and (3) in that other file, *fred* is also global. In other words, global **extern** declarations facilitate communication between files of a multi-file program.

Some linkage editors resolve multiple global declarations of a variable into a single one, thus eliminating the need for the **extern** storage class. In most cases, however, it is necessary to declare all shared global variables in one of the program files that uses those variables. The rest of the program files declare these to be **extern** variables. If the global variables in question are declared in a header file, they are declared the same way in all program files that **#include** the header file. One solution is to declare the variables as **extern** in the header file, and then add an extra program file that does not include the header file and serves only to declare the global variables. This extra file then is linked with the others in the normal way.

More on the static Storage Class

We have seen that, if a local variable is declared as **static**, it remains in existence throughout program execution. Since a global variable automatically possesses this quality, it is not necessary to declare global variables as **static**. When global variables are declared to be **static**, however, this has a special significance. A **static** global variable cannot be accessed by functions in any program file other than the one in which it is declared.

Global variables declared as **static** are useful when a program file contains a group of functions that share information with one another by way of global variables, but that information is not needed by other functions. (Such a self-contained program file often is called a *module*.) If a global variable in one program file is declared to be **static**, another program file can declare a global variable with the same name as the **static** one without any conflict.

A function also can be declared as **static**. Such a function can be called by other functions within the same program file, but not by functions in other files.

Neither a global variable nor a function can be declared to be of the **auto** storage class.

The continue Statement

The **break** statement, when executed, causes the immediate termination of the loop containing it. C also provides a statement, called **continue**, which terminates only the current iteration of the loop that immediately encloses it, thus causing execution to resume with the next iteration.

For example, the following function prints out all numbers in the range 1 through 100 which are not multiples of 7:

```
non_7 ()
{
    int i;

    for (i = 1; i <= 100; i++)
    {
    if (i % 7 == 0) continue;
    printf("%d\n", i);
    }
}
```

The **continue** statement can easily be replaced by an **if** statement, but in a loop with a more complex body, sometimes it is easier to use **continue**. Many proponents of structured programming criticize the use of **continue** because it can always be replaced by an **if** statement, whereas others approve of its use for the same reason. Many programmers believe that both **break** and **continue** are acceptable in structured programs, since they permit control to be transferred only locally (within the immediate neighborhood of the loop).

Unlike the **break** statement, **continue** has no meaning in the context of a **switch** statement. If it is used inside one, it causes termination of the iteration of a loop enclosing the **switch**. If a **continue** statement is not enclosed within a loop, a syntax error is indicated by the compiler.

Labels and the goto Statement

The **goto** statement is loathed by advocates of structured programming. It allows control to be transferred from one point in a function to any other point in that function. This action is called *branching*. If misused, the **goto** can make a program virtually impossible to understand. It permits wild and spasmodic transfers of control. Within such "spaghetti code," all sorts of errors become possible. Here is an extreme example of what might be done with the **goto** statement:

```
        goto first;
fifth:  goto sixth;
second: goto third;
third:  goto fourth;
sixth:  goto last;
first:  goto second;
fourth: goto fifth;
last:   printf("All that work for one lousy printf!\n");
```

In spite of all the negative aspects of the **goto**, the fact remains that it is included in the repertoire of C. Unlike Pascal, C was designed not to enforce structured programming but to provide a versatile and convenient programming tool. Some programmers feel comfortable using the **goto** statement when the occasion demands. They believe that it is arbitrary to enforce any sort of programming style. (Even Pascal grudgingly includes a **goto** statement.)

A **goto** statement merely instructs the computer to resume execution at a specified statement. The location of this statement is specified by a *label*, which is an identifier followed by a colon. For example, if the computer encounters the statement

```
goto there;
```

then the function which contains this statement must also contain one (and only one) instance of the label

```
there:
```

A label must be placed immediately before a statement and within the bounds of a function. When the statement

```
goto there;
```

is encountered, the computer resumes execution at the statement immediately following the label *there:*. A label can occur before or after the **goto** statement that references it; in other words, the jump can be either forward or backwards.

The naming rules for labels are the same as those for variables, except that a label is not declared. Of course, a label should not have a name that is the same as a preprocessor symbol.

Here is an example in which the **goto** statement might be considered useful, because it makes it possible to exit from a complicated nest of loops:

```
for (i = 0; i < 100; i++)
{
        . . .
    for (j = 0; j < 100; j++)
    {
        . . .
    for (k = 0; k < 100; k++)
    {
            . . .
        for (l = 0; l < 100; l++)
        {
                . . .
            if (error) goto escape;
                . . .
        }
      }
     }
}

escape:    printf("Can't continue nested loop\n");
```

Function Pointers

C contains a type that corresponds to a function pointer. Since every function is compiled into a series of instructions in memory, a function can be associated with a pointer to its first instruction. This permits an indirect call to a function, by stating in effect: "Call the function pointed to by this variable."

To declare a variable called *fun_pointer*, which points to a function that returns an integer, you would write

```
int (*fun_pointer)();
```

Notice the first pair of parentheses around *fun_pointer*. If these were not present, the declaration would be

```
int *fun_pointer();
```

which would mean: *"fun_pointer* is the name of a function that returns a pointer to an integer."

To declare a variable *point_point*, which is a pointer to a function that returns a pointer to an **int**, one would write

```
int *(*point_point)();
```

In order to assign a function's address to a pointer variable, it is first necessary to declare the function, even if it returns an **int**. We shall therefore declare the function *strlen* as follows:

```
int strlen();
```

Now the address of *strlen* can be assigned to *fun_pointer*:

```
fun_pointer = strlen;
```

Notice that the address operator is not used, since only a function's address can be assigned to a variable, never the function itself. The assignment also shows why the function whose address is being assigned must be explicitly declared. No parentheses can be used after the function name *strlen*. If they were, as in

```
fun_pointer = strlen();
```

then the compiler would call *strlen*, and would assign the returned value to *fun_pointer*. When no parentheses are used, the address of the function is assigned to *fun_pointer*. The compiler must be informed, however, that *strlen* is a function rather than a variable.

To call *strlen* indirectly by way of *fun_pointer*, one would write

```
(*fun_pointer)(a);
```

where *a* is a string. Notice again the first pair of parentheses. If these were omitted, the meaning would be: "Call *strlen* and then access the address pointed to by the returned value."

The purpose of a function pointer is illustrated by the functions *printf*, *fprintf*, and *sprintf*, all of which operate in basically the same way. They differ only in what is done with the characters generated by the function. The *printf* function sends its characters to the standard output, *fprintf* sends them to a specified file, and *sprintf* stores them in a string. All three functions call a common function, say *print* (the name varies from one function library to another). This function is passed a control string, a variable list, and a pointer to a function which is used to output characters to the proper destination. When the *print* function is ready to output a character, it merely calls the passed function, which sends the character to the appropriate location (standard output, a file, or a string).

To pass a function address to another function, the programmer can pass the value of a function pointer variable, or the function name (without parentheses) can be included directly in the argument list (if the function type has been declared). In the function that is being passed the pointer, the corresponding formal parameter (call it *func*) is declared as

```
int (*func)();
```

assuming that the function returns an integer. This is the same way a regular function pointer variable is declared.

If it is necessary to cast a value into a pointer to a function returning an integer, the cast operator is

```
(int (*)())
```

Also, if you wish to define a type named *funpt*, which represents a pointer to a function returning an **int**, the **typedef** declaration would be

```
typedef int (*funpt)();
```

Consider the following illustration of the use of function pointers. An array contains several floating point values, each of which is to be processed by some function. The returned floating point values are to be stored in the corresponding element of a second array. We wish to create a general function *multi* which can perform this operation, given any function and array. The function call

```
multi(update, x, y, 7);
```

is interpreted as: "Pass each element of array x to function *update* and store the returned values in array y, where x and y both have 7 elements." The *multi* function must assume that x and y are floating point arrays, and that *update* accepts a single, floating point argument and returns a floating point result. The type of *update* must be defined in the calling function. The function *multi* might be written like this:

```
multi(func, in_array, out_array, size)
double (*func)(), in_array[], out_array[];
int size;
{
    int i;
    if (size < 1) return (-1);    /* error code */
    for (i = 0; i < size; i++)
        out_array[i] = (*func)(in_array[i]);
    return (0);                   /* OK code */
}
```

Recursion

Recursion is a technique that has been implemented in most high-level languages, particularly the more recent ones. A recursive function is one that calls itself, but which halts at some definite point to avoid infinite recursion. This concept can be explained by reference to the factorial function in mathematics. Given a positive number n, the factorial of that number can be defined as

```
1! = 1
n! = (n)((n-1)!)
```

which in turn means

```
n! = (n)(n-1)(n-2) ... (1)
```

Suppose we wish to find the factorial of 7. Note that the second line in the first formula makes reference to itself, which is what we mean by recursion. Therefore,

```
7! = (7)(6!)
```

But 6! is equal to (6) (5!), so 7! is equal to

```
(7) (6) (5!)
```

If this process is continued, we end up with

```
7! = (7) (6) (5) (4) (3) (2) (1!)
```

Since 1! is equal to 1, 7! is equal to (7) (6) (5) (4) (3) (2) (1), which equals 5040.

In C, a recursive function that calculates a factorial can be written as follows:

```
factorial(n)
int n;
{
    if (n == 1)
        return(1);
    else
        return(n * factorial(n - 1));
}
```

Local variables in C are **auto** by default. Therefore, when a function calls itself, a new set of local variables is created (except for those variables declared as **static**). The variable names are the same as those in the calling function, but the memory locations associated with them are different.

Suppose the preceding function is called with the parameter 7. The series of recursive calls may be thought of as a hierarchy of nodes, as shown in Figure 16-1.

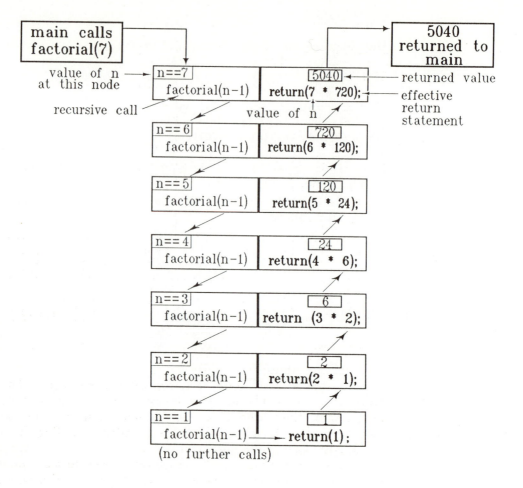

Figure 16—1

The **if** statement in this function ensures that, when the function is called with 1 as the argument, it returns the value 1 immediately instead of calling itself recursively again.

The value of the expression

```
(n) (n-1) (n-2) ... (2) (1)
```

can be calculated in C with a **for** loop, but some problems are easier to program by using recursion than linear or non-recursive methods. One such example is the so-called Towers of Hanoi problem. Assume that there are three pegs, A, B, and C. On peg A there are 64 disks, each one smaller than the one below it, as shown in Figure 16-2.

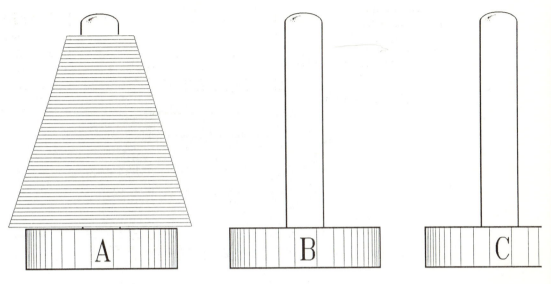

Towers of Hanoi — initial setup

Figure 16—2

The object is to move all the disks from peg A to peg C so that they are in the same order as before, with each disk atop a larger one. Only one disk can be moved at a time, and a disk can never be placed on top of a smaller one. Peg B is provided as intermediate storage.

Figure 16-3 illustrates a step of the solution, in which we move two disks from peg A to peg C. First, the smaller of the two disks is moved from peg A to peg B. The second-smallest disk (which is now atop the stack on peg A) then is moved to peg C. Finally, the disk on peg B is moved to C, as shown in Figure 16-3.

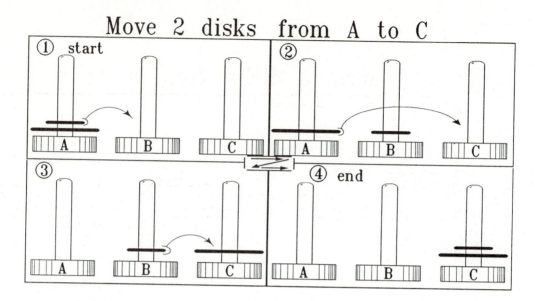

Figure 16—3

Throughout this process, we have followed the rule about never placing a disk on a smaller one. The process can be extended to moving three disks. Returning to the original configuration, first the smallest disk is moved from A to C, the second-smallest one is moved from A to B, and the smallest is moved from C to B. The result is that the top two disks are transferred to B. Then the largest disk is moved from A to C and the two smaller disks are moved on top of it, just as they were moved originally to peg B.

Move 3 disks from A to C

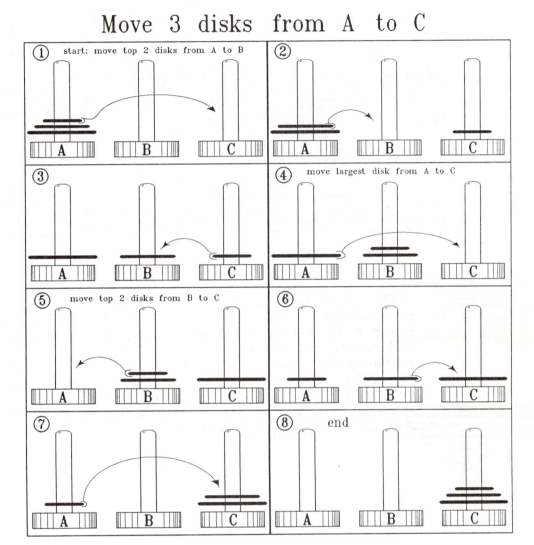

Figure 16—4

The problem of moving all 64 disks from peg A to peg C can be solved recursively as follows:

(1) Move the top 63 disks from peg A to peg B, using C as storage.
(2) Move the 64th (largest) disk from peg A to peg C.
(3) Move the 63 disks from peg B to peg C, using A as storage.

This solution obeys the rule that no disk may be placed on a larger one, because the largest disk is placed on peg C before any of those that were on top of it. Step (2) is straightforward, but steps (1) and (3) are merely smaller versions of the original problem, the only difference being that only 63 rather than 64 disks are being moved. In general, the problem of moving n disks from peg A to peg C can be specified recursively as follows:

(1) Move the top $(n-1)$ disks from peg A to peg B, using C as storage.
(2) Move the nth (largest) disk to peg C.
(3) Move the $(n-1)$ disks from peg B to peg C, using A as storage.

If there already are disks on any of the pegs when these steps are performed for any value of n, these disks will always be larger than the n disks in question. Therefore, any of the n disks may be placed on any of the three pegs, just as if those pegs were empty.

This recursive process ends when n reaches 1. At that point, only step (2), which has no recursion, is performed. The Towers of Hanoi problem differs from the factorial problem in that a function to solve the Hanoi problem would call itself twice each time, once for step (1) and once for step (3). The reader may wish to write such a function. Figure 16-5 illustrates the solution for four disks. Due to the two recursive calls, the picture takes the form of a binary tree, in which each node (representing a call to the function) branches out into two other calls.

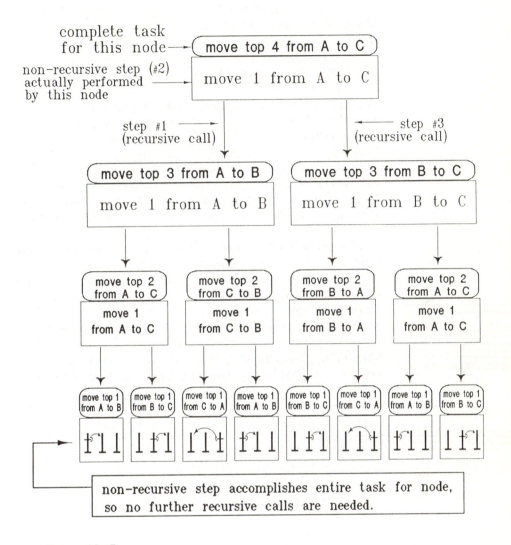

Figure 16—5

The Bitwise Operators

C differs from most other medium- to high-level languages in that it permits direct manipulation of the bits stored in memory which represent all data items. Thus C is the preferred language of systems programmers, who frequently need to manipulate these fundamental elements of data. C provides a full range of operators for this purpose.

All values stored in a computer's memory are represented as binary numbers. In the binary representation of integers, the rightmost bit represents the 1's place, the next represents 2's, the next 4's, and so forth. From right to left, each bit represents a successively higher power of 2. For example, the binary number 1001 represents, in decimal,

$$(1) \ (8) + (0) \ (4) + (0) \ (2) + (1) \ (1)$$

which equals 9. In bit parlance, a *set* bit is one that has the value 1, whereas a *clear* bit has the value 0.

In some previous programs, we have used variables as flags, which store the value *true* or *false* as represented by a non-zero value or zero. A truth value also can be represented by a single bit, rather than by the eight (or more) bits that make up a C variable. If the bit is 0, it indicates a value of *false*, and if it is 1, it represents *true*. Even if a **char** variable is used as a boolean flag, all but one of the bits making up that variable are wasted. Programs that use many flags usually pack these flags economically at the rate of eight per byte. Structures make use of this facility to minimize their size. For example, in the FILE structure used to represent an open file, one member contains flag bits that represent various features or states of the file. A bit set to 1 means that the feature or state applies to the file.

If eight flags are packed into a byte, it is necessary to be able to manipulate one bit without affecting the others. To do this, it is necessary to use the bitwise logical operators. Two of these operators are represented by the symbols & and |, which represent the AND and OR operations respectively. These are the same symbols used by the logical operators in conditional expressions, but their roles should not be confused. The bitwise AND and OR operators are represented by single characters. Also, the logical operators test the truth values of two variables and produce a value of *true* or *false*, whereas the bitwise operators perform their operations on each individual bit of their operands.

The bitwise operators can be used on any integer-compatible scalar variable, but for ease of explanation we shall confine ourselves to eight-bit **char** variables. Suppose the variables a and b have the values 7 and 12 respectively. The binary representations of these variables are

```
0 0 0 0 0 1 1 1      <-- a
0 0 0 0 1 1 0 0      <-- b
```

If we then execute the statement

```
c = a & b;
```

The bit patterns are

```
0 0 0 0 0 1 1 1      <-- a
0 0 0 0 1 1 0 0      <-- b
-----------------
0 0 0 0 0 1 0 0      <-- c  (a & b)
```

Each bit in c is set to the result of ANDing the corresponding bits of a and b. An AND operation returns a *true* result only if both of its operands are *true*, so a bit in c has the value 1 only if the corresponding bits of both a and b are 1.

In the diagram, all the bits in a single column are corresponding bits. Only one column, the third from the right, contains bits with the value 1 for both *a* and *b*. Therefore, only one bit of *c*, the third from the right, has the value 1. If *c* is interpreted as an integer, it has the decimal value 4, but on that level there is no apparent connection between the values of *a* and *b* and the result assigned to *c*. The bitwise AND operation has meaning only on the bit level.

The rules for the bitwise OR operation state that the result is 1 if *either* operand is 1 (or if both are 1). Therefore, if we execute the statement

```
c = a | b;
```

The result is

```
0 0 0 0 0 1 1 1        <-- a
0 0 0 0 1 1 0 0        <-- b
---------------
0 0 0 0 1 1 1 1        <-- c  (a | b)
```

A bit in *c* is set to 1 if either of the corresponding bits of *a* and *b* is set. That is, any column that has a 1 bit for *a* or *b* also has a 1 bit for *c*. The integer representation for *c* in this case is 15.

Now we can approach the question of how to set a single bit in a variable. To do this, we shall start with the desired result:

```
0 0 1 0 0 1 0 1        <-- a
0 0 0 0 1 0 0 0        <-- b
---------------
0 0 1 0 1 1 0 1        <-- c
```

The preceding diagram shows the result of the operation

```
c = a | b;
```

Our goal was to assign to *c* the bit pattern contained in *a*, but with the fourth bit from the right set. We did this by using *b*, whose bits are all clear except for the fourth from the right, which is set. When this variable is ORed with the value of *a*, the clear bits in *b* have no effect on the result; any value ORed with zero yields the original value. The set bit in *b* ensures that the corresponding bit in *c* is always set. If the bit in *a* corresponding to the set bit in *b* is already set, then no change takes place:

```
0 0 1 0 1 1 0 1        <-- a
0 0 0 0 1 0 0 0        <-- b
---------------
0 0 1 0 1 1 0 1        <-- c  (a | b)
```

In this case, *c* == *a*.

Variables such as *b* in these examples often are called *masks*, because they selectively mask or filter the bits of another variable, allowing some of the bits to remain unaffected while changing others. Usually the mask is specified as a constant value, since the programmer usually knows which bits are to be set. Often the bit pattern in a variable is changed within that variable, so that the result is stored in the variable being operated upon. Consider the following statement:

```
a |= 0x08;
```

where the number to the right of the |= operator is represented in hexadecimal notation. This statement is equivalent to

```
a = a | 0x08;
```

since |= is an updating assignment operator. (Notice that logical operators are commutative, meaning that *a* | 0x08 is the same as 0x08 | *a*.) The mask 0x08 is the same value contained in *b* in the previous diagram, only represented as a hexadecimal constant. The statement sets the fourth bit from the right in *a*, thus changing the value of *a*. If *a* is thought of as containing eight flags, then this operation sets the fourth flag from the right to the value *true* (regardless of its original value).

Hexadecimal or octal notation is used for masks more frequently than decimal. The reason is that the first two radices more directly reflect bit patterns than does decimal notation. For example, if we start with the bit pattern

```
1 0 0 1 1 0 1 0
```

and then divide it into two groups each containing four bits, the result is readily converted to hexadecimal as follows:

```
1 0 0 1        1 0 1 0
    9              A
```

This bit pattern is represented in hex as 0x9A. To represent the pattern in octal, the bits are split into groups of three instead. The octal equivalent is assigned to each of these groups:

```
1 0        0 1 1        0 1 0
  2          3            2
```

The grouping is done starting from the right, so the leftmost group only contains two bits. The result is the octal representation 0232. By the reverse process, the octal and hexadecimal representations can be converted into binary much more easily than could the decimal representation, which happens to be 154 (or -66 if it is interpreted as a signed value).

Another disadvantage of decimal notation for bit patterns is that the sign must be specified. If a bit pattern is assigned to a **char** variable, for example, any pattern in which the leftmost bit is set represents a negative number, unless the variable is declared to be an **unsigned char**. If decimal notation is used, the signed representation must be employed. When the constant is specified in octal or hex notation, however, a sign is never needed and this complication is avoided.

The method used to set a single bit can easily be extended to setting several bits at once. The statement

```
a |= 0x09;
```

sets both the fourth bit from the right and the rightmost bit in *a*, leaving the remaining bits intact.

To *clear* a single bit, we use the bitwise & operator. When any bit is ANDed with a zero bit, the result is zero (since the AND operation yields *true* only when both operands are *true*). When a bit is ANDed with 1, the result is the original value of the first bit.

As an example, let us again make use of the variable *a*, which contains the following bit pattern:

```
0 0 1 0 1 1 0 1
```

Suppose we wish to clear the third bit from the left. We use the operation

```
a &= 0xDF;
```

which is reflected in the following AND operation:

```
0 0 1 0 1 1 0 1      <-- a
1 1 0 1 1 1 1 1      <-- 0xDF  (mask)
---------------
0 0 0 0 1 1 0 1      <-- new value of a
```

The new value of *a* is the same as the old value, except that one bit has been cleared. That bit corresponds to the only clear bit in the mask. The result is independent of the original value of the bit being cleared. If the third bit from the left in *a* was already clear, no change would take place, and the new value of *a* would be the same as the old one.

If you wish to clear more than one bit, the mask must contain clear bits in all positions corresponding to the ones to be cleared.

The bitwise operators need not be confined to variables. For example, the expression

```
(0x07 & 0x04)
```

returns a value that is the bitwise AND of the constants 0x07 and 0x04. The returned constant can be used anywhere an integer value is permitted, even as a subscript.

The mask used to clear bits with the bitwise & operator may be somewhat confusing, because it requires a bit for each position that is *not* to be changed. It is relatively easy to see that the mask 0x20 sets the third bit from the left, in a **char** variable using the | operation. It is less obvious, however, that 0xDF contains a clear bit in the third position from the left. To help clarify and expedite matters, we can make use of the bitwise NOT operator.

The bitwise NOT operator (sometimes called the ones complement operator) is analogous to the logical NOT (!) operator. The bitwise ˜, represented by a tilde (˜), also is a unary operator. When it is applied to a value, it flips or complements each bit. In other words, each set bit is cleared and each clear bit is set. For example, if *a* has the value

```
0 0 1 0 1 1 0 1
```

then the value of ˜a is

```
1 1 0 1 0 0 1 0
```

The bit pattern within *a* can be complemented with the statement

```
a = ˜a;
```

The bitwise ˜, like the unary negation operator, cannot be used within an updating assignment operator. There is no such operator as ˜=. Updating assignment operators are available only for binary operators.

To make use of the bitwise ˜ operator in conjunction with clearing a bit, the programmer first develops a mask with a *set* bit in each position to be cleared. For example, to clear the first and fourth bits from the left, we use the mask value

```
0x90
```

which in binary notation is

```
1 0 0 1 0 0 0 0
```

When the bitwise ˜ operator is applied to this mask, as in

```
˜0x90
```

The resulting bit pattern is

```
0 1 1 0 1 1 1 1
```

in which each bit position to be cleared contains a 0, and every other position contains a 1. This is the proper mask to use to clear the first and fourth bits, as in the following statement:

```
a &= ˜0x90;
```

The ˜ operator can operate only on entire constants or variables, not on individual bits. To complement an individual bit in a variable, we use the bitwise EXCLUSIVE OR operator.

The EXCLUSIVE OR operation yields a *true* value if either of its operands is *true, but not both*. It is called *exclusive* because it excludes the case in which both operands are *true*. By this definition, the | operator introduced earlier sometimes is called the *inclusive* OR.

The bitwise EXCLUSIVE OR operator in C is the caret (ˆ). (On a few computers, this symbol is represented as an upward-pointing arrow, but according to the ASCII standard it is the caret.) The truth table for the ˆ operation is as follows:

```
A          B          A ^ B
---        ---        -----
0          0          0
0          1          1
1          0          1
1          1          0
```

Notice that the result of the ˆ operation is a 1 bit if and only if the two operand bits are different. When B is clear, C has the same bit value as A. When B is set, however, C is the opposite of A. To complement individual bits of a bit pattern, the exclusive OR operation is used, with the mask containing a set bit in each bit position to be flipped.

As an example, let us say *a* has the value

```
1 0 1 1 0 0 1 1
```

and we wish to flip the first and fifth bits from the left. The required mask is

```
1 0 0 0 1 0 0 0
```

which is represented in hexadecimal as 0x88. The statement used is

```
a ^= 0x88;
```

and the resulting operation is

```
1 0 1 1 0 0 1 1     <-- a
1 0 0 0 1 0 0 0     <-- 0x88 (mask)
---------------
0 0 1 1 1 0 1 1     <-- new value of a
```

There are two more operations that facilitate manipulation of bit patterns. These are the left and right shift operators, represented by the symbols << and >> respectively. Do not confuse these shift operators with the unrelated < and > operators.

Sometimes it is necessary to move bit patterns either to the right or to the left. Usually this is done for computational purposes or to extract a single bit. Each shift operator has two operands. The left operand is the value to be shifted (always an integer-compatible type), and the right operand is the number of bit positions by which the value is to be shifted. As an example, suppose *a* has the value

0 0 1 1 0 1 0 0

and we execute the statement

```
b = a >> 3;
```

The value of *a* is shifted to the right by three bits, and the result is stored in *b* (*a* remains unaffected). The value of *b* is now

0 0 0 0 0 1 1 0

To demonstrate more clearly what is happening, let us start with the original, unshifted value of *a*:

0 0 1 1 0 1 0 0

The first shift to the right produces the following:

0 0 0 1 1 0 1 0

Each bit is shifted to the right by one bit position. After the leftmost bit is shifted right, its former position is filled with a zero. The rightmost bit is shifted out completely and vanishes. The second shift produces the value

0 0 0 0 1 1 0 1

The third and final shift produces the value

0 0 0 0 0 1 1 0

Different versions of C handle right shifts differently. Some compilers implement a *logical shift*, in which zeroes are shifted into the leftmost position as shown in the example. On other compilers, the shift is *arithmetic*, meaning that if the variable or constant being shifted is a signed integer, the bit shifted in from the left is the same as the bit value formerly occupying the leftmost position. For example, the pattern

0 1 1 0 0 0 1 1

shifted one bit to the right in an arithmetic shift, yields the following:

0 0 1 1 0 0 0 1

whereas the pattern

```
1 1 0 0 1 0 1 0
```

shifted one bit to the right produces

```
1 1 1 0 0 1 0 1
```

Shifting a bit pattern to the left causes the leftmost bit to be shifted out the left side, and always shifts a zero bit in from the right. Therefore, if the preceding C statement were replaced with

```
b = a << 3;
```

where *a* still has the value

```
0 0 1 1 0 1 0 0
```

but the shift this time is three positions to the *left*, then the value of *b* is

```
1 0 1 0 0 0 0 0
```

Both operands of the shift operators can be either constants or variables. The right-hand operand is always the shift count, however, so the shift operators are not commutative. The shift count must be an integer, and the results of the shift are undefined if the shift count is equal to or greater than the number of bits in the value being shifted.

Suppose we wish to extract the third bit from the right from variable *a*, and store it, as a 1 or 0 value, in another variable called *bit*. In effect, we are unpacking a flag and storing it in its own individual variable. The statement

```
c = a & 0x4;
```

would extract the correct bit, but since it is the third bit from the right, its value is either 0 or 4, rather than 0 or 1. One solution would be to use an **if** test but a more elegant (and sometimes faster) method is to shift the value of *c* two positions to the right, making the extracted bit the rightmost bit of *c*. This can be accomplished by rewriting the preceding statement as

```
c = (a & 0x4) >> 2;
```

In this statement, the shift count is related to the bit position being extracted.

To unpack all eight bits of a **char** variable into, say, an array of eight elements, we could perform a series of operations eight times: extract the rightmost bit by ANDing the variable with 1, then shift the number right one bit. This could be done in a loop whose index also indexed the destination array. Of course, the bits are extracted right-to-left, so the loop would have to count down.

Shift operators often are used for multiplication and division by powers of two. For example, to divide an integer by two, we shift the variable right by one bit. To divide by four, shift it right by two bit positions, and so on. If the compiler implements the right shift as a logical shift, however, correct results are produced only if the value being shifted is unsigned or positive. To multiply integers by powers of two, the left shift can be used. This operation produces correct results only if the shift never causes a bit with a value of 1 to be shifted out the left side and lost.

Unions

Sometimes it is helpful to be able to treat a single area of memory as if it contains, at different times, values of different types. An example is Program 14-11, in which a single area of memory was referred to as both a structure variable and an array of characters. C provides a facility for accomplishing this: the **union** construct.

The syntax for unions is identical to that for structures, except that the keyword **struct** is replaced with the keyword **union**. Here is a sample **union** declaration:

```
union sample
{
    int integer;
    float real;
}
example;
```

This declares a variable *example* of type **union** *sample*. The members of *example* are referred to as *example.integer* and *example.real*. The members also can be referred to by pointer. Rather than containing enough room for two members, however, *example* contains memory for *one* value, either an **int** or a **float**, as specified in the body of the union. Assuming that both **ints** and **floats** are four bytes long in the computer being used, the variable *example* contains four bytes. It can be referred to as either a **float** variable, *example.real*, or an **int** variable, *example.integer*.

If a value is assigned to *example.integer*, then the value is placed, in integer format, in the memory locations belonging to *example*. The resulting bit pattern can be accessed as *example.real* and interpreted as a floating point number, but the results probably will be meaningless since no conversion is performed. Since they share the same memory location, changing *example.real* also changes *example.integer* and vice versa.

A union can contain as many members as desired, of any type, but it allocates only enough memory to hold the largest member. For example, if a union template named *two* is defined as

```
union two
{
    int big;
    char small;
};
```

then a variable declared to be of type **union** *two* contains enough room for a regular **int**, since an **int** is larger than a **char**. When member *small* is referred to, however, only a single byte is accessed.

Returning to the example of Program 14-11, the structure *inv_item* could share a union with array *inv_bytes*:

```
union
{
    struct inventory inv_item;
    char inv_bytes[sizeof(struct inventory)];
}
both;
```

Now both *inv_item* and *inv_bytes* are members of the union named *both*. Notice that *inv_bytes* is not defined as a pointer to **char**, but as an actual, explicitly dimensioned array. This is the only way to make the array *inv_bytes* actually occupy the same memory as the structure *inv_item*. The program must be modified to refer to *inv_item* as *both.inv_item* and *inv_bytes* as *both.inv_bytes*. To refer to a member of *inv_item*, such as *count*, one would write *both.inv_item.count*. To refer to an element of *inv_bytes*, say element 5, one would write *both.inv_bytes[5]*.

The union member *inv_item* cannot be subscripted (since it is not an array), and the member *inv_bytes* cannot be referred to as a structure. The two data items still are separate in terms of syntax; the only association between them is that they share the same portion of memory.

Unions are treated syntactically the same as structures. Their members can be referred to in the same manner, and the address, period, and arrow operators can be applied to both in the same way. The nesting rules (unions in structures, unions in unions, etc.) are the same. The only difference is that union members occupy the same memory and behave accordingly.

Bit Fields

Structures can contain special members called *fields* or *bit fields*. These are members whose type is **int** (or **unsigned int**), but whose length is specified in bits rather than bytes. For example, a member declared as

```
unsigned three_bits : 3;
```

is treated as a variable made up of only three bits. The number of bits in a field is specified by following the name of the field with a colon and a non-negative integer, which is the bit count. The size of a field cannot exceed the number of bits in an **int** variable on the machine for which the program is written.

Some C compilers implement all fields as unsigned integers, so they can be declared as **int**, **unsigned int**, or **unsigned**, all three being treated as equivalent. Other compilers allow signed bit fields, in which case an **int** declaration indicates a signed field. No C compiler permits fields to be declared with non-integral types, such as **float**, and no compiler permits arrays of fields.

Bit fields can be accessed and operated upon in the same way as integers, except that they cannot contain values larger than can be represented by the specified number of bits, and the address and **sizeof** operators cannot be applied to them.

The advantage of bit fields is that they force the computer to perform bit packing and unpacking automatically. For example, eight flags can be defined as eight one-bit fields in a structure, as follows:

```
struct
{
    unsigned first_flag   : 1,
             second_flag  : 1,
             third_flag   : 1,
             fourth_flag  : 1,
             fifth_flag   : 1,
             sixth_flag   : 1,
             seventh_flag : 1,
             eighth_flag  : 1;
}
pack;
```

On most computers, the eight fields are stored as individual bits of a byte. If an individual field value is assigned to a variable, however, as in

```
c = pack.third_flag;
```

then the accessed value will always be either 0 or 1. This operation avoids the need for shifting. Be aware that in a series of bit fields such as this, the first bit can be either the leftmost or rightmost bit of the byte in which the fields are packed. Fields cannot be members of unions, but they can be members of structures which are themselves members of unions.

As mentioned in Chapter 13, the size of a structure often is greater than the total size of its members. With bit fields, the difference may take the form of unused bits. Suppose that a structure contains, among other members, a bit field of size 5. If that bit field is followed by, say, an integer member, the integer must start at the beginning of a new byte. That means that the three bits left over in the byte occupied by the bit field of size 5 must go unused. Furthermore, fields cannot cross **int** boundaries, so if a field of 10 bits is followed by a field of 8 bits (on a machine where an **int** has 16 bits), the second field begins on the next **int** boundary, leaving 6 unused bits after the first field.

The programmer has some control over alignment within a structure declaration. When only the size of a bit field is specified, with no name, such as

```
:3;
```

then a field of the specified number of bits is reserved in the structure, but it cannot be accessed because it has no name. If the size specified is zero, then the following member in the structure is aligned on the next **int** boundary.

The *argc* and *argv* Parameters

The C language was developed under the UNIX operating system, in which every command is a program and every program is a command. Under UNIX, when the name of a file containing a compiled program is typed into the computer, the program in that file is executed. The program name, like a command, can be followed on the same line with various arguments that specify how the program is to operate. Virtually all computers with C compilers allow C programs to be executed in this manner, and provide a facility whereby the program can access command-line parameters.

In order to be able to access command-line arguments, the *main* function of the program must be defined as having two arguments, as shown here:

```
main(argc, argv)
int argc;
char **argv;
{
    /* Body of function goes here */
}
```

Like all parameters, the two parameters of *main* can be given any valid names; the names *argc* and *argv* used here are conventional. They must, however, be declared to have the types shown. The parameter *argv* can be declared equivalently as:

```
char *argv[];
```

since it is an array of pointers to characters, or simply an array of strings. These two arguments are generated by the computer whether or not the *main* function declares them. If the *main* function does not declare *argc* and *argv*, however, it does not have access to them.

The argument *argc* specifies the number of strings in *argv*, and *argv* contains the command-line arguments. For example, suppose the program *multiply* were executed with the command

```
multiply 2 3
```

The command line shown above is broken up automatically into words. A word is defined as a string of non-white space characters delimited by white space, just as if the %s conversion specification were being used. Usually, however, white space characters can be included in the arguments if quotes or backslashes are used; the exact rules vary, depending on the compiler or operating system. The command line shown previously contains three arguments:

```
multiply
2
3
```

The command word used to execute the program (in this case *multiply*) is included as one of the arguments. When *main* is executed, the value passed for *argc* is 3, and *argv* contains 3 strings:

```
argv[0] == "multiply"
argv[1] == "2"
argv[2] == "3"
```

If the purpose of the *multiply* program is to multiply its two arguments and print the result, it can accomplish this task by converting *argv[1]* and *argv[2]* into integers, multiplying their values, and printing out the result. The value of *argc* can be tested first to determine that the correct number of arguments has been provided. The program should also make sure that the arguments are strings representing integers.

The fact that the program name is the first argument is useful. For example, UNIX has an editing program that can operate in three different modes. The same program is compiled and stored in three separate files, with names that represent the available modes. When one of the three copies of the program is executed, it checks its first command-line argument to see with what name it was executed. Based upon this name, it enters one of the three modes.

You have now been exposed to all of the major facets of the C language. The material presented up to this point includes all of the important features of the language, regardless of the compiler you will be using. We hope you have benefited from the exposure to C, and we wish you every success with any work you may do in the future with this most interesting and flexible of languages. C you!

The Spirit of C

In this section we will demonstrate a practical use of the bitwise operators. The algorithm described here can be used in almost any language, but only in a language like C can it be made efficient on computers that can execute fast bitwise operations.

It is possible to raise a value *x* to a power *a* by multiplying *x* together *a* times. That is, a function to raise *x* to the *a*th power requires about *a* multiplications. It is possible, however, to write a function that performs the same operation faster with fewer multiplications, by adding a few bit operations.

Suppose we wish to raise the number 3 to the power of 6. This operation can be represented as

(3) (3) (3) (3) (3) (3)

or as

(34) (32)

or

((32)2) (32)

The implication is that raising a number to any power can be interpreted as the product of a series of squarings of the number. As an example, here is the number 6 in binary. (We show only the significant bits of the number, with no leading zeroes.)

1   1   0

The following table shows the binary value of each bit:

```
bit:   1  1  0
value: 4  2  1
```

For each bit that is a 1, we raise the number 3 to that power. We get 3^4 and 3^2. Multiplying these together gives us

(34) (32) = 36

It is necessary only to calculate 3^4 and 3^2. But since 3^4 is $(3^2)^2$, only two multiplications are needed: one to calculate $3^2 = (3)(3)$, and one to calculate $3^4 = (3^2)(3^2)$.

This algorithm can be extended to raise any value to a positive, integer power. Notice that the number of multiplications is no greater than the number of bits representing the exponent. The maximum is the number of bits in an **int** (usually 16 or 32). Therefore, to raise a number to an exponent ranging in the billions, only 32 multiplications would be necessary. Note, however, that even a small number raised to the billionth power would require an enormous amount of memory to store it—certainly more than can fit in a **long int**.

To make this method more general, we take the original value of a (the exponent) and examine its rightmost bit. If it is a 1, we multiply x into an accumulator that was initialized to 1. Whatever the value of the bit, we then shift a to the right by 1 place, thereby losing the first bit and moving the second bit into the rightmost position. We also square x. The process is then repeated until a runs out of bits. At that point, the accumulator holds the result. The best way to understand this algorithm (called *shift–and–multiply*) is to try it yourself.

To write a function using this method, we will need the following variables:

1) A variable *accumulator* to hold the accumulated result.
2) One to hold the power of x being used at any point. This can be the formal parameter for x, assuming that x is passed by value and changing its value will not affect any other variable.
3) One to hold the value of a, which is shifted at each step. This can be the formal parameter for a, which also is passed by value.

Without actually performing the exponentiation, it is not an easy task to check whether any given values of x and a will cause a **long int** to overflow, that is, to run out of room. Therefore, we will assume the user of the function will make sure the arguments are within reasonable bounds. Note that a real number smaller than 1 sometimes can be raised to a power greater than 31. The function we show, however, deals only with integers.

The loop used in the function is simple. The first step is to check the rightmost bit of a. As you may recall, this bit can be extracted and tested using the & operator and a mask. The test

```
if (a & 1)
```

will succeed if the rightmost bit of a is 1 (non-zero). This test could be done using the % operator instead, but that would be slower, because it requires the performance of a division operation. If the test succeeds, we multiply x into *accumulator*:

```
accumulator *= x;
```

Finally, whether or not the test succeeded, we shift a right by 1 bit and square x:

```
a >>= 1;
x *= x;
```

The loop iterates as long as there are bits set in a; that is, so long as a is non-zero:

```
while (a)
{
    if (a & 1)
        accumulator *= x;
    a>>=1;
    x *= x;
}
```

All that needs to be added is a test to ensure that the exponent a is non-negative. (An exponent of 0 will cause a result of 1 to be returned, which is correct). We can also ensure that a is not greater than 31, since an exponent larger than 31 will cause overflow for any value of x other than 1:

```
if (a < 0 || a > 31) return (0);
```

Here is the completed function:

```
long x_to_a(x, a)
int x, a;

/* Raise "x" to the power of "a". Both are integers, with "a" being
   non-negative. The shift-and-multiply technique is used. */

{
    long accumulator = 1;       /* Used to accumulate the value of "x"
                                   to the power of "a". */
    int i;                      /* Loop index */

    /* Make sure "a" is non-negative and has only 5 significant bits */

    if (a < 0            /* Error if "a" is negative */
        || a > 31)       /* Error if "a" is greater than 31 */
      return (0);        /* Error code; ambiguous only if "x" is 0 */

    else
    {

  /* Loop until "a" is zero */

while (a)
{

    /* If rightmost bit of "a" is 1, multiply "x" into accumulator */

    if (a & 1)
        accumulator *= x;

    /* Shift next bit of "a" into rightmost position */

    a>>=1;
                /* Square "x" */

    x *= x;

    /* Now repeat loop on next bit of "a" */

  }

  return(accumulator);
    }
}
```

Notice that the function returns a **long** value, since exponentiation tends to generate large numbers. Also notice that the error return code will be ambiguous if x is zero, because zero raised to a non-zero power yields zero. Therefore, the function should not be called with a value of zero for x.

Programming and Debugging *Hints*

The C language uses a small set of symbols to perform many different roles. For this reason, several C operators can be mistaken for other operators without causing a syntax error. These include the logical and bitwise AND (&&, &) and OR (||, |) operators, which are syntactically interchangeable but operate differently. We have already made mention of the notorious confusion between the = and == operators. All that can be said about these operators is, be careful.

Some Final Words on Debugging

Every programmer should be aware of the following fact: No matter how much debugging and testing is done, and no matter how thoroughly it is carried out, the best that one can say at any time is that all known bugs have been eliminated. It is never 100 per cent certain, except in the most trivial programs, that the program is completely error-free. In other words, one can always prove the presence of errors, but never their absence. That is why, as we mentioned earlier, programmers say that "there is no such thing as a debugged program." Yet a diligent programmer, by dint of concentrated effort, can produce a program almost totally devoid of errors. That is the ideal to which we must all aspire.

C Tutorial

1. Suppose you wanted to define *bingo* to be equivalent to type **float**. How would you accomplish this using the **typedef** declaration?

2. What is wrong with the following declaration?

   typedef static float floating_point[5];

3. What advantage is there in writing the following?

   typedef char *string;

4. What restrictions are placed in C on **register** class variables?

5. What advantage do operations on registers have over those performed on memory?

6. Why are there relatively few registers in a computer?

7. What does the **extern** storage class accomplish?

8. Why are **extern** declarations seldom used within functions?

9. Why are global variables sometimes declared as **static**?

10. What is the difference between the **break** and **continue** statements?

11. Why is the use of the **break** and **continue** statements so controversial?

12. Do proponents of structured programming favor the goto statement?

13. What is meant by "spaghetti code?"

14. In any given program, how many labels with the same name can be used?

15. In what situation is the **goto** considered most acceptable?

16. What is a function pointer?

17. What is meant by *recursion*?

18. How is a C function declared to be recursive?

19. Why is it sometimes useful to manipulate bits rather than bytes?

20. If x contains the bit pattern 1001 and y contains the pattern 1110, what are the results of the following bit operations?

    a) x & y
    b) x | y

21. What logical operation is associated with the ˜ operator, and what is the name of the symbol used?

22. Distinguish between the inclusive and exclusive OR operations.

23. What symbols are used in C for the following?

    a) left shift
    b) right shift

24. Distinguish between a logical and an arithmetic right shift.

25. How are the shift operators used in computation?

26. What is the **union** construct?

27. What are bit fields?

28. What is the meaning of the following definition?

    int four_bits : 4;

29. What is meant by *alignment*?

30. How are command-line arguments accessed?

31. What is always the first string in *argv*?

ANSWERS TO C TUTORIAL

1. typedef float bingo;

2. A storage class such as **static** cannot be used in a **typedef** declaration, since **typedef** itself is considered to be a storage class.

3. It aids in program documentation, because it is clear to the reader that a variable declared as type *string* is in fact a string pointer (as opposed to, say, just a pointer to a character).

4. (1) The address operator cannot be applied to such variables.
   (2) The **register** class can be applied only to local variables (or formal parameters).
   (3) Only scalar variables may be declared of the **register** class.

5. Operations on registers are faster.

6. Registers are more expensive to produce than memory.

7. When used in declarations outside any function, **extern** indicates that the variable in question is declared (has memory allocated to it) in another program file. When **extern** is used within a function, it specifies that the named variable is a global variable.

8. The **extern** class rarely is specified within functions because it can be omitted when the global variable being referred to is defined earlier in the program (which is usually the case).

9. When this is done, the global variable cannot be accessed outside the program file in which it is declared. This allows the variable to be used for communication between functions in the same file, while preventing it from being global to the entire program.

10. Whereas **break** terminates a loop entirely, **continue** merely terminates the current iteration of the loop, allowing execution to continue with the next iteration (if any). Also, **continue** cannot be used to terminate a **switch** statement.

11. The **break** and **continue** statements often are criticized because they allow execution to jump from one part of a program to another, and because they can be replaced by more acceptable statements such as **if**s. Their advantages are that they allow jumps to specifically defined points within the program, and sometimes simplify the logic of a program if properly used.

12. No.

13. Spaghetti code usually means program code that involves many **goto**s jumping all over the place, making it extremely difficult to follow the logic of the program.

14. A specific label name can be used only once in a function.

15. When it is used to jump out from a deep nest of loops (though only in cases of extreme necessity).

16. A function pointer points to the location of a function in memory, in much the same way that other pointers point to data in memory.

17. Recursion is a technique whereby a function calls itself. It is useful in problems that can be defined in terms of smaller versions of the same problem.

18. No such declaration is needed in C.

19. A byte or variable might contain individual bits or bit fields, each of which represents a different flag or value. In such a case, it is necessary to be able to manipulate the bits individually.

20. a) 1000
    b) 1111

21. The tilde (˜) represents the logical NOT (or logical inversion, or ones complement) operation.

22. In the inclusive OR operation, the result is *true* (1) when one or both operands are *true* (1). In the EXCLUSIVE OR, the result is *true* when one of the operands is *true*, but not both.

23. a) <<
    b) >>

24. In the logical right shift, zeroes always are shifted in from the left. In the arithmetic shift, the bit value shifted in from the left is the same as that which formerly was the leftmost bit (the leftmost bit is propagated).

25. The left shift can be used for multiplying by powers of 2, and the right shift can be used for division by powers of 2. The restrictions on these operations vary slightly from one machine to another.

26. The **union** construct allows the same portion of memory to be accessed as different data types.

27. Bit fields are structure members whose sizes, in bits, are explicitly specified and are less than the size of a word or **int**.

28. This definition can be used only in a structure template. It defines a bit field named *four_bits*, which is four bits in length. Since the field is not explicitly defined as **unsigned**, some compilers treat it as an unsigned variable and others treat it as signed.

29. Alignment is the requirement that a data item must begin on a specific memory boundary, such as the beginning of a byte (for bit fields) or the beginning of a word. This requirement may cause structures to contain "holes," or unused bits or bytes.

30. Through the *argc* and *argv* parameters of the *main* function.

31. The name used to execute the program, usually the name of the file containing the compiled and linked program.

Keywords

auto	break	case	char	**continue**	default
do	double	else	**extern**	float	for
goto	if	int	long	**register**	return
short	sizeof	static	struct	switch	**typedef**
union	unsigned	while			

Exercises

1. Use the **typedef** storage class to define a type that is equivalent to an array of 15 pointers to a structure whose members are an integer and a pointer to **char**.

2. Rewrite the calculator program (you may use the simplest version, from Chapter 11, Exercise 1) so that it uses a special function to do the calculation. The function takes three arguments: the two operands, and a pointer to a function that performs the proper operation (addition, subtraction, etc.) This requires that each operation have a corresponding function, which takes two arguments and returns the result of the operation. You may wish to store the pointers to these functions in an array. Constructing your program in this manner will make it easy to add additional binary operators at a later time, such as an operator to raise a number to a power.

3. A famous dilemma is stated as follows. A man wishes to cross a river. He has with him a goat, a cabbage, and a wolf. The man's boat can hold only him and one of his possessions at any given time. Therefore, the man must leave two of his possessions on the shore at any given time, as he brings the third item across. He cannot leave the goat with the cabbage, because the former will eat the latter; for similar reasons, he cannot leave the wolf with the goat. The question is: How many trips must the man make across the river, and what item must he bring with him on each trip? Try to write a recursive function to solve this puzzle.

4. An early method used to represent numbers in computers is called BCD, or *binary coded decimal*. In this system, two digits of a number can be packed into a single byte. This is possible because it takes no more than four bits to represent a decimal digit. For example, consider the number 92. The value 9 is represented in four-place binary as 1001, whereas 2 is represented as 0010. Therefore, in BCD the number 92 is represented by the byte 10010010. (In reality, BCD includes a method of representing signed numbers, but for this exercise we shall restrict the problem to unsigned integers.) The number of bytes needed to represent an n-digit number in BCD is $n/2$. Since a value with an odd number of digits would

require a fractional number of bytes, it is encoded with a leading zero. For example, 927 would become 0927.

Write a set of functions to pack an integer represented in ASCII (one byte per digit, with the digits stored as characters) into BCD, and another function to unpack it. Also, write a function to convert a BCD integer into a binary integer (the way it is stored in an **int** variable) and another to convert a binary integer to BCD. The latter pair of functions is very machine-dependent, so it might be desirable to use *sprintf* and *sscanf* to do the actual conversion to and from binary representation. The rest of the required operations, however, can be done in a virtually machine-independent manner. Hint: It may be easiest to implement the BCD-to-binary functions by using ASCII representation as an intermediate step between BCD and binary notation. Though this might not be the most efficient method, it permits the use of *sprintf* and *sscanf* to perform the ASCII-to-binary conversions. Also, since the handling of variable-length arrays to represent BCD numbers may be problematic, you may wish to handle only values with a fixed number of digits, padding them with leading zeroes if necessary.

5. Rewrite the program from Exercise 7 and/or the one from Exercise 8 in Chapter 14 so that, when the records are read into memory, the nodes of both linked lists are described by a single *union* whose members are the two different structures being dealt with. In this way, the functions to read in and write out the records can be independent of the file being handled; you merely pass them the appropriate FILE pointer and linked list pointer. Remember that **sizeof** for the union will be the size of the larger of the two structures. So outputting this number of bytes will always store the entire union. The smaller structure will have some unused bytes stored along with it.

6. Write a program that prints out all of its command line arguments.

7. Write a version of the calculator program (from Chapter 13, Exercise 6, or Chapter 12, Exercise 8) which evaluates only a single expression per run of the program. The expression is to be specified on the command line.

8. Here is a challenging problem. Assume you are writing a program to be used to handle electronic mail. A user who is sending a message to a foreign country specifies the country as a two-letter code. Every country is represented by exactly two uppercase letters. The program must convert this code into an integer, which is used by the hardware that actually routes the message. The program should look up the integer code in some sort of table, based on the two-letter code. Your job is to figure out what sort of data structure (array, structure, linked list, etc.) is most appropriate for this table, as well as an algorithm to do the conversion between a two-letter code and an integer.

Since the program is to be used for communications, it must be as fast as possible, and your chosen data structure should help achieve this speed. Assume that memory is not at a premium. This means your algorithm should be as fast and efficient as possible, even if it means wasting some memory. Remember that there is no one right way to solve this problem, so have fun with it.

Appendix A

C Reference Guide

This guide arranges all the elements of the C language in approximate order of complexity, beginning with the smallest elements such as keywords and constants, and building up to functions. It ends with a description of the preprocessor directives and a discussion of several extensions to the original C language.

Comments

A comment can be placed anywhere that white space (blanks, tabs, or *newlines*) can appear, except within a character or string constant. A comment consists of any text at all, delimited by /* and */, and may occupy more than one line. It has no effect on program execution. Comments cannot be nested.

Keywords

The following identifiers, written as shown without embedded blanks and in lowercase, are reserved by the compiler and cannot be used for any purpose other than those for which they are defined:

auto	break	case	char	continue	default
do	double	else	extern	float	for
goto	if	int	long	register	return
short	sizeof	static	struct	switch	typedef
union	unsigned	while			

Some C compilers also reserve the following words:

asm	const	entry	enum	fortran	signed
void	volatile				

Identifiers

Identifiers are names for entities in a C program, such as variables, functions, and labels. An identifier can be composed only of upper- and lowercase letters, the underscore, and digits. There can be no embedded blanks. The only syntactical restriction is that an identifier cannot start with a digit. It is not advisable to start it with an underscore, because of possible conflicts with names used by the system. There is no limit on the size of an identifier, but some compilers recognize only the first eight or so characters of an identifier, so the first eight letters of an identifier should be unique.

Scope of Identifiers

The scope of an identifier is the part of the program in which it is recognized. A variable name is recognized within the block (function or compound statement) in which it is declared, plus all enclosed blocks. If a variable name is declared outside any function, its scope is the entire program file following its declaration, as well as any other part of the file or another program file in which it is declared to be **extern**. A function name is recognized throughout the program. (A global variable or function is recognized only within its program file if it is declared to be **static**.)   A label's scope is the function in which it is defined. Some compilers allow a label to be redefined within a compound statement, but in general a label should be unique to the function in which it is defined.

It is best to use an identifier for only one purpose. For example, the same name should not be used for a label and a variable within the same function, although this may not be regarded as an error by the compiler.

Constants

C contains five basic types of constants.

1) **Integer constants**

An integer constant consists of one or more digits. An integer preceded by a unary minus may be considered to represent a negative constant, although it is actually a constant expression (see below). A **long** constant is followed by a letter l or L:

```
12345678L
```

or

```
123456781
```

Some C compilers require an unsigned constant to be followed by the letter u or U.

An integer beginning with the digit 0 is taken to be octal, and can contain the digits 0 through 7. An integer beginning with 0x or 0X is taken to be hexadecimal, and can contain 0 through 9 and the letters a through f and/or A through F:

```
37
0423
0x3f
```

2) **Floating point constants**

A floating point constant has two forms.

a) Decimal notation

This consists of a series of digits representing the whole part of the number, followed by a decimal point, followed by a series of digits representing the fractional part. The whole part or the fractional part can be omitted, but never both. The decimal point cannot be omitted.

Example:

```
3.27
```

b) Scientific notation
This consists of a mantissa in decimal notation, followed by the letter e or E, followed by an exponent. The exponent consists of an optional plus or minus sign, followed by a series of digits (forming a whole number).
Example:

23.91E-45

3) **Character constants**
A character constant consists of a character within single quotation marks. The character can be any in the ASCII character set. It can be represented either directly or as an escape sequence. An escape sequence is a multi-character combination, with a backslash as the first character, representing a single character. It may be one of the following special sequences:

Escape Sequence	Character Represented
\b	backspace
\t	tab
\n	newline
\f	form feed
\r	return
\'	single quote (apostrophe)
\\	backslash

An escape sequence also can be a backslash followed by up to three octal digits (no leading zero needed), representing the ASCII value of the character. For example, uppercase A has the ASCII value 65, which is 101 in octal, so the escape sequence representing it would be

\101

Usually octal escape sequences are used to represent non-printing characters, such as the bell or *null* character.
Examples:

'a'   'Z'   '8'   '.'   '"'   '\n'
'\''   '\\'   '\123' '\7'

The value of a character constant is the ASCII value of the character represented.
A character constant can consist of more than one character. For example, a **long** integer usually can hold four characters, so the following is valid:

long sample = 'abcd';

In such a case, the characters are placed in the variable in a machine-dependent order.

4) String literals

A string consists of double quotation marks containing any number of characters (including none). Escape sequences are permitted. The representation of double quotation marks within the string requires the escape sequence

\"

whereas single quotes can be written directly. Also, an octal escape sequence should contain three digits; otherwise, any digits immediately following the escape sequence may accidentally be included. A string constant always is stored in a specific location in memory, meaning it has an address. It contains all the characters specified in the string, followed by a *null* character as a terminator. For this reason, the string itself should not contain a *null*. The type of a string literal is **char ***.

5) Pointer constants

These include the name of an array without subscripts and the name of a function without parentheses. A string literal actually is an instance of a constant pointer, since its value is a pointer to the string.

Expressions

An expression consists of one or more constants, variables, function calls, or operations. For example:

constant: 4
variable: a
function call: sqrt(a)
operation: a + 4

These can be joined by operators and parentheses to form more complex expressions. Every expression has a value.

Operators

This section lists operators available in C. They have been grouped into several categories. Note that the operands generally come from the set of types consisting of integers, real (floating point) numbers, and pointers of any sort. There are some special cases, for example, when the operand must be an address or a variable. Unless otherwise specified, both operands of a binary operator are of the same type. Note that a truth value is an integer, with zero specifying *false* and any other value meaning *true*.

Except for (), [], and ?:, the two characters of a two-character operator must be contiguous, with no characters or white space between them.

Unary Operators

Operator: -
Operation: Negation
Operand type: Integer or real
Meaning: Negates operand
Examples: -3   -1.2   -456L

Operator: *(type)*
Operation: Casting
Operand type: Any
Meaning: Casts operand into specified *type* (returns a value)
Examples: (int)4.2   (char *)&a

Operator: !
Operation: Logical NOT
Operand type: Integer
Meaning: Reverses truth value of operand
Examples: !(a==b)   !x

Operator: &
Operation: Address
Operand type: Any variable (except one of the **register** storage class).
Meaning: Returns address of operand
Examples: &a   &b[7]   &d.e

Operator: *
Operation: Indirection
Operand type: Address
Meaning: Returns contents of location whose address is the operand. Can be used on left side of assignment operator, where the value is assigned to the location pointed to by the operand, which may be any pointer expression
Examples: *b   *(a+1)   *x = 4

Operator: **sizeof**
Operand type: Any variable, value, parenthesized type
Meaning: Returns size (in bytes or **char**s) of the operand
Examples: sizeof a   sizeof(int)

Operator: ~
Operation: Bitwise NOT or inversion
Operand type: Integer
Meaning: Reverses each bit in the operand from 1 to 0 and vice versa
Examples: ~w   ~(0x1f)

Binary Operators

Operator: +
Operation: Addition
Operand type: Integer or real
Meaning: Returns the sum of the two operands
Examples: `a + 2    4 + 5    3.1 + 2.7`

Operator: +
Operation: Address addition
Operand types: A pointer and an integer
Meaning: Returns the pointer plus the size of the pointer target type multiplied by the integer
Examples: `p + 2    p + a`

Operator: -
Operation: Subtraction
Operand type: Integer, real, or pointer
Meaning: Returns the difference of the two operands (for pointers, the difference is in target type units)
Examples: `a - b    4 - 2`

Operator: -
Operation: Address subtraction
Operand types: A pointer and an integer
Meaning: Returns the pointer minus the size of the pointer target type multiplied by the integer
Examples: `p - 2    p - a`

Operator: *
Operation: Multiplication
Operand type: Integer or real
Meaning: Returns the product of the two operands
Examples: `21.1 * 2.4    x * y`

Operator: /
Operation: Division
Operand type: Integer or real
Meaning: Returns the quotient of the two operands. If the operands are integers, the integer quotient is taken, with any remainder discarded
Examples: `3 / 2    1.4 / 2.8`

Operator: %
Operation: Modulus
Operand type: Integer
Meaning: Returns the integer remainder if the first operand is divided by the second
Examples: `23 % 7    14 % 2`

Operators: `<`   `>`   `<=`   `>=`   `==`   `!=`

Operations: Relational (less than, greater than, less than or equal to, greater than or equal to, equal to, not equal to)

Operand type: Any

Meaning: The specified test is performed on the operands, with the result returned as a truth value

Examples: `a < 3   b >= c   x == 0`

Operator: `&&`

Operation: Logical AND

Operand type: Integer

Meaning: Returns *true* if both operands are *true*, otherwise *false*. If the left-hand operand is *false*, the right-hand one is not evaluated

Examples: `a < 4 && b > 5   t == u && u == v`

Operator: `||`

Operation: Logical OR

Operand type: Integer

Meaning: Returns *true* if at least one of the operands is *true*. If the left-hand operand is *true*, the right-hand one is not evaluated

Examples: `a > 50 || a < 10   x == 2 || y == 2`

Operator: `,`

Operation: Comma

Operand type: Any (the two may be different)

Meaning: Evaluates the left-hand operand for its side effects, then evaluates the right-hand operand and returns its value. This operator is used most frequently in **for** loops

Example: `for(a = 1, b = 2; a < 20; a++, b++)`

Operator: `&`

Operation: Bitwise AND

Operand type: Integer

Meaning: Each bit of the result is 1 if and only if the corresponding bits of both operands are 1

Examples: `a & 7   b & 8`

Operator: `|`

Operation: Bitwise OR

Operand type: Integer

Meaning: Each bit of the result is 1 if and only if the corresponding bit of at least one operand is 1

Examples: `x | 8   y | 0x81`

Operator:	^
Operation:	Bitwise EXCLUSIVE OR
Operand type:	Integer
Meaning:	Each bit of the result is 1 if and only if the corresponding bit of one, but not both, of the operands is 1
Examples:	`a ^ 0x80    x ^ 0xff`

Operator:	<<
Operation:	Bitwise left shift
Operand type:	Integer
Meaning:	The bits of the left-hand operand are shifted left by as many bits as indicated by the right-hand operand. Zero bits are shifted in from the right side. The right-hand operand must be nonnegative and not greater than the number of bits in the left-hand operand
Examples:	`a << 4    x << a`

Operator:	>>
Operation:	Bitwise right shift
Operand type:	Integer
Meaning:	The bits of the left-hand operand are shifted right by as many bits as indicated by the right-hand operand. Zero bits are shifted in from the left side if the left-hand operand is unsigned; otherwise, the bit shifted in depends on the implementation. The right-hand operand must be nonnegative and not greater than the number of bits in the left-hand operand
Examples:	`a >> 4    x >> a`

The Conditional Operator

This operator takes the form

    test-operand ? operand-2 : operand-3

The test-operand is an integer. The other two operands can be any values or variables, so long as they are of the same type. If the test-operand is *true*, operand-2 is returned and operand-3 is not evaluated. Otherwise, operand-3 is returned and operand-2 is not evaluated.
Examples:

```
a < b ? a : b
x >= 0 ? a[x] : -1
```

Assignment Operators

These operators change the value of one of their operand variables.

Operator: ++
Operation: Increment
Operand type: Any scalar variable
Meaning: The value of the variable is incremented by 1, with the new value reassigned to the variable. (Pointer incrementing adds the size of the target type to a pointer.) If the operator precedes the variable, the new value is returned as the value of the operation. If it follows the variable, the original value of the variable is returned
Examples: a++   ++x

Operator: --
Operation: Decrement
Operand type: Any scalar variable
Meaning: The value of the variable is decremented by 1, with the new value reassigned to the variable. (Pointer decrementing subtracts the size of the target type from a pointer.) If the operator precedes the variable, the new value is returned as the value of the operation. If it follows the variable, the original value of the variable is returned
Examples: a--   --x

Operator: =
Operation: Assignment
Operand type: Any scalar type, with the left-hand operand being a variable
Meaning: The right-hand operand is evaluated, assigned to the left-hand operand, and returned as the value of the operator
Examples: a = 4   b = 3 * x   u = v = w *j = k

Operators: +=   -=   *=   /=   %=   &= |=   ^=   <<=   >>=
Operations: Updating assignment
Operand type: Any scalar type, but must meet the requirements of both the assignment operator and the updating operator. For example, in the expression a += b, a must be a variable and either a and b must be of the same type, or a may be a pointer with b an integer
Meaning: The updating operator is applied to the two operands, and the result is assigned to the left-hand operand and returned. For example, a *= b is equivalent to $a = a * b$
Examples: a *= b   x <<= y

Selection Operators

Operator:
  [ ]
Meaning:
  Square brackets are used to subscript an array. For example, if a is a one-dimensional array (or a pointer to an array), $a[0]$ selects the first element of the array. If a is two-dimensional, $a[0]$ selects the first row of the array, and $a[0][1]$ selects the second element of the first row of the array.

Operator:
  .
Meaning:
  The structure member or period operator selects a member of a union or structure. If a is a structure whose template includes a member named b, then $a.b$ selects member b of structure a.

Operator:
  ->
Meaning:
  The structure pointer or arrow operator selects a member from a structure or union pointed to by a variable. For example, if a points to a structure that contains a member b, then $a->b$ selects member b of the structure pointed to by a. In other words, $a->b$ is equivalent to $(*a).b$.

Function Call

Operator:
  ( )
Meaning:
  This operator appears to the right of a function name or any expression evaluating to type "function returning ..." it indicates that the function is to be called. The parentheses enclose the parameters to the function, if any.

Examples:
  `sqrt(7.0) (*func_ptr)()`

Operator Precedence, Associativity, and Order of Evaluation

Precedence

When an expression is evaluated, certain operators are performed before others. The following table lists the C operators in descending order of precedence.

( ) {function call} [ ] . ->									
- {unary} (*type*) ! & {unary} * {unary} sizeof ~ ++ --									
* {binary} / %									
+ - {binary}									
<< >>									
< <= > >=									
== !=									
& {binary}									
^									
|									
&&									
||									
?:									
= += -= *= /= %= &= |= ^= <<= >>=									
,									

Operators with the highest precedence are performed first. For example, in the expression

```
a + b * c
```

the multiplication is performed before the addition. Parentheses can be used to override the precedence. For example, in the expression

```
(a + b) * c
```

the addition is performed first.

Associativity

When operators of the same precedence appear in an expression, usually they are evaluated from left to right. For example, the expression

```
a * b / c
```

is evaluated as

```
(a * b) / c
```

There are some exceptions. Unary operators associate from right to left. In other words,

```
-*a
```

is evaluated as

```
-(*a)
```

and

```
*p++
```

is evaluated as

```
*(p++)
```

The regular and updating assignment operators also associate from right to left, meaning that

```
a = b += c
```

is evaluated as:

```
a = (b += c)
```

Finally, the conditional operator evaluates from right to left, meaning that

```
a > 2 ? b : c < 7 ? a : c
```

is evaluated as

```
a > 2 ? b : (c < 7 ? a : c)
```

Order of Evaluation

Associativity applies only to consecutive operators. Otherwise, the order of evaluation of subexpressions is unspecified. In the expression

```
(a + x) * (b + y)
```

there is no rule as to which addition is performed first. Usually this fact causes no difficulty, unless function calls with side effects or assignments are involved. For example, in the expression

```
(a = x) * a
```

is the value of *a* on the right side of the multiplication operator the original value of *a*, or is it the new value that is assigned on the left side of the operator? This depends on which operand of the multiplication operator is evaluated first, and there is no rule for this. If a function call were used instead of an assignment there would be no problem. Function calls have a higher precedence than multiplication and would therefore be performed before the multiplication.

Consider the following expression:

```
f(&a) + g(&a)
```

in which both functions change the value of *a*. Either function could be performed first. This is one reason that side effects should be avoided.

The exceptions to this rule are the operators &&, || and the comma operator, which guarantee left-to-right operand evaluation; and the ?: operator, which guarantees that its first operand is evaluated first, and then either its second or third operand (but not both). Also, a function call is performed after all its arguments have been evaluated. The order of evaluation of a function's arguments is unspecified.

Note that these rules apply to array subscripts and the arrow and dot operators as well.

The compiler recognizes the operators *, +, &, |, and ^ as being commutative and associative. Therefore, the expression

```
a + b + c
```

might be evaluated as

```
(a + b) + c
```

or as

```
a + (b + c)
```

or even as

```
a + (c + b)
```

Even the use of parentheses may not change this order. That is, the expression

```
a + (b + c)
```

might still be evaluated as follows:

```
(a + b) + c
```

Problems may result if side effects are used, as in the following example:

```
(x = a) + b + x
```

Notice that this special case occurs only when the same operator is used several times consecutively, and only in the case of the five operators mentioned previously. Since no two of the five operators have the same precedence, combining different operators results in an umambiguous expression.

Conversions

The following rules apply when a value of one type is converted to another type through assignment, casting, or mixed-mode conversion.

An integral type can be converted to a longer integral type. It is also possible to convert an integral type to a shorter one, provided that the number also can be represented in the shorter length. Otherwise, the value will be truncated and the result will be meaningless.

An unsigned integer can be converted to a longer signed one. It also can be converted to a shorter signed integer, if it can be represented in the shorter length. Since unsigned variables usually can represent larger positive values than signed ones of the same length, it may not be possible to convert an unsigned value to a signed one of the same size without erroneous results. A positive signed integer can be converted to an unsigned integer of the same size or longer. It also can be converted to a shorter one if it can be represented in the shorter length. If a negative integer is converted to an unsigned integer, the result is an unsigned integer with the same bit pattern as the signed integer. Usually there is no direct relationship between these two numbers, unless they represent characters.

A **float** value can be converted to **double**. A **double** value may be converted to **float** if its exponent (if any) is within the range that can be represented in a **float** value. In the latter case, the mantissa is rounded to a size that can be represented by a **float** value.

An integer can be converted to a floating point value, if it can be represented in the chosen floating point type. When a floating point value is converted to an integer type, the fractional part is truncated. Again, the integer must be large enough to hold the entire non-fractional part of the number.

Mixed mode

An expression may consist of subexpressions of more than one type. In the following discussion, we refer to the case in which a binary operator combines two values of different types. The exceptions are pointer addition and subtraction, bitwise shifts, assignment, the comma operator, function calls, and the selection operators. All the following conversions are automatic and are performed in the order specified:

1) All integer constants and variables in an expression that are shorter than an **int** are expanded to **int**s, and all **float** values are expanded to **double**s.
2) If one operand of an operator is a **double**, the other is converted to a **double** and the operation is performed.
3) If neither operand is a **double**, then if one operand is a **long**, the other becomes a **long** and the operation is performed.
4) If neither operand is a **double** or a **long**, then if one operand is **unsigned**, the other becomes **unsigned** and the operation is performed.
5) If both operands are **int**s, the operation is performed with no conversion.

The first rule, involving the "enlargement" of integer and floating point values, also applies to each argument in a function call. In an assignment, the right-hand operand is always converted to the type of the left-hand operand. The comma operator performs no conversion.

In some versions of C, operations can be performed on **short**, **char**, and **float** operands directly. In this case, the first step might not be performed. The general rule will be that the shorter operand is converted to the type of the longer one, and that if one operand is a floating point type and one is an integer, the integer is converted to floating point. If there are **unsigned** types of more than one size, the rule concerning unsigned values still applies.

Constant Expressions

A constant expression is one that evaluates to a constant, and consequently can be fully evaluated at compilation time.

An integer constant expression can contain integer or character constants, and any operators except for the following:

```
( ) {function call}    [ ]    ->      .
++     --
* {unary}    & {unary}
```

The **sizeof** operator can be applied to any expression (even a non-constant expression, since the **sizeof** operator cares only about the size of the result, not the value).

The only constant expressions other than integer ones that we are interested in are those used for initializing static variables. In those cases, the constant expression may include any sort of constant at all, all operators permitted in integer constant expressions, plus the unary & operator applied to any of the following:

1) An **extern** or **static** variable.
2) An element of an **extern** or **static** array, provided the subscript is an integer constant expression.
3) A member of an **extern** or **static** structure or union, provided the dot operator is used to reference the member.

Types

The following simple types are used in C:

```
char
double
float
int
long
short
unsigned
```

where **long** is the same as **long int**, **short** is the same as **short int**, and **unsigned** is the same as **unsigned int**. Most compilers also recognize **unsigned char**, **unsigned short**, and **unsigned long**, although they are not part of the original definition of C. The **unsigned** variables can hold only positive numbers. All these types are integers except for **float** and **double**, which are floating point.

Some compilers recognize the type **signed char**, which usually is the same as **char**, and **void**, which usually is used as the type of a function that returns no value. Some compilers have a type **long double**, which is a floating point number twice the length of a **double**.

The following table shows the standard sizes in bytes of the various data types:

type	size
char	1
int	2 or 4
short	2
long	4
float	4
double	8

An **unsigned** variable is the same size as its signed equivalent. The more bytes a variable occupies, the larger its magnitude or the number of significant digits it can hold.

Other types can be derived from these types. One such group of types is pointers. The programmer can declare a pointer to **int**, a pointer to a pointer to **int**, and so forth. The same can be done with any other type or C construct. The size of a pointer usually is the same as the size of an **int**. The programmer also can build these types into arrays, structures, and unions. It is possible to combine such *aggregate* types with one another, so that one can have, say, a pointer to an array of structures containing **ints**.

The following are examples of some compound types with their associated cast operators:

pointer to **int**	(int *)
array of 3 pointers to **int**	(int *[3])
pointer to an array of 10 **chars**	(char (*)[10])
pointer to function returning **long**	(long (*) ())

Duration of Variables — Storage Classes

The Five Storage Classes

C provides five storage classes for variables: **auto**, **static**, **register**, **extern**, and **typedef**.

1) auto

An **auto** variable is created each time the block in which it is declared is entered, and is destroyed each time the block is exited. Such variables can be declared only within functions. A local variable is by default **auto**, but it can be declared to be of another storage class by the use of an explicit storage class in its declaration. A formal parameter also is **auto** by default, but cannot be declared as such explicitly. A function cannot be declared as **auto**.

2) static

These variables remain in existence throughout the execution of the program. Global and local variables can be declared to be **static**, but not formal parameters. When a global variable or a function is declared explicitly to be **static**, its scope is restricted to the file in which it is declared.

3) register

A local variable or formal parameter can be declared to be **register**. The declaration means that, if possible, the variable is stored in a machine register rather than in main memory. It is like an **auto** variable, in that it disappears when the function exits. The only restrictions are that a **register** variable must be of a type whose size is not larger than the size of a register. Usually these types include **char**, **short**, **int**, and pointers, and sometimes also **long** and **float**. The address of a **register** variable cannot be taken (the & operator may not be used). A function or global variable cannot be declared to be **register**.

4) extern

This storage class does not allocate any memory for a variable, but merely declares it to have been created elsewhere in the program. This declaration must be used to access a global variable declared in another file, in which case it may be used in either a global or local declaration. It also must be used when a function wishes access to a global variable that is declared later in the same program file. It may optionally be used when the global variable was declared earlier in the file, but it is not necessary in that case. A formal parameter cannot be **extern**. A function is by default **extern**, although this storage class need never be used in a function definition or declaration.

5) typedef

This storage class is used to create new data types. It will be described later in this appendix, in the section headed **typedef**.

Global variables

A global variable is of a unique class. It is not an **auto** or **register** variable. It is not a **static** variable, because when a global variable is declared to be **static**, it is not accessible through an **extern** statement in another program file. A global variable is, by default, externally accessible. It is not itself **extern**, because declaring a global variable to be **extern** allocates no space for it, whereas the definition of a global variable normally allocates space in memory. A global variable therefore is static in nature, except that it can be accessed in another program file.

Declaration of Variables

A variable declaration consists of an optional storage class, a type, a variable name, and sometimes an optional initialization. An example of a declaration without initialization is

```
static unsigned char bingo;
```

An example of a declaration with initialization is

```
register int fred = 1;
```

where the initialization consists of an equal sign followed by an initializer, which we will describe for each case.

The type can be any of the simple types we have described, or it can be a structure or union tag and/or template, or a name defined in a **typedef**. The data type can be enhanced further by using one or more asterisks before the variable name, to make it a pointer of the desired level of indirection, or by following the name with one or more dimensions to make it an array of the desired dimensions. If the name is followed by a pair of parentheses, it declares the existence of a function with the specified name which returns the declared type.

A single storage class and type specifier can be used to declare several variables. For example, the declaration

```
static int a, b, c = 7;
```

declares *a*, *b* and *c* all to be **static int**s. Each variable can have its own initializer, or none at all. Also, subscripting and pointer specification is individual for each variable, so the declaration

```
int a, *b, **c, d[7];
```

declares *a* to be a simple **int**, *b* to be a pointer to **int**, *c* to be a pointer to pointer to **int**, and *d* to be an array of seven **int**s.

In all the following cases, a variable declared as **extern** cannot be initialized, and its type, dimensions, template, and so on must exactly match those used to declare the non-**extern** version of the variable named. If a **static** or global variable is not initialized, it is guaranteed to contain 0. The value of an uninitialized **auto** or **register** variable is undefined.

Simple variables

If the variable is declared as **auto** or **register**, the initializer can be any expression, as long as all variables and functions referred to in the expression have already been declared, are within the scope of the declaration, and will have a value at the time the variable being declared will be allocated. The initialization is performed each time the variable is allocated, so the initializing value can be different each time. A **static** or global variable can be initialized only to a constant expression, and this initialization is performed only once, at the beginning of execution.

Pointers

When a pointer variable is declared, the variable name is preceded by an asterisk for each level of indirection desired. For example, a pointer to **int** might be declared as

```
int *herb;
```

whereas a pointer to pointer to **int** might be declared as

```
int **herb;
```

The initialization rules for pointers are the same as those for simple variables. Remember that the initializing value must be a pointer, so it must point to a variable already declared. For example:

```
int henry;
int *herb = &henry;
int **malka = &herb;
```

A **char** pointer also can be initialized as a pointer to a string literal, as in

```
char *s = "bingo";
```

In this example, the **char** pointer s is assigned the address of the literal "bingo".

Arrays

An array declaration is similar to a variable declaration, except that the variable name is followed by one or more subscripts. A subscript takes the form of a integer constant expression within square brackets. For example, a one-dimensional array of seven pointers to **int** might be declared as follows:

```
int *arnold[7];
```

If multiple dimensions are desired, each subscript is placed within a separate pair of brackets, as in the following:

```
int *arnold[7][4];
```

All dimensions must be explicitly specified, with the following two exceptions: (1) If the array is a formal parameter, its first subscript can be omitted, meaning it is represented by an empty pair of brackets. (2) One or more dimensions can be omitted if the array is initialized (see below). The subscripts for the array elements range from 0 to n-1, where n is the dimension.

An array can be initialized only if it is **static** or global. The initializer to a one-dimensional array consists of a pair of braces containing a series of constant expressions separated by commas, which are assigned to the array in order of increasing subscript. If there are fewer initializing values than elements, the remaining elements are set to 0. There can never be more initializers than array elements. If the array's dimension is omitted (an empty pair of brackets is specified), the number of dimensions is equal to the number of initializing values.

When a multi-dimensional array is initialized, a group of initializing values representing a row of the array can be enclosed in braces. For example:

```
int joe [2][3] = { { 1, 2 }, { 3, 4 }, { 5, 6 } };
```

The inner braces are not necessary, unless some elements in each row are not initialized. For example, if the array is declared as

```
int joe [][4] = { { 1, 2 }, { 3, 4 }, { 5, 6 } };
```

then the array is declared as having three rows and four columns, where only the first two elements of each row are initialized. When one or more dimensions are omitted, the compiler must be able to deduce the implicit dimensions.

If the inner pairs of braces are not used, the array must be explicitly dimensioned. The declaration

```
int joe[2][3] = { 2, 3, 4 };
```

specifies initial values only for the first row and half of the second. The remaining elements are set to 0.

Strings can be used to initialize **char** arrays. The notation

```
char s[10] = "bingo";
```

is equivalent to

```
char s[10] = { 'b', 'i', 'n', 'g', 'o', '\0' };
```

whereas the statement

```
char s[] = "bingo";
```

where the dimension is not specified, is equivalent to

```
char s[] = { 'b', 'i', 'n', 'g', 'o', '\0' };
```

where the array is given six elements so that the *null* character will fit. In most cases, if the dimension is specified, it cannot be less than the number of characters in the string plus the terminating *null*.

A two-dimensional array of type **char** can be initialized to an array of strings, as in the following example:

```
char s[][10] =
{
    "Henry",
    "and",
    "Malka",
    "Mullish"
};
```

In this statement, each string is assigned to a row of the array. The number of columns must be large enough to hold the longest string plus the *null* character, and the number of rows is equal to the number of strings. (The number of rows also can be specified explicitly, in which case it can be as large as desired.)

An array of **char** pointers can be initialized in a similar way. The declaration

```
char *s[] =
{
    "Henry",
    "and",
    "Malka",
    "Mullish"
};
```

assigns to each element of *s* a pointer to the corresponding string literal.

Structures

When a structure is declared, its type is the keyword **struct** followed by one of these options:

1) a previously defined structure tag
2) a structure template
3) a previously undeclared structure tag followed by a template

The format for structure templates and the definition of structure tags is described later. An example of a structure declaration is

```
static struct plate bingo;
```

where *plate* is the structure tag and *bingo* is the variable name.

A structure can be initialized only if it is **static** or global. The procedure is similar to initializing an array, except that each initializing constant expression must be of the type of the member it initializes. If the structure contains a nested structure, the initializing expression for that inner structure should be contained within braces, as in the following:

```
struct malka
{
    int x;
    char y;
};

struct henry
{
    int i;
    float j;
    struct malka k;
}
herb = { 4, 3.2, { 7, 'c' } };
```

An array of structures is initialized in an analogous manner to a two-dimensional array, except that each "row" of the initializer represents a structure.

Unions

A union is declared exactly like a structure, except that the keyword **union** is used instead of **struct**, and a union can never be initialized.

Functions

A function is declared in the calling function by specifying the type, the function name, and an empty pair of parentheses. (Some versions allow the specification of the parameter types within the parentheses, which are used for type checking. See *Extensions to C* below.)   The type should match the type specified as the function's return value in its definition.

A function need not be declared in the calling function if either the definition of the called function precedes the calling function, or the type of the called function is declared globally (outside any function) at a point in the file preceding the calling function. Also, a function need not be declared if it returns **int**. The exception to all these rules is when a function's address is being taken, in which case it must always be explicitly declared in the function that refers to it.

Structures and Unions

A structure or union template takes the form of a pair of braces enclosing a series of member definitions. Each member definition has the same form as a top level variable declaration, except that no storage class or initializer can be specified. Here is an example:

```
{
    int a;
    float b;
    char *c;
    long int d[17];
}
```

A structure variable contains each of the named members, and its size is large enough to hold all the members (plus possibly a little more for alignment). A union contains one of the named members at any given time, and is large enough to hold the largest of the members.

A template can be given a tag by preceding it with the keyword **union** or **struct**, as appropriate, and the tag. For example:

```
struct henry
{
    int a;
    float b;
    char *c;
    long int d[17];
};
```

Notice that the template is followed by a semicolon. A tag definition allocates no variables, but merely associates the tag with the template. The tag can be used to declare a structure (in this case) or a union. Note that, if the tag is defined as a structure tag, it cannot be used to declare a union, and vice versa. Thus it is not permissible to write

```
union henry mullish;
```

where *mullish* is the variable name.

A template can appear directly in a variable declaration. For example, a union named *joe* could be declared as

```
union
{
    int a;
    float b;
    char *c;
    long int d[17];
}
joe;
```

Note that the variable name appears after the template, and that there is no union tag. An identifier appearing before a template is a tag, whereas one appearing after a template is a variable name.

A tag can be defined at the same time that a variable is declared. For example, the declaration

```
union henry
{
    int a;
    float b;
    char *c;
    long int d[17];
}
q, mullish;
```

associates the tag *henry* with the specified template, and also declares *q* and *mullish* to be variables of the specified union template.

Two structures or two unions are equivalent if they have identical templates, even if their tags are different.

A union or structure template cannot contain as a member a structure or union with the same tag as itself—that is, it cannot contain itself. Also, it cannot contain another structure or union which in turn contains it, and so forth. A structure or union can contain a *pointer* to a structure or union of the same template, as in the following example:

```
struct cooper
{
    int herbert;
    struct cooper *me;
};
```

Except for these restrictions, structures or unions can contain structures or unions as members.

An individual member of a structure or union can be accessed using the period operator. For example, if the structure variable *belinda* has a member called *cooper*, that member is referred to as

```
belinda.cooper
```

If that member is itself a structure with a member called *ear*, that member can be accessed as

```
belinda.cooper.ear
```

Since the period operator associates from right to left, this is evaluated as

```
(belinda.cooper).ear
```

The arrow operator is used with a pointer to a structure or union. If *peter* is a pointer to a union with a member *piper*, that member can be accessed as

```
peter->piper
```

which is an abbreviation of

```
(*peter).piper
```

Arrow operators can be used to access multiple nested structures or unions the same way the period operator can. When a pointer to a structure or union is involved, the arrow is used. When a structure or union itself is involved, the period is used.

Some compilers allow a structure or union to be assigned as a unit, and to be passed by value to and returned by a function. Many others, however, permit only their addresses to be taken and their members to be accessed.

A structure (but not a union) also can contain a *field*, which is a member whose length is a number of bits. This is specified by following the member name with a colon and the bit count:

```
int fred : 3;
```

This example defines a field of three bits. A field must be of type **int**, **unsigned int**, or (where permitted) **signed int**. If a field is defined to be of type **int**, this may imply a signed or an unsigned **int**, depending on the compiler. The size of a field cannot be larger than the number of bits in a machine word, which usually is the size of an **int** on whichever machine you are using.

If one field immediately follows another, the two are packed into the same machine word if possible. Some compilers do not allow a field to straddle a word, and may therefore place the second field in the following word. For example, if a word is 16 bits long, and a structure contains these consecutive fields (as the first fields in the structure):

```
int henry : 8;
int malka : 10;
```

then one of these two options is taken:

1) The first eight bits of the current word become *henry*, the second eight bits become the beginning of *malka*, and the first two bits of the next word become the end of *malka*.
2) The first eight bits of the current word become *henry*, the second eight bits are left unused, and the first ten bits of the next word become *malka*.

The option selected depends on the compiler: most choose the second one. Note that, if the total of the two fields were 16 or less (for example, if *malka* were only eight bits), both fields would fit into the same word. The order in which fields are packed into a word (low bits first or high bits first) is machine-dependent.
    A field can consist of only a colon and a size, as in

```
: 7;
```

This statement creates an unnamed field that merely occupies the specified number of bits. If the bit count is 0, as in

```
: 0;
```

then the remainder of the current word is skipped and the next member starts at the beginning of a new word. (Another way of saying this is that it *word-aligns* the succeeding member.)
    There can be no arrays of fields, and the address of a field cannot be taken.
    As mentioned previously, a union contains only one of its members at any one time. That is, if a value is stored in one of the members, it should be read under that name until another value is written to the union. The exception is if the union is used to convert a bit pattern from one type to another, such as accessing a structure as an array of characters. This operation requires knowledge of how various types are stored and defined. When a value is written to a union member, it is converted (if necessary) to that member's type and then stored in the union, starting with the union's first byte. If it is read under the same member name, the stored value is returned. If it is accessed under a different member name, the stored bits are read as if they were a value of the new member's type, without any conversion.

typedef

The **typedef** storage class does not allocate a variable, but associates an identifier with a particular simple or compound type. The new type name is specified where the variable normally would be. For example, the statement

```
typedef int fred;
```

makes *fred* a synonym for **int**, whereas

```
typedef int *joe[27];
```

makes *joe* a name for the type "array of 27 pointers to **int**." Thus the declaration

```
joe bingo;
```

is equivalent to

```
int *bingo[27];
```

This is useful for creating single identifiers to specify types that normally would require several keywords or symbols.

A **typedef** can refer to a previously-defined type, as in

```
typedef int henry[27];
typedef henry *malka;
```

where *henry* is defined as "array of 27 **ints**" and *malka* is defined as "pointer to *henry*" which is the same as "pointer to array of 27 **ints**." (Note that this is not the same as the previous definition of *joe*.)

Since **typedef** is a storage class, it cannot include another storage class. Therefore, the definition of a type cannot tie that type to a specific storage class. Also a **typedef** declaration can never include an initializer.

A typedef can be used even to specify a structure, as in

```
typedef struct
{
   int a;
   float b;
   char *c;
   long int d[17];
}
mullish;
```

This declares *mullish* to be equivalent to the structure template, so it can be used in a declaration such as

```
mullish henry;
```

where the keyword **struct** should not be used, since it was part of the **typedef**. In a **typedef** involving a structure or union, a template or a tag or both can be used.

Two defined types are equivalent if they are defined to be exactly the same combination of simple types. For example, the following two types are equivalent:

```
typedef int *x[4];
typedef int *y[4];
```

Both *x* and *y* are "array of four pointers to **int**," so a variable of type *x* can be assigned to one of type *y* and vice versa. They would be equivalent even if *y* were declared as

```
typedef int *q;
typedef q y[4];
```

because both *x* and *y* would still be of the same type in terms of both being
arrays of four pointers to **int**.

Statements

A simple statement in C can be a declaration, an expression (possibly empty)
followed by a semicolon, or one of the statements described in the following
sections (**if**, **while**, etc.)   Examples:

```
c = a + b;            /* Expression    */
if (a < b) c = 1;     /* "if" statement */
;                     /* Null statement */
```

A compound statement consists of one or more simple statements enclosed within
the braces { and }. Examples:

```
{ a = b; }

{
    c = a + b;
    if (a < b) c = 1;
}
```

A compound statement need not be followed by a semicolon, but it is usually
not an error to include the semicolon. For that reason, the following syntax
summaries show a semicolon after each statement, even if the statement is
compound. This usage will remind you to include the semicolon where it is
required.

A compound statement can begin with variable declarations which must
appear before any other statements. Example:

```
if (a == b)
{
    int c;

    c = b;
    b = a;
    a = c;
}
```

A statement can be preceded by a label, which consists of a unique identifier
followed by a colon. Examples:

```
bingo: a = 7;
```

```
test:  {
           int c;

           c = b;
           b = a;
           a = c;
       }
```

The only statement within which a label can appear is a compound statement. A label may also be a **case** or **default** label if it appears within a **switch** statement.

A statement can appear only within a function body. (Note that a compound statement constitutes the function body itself.)

In the following sections, an *int-expression* is an expression that evaluates to a value of an integer type.

if and if...else statements

Syntax:
  if (int-expression) statement-1;
  if (int-expression) statement-1; **else** statement-2;

Semantics:
  The *int−expression* is evaluated. If it evaluates to *true*, *statement−1* is executed. Otherwise, *statement−1* is ignored. In the second form, *statement−2* is executed if the *int−expression* evaluates to *false*.

  In the second form, if *statement−1* is a compound statement, its closing brace should *not* be followed by a semicolon. Such a semicolon is interpreted as a null statement between the **if** and **else** clauses. It is illegal to place a statement between the two clauses.

while statement

Syntax:
  while (int-expression) loop-body-statement;

Semantics:
  The *int−expression* is evaluated. If it evaluates to *true*, the *loop−body−statement* is executed. Then the *int−expression* is evaluated again. As long as the *int−expression* is true, the *loop−body−statement* is executed repeatedly. As soon as the *int−expression* becomes *false*, the loop terminates and the next statement following the **while** loop is executed. Note that if the *int−expression* is initially *false,* the *loop−body−statement* is not executed at all.

do...while statement

Syntax:
    do loop-body-statement; **while** (int-expression);

Semantics:
    The same as the **while** loop, except that the *loop−body−statement* is executed before the *int−expression* is evaluated. This means that the *loop−body−statement* is executed once even if the *int−expression* is initially *false.*
    If the *loop−body−statement* is a coupound statement, its closing brace should *not* be followed by a semicolon.

break statement

Syntax:
    break;

Semantics:
    Immediately exits from the innermost enclosing loop or **switch** statement.

continue statement

Syntax:
    continue;

Semantics:
    Skips the remainder of the current iteration of the *loop−body−statement* in which it is contained, and continues the loop with the next iteration.

return statement

Syntax:
    return;
    return expression;

Semantics:
    The first form causes a function to return immediately. The value of the function is undefined. The second form returns the expression as the value of the function. If the type of expression is not the same as the function's declared type, the expression is cast into the appropriate type.

for statement

Syntax:
  for (expression-1; int-expression; expression-3)   loop-body-statement;

Semantics:
  Exactly equivalent to

```
    expression-1;
    while (int-expression)
    {
        loop-body-statement;
        expression-3;
    }
```

All three expressions are optional, although the semicolons are not. If the *int−expression* is omitted, it defaults to 1. This means that the equivalent **while** loop would be

```
    while(1)
```

which can be terminated only by a **break** or **return** statement.

switch statement

Syntax:
  switch (int-expression) compound-statement;

  The compound-statement contains labels of the form:

  case int-constant-expression :

and optionally a label of the form

  default :

The *int−expression* is first evaluated, and then a search is made for a **case** label whose *int−constant−expression* has the same value as the *int−expression*. Note that no two **case** labels can have expressions that evaluate to the same integer constant. If a match is found, control passes to the statement following the matching label, and continues until the end of the *compound−statement* or until a **break** statement is encountered. If no match is found and there is a **default** label, execution continues at the statement after the **default** label. If there is no matching **case** label and no **default** label, the entire *compound−statement* is skipped.
  Note that a **switch** statement can contain a nested **switch**. This, in turn, can contain its own **default** label, as well as **case** labels identical to those of the outer **switch** statement. The **case** and **default** labels can be used only within the body of a **switch** statement.

goto statement

Syntax:
    goto label-identifier;

This statement immediately transfers execution to the statement labeled with the *label—identifier*. The *label—identifier* must be declared within the same function as the **goto** statement.

Functions

A function definition consists of three main parts:

1) Function header
2) Declaration list
3) Function body

The function header contains a storage class, a type, the function name, and an argument list. The storage class, if included, must be either **extern** or **static**. The type can be any simple type or a pointer, but never an array (it can be a pointer to an array). Some compilers also permit a function to return a structure or union. If the type is omitted, it defaults to **int**. The argument list is a pair of parentheses containing the names of the formal parameters to the function, if any. The parameters must be identifiers unique to the function, and they are separated by commas. If the function takes no arguments, the parentheses still must be included. The function header is *not* terminated by a semicolon.

The function header is followed by a declaration list, which declares the types of the formal parameters. No other variables can be declared at this point. The parameters need not be declared in the order in which they are specified in the function header. Any parameters not explicitly declared default to **int**. The only storage class that can be specified explicitly for formal parameters is **register**.
Here is an example of a function header and declaration list:

```
float mullish (henry, malka)
int henry;
long malka;
```

This specifies that the function takes two parameters: *henry*, which is of type **int**, and *malka*, which is of type **long**. The function returns a value of type **float**. Note again that the parameter list in the function header is *not* followed by a semicolon, whereas the declarations are. In fact, the formal parameter declarations have exactly the same syntax as regular declarations, except that they cannot contain initializers. The scope of the function's formal parameters is the function body.

The function header and declaration list are followed by the function body, which is merely a compound statement. When the function is called, the formal parameters are automatically initialized to the actual parameters used in the function call operator. The first actual parameter is assigned to the first formal parameter in the function header, the second actual parameter to the second formal parameter, and so forth. The number of actual and formal parameters must be equal.

Next, the function body is executed. During execution, the formal parameters can be used exactly like local variables. Changing their values has no effect on the actual parameters (although changing the memory location pointed to by a pointer argument affects the location pointed to). If a return statement is encountered during execution of the function body, the function terminates execution, returning the value specified in the return statement (if any), as the value of the function. If the end of the function body is reached without the execution of a return statement, the function terminates without returning a meaningful value.

A function must always be defined in the global environment; that is, a function cannot be defined within another function.

The function named *main* is always special. It is the function that executes first when the program is run. Therefore, a complete program must have one non-**static** function named *main* in order to be able to run. The function header of *main* can be written as

```
main (argc, argv)
int argc;
char **argv;
```

where *argc* is an integer indicating the number of words used in the command that runs the program, and *argv* is a pointer to an array of pointers, each of which in turn points to a string representing one of the words in the command line. The programmer can use names other than *argc* and *argv*; the example merely indicates which arguments are passed to the *main* function. The arguments can be ignored, but it is not a good idea to list only one of them in the function header.

A function can be *declared* inside a function or outside any function. This declaration specifies the function's returned type, the function name, and an empty pair of parentheses. Its purpose is to specify the returned type of the function, and also to allow the function's address to be assigned to a pointer variable or passed to another function.

The Preprocessor

The C preprocessor permits the insertion of files into a C program, the definition of macros, and the conditional compilation of sections of code. A preprocessor directive begins with a # sign. Some preprocessors require this to begin in the first column of a line, whereas others permit it to be preceded by blanks or tabs. This sign is followed by a directive word. Again, some preprocessors permit this word to be separated from the # sign by blanks or tabs and others do not. A preprocessor directive is terminated by the end of the line it occupies, but if necessary it can be continued onto one or more lines by ending all but the last line with backslashes.

File Inclusion

Syntax:
    #**include** <filename>
    #**include** "filename"

The first form causes the preprocessor to look for a file with the specified
<filename> in one or more specially designated places on disk, such as special
directories set aside for header files. In the second form, the "filename" should
specify the exact location of the desired file. On some computers, a user has a
default disk directory, so the file name can be the name of a file in that
directory. The last places in which the preprocessor searches for the "filename"
are the same directories in which it searches for a <filename>.
    The <filename> or "filename" can be a predefined macro.
    The file, if found, is inserted into the program file containing the #**include**
directive, at the point where the directive is specified. The included file can
contain other preprocessor directives, even #**include** directives, but a file cannot
#**include** itself.

Macro Definition

Syntax:
    #**define** identifier   characters
    #**define** identifier(parameters)   characters
    #**undef** identifier

The first form of #**define** defines the identifier to represent everything from the
first non-blank character following the identifier to the end of the directive.
Everywhere the identifier occurs in the program file following its definition (even
in #**include**d files), the identifier is replaced by the string it represents. The
identifier should not be the same as one used in the program for a variable,
label, etc.
    The identifier is not replaced if it is part of another identifier or a string.
That is, if a macro named FRED is defined, then it is replaced in

    FRED+1

but not in

    FREDDY

or

    "FRED"

A macro definition can include a previously defined macro. For example, if a
program contains the following lines, then all instances of FRED are replaced
with 3 + JOE, which in turn are replaced by 3 + 7:

    #define JOE 7
    #define FRED 3 + JOE

A macro cannot include itself in its definition.

If a line other than a preprocessor directive contains a macro, and if it expands to something that looks like a directive, it is *not* processed by the preprocessor.

The second form of **#define** is similar to the first, except that it can have arguments, just as a function does. The macro identifier is followed immediately by an open parenthesis (with no intervening blanks or tabs), which in turn is followed by a list of comma-separated identifiers, used as parameters. These are in turn followed by a close parenthesis. The argument list is followed by at least one blank or tab, which is followed by the macro definition: all characters until the end of the directive.

When the macro is used on subsequent lines, the macro name is followed by an argument list similar to the one in the definition, except that actual parameters are supplied rather than the names of the formal parameters. The supplied parameters can be any strings of characters, can include blanks and tabs, and are separated by commas. Each supplied parameter is bound to a formal parameter in the macro definition, so there must be the same number of supplied parameters as formal ones. The macro name and argument list are replaced by the macro definition, except that each instance of a formal parameter is replaced by its associated supplied parameter. For example, if a macro is defined as

```
#define   ADD_TO_A(x)   (a += (x))
```

Then an expression of the form

```
ADD_TO_A(23 + 7);
```

is replaced by

```
(a += (23 + 7));
```

When the macro is expanded, the string passed to the argument x, namely $23 + 7$, replaces all occurrences of x in the symbol's value.

The argument names used in a macro are local to the macro. That is to say, there is no conflict between a macro's formal parameter names and identifiers used in the program proper. This means a macro argument should not have the same identifier as one that is used in the non-varying part of the macro definition.

A macro expansion *will* substitute its actual parameters within quotation marks that are part of the macro definition.

The comma is the delimiter that separates arguments in a macro. Therefore, there are only three cases in which a comma can be included as part of an argument: (1) when the comma is located between quotation marks, (2) when the comma operator is used within parentheses, or (3) when a function call or macro invocation is used as an argument.

The preprocessor does not parenthesize arguments. If a macro is declared as

```
#define   sqr(a)   a * a
```

and invoked as

```
- sqr(x + 4)
```

the result is

```
- x + 4 * x + 4
```

The compiler interprets this as:

```
(- x) + (4 * x) + 4
```

when what is intended is

```
- ((x + 4) * (x + 4))
```

The macro should have been defined as

```
#define   sqr(a)   ((a) * (a))
```

Macro arguments can include other macro names, which are replaced appropriately. The exception, however, is if an argument includes the name of the macro being invoked. Also, if a parameter that is itself a macro expands to a string containing a comma, this comma is *not* interpreted as an argument separator.

The **#undef** directive removes the definition of the named macro, so that on all lines following the **#undef** directive, the identifier is not recognized as having been defined at all. The identifier can be redefined later. The identifier named in the **#undef** directive must have defined status at the point at which the directive is encountered.

Some C preprocessors allow macro definitions to be stacked. This means that a macro can be redefined without being undefined first. The old definition is saved until an #undef directive is encountered. For example, the code

```
#define FRED 1
a = FRED;
#define FRED 2
b = FRED;
#undef FRED
c = FRED + b;
```

results in the statements

```
a = 1;
b = 2;
c = 1 + b;
```

Some preprocessors, however, require that a macro be undefined before being redefined, in which case the old definition is lost.

Conditional Compilation

Syntax:
  #if int-constant-expression
  #ifdef identifier
  #ifndef identifier
  #else
  #endif

Each **#if**, **#ifdef**, and **#ifndef** must have a matching **#endif** directive in the program file. They may be nested, just like if statements. Each **#if**, **#ifdef**, and **#ifndef** directive also can have a single matching **#else** directive between itself and its **#endif**.

The **#if** directive tests the integer constant expression. This expression cannot contain any references to variables, so it cannot contain the **sizeof**, cast, or address operators. This expression can contain preprocessor identifiers, and virtually always does. If the expression evaluates to a non-zero value (*true*), all the lines following the directive are compiled, up to the matching **#endif** or **#else**. If a matching **#else** exists, all lines following the **#else** directive up to the matching **#endif** are ignored (not compiled).

After the **#endif** directive, all lines are compiled until another conditional compilation directive is encountered. If the expression in the **#if** directive evaluates to zero (*false*), the opposite occurs: all the lines following the directive are ignored, up to the matching **#endif** or **#else**. If a matching **#else** exists, all lines following the **#else** directive up to the matching **#endif** are compiled. After the **#endif** directive, all lines are compiled until another conditional compilation directive is encountered.

Where the term "compiled" is used in the preceding paragraph, it refers also to the processing of nested directives. For example, if an **#if** directive is followed by an **#include** directive, and the **#if** directive's expression evaluates to zero, the **#include** directive is ignored, along with any code that occurs between the **#if** directive and the associated **#else** or **#endif**.

Any undefined preprocessor symbol used in the **#if** expression is treated as if it has the value 0. A symbol that is defined with no value usually cannot be used, however, and an attempt to do so results in a preprocessor error. The same applies to macros whose expansions do not take the form of an integer constant expression.

The **#ifdef** directive compiles code depending on whether the specified preprocessor identifier is defined at the time the directive is encountered. If it is, it behaves like an **#if** directive whose expression is *true*. Otherwise, it behaves like an **#if** with a *false* expression.

The **#ifndef** directive is analogous to **#ifdef**, except that it behaves like a true **#if** directive if the identifier is *not* defined, and like a false **#if** directive if it *is* defined.

Extensions to C

Since the original definition of the C language in *The C Programming Language* by Kernighan and Ritchie, many new features have been added by the writers of various C compilers. An attempt has been made to include these changes in the proposed C standard. Some of these new language elements have been mentioned in this book and in this appendix. Several features, however, merit special mention. These are function prototypes, enumerated data types, the class **const**, and several new preprocessor features.

Function Prototypes

A function prototype is an extension to the function declaration. Thus it can occur inside another function or outside any function. It takes the form of a function definition header except that instead of specifying parameter names, it lists the types of the identifiers. An example would be

```
extern int myfunc(int, float, int *);
```

The storage class should match that of the actual function, and the returned value and argument types also should match those in the actual function definition.

A prototype has the same scope as a function definition. If a function call is made within the scope of a prototype for that function, each actual argument has its type compared to the corresponding type in the prototype. The types need not be identical, but should be compatible for conversion. That is, a char can be passed instead of an int, but not a pointer instead of a float. An unacceptable argument causes an error. The arguments are converted as necessary before being passed to the called function.

Note that the automatic widening conversions (**char** and **short** become **int**, **float** becomes **double**) are *not* performed if a function is called from within the scope of a prototype. All conversions are determined by the arguments in the prototype.

If the function prototype does not match the function definition, the type testing and conversion are performed according to the prototype.

The prototype can contain identifiers following the types, as in the following example:

```
extern int myfunc(int a, float b, int *c);
```

The scope of these names is restricted to the prototype.

Normally, the number of arguments in the prototype must match the number of arguments in the function call. A prototype supplying an argument of **void**, as in

```
int newfunc(void);
```

specifies that no parameters should be passed to the function. If the parentheses are left empty, as in

```
int newfunc();
```

no check of the argument types and numbers is performed. Furthermore, if the parameter list of a prototype ends in an ellipsis (...), as in

```
extern int myfunc(int, float, ...);
```

then no check of the number of arguments is made, and type checking is performed only for the initial arguments that are supplied in the prototype.

If a function is defined within the scope of a prototype for that function, all calls to that function must be within the scope of the same prototype. Also, in this situation, the function expects its arguments to be of the types they are actually defined to be, rather than widened types. That is, if a parameter is declared as char, it expects a char to be passed rather than an int. If a function is defined within the scope of its prototype, the type and number of its parameters must exactly match those specified by the prototype.

Enumerated Data Types

This feature was inspired by the enumerated types of Pascal. Its purpose is to allow the manipulation of symbols as new types of constants. A sample declaration of an enumerated type will best serve to clarify this.

```
enum weekdays
{
      Saturday, Sunday, Monday, Tuesday,
      Wednesday, Thursday, Friday
}
day_1, *day_2;
```

This declaration begins with the keyword **enum**, indicating that an enumerated type is being defined or that a variable of that type is being declared. The statement creates a type called *weekdays*, which is the name following the **enum** keyword. This is followed by a pair of braces enclosing a list of all the values (expressed as identifiers) which variables of this type may take on. These identifiers must be valid C identifiers, and must be unique within the scope of the declaration. The closing brace is followed in the example by the names of two variables. The variable *day_1* is declared to be of type *weekdays*, whereas *day_2* is of the type "pointer to *weekdays*."

Just as with structures and unions, the type name weekdays can be omitted:

```
enum
{
      Saturday, Sunday, Monday, Tuesday,
      Wednesday, Thursday, Friday
}
day_1, *day_2;
```

In this case, the enumerated data type has no name, and no other variables can be declared with that type unless the value list (the braces and enclosed constant names) is repeated. Alternatively, the variable names can be omitted, in which case a data type is defined but no variables are declared. Just as with structures and unions, once a type name has been defined, it can be used to declare other variables:

```
enum weekdays day_3;
```

An assignment statement involving an enumerated type would look like this:

```
day_1 = Saturday;
```

In this statement the constant *Saturday*, of type *weekdays*, is assigned to variable *day_1*, which is also of type *weekdays*. Since a constant of any enumerated data type must take the form of a C identifier, there is no clear way to distinguish constants of this type from variables unless one looks at the declarations.

Enumerated data types are useful if we wish to manipulate values that are, at least conceptually, not numbers or characters. It is comparable to the declaration of preprocessor constants to lend meaning to otherwise anonymous numeric values. The difference is that enumerated data types are part of the C language itself.

Enumerated data types should be treated as incompatible with any other data type. That is, only constants of enumerated data types should be assigned to variables of enumerated data types. Furthermore, those constants should be of the same type as the variables to which they are assigned. Enumerated data type constants should not be assigned to variables of other types. In reality, however, enumerated data types in C are always implemented as **ints**. Each constant is assigned a sequential positive integer, starting with 0. In effect, the **enum** type declaration given earlier is equivalent to the following preprocessor macro definitions:

```
#define weekdays   int
#define Saturday   0
#define Sunday     1
#define Monday     2
#define Tuesday    3
#define Wednesday  4
#define Thursday   5
#define Friday     6
```

Thus integers can be assigned to variables of enumerated types, and constants of enumerated types can be assigned to **int** variables, without casting. Some compilers do not even display a warning. Of course, a cast can be used if the type is given a name. For example, if *n* is an **int** variable, the following statements are valid:

```
n = (int)Sunday;
day_1 = (weekdays)3;
```

A value of one enumerated data type can be assigned to a variable of another enumerated type, since the integer values given to enumerated constants of different types all range from 0 on up. In fact, it may be possible to assign a value to an enumerated variable which is not represented by any constant of its type. For example:

```
day_1 = 99;
```

A cast could not be used in that case, since the compiler probably would then check the integer. The only restriction is that some compilers may make each enumerated data type equivalent to an integer of a different size, depending on how many constants of that type need to be represented.

The programmer has control over what integers are associated with each constant. This is accomplished by following the constant in the type definition with an equal sign and a non-negative integer. Here is an example:

```
enum fish { trout, bass, tuna = 7,
            salmon, herring, halibut = 12 };
```

The constant *trout* is given the value 0 and *bass* is given the value 1. The constant *tuna*, however, is given the value 7. After that point, until any more assignments are encountered, the assignment of consecutive values is continued from the assigned value. That means that *salmon*, which follows *tuna*, is given the value 8, and *herring* is given the value 9. Then *halibut* is assigned the value 12. (Constants cannot be assigned values in the program.)

Since constants can be associated with any values by using the equal sign, the programmer can give the same value to more than one constant of an enumerated type, although this is discouraged.

Because enumerated constants are equivalent to integer constants, they can be used in integer constant expressions.

C Constants

Some C compilers include constants as part of the language, rather than as symbols defined in the preprocessor. These should not be thought of in terms of the preprocessor at all, but as variables whose values cannot be changed. (Admittedly, "constant variables" is a contradiction in terms.)

A constant is declared by including the keyword **const** in the declaration. It may come before or after the type name. Here are some valid constant declarations:

```
int const a = 7;
const float x = 1.2;
const c = 4;
const struct f
{
    int integer;
    long longer_int;
}
f_var = { 4, 23L };
typedef int *int_ptr;
const intptr x;
```

Note that **const** without a type implies **int const**. Every constant variable must be initialized, because that is the only way to give a value to a constant.

Pointers have an interesting place in the world of constants. Consider the following two declarations, both of which are valid:

```
const int *point_to_const;
int *const const_pointer = &a;
```

We are assuming *a* is an **int** variable. The first declaration establishes a pointer to a constant **int**. That means *point_to_const* can be assigned a pointer to any **const int** variable. The **const** variable cannot be assigned a new value through indirection, but *point_to_const* can be assigned to point to another **const int** at any time, since it is not a constant itself.

The second declaration employs an unusual construction: an asterisk before the keyword **const**. The meaning is that *const_pointer* is itself a constant, which points to a variable **int**, and is initialized to point to *a*. Since *a* is not a constant itself, it can have its value changed, in an expression such as

```
*const_pointer = 7;
```

Since *const_pointer* is a constant, however, it must always point to *a*.

These declarations could be clarified by thinking of them this way:

```
(const int) (*point_to_const);
(int) (*const const_pointer) = &a;
```

If the address of a non-constant variable *a* is assigned (through a cast) to a pointer to a constant, such as *point_to_const*, the value of *a* cannot be changed by indirection through *point_to_const*, but it can be changed through direct assignment or by indirection through a regular pointer. If the address of a constant variable *c* is assigned to a regular pointer variable, the value of the constant can be changed through indirection; the compiler might not prevent you from doing this, but such a change could wreak havoc with your program.

A constant variable cannot be used in a constant expression, because its value is stored in memory and can be retrieved only during execution. This is one reason why a constant in C should be thought of as a constant variable.

Extensions to the Preprocessor

Some preprocessors include the special preprocessor operators # and ##. In a macro definition with parameters, if a formal parameter appears in the macro definition preceded by a #, then after the formal parameter is replaced by the actual parameter, it is enclosed within double quotation marks to form a string. That is, if a macro is defined as

```
#define   print_int(x)   printf("%s = %d\n", #x, x)
```

then the statement

```
print_int(some_integer);
```

is replaced by

```
printf("%s = %d\n", "some_integer", some_integer);
```

The symbol ## concatenates two symbols in the interpreted macro. For example, if a macro is defined as

```
#define   print_an_x(n)   printf("%d", x ## n)
```

then the line

```
print_an_x(7);
```

is translated to

```
printf("%d", x7);
```

The **#elif** directive is an abbreviation of

```
#else
#if ...
```

The difference is that the **#elif** does not need its own **#endif**, but uses the one corresponding to the original **#if**. That is, a section of code could take the form

```
#if (VERSION == 1)
    printf("This is the first version\n");
#elif (VERSION == 2)
    printf("This is the second version\n");
#elif (VERSION == 3)
    printf("This is the third version\n");
#else
    printf("This is the fourth version\n");
#endif
```

The **#if** directive may include a special preprocessor function, **defined**. This is a boolean function that returns *true* if its argument is a defined preprocessor symbol. An example is

```
#if defined(DEBUG) && (VERSION == 1)
```

The following two directives are equivalent:

```
#if defined(DEBUG)
#ifdef DEBUG
```

and so are these two:

```
#if !defined(DEBUG)
#ifndef DEBUG
```

The advantage of the **defined** function is that it can be used in conjunction with other tests in an **#if** directive.

Appendix B

Common Library Functions

T*his appendix lists the most common functions available to the C standard and math libraries. You should check your user's manual to find out which functions are available with your compiler.*

To use functions in the math library, you may need to give special instructions to the compiler or linker or operating system.

The functions in this appendix are grouped into several categories. Except for the math functions, they are always available in the standard library. Associated with each group of functions is a header file, which you should include in your program by using the **#include** preprocessor directive. These header files declare various constants that are necessary for the proper use of the functions, and also declare the types returned by the functions (and the types of the arguments, if this feature is supported by your compiler). Some of the functions listed here are implemented as preprocessor macros rather than functions. These macros are defined in the header files.

If functions from more than one group are used in a program, more than one header file can be **#include**d, and they can be specified in any order. Header files should be placed at the beginning of each program file in which they are required.

Several header files declare the constant NULL, which usually has the value 0. It is used to refer to the NULL pointer. Functions that normally return a pointer will return NULL in case of error, or to indicate some other condition (for example, if a search fails).

With most compilers, a program can access a special external variable *errno* by including the declaration

```
extern int errno;
```

Usually this declaration is made in each header file. Storage for this variable is allocated by the compiler in some unspecified location outside the program. It is accessible by the library functions so they can use it to communicate special information to the program.

When an error occurs in a function, usually it returns a value specifying that an error occurred, but not specifying the particular error. Some functions, especially the mathematical ones, can return any value as a normal result, so it is difficult to distinguish normal return values from error values. For these reasons, many functions store in *errno* a special value that indicates the nature of the error. One or more functions usually are provided to interpret these values. For example, the *perror* function, described among the I/O functions later in this appendix, produces an error message based upon the value in *errno*.

A function can set *errno* in case of error, but never clears it to zero in the absence of an error. Therefore, a program that uses the value in *errno* should clear it to zero before calling each library function for which *errno* may need to be used.

In this appendix, the function descriptions are provided as function prototypes (see *Extensions to C* at the end of Appendix A), thus allowing the types of the arguments and returned values to be specified. Unless otherwise stated, a function that normally returns a non-negative integer will return a negative value in case of error, and a function that normally returns a pointer will return NULL if an error occurs.

Input/Output Functions

The header file associated with these functions is <stdio.h>. It defines the macros, FILE, EOF, *stdin*, *stdout*, and *stderr*, among others. These are discussed in the following sections.

```
FILE
```

This is a defined type representing a structure used to store information about a file. Associated with each open file is a pointer to a FILE variable, which can be declared with a statement such as

```
FILE *fpointer;
```

A file is opened by specifying the file name as a string, but operations on an already opened file always are performed by specifying the FILE pointer.

```
EOF
```

This is the value that is returned when an end of file is encountered on a read, and sometimes also on a write when an error occurs. (Usually it is equal to -1.) In general, functions that write to or read from a file directly return EOF when an error occurs, whereas other functions return 0 if they succeed and non-zero otherwise. Functions that are expected to return a non-negative value return a negative value if an error occurs. Often a function returns EOF when an error occurs, even though this fact may not be stated in the following descriptions.

```
stdin
stdout
stderr
```

These are constant FILE pointers which represent standard input, standard output, and the standard error file respectively. These files always are open at the beginning of program execution, and usually are associated with a terminal when a program is interactive. They are specified in calls to functions in which a FILE pointer is needed and I/O to the standard files is desired.

Some of the functions described in the following sections also can be implemented as macros and should be treated accordingly.

A function returns an error if a FILE pointer passed to it does not correspond to an open file. Once a file is closed, its associated FILE pointer becomes meaningless. (This same pointer might later turn up representing another file that was opened after the first one was closed.) If a call is made to an input function, and it is passed a valid FILE pointer to a file that is open only for output, an error occurs. The same is true for output on an input file. An I/O error also may occur if an attempt to write to or read from a file fails. This might occur, for example, if the disk containing the file is removed from the drive while the program is running.

- `void clearerr(FILE *fpointer);`

The end of file and error flags associated with the file are cleared (see *feof* and *ferror*).

- `int fclose(FILE *fpointer);`

This function closes the file whose pointer is *fpointer*, flushing the buffer if there is one. It returns EOF if the file is not open or if the argument is not a valid FILE pointer.

- `int feof(FILE *fpointer);`

This is a boolean function that returns non-zero if an end of file was detected on the file associated with *fpointer* during the last I/O operation. Once the end of a file is reached, a special flag is set for the file and is not cleared except by *clearerr* or another function defined explicitly to do this. The *feof* function usually is implemented as a macro.

- `int ferror(FILE *fpointer);`

This is a boolean function that returns non-zero if a read or write error occurred on the last I/O operation attempted on the file associated with *fpointer*. Once an I/O error occurs, a special flag is set for the file and is not cleared except by *clearerr* or another function defined explicitly to do this. The *ferror* function usually is implemented as a macro.

- `int fflush(FILE *fpointer);`

This function flushes the buffer associated with the file whose pointer is *fpointer*. If the file is not an output file or is unbuffered, the function has no effect.

- `int fgetc(FILE *fpointer);`

This function behaves the same as the *getc* macro, except that it is always a function and never a macro.

- `char *fgets(char *string, int num_chars, FILE *fpointer);`

This function reads *num_chars* - 1 characters, or up to a *newline* or end of file, whichever comes first. The source is the input file specified by *fpointer*. The characters are placed in *string*, and a *null* character is added to the end. If a *newline* is encountered, no more characters are read in, and the *newline* is the last character in the string (before the *null*). The function returns the address of *string*.

- `FILE *fopen(char *filename, char *mode);`

The file named in *filename* is opened in the mode specified in *mode*. The most common modes are as follows:

"r"	read (file must exist)
"w"	write (file is created or erased)
"a"	append (position file for writing at the end, or create a new file for writing)
"r+"	read and write (file must exist)
"w+"	write and read (file is created or erased)
"a+"	append and read (position file at end, or create a new file for writing)

The version of *fopen* on a specific machine may have additional modes. A FILE pointer associated with the open file is returned, and is used in all operations on the file which require such a pointer.

■ `int fprintf(FILE *fpointer, char *format, [expression, ...]);`

The values of the *expressions* are output to the file specified by *fpointer* using the *format* (or control string). Zero or more *expressions* can be specified.

The control string can contain characters and conversion specifications. The characters (including white space) are displayed as written. The conversion specifications, if any, are replaced in the output by their corresponding values from the expression list, converted to character strings according to the type of conversion specification used. At least as many expressions must be passed to the function as there are conversion specifications in the control string. The first conversion specification is matched with the first expression, the second with the second expression, and so on.

A conversion specification begins with a percent (%) character. This is followed by an optional minus (-) sign, indicating that the value is to be left-justified in the output columns allocated to it. If the minus sign is not specified, all values (including strings) are right-justified.

The next character is an optional zero (0). If present, the value is padded with zeroes if the output field has more columns than are needed. If the zero is not present, the field is padded with blanks.

Next is an optional minimum field width specifier. This number specifies the minimum number of columns to be occupied by the output value. If fewer columns are needed, the remaining columns contain the padding character. If more columns are needed, the field width is the number of columns required to display the full value. The minimum field width specifier is always interpreted as a decimal representation, even if it begins with a zero (which specifies a zero as the padding character).

An optional decimal point (.) follows. Next comes an optional precision (or decimal digits) specifier, which has two possible meanings: (1) If the value being displayed is a floating point number, this specifies the number of decimal positions to the right of the decimal point that are to be displayed. (2) If the value being displayed is a character string, the precision specifier determines the maximum number of characters from the string which are to be displayed (the rest are truncated).

This is followed by an optional letter *l*, which must be used when the value being output is a **long int**. (It can be used with formats *d*, *o*, *u* and *x*.)

The conversion specification ends with a single letter determining the type of the corresponding value and the output format. Here are the most common ones:

c — The value is a **char**, and is to be displayed as a single character.

d — The value is an **int** (or **short int** or **char**), and is displayed in decimal notation.

e — The value is a **float** or **double**, and is displayed in scientific notation. If the precision has not been specified, six digits are displayed to the right of the decimal point and before the exponent.

f — The value is a **float** or **double**, and is displayed in decimal notation. If the precision has not been specified, six digits are displayed to the right of the decimal point.

g — Uses *e* or *f* format, whichever is shorter.

o — The value is taken to be an **unsigned int**, and is displayed in octal notation without a leading zero (except for any padding, if zero padding is specified).

s — The argument is a pointer to a character string, which is displayed as such. If the precision has been specified, only that many characters from the string are displayed.

u — The value is an **unsigned int**, and is displayed in unsigned decimal notation.

x — The value is taken to be an **unsigned int**, and is displayed in hexadecimal notation without a leading 0x.

Some versions of *fprintf* allow other letters. For example:

E — Like *e*, except the letter E preceding the exponent is uppercase. If *e* is used, the exponent is preceded by a lowercase e.

G — Uses *E* or *f* format, whichever is shorter.

n — The argument is a pointer to **int**, and the total number of characters output up to this conversion specification is stored in the **int** variable being pointed to.

p — The value is a pointer, and is displayed in a manner determined by the specific version of *fprintf*.

X — Like *x*, except the hex "digits" A through F are displayed in uppercase. If *x* is used, they appear as lowercase.

In some versions of *fprintf*, a precision specifier used with *d*, *o*, *u*, and *x* determines the minimum number of digits to appear. A letter *h* used instead of a letter *l* may specify that the corresponding value is a **short int**. With compilers in which the type **long double** exists, a capital L preceding a format letter *e*, *f*, or *g* indicates the value is a **long double**.

Sometimes the minus sign can be followed or preceded by one or more of the following:

+ — When a value is displayed in a signed format, a plus or minus sign always precedes the number. (Without this, a minus sign precedes a negative number, but nothing precedes a positive number.)

A blank space — This specifies that a negative value is preceded by a minus sign, and a positive number is preceded by a space. (Without this, a positive number is displayed without a leading space, unless padding with blanks occurs.) A plus sign supersedes a blank space.

— used with the *o* format, the value is preceded by a leading zero. With *x*, the value is preceded by a *0x*, and with *X* the output is preceded by *0X*.

If the programmer wants to output a %, it must be specified as %% in the control string.

The *fprintf* function returns the number of characters output.

- `int fputc(int c, FILE *fpointer);`

This function behaves the same as the *putc* macro, except that it is always a function and never a macro.

- `int fputs(char *string, FILE *fpointer);`

This function writes the *string* to the output file specified by *fpointer*.

- `int fscanf(FILE *fpointer, char *format, [pointer, ...]);`

Values are read into the variables pointed to by the *pointers* from the file specified by *fpointer*, using the *format* (or control string). Zero or more pointers can be specified.

The control string can contain characters and conversion specifications. The characters are expected to occur in the input in the same positions in which they appear in the control string. An exception is that a string of white space characters in the control string causes a string of white space characters in the input (not necessarily of the same length or type) to be skipped over. If the programmer wants to indicate that a % should appear in the input, it must be specified as %% in the control string. The conversion specifications, if any, indicate that the input is expected to contain a string of the specified format, which is to be converted for storage in the variables pointed to by their corresponding pointer arguments. There must be at least as many pointers passed to the function as there are conversion specifications in the control string, excluding conversion specifications containing asterisks (*). The first conversion specification is matched with the first pointer, the second with the second pointer, and so on.

A conversion specification begins with a percent (%) character. The % symbol is followed by an optional asterisk (*), indicating that the value is to be read in but not assigned to a variable. There must be no corresponding argument in the pointer list.

Next is an optional maximum field width specifier. This number specifies the maximum number of characters to be read from the input when attempting to input the specified value. Normally (with the exception of the %c format), leading white space characters in the input are skipped over, and characters are then read in up to the next white space character. If a maximum field width is specified, input ceases after the indicated number of non-white space characters is read in, or until a terminating white space character is encountered, whichever comes first. Input for the next conversion specification begins with the next character in the input.

The field width specifier, if any, is followed by an optional letter *l*. This must be used with formats *d*, *o*, and *x* when the value is being input to a **long int**. It must be used with formats *e* and *f* when the value is being input to a **double** variable.

The conversion specification ends with a single letter, which determines the type of conversion to be performed on the input. Here are the most common ones:

c — A character is expected, and the corresponding pointer should be of type **char** *. White space characters are *not* skipped over with this format.

d — An integer in decimal format is expected, and the corresponding pointer should be of type **int** *.

e — A representation of a floating point number is expected. It can be in scientific or decimal notation, and an exponent can be preceded by a letter e or E. The corresponding pointer should be of type **float** * (unless a letter *l* was specified indicating **double** *).

f — This is synonymous with the *e* format.

h — An integer in decimal format is expected, small enough to fit into a **short int**. The corresponding pointer should be of type **short int** *.

o — A value in unsigned octal format is expected. A leading zero is not required. The corresponding pointer should be of type **int** *.

s — A character string is expected, and the corresponding pointer should be of type **char** *. Furthermore, it should point to a character array with enough space to hold the entire string plus the terminating *null* character.

x — A value in unsigned hexadecimal format is expected. A leading 0x or 0X is not required. Most *fscanf* functions permit either form. The corresponding pointer should be of type **int** *.

Some versions of *fscanf* allow additional letters. For example:

E, g, G — Synonymous with *e* and *f*.

i — An integer is expected. It can be in decimal, octal, or hexadecimal format (in the last case, the letters X and A through F can be in upper- or lowercase). It can be followed by a letter *l* or *L* (or *u* or *U*). A decimal value can be preceded by a sign. The corresponding pointer should be of type **int** *.

n — The argument is a pointer to **int**, and the total number of characters read in up to this conversion specification is stored in the **int** variable being pointed to.

p — A pointer in a format determined by the specific version of *fscanf* is expected. The corresponding argument must be a pointer to a pointer.

u — An unsigned integer in decimal format is expected, and the corresponding pointer should be of type **int** *.

With compilers in which the type **long double** exists, a capital L preceding a format letter *e* or *f* indicates the pointer is of type **long double** *.

If an input character is encountered which is unacceptable in the specified format (for example, a letter *q* while reading in an integer), input of the current value ceases, and the characters read up to that point are used to determine the input value. The next conversion specification begins input at the character that caused the previous input to terminate.

The *fscanf* function returns the number of items successfully input.

- `int fseek(FILE *fpointer, long offset, int typeflag);`

The file associated with *fpointer* is repositioned, if possible, as specified by *offset* and *typeflag*. If *typeflag* is 0, the file is positioned *offset* bytes from the beginning. If *typeflag* is 1, the offset is relative to the current position of the file at the time of the function call. A *typeflag* of 2 means that the file is to be positioned *offset* bytes from the end of the file.

- `long ftell(FILE *fpointer);`

This function returns the current position of the file specified by *fpointer*.

- `int getc(FILE *fpointer);`

This function usually is implemented as a macro in *<stdio.h>*. (The macro can evaluate *fpointer* more than once, so it should not have side effects; that is, an expression such as *fp++* might cause problems.) The next character from the specified input file is returned, or EOF at the end of file or if an error occurs.

- `int getchar(void);`

This is equivalent to *getc(stdin)* or *fgetc(stdin)*. It is often a macro when <stdio.h> is included, but it is also available as an actual function when the header file is not included or if *getchar* is undefined.

- `char *gets(char *string);`

This function is similar to *fgets*, with the following differences:

  a) It always inputs from *stdin*.
  b) It always reads up to the next *newline* or end of file, with no character limit.
  c) The *newline* is *not* stored in *string*.

- `char *perror(char *string);`

The value of *errno* is examined, and a message describing the error is generated. If *string* is not a NULL pointer, the message consists of *string* followed by a colon, a space, a system-defined message describing the particular error, and a *newline*. The whole message is written to *stderr*, and a pointer to it is returned. If *string* is NULL, the function only returns a pointer to the system-defined message and performs no output.

- `int printf(char *format, [expression, ...]);`

This is similar to *fprintf*, but it outputs only to *stdout* using the specified *format* and *expressions*.

- `int putc(int c, FILE *fpointer);`

This usually is implemented as a macro in <stdio.h>. (The macro can evaluate *fpointer* more than once, so it should not have side effects; that is, an expression such as *fp++* might cause problems.) The character *c* is written to the specified output file. The character is also returned, or EOF in case of error.

- `int putchar(int c);`

This is equivalent to *putc(c, stdin)* or *fputc(c, stdin)*. It is often a macro when <stdio.h> is included, but it is also available as an actual function when the header file is not included or if *putchar* is undefined.

- `int puts(char *string);`

This function is similar to *fputs*, with the following differences:

   a) It always writes to *stdout*.
   b) A *newline* is appended to the output.

- `int remove(char *filename);`

Deletes the file whose name is in *filename*. This may or may not succeed if the file is still open, depending on your implementation.

- `int rename(char *oldname, char *newname);`

Renames the file whose name is in *oldname*, assigning it the name stored in *newname*. This may or may not succeed if the file is still open, depending on your implementation.

- `int scanf(char *format, [pointer, ...]);`

This is similar to *fscanf*, but it inputs only from *stdin*, using the specified *format* and placing values in the locations specified by the *pointers*.

- `int sprintf(char *string, char *format, [expression, ...]);`

This is similar to *fprintf*, but it places its output in the *string*, followed by a terminating *null* character.

- `int sscanf(char *string, char *format, [pointer, ...]);`

This is similar to *fscanf*, but it takes its input from the *string*.

- `int ungetc(int c, FILE *fpointer);`

The character *c* is pushed back into the file specified by *fpointer*. This character is the next one read from the file, unless a call is made to *fseek* first. The character *c* is not actually stored in the file, so even seeking back by one character erases *c*. Only one character per file can be pushed back at one time. The function returns *c*, or EOF if a character cannot be pushed back.

Character Handling Functions

The header file associated with the following functions is <ctype.h>. All these functions usually are implemented as macros in the header file, and may not be available as true functions.

Character Testing

The following functions all test a character to determine whether it falls into a specific category. They take as an argument a character represented as an **int**. They return boolean **int** values: 0 if the test result is false, non-zero if it is true. The following table lists each function name and the question it asks about its argument.

Function	Test used
isalnum	Is it alphanumeric (a letter of either case or a digit)?
isalpha	Is it alphabetic (a letter of either case)?
iscntrl	Is it a control character (ASCII 0 through 31 or 127)?
isdigit	Is it a digit?
islower	Is it a lowercase letter?
isprint	Is it a printing character (not a control character)?
ispunct	Is it punctuation (not control, alphanumeric, or a space)?
isspace	Is it a space (or tab, carriage return, or *newline*)?
isupper	Is it an uppercase letter?

Some C implementations also include the following:

isascii	Is it a true ASCII value (between 0 and 127)?
isgraph	Is it a printing character (excluding a space)?
isxdigit	Is it a hexadecimal digit ('0' through '9', 'a' through 'f', or 'A' through 'F')?

Case Conversion

The following functions convert the case of an alphabetic character.

- `int tolower(int c);`

This function converts its argument, an uppercase letter, to lowercase. If this is implemented as a macro, a meaningless result might be returned if the argument *c* is not an uppercase letter.

- `int toupper(int c);`

This function converts its argument, a lowercase letter, to uppercase. If this is implemented as a macro, a meaningless result might be returned if the argument *c* is not a lowercase letter.

String and Memory Handling Functions

The header file associated with the following functions is <string.h>.
If a function calls for a character array that is to have a string copied into it, the array should be large enough to hold the largest possible string that could be written into it by the function (including the terminating null character). Of course, a constant string should never be written to.
If an attempt is made to copy part of a string into another part of the same string, as in

```
strncpy(string, string+7, 10);
```

the results may be other than what is desired. The outcome depends on how the function is implemented. The proper course of action would be to copy *string+7* into a temporary array and then back into *string*.

- char *index(char *string, int c);

This function locates the first occurrence in *string* of the character contained in *c*. The terminating *null* character also is tested, so *c* can be a *null* character. The function returns a pointer to the first occurrence of the character contained in *c*, or NULL if none is found.

- char *memchr(char *array, int c, int nbytes);

This function locates the first occurrence of the character contained in *c* in the first *nbytes* bytes of *array*. The pointer *array* can point to any memory location. It need not be a string, so no test is made for a *null* character; exactly *nbytes* bytes are tested. The function returns a pointer to the first occurrence of the character, or NULL if none is found.

- int memcmp(char *array1, char *array2, int nbytes);

The first *nbytes* bytes of *array1* are compared to those of *array2*. The two pointers passed to the function can point to any memory locations. They need not be strings, so no test is made for a *null* character; exactly *nbytes* bytes are compared. If the arrays of bytes being compared are identical, zero is returned. If *array1* is lexically less than *array2*, a value less than zero is returned. If *array1* is lexically greater than *array2*, a value greater than zero is returned.

- char *memcpy(char *copy, char *original, int nbytes);

This function copies the number of bytes determined by *nbytes* from *original* to *copy*. The two pointers passed to the function can point to any memory locations. They need not be strings, so no test is made for a *null* character; exactly *nbytes* bytes are copied. (Compare with *strncpy*.) The function returns *copy*.

■ `char *memset(char *dest, int c, int nbytes);`

This function copies the character stored in *c* into the first *nbytes* bytes of *dest*. No terminating *null* is written. The function returns *dest*.

■ `char *rindex(char *string, int c);`

This function locates the *last* occurrence in *string* of the character contained in *c*. (The *r* in *rindex* stands for *reverse*, since the search is made from the end of the string.) The terminating *null* character is also tested, so *c* can be a *null* character. The function returns a pointer to the first occurrence of the character contained in *c*, or NULL if none is found.

■ `char *strcat(char *string1, char *string2);`

This function concatenates the string *string2* onto the end of *string1*, overwriting the *null* character that originally terminated *string1*. Note that *string1* must be a variable character array, and must be long enough to hold both *string1* and *string2*. The function returns *string1*.

■ `char *strchr(char *string, int c);`

This function is identical to *index*.

■ `int strcmp(char *string1, char *string2);`

The string *string1* is compared to *string2*. If they are identical, zero is returned. If *string1* is lexically less than *string2*, a value less than zero is returned. If *string1* is lexically greater than *string2*, a value greater than zero is returned. If one string is identical to the beginning of the other (for example, "lever" and "leverage"), the larger string is lexically greater.

■ `char *strcpy(char *copy, char *original);`

This function copies the string *original* into *copy*, including the terminating *null*. The function returns *copy*.

■ `int strlen(char *string);`

This function returns the length of *string*, not including the terminating *null* character.

■ `char *strncat(char *string1, char *string2, int nchars);`

This function concatenates the number of characters indicated by *nchars* from the string *string2* onto the end of *string1*, or up to and including the *null* that terminates *string2*, whichever comes first. The *null* character that originally terminated *string1* is overwritten. Note that *string1* must be a variable character array, and must be long enough to hold both *string1* and *string2*. If *string2* is longer than *nchars* characters, only *nchars* characters are copied, and *string1* may not be automatically *null*-terminated. The function returns *string1*.

- `int strncmp(char *string1, char *string2, int nchars);`

The string *string1* is compared to *string2*, but not more than *nchars* characters from each string are used in the comparison. If the sections being compared are identical, zero is returned. If *string1* is lexically less than *string2*, a value less than zero is returned. If *string1* is lexically greater than *string2*, a value greater than zero is returned.

- `char *strncpy(char *copy, char *original, int nchars);`

This function copies the number of characters indicated by *nchars* from the string *original* into *copy*, or up to and including the *null* that terminates *original*, whichever comes first. If *original* is longer than *nchars* characters, only *nchars* characters are copied, and *copy* may not be automatically *null*-terminated. The function returns *copy*.

- `char *strrchr(char *string, int c);`

This function is identical to *rindex*.

Miscellaneous Functions

The header file associated with these general standard library functions is <stdlib.h>.

- `char *calloc(int nitems, int size);`

This function attempts to allocate dynamically a block of memory for *nitems* elements of *size* bytes each. That is, the total number of bytes allocated is *nitems * size*. The block of memory is cleared to zeroes. A pointer to the allocated block is returned. It can be cast into a pointer of any type.

- `void free(char *block);`

This function deallocates the block of memory pointed to by *block*, making it available for later allocation. The block must have been allocated by a previous call to *calloc*, *malloc*, or *realloc*, but not previously freed by a call to *free*. Once a block of memory is freed, it should not be referenced.

- `char *malloc(int size);`

This function attempts to allocate dynamically a block of memory of *size* bytes. The block of memory is not initialized. A pointer to the allocated block is returned. It can be cast into a pointer of any type.

- `long random(void);`

This function returns a random **long int** value. It may be restricted to only positive values, or to **unsigned** values.

■ `char *realloc(char *old, int size);`

This function extends or reduces the dynamically allocated block pointed to by *old* to the size specified by *size*. The block must have been allocated by a previous call to *calloc*, *malloc*, or *realloc*, but not previously freed by a call to *free*. The new block can begin at a different memory location than the old block. If *size* is larger than the original size of *old*, then the first *size* bytes of the new block have the same values as those of *old*. If the new size is smaller than the original one, then the new block contains the same values as the first *size* bytes of *old*. The function returns the address of the new block. For the sake of generality, the original value of *old* should be considered a pointer to a deallocated block, even if this pointer also happens to be the same as the pointer to the new block. If the attempt at reallocation fails, the value of *old* remains valid, and the old block can still be referenced.

■ `void srandom(unsigned int seed);`

The value of *seed* is used to start a new sequence of random numbers. This means that the value of *seed* determines the values returned by subsequent calls to *random*. If two programs call *srandom* with the same seed value, both programs generate the same random values from subsequent calls to *random*. This is useful if it is desired to rerun a random number-driven program with the same results, such as for debugging purposes.

■ `int system(char *command);`

This function executes the command contained in *command* as if it had been typed as a command to the operating system. The result of this function and the value it returns are operating system-dependent.

Math Library Functions

These functions frequently are kept in a separate library from the standard C library functions. The header file associated with these functions is <math.h>.
In all the following functions, a domain error usually occurs if an argument to the function is outside the set of values allowed for that argument (for example, if a non-negative value is expected but a negative number is passed). A range error usually occurs if the value calculated by the function is too large in absolute value to be represented by a double value. The error values returned by each function are different, so it is best to check the value of errno before examining the value returned by a function. Specific errno values are associated with domain and range errors, and constants with these values can be defined in the header file (usually EDOMAIN and ERANGE).
In all trigonometric functions, angles are expressed in radians.

■ `int abs(int i);`

The value returned is the absolute value of integer *i*. (This function may be available in the standard function library rather than the math library.)

- `double acos(double x);`

The value x must be in the range -1.0 to 1.0. The value returned is the arccosine of x in the range 0.0 to π.

- `double asin(double x);`

The value x must be in the range -1.0 to 1.0. The value returned is the arcsine of x in the range $-\pi/2.0$ to $\pi/2.0$.

- `double atan(double x);`

The value returned is the arctangent of x in the range $-\pi/2.0$ to $\pi/2.0$.

- `double atan2(double y, double x);`

The value returned is the arctangent of y/x in the range $-\pi$ to π. The signs of y and x are used to determine the quadrant of the angle returned.

- `double ceil(double x);`

The value returned is the smallest whole number not less than x. This does not refer to the absolute value of a number: *ceil(1.3)* is 2.0, but *ceil(−1.3)* is -1.0.

- `double cos(double angle);`

The value returned is the cosine of *angle*.

- `double exp(double x);`

The value returned is e^x.

- `double fabs(double x);`

The value returned is the absolute value of floating point number x.

- `double floor(double x);`

The value returned is the largest whole number not greater than x. This does not refer to the absolute value of a number: *floor(1.3)* is 1.0, but *floor(−1.3)* is -2.0.

- `double fmod(double x, double y);`

The value returned is the floating point "remainder" of x/y; that is, the fractional part (the portion to the right of the decimal point) of the floating point quotient x/y. The sign of the returned value is the same as the sign of x. If y is zero, the value of x is returned.

■ `double frexp(double number, int *exponent);`

This function normalizes the value of *number*, and interprets it as a mantissa in the range 0.5 (inclusive) to 1.0 (exclusive), multiplied by a power of 2. The power to which 2 is raised is stored in the **int** variable pointed to by *exponent*, and the mantissa is returned. In other words, the returned value multiplied by $2^{exponent}$ yields *number*. If *number* is zero, then zero is stored in *exponent* and is returned by the function.

■ `double ldexp(double mantissa, int exponent);`

This function is the inverse of *frexp*. It returns the value of *mantissa* multiplied by $2^{exponent}$.

■ `double log(double x);`

The value returned is the natural logarithm of x.

■ `double log10(double x);`

The value returned is the logarithm to the base 10 of x.

■ `double modf(double number, double *whole);`

The value of *number* is divided into an integer part (the portion to the left of the decimal point) and a fractional part (the portion to the right of the decimal point). The integer part is stored as a **double** value in the location pointed to by *whole*, and the fractional part is returned by the function. Both parts have the same sign as *number*.

■ `double pow(double x, double y);`

The value returned is x^y. A domain error occurs if x is zero and y is negative or zero, or if x is negative and y is not a whole number.

■ `double sin(double angle);`

The value returned is the sine of *angle*.

■ `double sqrt(double x);`

The value returned is the non-negative square root of x.

■ `double tan(double angle);`

The value returned is the tangent of *angle*.

Appendix C

The ASCII Character Code

This appendix provides an easy reference to the ASCII character codes. Note: The caret (ˆ) represents the control key. That is, ˆA is the key combination control–A, whereas ˆˆ is control caret.

Dec	Oct	Hex	Symb	Name
0	000	00	^@	(null)
1	001	01	^A	
2	002	02	^B	
3	003	03	^C	
4	004	04	^D	
5	005	05	^E	
6	006	06	^F	
7	007	07	^G	(bell)
8	010	08	^H	(backspace)
9	011	09	^I	(tab)
10	012	0A	^J	(newline)
11	013	0B	^K	
12	014	0C	^L	(form feed)
13	015	0D	^M	(RETURN)
14	016	0E	^N	
15	017	0F	^O	
16	020	10	^P	
17	021	11	^Q	
18	022	12	^R	
19	023	13	^S	
20	024	14	^T	
21	025	15	^U	
22	026	16	^V	
23	027	17	^W	
24	030	18	^X	
25	031	19	^Y	
26	032	1A	^Z	
27	033	1B	^[	(ESCAPE)
28	034	1C	^\	
29	035	1D	^]	
30	036	1E	^^	
31	037	1F	^_	

Dec	Oct	Hex	Symb	Name
32	040	20	space	
33	041	21	!	
34	042	22	"	
35	043	23	#	
36	044	24	$	
37	045	25	%	
38	046	26	&	
39	047	27	'	(apostrophe)
40	050	28	(	
41	051	29	)	
42	052	2A	*	
43	053	2B	+	
44	054	2C	,	(comma)
45	055	2D	−	
46	056	2E	.	
47	057	2F	/	
48	060	30	0	
49	061	31	1	
50	062	32	2	
51	063	33	3	
52	064	34	4	
53	065	35	5	
54	066	36	6	
55	067	37	7	
56	070	38	8	
57	071	39	9	
58	072	3A	:	
59	073	3B	;	
60	074	3C	<	
61	075	3D	=	
62	076	3E	>	
63	077	3F	?	

Dec	Oct	Hex	Symb	Name	Dec	Oct	Hex	Symb	Name
64	100	40	@		96	140	60	`	(grave accent)
65	101	41	A		97	141	61	a	
66	102	42	B		98	142	62	b	
67	103	43	C		99	143	63	c	
68	104	44	D		100	144	64	d	
69	105	45	E		101	145	65	e	
70	106	46	F		102	146	66	f	
71	107	47	G		103	147	67	g	
72	110	48	H		104	150	68	h	
73	111	49	I		105	151	69	i	
74	112	4A	J		106	152	6A	j	
75	113	4B	K		107	153	6B	k	
76	114	4C	L		108	154	6C	l	
77	115	4D	M		109	155	6D	m	
78	116	4E	N		110	156	6E	n	
79	117	4F	O		111	157	6F	o	
80	120	50	P		112	160	70	p	
81	121	51	Q		113	161	71	q	
82	122	52	R		114	162	72	r	
83	123	53	S		115	163	73	s	
84	124	54	T		116	164	74	t	
85	125	55	U		117	165	75	u	
86	126	56	V		118	166	76	v	
87	127	57	W		119	167	77	w	
88	130	58	X		120	170	78	x	
89	131	59	Y		121	171	79	y	
90	132	5A	Z		122	172	7A	z	
91	133	5B	[		123	173	7B	{	
92	134	5C	\		124	174	7C			
93	135	5D	]		125	175	7D	}	
94	136	5E	^		126	176	7E	~	
95	137	5F	_	(underscore)	127	177	7F		DELETE

Appendix D

The UNIX Operating System

T*his appendix contains some basic information that will help you compile and run C programs under the UNIX operating system. It is not a complete description of the operating system. You should obtain documentation on the UNIX operating system and the computer system you are using. There are several versions of UNIX, as well as many UNIX "clones," so your system may operate a bit differently from the one described here. Also, you will need to learn how to use a text editor in order to be able to enter programs and other files into your computer.*

UNIX Commands

Even if your computer does not run UNIX, several versions of C run in an environment that mimics UNIX. Therefore, some of the commands and syntax described here may be of use to you, even though they may be applicable to your machine only when you are running C.

Under the UNIX operating system, almost every command—such as that to compile a program or produce a list of files—is carried out by a program. For example, when you type *ls* (for listing files), the system runs a program called *ls*. A C program, once compiled, is run the same way as a command is executed.

The UNIX File System

UNIX files reside in conceptual structures called *directories*, which can be thought of as "boxes" that contain files. These directories, in turn, can be contained in other directories, forming a tree structure as shown in Figure D-1.

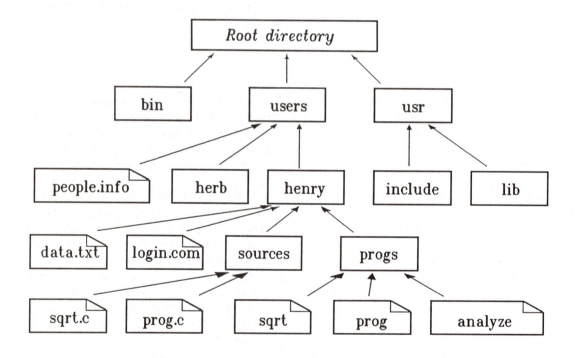

Figure D—1

In this figure, the file *prog.c* is contained in the directory *sources*. That directory is contained in a directory called *henry*, which is contained in the directory *users*, which finally resides in what is called the *root directory*. Each of the directories shown here can contain other directories as well, and some of them contain files. Any directory can contain either files or other directories.

Notice that directory structures are diagrammed as trees rather than as boxes within boxes. This is done for clarity, and also because a directory does not literally contain other directories or files, but merely points to them. In fact, a UNIX directory is a type of file that lists the names and locations of other files.

At any given time, a user is *connected* to a directory. This means that, when the user specifies a program or a file name in a command, the system first looks for that file in the directory to which the user is connected, unless the user specifies otherwise. This directory is called the *current directory*. If the file is not found there, the command produces an error message unless the file is being created. (When the file in question is the command name, the system searches in several alternate directories.) When the user creates a file, it is placed in the current directory, again unless otherwise specified. Typing the command *ls* alone on a line produces a list of the files and directories in the current directory.

When you log onto a UNIX system, the current directory initially is your *home directory*. In Figure D-1, *henry* might be the home directory of a user named *henry*. In this directory would be located most of the files belonging to *henry*. A user might also create subdirectories in order to organize these files. For example, a subdirectory called *sources* might be used to contain all source program files, whereas another subdirectory called *progs* might hold all compiled, executable program files. The parent directory, *henry*, might contain miscellaneous files. (A directory's *parent* is the one that immediately contains it.)

The user can specify the location of a file outside the current directory by identifying the file by its *path name*. For example, suppose our current directory is *users*, and we wish to access the file called *prog.c*. This file could be specified as

```
henry/sources/prog.c
```

The path name is a description of the "path" that must be taken from the current directory to the desired file. The current directory is not specified in the path name. In this example, the system looks for a directory called *henry* in the current directory, then for a directory called *sources* within *henry*, and then for a file called *prog.c* in *sources*. The directories and the file name are separated by slashes. The name of the file is always specified last. The rest of the names making up the path name must be directories, and must form an actual path in the directory structure. In the example, *sources* must be a subdirectory of *henry*, which in turn must reside in the current directory. The file *prog.c* must be in the *sources* directory, unless it is being created. Some commands require the specification of a directory, in which case the last file in the path name must be a directory. A path name cannot contain the name of more than one non-directory file, and if specified, the file name must appear at the end of the path.

The type of path name shown in the example is *relative*, in that it is meaningful only if the current directory is *users*. It is possible to specify an *absolute*, or *full*, path name that uniquely identifies a file regardless of the current directory. This is done by specifying the path to the file from the root directory. The file *prog.c* could be specified as

```
/users/henry/sources/prog.c
```

The slash at the beginning of the path name tells the system that the path starts at the root directory. The directory *henry* must be in the root directory. The rules that apply to a relative path name also apply to an absolute one.

Each directory contains a special subdirectory called .. (two consecutive dots). This is a pointer to the parent directory; conceptually, a directory can contain itself. The tree model of the file system can be used to illustrate this concept, as shown in Figure D-2.

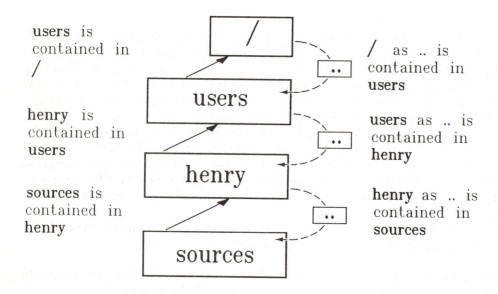

users is
contained in
/

henry is
contained in
users

sources is
contained in
henry

/ as .. is
contained in
users

users as .. is
contained in
henry

henry as .. is
contained in
sources

Figure D–2

This arrangement makes it possible for a relative path name to specify a file that is not a descendant of the current directory. For example, if the current directory is *progs*, the file *prog.c* may be specified as

```
../sources/prog.c
```

The path starts at the *progs* directory, leads (by way of ..) into the parent directory *henry*, then into *sources*, where *prog.c* is found.

The *cd* command is used to establish or change the current directory. Its argument is the path name of a directory. For example, to make *henry* the current directory, the programmer would type

```
cd /users/henry
```

If the current directory were *sources*, the following would be equivalent:

```
cd ..
```

Typing merely

```
cd
```

connects you to your home directory.

Compiling a C Program: The cc Command

Consider the following UNIX command, used to compile a C program:

```
cc sqrt.c
```

The first word, *cc*, is the command that invokes the C compiler. That is, it runs a program called *cc*. As with all UNIX commands, the command name is specified first, before any parameters. The system looks in the current directory first for *cc*, so you should not assign this name to one of your files. If *cc* is not in the current directory, the system looks in a common directory, usually */bin*.

The parameter to the *cc* command shown here is the name of the file containing the program to be compiled. The file name is separated from the word *cc* by a space. In this case, the file's name is *sqrt.c*. The name of a C program file must end with the suffix *.c*, so that the *cc* command can recognize it as a C source program (as will be seen shortly, other types of files also can be passed to *cc*). The beginning of the file name, in this case *sqrt*, should be chosen to describe the program.

Producing an executable program file from a source file requires three basic steps under UNIX, mediated by the *cc* command:

1. The C compiler is called. This step produces a file containing an assembly language source program, which is a translation of the C program.
2. The assembler is called to convert this program into an object file, which is the machine language version of the program. It is not yet executable, however.
3. The object file must be linked, or loaded, together with other routines such as library functions. This last step is accomplished by the *loader* and results in an *executable* file.

All these steps are invoked automatically by the *cc* command. If an error is detected at any stage, processing ceases immediately, and no subsequent steps are carried out.

If there are no errors, the *cc* command produces an executable file called *a.out*. This program can be run merely by typing

```
a.out
```

as a UNIX command. It is not a good idea to leave the program with this name, however, because the next time you compile a program, the new executable file also will be named *a.out* and the old one will be destroyed. One solution is to rename the executable file by using the *mv* command. It can be used to move a file to another directory, but in this case we use it merely to rename a file. Typing

```
mv a.out sqrt
```

changes the name of the executable file from *a.out* to *sqrt*. We chose *sqrt* because that is the *base name* (the name minus the suffix) of the source program file. To run the program, we type

```
sqrt
```

Another way of changing the name of the executable file is by specifying it in the *cc* command. The command

```
cc -o sqrt sqrt.c
```

causes the executable file to be renamed *sqrt* by the loader. The −*o* is called an *option*, because it enables the user to make choices about how the *cc* command works. Most options are specified before the file name(s). The *cc* command can distinguish options from file names by the fact that options begin with a dash. Notice that the −*o* option (for "output") is followed by a space, then by the name chosen for the executable file, and then another space.

Suppose a program is made up of more than one source file. If a program consists of the files *sqrt1.c* and *sqrt2.c*, we could compile it by typing

```
cc -o sqrt sqrt1.c sqrt2.c
```

Notice that the two file names are separated by a space. In a UNIX command, all parameters are separated from one another and from the command name by blanks or tabs. This command compiles and assembles the two sources separately, but loads them together into a single executable file (named *sqrt* by the −*o* option). It does not matter in what order you specify the files, because the *main* function always is called first.

It is possible to control the steps that the *cc* command performs. The −*c* option (for "compile only") stops the *cc* command after compilation and assembly, but before loading. The product is object files ending in *.o* (for "object"). If you type the command

```
cc -c sqrt1.c sqrt2.c
```

you will find two object files, *sqrt1.o* and *sqrt2.o*, in the current directory when the command is finished, if there were no compilation errors. If you then wish to load those two files into an executable program, you can type

```
cc -o sqrt sqrt1.o sqrt2.o
```

The *cc* command detects (by means of the *.o* suffixes) that object files are specified, so it skips the compilation and assembly steps and goes directly to the loading stage. (It is also possible to call the loader directly, using the *ld* command, but *cc* automatically loads in the necessary modules, such as functions from the standard C library.)

A reason for producing object files is that you may have a function or group of functions that are used by several different programs. If you place them in a file and compile them, they can be loaded with other program modules without having to recompile the object files. The command

```
cc numbers.c sqrt.o
```

compiles the source file *numbers.c*, assembles it, and then loads the resulting object file with *sqrt.o* to produce an executable *a.out* file.

If you compile a C program and then make a change to the source (perhaps because of a bug), it is necessary to recompile the program in order for the change to be reflected in the executable program. If the program consists of several modules (source files), however, and the source code change was made in only one module, then only the modified file need be recompiled. This is true only if object files have been created by compiling all the modules with the $-c$ option.

It is also possible to compile but not assemble a C program, using the $-S$ option. (In UNIX, as in C, uppercase and lowercase are differentiated, so $-S$ is not the same as $-s$.)   The command

```
cc -S sqrt.c
```

produces an assembly language program *sqrt.s*. You might wish to try this, to see how the compiler translates your C program. A *.s* file can be passed to the *cc* command, in which case compilation is skipped for that file; it is passed directly to the assembly stage.

It is possible to name a file in a *cc* command which is not in the current directory. For example, you could type

```
cc ../distant.c
```

which compiles a file in the parent directory. The executable file and any intermediate ones, such as the assembler or object file, always are created in the current directory.

All the options we have covered so far precede the file names in the *cc* command. There is one option, however, that follows the file names: $-l$. This option is used to specify libraries to be loaded with the C program. It is specified after the file names because it is necessary for the loader to determine which modules are needed from the library before the library is processed.

Under UNIX, function libraries are groups of object modules packed into a single file for easier and (sometimes) quicker access. The standard format of a library name is *lib?.a*, where the ? is replaced by one or more letters. (The *.a* stands for "archive.")   For example, the standard C library file is named *libc.a*, whereas the math library is named *libm.a*. These libraries are placed in a standard location, the directory */usr/lib*.

The standard C library is loaded automatically along with a C program. Actually, the entire library is not loaded, only the modules containing functions or variables explicitly referenced by the program, as well as other modules referenced by those modules. It is necessary to request the loading of the math library explicitly. The names of library files are standardized, so the *lib* and *.a* are omitted when the $-l$ option is used. To load *libm.a*, you specify $-lm$ as shown here:

```
cc sqrt.c -lm
```

Notice that, unlike the $-o$ option, the string (m in this example) specified with the $-l$ option follows *immediately* after the $-l$, with no intervening spaces. If there were a library file named *libjoe.a*, you would load it with the option $-ljoe$.

Your UNIX system may have other specialized libraries. You may also have your own library in your own directory. The method of creating a library is beyond the scope of this appendix. If it is necessary to load a library that is not in the */usr/lib* directory, or one that does not have a standard name, you can do so by specifying the library name in the *cc* command. For example, if there is a library file called *funny.a*, you could enter

```
cc sqrt.c joe.o funny.a
```

The *cc* command recognizes the library by its *.a* suffix and passes it on to the loader. Like the *−l* option, the library name should come after the names of any C, assembler, and object files. It is permissible to include both a library file name and the *−l* option in a *cc* command, or even more than one library file or *−l* option. Usually it is not necessary to specify the name of a library more than once, either explicitly or with the *−l* option. If a function in a library refers to one in another library, however, you should specify the library containing the calling function before that containing the called function.

The Preprocessor

The C preprocessor can be influenced by the UNIX environment in at least two ways. The first has to do with the **#include** directive.

If the file name specified in the **#include** directive is a simple file name or a relative path name in quotation marks, the preprocessor looks for that file in the same directory as the program file that contains the directive⎯not necessarily the current directory. Failing that, the preprocessor looks in one or more special directories, the identities of which can be changed at a particular site. If the preprocessor still cannot find the file, it produces an error message. If the name specified within quotes is a full path name, the preprocessor has only one option: It follows the path to look for the required file, and either finds it or doesn't. (The preprocessor invokes the UNIX system to search for the file, since UNIX contains a facility to interpret path names and to locate files.)

If the file name in the **#include** directive is enclosed within angle brackets < >, the file is *not* searched for in the directory containing the source file. The first special directory that UNIX looks in usually is one called */usr/include*. If a program includes the directive

```
#include <math.h>
```

the preprocessor looks for the file */usr/include/math.h*. A relative path name also can be specified. The directive

```
#include <sys/types.h>
```

causes the file */usr/include/sys/types.h* to be inserted into the source program.

The *−I* option of the *cc* command affects the search sequence for a file mentioned in an **#include** directive. If the file name is enclosed in quotes and is not a full (absolute) path name, the preprocessor searches for the named file in the source file's directory. The *−I* option provides the preprocessor with another directory to search if the file is not found there, before any system-defined directories are searched.

For example, suppose a user has a collection of personal header files in the directory */users/henry/headers*, and has a program file */users/henry/junk.c* which contains the directive

```
#include "stuff.h"
```

If the program is compiled with the command

```
cc junk.c
```

when the current directory is */users/henry*, then the file *stuff.h* will not be found. If, however, the program is compiled with the command

```
cc -I/users/henry/headers junk.c
```

then, after the search of the current directory fails, the preprocessor looks for */users/henry/headers/stuff.h*, and finds it. (As with the −*l* option, the string follows the option name with no intervening blanks.) Note that the directory name is appended to the file name with an intervening slash, so that a directive

```
#include "sub/stuff.h"
```

would cause the preprocessor to search for */users/henry/headers/sub/stuff.h*.

In the original example, it also would have been possible to change the directive to

```
#include "headers/stuff.h"
```

since the header file could have been reached from the current directory. Using the −*I* option saves typing in the program file, however, especially if many **#include** directives are used, and also makes it possible to specify a file name without needing to know where it will be located.

Another way the preprocessor can be affected by the *cc* command line is with the −*D* option. This option makes it possible to predefine a preprocessor symbol, so the symbol definition exists before any preprocessor directives in the program are processed. This simplifies the case in which the value of a symbol, or its existence or nonexistence, determines which of two blocks of code is to be compiled. It is not even necessary to remove or insert a **#define** directive from each file affected, merely to specify or omit the −*D* option from the command line. For example, suppose a program file named *junk.c* contains a directive

```
#ifdef EASY
```

Assuming no preceding **#define** directives define EASY, the command

```
cc -DEASY junk.c
```

causes the preprocessor to process the file *junk.c* as if the first line contained the directive

```
#define EASY 1
```

If more than one C file is specified in the *cc* command, this applies to all the files. If the −*D* option is omitted, the preprocessor proceeds normally. If there are no **#define** directives for the symbol EASY, it is treated as undefined. Of course, any **#define** directives within the program supersede the −*D* option.

The $-D$ option also can be used to equate a symbol with an explicit value. The command

```
cc -DEASY=23 junk.c
```

is equivalent to beginning the file *junk.c* with the directive

```
#define EASY 23
```

A symbol can be defined with the $-D$ option to have any string as its value, provided there are no imbedded blanks. For example, the following is valid:

```
cc -DEASY=hello junk.c
```

Since the $-D$ option contains an uppercase letter, and preprocessor symbols usually are uppercase, an interesting error is possible. If we wished to define a symbol named DO_IT, we might erroneously type:

```
cc -DO_IT junk.c
```

where one D is omitted.

This completes our coverage of the *cc* command. It has other options that are less frequently used; for a full description, see your UNIX guide, or the online documentation of *cc* if you have the *man* command.

cc Command Summary

Options

All options are specified before any file names, except for $-l$.

$-c$	Compile and assemble any *.c* files, and assemble any *.s* files, leaving object (*.o*) files.
$-D$symbol	Define a preprocessor symbol as having the value 1.
$-D$symbol=string	Define a preprocessor symbol as having the specified string as its value.
$-I$directory	Have the preprocessor search the specified directory for **#include** files, after searching for them in the source file's directory.
$-lx$	Load required modules from the library named *libx.a* (where *x* is the string following the $-l$) in the standard directory (usually */usr/lib*).

-o file   Place the executable program in the named file
                            (note the   space between the *—o* and the
                            file name). If this option is not specified, the
                            executable file is named *a.out.*

-S   Compile any *.c* files, leaving assembler
                            (*.s*) files.

Files

The following list shows which file suffixes match which types of files:

.c   C source file
.s   assembly language file
.o   object file
.a   library file

Redirection, Pipes, and Background Jobs

This section describes operations that can be performed on executable programs. The first feature is I/O *redirection*. When you run a program, you can redirect the source of the standard input and the destination of the standard output.

Normally a program expects standard input and output to be a terminal, but often the program wants input to come from a prepared data file. Since a single program can take its input from either a file or a terminal at different times, it may not be practical to code a program to handle both cases. In fact, it is not necessary under UNIX. Suppose a program named *sqrt* gets its data from the standard input. If you run it by typing

```
sqrt
```

then it waits for data to be typed at the terminal. If, however, you type

```
sqrt <data.txt
```

then the system automatically connects the file *data.txt* to the standard input of *sqrt*. The program itself cannot tell the difference. The string *<data.txt* says: "Get the program's standard input from the file *data.txt.*" The named file must already exist. When the end of the file is reached, the program detects an end of file condition.

Regardless of where a program's standard input comes from, it can use the *fopen* function to open files explicitly for input. Such files cannot be redirected. It is even possible for a program to open the terminal explicitly as an input device. Under UNIX, there is a "fake" file that corresponds to the user's terminal. This file is called */dev/tty.*

If a program prompts for interactive input, it still displays its prompts if the input is redirected. There is, however, a function called *isatty* which can be used to determine if a file is attached to a terminal. A program can use this function to decide whether or not to display prompts. Certain operations, such as the *fseek* function, cannot be performed on terminals, so before a program attempts to use such a function on the standard input (or output) it should determine that the file is not a terminal.

It is also possible to redirect output. Typing

```
sqrt >results.txt
```

causes the standard output of the program *sqrt* to be written to the file *results.txt*. If the named file does not exist, it is created. If it exists, it is erased and written over. The alternative syntax

```
sqrt >>results.txt
```

in which the greater-than sign is doubled, causes output to be *appended* to the end of the file if the file already exists.

As with input, output redirection has no effect on other files explicitly opened by the program. A program also can open the terminal for output by opening the file */dev/tty*.

It is possible to redirect both input and output in the same command. For example, the command

```
sqrt <data.txt >results.txt
```

runs the program *sqrt*, redirects its standard input from the file *data.txt*, and redirects its output to the file *results.txt*. The redirection specifiers can be typed in either order. That is, it is also valid to type

```
sqrt >results.txt <data.txt
```

and the results will be identical. It is illegal, however, to place more than one input redirection or more than one output redirection in a single command. It is also illegal to use both > and >> in the same command, and it is erroneous to attempt to redirect output back to the same file from which input is being redirected.

You can specify command line arguments along with redirection, as in the following example:

```
cc -c test.c >cc.out
```

which compiles the file *test.c* and places any output from the *cc* command into the file *cc.out*. All parameters must be specified before redirection. (Do not confuse a file specified in a redirection with one used as an argument to a command.)

Redirecting the standard output has no effect on the standard error file. It is possible to redirect standard error output, though the exact technique depends on which *shell* (a program which intercepts and interprets user commands) is interpreting your commands. It rarely is desirable to redirect standard error, however, because that file often is used as a last-resort communications link to the user. For example, suppose you are redirecting a program's output to a file, but you are typing input interactively. It is desirable for the program to be able to notify you immediately, by way of the terminal screen, of any errors in the input so that they can be corrected. The program could open the terminal as an extra file, but that is extra work that should be avoided.

If you wish to discard the output of a program, redirect it into a file called */dev/null*. As its name suggests, this sends the output into nothingness. Redirecting input from this file causes an end of file condition to be detected immediately.

An interesting mechanism provided by UNIX is the *pipe*, a conceptual device by which the standard output of one program can be redirected directly to the standard input of another one. As an example, one might type the following command:

```
sqrt | analyze
```

This executes the programs *sqrt* and *analyze*, with the standard output of *sqrt* redirected to the input of *analyze*. The program *sqrt* might generate the square roots of numbers entered by a user, and *analyze* might be employed to generate and display statistics about numbers that it inputs. You may think of both programs running at the same time, with *analyze* being fed data as it is generated by *sqrt*. Or you could think of *sqrt* running, with its output stored in a special file, and then *analyze* being run with its input redirected from this special file. Either way, the result is that the input for *analyze* is the output from *sqrt*.

When a pipe is used, command-line arguments still can be provided. One could type

```
sqrt xy | analyze ab
```

where the string "xy" is passed to *sqrt* and "ab" is passed to *analyze* (see the section headed *Command Line Arguments*).

It is permissible to string several programs together in a series of pipes, as in the following example:

```
sqrt | analyze | pr
```

As before, the output of *sqrt* becomes the input for *analyze*. Now, however, the output of *analyze* is not displayed, but is passed as input to the program *pr*. (The *pr* program sends its input to a printer, which is useful if the printer is not attached to the user's terminal.)

It is possible to combine regular redirection with pipes. For example, consider the following:

```
sqrt <data.txt | analyze | format >display.txt
```

The program *sqrt* gets its input from the file *data.txt*. Its output is passed as input to *analyze*, and the output of *analyze* becomes input for *format*. The output of *format* is redirected to the file *display.txt*. The rules for redirection with pipes are the same as if only a single program were specified. That is, only one input redirection can appear in a command; the input goes to the first file in the pipe chain. Only one output redirection, with or without appending, may appear; the output comes from the last program specified. The same file cannot be used for both input and output redirection in the same command.

The final feature of UNIX which we shall mention is running a program in the background. Normally, when you type a command, the command program takes over control of the terminal, and no more commands can be issued until the program terminates. If the program does not use the terminal—for example, if its input and output are redirected—you still cannot issue any more commands until the program is finished. It is, however, possible to run a program in the background. In this mode, as soon as a command is issued, the program begins running but frees up the terminal so that the user can issue another command. The command to be run in the background must be followed by an ampersand, as in:

```
sqrt <input.file >output.file &
```

Command Line Arguments

As we mentioned in Chapter 16, the *main* function is passed two arguments: *argc* and *argv*. The first parameter, *argc*, is an **int** that specifies how many strings are in the second parameter, *argv*, which is an array of string pointers. Each string is a string from the command used to run a program. For example, if you type

```
myprog a bcd ef
```

then, if the program specifies *argc* and *argv* as parameters to its *main* function, *argc* has the value 4, and the strings pointed to by *argv* will be

```
myprog
a
bcd
ef
```

Notice that the first string is the name of the executable file, since that is always specified first in a command. In this way, a program can discover the name of its executable file. Note that the strings in *argv* have no innate meaning. The programmer can interpret them as file names if he so desires, but can give them any other meaning. Thus the *cc* command interprets strings beginning with a dash as options, and all other strings as file names.

The separator between command line arguments is one or more blank spaces or tabs. If it is desired that an argument contain these characters, or other special characters such as "<", ">", "|", or "&", each of these characters can be preceded by a backslash. Another possibility is to enclose the special characters within quotation marks, as in

```
sqrt "a b" c"|"d
```

Single quotation marks also can be used. Quotes and backslashes used to indicate special characters are removed from the arguments before they are passed to the program. You should consult the manual for your command shell for more information on command line arguments. Note that I/O redirection specifiers, the pipe character (|), and the background character (&) are *not* passed to a program. Also, when a command is part of a series of pipes, its arguments are only those strings between the command (executable file) name and the next vertical bar.

Summary of Useful UNIX Commands

Command	Example	Description
cc	(see cc command summary)	Compile a C program
mv	mv file newname	Give "file" the name "newname"
	mv path1 path2	Move the file specified by "path1" to the new directory and name specified by "path2"
	mv file1 dir	Move "file1" to directory "dir"
	mv file1 file2 ... dir	Move all named files into directory "dir"
cp	cp file newname	Copy "file" to one named "newname"
	cp path1 path2	Copy the file specified by "path1" to the new directory and name specified by "path2"
	cp file1 dir	Copy "file1" to one with the same name in directory "dir"
	cp file1 file2 ... dir	Copy all named files into directory "dir"
ls	ls	Display listing of files in current directory
	ls filename	List named file, if it exists
	ls directory	List all files in named directory
cd	cd directory	Change current directory to "directory"
	cd	Change current directory to home directory
pwd	pwd	Display full path name of current directory
cat	cat	Copy standard input to standard output
	cat file	Display contents of "file"
	cat file1 file2 ...	Display contents of all named files, one right after the other

pr	pr	Print standard input
	pr file	Print "file"
man	man topic	Display online documentation on the named topic (or command)

All these commands have other options, which are described in your UNIX guide or online documentation.

You will also need to use an editor such as *vi*, *ex*, or *ed* to compose text, data, and source program files.

Appendix E

Keywords

This appendix contains keywords used by C compilers, written as shown without embedded blanks and lowercase, are reserved by the compiler and cannot be used for any purpose other than those for which they are defined.

Keywords

auto	break	case	char	continue	default
do	double	else	extern	float	for
goto	if	int	long	register	return
short	sizeof	static	struct	switch	typedef
union	unsigned	while			

Some C compilers also reserve the following words:

asm	const	entry	enum	fortran	signed
void	volatile				

Appendix F

Programming and Debugging Hints Reference Guide

This guide arranges all the elements mentioned in the Programming and Debugging Hints section in most of the chapters throughout the book. Use this appendix to quickly locate that Programming and Debugging section most applicable to your problem.

Chapter	Topics Covered	Page
1—4	No Programming and Debugging Hints	N/A
5	Syntax errors, Logical errors, Clarity in Programming, Comments, Choosing identifiers, Messages to the user, Program Output	78
6	Basic Debugging Techniques, Walk-through, Tracing execution, Possible Sources of Error in C (see Chapters 11,13), Updating assignment operators, Assignment operator, Equals operator, Assignment within an expression, Pascal errors, Semicolon, Omission of closing, comment delimiter, Commenting out a Section of Code, Formatting, Backslash, Name truncation	110
7	Robust Programming, Validating input, Runtime errors (Chap. 13,14), Execution errors (Chap. 13), Divide by zero error, Recovering from errors (Chap. 13), Error detection, Informing the user of the cause of an error, Selecting Test Data, Edge data	140
8	No Programming and Debugging Hints	N/A
9	Modular Programming (Chap. 10), Interfaces between functions, Global variables, Preprocessor constants, Comments, Returning error codes	214
10	Modular Programming (Chap. 9), Top-down programming, Test data, Bottom-up programming, Stubs, Stepwise refinement	266
11	Possible sources of error in C (Chap. 6,13), The precedence and associativity rules of C, Parentheses, lint program, Passing the wrong number of arguments, Data types of parameters, Omission of the address operator, Address operator, Indirection operator	317
12	No Programming and Debugging Hints	N/A
13	Runtime errors (Chap 7,14), Execution errors (Chap 7), malloc, Recovering from errors (Chap. 7), Possible sources of error in C (Chap. 6, 11), Semicolon, Closing brace, Error messages, if...else statement	403
14	Execution error, Tracing execution (Chap. 15), Tracing printf statements, Runtime error (Chap. 7, 13), fflush, Buffered output, stdout, stderr	451
15	Tracing execution (Chap. 14), Conditional compilation	480
16	Possible sources of error in C	522

Index